THE CHANGING FAMILY
COMPARATIVE PERSPECTIVES

THE CHANGING FAMILY

COMPARATIVE PERSPECTIVES

MARK HUTTER
Glassboro State College

JOHN WILEY & SONS
New York • Brisbane • Chichester • Toronto

Cover Photo of ''The Family'' by Gustav Vigeland.
This granite sculpture is located in the Vigeland
Sculpture Park, Oslo, Norway.

Library of Congress Cataloging in Publication Data:

Hutter, Mark, 1941–
    The changing family.

Includes index.
    1. Family. 2. Social change. 3. Cross-cultural
studies. I. Title.
HQ515.H87   306.8   80-28829
ISBN 0-471-08394-1

Printed in the United States of America

10 9 8 7 6 5 4 3 2 1

TO LORRAINE,
DANIEL, ELIZABETH,
AND MY PARENTS

PREFACE

This book reflects an increased concern by the American public and by social scientists to study change from both an historical and a cross-cultural perspective. Within the last 10 years, Americans have become more interested in their historical and cultural roots. In addition, in the light of worldwide revolutionary events that have had a dramatic impact on the lives of all of us, the desire to gain a better understanding of other cultures has grown significantly.

There has also been an impressive upsurge of significant information about the family from social history and cross-cultural scholarship. Sociologists, who in the past narrowly focused on the contemporary American family, have now broadened their approach to include comparative material from other cultures as well as from our own historical past. This textbook reflects these developments and provides students with new insights and a wealth of new information on the dynamics of family change and the making of the contemporary family.

Mirroring this development, instructors in courses on the family are devoting more time to historical and cross-cultural material. They are also finding that their students are interested in how the American family system differs from and is similar to family systems in other cultures. For example, students may ask if there is also a sexual revolution in Japan or India or how the elderly are treated in China when they examine these topics in their study of the American family.

It has been my aim to write a sociology of the family textbook that addresses these interests. Therefore, I have systematically presented historical and cross-cultural materials *throughout* the book. Yet I am aware that this is a textbook, not an encyclopedia; it is not my intention to cover the entire range of differences that exist and have existed. My objective is to enhance the students' understanding of the American family through comparative illustrations of family systems, their similarities and differences. Thus, I focus on certain selected societies to reveal both general trends as societies modernize and certain unique variations that are a product of specific historical circumstances. I wish to present comparative materials that have inherent interest of their own and that will also illuminate American family dynamics.

Two chapters are exclusively devoted to examining changing patterns of family life in non-Western societies: Chapter 5 discusses family life in sub-Saharan African cities and Chapter 16 examines the Chinese family. These more detailed analyses provide three-dimensional portraits of the impact of family change in diverse contemporary situations as well as some fascinating insights.

A distinctive feature of this text is the use of newspaper articles. They illustrate concepts and theories in everyday language. There are also case studies, which serve a useful pedagogical purpose and add to the relevance of the text. These materials reveal the impact of change on a personal level and add the human dimension to the analysis of family dynamics.

This book should be seen as a logical evolution in the sociology-of-the-family textbook. It does not break with the past; instructors do not have to revamp their courses since the book follows traditional topical patterns. Its outstanding feature is its extensive coverage of cross-cultural and historical materials from beginning to end. Most instructors will welcome this emphasis. Those instructors who do not emphasize the family systems of other societies will be able to elaborate on the American family in their own class lectures with the full knowledge that the comparative perspective presented in this textbook will complement and enhance their own presentation. A teacher's manual is also available for the convenience of instructors.

MARK HUTTER

ACKNOWLEDGMENTS

I owe a life-long intellectual debt to Alfred McClung Lee and Murray A. Straus, and my point of view has been influenced by Sidney Aronson, Peter L. Berger, Reuben Hill, Gregory P. Stone and other members of the Department of Sociology at Brooklyn College and at the University of Minnesota. Their insights and knowledge are inevitably reflected in this book.

The following colleagues and friends enlightened me on one or more occasions about sociology and on how it should be taught: Charles Auslander, David Bartelt, Pearl W. Bartelt, Jay Chaskes, R. Frank Falk, Richard N. Juliani, Patrick Luck, John Myers, Wilhelmina Perry, Manju Sheth, Margaret Tannenbaum, Richard V. Travisano, Flora Dorsey Young, and Margaret Zahn. I am most grateful to the many students who have strengthened and modified portions of this book through classroom and seminar discussions.

I am also deeply indebted to those who read part or all of this manuscript and who made valuable and helpful suggestions. I wish to especially thank Ted Tannenbaum, friend and colleague, for his critical reading and his keen judgment that improved many a chapter. Those involved in the John Wiley & Sons editorial review process include Michael Gordon, University of Connecticut; Paula M. Hudis, Indiana University; Elizabeth Huttman, California State University, Hayward; David Kent Lee, California State University, Sacramento; and Hallowell Pope, University of Iowa.

The professional staff at John Wiley & Sons has been most helpful in the publication of this book. A special thanks to Carol Luitjens, Sociology Editor, whose enthusiasm and creative suggestions have been most gratifying. I am grateful to Geraldine Ivins who attended to interminable and often tedious details and reminded me of dozens of chores I surely would have neglected otherwise. Rosemary Wellner and Andrew Yockers made important editorial comments that have immeasurably improved the text.

Lastly and typically, I too often took for granted but nevertheless fully appreciate the tolerance and forbearance displayed by my wife, Lorraine, and our children, Daniel and Elizabeth, for what must have seemed like an endless number of years as I worked on this book. I sincerely hope that they feel that the sacrifice was justified.

M.H.

CONTENTS

PART TWO THE FAMILY IN THE COMMUNITY: COMPARATIVE PERSPECTIVES

PART THREE SEX ROLES, COURTSHIP, AND MARITAL RELATIONSHIPS

PART FOUR   GENERATIONAL RELATIONSHIPS

PART FIVE   FAMILIES IN CRISIS AND CHANGE

Boxes

One

COMPARATIVE AND THEORETICAL PERSPECTIVES

CHAPTER 1

Introduction to Comparative Family Study

Change seems to be the most permanent feature in the world today. Dramatic and revolutionary changes that affect all of humanity are occurring in the contemporary world in attitudes and behavior regarding politics, economics, and social life. Fundamental ideas and values pertaining to religion, morality, and ethics are being questioned, examined, and—in some cases—reevaluated. Massive modifications and breakdowns of societal structures and cultural values are associated with social and individual crises in which customary experience and meaning are no longer taken for granted. The conventional assumptions regarding sex-role relationships, marriage, and the family are being challenged.

Politically, we have seen the final dissolution of the colonial empires of Western European societies, some of which began over 500 years ago. In the last 50 years new nations have arisen and have begun to establish viable governmental systems; to integrate and consolidate diverse and, in some cases, antithetical cultural and social groups; and also to make themselves felt as important political entities on the world scene. In addition, advanced industrially developed nations have been undergoing major political changes with resultant national identity crises and reexaminations in the light of world economic and political realignments.

Economically, the forces of industrialization and urbanization are making themselves felt in both the developed and the undeveloped nations of the world. The ramifications of these forces affect all of humanity and transcend political, cultural, and national boundaries. Further, the dynamic interrelationship of energy sources is becoming so obvious that many express surprise at the myopia of those in the recent past who failed to recognize this fundamental fact of world life. The rapidity of the economic changes that are sweeping the contemporary world is almost beyond comprehension.

Social and individual changes have been as radical as those that have been occurring in the political and economic spheres. In developing societies there is a transitory quality to all patterns of social life. The following quote from the New York Times—datelined Teheran, Iran, January 16, 1975—illustrates this point:

> Haji Mahmud Barzegar, a seller of songbirds, scowled at the new cars that streamed unceasingly along the avenue past his neglected shop. "The people do not buy nightingales these days," he intoned glumly. "They are too busy doing other things." (Pace, 1975)

Cross-culturally, the family is undergoing massive changes. The opening statement of William J. Goode's seminal work, *World Revolution and Family Patterns*, states:

> For the first time in world history a common set in influences—the social forces of industrialization and urbanization—is affecting every known society. Even traditional family systems in such widely separate and diverse societies as Papua, Manus, China, and Yugoslavia are reported to be changing as a result of these forces . . . . (Goode, 1963:1)

Goode emphatically declares that the worldwide changes spell the doom for the old social orders and the traditional family systems. The recent social revolutions in Iran and China reflect the continued instability and nonpermanence of much of the changes.

These revolutionary changes have not been restricted to non-Western societies. Equally radical events have occurred in the family of Western industrial societies, particularly in the United States. In recent years the nature of marriage, family, and kinship systems in American society has been the subject of intensive scrutiny and analysis. Questions have centered on the conventional assumptions about the necessity of maintaining kinship relations and the role of the nuclear family, the inherent nature of male-female sex-role relationships, the marital relationship, and the importance and desirability of parenthood. A new, more permissive sexual morality—in part precipitated by the activities of the women's movement and some segments of the youth counterculture—is reflected in the reexamination of previously held attitudes opposed to premarital and extramarital sexual relations, out-of-wedlock pregnancies, and abortions. In fact, the very necessity, desirability, and relevancy of marriage and the family have been challenged.

Concomitantly, there has been a dramatic change in behavioral practices relating to family structure. One of the starkest of these is the continued rise in the divorce rate. In 1920 there was one divorce for every seven marriages, in 1960 one divorce for every four marriages, and today one divorce for every three marriages. Another major area of change has been the drastic decline in fertility rates. The national birthrate has dropped to the lowest point since federal statistics began being compiled in 1917; it is even lower now than during the depression years of the 1930s. The rate is close to a replacement level of population growth.

Also having some impact on the nation's attitudes and values concerning marital and family dynamics has been the U.S. Supreme Court decision of 1973 that allows a woman anywhere in the United States to have a legal abortion if she so desires. Although it seems evident that the legalization of abortions has had relatively little impact on the national birthrate (one demographer states that two-thirds of all legalized abortions would have been performed illegally), the law reflects the striking attitudinal changes occurring in America not only regarding this issue but also many related ones concerning sexual, marital, and familial attitudes.

As a result of all these changes there has been great discussion about the future of the family. A widespread view declares that the family is a dying institution and expresses much concern about the consequent implications for the "American way of life." The aim of this book is to aid in the understanding of the causes, conditions, and consequences of these changes for the individual, the family, and society. It seeks to answer questions on the contemporary status of the family.

We believe that it is futile to examine the family without attending to the almost continuous and radical family changes occurring not only in the United States but also throughout the world. Thus our entire analysis of the family must be grounded in change, and it particularly must be linked with the universal concomitant changes in conjunction with processes of modernization, industrialization, and urbanization.

THE WHYS OF COMPARATIVE ANALYSIS

Americans have been notorious for their lack of understanding and ignorance of other cultures. This is compounded by their gullible ethnocentric belief in the superiority of all things American and has made them not only unaware of how others live and think but has also given them a distorted picture of their own way of life. In the light of today's startling changes in personal value systems and interpersonal relationships, we would argue that by using a comparative perspective not only can we gain a better understanding of other people but also a better understanding of ourselves.

The basic aim, then, in the comparative analysis of the family is to further the

---

[1]Public concern about changes in the family has become centered on the abortion issue. In the seven years since the Supreme Court declared that women have a constitutional right to choose abortions, the Justices have decided five major abortion cases and several secondary ones. These cases reflect local, state, and Federal government efforts to undermine the 1973 Roe v. Wade decision by making it more difficult and expensive for a woman to terminate her pregnancy. The majority ruling of June 1980 upholding the Hyde Amendment left intake the constitutional freedom recognized in the 1973 case but ruled that the freedom to have an abortion does not encompass a constitutional right to public funding.

understanding of the family in both our own society and in other societies. The sociologist, William F. Kenkel (1977:6−8) outlines four major objectives of cross-cultural comparative analysis:

1. *Appreciation of intercultural family variability and uniformity.* An examination of other societies' family systems provides knowledge about the diversity of family institutions and helps develop our own insights into the meanings a practice has for the peoples involved. For example, by studying polygyny (the marriage of one male to two or more females), a practice that has had worldwide popularity as a preferred marriage form, we see its importance to the people who practice it in their everyday life, and thus it is taken out of the realm of an ethnocentric "playboy" fantasy.

2. *Increasing objectivity.* Kenkel argues that comparative analysis developes one's objectivity by placing a familiar phenomenon in an unfamiliar setting. For example, most people are able to make more objective analytical statements about the status of other people's relationships with their parents than they are about *their* relationships with *their* parents. Likewise, a greater degree of objectivity can be gained in the comparative study of family systems than in the study of the family system of one's own society. We gain much objectivity and emotional detachment through comparative analysis, and thus the task of self-examination becomes easier.

3. *Increased sensitivity toward the American family.* The diverse and idiosyncratic features of contemporary American society come into greater focus when one compares it with other societies. For example, one can gain a better understanding of the dating and courtship patterns of Americans by comparing these patterns with the different customs and practices surrounding mate selection in other societies.

4. *Formulation and Hypotheses.* Comparative analysis gives one a different perspective and increases both perception and the analytical ability to examine the family. Through the process of comparative analysis, the observer begins to be able to develop hypotheses concerning the family in its relationship with other institutions in society and also in the relationship that family members have with each other. For example, the study of the family life of the Hutterites or the Amish may provide us with insights into the development of hypotheses concerning the relationship between religion and the family. Kenkel concludes that whether hypotheses that are developed through comparative analysis "prove to be original, or commonplace, testable or untestable, is not nearly so important as the fact that scientific curiosity about the family has been stimulated and an attempt has been made to channel it" (Kenkel, 1977:8).

John Sirjamaki succinctly summarizes the major rationale for the use of the comparative method in the sociology of the family:

Used in family studies, the comparative method makes possible a cultural and historical analysis of family organization and institutions in societies. It permits cross-cultural generalizations about families which reveal their universal character in world societies and their particular character in individual societies in the same or different regions or periods. It provides a means to interpret historical changes in families, and to relate these to other social and cultural changes in societies. These functions of comparative analysis are of enormous importance; they make the comparative method indispensable to the scientific understanding of the family. (Sirjamaki, 1964:34)

Robert Marsh (1967) has made a similar point. He argues that many of the sociological propositions that have been treated as universal explanatory relationships and generalizations were based on data gathered in the United States and thus may have validity only in the United States and may not be applicable cross-culturally. However, many persons view these propositions as being universal. This criticism seems particularly true for the sociology of the family. Systematic comparative analysis of the family is vital; many of the assertions about the family must be examined and investigated with data from cross-cultural societal settings. This is of crucial importance in testing generalizable assertions about family processes and structures.

The main reason, then, for the comparative analysis of the family is to see which assertions are universal and which are unique. And, if the latter, what accounts for their uniqueness. This is of crucial significance if one wishes to answer questions about family processes and structures and their relationships to other societal institutions. Brigitte Berger (1971) has stated that the marked rapid economic, political, and social changes characteristic of the contemporary world have forced social scientists to understand these changes—not only for pragmatic and political reasons but also because comparative sociology contributes to the development of sociological theory even for those who are not primarily interested in the problems of social change. It is our firm belief that the wisdom of her remarks are of particular relevance to the sociology of the family.

AIMS OF THIS BOOK

This book does not claim to present an encyclopedic account of comparative family forms. Our selections and illustrations are designed to aid in the understanding of present-day family structure and processes in a world of change. Further, they are used to highlight such changes and to indicate the similarities and diversities of families and individuals in the United States and other societies.

This book is not intended to be exhaustive, it does not contain an account of every society in the world today. We have been selective in our choice of the societies we discuss, preferring to deal with a few in depth rather than provide a comprehensive cross-cultural account. Our aim in this approach is to establish some general themes, to identify the nature of family change, and to provide the means for a better understanding of future changes.

Another aim of this selective approach is to bring to life in the mind of the reader the family systems we discuss. For many, the image of a different society is so abstract and "foreign" that they cannot relate to it. We discuss different family systems so that the reader will have a fuller and deeper understanding of them and will be able to use them comparatively in the analysis of American society. Thus, by attempting to examine other family systems in comparison to our own, we hope to shed light on the worldwide changes that are affecting all family systems.

It is not our intention to overburden the reader with a seemingly endless presentation of family and kinship classification terms. Rather, we will sketch out the variations in kinship systems to highlight how family relationships have implications not only for the individual but also for the preservation and continuation of societal patterns. We must also caution the reader to keep in mind that some of this discussion may not be of immediate apparent usefulness; however, the material introduced here will be elaborated on in the chapters that follow. With this cautionary note, let us proceed.

THE FAMILY IN CROSS-CULTURAL PERSPECTIVE: A BRIEF SKETCH

Throughout history the family has been the social institution that has stood at the very center of society. For most individuals the family is the most important group to which they belong. It provides intimate and enduring interaction and acts as a mediator between themselves and the larger society from birth until death. The family transmits the traditional ways of a culture to each new generation. It fulfills human needs as few other institutions can. It is the primary socializing agent as well as a continuous force in shaping the course of one's life. It is through the family that men and women satisfy most of their sexual, emotional, and affiliational needs. Children, inevitably raised in their families, provide a tangible link with future generations. For the society, the family provides the necessary link between it and the individual; the family motivates the individual to serve the needs of the society and its members. It is through the family that the society determines the everyday interactional patterns of the individual. In many societies it is the family that provides the bonds of mutuality that define their members' occupation, religious life, political role, economic position (Keniston, 1965).

It is true that every society may develop its own variations on these universal themes. Yet, as the French anthropologist, Claude Levi-Strauss (1971), has so astutely observed, one central feature emerges in all structural variations of the family: the family links individuals into an intermeshed network of social relationships. The family regulates and defines social relationships through contractual marital relationships. The incest taboo may be seen as functioning to assure patterned forms of marital exchange between families instead of within families. The division of labor between husband and wife serves to enhance their dependency on one another, just as the marriage of man to woman serves the development of reciprocal ties between family groups. The continued accumulation of reciprocal obligations linking man to woman, family to family, and kinship groups to the wider social system is seen as the very basis for the social structure of a given society.

One can get a better appreciation of this perspective by examining the cross-cultural variations of the family. By paying particular attention to how the family interrelates the individual to the societal matrix through kinship structures, the importance of the orientation becomes clear. Further, if one keeps in mind that there is now occurring what Goode (1963) has called a ''world revolution in family patterns,'' one can more readily understand why it is so vitally necessary to understand the role of the family in the world today.

Family, the first and most important term in our study, is so familiar that it does not seem to warrant clarification. However, when one takes a closer look at family systems in other societies as well as the diversity of forms in our society, we come to realize that the familiar can be rather complex; there is no universal family form, but many forms and variations. However, each form and structure of the family serves important functions for a given society and its members. The student, while noting these variations, should pay close attention to the purposes these forms serve rather than simply to memorize and catalog them.

George Murdock suggested that, ''The family is a social group characterized by common residence, economic cooperation, and reproduction; it includes adults of both sexes, at least two of whom maintain a socially approved sexual relationship, and one or more children, own or adopted, of the sexually cohabitating pair'' (Murdock, 1949:2−3). This definition has been questioned in that there are families that contain neither cohabitating adults nor adults who work and live together.

Exceptions ot Murdock's definition have led sociologists to modify the definition and to stress the predominant characteristics of the family arrangement. These definitions usually refer to the fact that the family finds its origin in marriage, which is an institutionally sanctioned union between a man and a woman that assumes some permanence and conformity to societal norms. A primary function of the family is the reproduction of legitimate offspring, their care and their socialization into the traditions and norms of the society, and the acquisition of a set of socially sanctioned statuses and roles acquired through marriage and procreation.

The definition lays down guidelines that emphasize the social arrangements relating to marriage and the family and the deemphasis on the human biological aspects of the family. For humans, unlike animals, social determinants set limits, constraints, and meanings on biological determinants. Marriage and the family should not be confused with biological mating and resultant offspring.

> The mating phenomenon is shared with other animals, whereas marriage is strictly human. Mating, even on the human level, may be quite impersoal, random, and temporary. Marriage, on the other hand, is a social institution, and it assumes some

permanence and conformity to societal norms. Marriage is society's way of controlling sex and fixing responsibilitiy for adult sexual matings. In this connection it is worth noting that all societies, both past and present, prescribe marriage for the majority of their members. Marriage, in other words, is a universal social institution, and, although extramarital sexual contacts frequently are permitted, it is the marriage arrangement that is most strongly sanctioned for most men and women during most of their life spans (Christensen, 1964:4).

Thus, although the family is based on biological processes, these processes are channeled by a society to conform to its traditions, rules, and attitudes.

Sexual interaction and children occur biologically, but they are socially defined. The family can also be analyzed from several vantage points, depending on its structural characteristics.

1. The family can be classified according to the form of marriage allowed by a given society:

Monogamy: one man to one woman

Polygamy: a plurality of mates

Polygyny: one man to two or more women

Polyandry: one woman to two or more men

Group Marriage: two or more men to two or more women

Murdock (1949, 1957) has found that polygyny existed in 193 (81 percent) of the 238 societies he sampled in 1949 and 415 (75 percent) of the expanded sample of the 554 societies comprising his world ethnographic sample fo 1957. Monogamy, although the preferred and exclusive form of marriage for only 43 (18 percent) of Murdock's 1949 sample and 135 (24 percent) of his 1957 sample, is and has always been the most widely practiced form of marriage. For the man of polygynous-allowing societies, the privilege of having multiple spouses is restricted to a small minority, usually composed of members of the higher social strata. William N. Stephens (1963) states that polygyny serves as a status distinction, a mark of prestige, by virtue of the economic and political advantages of having several wives. That is, when women have economic and political value, there is a greater demand for polygyny than monogamy.

Polyandry, which is relatively rare (only 1 percent—two and four societies respectively in Murdock's two samples), tends to be prevalent where there is a limited amount of land, conditions are hard, and wives are not economic assets. Where it occurs, the society is characterized by severe economic conditions, female infanticide, and a marked lack of jealousy among the cohusbands, who frequently are related. In the polyandrous marital system there is a patriarchal (male dominant) organization in which one male agrees to share his wife in common with other men in exchange for the men's work services. Group marriage has not been a permanent characteristic of societal family patterns. Frequently, a polyandrous-allowing community takes on this form. It occasionally occurs during periods of societal turmoil and transition or in short time-span experimental forms, as was the case of the Oneida community in New York State from the 1840s to the 1880s and during briefer but well-publicized hippie communal groups of the late 1960s and early 1970s.

The family can be classified according to one point of reference. The family that one is born into and from which the individual receives his or her initial and most basic socialization is called the family of orientation. The family of procreation refers to the family established by the individual through marriage and having children. The salience of these different family forms leads us to our next categorization.

2. The family can be categorized in terms of the family formed:

Nuclear Family: husband, wife, and child(ren)

Extended Family: persons related by common descent

The other classifications of the family are based on the dominance and authority of family members, on the manner in which descent is reckoned, and on the residence of the nuclear family:

3. Authority:

Patriarchal   authority held by the male (eldest male, usually the father)

Matriarchal   authority held by the female (eldest female, usually the mother)

Equalitarian   husband and wife share equally

4. Descent

Patrilineal   names, property, obligations, and duties descend through father's line

Matrilineal   names, property, obligations, and duties descend through mother's line

Bilineal   names, property, obligations, and duties descend through both lines

5. Residence

Patrilocal   newly married couple reside with husband's consanguineal family

Matrilocal   newly married couple reside with wife's consanguineal family

Neolocal   newly married couple set up own household

In the structure of kinship, priority can be given to either marital relationships or generational relationships. The nuclear family is composed of a husband and wife and their children. An extended family is composed by combining nuclear families through the parent-child relationship. This results in family units of three or more generations—at least grandparents, parents, and children. Although the nuclear family is a recognizable unit in most societies, there is great variation in its autonomy. When it is relatively autonomous from extended family ties and when the marital bond is of primary importance, it is referred to as a *conjugal* family.

In contrast, when there is an emphasis on blood ties between generations or between siblings, the extended family is referred to as a *consanguineal* family. The nuclear family has less autonomy when it is part of a functioning consanguineal family system. In such circumstances it is inappropriate to refer to the nuclear family as a conjugal family.

Patriarchy, by far, is the most common authority arrangement. Older men have the right to make those decisions that affect the overall operation of the family and the community at large. Its prevalence is attributed to the males' size and strength and perhaps, most important, to the fact that men are not encumbered by pregnancy and the burdens of infant and child care.

Patriarchy does not only mean the subservience of women to men. It also means the submission and obedience of the young, both boys and girls, to the old. Where authority is based on age and kinship, children have little freedom and can take little initiative in determining their future. This includes the freedom of choosing marriage partners.

Bernard Farber (1964) points out that individuals' rights and obligations are specified through lineage membership. The reckoning of descent determines inheritance, authority, economic privilege, ceremonial and ritual rights of participation, choice of marital partners, and warfare and conflict alliances and opponents.

The most common form of descent, patrilineage, focuses on the man's lineage only. Men reckon their kinship obligations and duties through their father's relatives. They have minimal formal involvements with their mother's kinship groups. Women marry into their husband's family and their male children belong to their spouse's family.

Matrilineage is *not* the mirror image of patrilineal descent. Even though lineage is traced through the female line, authority and responsibility for the maintenance of the line is held by men (especially the mother's brother). The marital relationship has little significance. The biological father-ties to children are solely through affectional bonds. The maternal uncle serves as the predominant authority figure and is in fact the child's social father.

A second variation, pointed out by Farber (1964), that contrasts matrilineage from patrilineage is the role of the women vis-à-vis the man. The man in a matrilineal society retains supervisory obligation over his own lineage. However, the woman in a patrilineal system does not have these same rights. She does not take part in any of the decisions of her own lineage after she marries. The rationale is to enhance her incorporation into her husband's lineage group. Thus the woman in a patrilineal society does not have authoritative influence, nor does she have it in a matrilineal society.

Children, in the patrilineage, are the property of the father's lineage. They thus serve as the replacement population for that lineage. The wife's lineage has no rights to these children. In contrast, in matrilineal societies the wife's lineage in the person of her brother controls her children. Further, although the husband has the right of sexual access to his wife, he does not have the right to raise his children; he must raise his sister's children.

In societies characterized by consanguineal family relationships, upon marriage, which is usually arranged by the respective extended family systems, the couple usually resides in the residence of one of their families. The residential pattern is patrilocal when the couple resides within the husband's family home, or matrilocal when the couple resides within the wife's family home. In either case the married couple and their children are subservient to the larger extended family system. The emphasis is on the consanguineal organization and its continuation, as opposed to the autonomy of the nuclear family.

Farber (1964) sees marital rules of residence along with lineage as instrumental in delineating kinship continuity. Marital residence is important in that children can be supervised and socialized by the given lineage group. In the patrilocal situation, the wife comes as a stranger to live with her husband and his family. As a result she is at a distinct disadvantage in maintaining control over her children. The children are thus raised in the social traditions and the norms and values of her husband's family. The children have minimal contact and involvement with their mother's lineage. The reverse holds true in the matrilocal situation.

There are also rules of residence governing where children and youths are to reside. In some societies children are separated from their families as they mature. These societies are characterized by marked differentiation of age groups. During their earlier years boys reside with their parents. But as they get older they are separated from their parents and are reared in villages populated solely with their age cohorts. Such age differentiated societies are characterized by rigid rules, obligations, and duties that govern generational relationships with the younger generations subsumed under the authority of the older ones.

In summary, according to Murdock (1949), the majority of the world's societies have been characterized by an emphasis on the consanguineal family form and have extended kinship structures organized in blood-related clans or tribes. These extended kinship organizations have served as the major structural units in most societies of the world. Through kinship lineages, and authority and residence patterns, inheritance, economic and status patterns are determined. These controlled marital and sexual partnerships and relationships determine child rearing patterns.

CONCLUSION

This prefatory examination outlines the major cross-cultural variations and normative patterns governing family systems. It suggests why the family is of vital importance to the society and to the individual. It should be apparent that changes in the family either precipitated by internal factors or influenced by external processes of social change will have serious ramifications for a given society and its people. Social scientists have increasingly observed that there is now a worldwide trend toward varients of the conjugal family. These families are characterized by equalitarian patterns of authority, bilineal descent, and neolocal residence.

The sources of these changes stem from the major social, economic, religious, political, and familial upheavals that began making themselves felt on a universal scale in the nineteenth century. Our study begins with the examination of social change and the family systems existing in Western societies a century ago. Integral to this discussion is the analysis of sociological thought that not only sought to understand these changes but also became influential in directing that change in the nineteenth as well as in the twentieth century.

The Changing Family: Comparative Perspectives is divided into three main parts. In the first part, Chapters 2 and 3, we examine the main issues in the sociology of comparative family systems that have influenced both the discipline and the very phenomena it seeks to study: the family. An historical account of the development in comparative family analysis will be presented and related to the historical developments of Western societies. In addition, we will look at the major theoretical orientations used by sociologists to study social change, modernization, and the family.

Part Two of our discussion focuses on the family in relation to the community. We will be applying the theoretical orientation presented in the first three chapters to our later discussions. Chapter 4 is concerned with the family in cities of the Western world, with particular emphasis on the family in England and the United States. Chapter 5 aims to increase our understanding of urban family dynamics by seeing how they operate in a non-Western context in Africa. The family in Lagos, Nigeria, serves as the case in point. Chapter 6 looks at poverty conditions cross-culturally and their impact on the family. Poverty families in the United States and in Latin America are the center of attention here.

The third part of the book, Chapters 7 through 10, takes an in-depth look at sex roles, courtship, and marital relationships in changing societies. These chapters focus on topics of current interest. The first two chapters examine sex-role relationships in the context of dating, cohabitation, courtship, and mate-selection patterns. The following two chapters are concerned with sex-role relationships in the world of work and the world of the home. In addition to looking at preliterate societies, Africa, the Soviet Union, Sweden, and Israel provide the comparative illustrations in Chapter 9. Chapter 10 deals with the same issues but places particular stress on family patterns in the Western world. It builds on previous chapters and takes an historical approach to a better understanding of contemporary American marital relationships.

Part Four is composed of three chapters that deal with different aspects of generational relationships within the family. Chapter 11 examines changing fertility patterns and their influence on family dynamics. The headline-grabbing events of recent years in India regarding population-planning programs comes under scrutiny here. We then shift gears and examine what may be the most crucial stage of the family life cycle—the transition to parenthood. American social class variations are discussed and analyzed. Chapters 12 and 13 are centered around the theme of generational relationships as expressed through age differentiation and age stratification processes. First, we study childhood and adolescence, then in Chapter 13 we examine the elderly. The discussion of the relationship of the individual to the family and, in turn, to the community serves as an additional anchoring theme. Contrasts and comparisons between historical preliterate societies and industrial societies in the West are made. Historical changes in the West are also analyzed to help our understanding of contemporary American patterns.

The last part of the book is concerned with families in crisis and change. The emphasis in Chapter 14 is on two of the most dramatic manifestations of family violence—wife battering and child abuse. In our handling of family violence we emphasize how the structure of the contemporary Western conjugal family system plays a role in the manifestation of violence. The following chapter deals with divorce, single parenthood, and remarriage. We begin by examining the Arabic Islamic attitude and behavior toward divorce and contemporary changes in Egypt are analyzed. This is followed by a detailed investigation of changing divorce patterns in the United States. Such emerging issues as no-fault divorce, changing adjudication decisions on child custody, and the effects of divorce on children are discussed and analyzed. Single-parent households, the problems they face and solutions to these problems next gain our attention. We close this discussion with a detailed look at remarriage after divorce.

The concluding chapter of the book differs from the perfunctory summary chapters found in most textbooks. We apply the themes discussed in previous chapters to an analysis of a family system that we have only briefly discussed previously—the Chinese family. The usefulness of the theories introduced earlier in the book are put to the test by looking at changes in the Chinese family system. The analysis is on modernization processes, the family's relationship with the wider kinship networks and surrounding communities, premarital and marital relationships, divorce, and age and sex differentiation and stratification patterns. The subject matter is seen within the framework of one of the most significant and intriguing events of the twentieth century—the social revolution and cultural upheaval in China. However, we emphasize the need for caution in using China as the model for predicting the future of all family systems. China demonstrates the complexity of issues that underlie the study of social change and the family and provides a dramatic contrast to the American family.

This book is about families in change. We hope that it makes a contribution to the understanding of this phenomenon.

2

Comparative and Theoretical Perspectives: The Nineteenth Century

Sociological interest in the study of social change and the family was very strong in the mid-nineteenth century in Western Europe. There are a number of important factors to help account for this involvement. First, the social fabric of Western Europe and American society was undergoing major changes. Societies were rapidly industrializing and urbanizing. The old social class systems were being reworked and a new class structure was developing. Family relationships were also undergoing radical changes. The individual rights, duties, and obligations to the family and, in turn, to the larger community were being questioned and challenged.

A second impetus was the full development of Western colonial expansionism and imperialism. Unknown and hitherto unsuspected cultural systems with strange and diverse ways of life were being discovered and analyzed. Family systems were found to have differences almost beyond imagination.

Third, an intellectual revolution was occurring. The controversy surrounding evolutionary theory was sweeping Western Europe and America. It led to ramifications on the nature and place of the human species. It affected the traditional institutions of the church, the state, and the family. Coinciding with the doctrine of evolutionism was the development of individualism and democracy.

Developing out of this social and intellectual ferment was the application of evolutionary throught to the analysis and understanding of the social origins of the human species. This chapter is concerned with the resultant theories of social change and their applicability to the study of family change.

EVOLUTIONARY THEORY: THE SOCIAL DARWINISTS

Social Darwinism was characterized by nineteenth-century evolutionary theories and was associated with among others, the names of Herbert Spencer (*The Principles of Sociology*, 1897), J. J. Bachofen (*Das Mutterecht* [The Mother Right], 1861/1948), Henry Sumner Maine (*Ancient Law*, 1861/1960), and Lewis Henry Morgan (*Ancient Society*, 1877/1963). As Robert H. Lowie (1937) has pointed out, the idea of progressive development from stages of savagery to civilization was much older than Charles Darwin's *Origin of Species* (1859/n.d.). However, once the theory of evolution became the dominant force in explaining biological principles and prehistoric artifacts and fossils were also discovered, the social scientists of the nineteenth century quickly assimilated their earlier speculations about cultural changes into the evolutionary model. Thus both biological theory and archaeological research provided powerful stimulating forces to the study of society and culture. The basic argument was that since biological evolution proceeded by a series of stages (from the simple to the complex), the same process would hold for cultures. Thus the Social Darwinists shared in the basic assumption of unilinear evolution (the idea that all civilizations passed through the same stages of development in the same order); they, then, sought to apply the ideas of progressive development to social forms and institutions—a primary concern being the development of explanatory schemas on the evolution of marriage and family systems.

A second theme underlying the works of the Social Darwinists was the attitude that regarded civilized man as the antithesis of primitive man; if monogamy is the state of modern man, then, polygamy is the state of primitive man. Lowie (1937) believes that the theoretical position of the Social Darwinists was a rebuttal against the theologians who argued that primitive peoples had retrogressed from a higher level of civilization. The evolutionists argued, in rebuttal, that the history of organisms is one of progressive evolution from lower to higher forms. In the nineteenth century, evidence of the "backward" nature, or lower state of civilization, was seen in the newly discovered archaeological artifacts and in the institutions of nineteenth-century primitives—the Australian aborigines, the Indians of the Americas, or the black natives of Africa. Lowie's (1937) quotation from the works of the Darwinist, A. Lane-Fox Pitt-Rivers,[1] illustrates this:

> . . . the existing races, in their respective stages of progression, may be taken as the bona fide representatives of the races of antiquity. . . . They thus afford us living illustrations of the social customs, the forms of government, laws, and warlike practices, which belong to the ancient races from which they remotely sprang, whose implements,

---

[1]A. Lane-Fox Pitt-Rivers. 1916. *The Evolution of Cultural and Other Essays*. Oxford: Oxford University Press.

resembling, with but little difference, their own, are now found low down in the soil. . . . (Pitt-Rivers, cited in Lowie, 1937: 20−21)

The Social Darwinists differed concerning specific lines of development. Bachofen (1861/1948) argued that there was an historical stage of matriarchy where women ruled the society, whereas Maine (1861/1960) argued that a matriarchal stage of social evolution never existed. Yet the Social Darwinists generally agreed that the family evolved through certain natural stages. Their general approach was to search the literature—particularly the Bible, the Greek and Roman historians, and the existing cross-cultural literature gathered by rather unscientific and biased missionaries and travelers—in the hope of determining the origin and evolution of marriage, the family, and kinship systems.

The argument among evolutionists on the existence of a matriarchal stage of development went beyond academic historical interest. Ultimately, it centered on the nature of women's roles in nineteenth-century Western European and American societies. The different positions espoused by evolutionists reflected different beliefs on sex-role relationships and the differentiation of labor. These different theories had social and political implications for contemporary society. Feminists and socialists argued for the existence of the matriarchal stage to support their belief that nineteenth-century Western culture was exploitative of women. It would be instructive to present brief summaries of these arguments as expressed first in the patriarchal theory of Maine (1861/1960) and, then, in the matriarchal position of Morgan (1877/1963).

In 1861 Henry Sumner Maine (1822−1888) published *Ancient Law* in which he presented his patriarchal theory of the family. Maine took issue with the thesis on the historical existence of a matriarchal stage. He rejected the use of non-Western nineteenth-century primitive cultures as sources of data through which one could trace evolutionary universality. His analysis was limited to classical antiquity. From Greek, Roman, and Hebrew history, Maine concluded that the family's origin was patrilocal, patrilineal, and formally or informally polygymous.

On the basis of the evidence he found in ancient law, Maine advanced the patriarchal theory of society. Basically, it states that in classical antiquity society was organized in male-dominated households. The eldest man had supreme power, which extended to life and death decisions over his wife, children, and slaves. With changes in the Roman legal system (Justinian law), there was a gradual decline in the authority of the male head, which led to the increased freedom of the some from the father's influence and, ultimately, to the gradual freedom of women. Maine saw male-centered families as primitive and natural; female-centered families as a more recent phenomenon.

Maine's primary contribution lies in his analysis of the changing importance of kinship in the social evolution of societies from "status to contract." In primitive society, kinship provided the basic principle of organization. These kinship-dominated societies were characterized by group relations and tradition-determined rights and obligations. Over time, there was a movement to greater urbanization, with an accompanying lessening of the kinship bond. ''The contrast may be most forcibly expressed by saying that the unit of an ancient society was the Family, of a modern society the Individual'' (Maine, 1861/1960:99). Ancient societies were seen as emphasizing collectivity and were organized around the family. The individual was defined as one whose primary purpose was to support the collectivity and assure its continuity in succeeding generations. The family had collective ownership of property. Societies organized around individuals, individuals gained power at the expense of the family.

With the decline of familism, the state became stronger. Civil law began to take account of the individual, the family no longer was considered as the basic unit. According to Maine, the growth of power of the state combined with the ascendancy of the ideology of individualism would lead to the further demise of the family.

Maine sums up his position in his famous aphorism that the movement of progressive societies has hitherto been a movement from ''status to contract'' (Maine, 1861/1960:100). By *status* Maine means that members of the family have no power to acquire property, or bequeath it, or to enter into contracts in relation to it. By *contract* he refers to the capacity of the individual to enter into independent agreements with strangers. The individual no longer is legally bound and restricted by the family.

Maine elaborates on the changes in the roles of women as a consequence of this movement from status to contract. In ancient law a woman was subordinated to her blood relations. In modern jurisprudence she became subordinated to her husband. Maine believes that initially under Justinian law women gained personal proprietary independence. But with the advent of Christianity, there was a noticeable diminishing of women's liberty. Reacting against the perceived excesses of Roman society and favoring asceticism, the new faith strongly restricted the freedom of women and equality within marriage. Ultimately, however, Maine argues that, with the development of the state and the ascendancy of contract-based relations, both sexes will gain greater independence as the ideology of individualism gains in popularity.

In opposition to the patriarchal theory of Maine, Bachofen (1861/1948) and Morgan (1877/1963) formulated theories of evolution that postulated the existence of a matriarchal stage in which women dominated the family and the society. Unlike Maine, Bachofen and particularly Morgan incorporated the study of nineteenth-century primitive peoples into their developing theories. Their evolutionary theory was based on the convergence reported by ethnologists in the existence of matrilineal systems of relationships and matrilocal families among nineteenth-century hunting and gathering cultures. This fact as well as the classical historical documents [e.g., the Bible] that reported on the frequency of paternal families among pastoral peoples and in early civilizations led these scholars to hypothesize that the matriarchal family preceded the patriarchal family.

Lewis Henry Morgan (1818–1881) was an anthropologist who, unlike many of the armchair evolutionists of Europe, conducted field work among the Iroquois and other American Indian groups. Morgan saw societies moving through fixed series of stages, and he shares with other evolutionary theorists the notion of progress cumulating in Western industrial society. Morgan divided all human history into three broad stages of human progress: savagery, barbarism, and civilization. Each stage is characterized by the type of inventions that man used to gain subsistence. Morgan further argued that the development of technology, government, kinship and family patterns, and other institutions were traced through these stages and their substages. Thus the three substages of savagery range from the development of a fish subsistence to the knowledge of fire, to the invention of the bow and arrow. The three substages of barbarism proceed from the invention of the art of pottery to the domestication of animals, to the cultivation of maize and plants, to the invention of the process of smelting iron ore and the use of iron tools. Finally, the stage of civilization begins with the invention of a phonetic alphabet and the use of writing and proceeds to the present. A parallel classification is made of marriage and family forms. The family followed the following stages: promiscuity, punalua (group marriage), polygamy, and monogamy.

Richard P. Appelbaum (1970) has noted that Morgan's theory is descriptive rather than explanatory and that the descriptive analysis is frequently erroneous. Subsequent empirical research indicated that many societies do not fit the schema, that Morgan underemphasized cultural diffusion, and that some of the examples cited were incorrect. Marvin Harris (1968) criticizes Morgan for failing to link systematically the stages of kinship with the stages of technology and for not explaining why there should be a particular form of technology associated with a particular form of family system. More fundamentally, Morgan shares the same bias as the other Social Darwinists in believing that the apex of human civilization is found in Western industrial society.

In summary, the evolutionary theory of the Social Darwinists ostensibly dealt with such nonimmediate concerns as the origins and historical development of the family. But underlying their theorizing were implications for the roles of men and women in contemporary nineteenth-century family systems. Indeed, their twentieth-century evolutionary theory counterparts continue to put forth these same arguments—over a century later. The initiative for this rebirth of interest in the evolutionary reconstruction of family forms has been the development of arguments and counterarguments stemming from the concern of the women's movement with origins of patriarchy and male sexual dominance.

However, it was the nineteenth-century founders of communistic thought, Karl Marks (1818–1883) and Friedrich Engels (1820–1895), who made sex-role relationships the central and dominating concern of evolutionary theory. Although Engels was strongly influenced by the work of Morgan, he used it to address his primary concern—the social condition of the poor and working classes and the exploitation of men, women, and children.

Cavemen May Not Have Been All M.C.P.

Scholarly as well as popular thinking about the evolution of the male-female relationship has been that it started with the caveman dominating his mate. That may not be so; there is now an accumulation of evidence indicating that early man and woman may have shared power.

The evidence is in studies of hunter-gatherers, such as the Australian Aborigines, the !Kung bushmen in Africa and some Eskimos, all groups that live without agriculture and domestic animals. Because the culture of these groups is similar to that of man throughout much of human history, they are used by many anthropologists as models for clues about early social forms.

The latest to question the traditional thinking is anthropologist Richard Borshay Lee of the University of Toronto, who has done field work with the !Kung bushmen in Botswana. In a report in *The Archives of Sexual Behavior,* Mr. Lee writes that in hunter-gatherer groups, the men do the hunting but the women do the gathering of plant foods and fish, and are therefore neither economically nor politically dependent on the men.

Bushmen often take brides outside their own groups and, by custom, join the brides' groups as outsiders without influence based on blood kinship. The result, he says, is not a single male dominance but a multiplicity of aspects in male-female relationships.

Mr. Lee agrees that any attempt to reconstruct prehistoric society must be inexact, but he contends that "the hunter-gatherer data should make us view with suspicion any theory that seeks to prove that the male dominance in our present social order is part of an evolutionary heritage."

EVOLUTIONARY THEORY: THE MARXISTS

During this same period Karl Marx and Friedrich Engels shared and borrowed some of the evolutionary ideas of the Social Darwinists. They developed their own historical theory of the family. Marx and Engels, like the evolutionists, believed that structural differences among societies were to be accounted for by assuming they existed at different stages in the evolution of human civilization. Unlike their contemporaries, they placed primary emphasis on economics as a causal variable rather than on the ideational variables of art, magic, or religion.

Engels' work, *The Origin of the Family, Private Property and the State,*

(1884/1972) was profoundly influenced by Morgan's *Ancient Society* (1877/1963), for here was an independent corroboration of the materialistic interpretation of history. Morgan's work seemed to confirm the Marxist principle that social institutions change as a result of specific socioeconomic conditions at certain periods of history. Following Morgan's schema of the three main epochs of human history—savagery, barbarism, and civilization—Engels also borrowed Morgan and Bachofen's theory of the existence of an evolutionary theory linking the particular forms of technology with a particular form of family system.

Engels postulated a primitive natural democracy occurring in the first stage— savagery. Savagery was characterized by a primitive commune with no economic inequalities and no private ownership of properties. The family form was group marriage based on a matriarchy. This was followed by the overthrow of the matriarchally based society when men gained economic control over the means of production during the state of barbarism. Women, then, became subjugated to the masculine-dominated economic system in civilization. In this conceptualization such social institutions as the family were seen as almost totally dependent on economic relationships and as a means to combat the evils of prostitution (hetaerism); children and women were subjugated and forced to labor as a result of capitalistic exploitation. Engels argued that rather than monogamy being the apex of marital and family forms, it represented the victory of private property over original naturally developed common ownership; group marriage, and polygynous marital arrangements.

> Thus, monogamy does not by any means make its appearance in history as the reconciliation of man and woman, still less as the highest form of such a reconciliation. On the contrary, it appears as the subjection of one sex by the other, as the proclamation of a conflict between the sexes entirely unknown hitherto in prehistoric times. In an old unpublished manuscript, the work of Marx and myself in 1846, I find the following: "The first division of labour is that between man and woman for child breeding." And today I can add: the development of the antagonism between man and woman in monogamian marriage, and the first class oppression with that of the female sex by the male. Monogamy was a great historical advance, but at the same time it inaugurated, along with slavery and private wealth, that epoch, lasting until today, in which every advance is likewise a relative regression, in which the well-being and development of the one group are attained by the misery and repression of the other. (Engels, 1884/1972:74–75)

Engels goes on to speculate that with the coming of the socialist revolution and the next stage in the evolutionary division of labor, family relationships would be characterized by independence from property rights and women would have equal rights with men in decisions on the persistence and dissolution of their marriage. Shulamith Firestone (1970) has developed a table depicting Engel's evolutionary schema (Figure 1).

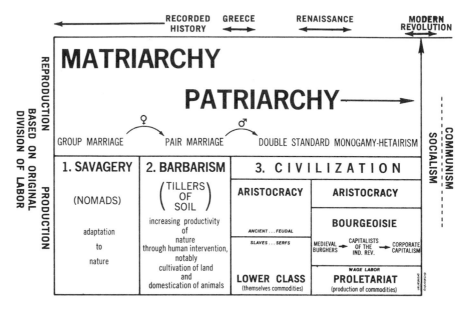

Figure 2.1 Shulamith Firestone's schematic presentation of Friederich Engel's interdevelopment of matriarchy to patriarchy and the division of labor on a time scale. (*Source:* Shulamith Firestone. 1970. *The Dialectic of Sex: The Case for Feminist Action.* New York: William Morrow, p. 5. Copyright © 1970 by Shulamith Firestone. Reprinted by permission of William Morrow & Company.

Engels' work has attracted the attention of some feminists who see in his analysis of patriarchal marriage and the family a positive statement addressed to the problems of women's liberation. Kate Millett (1970) states that Engels' theory of the existence of ancient matriarchies demonstrates that patriarchy is not inevitable and that the family must be treated as other historical institutions and social phenomena—subject to alteration and processes of evolution and change. Marxist-oriented feminists directly link the women's liberation movement with calls for a socialist revolution. Evelyn Reed,[2] a leading Marxist, writes:

> The renewed interest of women in his book is also a tribute to the value of the author's Marxist method. The outstanding merit of Engels's exposition is that he shows the real historical causes behind the catastrophic downfall of women and thereby illuminates the road ahead for female emancipation. The oppression of women came into existence for the same reasons and through the same forces that brought private property and class society into existence. It did not exist before that. But, as Engels indicates, class society is itself a transitory phenomenon, the product of specific economic

[2]*The Origin of the Family, Private Property and the State* by Friedrich Engels. Introduction by Evelyn Reed. Reprinted by permission of Pathfinder Press, Copyright © 1972.

conditions at a certain stage of social evolution. It has been—and will be—only a brief interlude in the forward march of humankind. Through further evolution—and socialist revolution—this oppressive system and its degradation of women will be done away with. (Reed in Engels, 1884/1972:22)

Engels' achievement is the exploration of the family as an economic unit and is of great theoretical importance in the study of the sociology of the family. But as Harris (1968) states, insofar as the Marxist orientation constituted a branch of evolutionary thought it was subjected to many of the same objections raised against it.

EVOLUTIONARY THEORY: CRITICISM

Evolutionary theory with its emphasis on large-scale, grand historical theorizing on the origins, evolution, and development of family forms lost its popularity by the end of the nineteenth century. Such theorists were criticized on a number of grounds. The concern of evolutionists with establishing evolutionary stages in the family form was rejected because of methodological weaknesses. The data collection was provided by inexperienced travelers and missionaries with minimal training in the social sciences. For many critics much of the ancient historical data was worthless:

> Considering how uncertain the information is which people give about the sexual relations of their own neighbours, we must be careful not to accept as trustworthy evidence the statements made by classical writers with reference to more or less distant tribes of which they evidently possessed very little knowledge. In the very chapter where Pliny states that among the Garamantians men and women lived in promiscuous intercourse he tells us of another African tribe, the Blemmyans, that they were said to have no head and to have the mouth and eyes in the breast. I have never seen this statement quoted in any book on human anatomy, and can see no reason to assume our author was so much better acquainted with the sexual habits of the Garamantians than he was with the personal appearance of the Blemmyans. (Westermark cited in Bardos, 1964:406–07[3])

Theoretically, the belief in unilinear evolution—that every society develops on a single continuum of evolution—is wrong. There are a great many evolutionary tracks that societies can follow. Evolutionary theory by its very nature tends to be ethnocentric and often racist. The decision as to which factor in society represents the greatest advancement of civilization is subjective. That is, if you measure the apex of civilization by examining technological criteria, Western society obviously

[3]Edward A. Westermarck. 1922. *The History of Human Marriage.* (Fifth ed, 3 vols.) New York: Macmillan. First published in 1891.

ranks on top; however, if you judge advancement by development of kinship classificatory systems, a hunting and gathering society (e.g., the Arunta of Australia) would rank at the top with Western society pretty low on the continuum. The kinship classificatory system of Western civilization is comparatively undeveloped compared to the Arunta. Not surprisingly, the Social Darwinists measured the advancement of civilization on a unilinear scale based on criteria that placed their own society as the most advanced.

The Social Darwinists made the fatal error of equating contemporary nonliterate cultures with the hypothetical primeval savage. They failed to understand that *all* contemporary peoples have had a prolonged and evolved past. The failure of many of them to have a written record of the past led the Social Darwinists to assume erroneously that they had none. Further, they did not understand that many nonliterate societies deemphasize changes in the past to stress their continuity with it. This is especially the case in cultures that glorify tradition and reify their sameness with their ancestors. Social Darwinists made ethnocentric and subjective pronouncements. They viewed their own society's art, religion, morals, and values according to their notions of what was good and correct. They explained such ''barbaric'' practices as polygamy and sexual promiscuity based upon their own national and individual norms. They biased their analysis with their own moral feelings on such customs.

Another factor in the decline of comparative analysis was the fact that the Marxists incorporated the evolutionary schema in their own theoretical framework. Contemporary evolutionary anthropologists, like Leslie White and Marvin Harris, believe that the linkage of Marxism and evolutionism—Engels' *The Origin of the Family, Private Property and the State* being a prime example—gave cause for anti-Marxist-oriented anthropologists to reject the evolutionary schema and the method that it was based on—comparative analysis.

One final factor in the decline of the evolutionary theory was that it was involved with an irrelevant set of questions. What difference does it make which theory you propose on the origin of marriage and family systems or which society represents the apex of civilization and which the nadir if it does not aid in understanding contemporary marriage and family systems? This is especially the case in a world undergoing revolutionary changes and one in which formerly isolated cultures are becoming more and more involved with Western civilization as a result of colonization. Anthropologists, particularly those representing the dominant school in America, the Boasian diffusionists, felt that attempts to theorize about the historical evolutionary process was not as important as examining the influences cultures had on each other. The basic position taken was that societies did not evolve in isolation but rather that they continuously interacted with each other and were constantly influencing each other. Thus it was felt to be imperative to examine cultures that were being increasingly Westernized. Margaret Mead, in her autobiography, underscores the basic motivation of Boas and his followers:

. . . the materials on which the new science depends were fast vanishing, and forever. The last primitive peoples were being contacted, missionized, given new tools and new ideas. Their primitive cultures would soon become changed beyond recovery. Among many American Indian groups, the last old women who spoke a language that had developed over thousands of years were already senile and babbling in their cups; the last man who had ever been on a buffalo hunt would soon die. The time to do the work was *now*. (Mead, 1975:138)

Many European and American social scientists of the later nineteenth and early twentieth centuries had a more immediate concern. They were appalled by the excesses of industrial and urban society and the calamitous changes in the family system. The study of social change and the family centered on this concern. It is these concerns and how social scientists analyzed and dealt with them to which we now address our attention.

CONTEMPORARY CRITICS OF NINETEENTH-CENTURY WESTERN SOCIETY

European societies during the nineteenth century were undergoing massive changes. The old social order anchored in kinship, the village, the community, religion, and old regimes was under attack and falling to the twin forces of industrialism and revolutionary democracy. The sweeping changes had particular effect on the family. There was a dramatic increase in such conditions as poverty, child labor, desertions, prostitution, illegitimacy, and abuse of women. These conditions were particularly evident in the newly emerging industrial cities. The vivid writings of such novelists as Charles Dickens in *Oliver Twist* and *Hard Times* provide startling portraits of a harsh new way of life.

Both radical and conservative critics of the new social order saw the decline in the importance of kinship and community involvements and the changes in the makeup of the nuclear family as more important areas of investigation than the study of the evolutionary transformations of the family. The radicals, as typified in the writings of Marx and Engels, saw the necessity for the overthrow of the new capitalist-based industrial system to establish equality between the sexes. The conservatives, Frédéric Le Play (1806–1882) being the most important to family study, called for the reestablishment of the old social order. Many of the family issues raised by these ideologically opposing camps are relevant to the analysis of the contemporary family system. It is highly important to see how these theorists examined the pressures on the family created by the social changes that were transforming Western European and American societies.

If one removes the evolutionary trappings from the works of Marx and Engels, especially the Morgan-derived anthropological analyses and speculations on the family in antiquity, one is left with an outstanding critique of mid-nineteenth-century family life. Indeed, this insightful analysis has been most influential in the understanding of later twentieth-century family dynamics.

Marx and Engels examined changes on the nuclear family that were instituted with the rise of industrial and monopolistic capitalism. The new economic system separated work from the home. In the domestic economy of preindustrial Europe, work and family activities were integrated in the household. Husband, wife, and children were all involved in economic production. With the change in the economic order, small landholdings and businesses were lost and the men became wage earners in factories. As men became dependent on their bosses, the more fortunate women and children became dependent on their husbands and fathers. The poorest and most unfortunate women and children worked as marginal laborers in the mills, factories, and mines under exploitative condtions for wages that were barely subsistent.

The new economic system was particularly harsh on women. Those who had husbands to provide for them were domestically confined to household tasks and child-care chores. The gradual loss of women's economic independence led to an increased division of labor between men and women and to the subservience of women to men. In the domestic economy of preindustrial society, women had a public role; in the capitalistic industrial society, women had a private role. In the following passage, Engels spells out the implications of the development of the ''private'' family for women and what is necessary to assure the independence and equality of women:

> . . . her being confined to domestic work, now assured supremacy in the house for the man: the woman's housework lost its significance compared with the man's work in obtaining a livelihood; the latter was everything, the former an insignificant contribution. . . . the emancipation of women and their equality with men are impossible and must remain so long as women are excluded from socially productive work and restricted to housework, which is private. The emancipation of women becomes possible only when women are enabled to take part in production on a large, social scale, and when domestic duties require their attention only to a minor degree. (Engels, 1884/1972:152)

In summary, the privatization of the family becomes the key conceptualization in the Marxian analysis of the family. The withdrawal of the family from economic and community activities led to the development of inequality within the family. This inequality was based on the sexual differentiation of labor and the different family roles for men and women. As we will see throughout this book, the study of privatization in the family becomes for us, too, a key conceptualization in the analysis of social change and the family.

Frédéric Le Play, a leading exponent of political conservatism, was profoundly influenced by the effects of the industrial and democratic revolutions on Western society. A devout Catholic, he was appalled by the loss of power and prestige of the family, church, and local community. He strongly reacted against what he saw as the atomizing effects of such forces as technology, industrialization, and the division of labor. He cared less to develop grand evolutionary theories than to react against the growing decline of the extended family and the instability of the nuclear family.

Le Play was a French engineer, administrator, and social reformer. He and his followers, in a half century of unbelievably ambitious work, studied the nature of the family and its relationship to the surrounding community. His magnum opus, *Les Ouvrier Européens (The European Workers)* was published in 1855 and is a comprehensive comparative analysis of more than 300 working-class families who are representative of those who labor in characteristic industries and are from typical localities all over Europe and parts of Asia. Le Play's work was a forerunner of many twentieth-century methodological techniques. He created his own instruments of data collection. These included social surveys, research interviews, family-budget questionnaires, participant-observation methods, and case-history methods. The contemporary American sociologist, Robert A. Nisbet, refers to this work as "the supreme example in the nineteenth century of actual field study of the traditional community, its structure, relation to environment, component elements, and disorganization by the economic and political forces of modern history" (Nisbet, 1966:62).

The European Workers places great stress on the familial form and seeks to demonstrate that the major outlines of any society are set by its underlying type of family. The family types that are characterized by a high degree of stability, commitment to tradition, and security of the individual are delineated. Also dealt with are family systems undergoing disorganization. In the analysis of French families, secularism and individualism are seen as destroying the bases of tradition and community and rupturing the relations between tradition and the family.

Three dominant types of families are recognized by Le Play: (1) the patriarchal or extended family, (2) the unstable or nuclear family, and (3) the stem family. The patriarchal family is authoritarian and based on tradition and lineage. It is common among pastoral people, such as the Russian peasants and the Slavonic peasants of central Europe. The father has extensive authority over all his unmarried sons and daughters and is the sole owner of the family property. The patriarchal authority of the family occurs where there is a minimal of extended political and social authority. Such a family system is seen as incompatible with political and modern systems.

The unstable family is seen to prevail among working populations who live under the factory system of the West. This type of family was also common during other historical periods of great instability, such as in ancient Athens after its disastrous wars with Sparta and other Greek states and in the later Roman Empire. This family type is seen to be inherently disorganized and is the prime cause of social disorganization. It is strongly individualistic, mobile, and secular. "Where individualism becomes dominant in social relations men rapidly move towards barbarism'' (Le Play cited in Zimmerman and Frampton, 1966:14).

The unstable family shows little attachment to family lineage. It has no roots in property and is an unstable structure from generation to generation. It is associated with the pauperization of working-class populations under the new manufacturing regime in the West.

> Under this regime the individual, single or married, finding it no longer necessary to provide for the needs of his relatives, rapidly attains a high position, if he is capable. On the contrary, if he is incapable or unfortunate he is not able to call upon any family help in case of need. Thus, he falls more quickly into a miserable condition. Unhappily, this depraved condition tends to perpetuate itself because parents can no longer contribute further to the establishment of their children, or because the children are not under parental guidance. Thus is formed that peculiar social state which history has not often disclosed before—pauperism. (Le Play cited in Zimmerman and Frampton, 1966:15)

The stem family is seen as the happy compromise between the two other types. It is free of the authoritarianism of the patriarchal family, but it is still rooted in traditionalism. It is stable in structure and committed to perpetuating the family lineage. It, however, joins only one married child to the household, the others are independently established with shares of the inheritance and are free to found their own households or to remain in an unmarried state on the family land. The stem family is seen to arise partly from traditional influences of patriarchal life, but it finally forms itself under the influence of individually owned property. It is found in Scandinavia, Hannover (West Germany), northern Italy, and to some extent in England. This system ensures the continuation of the ancestral household and also encourages individual autonomy, new enterprises, and new personal property. Le Play sees it as combining the best features of the patriarchal system with the individualism of the unstable family form.

> It satisfies both those who are happy in the situation of their birth and those who wish to advance socially or economically. It harmonizes the authority of the father and the liberty of the children. . . . The stem-family satisfies both tendencies and harmonizes two equally imperative needs—the respect for tradition and the yearning for the new. . . . The stem-family, indeed, answered all the legitimate instincts of humanity. This is the reason why public order prevails everywhere it exists in strength. (Le Play cited in Zimmerman and Frampton, 1966:15−16, 20)

Each family type, then, is seen to be related to other types of institutions in the community. Le Play's central concern is the ties uniting the family with other parts of the community—religion, government, education, and economy. His analysis of the family is intertwined with the analysis of the community in which the family finds itself. It is this insightful perspective that has made Le Play's work stand out in the history of family analysis. His conservative orientation, although distasteful to many contemporary social scientists, should not obscure the importance of his empirical findings on the economic basis of family and community life.

The family issues raised by Marx and Engels and by Le Play still are the central core of contemporary analysis of social change and the family. Both the radical perspective and the conservative perspective are highly critical of the emerging family form of the nineteenth century. Marx and Engels refer to it as the monogamous family characterized by the privatization of family life. Le Play refers to it as the unstable family.

Robert A. Nisbet (1966) has provided us with a highly useful comparison of Le Play and Marx. His work provides a concise summary of their respective positions. Both were aghast at the bourgeoisie democracy of the nineteenth century. Rather than providing for liberty and prosperity, it was seen as leading to disabling competition and strife. Both sought social orders that would remove the excesses of bourgeoisie democracy and the evils of industrialism. Yet the differences stemming from their opposing ideologies lead to different assessments and conclusions.

> Both Le Play and Marx were sensitive to the institutional component in history, but beyond this generic likeness there is only stark contrast. For Marx the key institution is social class. For Le Play it is kinship: the structure of society varies with the type of family that underlies it. Marx detested private property, Le Play declared it the indispensable basis of social order and freedom. Marx treated religion as something superfluous to an understanding of human behavior and, in its effects, an opiate. For Le Play religion is as essential to man's mental and moral life as the family is to his social organization. For Marx, the whole rural scheme of things is tantamount to idiocy as far as its impact on human thought is concerned. Le Play, for all his conscious acceptance of industry, plainly prefers rural society, seeing in it the haven of security that urban life, by its very nature, must destroy. Marx was socialist; Le Play put socialism, along with mass democracy, secularism, and equalitarianism, among the major evils of his time—all of them unmistakable signs of social degeneration. (Nisbet, 1966:67)

It is the tensions between the radical perspective and the conservative perspective that echoes throughout the contemporary analysis of the family in change. It takes different forms depending on different substantive issues. But, taken together, they can be seen as critical perspectives questioning the nature and makeup of contemporary family systems and their relationships with the individuals that compose them and the communities that surround them.

The concerns voiced by conservatives and radicals in the nineteenth century have their counterparts in the twentieth century. One notable attempt to update the conservative position of Frédéric Le Play in the mid-twentieth century was the position represented in the works of Carle C. Zimmerman (1897–   )

Zimmerman: Family and Civilization (1947)

Carle C. Zimmerman's (1947) theory of social change and the family differs from that of the evolutionists in that he posits a cyclical theory of change. He opposed the view that family systems can be analyzed in terms of evolutionary stages. Rather, he proposes a theory of cyclical movements of families occurring in giant historical swings or cycles. Zimmerman also differs from the Social Darwinists in his rejection of cross-cultural comparative analysis; instead, he posits that the study of contemporary non-Western family systems is irrelevant to the study of Western civilization. He believed that the study of non-Western family forms would not aid in the explanation of the social and family changes of Western civilization in that they were not predecessors of Western society nor did they represent earlier stages of development—an explicit rejection and refutation of the notion of unilinear evolution.

Zimmerman postulated a theory of a cyclical movement of families through a sequence of three main family types—the trustee family, the domestic family, and the atomistic family. He argues that the cycle of development is reversible, especially in the case of atomistic and domestic families, and that the three family types can coexist at a given point in time. He believes that these three types of family systems differ primarily in the power of the family, the width of its field of action, and the amount of social control it can exercise in the given society. As J. Ross Eshleman states, the questions with which Zimmerman was concerned take the following form:

> . . . of the total power in the society, how much belongs to the family? What role does the family play in the total business of society? If individuals want to marry or break up a family, whom do they consult—the family, the church, or the state? If a rule is violated does the family, the church, or the state dispense the punishment? (Eshleman, 1978:116)

Zimmerman (1949) graphically depicted the cyclical theory in his book, *The Family of Tomorrow: The Cultural Crisis and the Way Out* (see Figure 2.2) He pegs his theory to Western historical epochs.

The trustee family controls through power and dominates the individual. The individual's rights and privileges are subordinate to the family group. Individuals owe their primary obligations and duties to the family. The family and kin groups control the wealth, property, and rights of its members. In societies where the trustee family is dominant, the state is organized primarily in terms of kinship obligations, with the family taking on the responsibility of governing, protecting, supporting, and disciplining its members. Historically, this type of family system is seen to have been predominant in ancient Greece and Rome and in the period after the decline of the Roman Empire.

The domestic family, is seen as the second family type, one that shares power

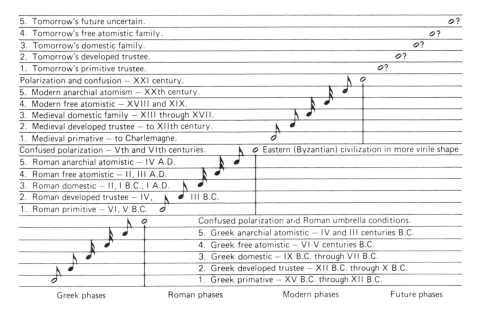

Figure 2.2. Carle C. Zimmerman's cycles of cultural determination for the Western family system since 1500 B.C. Change occurs in giant historical cycles—Greek, Roman, Medieval, Modern, and Tomorrow's. All end on a "whole note" of confusion with no cultural pattern predominating. As a given cycle wanes, the centrality of the family diminishes. *Source:* Carle C. Zimmerman. 1949. *The Family of Tomorrow: The Cultural Crisis and the Way Out.* New York: Harper & Row, p. 218. Copyright 1949 by Harper & Row, Publishers, Inc. (Reprinted by permission of the publisher.)

with the state or church. The family still remains a strong unit, maintaining many of the powers over the individual that it had under the trustee-type system. When the domestic family type is in ascendancy there is a balance between the power of the state and the power of the family; the state does not replace the family but rather restricts the rights of the family to punish its members. The development of individual rights and the conceptualization of divorce, both limiting family authority, characterize domestic family ascendancy.

The third family type, the atomistic family, is a resultant of the emergence of state power and the philosophy of individualism; the power and latitude of the family is reduced to a minimum. Atomistic family systems arise when the individual is freed from the controls of the family and the church and when the cultural incentive of the society is the pursuit of private and public goals of individualism. A prime illustration for understanding this type of family system is the attitude toward illegitimate children versus legitimate children. In the trustee family system the negative stigma attached toward illegitimacy results frequently in the destruction of the bastard; whereas in the atomistic family system, the bastard is now legally afforded the same rights and privileges of the legitimate child by the state.

Zimmerman believes that the atomistic family is characteristic of contemporary society, with marriage and family obligations having minimal obligations on the individual and where the individual's major responsibilities are linked to the law and the government. The following quote summarizes his basic view on the atomistic family system:

> The Zimmerman theory is that the climax of a modern civilization is one in which the family system has lost much of its power to control the individual. In such a case there tends to rise an inability or unwillingness of the family to control the individual to sacrifice for the family. Hence a vast increase of confusion arises which is associated with desertions, divorces, juvenile delinquencies, the increased dependency of individuals upon public relief, the decay of former sex mores, and the inability of larger and larger portions of the social system, keyed to family life, to function at all well. This, according to Zimmerman, is a state of social distress which can only lead to one or the other of two logical ends. One of these is suggested as a vast increase in alienation and anomie. These spread like epidemics in all parts of the culture, weakening it and, in time, making social survival extremely difficult. The other is that many members of the society recognize the impending condition and try to avoid it. This leads to a condition called "Polarization" in which one part of the society tries to avoid the other so that necessary family life can be held together. If this movement succeeds eventually new leadership takes over in the society and the social system gets a new lease upon life. But, in the meantime, there are the most violent differences between the segments of the system. One part of the society becomes more and more creative and the other part tries to make all former types of "abnormalities" normal and acceptable. Thus one can witness the greatest "good" and the greatest "evils" appearing simultaneously. The word "atomistic" family applies to this situation in that the conventional mores lose their general significance and each family and individual has to make its own choice. (Zimmerman, 1970:11)

In critiquing Zimmerman's work we should first make note of the great sweep of his historical analysis—the history of Western society from approximately 1500 B.C. to the present. Gerald R. Leslie (1979) observes that the very vastness of this erudite analysis prevents lesser men from adequately assessing the adequacy and reliability of his work. Thus there is reluctance to accept it as adequately proven. Leslie further argues that Zimmerman's exclusion of cross-cultural comparative data from preliterate societies in his examination of social origins of family systems is open to question; that is, it cannot be proven that Zimmerman is correct or that he is wrong in his judgment that cross-cultural data is irrelevant.

Zimmerman can be taken to task based on another criterion. Although Zimmerman's basic theory of social change falls into the cyclical model, he also posits what Don Martindale describes as "the fall from the Garden of Eden" theory:

The theory has been entertained that social and cultural changes do occur, but primarily for the worse. The Golden Age (Garden of Eden) of society and culture is in the past. Mankind is moving step by step toward some horrible end. (Martindale, 1962:1)

Zimmerman is a prime defender of the nonatomistic family system. Reading Zimmerman one gets the feeling that the atomistic family system will lead to the downfall of civilization. This rather explicit value position has "turned off" many of his contemporaries especially those who believe that the more traditional family system, rather than being on the whole positive, was the primary source denying individual rights and freedoms. The problem in assessing Zimmerman, then, is compounded by his valuational orientation in his theory of social change and the family.

AMERICAN FAMILY SOCIOLOGY: LATE NINETEENTH AND EARLY TWENTIETH CENTURY

Toward the end of the nineteenth century and through the early twentieth, sociology in the United States shifted its emphasis away from the study of evolution to the study of social problems and the advocacy of social reform. The social reform movement's paramount concern was the study of the family in the context of the abuses of rapid industrialization and urbanization. The emphasis switched from the development of theories of family systems to the more urgent concerns of individual families and their members—illegitimacy, prostitution, child abuse, prostitution, and other resultant abuses, which were seen as arising from nongovernmental supervision of industrial and urban institutions. This underlying assumption about the causes of social problems was held by the social reform movement's major advocate, the Chicago School of Sociology, and is reflected in the following quotation from its journal, the *American Journal of Sociology* (founded in 1894): "we understand both the family and the effects of urban and industrial developments; what we must do is solve the resulting problems and strengthen the family" (cited in Adams, 1975:5).

The University of Chicago dominated much of twentieth-century American sociology. The Chicago School of Sociology—under the chair of Robert E. Park and with such important sociologists as Ernest W. Burgess, E. Franklin Frazier, Louis Wirth, W. I. Thomas, and Florian Znaniecki—played a pivotal role in the development of American family sociology and urban sociology. In addition, Chicago was blessed by the presence of such important intellectuals as Thorstein Veblen, John Dewey, and George Hebert Mead. Chicago also saw the blossoming of the social welfare and social reform activities of Jane Addams, Graham Taylor, and other settlement workers. Their work increased the empirical data base on city life. The Chicago School served as the intellectual nexus for the study of urban life and dynamics.

We will devote much of Chapter 4 to the analysis of the contributions and limitations of the Chicago School in the study of urban family systems. Here, let us briefly acquaint the reader with the Chicago School's general theoretical orientation. The Chicago School developed a distinct contrast between urban life and rural life. Following intellectual biases in sociology as well as in the larger society, the Chicago School developed an implicit antiurban model of city life. They saw traditional patterns of life being broken down by debilitating urban forces. The result was social disorganization, with the family being particularly affected.

One theme picked up by the Chicago School was the loss of family functions as a result of urbanized and industrialized society. Its leading exponent was William F. Ogburn (1886–1959). The breakdown of traditional culture saw the development of a new type of family life, one divested of much of its functions—economic, educational, religious, protective, and recreational. This new family emphasized personality functions. This position on the transformation of family functions was developed and expanded so that it became a major cornerstone in much of structure functionalist analysis of the family.

Ogburn's Theory of Social Change and the Family

William F. Ogburn's work has had an important impact on American sociology— the sociology of the family in particular—from the publication in 1922 of *Social Change*, to 1955 when his last major work, *Technology and the Changing Family*, was published with the collaboration of Meyer F. Nimkoff. Ogburn's primary concern was with the processes of social change. His contribution to sociology lies in the distinction he made between *material* culture (technology, factories, machines, transportation, etc.) and *adaptive* culture (values, ideas, attitudes, customs, etc.). He argued that the real sources of progressive change were found in material innovations with customs, beliefs, and philosophies adapting themselves to the material substructure. The fact that the adaptive culture follows the material culture led Ogburn to postulate the hypothesis of *culture lag*—changes in the material culture occur and cause changes in the adaptive culture that result in continuous social maladjustment between the two types of culture.

The particular interest of this for students of the family lies in Ogburn's ideas about the processes of social change and the impact of technology, innovations, and ideologies on family systems. Applying this theory to the family, the argument is made that the family system changes as a result of technological changes; the family, then, is an example of adaptive culture. This is the dominant theme of the Ogburn and Nimkoff historical study of the American family: "In this book . . . a single institution, has been chosen and upon it are recorded the influences coming from many different inventions and scientific discoveries" (Ogburn and Nimkoff, 1955:iv).

Ogburn and Nimkoff present the argument that inventions and discoveries of modern technological society have led to the decline of the family's economic, educational, recreational, religious, and protective functions. This was in disaccord with the satisfactory adjustment of the family during the earlier history of America, which was dominated by an agricultural economy. In their text, after consultation with 18 prominent American sociologists, a virtual "who's who" of family sociology, they presented a list of the significant changes in the American family systems. This list served as a prime illustration of the effect of cultural lag:

1. Increasing divorce rate.
2. Wider diffusion of birth control and decline in family size.
3. Decline in authority of husbands and fathers.
4. Increase in sexual intercourse apart from marriage.
5. Increase in number of wives working for pay.
6. Increasing individualism and freedom of family members.
7. Increasing transfer of protective functions from family to state.
8. Decline of religious behavior in marriage and family.

In summarizing the work of Ogburn and Nimkoff we concur with the assessment of Leslie (1979). Leslie believes that the strength of Ogburn's work does not lie primarily in his theoretical formulations but in his exhaustive descriptions of the changed relations of the family and other institutional structures, which he documented for more than three decades: the increased participation of government, economic enterprises, education, and so on, in the once private domain of the family.

The major theoretical criticism of Ogburn's works lies in his oversimplification of the notions of material and adaptive cultures, his overemphasis on resistances to changes in the area of adaptive culture, and his under-emphasis on the resistances in the area of material culture. Sociologists of the family have particularly criticized his work because it views the family as a passive recipient adapting to changes in the materialistic culture which is viewed as the active causal agent. They believe[4] that the family may itself be a causal faction in the rate and growth of materialistic culture. One final point—Ogburn and Nimkoff's position on the loss of family functions has become a primary investigatory concern in the study of the family and social change, as we will see in subsequent chapters.

Ernest W. Burgess and Symbolic Interactionism

At the same time that the Chicago School was making its influence felt in American sociology, another approach was developing that focused on the examination of the internal relationships of family members. This new orientation centered on the

---

[4]See in particular William J. Goode's 1963 study, *World Revolution and Family Patterns.*

organization of roles in family life; for example: What is the role of the father or mother in the family structure? Two major conceptual frameworks developed during this period—structure functionalism and symbolic interactionism. Symbolic interactionism dominated much of early twentieth-century sociology with structure functionalism serving a similar role in the period after World War II.

Symbolic interactionism as applied to the study of the family is a social psychological perspective that emphasizes the various forms of family interactional patterns: courtship, the honeymoon period, child-rearing practices, divorce and separation, the role of the elderly, and so on. Charles Horton Cooley, George Herbert Mead, W. I. Thomas, and especially Ernest W. Burgess (who spoke of the family as ''a unity of interacting personalities'') developed this perspective. Symbolic interaction made important methodological contributions to the study of the family. These include the social survey, interview and questionnaire schedules, and participant observation.

The focus of symbolic interaction is on the study of the family as a small-scale social phenomenon. It became almost completely devoted to the study of the American middle-class family structure. Symbolic interactionists were not as involved with the impact of larger societal institutions and processes on the family. Ernest W. Burgess (1886–1965), however, does pick up on the work of his colleague, William F. Ogburn, to explain the shifting of traditional functions of the family to outside agencies. Industrialization and urbanization are seen as primarily responsible for this shift. Burgess observes that the economic, educational, recreational, health-protection, and religious functions of the family were being transformed to other institutions. The family was left with the functions of achieving the happiness and the personal growth of its members. The family now rested on ''mutual affection, the sympathetic understanding, and comradeship of its members' (Burgess and Locke, 1945:vii).

This shift in family functions led to Burgess's famous classification of family types as moving from ''institution to companionship.'' According to this conceptualization, the institutional family is one in which the unity is determined entirely by traditional rules and regulations, specified duties and obligations, and other historical social pressures impinging on family members. The extended patriarchal type of family most closely approximates the institutional family. It is authoritarian and autocratic. It demands the complete subordination of each family member and their spouses and children to the authority of the husband or eldest male (the patriarch). The emphasis is on compliance with duty and the following of tradition. Marriages are arranged with the emphasis on prudence, on economic and social status, and the subordination of the married couple to the extended family group.

The companionate or democratic family is the recently emerging family type. It has moved away from an institutional character towards a ''unity which develops out of mutual affection and intimate association of husband and wife and parents and children'' (Burgess and Locke, 1945:27). This type of family includes affection as a basis for its existence, equal status and authority between the spouses, equalitarian decision making, and the sharing of common interests and activities, coexisting with divisions of labor and individuality of interests. According to Burgess, the institutional family is sustained by external community pressures and involvements. The companionate family, on the other hand, is sustained by the emotional attachments among its members.

CONCLUSION

This chapter is concerned with the development of sociological interest in the study of social change and the family. For almost 50 years (1850–1900), Social Darwinism dominated the study of the family. It applied an evolutionary perspective to the analysis and understanding of the social origin of the human species. Social Darwinsin was concerned with comparative analysis through the emphasis on large-scale historical and cross-cultural theory on the origins, evolution, and development of family forms.

This theoretical perspective had social and political implications. It provided "scientific" legitimation for Western imperialistic colonization and exploitation of "primitive" peoples. It provided supportive guidelines for the treatment of the poorer classes of American and Western European societies. It also had implications for the roles of men and women in nineteenth-century family systems. We pointed out how the communistic theory of Karl Marx and Friedrich Engels made sex-role relationships the dominating concern of evolutionary theory. They provided an alternative evolutionary explanation that reflected different beliefs on the nature of women's roles, on sex-role relationships, and on the sexual division of labor.

By the end of the nineteenth century, Social Darwinism was no longer the primary theory of students of the family. The methodological weaknesses of the approach, its explicit value assumptions on the superiority of Western family forms, and the rejection of the theory of the unilinear evolutionary development of the family were all contributing factors. The Marxist branch of evolutionary theory was likewise rejected when it was subjected to many of the same theoretical and methodological objections. However, it has reappeared in recent years through its proponents in the women's movements who link the subjugation of women with capitalism and the privatization of the monogamous family.

Towards the later nineteenth and early twentieth century the focus of the sociology of the family shifted. It was now dominated by the issues of social reform, which was an outgrowth of what was viewed as the excesses of industrial and urban society and the calamitous changes in the family system. We highlighted our discussion by comparing the conservative perspective of Frédéric Le Play with the radical perspective of Marx and Engels. We indicated how these two schools developed alternative and opposing viewpoints and solutions to their common perception of the evils of the emerging family form—Le Play's unstable family and

Marx and Engels' privatized family. Both were highly critical of the emerging family form, its treatment of family members, and its relationship to the surrounding community.

We concluded by noting that American sociologists turned to the study of internal family dynamics, paying little attention to the broader issues of social change during the first 50 years of the twentieth century. Yet a significant segment of American sociology continued to wrestle with the themes and issues raised by conservatives and radicals in the nineteenth century. The theories of Carle C. Zimmerman, William F. Ogburn, and Ernest W. Burgess (with Harvey J. Locke) were discussed for their contemporary significance.

In summary, until the end of World War II American sociology was characterized by an almost complete cessation of interest in large-scale comparative analysis. The interests and concerns of the Chicago School and of the symbolic interactionists was picked up and developed by the dominating perspective of the postwar era, that of structure functionalism. An offshoot of structure functionalism, "modernization theory," attempted to reestablish the importance of cross-cultural and historical analysis of social change and the family. In the next chapter we will examine this perspective.

3

Comparative and Theoretical Perspectives: The Twentieth Century

In the previous chapter we presented an historical overview of the development of comparative family sociology. Since the mid-nineteenth century there has been a vacillation of interest in cross-cultural family research. It reached a peak during the second half of the nineteenth century, a drop in interest during the first half of the twentieth century, and a return to comparative study since World War II. In this chapter we will investigate some of the factors that help to account for the current interest in cross-cultural study. We will be looking at the dominant perspective, modernization theory, and at its strengths and weaknesses. We will conclude the chapter with the presentation of what we believe are the most profitable conceptualizations for the examination of processes of social change and the family.

The rebirth of interest in comparative studies has two prime sources. The first is an intellectual rebellion against the limitation of the rigorous empirical methods emphasized during the early twentieth century. The development of this methodology, frequently statistical in nature, was used to investigate small-scale social phenomena and paid little attention to social change and its consequences for the family. American sociologists limited their analysis to their own society, ignored other societies and cultures, and left comparative analysis to the other social sciences, particularly anthropology. The second factor that stimulated comparative analysis was the revived interest in social change. The postwar period was marked by rapid dissolution of the colonial empires of the Western industrial societies and the concomitant transformation of what Westerners called underdeveloped or backward societies. In addition, Western societies were also undergoing processes of social change. What was becoming particularly clear was that "scientific" sociological study of the family was not able to come to grips with the dominant social issues and problems of contemporary times. The sociology of the family was dominated by two conceptual frameworks, structure functionalism and symbolic interactionism. The symbolic interaction framework has not been involved with the study of social change. It has, by and large, focused on internal family dynamics as opposed to examining the family in relation to other institutions in a given society. Structure functionalism, on the other hand, and its offshoot, modernization theory, have been involved in this endeavor as well as in cross-cultural and historical analysis of social change and the family. However, as we will demonstrate, its frame of reference is inadequate to study family change.

STRUCTURE FUNCTIONALISM, MODERNIZATION THEORY, AND FAMILY CHANGE

The structure functionalist perspective tends to see society as an organism that strains toward maintaining itself in some form of balance—it is an equilibrium model. The concern is with the functional connections among the various parts of a system, whether the society or the family. For example, it views the family as a social system. Its constituent parts, husband-father, wife-mother, and children are bound together by interaction and interdependence. It is concerned with whether any given part is either functional or dysfunctional to the family. That is, whether it adds or subtracts from the system's operation. Stability and order are implicitly viewed as being natural and normal. Conflict and disorder are seen as being deviant phenomena and as evidence that the system is not working properly.

The inherent problems of structure functionalism is in its handling of social change. It stems from its emphasis on consensus and cooperation, its failure to acknowledge the possibiltiy of conflicting interests of constituent elements in a social system, and its reification of the status quo. The structure functionalist perspective does not lend itself readily to explain or describe the phenomena of social change. When the system, whether it is a society or the family, is reified and is seen as being in a state of equilibrium, one can only emphasize slow, orderly change. Conflict and rapid social change are regarded as pathological trends and the only source of change is by outside agents. Marvin Scott states that structure functionalism is its attempt to study social change falls prey to the evolutionary hangover of "functional ahistoricism" (Scott, 1970:22). Structural functionalists proceed by taking a spatial sequence (cross-cultural analysis). Evolutionists, for example, observed that axes in country Z were more advanced than in country Y, which, in turn, were more advanced than in country X. They concluded that the evolution of the axe followed the time sequence of X, Y, Z. Structure functionalism, although in the forefront of cross-cultural family study, has not been able to handle satisfactorily the problem of social change because of its emphasis on studying societies in the ahistorical present and, then, making cross-cultural historical comparisons, much in the same manner as the Social Darwinists.

Modernization theories were developed from a combination of conceptualizations derived from evolutionary theory and structure functionalism. Modernization theories have been widely used in sociology since World War II. However, the basic conceptual problems of both evolutionary theory and structure functionalism in their handling of social change have also led to similar problems in the development of adequate conceptual tools by the proponents of modernization theory.

The concept of modernization and the theories stemming from its conceptualization have been the dominating perspective in the analysis of global social change and the family. *Modernization* is usually used as a term in reference to processes of change in societies that are characterized by advanced industrial technology. Social scientists have attempted to make the development of Western European and American technological society the model for the comparative analysis of developing countries. Daniel Lerner in his influential study, *The Passing of Traditional Society: Modernizing the Middle East,* presents a model of universal process that all developing societies must pass through to become modernized.

> The Western model of modernization exhibits certain components and sequences whose relevance is global. . . . The model evolved in the West is an historical fact. That the same model reappears in virtually all modernizing societies on all continents of the world, regardless of variations in race, color, creed, will be shown. . . . (Lerner, 1958:46).

Marion J. Levy, Jr., defines modernization in relation to technology: "I would consider any society the more modernized the greater the ratio of inanimate power sources and the greater extent to which human efforts are multiplied by the use of tools" (Levy, 1967:190). Levy's definition emphasizes that the transformation of the world by technology is the principal cause of everything connected with modernization. Other theorists expand on this meaning and link the term with a wide range of concomitant institutions in the political, economic, social, and individual spheres. Neil J. Smelser indicates that modernization includes more than technological development:

> The term "modernization"—a conceptual cousin of the term "economic development," but more comprehensive in scope—refers to the fact that technological, economic, and ecological changes ramify through the whole social and cultural fabric. In an emerging nation, we may expect profound changes (1) in the *political* sphere as simple tribal or village authority systems give way to systems of suffrage, political parties, representation, and civil service bureaucracies; (2) in the *educational* sphere, as the society strives to reduce illiteracy, and increase economically productive skills; (3) in the *religious* sphere, as secularized belief systems begin to replace traditionalistic

religions; (4) in the *familial* sphere, as extended kinship units lose their pervasiveness; (5) in the *stratificational* sphere, as geographical and social mobility tends to loosen fixed, ascriptive hierarchical systems. (Smelser, 1973:748)

The main tie between modernization theory and structure functionalism is the key concept of structural differentiation. Smelser defines the process of structural differentiation as:

> When *one* social role or organization . . . differentiates . . . into *two or more* roles or organizations which function more effectively in the new historical circumstances. The new social units are structurally distinct from each other but taken together are functionally equivalent to the original unit. (Smelser, 1959:2)

In a later work Smelser (1973) explains structural differentiation as the manner in which, after industrialization, family functions lose some of their former importance in matters of training and economic production and schools and economic organizations begin to fill these functions. As the family ceases to be an economic unit of production, family members may leave the household to seek employment in the outside labor market. With the decline of the family's function in the economic sphere, the family (particularly in the figure of the father) loses its economic training function, which further leads to a decline in general paternal authority. The family's activities become more concentrated on emotional gratification and socialization, with the mother developing more intense emotional relationships with children because of the absence of the father in the job market. Smelser concludes:

> . . . modernization tends to foster the rise of a family unit that is formed on emotional attraction and built on a limited sexual-emotional basis. The family has been removed from other major social spheres except for the segmental, external ties of individual family members. The family, being thus isolated and specialized, impinges less on these other social spheres, nepotism as a basis for recruitment into other social roles tends to become at most corrupt and at least suspect, whereas in traditional society it was the legitimate basis for recruitment into roles. Finally, within the family the complex and multi-functional relations of family members to one another tend to be pared down to more exclusively emotional ties. (Smelser, 1973:752)

WILLIAM J. GOODE'S WORLD REVOLUTION AND FAMILY PATTERNS

The major work coming out of modernization theory, which centers on the family in change, is William J. Goode's *World Revolution and Family Patterns* (1963). This work has had a profound impact on the comparative study of social change and the family. Goode's major contribution is the comprehensive and systematic gathering and analyses of cross-cultural and historical data to attack the notion of unifactoral hypotheses, which viewed family systems as dependent variables affected by such phenomena as industrial and economic development. Goode concluded that changes in industrialization and the family are parallel processes, both being influenced by changing social and personal ideologies—the ideologies of economic progress, the conjugal family, and egalitarianism. Finally, Goode proposes that in the "world revolution" toward industrialization and urbanization, there is a convergence of diverse types of extended family forms to some type of conjugal family system.

Goode's conceptualization of modernization processes and of the classification of societies and family systems stems from an implicit linear developmental orientation that sees societies moving from traditional systems to modern systems and the family moving from extended kinship family systems to the conjugal family form. Thus at the same time that Goode criticizes unifactoral hypotheses of social change he, himself, has developed a unilinear evolutionary schema.

Goode takes issue with theories that view change in family patterns as a simple function of industrialization. Rather, he sees modernization represented by ideological value changes as being partially independent of industrialization as well as having important impacts on both the family system and on industrialization itself. Following a structure functionalist framework, Goode takes issue with the position that the conjugal family emerges only after a society is exposed to industrialization. This position ignores the theoretical "fit" (empirical harmony) between the conjugal family and the modern industrial system. For example, the independence of the conjugal family from extended kinship ties permits the family to move where the jobs are. The increased emotional component of the conjugal family relationship provides a source of psychological strength in the face of pressures from the industrial order and the absence of extended kin relations. This seeming "fit" is not seen as obscuring either the importance of ideological factors or the fact that the family itself may be an independent factor influencing the industrialization process.

Goode believes that the ideology of economic progress and technological development as well as the ideology of the conjugal family occurred in non-Western societies prior to industrialization and family changes. The significance of the ideology of economic progress lies in its stress on societal industrial growth and change and its relegation of the issue of tradition and custom to a lower level of importance. The ideology of the conjugal famliy asserts the worth of the individual over the lineage and personal welfare over family continuity. A third ideology is that of egalitarianism between the sexes. The emphasis is on the uniqueness of each individual within the family with lesser importance given to sex status and seniority. This ideology reduces the sex-status and age inequalities of families and also undermines the traditional subordination of the young by the old.

All three modernization ideologies aim directly or indirectly at ending the dominance of the extended family system over the conjugal family and, in particular, over the young and of women. Further, all three ideologies minimize the traditions of societies and assert the equality of the individual over class, caste, or sex barriers.

Goode's theoretical position centers around two major functional fits. The first is that between the desire of the individual to maximize his or her need for equality and individualism and the type of family system that can best satisfy those needs as well as the type of family system that can best serve the needs of an industrial and technological social order.

Goode argues that the ideology of the conjugal family system, which emphasizes the relationship of husband and wife and their children and deemphasizes the obligatory relationship with extended kinship systems, is best able to maximize the values of individualism and equalitarianism. The extended family system tends to subordinate the individual to the family group—family continuity is more important than individual welfare and desires—whereas the ideology of the conjugal family asserts the equality of individuals over sex, kinship, caste, and class barriers.

> The ideology of the conjugal family proclaims the right of the individual to choose his or her own spouse, place to live, and even which kin obligations to accept, as against the acceptance of others' decisions. It asserts the worth of the *individual* as against the inherited elements of wealth or ethnic group. The *individual* is to be evaluated, not his lineage. A strong theme of "democracy" runs through this ideology. It encourages love, which in every major civilization has been given a prominent place in fantasy, poetry, art, and legend, as a wonderful, perhaps even exalted, experience, even when its reality was guarded against. Finally, it asserts that if one's family life is unpleasant, one has the right to change it. (Goode, 1963:19[1])

The second functional fit is between the family system and industrialization. Goode states that the ideology of the conjugal family and industrialization fit each other through the sharing of common ideas and values intrinsic within both systems. In addition, he argues that these shared ideas and values are necessary for the development of both types of systems. The conjugal family system, which emphasizes the independence and equality of each family member and urges the freedom of the individual from old restrictions in traditional extended family systems, is closely tied with the ideology of economic progress and technological development, which stresses industrial expansion and the freedom of economic activity that is demanded in a rapidly changing industrializing economy.

Goode (1963, 1964) assembles a massive amount of comparative data, both historical and cross-cultural (the West, Arabic Islam, sub-Saharan Africa, India, China, and Japan) to test these hypotheses. The conclusion reached is that *all* the family systems examined are moving towards some form of conjugal family system. The trends and changes that are occurring take on the following characteristics.

1. *Free choice in mate selection.* In extended family systems marriages are arranged by family elders, frequently without the marrying couple meeting prior to the actual marriage. This is to minimize the development of potentially conflicting emotional and obligatory ties between spouses and to maintain control over the future generational development of the extended kinship system. Marriages today, Goode concludes, are being based on love; dowry and brideprice arrangements are disappearing.

2. *Emphasis on individual welfare as opposed to family continuity.* The authority of parents over children and husbands over wives is diminishing and greater sexual equality is becoming manifest in changes in legal systems regarding such matters as divorce and inheritance. Further evidence is the weakening of sex, kinship, class, and caste barriers and the assertion of the equality of individuals in various substantive legal actions.

3. *Greater emphasis on the conjugal role relationship.* Husbands and wives are moving more and more in the direction of setting up their own independent households (neolocal residences) as opposed to living within the confines of either the husband's family's residence (patrilocality) or the wife's family's residence (matrilocality) thus diminishing the everyday interaction control of either extended family system. Another development that tends to support the independence of the conjugal family system is the development of bilineal descent systems (tracing lineage equally through both family lines) in contrast to a unilineage descent system (either patrilineal or matrilineal). Goode shows that the development of a bilineal descent system results in the loss of power for both unilineage systems and changes the nature of extended kinship ties to one based on affection and choice rather than an obligation. Thus neolocality and bilineality aid in the development of relative freedom of the conjugal family system from the extended family system and prevent the continuation or the development of powerful unilineage systems that dominate the husband-wife marital relationship.

Goode observes that, whenever a country moves toward industrialization, there is some concomitant change in the family system toward some type of conjugal system. He suggests that the family system may hinder or facilitate industrialization in important ways. He argues that the development of Western economic and technological systems would have been severely handicapped if Western family systems "had been patriarchal and polygynous, with a full development of arranged child marriages and a harem system" (Goode, 1963:23). In his chapters on China and Japan and in a later work (1964) Goode compares the Chinese and Japanese family systems during the late nineteenth and early twentieth centuries to illustrate the importance of family patterns in facilitating or hindering industrial social change. In Japan patterns of inheritance, attitudes toward nepotism, narrow patterns of social mobility within the merchant class, and a feudalistic loyalty of individuals to their extended families, and, in turn, the feudalistic loyalty of the extended families to the state imperial system all assured the rapid industrialization of the society. In China, the patterns of inheritance—equal inheritance as opposed to the

Japanese system of the eldest inheriting all—prevented the accumulation of family capital. The Chinese, unlike the Japanese, accorded a low social rank to the merchant status. Thus, when wealth was gained, individuals sought to achieve prestige and power by becoming members of the gentry; this prevented the steady accumulation of financial and technical expertise. Finally, the relationship of the family to the state was familistic not feudalistic. That is, an individual owed loyalty to both the extended family and the state personified in the Emperor. However, in the case of conflict between the two, the individual's first loyalty was to the family. Goode concluded that these different family systems played an important part in the industrial achievement of Japan and the lack of such achievement in China.

Goode believes that this analysis emphasizes the independent effect of family variables. But more important, he is demonstrating that family patterns cannot be solely predicted from a knowledge of economic or technological facts alone. The analysis further demonstrates that even when the family is confronted by antithetical forces it does have the capability of resistance and thus it must be taken into account in any work on societal social change. Finally, his stress on the commonality of ideological factors in both industrialization and in the conjugal family demonstrates the inadequacy of unilateral causality, which exists in the evolutionary theories of Social Darwinism and Marxism:

> To be avoided are all theories that turn out to be only unifactorial hypotheses, suggesting that all change and all causal relations flow from some single, global factor, such as race, environment, technology, or industrialism. In the past these seemed plausible only because analysts who proposed them usually included within such global variables almost everything that needed to be explained. (Goode, 1964:116)

In summarizing Goode's work one sees that the basis of his argument revolves around the legitimacy of extended family systems in terms of their domination over the individual and the belief that the conjugal family system maximizes the ideology of equality and individuality. This desire for egalitarianism results in a power conflict between the individual and the traditional extended family systems. Further, the ideology of the conjugal family links up with the ideology of economic progress associated with industrial and economic development. The ideology of economic progress runs counter to the ideology of traditionalism, which emphasizes the continuity of historical traditional patterns. Both ideologies operate to foster change in the society and interaffect one another. At the end of his seminal work (1963), Goode gives his own evaluation of the changes that are occurring. Although he is aware of the dysfunctions these changes may have—particularly to the elders of extended kinship systems—Goode welcomes them:

> . . . I welcome the great changes now taking place, and not because it might be a more efficient instrument of industrialization, for that is irrelevant in my personal schema. Rather, I see in it and in the industrial system that accompanies it the hope of greater freedom: from the domination of elders, from caste and racial restriction, from class

rigidities. Freedom is *for* something as well. the unleashing of personal potentials, the right to love, to equality within the family, to the establishment of a new marriage when the old has failed. I see the world revolution in family patterns as part of a still more important revolution that is sweeping the world in our time, the aspiration on the part of billions of people to have the right for the first time to choose for themselves—an aspiration that has toppled governments both old and new, and created new societies and social movements. (Goode, 1963:380).

Goode's great work stimulated a large amount of empirical studies in social change and the family. Soon after the publication of his monograph, a series of comparative studies, both cross-cultural and historical, presented evidence contrary to his hypothesis that there was a worldwide trend toward the conjugal family system. In recent years new developments in the analysis of modernization processes and in the sociological study of the family have pinpointed limitations in modernization theory and have begun to show how these limitations can lead to distortions in the comparative analysis of social change and the family.

To fully understand these developments, it is vitally necessary to understand the inherent limitations of modernization theory. Goode's *World Revolution and Family Patterns* (1963) comes out of this perspective. Although it transcends some of these deficiencies, it too suffers from its distortions.

Indian Scientist Discovers Bride in Ad

Sydney H. Schanberg

NEW DELHI, July 11—A young research metallurgist who works for International Business Machines in Fishkill, N.Y., was married in New Delhi the other night in an ancient Hindu ceremony in which the dhoti-clad priest invoked the deities of earth, air, fire and water.

It was not a marriage of West and East, as the contrast of I.B.M. and the Hindu priest might suggest, but rather a marriage of modern-India and traditional India.

The 29-year-old bridegroom, Rajendra Dhir, had won his Bachelor of Science degree in Bombay, but had then gone abroad—first to Canada and finally to the United States—to seek, and find, success.

After four years away, Mr. Dhir traveled the 8,000 miles home for a family visit. To his surprise—partly because of a matrimonial advertisement placed in the New Delhi newspapers by his eldest sister without his knowledge—he found himself quickly engaged to an Indian girl who had been traditionally reared and who had moved in circles so close to home that she had never even seen the southern part of India. They are spending their honeymoon there.

Matrimonial ads placed by the families of potential brides and bridegrooms are a relatively new phenomenon on the Indian social scene, having cropped up only in the last decade or two. Even more recent are the growing number of ads placed by the families of young men who, like Mr. Dhir, have gone to Western countries to make a better living but return to India briefly to claim an Indian bride, get married in the traditional religious rites and then hurry back with her to the foreign home.

These ads usually require the woman be "beautiful" and "educated," generally mention the man's salary and sometimes break with custom by saying "caste no bar." (Although the caste system has been outlawed for decades, it is still a powerful force, especially in seeking a marriage partner.) The ads also offer such lures to a potentially homesick bride as "she will be able to come to India every year if desired."

On the day before his wedding, Mr. Dhir—with only a touch of 20th-century embarrassment about his family's advertising for a wife—discussed quite freely the process by which he had selected his bride, Renu Singh, who is 21 years old and just graduated from Delhi University with a Bachelor of Arts degree in economics.

"I felt quite strange. You can't decide something like this in a short time," he said to describe his initial reaction when he arrived here and learned that several potential wives were waiting to be inspected.

The shock apparently wore off soon, as his emotions—amid the familiar Hindu background—accepted his family's role in his marriage. His was, in fact, more modern than most Hindu marriages, in which the families make all the arrangements and the bridegroom does not get to look at his bride until the wedding day.

At least he would interview the eligibles and make the final decision. "I talked to six or seven of them," he said. "But it didn't click. When I met Renu, something clicked. That's the only answer I can give."

Her mother and father had not literally answered the newspaper ad, but they were old friends of Mr. Dhir's family, knew about the ad and were also looking for a husband for their demure, attractive daughter.

"I had never taken her out," said Mr. Rhir, who is slightly chubby, bespectacled, very serious and very outgoing. He continued:

"But I had met Renu before, I knew her and knew her family. She was approved by my family. It has to be mutual. Also, my father told me our horoscopes matched, so that was okay."

"And we assume that a girl from that social setup will have a normal, healthy, background."

Miss Singh's father, V. J. Singh, is director of the Delhi Planning Commission. Mr. Dhir's father, K. L. Dhir, is a doctor with a clinic in Gwalior, about 200 miles south of Delhi. There is a heavy emphasis on college and graduate education in both families.

Rajendra, who is called "Raj" at I.B.M., won a master's degree in metallurgy at the University of Toronto and is working part-time now for his doctorate at Brooklyn Polytechnic Institute. A recent raise at I.B.M. put his salary at more than $13,000 a year.

After he made up his mind about Miss Singh, he took her out a few times—another departure from Indian tradition—to tell her about the United States.

"When you're taking a girl to a strange country, you've got to tell her what to expect," he explained. "It's not fair otherwise."

Mrs. Kamala Passi, the sister who placed the matrimonial ad, was asked why she had not told him in advance. Before she had a chance to answer, the eldest brother in the family, Prem, an ophthalmologist, said, laughing: "We thought he might run away. As soon as he landed, we wanted to push the girls on him so he'd have to select one of the bunch. There wasn't much time. He said he wanted to go back on July 30."

Mr. Dhir said he saw flaws in both the wide-open American tradition of choosing mates and the family-arranged tradition in India, but said he was at a loss to suggest a perfect method.

The outdoor Hindu marriage ceremony juxtaposed the old and the new in this country's changing culture. Miss Singh's father was dressed in a Western business suit, but wore sandals, without socks. Mr. Dhir also wore a western suit, but his head was swathed in a turban decorated with tinsel and flowers.

An electric fan cooled the wedding party—the priest and his assistant wearing dhotis, or long loincloths, the bride in an elegant sari and the bridegroom in his business suit—as they sat on their haunches under a jasmine-covered wedding canopy through the elaborate two-hour ceremony at a social club here.

Mr. Dhir, as is the custom in his Khatri, or martial, caste, rode part of the way to the wedding on a horse. Then he switched to a blue 1959 Plymouth, which arrived at the social club preceded by a peppy marching band.

Since much of the ceremony was chanted in Sanskrit would be abruptly broken by phrases like "permission from the father" and "bank balance"—bringing gleeful chuckles from the guests.

Sydney H. Schanberg, *The New York Times*, July 16, 1969. © by The New York Times Company. Reprinted by permission.

MODERNIZATION THEORY AND THE FAMILY: ASSESSMENTS AND DEVELOPMENTS

Modernization theory's reliance on an evolutionary model grounded in the notion of progress leads implicitly to the idea that progress is a more valued phenomenon than traditional stability and that modern societies, that is, Western industrial societies, are somewhat superior to traditional nonindustrial societies. This has resulted in a deemphasis on problems in modern industrial societies and an emphasis on the dysfunctional characteristics of traditional societies in regard to industrialization.

Richard P. Appelbaum (1970) characterizes modernization theories as "diachronic theories of unilinear change." He argues that modernization theories, basically concerned with the correlates of industrialization develop before-and-after models of societies, which contrast preindustrial characteristics of traditional societies with the corresponding set of characteristics that have evolved in highly industrialized modern societies:

> The theories are said to be diachronic, therefore, in that they attempt to infer process from a methodology of comparative statics. They are held to be unilinear in that all societies are held to undergo a parallel series of transformations during the process of industrialization that results in a highly homogeneous final product. (Appelbaum, 1970:36)

The concept of structural differentiation has been attacked for regarding society as a mechanistic, equilibrating system. The basic characteristics of this type of system is that new structures develop from old ones that no longer perform their functions adequately. Further, when processes of structural differentiation proceed unevenly, the system experiences tensions and imbalances and there is a need to reestablish an equilibrial system. As Marvin Scott (1970) observed, this is the conservative bias of structure functionalism, which emphasizes slow, orderly change within the system and regards conflict and deviance as pathological tendencies that disturb the social equilibrium. Further, although structure functionalists find the source of change in deviance, they have no systematic theory of deviance to account for change. Scott also observes that this perspective of social change—clearly stated in the concept of structural differentiation—posits the idea of progress, with new structures being superior to old ones:

> To this way of thinking, the loss of traditional functions of (say) the family is an indicator of good tidings: now the family can better perform its *real* function (which, alas, is real by heuristic assumption). Such optimistic apologetics assume the workings of an invisible hand of progress: dissatisfaction of alienate groups, for instance, is viewed as a temporary condition resulting from increasing differentiation. Structural differentiation illustrates what Gouldner has called the "Pollyanna fallacy," which proclaims that every day in every way we are becoming better and better integrated. (Scott, 1970:24)

There has been widespread dissatisfaction with these assumptions of modernization theory which dominated comparative sociology in the 1950s and 1960s. Wilbert E. Moore (1964) has stated that the three-stage model—tradition, transition, and modern—has inherent problems. By focusing on societies in transition, the theory implies a static traditional stage with a societal social structure persisting in an equilibrated balance without change as well as a modern society that is also static and unchanging. Moore argues that "change is an intrinsic characteristic of all societies and the historic paths to the present inevitably and significantly affect the continuing paths to the future'' (1964:884). He also states that owing to temporal myopia and the lack of historical perspective the fact is overlooked that most of the world has been under some form of Western influence for extended periods of time (e.g., for over 400 years in Latin America and parts of Africa). This has resulted in a great intermixture of cultural forms and social organizations that have affected the modernization processes of all the world's societies.

The Winter 1973 issue of *Daedalus* was devoted to this topic. The issue was titled "Post-Traditional Societies" by S. N. Eisenstadt to emphasize the continuity and reconstruction of tradition. The general argument made by the contributors to the issue was the need to look at developing, modernizing, and modern societies in terms of processes of change rather than being concerned with elements of congruence and uniformity that would eventuate into a world of societies, all modern—societies that would resemble each other to the extent that earlier cultural identities and traditions would be virtually absent.

The dominant theme of this *Daedalus* issue is (1) that tradition is not a static and unchanging entity with no changes occurring in the given traditional society and (2) that it is wrong to assume that tradition and modernity are conflicting alternative polarities. S. J. Tambiah (1973) addresses himself to the first point—that the concept of tradition applied in an uncritical ahistorical sense denotes a collective heritage virtually unchanged from the past:

> By conceiving of tradition in this way, two things tend to be forgotten: that the past was, perhaps, as open and dynamic to the actors of that time as our own age appears to us; and that the norms, rules, and orientations of the past were not necessarily as consistent, unified, and coherent as we tend to imagine. (Tambiah, 1973:55)

J. C. Heesterman (1973) argues that tradition itself is full of paradox. It has to do with the way in which a society deals with fundamental questions, including the meaning of life and death, and, therefore, there can be no final formulations that are totally inflexible.

The second theme of this issue of *Daedalus* was that tradition and modernity do not necessarily have to be exclusive and conflicting categories. On examination of given societies, the contributors reached similar conclusions: in many societies tradition and modernity are inseparable and there exists an interactive relationship with modernity and traditional culture that permeates the emerging social and political structures and exercises influence on the economic development of given societies.

If we accept the findings of the critics of early modernization theory, how can we explain why the theory of the incompatibility of tradition and modernity was voiced in the first place? Or, how was it held that traditional societies were basically static and nonchanging? Constantina Safilios-Rothschild (1970) provides one possible explanation. She argues that the conceptualization of "modern man" and the "modern attitude" are specifically defined with the contemporary, middle-class American as a model. This conceptualization was broadened to assume that all modern people will become the same regardless of the society of origin or their cultural heritage. It would logically follow, then, that non-Western "traditional" societies and Western "modern" societies are polar opposites in a linear theory of social change and that the content of tradition—institutions and value systems— would be impediments to changes and obstacles to modernization. Safilios-Rothschild follows Joseph R. Gusfield (1967) in arguing that modernity may be differentially expressed from society to society as a particular blend of tradition and modern ideas, values, and behaviors. In Gusfield's (1967) influential paper he outlines six fallacies relating to the misplaced polarities of tradition and modernity:

1. Fallacy: Traditional culture is a consistent body of norms and values.
2. Fallacy: Traditional society is a homogeneous social structure.
3. Fallacy: Old traditions are displaced by new changes.
4. Fallacy: Traditional and modern forms are always in conflict.
5. Fallacy: Tradition and modernity are mutually exclusive systems.
6. Fallacy: Modernizing processes weaken traditions.

Gusfield argues that tradition becomes an ideology, a program of action that provides a justificatory base for present behavior. He notes that a desire for the preservation of tradition and the desire to modernize do not necessarily have to be in conflict. Modernity depends on and is often supported by traditional ideology: "In this process, tradition may be changed, stretched, and modified, but a unified and nationalized society makes great use of the traditional in its search for a consensual base to political authority and economic development" (Gusfield, 1967:360). Gusfield concludes that the treating of tradition and modernity as conflicting opposites itself leads to the development of an antitraditional ideology, which is manifested in the denying of the necessary and usable ways in which the past may serve as a support to the present and the future.

A basic problem, then, of modernization theory is the tendency to view traditional society and modern society as static entities. It focuses solely on the transitional stage of a traditional society modernizing in terms of process. Traditional society is conceived as a relatively stable social order that does not change over long stretches of historical time periods. Further, modern industrial societies are seen as the end product of societal evolutionary development and this has led to a tendency to overlook and discount changes in modern societies as minor readjustments in the social order. One can readily visualize the intellectual predecessors of this orientation in Social Darwinism, which believed that non-Western stone-using, hunting-and-gathering societies were social fossils from the Neolithic or Paleolithic periods and that Western industrial society was the apex and culmination of human civilization. Although modernization theory was more sophisticated, both theoretically and methodologically, than Social Darwinism and was quite critical of such simplistic unilinear evolutionary schemas, vestiges of the earlier position remained partly as a result of the continuation of Western ethnocentric biases.

This manifests itself in the model used by modernization theorists in which modern industrial man and society are based on the Western archetype. It led to the conclusion that human beings who did not share Western ideologies and value systems were antithetical to modernization and their traditional societies were opposed to modernization. Myron Weiner (1966) suggests that the problem of conceptualization of traditional societies as static entities opposed to modernization and the development of industrial and economic systems stems from a confusion between traditionalism and tradition.

> Tradition refers to the beliefs and practices handed down from the past; as we reinterpret our past, our traditions change. In contrast, traditionalism glorifies past beliefs and practices as immutable. Traditionalists see tradition as static; they urge that men do things only as they have been done before. This distinction between tradition and traditionalism calls attention to a fundamental issue in development: how do people see their past? Are the values and practices of the past to be preserved or adapted? . . . When people are attached to the past in such a way that they will not adopt new practices that modify past behavior, we are confronted with an ideology of traditionalism. Traditionalism, by virtue of its hostility to innovation, is clearly antithetical to the development of modernization; traditions, which are constantly subject to reinterpretation and modification, constitute no such barrier. (Weiner, 1966:7)

Interestingly, both Weiner and William J. Goode illustrate this difference between traditionalism and tradition in their respective discussions on the differences between nineteenth-century China and Meiji Japan. Goode's discussion of the differential relationship of the family systems in China and Japan makes it evident that the family system in China was a hindrance to rapid industrialization, whereas the family system in Japan aided in the industrialization of that country. Weiner states that, "while the Japanese sought to reinterpret their past so as to make it congruent with their efforts to modernize, many Chinese leaders were hostile to innovations that violated previous practices" (Weiner, 1966:7). In Japan *tradition* was subject to reinterpretation and modification and thus constituted no barrier to industrialization, in China *traditionalism* was hostile to innovation and was opposed to the development of modernization.

Unfortunately, Goode does not systematically develop the idea that tradition and modernity may *not* be conflicting and polar opposites. This is partly attributable to his conceptual model of modernization (evolutionism and structure functionalism) and to his substantive hypothesis that the family is evolving worldwide to some form of conjugal family system. Recently many others (Moore, 1964; Bendix, 1967; Gusfield, 1967) have reached the similar conclusion that tradition and modernity can be inseparable: modernity can be incorporated into the traditional order, and the traditional culture can permeate and have an impact on the individual, social, economic, and political spheres of modernization. Indeed, as we saw, an entire issue of *Daedalus* (Winter 1973) was devoted to this question under the title, "Post-Traditional Societies."

One of the most exciting developments in the analysis of modernization processes is the attempt to delineate different forms of modernization that are characteristic of advanced industrial societies (the Soviet Union, Eastern and Western Europe, and the United States) and the Third World (the less modernized societies of Asia, Africa, and Latin America). Two monographs stand out in their sociological insight into modernization: Szymon Chodak's *Societal Development: Five Approaches with Conclusions from Comparative Analysis* (1973) and Peter L. Berger, Brigitte Berger, and Hansfried Kellner's *The Homeless Mind: Modernization and Consciousness* (1973). Chodak's work is a macrolevel analysis of societal development and modernization. Berger et al. is concerned with the utilization of the "social construction of reality" thesis developed earlier (Berger and Luckmann, 1966) to examine the modernization processes and the way individuals see themselves and their roles in life. They attempt to "link the structures of consciousness to particular institutions and processes" (Berger et al., 1973:16). We will first discuss Chodak's schema and then link it with that developed by Berger and his associates. Finally, we will tie them together to examine their implications for the study of modernization and the family and how they relate to Goode's *World Revolution and Family Patterns*. (1963)

Basis of Iranian Conflict: A Mishandling of Modernization

Nicholas Gage

QUM, Iran, Dec. 19—Iran is a country of two worlds that are locked in a battle for supremacy.

One is the modern, secular world largely created by Shah Mohammed Riza Pahlevi, with its capital in Teheran. The other is the traditional, religious world of the mosques and the mullahs, with its capital here in the holy city of Qum. Everywhere in the country the stark contrasts are visible.

In Qum the women are draped in the black all-enveloping chador and stay home weaving decorous silk carpets; in Teheran many women wear Western dress and work in shops and offices. In Qum a pristine skyline is dominated by the sharp needles of the minarets; in Teheran the dominant motif is skyscrapers obscured by the clouds of exhaust fumes from hordes of automobiles.

Even in Teheran the schism is clearly marked. In the northern suburbs are the modern office buildings and the sumptuous villas of wealthy Iranians, crowned by two imperial palaces. In the southern sectors are the squat homes and cell-like shops of the working classes, with a bazaar and a mosque in every neighborhood. This area is more Qum than Teheran, and here live the opponents of the Shah, including the mullahs and their allies, the bazaaris, or merchants.

In all Iranian cities the same schism is evident, the secularized Iranians and foreigners living in districts that could as well be in Europe or America, while around them dwell the Moslem faithful in a humming maze of bazaars and twisting streets. Some of the bazaaris are just as wealthy as the Westernized people, but they are devoted to Islam.

Every day the two worlds clash, the faithful, unarmed, pouring into the streets out of the mosques and defying the soldiers to shoot, ready to heed the injunction of their exiled leader, Ayatollah Ruhollah Khomeini, to sacrifice their blood to restore the Islamic world that, they feel, the Shah and his father before him, Riza Shah, tried to destroy.

"The efforts to separate religion and politics over the past 50 years struck at the very heart of Islam, which recognizes no divisions but embraces the whole of human activity," said Ayatollah Sharfat Madari, the most prominent religious leader living in Iran, during an interview.

The breach between the two worlds was opened and considerably widened by Riza Shah. Born of a poor family and rising through the ranks as a soldier, he tried to give prestige, support and justification to this position as ruler by identifying it not with Islam but with ancient Iran, dating from the creation of the monarchy by Cyrus the Great in the sixth century B.C.

While de-emphasizing the historical role of Islam, Riza Shah, who died in 1941, moved against the traditional power of the mullahs by starting a campaign to lay the foundations of a modern, essentially secular nation. He took away their authority over legal disputes and education and even undermined their control of religious traditions by forbidding passion plays, allowing foreigners in mosques and removing the veil from women.

A tall, imposing, ruthless man, Riza Shah once came to Qum, entered the holy shrine here without bothering to remove his boots and whipped the country's foremost religious leader because he had criticized the Queen for not wearing the veil.

The present Shah continued his father's policies. He too emphasized the pre-Islamic past to provide the psychological groundwork to build a modern state, even changing the Islamic calendar to one beginning with the establishment of the monarchy by Cyrus. The glorification of the ancient past culminated in 1971 in a celebration of the empire's 2,500th anniversary, which cost $100 million and brought the Shah considerable criticism for his extravagance while at the same time fascinating the world with the spectacle.

The Shah resolved to modernize the country even more dramatically than his father. But the Western technology he bought with oil money brought with it Western influences that offended the faithful, as the burned ruins of liquor stores, nightclubs and movie theaters now testify.

The policies of the Rizas, father and son, left the traditional religious world squeezed between the emphasis on the pre-Islamic past on one side and the modernization drive and its Western accompaniments on the other. "All the changes made by the Shah and his father that go against Islamic law are an affront to every Moslem in Iran and we never accepted them," said Ahmad Mollael, a 53-year-old mullah.

Though the religious world represented by Qum resisted the changes every step of the way, it lost most of the battles to the secular world of Teheran and the might of the palace. The mullahs did not give up, however, and when the Shah was forced by economic and international pressures to relax his iron hold on the country last year, the mullahs redoubled their attacks, so that today small, austere Qum has modern, powerful Teheran under siege.

The success of the mullahs is a direct result of a mistake made by the Shah and his father in their single-minded drive for modernization. Unlike the neighboring great modernizer, Kemal Ataturk of Turkey, they failed to establish the kind of democratic institutions—a free press, independent political parties—that would stand as a bulwark against the traditional and religious forces opposed to change. To make things worse the present Shah blocked all avenues for expressing dissent and forced the liberals and intellectuals, who could have been a counterweight to the mullahs, to form alliances with them instead.

Still, the vast wealth brought into Iran after the Shah quadrupled oil prices in 1973 gave him a great opportunity to win popular support and restrict the growing strength of the mullahs. He ruined his chance by imposing an extensive and often wasteful development program without bothering to find out how fast and in what direction the people wanted to go.

As a result, though the program improved the lot of most Iranians, they felt alienated from it and saw only the tremendous corruption it generated in the ruling class. The people also blamed the Shah for every mistake in the way it was administered because he insisted on pulling all the strings himself. It seemed to most people that they would have more voice and more chance of participating in their destiny if they shifted their support to the mullahs, who have to be responsive to popular sentiment because they depend on the gifts for their livelihood.

That dependence was fostered by the Shah, who denounced the wealth of the clergy, Iran's second largest landholder until the 1961 land-reform program, as well as their power, eliminating a source of corruption that had kept the faithful suspicious of the mullahs.

As resentment against the Shah has increased the strength of the opposition forces, he has been looking in vain for the popular support he feels he deserves. Even the most wealthy, whose luxurious new homes, cars and Western wardrobes have been bought with money made in the oil boom the Shah set off, are deserting him en masse, moving to Europe and taking their money with them. Only the military men remain committed to defending the order he has established.

That is powerful backing, but in the clash between the two worlds of Iran, theocracy has already gained the upper hand, whether the mullahs ultimately manage to drive out the Shah or not. The country is back on the Islamic calendar; the chador is seen everywhere. Here in Qum, the religious capital of the mullahs, there are no movie theaters because it is felt that films corrupt the people. In the secular capital, Teheran, there were 118 cinemas only a year ago; just seven remain, the rest having been burned by demonstrators.

Nicholas Gage, *The New York Times,* December 22, 1978. © 1978 by the New York Times Company. Reprinted by permission.

Szymon Chodak's Conceptualization of Modernization

Chodak, building on the accumulating body of empirical studies and theories on modernization, develops a fourfold classification of forms of modernization. He is primarily interested in comparing three forms of modernization: industrial (combining industrial modernization in both capitalist and communist countries), acculturative, and induced. Chodak's classification schema is depicted in Table 3.1.

Industrial modernization—found in both Eastern and Western Europe, the Soviet Union, the United States and Canada—created new material conditions and needs. This stimulated the adoption of new attitudes and value orientations and produced a new social division of labor and the exchange of services. Developing concomitantly with industrialization were new roles, organizations, and systems of activities (social and political) that were complementary and interdependent.

Chodak compares industrial modernization with accultural and induced modernization and finds that in Third World societies the later types of modernization are characterized by the absence of industrialization. These societies aim at the

Table 3.1   The Forms of Modernization

Modernization	*Spontaneous*	*Organized by Government*
Based on industrialization	Industrial modernization in capitalist societies	Industrial modernization in communist societies
Based on cultural contact	Acculturative modernization	Induced modernization

Source: Szymon Chodak. *Societal Development: Five Approaches with Conclusions from Comparative Analysis.* 1973. New York: Oxford University Press, p. 268. Copyright © 1973 by Oxford University Press. Reprinted by permission.

transformation of their social structures through the education system and the propounding of new norms and values. "While industrialization in Europe gave birth to modernization, in Africa and Asia the present modernization processes— may—though not in all cases—create favorable conditions for the industrialization that will come" (Chodak, 1973:259). Accultural modernization, which was typical of the African colonial systems, emerged from a direct confrontation and superimposition between European colonial culture and the traditional African culture. This created a new semidevelopmental buffer culture that was marginal to both and that promoted duality in norms, patterns of behavior, attitudes, and structural affiliations (Chodak, 1973:263). Colin Turnbull (1962) describes his experiences with one individual who led a dual existence in two cultural worlds:

> In Accra I stayed in the town household of a Kwahu family, their home residence being between Accra and Kumasi, in the depths of the countryside. In his country home the family head was a chief—"*Kwame,*" or "He who was born on Saturday." In his Accra house the chief became Harold, a prosperous merchant and a politician. His town house was large and rambling, on two floors. He occupied the upper floor with his wife by Christian marriage and their small children. It was a magnificent apartment, with every possible luxury—including a well stocked cocktail cabinet, for the one tradition that dies the hardest is the tradition of hospitality. In this apartment lived a happy, settled, thoroughly westernized family. But downstairs lived his other family, the family of Kwame as opposed to that of Harold—all his nephews and other appendages of his extended Kwame family which, as Kwame, he felt obliged to support, even in Accra.
>
> It was like going from one world to another, and I lived a completely double life with ease and pleasure in that household. Upstairs we drank whisky, danced the cha-cha and the mambo, ate bacon and eggs for breakfast and drank tea at tea time. From upstairs, we sallied forth for evenings at the various smart night clubs (evening dress compulsory), or to elegant private dinner parties. But downstairs I ate *fufu* (a kind of unsweetened dough made from manioc flour, from which one tears pieces to dip in a sauce) with my fingers, drank palm wine, danced Abalabi, and learned what real family life is like. (Turnbull, 1962:32[2])

But Chodak sees the acculturative process as a process of alienation. He reports that Colin Turnbull calls these individuals alienated, whereas Frantz Fanon (1968) in his book, *The Wretched of the Earth,* sees them as men and women with a black skin and a white mask. Chodak views the acculturated alienated individual as being transformed into a "superior inferior" (Chodak, 1973:265). Although such alienated individuals acquire the habits of the European colonizers and are told that they are superior to nonacculturated individuals, they are at the same time treated as inferiors by Europeans. Chodak provides a powerful illustration of this situation in

---

[2]From *The Lonely African* by Colin M. Turnbull. Copyright © 1962 by Colin M. Turnbull. Reprinted by permission of Simon & Schuster, a Division of Gulf & Western Corporation.

the writings of an African, Robert Mueme Mbate, who, as he searches for his identity, asks: "Who am I?"

> I am not a Mkamba, yet I am Mkamba, I was born of Kamba parents. In my veins there flows Kamba blood. . . . I know a number of Kamba customs, but what I know is so little that I am ashamed. . . . Can I claim to be a European? A black European? Now wait a minute! In my veins, there flows Kamba blood. My skin is black like a Mkamba's. . . . And when I eat European food my stomach rebels. It wants most of all the Kamba dish—*isye*—maize with beans and green vegetables. . . .
>
> I speak the English language. I write in English. I even dress like English people. In my best clothes, I look like an Englishman. I struggle hard to learn the manners of the English' people. . . . I fall short of European customs and culture. When they say, "Don't be silly," I feel I have been insulted. Yet it's not so. When a daughter kisses her father, my blood says, "Oh no!" It is odd to me. . . .
>
> When I was a young boy, I was "Kambanized." I learned how to make bows and arrows, the Kamba traditional weapons. . . . I don't know how to dance the traditional Kamba dances. I went to school too early to learn them. At school I learned English and Scottish dances. Yet I don't know why the English and Scottish dances are danced. . . .
>
> What then, am I? A conglomeration of indigeneous and borrowed ideas and ideals. As such, I must find my footing in the whole nation, and indeed in the whole human race. I am not a Mkamba, yet a Mkamba, in whose veins Kamba blood flows. (Mbate, cited in Chodak, 1973:266[3])

Finally, Chodak perceives the process of acculturative modernization as a process of detribalization; a process in which there is a gradual substitution of traditional roles and an ascriptive allocation of roles and positions based on individual achievements within a new social and political organization of the society.

The third form of modernization is induced modernization, which consists of introducing Western patterns of government and administration, education systems, and value orientations to the still nonindustrialized country:

> I call it induced modernization because the changes and transformations—particularly in the sphere of social relations—which are involved, and which are usually government-initiated, lead to the acceptance in the new society of the norms, values, and organizations of the industrial socieites. Thus this is a process induced by the existence of industrial societies elsewhere in the world. (Chodak, 1973:267)

Chodak identifies induced modernization as a process of nation building and the generation of national identities. Its primary aim is the transformation of the societal population into a new, national entity while retaining significant parts of the traditional culture (norms, symbols, patterns of behavior, and aspects of the social structure) and trying to integrate these parts into the new social order. The process of induced modernization is not seen as a procedure by which there is growing mass

[3]Robert Mueme Mbate, 1969. "Identity." *Bursara* (Nairobi) 2:31–34.

participation in the decision-making processes of the new states but rather as one in which the government and the ruling political party are the chief organizers and implementers.

The process of induced modernization, then, aims at the development of what Chodak calls a "stratified supratribal national society" that is superimposed on the traditional tribal structure. Further, different groups of individuals within the society can be distinguished in terms of the different degrees of their belonging in the new national state. Chodak goes on to distinguish the differential relationships that societal groups have with induced modernization processes—the elite, the working class, the class of entrepreneurs, and the peasantry—as well as the geoegraphical areas in which they reside—urban or rural. He finds that the detribalized urban dwellers, especially those who have earlier generational ties with the urban areas and who are intertribal offspring, are more assimilated to the supratribal society than those individuals who reside in rural tribal areas and who think of themselves primarily in terms of their tribal membership.

Berger, Berger, and Kellner's The Homeless Mind

This theme is continued and expanded in Berger et al. *The Homeless Mind: Modernization and Consciousness* (1973). In this work the argument is made that the process of modernization and the institutions that accompany it have had a negative impact on human consciousness of reality not only in the non-Western Third World but also in the industrialized world, especially in the United States. The modernization process, which was supposed to free individuals, is seen instead as increasing feelings of helplessness, frustration, and alienation that beset individuals with threats of meaninglessness. Berger et al. examine the processes of modernization in the Third World and its effect on traditional ways of life, kinship patterns, and "social constructions of reality" and find them being changed. In industrial societies they see the development of processes of "demodernization" being manifested in various forms of counterculture movements. Like Chodak, they emphasize the differential impact of modernization on individuals within both categories of societal orders. They, too, see the relationship between tradition and modernity, modernization and consciousness, as having differential relationships, which are dependent on particular individual and group positions within a given society, whether they are of the Third World or of the Western industrialized social order. The arguments that they make extend the earlier positions on whether or not tradition and modernity may or may not be conflicting and polar opposites.

Modernization is seen to consist of the growth and diffusion of a set of institutions (bureaucracy, technological economy, political systems, and social and cultural pluralism) that stem from the transformation of the economy by technological innovations. Modernization has helped lead the individual away from the domination of the extended family, clan, and tribe and has given the individual the opportunity to pursue previously unheard of choices and options. Both geoegraphical mobility (the movement from the rural small community to the larger urban community) and social and occupational mobility have freed the individual from these previously dominating institutions. As is readily apparent, this position parallels that of William J. Goode who welcomed these changes in that they provided men and women the potential for greater individual freedom and the "unleashing of personal potentials, the right to love, to equality within the family, to the establishment of a new marriage when the old had failed . . . the right for the first time *to* choose for themselves . . ." (Goode, 1963:380). However, Berger et al. (1973) go beyond Goode and see that modernization has, in fact, not led to freedom and the maximization of individual potentialities but, instead, has led to a condition of "homelessness' and to feelings of helplessness, frustration, and alienation. The focus of *The Homeless Mind: Modernization and Consciousness* is to determine the factors in modernization that have had this effect on individuals.

Although Berger and his associates' examination of the modernization processes in the Third World does not explicitly make the distinction between Chodak's acculturated modernization and induced modernization, they reach a similar conclusion by emphasizing that these forms of modernization are experienced in terms of cultural contact and imposition. They extend the argument by noting that even when modern technology is encountered, most people in the Third World are related to it in terms of low-skill labor without experiencing the ideologies of modernity. "What frequently happens in such cases is that there are very destructive effects on traditional patterns of life *without* any significant modernization of consciousness in terms of positively identifiable themes" (Berger et al., 1973:121). They illustrate this very persuasively by looking at how mining in South Africa has had the immediate consequences of weakening village life and its traditional cultural patterns. Men are separated from their families and their traditional way of life and are placed in an industrial life-world that is amorphous and composed of uprooted individuals:

> In such a situation the structures of modernity (in terms of institutions, patterns of everday life, cognitive and normative themes and anything else one may wish to name) must necessarily appear to the individual as an alien, powerful and, in the main, coercive force that completely uproots his life and the lives of those he most cares about. In such a situation, there is little if any direct identification with modernity. (Berger et al., 1973:122[4])

The development of an identification with modernization can only begin to occur when individual's begin to settle into a new life and if and when they are joined by their families. Berger et al. also observe that initially only a small number of individuals adapt to modernization. These people—who are labeled modern

---

[4]From *The Homeless Mind: Modernization and Consciousness* by Peter L. Berger, Brigitte Berger, and Hansfried Kellner. Copyright 1973 by Random House, Inc. Reprinted by permission.

types—are seen to have been marginal to the life of the traditional community. These are the people to whom Chodak refers in his concept of acculturated modernization and Colin Turnbull calls "the lonely African."

In their examination of what Chodak has called induced modernization, Berger and his associates view this phenomenon as representing a later stage of the modernization process occurring in the Third World. The earlier stages occur when both the modern state and the modern economy impose themselves as alien realities on traditional social situations, and it is in this earlier stage that the accultured modern man is found. In the later stage—particularly when the Third World society achieves political independence (in Africa or Asia) or gains a revolutionary government (in Latin America or Asia)—the state itself is presented as a mobilizing agent for development. This makes it easier for various people and groups, particularly the acculturated modern type, to identify with what Chodak has called the "supratribal national society" rather than with the traditional tribal structure as well as to identify with the state rather than with a particular economic system. Further, the state becomes the vehicle for accomplishment of the social ambitions of these people, especially for those who are involved with the governmental bureaucracy, which becomes the ladder for the attainment of status, privilege, and power. Berger et al. explain this phenomenon in the following passage:

> [It] is probably because the bureaucracy is able to accommodate itself to traditional patterns of social relations more easily than an increasingly technological economy can. Even a very modern bureaucratic structure can establish working relations with traditional power structures far better than a modern economic enterprise can with traditional patterns of production. Traditional patterns can actually be incorporated into the workings of the bureaucracy, as the importance of family, clan and tribal loyalties in the politics of Third World states clearly indicates. (Berger et al., 1973: 127–128)

This insight is broadened with the authors' understanding that bureaucracy in the Third World is frequently tied up with ideologies of nationalism and socialism. The aim of the state government is to make the governmental system combine the benefits of modernity within the traditional tribal community and offer the individual meaning and solidarity. Here Berger et al. integrate the idea that modernity and tradition do not have to be polar opposites since they see that the goal of socialism and state nationalism is to provide an answer to the problems of modernization:

> . . . we repeatedly emphasized that the dichotomization of private and public life is one of the crucial social characteristics of modernity. Modernization in contemporary Third World societies imposes this same dichotomization, and in most instances it is felt to be an extremely difficult and often repugnant ordeal, which gives birth to profound threats of anomie. Socialism presents itself as a solution to this problem. It promises to

reintegrate the individual in all-embracing structures of solidarity. *If modernization can be described as a spreading condition of homelessness, then socialism can be understood as the promise of a new home.* (Berger et al., 1973:138)

The goal of the socialist Third World society is to offer both modernity and traditional community and thus reverse the alienating, fragmenting, and disintegrating processes relating to the destruction of tribal and communal solidarities. The ambition of the Third World is the combination of development and modernization of society with the protection of traditional symbols and patterns of life. This is an extremely difficult task because, as we have seen, modernization brings with it reclassification schemas of social relationships based on economic status, occupation, and supratribal relationships rather than on social relationships based on tribal and kinship criteria. Thus nationalism is seen as being both a liberator and an oppressor: liberating individuals from colonialization and from the controls of family, clan, and tribe and oppressing individuals in the quest for modernization and the development of technological and bureaucratic institutions.

In the advanced industrial nations, Berger et al. see modernization as leading to a variety of discontents stemming from the technologized economy, the bureaucratization of major institutions, and the "pluralization of social worlds," resulting in a condition that they label as "homelessness."

These authors develop the argument that technology's primary consequence has resulted in the separation of work from private life. This condition has also had an impact on the individual's "levels of consciousness." Technological production, they say, is characterized by anonymous impersonal social relations where individuals interact with each other in terms of the functions they perform in their structured work tasks and where there is no need to be aware of each other's uniqueness as individuals. The consequence of this is that "the individual now becomes capable of experiencing himself in a double way; as a unique individual rich in concrete qualities and as an anonymous functionary" (Berger et al., 1973:34). The implication of this dichotomization of self is that it is only in their private lives that individuals can express elements of their subjective identity, which is denied them in their work situation. However, people are unable to find ample satisfaction in their private lives because their private lives tend to be composed of weak institutions, a prime illustration being the family.

The reason for this is that the nature of modern industrial society is characterized by a "plurality of life-worlds"—modern life is segmentalized (pluralized) to a high degree, and the different sectors of everyday life that an individual experiences are not related and may represent vastly different worlds of meaning and experience. In contrast, according to these authors, traditional society is characterized by a life-world that is relatively unified, with a high degree of integration existing among the various groups in which the individual participates. Thus individuals do not experience the sense of segmentation of modern life and do not have the feeling that a particular social situation took them out of their common life-world, whether they are involved with their family, religious groups, or at work.

The pluralization of life-worlds is distinguished by the dichotomy of private and public spheres; furthermore, pluralization can take place *within* these spheres. Berger et al. examine the family to show the effect of pluralization within the private sphere:

> . . . the private sphere itself is not immune to pluralization. It is indeed true that the modern individual typically tries to arrange this sphere in such a way that by contrast to his bewildering involvement with the worlds of public institutions, this private world will provide for him an order of integrative and sustaining meanings. In other words, the individual attempts to construct a ''home world'' which will serve as the meaningful center of his life in society. Such an enterprise is hazardous and precarious. Marriages between people of different backgrounds involve complicated negotiations between the meanings of discrepant worlds. Children habitually and disturbingly emigrate from the world of their parents. Alternate and often repulsive worlds impinge upon private life in the form of neighbors and other unwelcome intruders, and indeed it is also possible that the individual, dissatisfied for whatever reason with the organization of his private life, may himself seek out plurality in other private contacts. This quest for more satisfactory private meanings may range from extramarital affairs to experiments with exotic religious sects. (Berger et al., 1973:66−67)

In summary, these authors put forth the argument that marriage, which was seen as providing a meaningful world for its participants, is, in fact, unable to overcome the homelessness resulting from the pluralization of life worlds in modern society. This conclusion is diametrically opposite to that reached by William J. Goode. Where Goode welcomes the changes and is optimistic about the actualization of individualism and equalitarianism, Berger and his associates are quite pessimistic. In their delineation of the public and private life, they hit at a key variable in explaining much of the tensions surrounding the contemporary American family system.

In essence we are in agreement with this latter position. The dichotomization of public and private spheres of activities is a main characteristic of contemporary Western family systems. It is this dichotomization that provides the key to the analysis of social change and the family. Much of cross-cultural and historical analysis of family change has ignored this characteristic. Influenced by modernization theory, scholars have overemphasized the need to investigate structural changes in the family. These theorists have built up the case that the distinctive feature of modern society is the predominance of the nuclear family and the prevalence of the large patriarchal extended kin group of traditional societies from the historical past of Western Europe and America.

Interestingly, William J. Goode (1963) debunks the myth that the ''classical family of Western nostalgia'' was the large extended family living happily in the large rambling house on the farm. But, in his emphasis on the close ''fit'' between industrialization and the conjugal family and in his emphasis on the retarding effects of the extended family with industrialization, his argument takes a different twist. It centers on changes in the structural nature of the family and limits the analysis of changes to the family's involvement in the community. His argument, then, becomes one aspect of the theme that industrialization means the end of the viable extended family and the development of the conjugal family, which has severed meaningful involvements with other kin.

Recently, family historians have taken issue with the conclusion that the history of the Western family is a movement from the consanguineal system to the conjugal one. And, in their historical analysis of the Western family form, they reach strikingly similar conclusions to such cross-cultural comparative sociologists as Peter L. Berger and to the conclusions of Karl Marx and Friedrich Engels on the privatization of the family. Let us now turn our attention to the family historians and examine their research findings and conclusions.

Switch to Bottle-Feeding Perils Third World Babies

Leonard Santorelli

LONDON.—A revolution without guns, flags, or slogans is profoundly changing the lives of many women and children in the Third World. It is the switch from breast bottle-feeding.

The switch has freed Arab, African, and Asian women, especially city-dwellers, from the home and enabled them to take jobs, often overcoming deeply-ingrained cultural taboos to do so.

But it has also brought in its wake a pitiful toll of malnutrition and disease among infants whose mothers used dirty water in the mixture or cut down on milk powder to make the packet last longer.

The bottle is already firmly established in many cities and towns and is slowly taking hold in rural areas. Clearly, Western ideas on female emancipation and even on what constitutes a shapely figure are key factors.

But controversy has also been stirred by the role of the firms that sell the milk products. Attention has focused on their sales techniques in places where water is scarce, conditions unhygienic, and costs of the products high.

In Berne, 13 young Swiss people have just been convicted of criminal libel against the giant Nestle Food Company for producing a pamphlet entitled "Nestle Kills Babies."

The booklet accused Nestle of responsibility for the deaths of thousands of children in developing countries by promoting powdered milk as preferable to breast-feeding. The court ruled that the title of the pamphlet was clearly defamatory.

"The death of small children is the fault of bad preparation of the products," the judge said. "I have come to this conviction. It is not the product, but the dirt, the germs."

But the judge, Juerge Sollberger, called on Nestle to make drastic changes in its publicity methods in the Third World, saying the misuse of its products had caused the deaths of children.

The defendants have said they will appeal.

A look at the background to the bottle-versus-breast debate in Asian and African countries shows that the bottle has gained a firm foothold, breaking down strong cultural and practical barriers in the process.

Many Asian women for instance, thought they would lose the love or respect of their infants if they went on the bottle. The average African child can spend up to two hours a day bringing home water that will be needed for mixing and sterilizing the baby formula.

Western ideas have had a big influence. One Kenyan social worker blames the "prudery" brought to Africa by colonial missionary doctors who discouraged the exposing of women's breasts and public feeding of babies.

The Western practice of putting a baby in a crib, he adds, instead of its mother's bed where it had a constant supply of milk has broken down feeding patterns, and often causes the mother's milk to dry up prematurely.

Even so, many Kenyan women will pay up to a third of their annual income on a product they could produce themselves and officials of international agencies in Nairobi say one of the reasons is that they believe this is the "modern way, the way of the white man."

The problem is that poor families will try to economize by using less powder. One U.N. Children's Fund official said: "If you buy a tin of milk powder for what is fundamentally a week's ration and stretch it to two weeks, the child is starving."

Most medical authorities agree that conditions in the majority of Kenyan homes are not conducive to the hygienic mixing of milk. The water, for instance, is sometimes brought straight from a muddy pond and few uneducated women would understand the need to boil it.

This, and over-dilution of powder result in a danger of bacterial infections and malnutrition.

In the Keynatta national hospital, 125 to 200 babies arrive each month dying from dehydration and severe diarrhea. A doctor said that most of them were bottle-fed.

It would appear, he said, that their condition was the result of poor hygiene and mothers' failing to follow the manufacturer's instructions.

"There are suspicions that most of these babies would not be here in this state if they were not being fed with unsterilized bottles and probably over-diluted milk," said a doctor. "But we just do not have the data."

This resulted in a steady drain on the income of poorer families, he said. Mineral water, for instance, needed to mix with the milk powder, could absorb up to a tenth of the monthly earnings of such a family.

Although the breast versus bottle debate is a non-issue in most of India because of widespread poverty, there is a gradual switch to the bottle among the rich.

Advertisements describing powdered milk as "as good as mother's milk" brought a riposte in a leading women's magazine, Femina, extolling the virtues of breast-feeding and emphasizing the risk of contamination during the powdered milk's journey from cow to baby.

Leonard Santorelli in the *Philadelphia Inquirer*, August 1, 1976.

SOCIAL HISTORY, MODERNIZATION THEORY, AND FAMILY CHANGE

In the last 15 years social historians have begun gathering evidence that seriously questions the assumptions that the emergence of the nuclear family in the Western world is a recent phenomenon. Research on the historical European and American family system has convinced most social scientists that modernization theory, which postulates the historical existence of the large extended patriarchal family and its transformation into the nuclear family, is wrong. Now social scientists are reaching realtive agreement that the nuclear family has predominated in western societies for the last 300 years.

Most interestingly, their historical investigation of the size and composition of the family has led them to a new research focus, one that is virtually the same as that expressed by Peter L. Berger et al. in *The Homeless Mind: Modernization and Consciousness* (1973). Family historians also emphasize changes in Western society, a society that has seen the development of private life and the private sphere. The great public institutions of the society, including work and the community, are seen as being separated from the private sphere of social life, particularly the most important one—the family. It is observed that this development is in striking contrast to the family's historical position in the nonindustrial and early industrial past. Historically, the family has served as the very foundation of social life and the center of the institutional order. There was no segregation between the family and the totality of the institutions in the society. It is precisely these changes in the texture of private family life and the family's involvement in work and the community that is seen as the outstanding feature of the contemporary family. It is this change rather than the transformation from the consanguineal extended family system to the conjugal nuclear family system that is the distinguishable characteristic of the modern family.

We will now briefly discuss the research findings that questioned the hypothesis that the Western trend was from the consanguineal to the conjugal family. Particular attention will be given to the emerging position that believes that the general concern over structural and size changes was misspent and that the new research concern should be with the examination of the familial texture of the nuclear family and its relationship to social, economic, and political changes in Western societies during the last 300 years.

We will begin our analysis by looking at the important contributions of Peter Laslett and the Cambridge Group for the Study of Population and Social Structure. Their concern has been in examining household size and composition and internal family relationships. They have employed a technique of data analysis, which has been given the name, *family reconstitution.* Essentially this technique uses demographic data culled from records of births, deaths, marriages, wills, and land transfers to establish lineages and relationships. The aim is to reconstruct family and household patterns of ordinary people who have directly passed down little information of their way of life. Although data on the wealthy and well born have been more readily available, family reconstitution is one way of retrieving information on people whose everyday life has heretofore been hidden from history.

Peter Laslett in *The World We Have Lost: England Before the Industrial Revolution* (1965) contrasts the small-scale, primarily rural and familial society of seventeenth-century England with the large-scale, industrial and urban English society of contemporary times. Laslett utilizes the family-reconstitution technique in examining the household size of preindustrial England. Parish registers provide him with data on household size of rural English villages. His findings indicate that although many English households contained servants, there was a general absence of extended kin. The data led him to conclude that the nuclear family was predominant in preindustrial England. It also led him to question the thesis that emphasizes the connection between industrialization and the small nuclear family.

Based on this conclusion, Laslett and the Cambridge Group used the family-reconstitution technique and examined historical census data from a number of societies. Laslett posited a series of questions and dictated the methodological format based on census lists to provide comparative evidence on changes in household size and organization. The resultant volume, *Household and Family in Past Time* (1972) consists of 22 articles written by different scholars who utilized Laslett's theoretical and methodological research design and who presented their findings at a conference that Laslett organized in 1969. These papers are concerned with the size and structure of domestic groupings over the last three centuries in England, France, Serbia, Japan, and the United States.

According to Laslett, research findings reveal that, except for Japan and possibly Serbia (part of present-day Yugoslavia), household size has not varied to a great extent in the last 300 years. The extended family system is found not to be particularly prevalent. Households contain nuclear families with the poor serving as servants of the rich. Laslett reaches the conclusion that these findings support his earlier one that the small nuclear family was an essential part of these societies long before industrialization.

Studies of colonial American family life has provided additional evidence on the prevalence of the nuclear family in Western history. Philip J. Greven, Jr.'s (1970) analysis of colonial Andover, Massachusetts, documents that newly married couples were expected to set up their own households. Greven examined four generations of settlers in Andover using family reconstitution techniques. His findings reveal the control parents had over children through their control and ownership of the farming land. Although patriarchal control was reinforced through inheritance patterns and the availability of land, Greven documents how children prevailed and how the nuclear family predominated family life.

John Demos (1970) found the family reconstitution technique instrumental in his study of Plymouth Colony, the settlement founded by the Pilgrims in the seventeenth century. Demos examined official records of the colony, the content of wills and physical artifacts, which included houses, furniture, tools, utensils, clothing and the like, to reconstruct family patterns. He sought to relate demographic and psychological approaches to demonstrate that the extended family system was by and large absent in the colonial era.

Demos analyzed the structure of the household and the relations between households and the larger community. He found that households were composed of nuclear families and that the basic structure of the family and the roles and responsibilities of family members were essentially the same as the American pattern of the 1960s: husbands were the dominating individuals in the family; women were given considerable authority in their own sphere of concern. Children were expected to take on adult responsibilities and activities by the age of 6 and 7—much earlier than in contemporary society.

The distinguishing feature of life in Plymouth Colony was the prevalence of nonkin related members of households. The presence of these individuals in the household is explained by a different conceptualization of the role of the family in relation to the community than the one we have today. Demos uses a structure functionalist perspective and develops the point that the range of functions preferred by the family contrast strikingly with contemporary patterns. He sees the family being charged with social responsibilities that have subsequently been taken over by institutions specifically designed for this purpose:

> The Old Colony family was, first of all, a "business"—an absolutely central agency of economic production and exchange. Each household was more or less self-sufficient; and its various members were inextricably united in the work of providing for their fundamental material wants. Work, indeed, was a wholly natural extension of family life and merged imperceptibly with all of its other activities.
>
> The family was also a "school." "Parents and masters" were charged by law to

attend to the education of all the children in their immediate care—"at least to be able duely to read the Scriptures." Most people had little chance for any other sort of education, though "common schools" were just beginning to appear by the end of the Old Colony period.

The family was a "vocational institute." However deficient it may have been in transmitting the formal knowledge and skills associated with literacy, it clearly served to prepare its young for effective, independent performance in the larger economic system. For the great majority of persons—the majority who became farmers—the process was instinctive and almost unconscious. But it applied with equal force (and greater visibility) to the various trades and crafts of the time. The ordinary setting for an apprenticeship was, of course, a domestic one.

The family was a "church." To say this is not to slight the central importance of churches in the usual sense. Here, indeed, the family's role was partial and subsidiary. Nonetheless the obligation of "family worship" seems to have been widely assumed. Daily prayers and personal meditation formed an indispensable adjunct to the more formal devotions of a whole community.

The family was a "house of correction." Idle and even criminal persons were "sentenced" by the Court to live as servants in the families of more reputable citizens. The household seemed a natural setting both for imposing discipline and for encouraging some degree of character reformation.

The family was a "welfare institution"; in fact, it provided several different kinds of welfare service. It was occasionally a "hospital"—at least insofar as certain men thought to have special medical knowledge would receive sick persons into their homes for day-to-day care treatment. It was an "orphanage"—in that children whose parents had died were straightaway transferred into another household (often that of a relative). It was an "old people's home"—since the aged and infirm, no longer able to care for themselves, were usually incorporated into the households of their grown children. And it was a "poorhouse" too—for analogous, and obvious, reasons. (Demos, 1970:183–184[5])

According to Demos, the family in America has increasingly over the years contracted and withdrawn from social responsibilities. The central theme is the gradual surrender to other institutions of functions that once lay very much within the realm of family responsibility. The result was that the family became more isolated and detached from the community as a whole. Replacing the declining social functions, it now took on more important psychological functions for its members. The inseparable and indistinguishable facets of social life—family and community, private life and public life—were cleaved.

Thus, although Demos differs from Goode in his stress on the historical prevalence of the nuclear family in the West, he shares Goode's viewpoint (and that of other modernization theorists) on the dominating characteristics of the contempo-

---

[5]From *A Little Commonwealth* by John Demos. Copyright 1970 by Oxford University Press. Reprinted by permission.

rary family. These characteristics include the decline in the functions of the family and the severing of the family's ties with the community, which has led to the development of the private family. This family form has turned inward; the home is seen as a private retreat. The emotional intensity of the ties between family members has heightened as the ties with the community have lessened.

The Family-Reconstitution Technique: An Assessment

The study of ordinary families through the use of family-reconstitution techniques has provided social science with fascinating information on the historical Western family. Taken together, these historical studies have led to the questioning of the thesis of the emergence of the nuclear family tied to recent industrialization processes. The extended-family historians generated much controversy in social science. It stems in part from their overemphasis on structural changes in the size and composition of the family and their neglect of the emotional arrangement of the family. And, when they do look at the emotional texture of the family, they do so from an inadequate base: census data and household size. Critics question how one can attribute emotional qualities of family life from the analysis of birth, death, and marriage records or from household size and composition or from the physical layout of the household. Let us examine these criticisms in more detail and, then, examine the new approach being put forth by social scientists interested in family change.

Peter Laslett and the Cambridge Group's conclusions have been open to criticism on both methodological and theoretical grounds. In a stinging critical review of the *Household and Family in Past Time* (1972) Lutz K. Berkner (1975) questions the almost complete dependence on census data in making household analysis. Berkner argues that this source of data is severely limited to the kinds of analysis that can be made and on the conclusion one can reach. He believes that the available cross-cultural data used is woefully deficient, incomplete, and noncomparable. Berkner seriously questions Laslett's decision of refusing to allow his contributors the right to consider family ideals of norms as part of the field of inquiry. He further decries the failure of the articles to differentiate household structures of different social classes within a given society. These researchers should have distinguished between the wealthier households, which have servants, and the households of poorer families, whose children were forced to leave to serve richer families. This leads Berkner to conclude that, because of these severe theoretical and methodological deficiencies, one can discard much of the Cambridge Group's conclusions.

Christopher Lasch (1975a, 1975b, 1975c), in his caustic reviews of Peter Laslett and the Cambridge Group, believes that their 15 years of laborious investigations into the structure of the household has only established the unimportance of the question to which they have devoted much of their attention. He criticizes the "empty" findings of those who seek answers by looking at census data and exclude from analysis the emotional nature of the family. The position taken is that sociologists cannot describe the family solely in terms of size or structure alone, they must take into accord the emotional dynamics of family life. Further, changes in the emotional character of the family must be seen in relation to the changes in the economic, social, and political activities occurring in given societies.

The argument against Demos (see, e.g., Rothman, 1971; Henretta, 1971) takes a similar stance. When Demos limits his analysis to examine the physical setting of colonial life in his chapters on the housing, furnishings, and clothing of the colonists, he is remarkably successful. However, when he attributes the crowded conditions of the household to fostering frustrations and aggression in child-rearing practices, he outstrips scientific plausibility. The physical characteristics of the household could have achieved the opposite results. For example, it could have developed closeness among siblings. Further, the aggressive behavior of childhood, which is seen to culminate in a large number of court cases, can be explained by other factors in the community. David Rothman (1971) observes that:

> Many historians have experienced that middle-of-the-night panic when contemplating how thin a line sometimes separates their work from fiction. But on this score the study of childhood seems especially nerve-racking, threatening to turn us all into novelists. (Rothman, 1971:181)

In summary, family historians have established the fact that the nuclear family has been prevalent for the last 300 years. These findings have convinced sociology that it was wrong to identify the distinctive feature of the modern family as its structural isolation from the larger extended kinship structure. The new position that has emerged believes that the modernization of the family can best be understood in terms of changes in nuclear family values and orientations and in the changing involvement of the family with work and the community.

Tamara K. Hareven (1971), picking up on John Demos's findings on the family's relationship to the community, has observed that the modernization of the family can be better estimated in terms of household membership. Modernization involves the gradual withdrawal of non-kin-related individuals from the household. As has been shown, extended kin were never present in significant numbers in the household. Family historians have provided the evidence on the relative nonimportance of extended kin in everyday household activities. They have also revealed the importance of non-kin-related individuals in the household. The involvement of the latter in the household reflect the different conceptualizations of the ideology of the nuclear family over the last 300 years. It is the implications of this fact that should have been studied but was not.

Unfortunately, too often family historians got caught up in asking structural questions on the size and composition of families within households in their attempt to investigate the thesis on the transformation of the Western family from extended to nuclear. They further confused the issue by failing to distinguish between household composition and family composition. They did not give proper attention to the fact that members of the same family may not live in the same household, nor are households restricted only to family members. The absence of extended kin in the household led them to dismiss the thesis of structural changes in the family. But they ignored the involvement of nuclear families with extended kin outside the household. Nuclear families were intertwined with a network of relatives, all residing in the same community. Further, although extended kin did not reside in the household, this did not mean that the nuclear family was not involved with them or that they had no influence on them. In summary, although the majority of households studied historically were composed of nuclear families, they did not conform to the characteristics of the conjugal family described in modernization studies by such sociologists as William J. Goode. The historical Western European and American nuclear family was not a conjugal family. It was not intimate. It did not encourage domesticity or privacy. It was not detached from the community nor was it highly mobile, either socially or geographically. The overemphasis on family structure variables, that is, from extended family to nuclear family, obfuscated the orientational and value variations of the historical nuclear family.

Why did this transformation take place? Why did the personal life in the eighteenth and nineteenth centuries move toward privation and domesticity? Why is the significance in the change of the historical family seen not so much in terms of size and composition of the household but in the detachment of the nuclear family from the outside world? Why did the family develop an ideology that saw it as the center for emotional support and gratification? What were the implications of these changes for the family, for the husband, for the wife, and for the children? How successful has the family been in becoming a private institution? We have only briefly sketched out some of the answers in this chapter. The answers to these historical questions on the Western family will be examined in greater detail in the ensuing chapters.

CONCLUSION

In this chapter we examined the post-World War II nature of interest in comparative family sociology. We began with an examination of the basic premises of structure functionalism, the theoretical perspective most influential in the comparative analysis of social change and the family. We argued that an inherent problem of structure functionalism is its basic assumption that social change is an "abnormal" phenomenon and detrimental to the functionality of the social system. This approach tends to reify the given social system, whether it is of the society or the family, and thus overlooks the inequalities that may exist within it.

Given the limitations of structure functionalism, it is somewhat surprising that it has been so dominant in American sociology. It has been incorporated with evolutionary theory into modernization theory. A main component of modernization theory is the construct of structural differentiation. This construct has been open to criticism for its tendency to view society as a mechanistic equilibrating system. In addition, modernization theory's use of Social Darwinist evolutionary theory has led to the biased viewpoint that Western industrial societies are superior to non-Western nonindustrial societies and to the deemphasis of the problems of Western societies.

The most significant and important representation of modernization theory in the comparative analysis of social change and the family is William J. Goode's *World Revolution and Family Patterns.* (1963. Goode's study is of pivotal importance in that it is the culminating work on both the strengths of modernization theory and its weaknesses in the analysis of family systems.

Goode's major contribution to the comparative analysis of the family is the comprehensive and systematic analysis of cross-cultural and historical data that attacks the unifactoral hypotheses of industrialization and the family. These hypotheses see the family as a dependent variable changing as a result of industrial processes. Goode emphasized the interaction of family and industrial processes of change, which are both influenced by ideological changes and, in turn, are influenced by them. Finally, Goode proposed that in the ''world revolution'' toward industrialization and urbanization, there is a convergence of diverse types of extended family forms with some type of conjugal family system.

We argued that Goode's theory suffers from the limitations of modernization theory. Modernization theory has a conservative bias developed out of the use of an equilibrium model that tends to deemphasize conflict and social change. The framework was seen to suffer from a simplified conceptualization of traditional and modern societies, seeing them primarily as static entities. Traditional societies were viewed as being antithetical with modernization processes. This is a gross distortion; it has been combated with a new emphasis on the positive nonproblematic nature of modernizing nonindustrial societies.

Further, the biases and inadequacies of structure-functionalist-based modernization theory were seen to be derived from its implicit reification of the societal social order or system and a deemphasis of the individual. In contrast, we presented the orientation of Szymon Chodak and Peter L. Berger and his associates. Chodak delineates different forms of modernization that are characteristic of advanced industrial societies and the less developed societies found in Asia, Africa, and Latin America. Berger is concerned with the manner in which modernization processes affect the way individuals see themselves and their roles in life. Both viewpoints examine society and the individual in terms of processes of change as opposed to being static entities. Both also view society as composed of ''active'' human beings who are conscious of their world and who take an active part in constructing their social reality and social world.

We concluded the chapter with an extensive examination of the recent research by family historians, who have taken issue with the conclusion that the history of the Western family was a movement from the consanguineal system to the conjugal one. We pointed out how their historical analyses of the Western family form were strikingly similar to the conclusions reached by such cross-cultural researchers as Peter L. Berger. We also indicated how the themes developed out of the social history of the family echo the position of Marx and Engels on the privatization of the family.

We emphasize the position that the modernization of the family can best be understood in terms of changes in nuclear family values and orientations. Thus, although the historical evidence seems to indicate that the nuclear family has been prevalent in the West for the last 300 years, there has been a fundamental change in the family's involvement with the world of work and with the community. This change draws our attention. In the next part of this book we will investigate changes in the family's relationship with the larger community. In Chapter 4 we will focus on Western communities with particular attention to the family in American cities. It will be followed by a comparative examination of the family in African cities (Chapter 5). Chapter 6, the concluding chapter of this part of the book, will be devoted to the impact of modernization processes and structures on poverty families. We will examine social policy implications on families living under poverty conditions and we will analyze the relationships that exist among families living in economically deprived communities. Subsequent chapters will investigate how these changes in the texture of private family life and the family's involvement in work and the community affects the relationships of family members with each other.

Two

THE FAMILY IN THE COMMUNITY: COMPARATIVE PERSPECTIVES

4

The Family in the City: The Western Experience

Sociologists studying historical changes and cross-cultural variations in family institutions have employed various methods of comparative analysis. Social scientists of the nineteenth century used the evolutionary progress conception of Charles Darwin. This approach was largely discarded by the turn of the twentieth century for numerous reasons: ethnocentric value judgments, biased and distorted methodological techniques, and erroneous theoretical assumptions head the list. A contemporary offshoot of Social Darwinist evolutionism is modernization theory, which combines evolutionary progress conceptualization with structure functionalism. In Chapter 3 we discussed the heuristic value of this approach and delineated its limitations. In this chapter we will focus on another major approach favored by social scientists in the comparative analysis of family institutions—the comparison of rural agricultural communities with urban industrial communities— by developing typologies, or ideal types, of communities. As we will demonstrate, this approach is a direct outgrowth of the antiurban bias of sociologists of the nineteenth and early twentieth centuries. Their ideological biases were coupled with a strong distaste for emerging urban family forms. Ultimately, their values distorted their analysis of the phenomenon that they sought to investigate—the family in the city.

THE IDEAL TYPE

The ideal type is a conceptual construct used in the analysis of social phenomena. The techniques for its use were developed by the German sociologist, Max Weber

(1949). The ideal type is constructed from observation of the characteristics of the social phenomena under investigation, but it is not intended to correspond exactly to any single case. Rather, it designates the hypothetical characteristics of a "pure" or "ideal" case. The ideal type, then, does not imply evaluation or approval of the phenomena being studied. No normative or evaluative connotations are implied—it is an analytically constructed model.

The ideal type does not conform to reality, being an abstraction that hypothesizes certain qualities or characteristics of the social phenomena under study. These qualities or characteristics are believed to be typical of that type of phenomenon and, then, the construct proceeds to describe and test hypotheses about actual empirical social phenomena. For example, an ideal type is constructed on the characteristics of cities. No cities would actually conform in an absolute sense to this ideal type, but the construct is useful in that it provides a focus point, a frame of reference, for the study of a given city. Or take the illustration of "the American family." No particular American family can match all the characteristics of a hypothetical construct of the American family, but such a construction can be useful in examining given families in comparison with this construct and in comparison with each other. The ideal type provides a hypothetical model against which real cities or real families can be contrasted, analyzed, and measured. The ideal type facilitates classification and comparison, and actual social phenomena may thus be compared on the basis of actual as well as hypothesized characteristics.

Social scientists have found ideal types highly useful as analytical tools. They make possible a conceptualization of social phenomena and facilitate cross-cultural and historical comparison among them. They aid in locating factors of social change in societies and enable the comparative investigation of institutions, such as the family, over time and space. Yet, they have severe limitations. In this chapter some ideal types of communities will be examined. For the purposes of this book, only a limited number of such conceptualizations will be considered, and they will be analyzed in terms of relevancy in the study of urbanization processes and the family.

THE IDEAL TYPE OF COMMUNITY

European sociology, which rejected the theoretical assumptions of Social Darwinism by the turn of the twentieth century, had developed the ideal type as an alternative procedure to account for and explain historical changes in Western societies—from agriculture-based economies to those based on industrialization.

The Industrial Revolution dramatically changed the nature of economic and social life. The factory system developed, and, with its development, there was a transformation from home industries in rural areas to factories in towns and cities of Europe and America. Rural people were lured by the novelty of city life and the prospects of greater economic opportunity. England became the first and prime example of the new society. In the great midlands of England, such cities as Birmingham, Leeds, Manchester, and Sheffield emerged. Manchester, which was probably the first industrial city in history, saw its population shoot up from some 70,000 people in 1801 to over 225,000 by 1830 and to slightly over 300,000 by 1850. In these new industrial cities large amounts of labor, raw materials, and capital were centered.

Neil J. Smelser (1959) describes the effects on the family of the mechanization of spinning and weaving in the cotton industry. The domestic economy of the preindustrial family disappeared. The rural and village-based family system no longer served as a productive unit. As a productive unit the cottage industry enabled the family to combine economic activities with the supervision and training of its children. The development of the factory system saw the differentiation of family roles. Members of the family performed separate tasks, frequently not even in the same factory or industry. Patriarchal authority was weakened with urbanization. Previously, in rural and village families, fathers reigned supreme; they were knowledgeable in economic skills and were able to train their children. The great diversity of city life rendered this socialization function relatively useless. The rapid change in industrial technology and the innumerable forms of work necessitated a more formal institutional setting, the school, to help raise the children. In response to the changing family situation, the British passed legislation to aid children. Separated from parental supervision, working children were highly exploited. Laws came into existence to regulate the amount of time children were allowed to work and their working conditions. The law also required that children attend school. These legal changes reflected the change in the family situation in the urban setting; families were no longer available or able to watch constantly over their children.

The separation of work from the home had important implications for family members. Increasingly, the man became the sole provider for the family. The women and children virtually developed a life comprised solely of concerns centered around the family, the home, and the school. Their contacts with the outside world diminished and they were removed from community involvements. The family's withdrawal from the community was tinged by its hostile attitude toward the surrounding city. The city was depicted as a sprawling and planless development bereft of meaningful community and neighborhood relationships. The tremendous movement of a large population into the industrial centers provided little opportunity for the family to form deep or lasting ties with neighbors. Instead, the family viewed their neighbors with suspicion and weariness. Exaggerated beliefs developed on the prevalence of urban poverty, crime, and disorganization.

The perceived chaotic world of the city was countered by the family turning in onto itself. What Marx has described as the privatization of the family reflects this development. A strong emotional transformation characterizes the nineteenth century. The emotional bounds that individuals held for the community, the village, and the extended family was transformed into the development of an exclusive emotional attachment to family members. With the work world seen as hostile and precarious, the family took on an image as a place of refuge. The home was seen as a place that provided security and safety from a cruel, harsh, and unpredictable industrial-urban society.

This antiurban state of mind was echoed in the works of contemporary social scientists. The revulsion to the city and the bemoaning of the loss of an idealized past naturally led sociologists to develop contrasting models of city life versus rural life. The city became identified with social disorganization, alienation, and the loss of community and meaningful relationships. In comparison, the small village and rural community was romanticized for its orderliness, noncompetitiveness, and meaningfulness for personal relationships.

As Robert A. Nisbet (1966) points out, both radicals and conservatives viewed the past with nostalgia and the urban present with distaste. Although the radicals eventually embraced the city, seeing in it the hope for the revolutionary future, they too were aghast at the social conditions existing in the emerging industrial cities of the nineteenth century. Such radicals as Friedrich Engels, albeit a romantic radical, was appalled by the urban prospect:

> We know well enough that [the] isolation of the individual . . . is everywhere the fundamental principle of modern society. But nowhere is this selfish egotism as blatantly evident as in the frantic bustle of the great city. (Engels cited in Nisbet, 1966:29)

One is struck with the similarity of Engels' view with that of the conservative Alexis de Tocqueville (1805−1859), who wrote the following after a visit to Manchester, England:

> From this foul drain the greatest stream of human industry flows out to fertilize the whole world. From this filthy sewer pure gold flows. Here humanity attains the most complete development and its most brutish, here civilization works its miracles and civilized man is turned almost into a savage. (cited in Nisbet, 1966:29).

Keeping in mind this antiurban bias, let us now look at some of the more famous and influential typologies that were developed during this period.

Henry Sumner Maine's (1862/1960) distinction of ''status to contract'' society was one of the earliest of such typologies. Maine postulated that *status* societies are characterized by group relations that are anchored in tradition. Tradition, in turn, determines the rights and obligations of individuals. The individual's status was fixed by his or her family and kinship system, which served as the foundation of social organization. The movement to *contrast* relations was fostered by urbaniza-tion, with kinship bonds becoming less strong. With the ascendancy of the state, civil law replaced traditional customs in enforcing and regulating social obedience and social control. Maine argued that with the increased power of the state, the influence of the family over the individual would decline and concomitantly women's social status, which was extremely low in status communities, would rise and familism would decline. The essence of Maine's argument was that the powers, privileges, and duties that were once vested in the family had shifted to the national state. Concomitantly, people's social relationships, which were based on their sta-tus, shifted to individually agreed *contracts*.

Maine's work had a great influence on his nineteenth-century contemporaries. Ferdinand Tönnies (1855–1936), whose *Gemeinschaft und Gesellschaft (Commu-nity and Society,* 1963) was originally published in 1887, has been an inspirational source for students of community analysis to the present day. *Gemeinschaft* and *Gesellschaft* are ideal types and refer to the nature of social relationships, basic social groups, and institutions.

Gemeinschaft (community) relationships are intimate, traditional, enduring, and based on informal relations determined by *who* the individual is in the community as opposed to *what* he or she has done—in sociological parlance, ascriptive status rather than achieved status. The culture of the community is homogeneous and the moral custodians are the family and the church. For Tönnies there are three central aspects of *Gemeinschaft*: kinship, neighborhood, and friend-ship. These institutions serve as the foundation for social life and activities.

Gesellschaft (society association) refers to the large-scale, contractual, imper-sonal relationships that Tönnies saw emerging in industrializing and urbanizing Europe in the late nine-teenth century. *Gesellschaft* includes business-oriented relations based on rational calculations geared to instrumental ends. Personal relationships are subordinate. In the *Gesellschaft,* family groups and institutions no longer serve as the basis of social life, rather, such societies are organized around work relationships and bureaucratic institutions.

Tönnies was antagonistic to the growth of individualism. He believed that acute individualism led to egotistic, self-willed individuals who sought friends only as means and ends to self-interested gains. He decried the involvement of women in the labor force, and he feared the loss of their involvement in the family.

As woman enters into the struggle of earning a living, it is evident that trading and the freedom and independence of the female factory worker as contracting party and possessor of money will develop her rational will, enabling her to think in a calculating way, even though, in the case of factory work, the tasks themselves may not lead in this direction. The woman becomes enlightened, cold-hearted, conscious. Nothing is more foreign and terrible to her original inborn nature, in spite of all later modifications. Possibly nothing is more characteristic and important in the process of formation of the Gesellschaft and destruction of Gemeinschaft. (Tönnies, 1887/1963:166)

Likewise, he saw the destructive effects of child labor on the family. Basically a conservative, Tönnies cites Karl Marx in documenting the ill effects of child labor. Taken together, these changes are seen as destroying the fabric of traditional society and the solidarity of its people. Old values and attitudes are no longer internalized by the young, and the intertwining rights and obligations that bound the traditional community together are weakened and gradually dissolve. The family, itself, becomes subordinated to personal interests. "The family becomes an accidental form for the satisfaction of natural needs, neighborhood and friendship are supplanted by special interest groups and conventional society life" (Tönnies, 1887/1963:168).

In summary, Tönnies' depiction of the *Gesellschaft* is strikingly similar to that of Karl Marx. But, unlike Marx, who sought future revolutionary changes, Tönnies yearned for the return of the romantic past destroyed in his ideal typification of the *Gemeinschaft*. In Table 4.1 a schematic representation of Tönnies societal types are delineated.

Emile Durkheim (1855–1917) also distinguished the nature of social relationships with these two contrasting types of social orders. Durkheim's doctoral dissertation, *The Division of Labor in Society,* was published in 1893. He compared societies based on *mechanical solidarity* with societies based on *organic solidarity* in regard to social integration. Mechanical solidarity describes the form of social cohesion that exists in small-scale societies that have a minimal division of labor. The type of relationships that link members of such small, stable communities are characterized as being overlapping and interrelated; they are cohesive because of shared bonds and habits. Social unity, Durkheim said, is mechanical and automatic in that the parts of the society are interchangeable. Close friendship groups and kinship groups are typical of mechanical solidarity in that they are secured by personal, stable, and emotional attachments.

In contrast, societies based on organic solidarity, which Durkheim believed was emerging in Europe, were founded on increased specialization and the division of labor. Organic-solidarity-type relationships are impersonal, transient, fragmented, and rational. The source of societal unity is the interdependence of specialized and highly individualized members and the complementary diversity of their positions and life experiences. In relationships marked by organic solidarity one does not relate as a whole individual, but one relates to those qualities that are relevant to the particular function one is performing in relation to others. Durkheim associated the shift in these two types of solidarities, from mechanical to organic, as resulting from the increased size and density of population, the ease and rapidity of

Table 4.1   A Summary of the Contrasts Between *Gemeinschaft* and *Gesellschaft*

	Societal Types	
Social Characteristic	*Gemeinschaft*	*Gesellschaft*
Dominant social relationships	Fellowship Kinship Neighborliness	Exchange Rational calculations
Central institutions	Family law Extended kin group	State Capitalistic economy
The individual in the social order	Self	Person
Characteristic form of wealth	Land	Money
Type of law	Family law	Law of contract
Ordering of institutions	Family life Rural village life Town life	City life Rational life Cosmopolitan life
Type of social control	Concord Folkways and mores Religion	Convention Legislation Public opinion

Source: Don Martindale. 1960. *The Nature and Types of Sociological Theory.* Cambridge, Mass.: Houghton Mifflin, p. 84. Copyright © 1960 by Houghton Mifflin Company. Used by permission.

communication, and especially with the increased division of labor. All of these factors are seen to be linked with the rise of industrialization and the growth of cities.

Durkheim mirrors the conservatism of Maine and Tönnies. In *The Division of Labor in Society* as well as in his other works, notably *Suicide* (1897/1951), Durkheim argues that the cohesive and stabilizing forces of European society are disintegrating. The destructive forces of industrialization, secularization, and revolution account for the alienation, anomie, and isolation of modern urban life. Indeed, in his *The Elementary Forms of Religious Life* (1912), Durkheim viewed the collective conscious as arising out of the individual's participation in the communal life. The origins of man's conceptualization of the universe and the categories of knowledge, he said, stem from this communal perspective. It is no wonder, then, that Durkheim reflects the concern of his contemporaries, both sociologists and lay people, about the problems inherent in the new modern industrial urban society.

In conclusion, the ideal type was developed to contrast the emerging industrial city with the predindustrial rural and village community. This typological approach was tinged with an antiurban bias that distorted the analysis of these authors, as well as many subsequent analyses of the city. Further, since typologies were too broadly based and too vague, rather than aid in the analysis of urban family-life patterns, they led to obfuscation and distortion. Finally, the typologies failed to deal with the wide range of variations within cities as well as with cross-cultural and historical variations. Our discussion of the works of the Chicago School, which follows, will illustrate this criticism.

THE CHICAGO SCHOOL

The typologies of urban-rural societies culminated in the works of the Chicago School and particularly in the writings of Louis Wirth and Robert Redfield. Wirth and Redfield's work can be best understood within the historical context of Chicago during the 1920s and 1930s and the University of Chicago's intellectual activities during this same period.

Chicago epitomizes the phenomenal population growth of American cities. In 1860 its population was 112,000; by the turn of the century (1900) its population was over 1.5 million, and it proceeded to grow at a rate of over 500,000 for each of the next three decades, culminating in a population of over 3.5 million by 1930. As Maurice Stein (1964) has stated, these statistics can give but a suggestion as to what it means in human terms to live in a city whose population swells at such a rapid rate. The unprecedented demands for the development of municipal services—street and transportation systems, sanitary water supplies, garbage disposal, and sewage systems, fire and police protection, schools, libraries, parks, playgrounds, and so on—must have been overwhelming. Further complicating the situation was the fact that the new urban population was comprised predominantly of an influx of European immigrants (who had little familiarity with American customs and language) and migrants from rural America, both groups were unfamiliar and unaccustomed to city life and to each other.

It is not surprising, given the momentous and unplanned changes taking place in American cities during this period, that social scientists emphasized the negative and opposed the positive qualities of urban life. They focused on social disorganization and its consequences—alienation, anomie, social isolation, juvenile delinquency, crime, mental illness, suicide, child abuse, separations and divorce—as inherent characteristics of urban life. "Small wonder that the Chicago sociologists focused on the absence of established institutional patterns in so many regions of the city, stressing that the neighborhoods grew and changed so rapidly that sometimes the only constant feature appeared to be mobility . . . *and* why 'disorganization' accompanied 'mobility' '' (Stein, 1964:16).

The study of the city flowered at the University of Chicago during the 1920s and 1930s. Under the leadership of Robert E. Park (1864–1944), a community of scholars was established who have had an unprecedented influence on the course of sociology to the present day. Such areas as urban sociology, the family, crime and delinquency, social disorganization, social change, the sociology of occupations, political sociology, and social psychology were developed and shaped by the intellectual activities at Chicago. Among the influential social scientists identified with the University of Chicago in addition to Park were W. I. Thomas, George Hebert Mead, Ernest W. Burgess, William F. Ogburn, Ellsworth Faris, Louis Wirth, and Robert Redfield. Among the classical sociological monographs arising out of Chicago during this period and concerned with various aspects of Chicago life are *The Hobo* (Anderson, 1923), *The City* (Park and Burgess, 1925), *The Gang* (Thrasher, 1927), *The Gold Coast and the Slum* (Zorbaugh, 1929), *The Ghetto* (Wirth, 1938a).

The essay, "Urbanism as a way of life" (1938b) by Louis Wirth (1897–1952) has become the classic and most influential statement on urbanism in American sociology. Further, his analysis of urban family life has had an equally important influence on the sociology of the family. Wirth was concerned with developing a sociological definition of the city that would focus on those elements of urbanism that mark it as a distinctive mode of human life that is, one that would focus on the human dimension of the city—what it does to people. In addition, his aim was to develop a definition that would transcend a given historical and cultural type of city and that would hold true for all cities, whether they were industrial or nonindustrial, American or foreign, contemporary or historical.

For Wirth, the main concern of the sociologist of the city was to discover the typical forms of social action and organization that characterize the city. Wirth argued that size, density, and heterogeneity were the key elements determining the social organization and behavior in the urban community. The consequences of these three variables are the relative absence of personal relationships; the depersonalization and segmentation of human relations, characterized by anonymity, superficiality, and transitoriness; and the breakdown of social structures and increased mobility, instability, and insecurity. Wirth summarizes his view of the influence of the city on the life of its inhabitants in the following statement: "The distinctive features of the urban mode of life have often been described sociologically as consisting of the substitution of secondary for primary contacts, the weakening of bonds of kinship, and the declining social significance of the family, the disappearance of the neighborhood, and the undermining of the traditional basis of social solidarty" (Wirth, 1938b:21–22). Wirth goes on to describe the impact of the city on the family:

. . . the low and declining urban reproduction rates suggest that the city is not conducive to the traditional type of family life, including the rearing of children and the maintenance of the home as the locus of a whole round of vital activities. The transfer of industrial, educational, and recreational activities to specialized institutions outside the home has deprived the family of some of its most characteristic historical functions. In cities mothers are more likely to be employed, lodgers are more frequently part of the household, marriage tends to be postponed, and the proportion of single and unattached people is greater. Families are smaller and more frequently without children than in the country. The family as a unit of social life is emancipated from the larger kinship group characteristic of the country, and the individual members pursue their own diverging interests in their vocational, educational, religious, recreational, and political life. (Wirth, 1938b:22)

Louis Wirth's essay has generated a vast amount of research to test the conclusions drawn from his ideal typification of the city and the urban family. We will discuss this research shortly, but we will first present Redfield's typification of the polar opposite of the urban society—the rural society, or as Redfield labels it, *folk* society.

The schema of Robert Redfield (1897−1958) the folk-urban typology, is of particular importance to the comparative study of the city and of family life. Redfield was an anthropologist who was strongly influenced by the Chicago School of Robert E. Park and the works of the earlier classical social scientists, Maine, Durkheim, and Tönnies. His employment of the ideal type approach in his conceptualization of folk societies stands as a polar opposite to his contemporary, Louis Wirth's conceptualization of urban societies. Unlike Wirth, whose conclusions are drawn primarily from an analysis of urban centers in the United States and particularly Chicago, Redfield's conclusions result from extensive field work outside of the United States.

Redfield analyzed the contrasting cultures found in the Yucatán and Guatamala. Among his major works are *The Folk Culture of Yucatán* (1941), *The Primitive World and Its Transformations* (1953), and *The Little Community* (1955).

Redfield comparatively studied contrasting cultures in Central America, ranging from relatively isolated small tribal villages to a large metropolitan city. The typology developed characterized the folk society as small, isolated, nonliterate, and homogeneous and one that had a strong sense of solidarity and intimate communication and stressed the importance of familial relationships and the sacredness of sanctions and institutions. Of paramount interest is Redfield's view that the folk society is a familial society:

. . . the personal and intimate life of the child in the family is extended, in the folk society, into the social world of the adult and even too into inanimate objects. It is not merely that relations in such a society are personal; it is also that they are familial. The first contact made as the infant becomes a person are with other persons; moreover, each of these first persons, he comes to learn, has a particular kind of relation to him which is associated with that one's genealogical position. The individual finds himself fixed within a constellation of familial relationships. The kinship connections provide a pattern on terms of which, in the ideal folk society, all personal relations are conventionalized and categorized. All relations are personal. But relations are not, in content of specific behavior, the same for everyone. As a mother is different from a father, and a grandson from a nephew, so are these classes of personal relationship, originating in genealogical connection, extended outward into all relationships whatever. In this sense, the folk society, is a familial society. (Redfield, 1947:193)

In contrast, Redfield delineates the process of what happens to persons as they live in cities. As communities become less isolated and more heterogeneous, they become more secular and individualistic and more characterized by cultural disorganization. The foundation of the folk society embedded in the family loses strength with a corresponding decline of patriarchal and matriarchal authority. Traditional customs, which helped anchor legitimate family relations, diminish in importance and extended kinship ties also diminish with a reduction of respect and obligations to extended kin. The sacred religious order gives way to secularized religious practices and the moral order gives way to the legal order.

Underlying all these typologies is an essentially negative view of the city and urban life, particularly in regard to the family. This antiurban bias tends to depict rural life as basically good, clean, and pure as opposed to the city, which is associated with social disorganization, decay, and filth. This emphasis on the negative aspects of city life is not peculiar to social scientists. It pervades the belief system about the city in social philosophy, religion, and popular music, art, and literature (Gist and Fava, 1974:573−595). Morton and Lucia White (1962) in tracing the intellectual portrait of American cities conclude that historically:

. . . enthusiasm for the American city has not been typical or predominant in our intellectual history. Fear has been the most common reaction. For a variety of reasons our most celebrated thinkers have expressed different degrees of ambivalence and animosity toward the city. . . . We have no persistent or pervasive tradition of romantic attachment to the city in our literature or in our philosophy, nothing like the Greek attachment to the *polis* or the French writer's affection for Paris. (White and White, 1962:1−2)

The fascination with the social disorganization aspects of urban life by these earlier sociologists led them to overlook the role of the city as a positive experience—a social integrator of people and families and with many positive qualities—and also led them to dismiss the social organizational aspects of urban ethnic working-class communities. Further, in their study of the urban poor, particularly the black and hispanic communities, they developed a conceptualization of the poor that viewed them as socially disorganized, pathological, and suffering from a "culture of poverty," which assured the perpetuation of their poverty-ridden existence.

The works of Wirth, Redfield, and the earlier classical social scientists who developed typologies on the urban-rural dichotomization of society shared a common orientation—a negative view of the city and of urban life, particularly in its impact on the family. Reaching similar conclusions on the nature of urban family life, but based on a more positive or functional view, was the work of Talcott Parsons.

TALCOTT PARSONS AND THE ISOLATED NUCLEAR FAMILY

Talcott Parsons (1902–1980) was one of the most predominant and influential sociologists of the twentieth century. Arguing from a structure functionalist model, Parsons proclaimed a theory of the American family that has generated extensive research both in the United States and elsewhere on the characteristics of the family system in cities. According to Parsons the isolation of the nuclear family "is the most distinctive feature of the American kinship system and underlies most of its peculiar functional and dynamic problems" (1943:28). The normal American household consists of a husband, wife, and children economically independent of their extended family and frequently located at considerable geographical distance from them.

Parsons views American society as highly differentiated, with the family system's previous educational, religious, political, and economic functions being taken over by other instituions in the society. Thus schools, churches, peer groups, political parties, voluntary associations, and formal occupational groups have assumed functions once reserved to the family. Unlike the social disorganization, anomic, and alienating assessments—made by such theorists as William F. Ogburn, Carle C. Zimmerman, and Louis Wirth among others—on the negative impact of industrialization on the family, Talcott Parsons sees the family as becoming a more specialized group, concentrating its functions on the socialization of children and providing emotional support and affection for family members.

Parsons further suggests that the isolated nuclear family may be ideally suited to meet the demands of occupational and geographical mobility that is inherent in industrial urban society. Unencumbered by obligatory extended kinship bonds, the nuclear family is best able to move where the jobs are and is better able to take advantage of occupational opportunities. In contrast, the traditional extended-family system bond of extensive, obligatory economic and residential rights and duties is seen to be dysfunctional for industrial society. (The classical Parsonian position that there is a close fit between the isolated nuclear family and the industrialized system is essentially similar to that of Goode who emphasized the fit between the conjugal family and industrial societies.)

Arguing against the social disorganization thesis on the breakdown of the contemporary family, Parsons (1955) finds support for the importance of the nuclear family in the high rates of marriage and remarriage after divorce, the increase in the birthrate after World War II, and the increase in the building of single-family homes (particularly in suburbia) during this time period. All these trends provide evidence of the continuing visibility *not* social disorganization of the family and *increased* vitality of the nuclear family bond. Thus a specialized family system functionally meets the affectional and personality needs of its members; it may be admirably fitted to a family system that is a relatively isolated and self-sustaining economic unit of mother, father, and children, living without other relatives in the house and without close obligations and ties to relatives who live nearby.

> . . . the family has become *a more specialized agency than before,* probably more specialized than it has been in any previously known society. This represents a decline of *certain* features which traditionally have been associated with families, but whether it represents a "decline of the family" in a more general sense is another matter; we think not. We think the trend of the evidence points to the beginning of the relative stabilization of a new type of family structure, in a new relation to a general social structure, one in which the family is more specialized than before, but not in any general sense less important, because the society is dependent *more* exclusively on it for the performance of its vital functions. (Parsons and Bales, 1955:9)

In summary, Parsons emphasizes the importance of the nuclear family—in the absence of extended kinship ties—in that it meets two major societal needs: the socialization of children and the satisfaction of the affectional and emotional demands of husbands and wives and their children. Further, the isolated nuclear family, which is not handicapped by conflicting obligations to extended relatives, can best take advantage of occupational opportunities and is best able to cope with the demands of modern industrial urban life.

QUESTIONING THE IDEAL TYPOLOGY: THE VIABILITY AND VARIABILITY OF URBAN FAMILY LIFE

In the remainder of this chapter we will examine research that questions the assumption that the city is antithetical to family life. In particular, we will discuss the accumulated research that postulates the existence of a modified extended family system among the urban middle classes. We will also look at ethnic groups, such as Italians, Irish, Jews, Puerto Ricans, and so on, who continue their ethnic cultural heritage in urban enclaves, who have extensive and viable family kinship ties, and who isolate themselves from the encroachment of the larger city. In addition, we will examine the research on the modified extended family in the cities of the United States within the context of mobility and kinship relationships.

Since 1950 a mass of empirical data has accumulated that questions the basic assumptions of theorists like Louis Wirth[1] and Talcott Parsons.[2] These studies have shown that viable relationships exist among relatives and that they constitute a family's most important social contacts. They also demonstrate that relationships with kin are a major source of recreational and leisure activities and that there is a considerable interchange of mutual aid among related families. The studies directly contradict the prevalent notions about the social isolation of the urban nuclear family and the underlying theme of social disorganization as a characteristic of urban life that leads to the disintegration of families and the alienation and anomie of individual city dwellers.

These studies of urban family relations in New Haven (Sussman, 1953), East Lansing (Stone, 1954; Smith, Form, and Stone, 1954), Detroit (Axelrod, 1956), Los Angeles (Greer, 1956), San Francisco (Bell and Boat, 1957), Philadelphia (Blumberg and Bell, 1959), Cleveland (Sussman, 1959) and Buffalo (Litwak, 1959–1960, 1960a, 1960b)—all provided evidence of the significant role played by extended kin on contemporary American families. Sussman and Burchinal (1962) summarized this relevant research and concluded that the urban nuclear family must be seen within the context of an interrelated kinship structure that provides services and aid in a reciprocal exchange system. They schematically summarize this research on the functional interrelationship of nuclear families in Figure 4.1. They find that the major forms of help and service include the following: help during illness, financial aid, care of children, personal and business advice, and valuable gifts. Social activities were found to be the principal functions of the interrelated family network—major forms being interfamily visits, joint participation in recreational activities, and participation in ceremonial activities, such as weddings and funerals, which are significant demonstrations of family unity. These findings led Sussman to conclude in an earlier paper that:

[1] "The family as a unit of social life is emancipated from the larger kinship group characteristic of the country, and the individual members pursue their own diverging interest in their vocational, education, religious, recreational and political life" (Wirth, 1938:21).

[2] "The isolation of the nuclear family "is the most distinctive feature of the American kinship system and underlies most of its peculiar functional and dynamic problems" (Parsons, 1943:28).

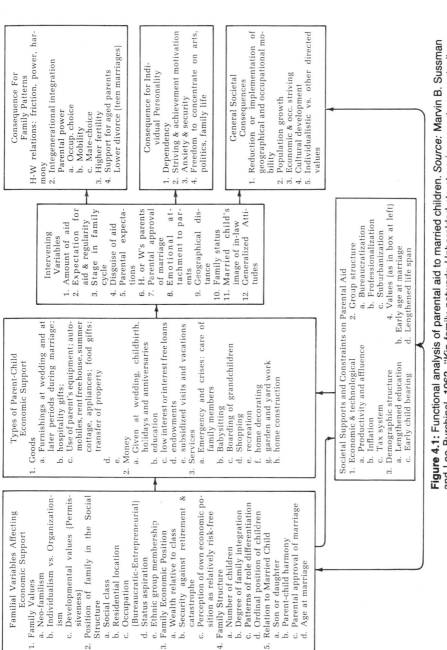

Figure 4.1: Functional analysis of parental aid to married children. *Source:* Marvin B. Sussman and Lee Burchinal. 1962. "Kin family network: Unheralded structure in current conceptualizations of family functioning." *Marriage and Family Living* 24:233.) Copyright 1962. Used by permission of the National Council on Family Relations. Reprinted by permission of the publisher and authors.

The answer to the question "The Isolated Nuclear Family, 1959: Fact or Fiction?" is, mostly fiction. It is suggested that kin ties, particularly intergenerational ones, have far more significance than we have been led to believe in the life processes of the urban family. While these kin ties by no means replicate the 1890 model, the 1959 neolocal nuclear family is not completely atomistic but closely integrated within a network of mutual assistance and activity which can be described as an interdependent kin family system. (Sussman, 1959:340)

Sussman (1953, 1959), Litwak (1960a, 1960b), and Sussman and Burchinal (1962) provide a theoretical explanation accounting for the existence of viable kinship relations in urban centers when the early theorists hypothesized that they did not exist. Whereas Parsons (1943) suggests that the isolated nuclear family is ideally suited to the demands of occupational and geographical mobility, which are in inherent part of urban industrial society, these researchers suggest that it may not be the most functional family type. They hypothesize that the modified extended family may be more functional than the isolated nuclear one.

Litwak (1959−1960, 1960a, 1960b) found that an extended family kinship structure existed in a modern urban center—Buffalo, New York. This extended family structure differed from the classical extended family in that there was no authoritarian leader, nor was it dependent on geographic mobility or occupational similarity to assure its viability. This modified extended family structure consisted of a series of nuclear families joined together on an equalitarian basis for mutual aid. It thus differed from the isolated nuclear family in that considerable mutual aid is assumed to exist among these family members, and thus the family does not face the world as an isolated unit.

The question naturally arises as to how these later findings reporting on the viability of extended kinship relationships can be reconciled with the earlier sociological accounts reporting the existence of isolated nuclear families and the absence of viable kinship networks.[3] Key (1961) suggested that the hypothesis on the disintegration of the extended family was focused on the experiences of immigrant groups coming to the city during the period of urbanization in Western society before these immigrants had the opportunity to establish families. In addition, this period of industrialization was characterized by rapid change and great geographical mobility from rural areas to newly urbanized ones. The events occurring in such American cities as Chicago during the first 30 years of the twentieth century dramatically illustrate this point.

It is our contention that the earlier theorists, particularly Wirth and Parsons, confounded the effects of differential socialization experiences on intergenerational families when they examined the relationship between industrialization and kinship

---

[3]The ensuing discussion follows an earlier presentation of this argument by Hutter (1970).

solidarity. That is, when they looked at that relationship, they did not control for the "transformation of identity" of family members as a result of their differential socialization experiences. This belief is shared by Peter L. Berger (1963) who notes that kinship ties are weakened by social mobility *when* social mobility has consequences in terms of the reinterpretation of one's life. Berger argues that individuals reinterpret their relationship to the people and events that used to be closest to them because their self-image changes as they move up the occupational and ethnic assimilation ladder. "Even Mama, who used to be the orb around which the universe revolved, has become a silly old Italian woman who must pacify occasionally with the fraudulent display of an old self that no longer exists" (Berger, 1963:60).

During this earlier stage of industrialization and urbanization, then, social mobility was accompanied by differential socialization experiences that accounted for the "transformation of identity" of the younger family members and the resultant weakening of kinship ties. This period of rapid social change—great geographical mobility from rural areas to newly urbanized ones and, in the United States, a great influx of Europeans emigrating from their homelands—caused great social and cultural mobility and separation among intergenerational families. Today, following Litwak (1960b), we contend that in the United States social class differences based on cultural diversity are moderate and shrinking. They are not growing larger. Litwak argues that social class similarities are sufficiently large to provide cross-class identification by extended family members. He maintains that among white Americanized groups, especially those of the middle class, upward mobility does not involve radical shifts in socialization and, therefore, does not constitute a real barrier to extended family communication. Here, then, is one key intervening variable between social mobility and kinship solidarity—transformation of identity caused by differential socialization experiences. It is because differential socialization experiences have been largely absent in urban America in the last 25 years that helps to account for the appearance of the modified extended family.

In summary, some would argue that the discovery of the viability of extended kinship ties, albeit modified, may be a post World War II phenomenon and may or may not have existed prior to that time. Recently, however, family historians have presented evidence that extended kinship ties may have existed during the latter part of the nineteenth century and the first half of the twentieth century. They believe that the conceptual straitjacket of the ideal typology led sociologists to concentrate their attention solely on examining the social disorganization of the city and the isolation of the nuclear family.

They argue that an important factor in the failure of sociologists to see the viability of urban kinship relationships stems from the oversimplification of the ideal typology, which contrasts urban and rural life and modern city families and traditional rural families. Sociologists failed to recognize the urban manifestations of extended kinship involvements. They failed to see that all too frequently traditional family systems also served as agents of modernization through example as well as by offering direct assistance to geographically mobile families. Tamara K. Hareven (1975) in her study of the industrial town of Manchester, New Hampshire, from the end of the nineteenth century through the first quarter of the twentieth, found that kin served as conveyers of individuals from preindustrial to industrial settings. They did not "hold down individuals" nor did they delay their mobility. Her research reveals that the kinship patterns of immigrant groups may be representative of a modern adaptation to new conditions. Kin relationships changed and were modified so that they could function within the industrial system, but such relationships were quite different from what they have been in their rural origins. Her findings led her to conclude that the ideal typology, with its either/or assumptions, might be a simplification of the historical process.

A further limiting aspect of the ideal typology was its failure to take into consideration differences in class and ethnicity. As we will soon see, the working-class family still served as a basic economic unit. It had a strong influence on the work and occupational careers of its individual members. Working-class and ethnic families banded together in their attempt to overcome their poor economic circumstances. The middle-class family with its values of privacy and individualism best approximates the ideal typology of the urban family. But, the working class developed their own "modern" and urban attitudinal value system to best allow them to cope with the vicissitudes of urban industrial life. Thus within the same historical period there was a myriad of urban adaptation processes. Herbert Gans (1962b) has presented the first and most important statement of this argument.

Herbert Gans's Urbanism and Suburbanism as Ways of Life: A Reevaluation of Definitions

Herbert Gans (1962b) took issue with the dominant sociological conceptualizations concerning cities and urban life held by the Chicago School as well as with the definitive summary statement in Louis Wirth's "Urbanism as a Way of Life." Gans makes the following points: (1) Wirth's urbanites represent not a picture of urban men and women but are rather a depiction of the depersonalized and atomized members of mass society; they are representative of society not of the city; (2) residents of the outer city tend to exhibit life styles more characteristic of suburbia than of the inner city; and (3) Wirth's description of the urban way of life fits best the transient areas of the inner city; here too it is best to view the inner city as providing a diversity of ways of life rather than a single way of life. Of immediate interest is Gans's argument that there are at least five urban ways of life that characterize the inner city (downtown) and that vary depending on the basis of social class as well as the stages in the family life cycle. Gans uses the following classifications:

1. Cosmopolites
2. The unmarried or childless
3. Ethnic villages
4. The deprived
5. The trapped and downward mobile

The cosmopolites place a high value on the cultural facilities located in the center of the city and tend to be composed of artistically inclined persons, such as writers, artists, intellectuals, and professionals. A large proportion of inner-city dwellers are unmarried or, if married, childless. This group is composed of the affluent and the powerful members of the city. The less affluent cosmopolites may move to suburban areas to raise their children while attempting to maintain kinship and primary group relationships and resist the encroachment of other ethnic or racial groups.

The deprived population find themselves in the city out of no choice of their own. This group is composed of the very poor, the emotionally disturbed or otherwise handicapped, broken families, and—in significant number—the nonwhite poor who are forced to live in dilapidated housing and blighted neighborhoods because of discrimination and an economic housing marketplace that relegates them to the worst areas of the city.

The fifth and final group are composed of trapped people who stay behind in the city as a result of downward mobility, who cannot afford to move out of a neighborhood when it changes, and who cannot economically compete for good housing. Aged persons living on fixed incomes and families that do not have a stable economic income fall into this category.

The first two groups described—the cosmopolites and the married and childless—and the last two groups—the deprived and the trapped—share a common residential characteristic—they live in transitional areas of the inner city. These areas are heterogeneous in population because they are either inhabited by transient types who do not require homogeneous neighborhood relations (the cosmopolites and the unmarried and childless groups) or by deprived or trapped people who are forced to live in transitory heterogeneous neighborhoods. The relationships these two groups have with their communities is the same—segmented role relationships that are necessary for obtaining local services and are characterized by anonymity, impersonality, and superficiality. However, these segmented role relationships have different consequences for the two groups. The cosmopolites and the unmarried and childless groups live in their neighborhoods by choice and frequently have positive psychological experiences; the deprived and trapped groups are forced to live in such communities and may suffer psychological damage resulting from their forced isolation.

Gans (1962b) does not address himself to Parsons's conceptualization of the isolated nuclear family, although it may fit to some degree the cosmopolites and the married childless or the affluent with young children, all of whom are found among the first two inner-city types. These individuals positively benefit from the occupational opportunities of urban industrial society and are not handicapped by economically detrimental obligatory ties with extended kin. The economically deprived and trapped groups share the negative impact of isolation from relatives; their isolated family system takes on all the negative characteristics of the family unit described by the social disorganization and alienation theories of urban life, which we have already discussed.

Gans goes on to describe a sixth urban way of life that is characteristic of individuals and families who live in the outer city and the suburbs. He describes the relationship between neighbors as *quasi primary,* "Whatever the intensity or frequency of these relationships, the interaction is more intimate than a secondary contact, but more guarded than a primary one" (Gans, 1962b:634). Although Gans does not describe the relationship these people have with their extended kin, we may conjecture (based on previously mentioned studies) that their relationship shares many of the characteristics of the modified extended family. Families residing in outer city and suburban communities tend to live in single-family dwellings, they are younger, more of them are married, they have higher incomes, and they hold more white-collar positions than their inner-city counterparts.

Urban Villagers and Closed Communities

Among the five inner-city resident groups, the ethnic working-class villages are the most highly integrated and tend to resemble small-town homogenous communities more than they resemble Wirth's characteristics of urbanism. Far from being depersonalized, isolated, and socially disorganized, emphasis in the urban villagers' way of life is "on kinship and the primary group, the lack of anonymity and secondary-group contacts, the weakness of formal organization, and the suspicion of anything and anyone outside their neighborhood" (Gans, 1962b:630).

John Mogey (1964) in his essay, "Family and Community in Urban-Industrial Societies," draws on the descriptive writings about urban villages in England, France, and the United States and develops a theoretical dichotomy between *open* and *closed* communities. The closed community is the urban village. It is characterized as one where schemes of intense interfamilial cooperation exists and as one that is cohesive, homogeneous in cultural values, and closed against outsiders. The open community, on the other hand, is similar to Gans's depiction of the urban way of life of the cosmpolites and the unmarried and the married without children. In these communities people have voluntary attachments to a variety of associations and secondary groups. Families who live in these communities interact with individuals from other areas as well as from their own.

An open community has an in-and-out migration of population, whereas the closed community is characterized by relatively little mobility. The closed community or urban village has families who are acquainted with each other and have extensive ties with neighbors. In the open community each family lives in relative anonymity and few personal relationships exist among members of the community.

Mogey states that the conjugal family is not prevalent in the closed community. No isolated nuclear family structure exists since it requires an open community structure, with secondary group relationships predominating over primary ones. Family mobility is also seen as leading to the abandonment of segregated family role patterns.

Young and Willmott (1957/1962) in their study of the working-class community of Bethnel Green in east London report that the extensive family ties, far from having disappeared, were still very much prevalent. They provide an interesting illustration of the extensiveness of family relations in Bethnel Green—the report by one of their children who was attending a local school. The child came back from school one day and reported that:

> The teacher asked us to draw pictures of our family. I did one of you and Mummy and Mickey and me, but isn't it funny, the others were putting in their Nannas and aunties, and uncles and all such sorts of people like that. (Young and Willmott, 1957/1962:14)

A similar observation is made by Gans (1962a). He reports that the family system of the Italian-Americans residing in the working-class community on the West End of Boston have a family system that shares some of the characteristics of the modified extended family and the classical extended family. Although each of the households are nuclear—composed of husband, wife, and children—there are extended family ties.

> But although households are nuclear or expanded, the family itself is still closer to the extended type. It is not an economic unity, however, for there are few opportunities for people to work together in commercial or manufacturing activities. The extended family actually functions best as a social circle, in which relatives who share the same interests, and who are otherwise compatible enjoy each other's company. Members of the family circle also offer advice and other help on everday problems. There are some limits to this aid, however, especially if the individual being helped does not reciprocate. (Gans, 1962a:46)

Mogey describes the impact of the closed community on marital roles as one characterized by husbands and wives each performing a separate set of tasks. The wife is in charge of household tasks and the raising of children, the husband is primarily responsible for being the breadwinner. Leisure-time activities are similarly segregated. In times of emergency aid for either the husband or wife is provided by same-sex relatives. Within families with segregation role patterns, mother-daughter relations tend to be stronger than father-son relations. This is particularly true when the husband has moved his residence at the time of marriage to the street of the wife's mother. Both Gans (1962a) as well as Young and Willmott (1957/1962) report that a particularly strong relationship exists between married daughter and mother:

> Marriage divides the sexes into their distinctive roles, and so strengthens the relationship between the daughter and the mother who has been through it before. The old proverb applies:
>
> My son's a man till he gets him a wife,
> My daughter's a daughter all her life.
>
> The daughter continues to live near her mother. She is a member of her extended family. She receives advice and support from her in the great personal crisis and on the small domestic occasions. They share so much and give such help to each other because, in their women's world, they have the same functions of caring for home and bringing up children. (Young and Willmott, 1957/1962:61)

Of particular importance to the working-class Italian-Americans of the West End of Boston are the peer group relations with friends and kin of the same generation. Social gatherings of married adults do not revolve around occupational roles as it does among the middle class but rather among the same-age kin and long-standing friends. Social gatherings tend to occur regularly, for example, once a week to play cards, and usually with the same people. These activities as well as major family events, such as christenings, graduations, and weddings, are all sex segregated—men staying in one group, the women in another group.

The working-class families are an adult-oriented family system. Children do not have center stage as they do among families of the middle class and upper middle class. Gans reports that, in the West End of Boston, the child is expected to develop and behave in ways satisfying to adults. Little girls are expected to assist their mother with household tasks by the age of 7 or 8; little boys are treated in a similar way as their fathers are, free to go and come as they please but staying out of trouble. Thus the children tend to develop a world for themselves that is relatively separate from their parents and in which the parents take little part:

> . . . parent-child relationships are segregated almost as much as male-female ones. The child will report on his peer group activities at home, but they are of relatively little

interest to parents in an adult-centered family. If the child performs well at school or at play, parents will praise him for it. But they are unlikely to attend his performance in a school program or a baseball game in person. This is his life, not theirs. (Gans, 1962a:56−57)

Of considerable interest are the studies that report the effects of social and geographical mobility—from the inner-city's ethnic villages to the outer city and the suburbs—on the family's way of life. Earlier, we suggested that Gans' description of middle-class families residing in these areas fits to some degree the characteristics of the modified extended family type. Now, we would like to turn our attention to a more detailed look at the family life of working-class and middle-class residents in this geographical area.

Young and Willmott (1957/1962) contrasted the working-class urban village of Bethnel Green in East London with the upwardly aspiring working-class suburban community of Greenleigh, located outside London. They found that the migrants from Bethnel Green did not leave because of weaker kinship attachments. Rather, they left for two main reasons: first was the attraction of a house with its modern conveniences as opposed to the antiquated, crowded flats that pervade Bethnel Green; second was that Greenleigh was generally thought to be "better for the kiddies." These migrants left their extended kin in Bethnel Green with regret. However, these people were not deserting family so much as acting for it, on behalf of their children rather than the older generation.

The effect of moving to Greenleigh was a significant drop in the frequency of visiting relatives in Bethnel Green, despite the close proximity of the two areas. Life in Greenleigh became much different than life in east London. In day-to-day affairs, the neighbors rarely took the place of kin. Even when neighbors were willing to assist, people were apparently reluctant to depend on or confide in them. For the transplanted Bethnel Greeners their neighbors were no longer relatives with whom they could share the intimacies of daily life. This had a particularly strong impact on wives, who were no longer in daily contact with their mothers and sisters; their new neighbors were strangers and were treated with reserve. The neighbors did not make up for kin. The effect on the family was that the home and the family of marriage because the focus of a couple's life, far more completely than in Bethnel Green.

Young and Willmott (1957/1962) conjecture that, since Greenleigh was a newly developed community populated by upwardly aspiring working-class couples, they neither shared long-time residence with their neighbors nor did they have kin ties to serve as bridges between themselves and the community. Young and Willmott believed that it would not have mattered quite so much in their neighborhood relationships if the migrant couples from Bethnel Green had moved into an established community. Such a community would have already been criss-crossed with ties of kinship and friendship, thus one friend made would have been an introduction to several.

Two research papers by Irving Tallman (1969; Tallman and Morgner, 1976) examined the effect of the move on working-class couples from inner-city communities in Minneapolis-St. Paul to a suburban community outside the Twin Cities. This research was concerned with what effect social and geographical mobility has on couples who had lived in urban villages and who were intimately tied to networks of social relationships composed of childhood friends and relatives. It found that, despite the considerable amount of neighborhood contacts established by these couples after they moved to the suburban community, the wives experienced a considerable amount of dissatisfaction and personal unhappiness and feelings of anomie and person disintegration. They believed that this resulted from the loss of contacts with their relatives and long-standing childhood friends in the city and the failure of the couple to reorganize their conjugal relationship. That is, the emotional and psychological supports that the wife received from her relationships with her relatives and friends was severed by the move to the suburbs and this required fundamental changes in the husband-wife relationship to make up for this loss. The working-class wife who was very dependent on extranuclear family, primary group relations was not able to make adequate adaptions to the suburban move:

> The disruption of friendship and kinship ties may not only be personally disintegrating for the wife but may also demand fundamental changes in role allocations within the family. Suburban wives may be more dependent upon their husbands for a variety of services previously provided by members of tight-knit networks. In addition, the ecology of the suburbs makes it necessary for the women to interact with strangers and to represent the family in community relations. Such a reorganization can increase the strain within the nuclear family and take on the social-psychological dimensions of a crisis in which new and untried roles and role expectations are required to meet the changing situation. (Tallman, 1969:67)

Tallman's work suggests, then, that the movement from working-class urban villages of the inner city to outer city and suburban open communities necessitates fundamental reorganization of conjugal and community roles of working-class couples to the middle-class type that emphasizes the importance of the conjugal role relationship. To support this contention, research indicates that the anomie and alienation characteristic of working-class couples does not exist to the same extent with middle-class families in suburban communities.

The study by Wendell Bell (1958) of 100 middle-class couples residing in two adjacent Chicago suburbs provides a vivid contrast to the working-class couples' experiences. Bell tested the hypothesis that the move to the suburbs expressed an attempt to find a location in which to conduct family life that is more suitable than that offered by inner cities. That is *familism*—spending the time, money and energy of the nuclear conjugal family—was chosen as an important element of the couples' way of life.

Bell devoted his concern to probing the reasons that the couples moved to the suburbs. Four-fifths of them gave reasons that had to do with bettering conditions for their children, a finding similar to Young and Willmott's (1957/1962) Greenleigh couples. Three-fourths of the respondents gave reasons that were classified as "enjoying life more." This classification was composed of such responses as being able to have more friendly neighbors, greater participation in the community, and easier living at a slower pace than in the city. A third major theme was classified as "the-people-like-ourselves" motive. These couples wanted to live in a neighborhood where people had the same age, marital, financial, educational, occupational, and ethnic status as themselves.

It is important to note that the latter two themes, "enjoying life more" and "the-people-like ourselves," were not given by the working-class couples of Young and Willmott's study of Greenleigh. The different social class compositions of these two suburban populations account for these differences; only one-third of Bell's couples were identified as blue collar, whereas all of Young and Willmott's couples fell into that category. It is particularly relevant in Bell's finding that only 14 percent gave as the reason for their moving to the suburbs more space inside the home; this was the major factor for the Greenleighers. Finally, the fact that the Greenleighers all had moved from the closed community of Bethnel Green as opposed to Bell's couples who moved from transitional inner-city neighborhoods or from the outer city may account for the differences in their attitudes toward the suburban community and their neighbors.

A most important variation in these two groups of people is the overwhelming familistic orientation of the Chicago suburban couples. This familism, as it enters into the suburban move, largely emphasizes the conjugal family system. This is indicated by the fact that only a small percentage of the respondents moved to be closer to relatives. In fact, in vivid contrast to the working-class couples described by Young and Willmott (1957/1962) and by Tallman (1969), several of the middle-class couples moved to get away from their relatives, a condition they considered desirable. In conclusion, Bell's (1958) findings support his hypothesis that the suburbanite couples have chosen familism as an important element in their life styles and, in addition, have a desire for community participation and involvement in neighborhood affairs. Both factors are absent as motivators for the blue-collar families of Greenleigh and the Twin Cities and may be the crucial reasons for the instability and unhappiness of the transplanted urban villagers.

In contrast to the adult-centered life of the urban villagers and the transplanted couples in the outer city and suburbs is the child-centered orientation of their middle-class counterparts. Wendell Bell has indicated the importance of familism and the involvement of parents with their children, as opposed to their extended family; a similar finding has been made by John Seeley and his collaborators (1956) in their study of an upper middle-class, outer-city suburban community in Toronto.

Seeley reports that the focus in these families is on the children; close, continuous attention is given to them. Tied with this is the extensive involvement of the couple with each other, a condition that is not present to the same degree in working-class couples of the city and suburbs. The Crestwood Heights suburban couple of Toronto is characterized by intense interaction and exchange by all family members, the family is viewed as a refuge from the trials and tribulations of the outside world. The dominant theme is home-centeredness; family members are expected to ask for and achieve psychic gratifications from each other.

Willmott and Young (1960) report a similar pattern in a predominantly middle-class suburban community (Woodford) in England. The young middle-class couples see little of their relatives and do not depend to any great extent on the extended family for regular help or companionship. Instead, they create social networks with people of their own age in the community. However, Willmott and Young believe that, although they have a larger circle of friends outside the family than do the urban villagers of Bethnel Green, their social relationships are not as closely knit nor are their loyalties as strong. The "friendliness" does not have the same characteristics in the two districts. In Bethnel Green people are seen to take each other for granted based on long-term friendship ties: in Woodford relations are not so easygoing. This results in sociality becoming a sort of how-to-win-friends-and-influence-people type, with a great amount of superficiality and noncommitment—and with people leaving out some part of their inner self in the process. This corroborates Gans's (1962b) observation that the common element in the ways of life of the outer city and suburban family is quasi primary: relationships that are more intense and occur with greater frequency than secondary contacts, but that are more guarded and less intimate than primary relationships. Gist and Fava (1974) have concluded that the vast literature on suburban family relationships makes similar observations. Finally, as with the research on suburban couples in America, Willmott and Young find that the area for intense emotional relationships for their English suburbanites lies not in contacts with friends, neighbors, or relatives, but within the nuclear family. The conjugal role organization of these families is home centered, couples share in many household tasks, including the raising of the children.

CONCLUSION

In summary, we compared and contrasted the different ways of family life of urban and suburban families. Our particular focus is on working-class families of the urban villages (closed communities) and the middle-class families of the outer city and suburbs (open communities). In addition, we looked at the impact of the movement to open communities by both middle-class and working-class couples. We were concerned with the variations in these two classes in regard to their relationships with their communities, their extended kin, and the internal family relationships of husband, wife, and children. In light of the opening discussion of the ideal typologies of urban-rural families and the position of Wirth and Parsons on the relative isolation of the nuclear family system in urban industrial societies, we saw that the issue is much more complicated than it was made out to be by these earlier theoretical schools of thought. Urban villagers have a family life that is a combination of traditional extended kinship ties and modified extended kinship ties, whereas the middle-class family system tends to have a family way of life that is a combination of relative nuclear family isolation with emphasis on the conjugal role relationship and the modified extended family form, which allows the conjugal family to take advantage of the extended family for mutual aid without giving up its structural independence.

In Chapter 5 we will examine in some detail the ways of life of family systems in urban centers that are located in nonindustrial countries to shed additional light on the relationship of the family to the city. In Chapter 6 we will turn our attention to poverty family systems that are located in industrial and nonindustrial societies' cities. By using this comparative approach we will best be able to grasp the complexity of the relationship of family systems undergoing processes of change in the contemporary world.

5

The Family in the City:
The African Experience

In Chapter 3 we examined various theories in sociology that were concerned with comparative cross-cultural analysis. The most influential was structure functionalism, which was limited by a theoretical bias that led it to underestimate the importance of social change. This bias stemmed from the emphasis of structure functionalism on an organismic model of consensus and cooperation and on its failure to acknowledge the possibility of conflicting interests among the constituent elements in a social system. In anthropology this theoretical position is labeled social anthropology. Like structure functionalism, social anthropology presents rather static models of society and tends to ignore change, even as it is occurring. Traditionally, social anthropologists in their study of nonliterate tribal peoples have tended to view their cultures as static entities and have, by and large, ignored the impact of colonial regimes on them. Instead, they have preferred to focus on the historical past prior to colonialism rather than on the transitional colonial era and the postcolonial present. This is evident by the limited number of studies that exist on tribal peoples outside their tribal communities. Peter C. W. Gutkind states that although contemporary social anthropologists are turning to urban studies, the previous generation of fieldworkers, as the noted social anthropologist, Max Gluckman, has pointed out, were "reared on the rural tradition of the tribe" (Gutkind, 1969:215). This attitude is reflected in the following report by a British anthropologist, Audrey Richards:

> In 1931 I first left the under-populated bush inhabited by the Bemba of north-eastern Rhodesia to study the men and women of this tribe who had migrated to the copper

mining towns of the south. My conduct was then thought rather unusual in a social anthropologist. I was even told by one of my professors not to meddle with these modern urban problems, but to stick to "really scientific work" in an unspoilt tribe! (Aubrey Richards cited in Gutkind, 1969:215)

Tied to this concern for study in the untampered past was an avoidance of both national political issues and the economic, political, and social forces accompanying colonialism. William Mangin (1970) believes that the dislike of anthropologists for the study of acculturation and the involvement of "their" people with cities and with national and international politics is shared by sociologists in their small-town and rural bias and their dislike of cities. Both orientations (as we have noted in the previous chapter) are part of the overall antiurban sentiments of intellectuals, artists, politicians, and lay people of western industrial societies. In recent years, however, an increasing number of anthropologists have turned from this traditional position and have concerned themselves with the transitions and changes in non-Western preliterate societies. Of particular interest to us is the accumulating research in urban anthropology that is concerned with the migration of peoples into the cities of colonial and postcolonial societies as well as their various adaptions and modifications of traditional family, religious, and political institutions and on the emerging new patterns of life.

In this chapter we will look at migrants to African cities south of the Sahara (black Africa) to shed comparative light on urban ways of life. We must warn the reader that the peoples and family patterns of sub-Saharan Africa vary a great deal and by necessity there will be a glossing over of these differences. Our main concern is to look at the profound effect urbanization has had on the family and to compare the adjustments, modifications, and new emerging patterns of these peoples with those that have occurred in Western industrial cities, particularly in the United States. In addition, we will be able to explore the validity of urban-rural ideal typologies and the isolated-nuclear-family theories of Louis Wirth and Talcott Parsons.

We will limit our attention to sub-Saharan African cities, but we do not claim to provide a complete comprehensive treatise on the family systems in this area owing to space limitations. Further, we wish to point out the great differences that exist in the different regions of tropical Africa. East, Central and South Africa are characterized by extreme racial intolerance. The various policies of apartheid have generated fear and hatred. Colin M. Turnbull (1962) observes that this has occurred in those regions where Europeans decided to settle and where they appropriated the tribal lands of the Africans. Ultimately, in all but the Republic of South Africa, the Europeans were forced out, leaving a feeling of hatred and dislike. In West Africa the situation was different, and this difference must be underlined. The Europeans did not have the desire to set up permanent residence; the mosquito problem partly accounts for this attitude. Further, there was less hostility between the African and the European because the European chose to live in the towns and cities of West

Africa, did not take over the tribal lands, and did not have the vast private farming estates characteristic of the other regions of sub-Saharan Africa. Turnbull (1962) believes that the Africans developed less antagonism toward European-dominated towns and cities because of these factors and owing to the greater economic opportunity and political equality of West Africa. Further, there were greater educational opportunities for the West African. The segregation occurring in these towns tended to be more social than racial, in contrast to the rigid segregated districts of cities in South Africa.

In the course of our discussion we will make note of these distinctions. For now, we want to alert the reader of their existence and to point out that in sub-Saharan cities and family life there are differences that exist based on these regional variations as well as on tribal and social class criteria.

SUBSAHARAN AFRICAN CITIES

African cities, especially the main cities in each country, are the centers of modernization. These cities, which anthropologists have labeled *primate* cities, are the intellectual and social capitals, the seats of government and political activity, and the economic capitals of their respective countries. The geographer, William A. Hance (1970), observes that the most notable characteristics of many African countries is the rapid fading away of modernity as one leaves these urban centers.

Figure 5.1 indicates great regional variations in the percentage of urban population in Africa, country by country. The most urbanized areas are the northern countries of Africa that border on the Mediterranean and the Republic of South Africa at the southern end of the continent. East Africa and west Africa vary in urban population. West Africa has a tradition of cities—with the Yourba cities of Nigeria being prominent—and east Africa is the least urbanized part of the continent.

African cities can be classified according to size and age as well as political, economic, tribal, social, and cultural functions. The most widely used system is one that classifies cities as to whether they were founded by Africans (indigenous cities) or by Europeans (expatriate cities). The anthropologist, Aidan Southall (1961), refers to the indigenous cities as Type A towns. These are old-established, slowly growing African towns whose social structure is basically traditional. Type B towns are of European creation, comprise rapidly expanding populations, and are mostly found in the industrialized areas that have the largest white populations.

Southall (1961:1−13) delineates the characteristics of Type A and Type B towns. Type A towns are composed of homogeneous indigenous populations. Although subsistence agriculture still plays a part in the economic life of the towns—with residents moving to the surrounding countryside for daily farm work and returning to the town in the evening—the dominant occupations tend to be clerical and commercial rather than industrial. Variations in social status are based

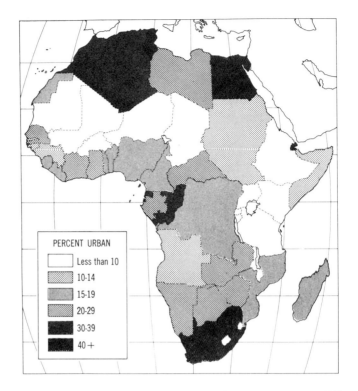

Figure 5.1. Estimated percentage of urban population by country. *Source:* William A. Hance. 1970. *Population, Migration and Urbanization in Africa.* (New York: Columbia University Press, page 221. Copyright 1970 by Columbia University Press. Reprinted by permission.)

on economic position, distance from rural origins, and length of time one has lived in the city. Kinship and tribal structures are not as extensive as in the rural areas, but they do exist and are sufficiently flexible to permit tribal and kinship concentrations.

In contrast, Type B towns are composed of an immigrant African population whose ties are severed from their rural origins. During the colonial period, the administrative control of the town was exercised by the white colonizers. The emerging independent African nations are developing managerial, entrepreneurial, landlord, and professional skills since they were little developed during the colonial period and the immediate preindependence period [when Southall wrote his essay (1961)]. Of economic and political importance to urban Africans are trade unions, political parties, and tribal welfare associations. In relation to the Type A town situation, there is little kinship and tribal concentration. Further, regional diversities of culture and social structure are minimized with emphasis being placed on the problems and solutions to the new urban condition.

The distribution of indigenous (Type A) and expatriate (Type B) towns and cities are mapped by Hance in Figure 5.2. Spatially, the Type A urban areas are centered around marketplaces, which are in open areas devoid of houses. Frequently, the quarters surrounding the market in North Africa take on the appearance of a rural village populated on the basis of tribal or religious affiliation, whereas they are likely to be of more homogeneous character in sub-Saharan Africa. The markets are devoted to the sale of farm produce and handcrafted items. In the towns that have fallen under modern influences, industrial crafts, mechanical and electrical repair shops, plumbing supplies, and so on, are present.

The Type B expatriate towns and cities differ in almost every respect from the indigenous town. Founded by Europeans, these colonial urban centers take on European architectural and street-layout styles and patterns. Populations are diverse, with Indians, Pakistanis, Syrians, Lebanese and other minorities residing exclusively in these European-oriented towns, as opposed to the indigenous ones. During the colonial period, the indigenous African population was separated and segregated in surrounding suburban areas called *Bidonvilles* ("tin-can towns"). The indigenous Africans migrated into the city to work and then, returned to their rather squalid shantytowns at night. This is the reverse of the American industrial city pattern. With independence, the more squalid of these communities have been replaced by low-cost housing in many sub-Saharan countries, but there is still a great need for adequate housing for these people. The amount of residential segregation has varied—from the extreme government policy of apartheid in the Republic of South Africa (where sections of the major cities are composed exclusively of the African, European, Indian, and Coloured, that is, mixed race populations) to the mixed residential patterns of such cities in West Africa as Lagos, Nigeria. However, as A. L. Epstein (1969) states, the tendency for Africans to be housed in strict segregation was almost universal in preindependence countries. The anthropologist V. G. Pons's description of Stanleyville (now Kisangani), Belgian Congo (now Zaire) is typical:

> The physical lay-out of the town could be seen as both an expression and a symbol of the relations between Africans and Europeans. European residential areas were situated close to, and tended to run into, the area of administrative offices, hotels, shops and other service establishments, while African residential areas were strictly demarcated and well removed from the town centre. (V. G. Pons cited in Epstein, 1969:249)

TYPE A INDIGENOUS TOWNS: YORUBA, NIGERIA

In this section we will first discuss the family and kinship systems existing in the traditional indigenous Type A towns south of the Sahara, using the towns of the Yoruba in western Nigeria as the illustrative case. We will then discuss and compare these towns with the family and kinship systems in the expatriate Type B towns that have developed as a result of direct European contact.

The anthropologist William Bascom (1968) describes the old historical Yoruba cities. These were based largely on agriculture and the populace were mainly farmers. The inhabitants commuted, not from the suburbs into the work places of the city, but rather from their city homes to the belt of farms that surrounded each Yoruban city. Kinship was the principal factor in and primary determinant of behavior in every aspect of community life and, most important—since farming itself was organized around family and kinship—these institutions set the way of life in both city and countryside.

Bascom describes the large number of urban centers that existed in western Nigeria prior to the slave-trade wars of the first half of the nineteenth century. A large number of these towns were destroyed or abandoned during this period. He quotes Bowen, the first American missionary in Nigeria, who traveled through much of the Yoruba country in 1849–1856:

> I have counted the sites of eighteen desolated towns within a distance of sixty miles between Badagry and Abbeokuta [sic]—the legitimate result of the slave trade. The whole of Yoruba country is full of depopulated towns, some of which were even larger than Abbeokuta is at present. Of all the places visited . . . only Ishakki (Shaki), Igboho, Ikishi (Kishi) and a few villages remain. Ijenna (Ijana) was destroyed only a few weeks after my arrival in the country. Other and still larger towns in the same region have lately fallen. At one of these Oke-Oddan, the Dahomey army killed and captured 20,000 people on which occasion the king presented Domingo, the Brazillian slaver, with 600 slaves. The whole number of people destroyed in this section of the country, within the last fifty years, can be not less than five hundred thousand. (Bascom, 1968:84)

Today these traditional cities continue to exist without industrialization. Farming, specialized production in woodcarving, metalwork, brass-casting, weaving and dyeing, the trade of domestic products, and so forth, are the cornerstones of the Yoruba town economy. The local retail trade has remained primarily in the hands of women, who tend to specialize in yams, corn, chickens, and other such commodities. They, like the artisans, are organized into guilds. The foundation of group activities is lineage, which involves reciprocal social and economic obligations. Thus there is little loneliness and insecurity. Yoruba society is pecuniary and highly competitive. Therefore, economic failure can lead to frustration, aggression, or suicide, but such outcomes are minimized because of social and economic lineage support.

Bascom contrasts this description of the Yoruban way of life with that of Louis Wirth, who argued that the bonds of kinship, neighborliness, and sentiments stemming from a common folk tradition would be absent or, at best, very weak in the city. Such is not the case in the Yoruba cities. Bascom (1968:90–91) emphasizes the fact that Yoruba cities, unlike Wirth's ideal type city, are not characterized by the substitution of formal control mechanisms for bonds of solidarity. Instead, formal control mechanisms were developed as mechanisms of political control on a

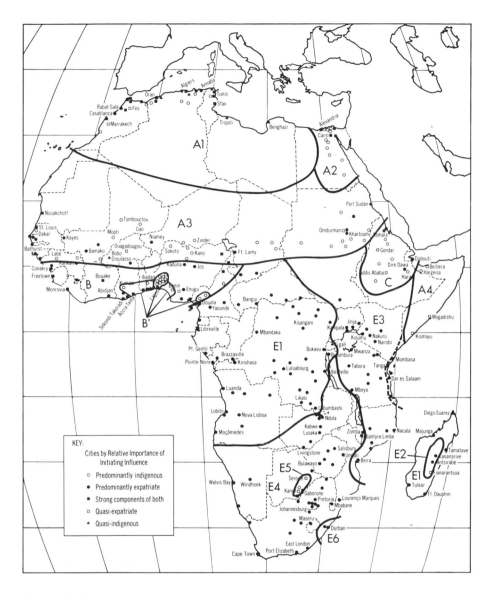

Figure 5.2. Selected towns and cities of Africa mapped according to the relative importance of indigenous and expatriate influence and tentative urban cultural regions. See key. (*Source:* William A. Hance. 1970. *Population, Migration and Urbanization in Africa.* New York: Columbia University Press, pp. 246–247. Copyright 1970 by Columbia University Press. Reprinted by permission.)

117

secondary, suprakinship level, transcending the primary groups, such as lineages. Kinship bonds were not weakened by urban life or, on a higher level, by the political control of city governments. Lineage *was* the basis of both urban and rural political structure.

Bascom concludes that in these indigenous cities the majority of the residents marry, raise their children, and live with their families throughout most of their lives. They die and are buried within the city and with their own lineage. Ties with family and lineage are not broken or even suspended by urban life. The authority of the family, lineage, and the chiefdom are maintained in the cities through the family and lineage and through the town chiefs and heads of the Yoruba states. As a result there are low rates of illegitimacy, juvenile delinquency, and crime in comparison to the newer African cities and to the cities of Europe and America.

Finally, Bascom notes the effects of European influence during the present century. Both the old residents of Yoruba cities and the new migrants from rural areas are forced to adopt to European acculturation. Yoruban religion was also undermined and its sanctions of behavior were sapped by Christian and Moslem missions and by schools and government. With the destruction of old belief systems and the substitution of western concepts of individual salvation and individual

---

Regions delineated on map in Figure 5.2:
A. Areas of Strong Muslim Influence
    A1. North Africa, Indigenous influence Arab-Berber; modern influence predominantly French in the Maghreb, Italian in Libya, Spanish in northern Morocco, Ceuta, and Melilla.
    A2. Egypt. Considerable European influence in modern cities.
    A3. Sudan belt. Emirate cities, old caravan centers; Arab and some Egyptian influence in east; modern influence French and British.
    A4. Somalia and East Coast. Arab influence strong.
B. Western Africa
    B. Modern cities dominate; French and British influence most important.
    B′. Subregions where indigenous cities are best represented.
C. Ethiopia. Mainly indigenous; Muslim and Italian influence in Eritrea; Italian influence in Addis Ababa, Gondar.
E. Middle, eastern, and southern Africa. European influence predominant in most areas.
    E1. Middle Africa. French, Belgian, and Portuguese influence dominant. On Madagascar [now the Malagasy Republic] French influence predominant in newer towns, some Arab influence at Majunga.
    E2. Merina and Betsileo towns of Malagasy Highlands; important French influence in new sections.
    E3. Eastern Africa. Modern influence primarily British; important Indian components in most towns; Arab influence on coast and islands.
    E4. Central and South Africa. Influence predominantly British; Afrikaner initiative in some South African towns.
    E5. Botswana. Agrotowns of Tswana.
    E6. Natal. Mainly British towns, strong Indian component.

responsibility, there has been a concomitant undermining of the traditional respect for elders, lineage responsibilities, and the strength of lineage controls. Bascom predicts that with the increasing industrialization and urbanization in Nigeria "that although African cultural features will be retained, . . . the new and old cities of Africa will tend to approximate each other and the cities of Europe and America in their sociological characteristics" (Bascom, 1968:93).

We will examine the transitions occurring in family life in indigenous Type A towns by reviewing in some detail the impact of family change in the increasingly industrial city of Lagos, which has its origins as a Yoruban town. We will then contrast the events occurring in these types of urban areas with those cities of Africa that are of European origin and influence in regard to family and kinship patterns.

TYPE A INDIGENOUS TOWNS: LAGOS, NIGERIA

In the study of family and kinship ties in indigenous Type A urban areas, a landmark research monograph was written by Peter Marris (1961), *Family and Social Change in an African City: A Study of Rehousing in Lagos.* Marris's aim was to replicate Michael Young and Peter Willmott's (1957) study of working-class families of Bethnel Green in East London, England, and the effect of the move to a suburban housing development, Greenleigh, located outside of London. As you recall from our discussion in the previous chapter, Young and Willmott found that Bethnel Green working-class families were characterized by widespread cohesive kin groups imbedded in a closed community with a strong sense of homogeneity and togetherness. The immediate effect of the move to Greenleigh was the loss of this sense of community, restrictions in contact with neighbors and friends, and a withdrawal of the husband and wife into their households—homecenteredness.

Lagos, Nigeria, the African city studied by Marris, is a city with a strong Yoruban traditional history that is being subjected to the demands of modernization and industrialization. Marris was fortunate in finding a parallel situation to that which occurred in East London; the central district of Lagos, which was inhabited by extended family systems, was undergoing a slum-clearance disruption. Marris was concerned with comparing the family life in the central area before people were forced to move with the life of those living in the newly established rehousing estate. He was also interested in people's assessments of life in the central district before they moved. Finally, he wished to compare his findings with those of Young and Willmott's London study.

Marris describes the traditional Yoruba family as residing in a family compound based on a lineage that traced its descent from the same male ancestor. The characteristic pattern of residence consisted of a group of sons and grandsons—with their wives, children, and descendants—of the man who established the compound. Although they resided in the same compound, the members of it did not form a single economic unit. Rather, each married man with his wives and unmarried children and any other kin for whom he was responsible (e.g., a widowed mother or unmarried brother) formed a separate household. Each household would become an independent economic unit centered around the farmland the man owned. In cases where the man had more than one wife, each wife and their respective children would form a subsidiary household within the larger one, with the mother as the focal point of the children's ties, loyalties, and affections. This, then, was the smallest family unit in the Yoruba pattern of kinship—the mother and her children. The mother and her children formed part of the husband's household. The husband's household, in turn, was incorporated within several that resided within the same compound under the dominance of a single senior male. These lineages, in turn, were part of a larger and more comprehensive lineage residing in separate dwellings. Ultimately, the whole lineage became part of still larger social groupings, with members recognizing the bonds of distant kinship with each other (Marris, 1961:12–16). The following account illustrates this traditional family compound arrangement that—although changing more in Lagos as a result of industrialization than in other parts of the Yoruba country—still had a profound influence on its members.

This house was built by a wealthy trader about a hundred years ago. It fronted on to a narrow lane, the walls patched with corrugated iron, the windows boarded with cream and black shutters, grimed with age. Inside the door on the right, a passage extended past two rooms to an open yard, where chickens and guinea fowls clattered in their pens. A second passage facing the entrance led past three more rooms to a larger yard at the back of the house, where the households cooked, washed and kept their stores. Sheds lined two sides of the yard, and lavatories were built into a corner. Inside the passage a narrow staircase gave access to the upper floor: the three lower steps were of concrete, the remainder thin wooden slats, worn away by years of use. At the head of the stairs was a landing with a gable window, where in the rainy season basins were spread to catch the leaks. On either side were sets of rooms, low-pitched under the iron sheeting of the roof. The walls and ceilings were of uneven, cream-painted boarding, and there was a gap between wall and floor, through which appeared the supporting poles of the eaves. On this floor were six more rooms, beside two small anterooms through which they were reached. Altogether, the house contained eleven rooms, each occupied by a separate household.

As with many of the old houses of Lagos, it seemed shabby and neglected. The furniture of each room was bare and functional—a bed, a few wooden stools or folding chairs, a cupboard, a pile of trunks and boxes, mats thrown on the floor. In the passage hung a mirror and a wall clock, no longer working. The only decorations were the calendars of commercial firms—the playfully exotic landscapes with which airlines like to match the months, or Coca Cola girls with their insatiable thirsts—and large wall almanacs put out by Lagos publishers, with inset photographs of chiefs and leading politicians. But in spite of their apparent indifferences to appearances, the family was deeply attached to their home.

The most senior member of the house, a vigorous woman in her seventies, was the only surviving child of the original owner. She spent most of her day in a corner of the passage which flanked the front of the building, where every visitor would pause to pay her their respects. Here she presided over the affairs of the house. She shared a room and parlour with her eldest son, his wife and the wife's twelve-year-old niece, who helped with the housework. Two other rooms were occupied by women of her generation; the widow of one of her brothers, with her daughter and grandchildren, and the widow of a half brother with three grandchildren. Most of the rest of the house was taken up by six of her nephews, with their wives and children, and usually one or two young girls of the wives' families. Lastly, one room was used by the granddaughter of one of her brothers, who was separated from her husband. In all, these ten households contained eighteen men and women, and sixteen children. The head of each was a child (or his widow), grandchild or great-grandchild of the original owner of the house. In this sense, they lived as a traditional Yoruba family. But there were many other grandsons and great-grandsons who, because of their work, or simply because there was no place for them, lived elsewhere, either with other relatives or in rooms they had rented. (Marris, 1961:17 – 19)

In summary, the traditional Yoruba extended family was composed of individuals with strong obligations to give economic assistance to kin while maintaining their social ties within the customary residential unit of a compound based on lineage. The extended family recognized the authority of a single head, usually the senior male member, and concomitantly the status of each family member was defined by his seniority. Finally, family relationships emphasized the importance and predominance of the family group over the individual.

The large family compound described is becoming more and more scarce with fewer houses in Lagos under common family ownership or entirely occupied by an extended family. The separate household has replaced the compound as the predominate unit of residence. However, the vast majority of the residents of the central district of Lagos interviewed by Marris still have strong family ties with their kin. And despite the predictions of such sociologists as Louis Wirth and Talcott Parsons, "the households are not isolated; their connections branch out into the neighborhood, and their lives are still centered on the affairs of their family group" (Marris, 1961:27). Friendship and kinship networks are maintained by daily meetings, which serve as communicative interchanges to pass on family news and to discuss family problems. Assistance patterns continue, with regular sums of money given for the support of kinfolk; the feeling is that the needs of relatives assume first obligatory priority. Individuals, rather than being primarily responsible and having first loyalties to themselves or to their conjugal nuclear families, see their prime responsibility to their extended family. Marris observed that the extended family also serves as the basis for some of the voluntary associations individuals joined to further their economic interests.

Of the families studied by Marris, two-thirds of them were Muslims, one-third Christian. Of the 126 marriages studied, 118 had a customary marriage solemnized by the consent of the bride's family, the bridegroom usually provides an agreed upon monetary sum and ritual gifts. Although traditionally these marriages are arranged between the kinsfolk of the couple, 8 of 16 men sampled chose their wives themselves. Of the remaining 8 marriages, 7 were performed in church and 1 was a civil ceremony. The significance of this is that to be married in church places one under the rights and penalties derived from English custom rather than Nigerian custom.

Two-thirds of the householders in central Lagos are Muslim and half had more than one wife. Polygyny was also found in the Christian households but to a lesser degree. Polygyny is correlated with wealth and social status, and most important, more children are beneficial for the extended famliy system (Marris, 1961:47−49). There are also practical and moral advantages associated with polygyny. The Yoruba consider it wrong to have sexual relationships with pregnant women and women who are breast feeding.

In the polygynous household, the senior wife enjoys a privileged position and has authority over the junior wives, especially in allocating heavy housework. The junior wives, in turn, can benefit from this household arrangement since the household can provide aid to them in times of need, for example, sickness. However, Marris observes that most women in Lagos do not prefer polygyny and that polygyny is particularly vulnerable to the precarious economic circumstances of the husband.

The disappearance of the extended family traditional compound has led to the weakening of the extended kinship control of the husband's family over the wife. This combined with the fact that most marriages are no longer arranged by the couple's kinfolk has led to greater freedom of the wife from the husband's lineage and at the same time has lessened the extended family's support, especially if some misfortune befalls the husband. Marris believes that the weakening of the traditional sanctions has also made divorce more prevalent than previously. This has led women to secure an independent income to replace the dependency on their husband's extended family—9 out of 10 wives work in some kind of trade.

The greater independence of the wife has had an effect on the raising of children. In the traditional family compound children were raised by all members of the lineage. Although kinfolk still care for each other's sons and daughters, the breakdown of the compounds has led to a lessening of this everyday contact. Grandparents still have grandchildren residing with them to help with the household chores since failure of the parents to respond to such a request is a serious breach of familial respect. Although there is an increase in the number of women who set up economically independent households from their husbands and the extended family of their husbands and although there is an increase in the divorce rate, children who live with only one parent may still see the other parent very often. The pattern emerging is one where, despite the breakdown of extended family solidarity, there are various accommodations made to maintain intimate and continuous relationships of children with their larger families.

Marris sees an evolution of the family resulting from the new urban patterns. There has been a gradual weakening of the extended family system and an increase in the independence of wives from family control and the control of their husbands. New patterns of marriage and kinship are beginning to be formed with the outcome still in doubt.

> In this discussion of some Lagos families, I have tried to bring out a theme which seems especially relevant to the evolution of urban patterns of life. In any society, people look for secure affection above all to their family relationships, and find there also much practical help. Without this fundamental assurance, they tend to lack confidence in other social roles. The stability of family relationships is therefore very important, but the emphasis varies according to whether ties of marriage or ties of blood command the strongest loyalties. Traditionally, in Nigerian societies, the households of husbands and wives were subordinate to a wider family grouping. But as this subordination was not questioned, and the family group shared a common dwelling, obligations of marriage and of kinship could, at least in principle, be reconciled within the values of the culture. In Lagos, as households tend more and more to live apart, the group reasserts its common interests by frequent meetings both formal and informal, by the acceptance of mutual obligations, and by caring for each other's children. But this pattern of family affairs does not seem to have reasserted so effectively the authority of the group over relationships between husband and wife, nor is the group so responsible for the women who have married into it. If wives have more freedom from the control of their husbands' family, they cannot at the same time depend on them so much. But they cannot instead depend more on their husbands, unless he can both ensure their welfare, and reconcile his obligations to her with those to his kin. She, for her part, may put more trust in an economic independence, and the support her own family can give her. So the dispersal of the family group is not necessarily compensated by the strengthening of ties of marriage. In a time of rapid social change, people may rely less on any relationship, and as this also affects the care of children, the next generation may grow up without the experience of secure attachments, and so less able to form them.
>
> The reconciliation of ties of marriage and kinship seems a crucial issue in the evolution of Lagos family life. . . . (Marris, 1961:65)

In contrast to family life in Lagos, a study of the rehousing estate outside the city highlights and accentuates the social dynamics of family processes and the dissolution of extended family ties. Here, families see less of their relatives and the characteristic qualities of these relationships also change. Although in central Lagos the communal family compound is gradually disappearing, there remains strong vestiges of the extended family. In the rehousing development extended family ties are disappearing; individuals find it more difficult to visit their relatives and to fulfill their familial obligations:

> We used to see them almost every day when we were in Lagos, sometimes two or three times. But they don't come because of the transport, and they think this place is far.
> The slum clearance has scattered us. Apart from those of the same father and

mother, I don't see my family again. All other family is scattered, some at Shomolu, some Agage, some of them have gone to the bush of their villages, I've not been able to see some of my family for two years, and I don't even know where they are.

I don't see my sister at all unless I force myself there. If you don't go to see them they don't come. Sometimes I visit them four times before they come—they don't like this side. They have to change bus six times.

When I was in Lagos they were with me. We live in the same street. Old wife's family, new wife's family, we see each other every day. In Lagos you see everybody nearly every day. Do you see any of my family visiting me here?

On Saturday I made 5*s* gain, and I ran to see my mother. I've not seen her since Saturday, and God knows when I shall see her again. She wept when I was to leave, because she didn't want to leave me, and she is afraid to come here. When I was in Lagos there was not a day I don't see her. (Marris, 1961:110−111)

Marris asserts that for some of the young married couples moving to the rehousing estate was a welcome occurrence as they became more independent from extended kin. Three main reasons were delineated: (1) they were able to free themselves from the controls of their elders; (2) they were free from the quarrels between wives and mothers, which divided their loyalties; and (3) they were free from the continual demands of extended kin for monetary aid. [The reader will be aware of the motivational similarities of these people with that of middle-class Americans who moved from the city to outer city and suburban areas in the United States (Bell, 1958)]. The Nigerians who welcomed this change tended to be Christian rather than Muslim, Ibo rather than Yoruba. Marris suggests that their occupations—many were civil servants provided with governmental security and perspective old age pensions—allowed them to be less dependent on their extended kin and thus helped them to repudiate the traditional kinship obligations.

However, the more traditionally oriented Yoruba who were forced to migrate to the rehousing development found their family life in turmoil—a similar reaction of the transplanted working-class Bethnel Greeners who were forced to move to Greenleigh. The increased costs of living in the rehousing estate led to the withdrawal of financial aid to their kinfolk and a decrease in their visits to them. The slum clearance scattered the family group. It may have pleased a few non-Yorubans, but for the Yorubans to be out of reach of their relatives was distressful. It was particularly disruptful for the elderly who had lived in family property and had been cared for by relatives and now found themselves isolated from them:

There's plenty of breeze and it's quiet here,'' said an old woman, who had been moved from her uncle's house. ''But this seems to be a sort of hidden place—some of my family have never been able to find me here. And if you think of going to see them, you have to think of transport. . . . There's a proverb says there's no good in a fine house when there's no happiness. It's by the grace of God that you find me still alive. I've tasted nothing since morning, and I'm not fasting yet. The money I'd have spent on food has all gone on light. I handed over six and threepence this morning.'' (Marris, 1961:112−113)

In the end, the isolation of the estate led to an impoverished social life and disruption of the family, and it did not increase the self-efficiency of the husband and wife. The greater expenses of suburban life led many husbands to send their wives to their families and distribute their children among relatives who could care for them. Further, the increased emotional dependence and intimacy necessary to cope with the loss of extended kinship supportive relations did not develop, leading to additional feelings of dependency. Again, the reader is alerted to the similar phenomena occurring among blue-collar suburban wives in the United States, who developed feelings of alienation and anomie as a result of the severing of their ties with their extended kin (Tallman, 1969; Tallman and Morgner, 1970).

Marris ends his discussion with the pleas that future city planners take into account the social and psychological needs of the populace. Drastic dislocations mean disruptions not only in economic activities but also in social lives; although good housing is a necessity, it must be provided without causing major disruptions in people's lives:

> There is a danger that their family life will be improverished as much as their livelihood, and in turn create new hardships as they are forced to abandon obligations to their kin. Good housing is very much needed in Lagos, and a nation naturally desires a fine appearance for its capital city. But unless these aims can be reconciled with the needs and resources of the people who must be displaced, the harm done will be disproportionate to the achievement. (Marris, 1961:115)

Despite the extreme dislocations of families resulting from the slum clearance of central Lagos, the overall picture of family life in the indigenous towns of western Africa continues to show the vitality of the extended family system. These family systems continue to exist because they serve useful purposes for its members. Joan Aldous (1968), reviewing existing research up to 1962, reports that extended family and kinship ties are important in meeting economic, religious, legal, and recreational needs owning to the absence of such services by the central government. As long as substitute institutions do not develop to satisfy the demands of the populace, the vitality of the extended family and kinship ties will play an important role in the urbanization of African cities. The continued viability of the extended family system form goes counter to the theoretical positions of such sociologists as Louis Wirth and Talcott Parsons, who suggested that the extended family would disappear in the urban milieu.

We will now turn our attention to exploring changes in the urban way of life existing in the European-influenced expatriate cities of Africa, especially in regard to family and kinship patterns.

TYPE B EXPATRIATE TOWNS

The expatriate towns and cities are a result of colonialism and economic interests requiring administrative centers. Nairobi, which is now the largest city in East Africa, began as a construction camp for the Uganda railway in 1899 (Little, 1973). The capital of Uganda, Kampala, and the capital of Tanzania, Dar es Salaam, were founded by the British and Germans, respectively. Europeans in West Africa established port cities at Accra, Ghana; Freetown, Sierra Leone; Dakar, Senegal; and Lagos, Nigeria. Other urban centers developed as communication centers; as collection points for local produced commodities, like cocoa and groundnuts; and for their convenience to the mining centers of gold, diamonds, iron ore, and tin.

The colonial period was marked by the forced movement of workers from tribal areas to areas where their labor was needed for agriculture, mining, and construction:

> The Belgians used forced labor to build the Congo-Ocean railway, which was completed in 1934 at a cost of over 15,000 African lives. The British also used, until the 1920s, a system of compulsory service known as the "Kasanvu System" (Palen, 1975:372−373).

Although the forced labor systems are disappearing in the newly independent African states, the large scale migration continues. Kenneth Little (1973) points out that the city sets the pace for the wider society, that city growth in Africa is proceeding at a more rapid rate than in other regions of the world, and that it exceeds the city growth of the western industrial nations, including the United States, during their own period of fastest urban growth:

> For example, of the original port towns on the west coast of Lagos had a population of 126,000 in 1930 and had more than doubled to 364,000 by 1960. (A recent estimate . . . puts the population of Greater Lagos in 1963 at 1.2 millions.) Accra had only 40,000 inhabitants in 1930, had doubled in population by 1950, and had a population approaching a half million by 1960. Similarly, in the Francophone countries, there was an increase of 100 per cent in the populations of the principal towns of Senegal between 1942 and 1952, while those of the Ivory Coast grew by 109 per cent during the same decade, and those in the Cameroons by 250 per cent between 1936 and 1952. In what is now Zaire, Kinshasa (formerly Leopoldville) was a large country town of 34,000 in 1930, but in 20 years it had a population of 402,000. On the other side of Africa, Nairobi doubled in size during the 1940−50 decade and rose from 119,000 inhabitants in 1948 to about half a million in 1969, while Dar es Salaam grew from 69,000 in 1948 to 128,700 in 1957, and to 272,500 in 1967. Also, not only have existing towns swelled in size, but in some cases entirely new urban centres and agglomerations have come into being. For example, Enugu, now one of the largest cities of eastern Nigeria was founded in 1914 on an empty site, had a population of some 10,000 by 1921, which rose to 138,457 by 1963; while the population of Port Harcourt—another "new" town grew to 208,237 by 1969. [Little, 1973:12−13 (sources omitted)]

It is no wonder, then, that social scientists, like William J. Goode (1963), observe that in the modern world it does not seem possible to distinguish clearly between urbanization and modernization and their effects on the individual, the family, and kinship and tribal groups. It is now time to examine these effects on the newly emerging urban centers of sub-Saharan Africa.

William A. Hance (1970) examines the differences between urban growth in Africa and in the West during a comparable period. Of note is the contrast in the greater rates of growth of the major cities of Africa with those in the West and the fact that the growth of urbanization in Africa is not accompanied by a comparable change in the rural areas. This has led to a greater dichotomy between the rural and urban areas that is reflected in individual behavior, social values, and economically—a factor has reduced the tempo of economic life. This is in contrast to the Western pattern, which is characterized by the Protestant ethic and its emphasis on hard work, achievement, and success. Hance takes note of the dual existence of tribal and Western structures in many African cities; a phenomenon that has not had an equivalent counterpart in Western industrial cities and one that is worthy of a longer look. This theme on the duality of value systems of African urbanites will be followed up later in our discussion.

Research on black Africans migrating to urban areas indicates that the social structure that emerges is not a simple modification and adaptation of rural life structures. Peter C. W. Gutkind (1969) views urbanism in Africa as a distinct way of life, with urban institutions exerting strong pressures on individuals and groups to adapt an urban model—"we are dealing with townsmen in town and not tribesmen in town" (Gutkind, 1969:217). The urbanization of sub-Saharan Africa has had a profound effect on the family life of the rural African. Although, as Goode (1963) has discussed, there is great danger in oversimplification and generalization of the sub-Saharan family system, an overall pattern does emerge: extensive extended kinship ties are articulated within the tribal system.

Goode (1963), while cautioning the reader on the variability of family systems, does outline some of the main African family patterns. Of particular importance is the high emotional significance of the son-mother relationship. Tied in with this is the importance of legitimate descendants and the focus on the birth and possession of children. Almost all kinship systems are unilinear, the tracing of descent through one lineage. Polyandry, the marriage of one female to two or more males, is quite rare. Polygyny, the marriage of one male to two or more females, has greater appeal in Africa than in any other part of the world. However, it is more common as an ideal (in 88 percent of the 154 African societies studied by Goode) than an actuality. Most African men have only one wife (Goode, 1963:168).

In polygynous families the most common living arrangement is setting up separate households for each wife and her children. Goode sees the importance of the mother-son relationship stemming in part from the existence of polygynous households and the fairly high percentage of children growing up in them. The son's emotional dependence on his own mother is heightened by the separate household existence of other mothers and other sons in the same family. In addition to her emotional support of her son, the mother provides assistance to the son in matters of advice, analysis, and teaching techniques. The second factor in explaining the importance of the mother-son relationship is the importance of the mother as seen in the reciprocal exchanging of bride prices by which two extended families or lineages are gradually united over time. "Marriage was not generally an event but a *process,* in which visiting, services, and gifts were exchanged over a period of time, as the marriage relationship was gradually strengthened, and each spouse was more fully accepted by his affinal relatives" (Goode, 1963:177 – 178). This factor tied in with the high value placed on children and lineage possession of children contributes to the importance of the relationship. Together, these all reinforce the importance of kinship in the tribal community, within which the primary bond of association is kinship descent.

The movement to the European-founded expatriate cities was stimulated by the industrial economy of the colonizing countries. The Western market economy was extended into these African urban areas and brought the indigenous African into a wider social system than the tribe. Industrialization and urbanization led to a greater specialization of institutions and gave rise to a new series of social groupings, networks, and relationships that transcended those based on family, kinship, and tribe. However, it would be erroneous to assume that these processes of modernization simply supplemented the traditional tribal arrangement; in many cases they were adapted to them. Viewed in this light, modifications of the traditional institutions combined with Western industrialization, technology, and economic and social values and practices gave rise to an emerging social structure that, although in the processes of change, still maintained cultural continuity with the past.

Gutkind (1969) describes two formative processes that influenced the individual's life in the city: (1) tribal and ethnic identities in the urban context and (2) a distinctive urban life style based on economic and political processes. Combined, these processes lead both to the development of new relationships that are components of the restructuring of traditional tribal roles and to the development of new roles derived from the industrial system.

The families Gutkind studied in Kampala, Uganda, constantly moved back and forth from the world of association—based on kin and ethnic similarity and familiarity—to participation in groupings that cut right across such association, particularly in economic and political activity and leisure pursuits. There is a constant convergence and separation of these two networks, and the conditions that produce them are mutually dependent and compatible. Together they contribute to the social and economic stability of urban family life. Family life, kin ties, and neighborhood associations or groups of friends are explicitly designed to assist and meet the social and psychological needs of their members and they act to support, protect, and guide their members. The complementary network of relations extends from the urban neighborhood community and is determined by economic and political processes based upon the broader urban, national and international marketplace. The result is an intertwining of these two processes in relation to individuals and families:

> Above all, in the local community, decisions which affect its life are taken by members who are known to one another. Not so in the larger social field of urban life, the structure of which is largely determined by agents external to it. Thus, while the social-psychological processes give the African urban family the opportunity to adjust to a new social environment, the urban institutions provide the same family with the opportunities of educational and economic mobility. But in either world African residents in towns are not merely rural residents transplanted who seek a conscious modification of rural ideas and habits suitable under new conditions. Rather, where for example, tribalism prevails, or tribal settlements come into being, the reason is that this form of association is as purposeful a part of urbanism and a style of life as it is for a New Yorker not to know his neighbor. Both styles of life are not incompatible with their opposites, i.e., the increasing importance of non-tribal and non-ethnic based associations in Africa, or the neighborhood associations aiming at a development of neighborliness and face-to-face contact in a New York city housing development. (Gutkind, 1969:218–219)

African migrant laborers finding themselves in a strange new urban area look to fellow tribal members already residing in the town to provide intimate and protective forms of association. Kinship and tribal affiliation serve as the linkage from the rural village to life in the city. Tribal membertship gives newcomers an immediate identification, furnishes the normative guidelines on how to behave, and gives them community supports with ties with people like themselves. The African who comes to the city does not come as a stranger. The situation of the migrant to Dar es Salaam, Tanzania, is typical:

> It would be difficult to find a single African who arrived in Dar es Salaam knowing not a soul. . . . Almost every African who decided to come [there] comes to a known address, where lives a known relation; this relation will meet him, take him in and feed him and show him the ropes, help him seek a job . . . until he considers himself able to launch out for himself and take a room of his own. (J.A.K. Leslie cited in Epstein, 1969:256)

The urban dweller tends, therefore, to be involved in a complex network of relationships based on tribal affiliation, which includes neighbors, friends, and fellow workers as well as kin. Tribal association can be seen as an adaptive device that eases the adjustments of migrants to the urban area. Thus, although urbanization is supposed to weaken traditional bonds, in the urban area it has strengthened rather than weakened tribal ties. Further, it gives migrants a new conception of their tribal culture that transcends the particular tribal community from which they come.

However, African urbanists (e.g., Epstein, 1969, and Southall, 1961) state that *supertribalism* is quite different in the urban setting than tribalism in the rural area.

In the city tribalism's main function is to classify Africans of heterogeneous tribal origins and to provide a limited number of meaningful social categories that serve as the basis for new groupings so that the new demands of city life may be met. "This form or urban tribalism is a category of interaction within a wider system, not the corporate and largely closed structure of social relationships provided by a tribe in its traditional areas" (Southall, 1961:3). A. L. Epstein (1969) observes that there are various forms of organizations that have their basis in urban tribalism. These organizations range from those that have institutionalized tribal eldership and headmanship to oversee various forms of social activity (e.g., arranging funerals; parties; marriages; or serving as arbitrators in disputes, which is characteristic in Dar es Salaam; the copperbelt, and Freetown) to associations that are no longer dominated by the conservative elders but rather by upwardly aspiring younger men looking for prestige and status; to pantribal federations of the Kenya Luo or some of the Nigerian groups, which developed the infrastructure for nationalist movements and competitive political parties; and to those tribal associations that approximate exclusive social clubs (Epstein, 1969:257).

Aidan Southall (1961) describes the various applications and outcomes of supertribalism in urban areas, especially as it affects kinship and family relationships. He reports that urban conditions have led to the diminished importance of the finer points of distinction in kinship systems and to the use of common denominators that are acceptable to all for intertribal dealings. But there has been little development of local kin groups; most urban dwellers still maintain strong rural ties, with the intention of eventually returning to their tribal homes in their old age. Life in the city is seen as an economic necessity and, although it may satisfy their financial ambitions and needs, their ultimate goal is to return home. Economic development, then, strengthens the tribal structure.

Southall delineates three phases in tribal associations. In the first stage recently arrived migrants are not interested in the formation of effective tribal associations, rather they are concerned with the ways that kinship and tribal bonds can be of mutual aid situationally. Second, the tribal associations are formed for general welfare purposes. Finally, Africans begin to move beyond a tribal basis to form associations for common interests and to express their similar achieved status. This cuts across tribal lines. Thus Southall sees tribal bonds developing new patterns; hampering and inappropriate close-knit traditional situations are being replaced by new ones that stress interpersonal relationships and association organizations appropriate for urban life:

> Evidence from the Copperbelt, from Dar es Salaam, and from Sierra Leone shows how tribal headmen or representatives have been important in the early stages of urban settlement but later were eclipsed. On the Copperbelt the formal way in is through tribal elders, but in Salisbury through friendly societies, usually of twenty to thirty tribesmen, which also act as burial societies. Immigrants later tend to join groups with a more

specific focus, such as friendship at work or common religion. Similarly, immigrants to Freetown come under the patronage of tribal headmen or notables and join voluntary associations with special interests later, entry to certain élite associations being the most difficult of all. Tribal associations are reported from East, West, and Central Africa. They mark a stage in which immigrant workers have become sufficiently used to town life to be able to organize themselves effectively in that context, yet on the basis of interest fundamentally centered in the countryside, indicating that they reject any irrevocable commitment to the town. (Southall, 1961:37)

In examining the relationship of kinship and tribalism on the individual and family, Southall emphasizes the need to distinguish between the experience of West Africa and the other regions of sub-Sahara Africa. As we described earlier the West African family is firmly established in both Type A and Type B cities, with a minimal break between family life in town and that in the rural areas. However, the proportionately smaller migrant population in the cities is characterized by similar characteristics as the more prevalent migrant population in the European-founded towns and cities of East, Central, and South Africa. Southall describes the conditions of migrant labor in East and Central Africa as having a "disproportion of the sexes, high mobility, lack of family life, and failure to achieve full integration in an urban existence" (1961:41). The disproportionate number of males and females varied by geographical area and by governmental policy. John J. Palen (1975) notes that the situation was reasonable in West Africa, where there was a ratio of 95 women to 100 men. However, in Central Africa it was only 85 women to 100 men; in parts of East Africa 55 to 75 women per 100 men was prevalent. The situation was aggravated to a larger extreme in South Africa, where government policy prevented workers from bringing their wives to the cities with them.

Goode (1963) reports that in Salisbury, (Zimbabwe) that the much greater number of men to women, seven to one, prevented most men from ever marrying as long as they remained in the city. Further, the women available for marriage found that prostitution provided more financial lucrative rewards than marriage. The result was an almost complete breakdown of stable family patterns and the substitution of prostitution, temporary sexual liaisons, and illegitmacy for legalized family arrangements. In these European-dominated cities urbanization had led to the separation of the individual from his family and lineage, with the consequent weakening of the family as an institution and the increase of extramarital relations and of illegitimate children, who are raised in poorly constructed housing with inadequate care and supervision. These processes are similar to those described by Louis Wirth in his examination of Chicago in the 1920s and 1930s. These disorganization patterns, rather than being indigenous to Africa, are the results of European colonial policies and, with the removal of the colonial governments, there has been a reestablishment of families and lineages and a subsequent decline in illegitimacy, juvenile delinquency, and crime similar to the pattern of urbanism found in the Type A traditional African city. The roles of the tribal associations have been partially responsible for this organizational stability. An additional organizational structure, which in some cases emerged out of the tribal association and in other cases was independent of it, is the voluntary organization.

TYPE B EXPATRIATE TOWNS: VOLUNTARY ASSOCIATIONS

Little (1965) believes that voluntary associations of men and women, institutions based on common economic and social interest, are of great importance in urban areas. They are seen to facilitate a transition from the rural village to the city, with its highly differentiated social system anchored by occupation-derived achieved statuses rather than by traditional-based ascribed statuses. The voluntary association assists the individual to adapt to urban life—to the behavioral patterns, the acquisition of technical skills, and the development of new social relationships. The voluntary association helps rural migrants to adjust to the town and to becoming members of a multitribal metropolitan community. By aiding in the establishment and validation of new urban values and norms, the voluntary associations develop controls over the behaviors of their members and, untimately, aid in the development of an overall system of relationships based on law and order for the heterogeneous populations of these towns and cities. This is particularly important because it provides a substitute for the traditional institutions of lineage and kinship that have not been established in the city or that need to be modified because of their dysfunctionality.

Little argues that the voluntary associations are particularly important because there are few agreed-on patterns and moral standards in the urban family for such concerns as the upbringing of children and marriage. The voluntary associations have developed policies of their own. For example, they all strongly support marriage as an institution; many forbid their members to divorce. Many of the associations condemn adultery, promiscuity, and treat abortion as a crime. Social control is obtained through formal controls such as liegislation, or in informal ways, such as the following song, cited by Michael P. Banton, that was sung to a chief's wife when she was estranged from her husband:

Oh Bom Posse, Oh Bom Posse, patience in marriage is a good thing,
Which God has given you,
When you grow old you will see how good is this thing,
Which God has given you. (Banton cited in Little, 1965:101)

Or in the following song used as a weapon of ridicule to ensure conformity:

The shame of it, Ai Kamara, the shame of it!
Ai Kamara bore a child:

He had no sooner grown up than she made him her husband.
Ah friends, let us come together
And consider if this is what is done in Temne-land?
(Banton cited in Little, 1965:98)

Finally, in addition to the functions of family and kinship groups, tribal associations and voluntary associations are the sources of the emerging literature of indigenous African writers in soap-opera novelistic contexts as well as Dear-Abbey type syndicated columns, published in indigenous newspapers, and providing suggested guidelines to reconcile the rural village tribal customs to the emerging norms demanded in city life. William Mangin (1970) cites the "Tell me, Josephine" column in East and South Africa. Two letters are presented; the first one tries to reconcile the conflict of a man and a wife; the second discusses the choice between loyalty to a mother's brother and a man's obligations to pay a matrimonial bride price. Mangin observes that Josephine's answers attempt "to bridge the gap but always on the side of adapting the traditional to modernization, westernization, and the new marketplace" (Mangin, 1970:xv):

[1.]*Q*. During the course of my marriage I find my wife belongs to a tribe which is maternal. When we divorce or one of us dies, our children will belong to her brothers. I rushed into marriage without learning of this custom.

I am afraid that if we divorce, I shall go to my village quite old and helpless while my wife's brothers will get every help possible from my children. So where should I get children to support me? My tribe does not do this. I find some difficulty in divorcing her now, before the children come, because I love her very much and she does the same to me. But what about this awful custom? When I mention my fears she tries to bluff me by saying her brothers will let me get my children, but I don't believe it. What have you to say before I sadly act?

A. That it would be foolish to break up a happy marriage for fear of an old custom that may no longer be practiced when you are old. Do not think of divorce, many people live happily together all their lives. Also, you may die before your wife. If you are good to your children they will not desert you in your old age. Twenty years from now, these customs may have died out completely.

[2.] *Q*. My uncle who is a charcoal-burner was taken to Native Court and told to pay 15 pounds for damaging two virgins.

He has written to me that according to our custom I must get money for him, and send it quickly to the Northern Province or he will go to prison. This will take all my savings which I had planned to use for marriage in two years. So must I send him the money?

A. If you wish to keep tribal custom, then you are obliged to help your uncle.

If you do not care about tribal custom any more and do not intend to visit your family in the rural areas again, then no-one can make you pay. Only you can decide.

I presume that according to the same custom you will inherit your uncle's property when he dies. (Josephine cited in Mangin, 1970:xv−xvi)

TYPE B EXPATRIATE TOWNS: THE URBAN ELITE

Our concluding discussion will consider the urban elite, who, although not a numerically significant number, are of vital importance to the independent sub-Saharan African states. Also the family system of these urban elite may provide clues to the eventual direction that African family and kinship patterns may move.

P. C. Lloyd (1969) states that the leaders of the precolonial African societies were the tribal chiefs and priests. During colonialism they served as the link between the Europeans and the indigenous people. Eventually, the Western-educated Africans, who led the nationalist movements, arose and achieved control of the newly independent African states. These individuals displaced the traditional elite and now serve as the mediators between Western and traditional African value systems. Lloyd discusses the various elite groups that have emerged and contrasts them in terms of their origins in a particular European colonial government and in the postindependence period. For our purposes, we will ignore these distinctions and treat these elite groups as unitary phenomena, focusing our attention on the overall marital, family, and kinship pattern.

The marital roles that have emerged find women in a rather egalitarian relationship, much to the dismay of traditionalist males. This particularly occurs when the educated wife is employed outside the home. The husband-wife relationship also features a segregated role pattern, with separate domestic activities and separate occupational spheres of activity and responsibility, Lloyd notes that the pattern is quire different from the Western one, where there is a greater sharing of roles and activities. The segregated role pattern is more similar to the working-class pattern in the West. It is derived from two sources: (1) the traditional marital relationship in African societies that emphasizes the separate social networks of husband and wife and (2) the continuation of the strong ties that men retain with their own parents and kin:

> Many educated husbands still say that their mothers are more important in their lives than their wives; one can always get another wife, never another mother. Men will first discuss matters such as building a new house or changing jobs with parents or brothers. Tension between the husband's mother and his wife, if the former lives with her son, seems to be even more acute in Africa than in the England of the music-hall jokes. (Lloyd, 1969:178–179)

The continuation of ties with one's own kin is frequently incompatible with loyalty to one's wife. The wife's response is to seek and maintain the more egalitarian form of marital relationship and to emphasize the segregation of marital roles.

The children of the elite are raised within the nuclear family with the aid of a few domestic servants, a vivid contrast to the involvement of extended kin in the raising of children in the Yourban family compound. Child-rearing practices for elite children are more tolerant of aggressive play, and the child is encouraged to realize his or her own potential. In contrast the traditional pattern emphasizes that the child follow parental expectations and discourages fighting among children. Cooperation among children is encouraged as it diminishes the possibility of quarrels and tensions between cowives residing in physical proximity to each other.

In examining the relationship between individuals and their kin, Lloyd acknowledges the tensions arising out of the different interpretations of a person's traditional ways and values. However, the relationships between the residents of the towns and their rural counterparts continue, as do the viability of extended kinship ties. Lloyd sees the expectations of the extended family for individuals as spurring them on to achieve economic success. Further, individuals may be judged by their success rather than by their censure of the elders in the extended family group. He concludes that the assertion that the extended family is an impediment to the modernizing process needs considerable qualification when applied to the African situation.

CONCLUSION

This chapter has examined the city in West Africa and sub-Saharan Africa and its relationship to urban family systems. Our discussion has sought to test the basic hypothesis of the urban sociologists who see family life in the city as gradually diminishing in importance, particularly causing the dissolution of the extended family system and the substitution of the isolated nuclear family type. William J. Goode shared this position: "If the new African nations follow the paths of many other emerging nations, the next decade will witness an accentuated move away from tribal family patterns, and toward a conjugal system" (1963:201–202).

In examining the evidence, we have found that in the traditional African city, for example, those found in the Yoruba of West Africa, the fundamental family pattern took on the pattern of the extended family. This runs contrary to the position of such social scientists as Louis Wirth and Talcott Parsons who believed that the extended family form would be nonexistence in cities, whether industrialized or not. When, in turn, we examined family, kinship, and tribal relationships in the more industrialized European-founded towns, family-based networks still remained visible and still provided needed resources for the populace. Finally, when we turned our attention to the urban elite, those who would most likely follow the Western model, we discovered a continued existence of extended kin ties. In addition, the nuclear family arrangement was characterized by a greater egalitarianism and independence of husband and wife than in their Western counterparts. This is a departure from what we would have expected from the dominant theoretical positions of the sociologists of the urban family.

The existence of extended family relationships, of tribal associations, and of voluntary associations all suggest that differential adaptations are possible when confronted with urbanization processes. Further, it is vital to understand the cultural context of the populace under study to predict in what manner urbanism as a way of life will evolve.

6

Poverty Families in Communities

In the preceding two chapters on the family and the city we discussed how the sociological model of the city that stresses the social disorganizational qualities of city life and its negative implications for the family has influenced sociologists in their descriptive analysis of the city. In particular, the dichotomization of rural and urban life through the use of various ideal-type conceptual constructs has led many sociologists to stress the positive qualities of rural life and to develop nostalgic views of the rural family system. Conversely, the model of urban life has been essentially negativistic, focusing on the social disorganization of the city and its consequences—alienation, anomie, social isolation, family isolation, juvenile delinquency, crime, child abuse, separation, and divorce.

In our examination of the family in American cities (and the working-class families of Bethnel Green, London), we saw that the previously held position was an oversimplification of reality. In particular, studies of working-class urban villagers residing in closed communities were seen to have an urban way of life. These studies emphasized the importance of neighborhood ties and relationships with relatives, friends, and neighbors in the tightly knit community organization that was relatively homogeneous and as far as possible excluded outsiders from involvement in the community. (As an aside, it is important to note that the contemporary controversies centering around the issues of school busing and the community control of schools may be seen as a manifestation of this closed-community-solidarity ethos of these urban villagers. Although racial undertones are also present; it would be an oversimplified distortion to analyze this conflict solely in racial terms.)

We also tested the validity of the social disorganizational model in the urban centers of sub-Saharan Africa. Unlike the predicted model described by Louis Wirth (1938b), these centers were not solely characterized by alienation, anomie, family disorganization and other forms of disorganization. For the vast majority of African city dwellers, the ties between the extended family and those between city and rural village were maintained and, instead of isolation and detribalization, comprehensive associational structures were developed for the purposes of mutual aid and to provide the necessary transitional supports for the new urban residents.

Although the model of Wirth and other proponents of the social disorganization school has lost validity for its oversimplifications and distortions in depicting a debilitating urban way of life for all city dwellers, the model has continued to be used in the analysis of the poverty classes. In addition, both in anthropology and sociology, a viewpoint has been developed that stems from this position and stresses the development of a *culture of poverty* by those individuals and families who live in poverty conditions. This culture exhibits all the negative qualities associated with social disorganization. This viewpoint argues that there exists a culture among the poor that transcends given societies and exists in the slums, ghettos, and squatter settlements of the United States, Latin America, Africa, and Asia—wherever a capitalistic economy exists. The people and families who exhibit this culture of poverty tend to share similar attitudinal and behavioral patterns relating to the family, work, and the given society. In this chapter, we will investigate the poverty family in light of the social policy implications of the contemporary social disorganizational framework—the culture of poverty. Our focus will be on the poor of the United States and of Latin America.

SQUATTER SETTLEMENTS AND POVERTY FAMILIES

The geographer, Brian J. L. Berry (1973) points out that it is in the Third World societies of Latin America, Africa, and Asia that the major thrust of urban growth is occurring. While the industrialized societies of the world have increased in urban population from 198 million to approximately 546 million in the last 50 years, the urban population of Third World societies has increased from 69 million to 464 million. While the Third World accounted for only 25 percent of the world's urban population in 1920, it is estimated that it will account for 51 percent in 1980.

It is important that we emphasize a major variation in the urban growth patterns of Third World societies and in industrial societies. The rapid urbanization of the industrial societies of Western Europe and North America occurred at the time when these societies had the highest level of economic development. In contrast, the contemporary accelerated growth occurring in the Third World is taking place in the countries with the lowest level of economic development. Berry (1973:74) also notes that this urban growth is occurring in countries with the lowest levels of life expectancy at birth, the poorest nutritional levels, the lowest energy-consumption levels and the lowest levels of education. In addition, Third World urbanization, although it involves greater numbers of people than it did for the industrial societies, is characterized by less industrialization. One consequence of this is that many of the population are unemployed or finding marginal employment in the cities.

A further striking variation in the Third World urbanization patterns is the development of peripheral settlements, squatter settlements, around a city; they serve in transforming rural societies into urban societies and account for a substantial percentage of the urban population. The squatter settlements are shantytowns that have sprung up around large cities, largely because of the inability of the governments in those cities to provide adequate housing for the overwhelming influx of migrants. The residents are migrants from rural areas who have banded together and have established squatter settlements by constructing their own houses on land, both publicly and privately owned, usually against the armed opposition of the government. Often these settlements, as in Latin America, disregard urban planning and building regulations, nevertheless they provide ''uniquely satisfactory opportunities for low income settlers'' in that they are built according to the needs of the inhabitants in terms of social and economic urban changes (Turner, 1970:10).

40,000 Squatters Live in Shanty 'Forest' in Bangkok

Bangkok, Thailand—Ten years ago floods and then drought forced Boomchuay Pomsakul off the patch of land that his family had worked for generations.

Hoping for something better than the future of a tenant farmer, he came to Bangkok.

Today he lives in a wooden shack on stilts in a swamp overlooking the Bangkok docks. There is no running water; there are no sewage facilities; public health care for his eight children is scant. He used to work as a stevedore, but with the shipping industry in a slump jobs are rare. What little money comes in is from a part-time job his wife has in a textile factory.

Boomchuay Pomsakul is among 40,000 people who live in a forest of shanties, creaking catwalks across green, scum-filled water, in a district called Klong Toey, named for the canal it borders.

A squatters' slum, it lies between the city garbage dump and the docks along the Chao Phraya River. It is a part of this capital that the government would like to forget. Officially, it does not exist as a community.

But Boomchuay Ponsakul and other residents of the slum, plan to visit Premier Kukrit Pramoj to plead that Klong Toey become an official part of the city.

"We need help," said Boomchuay Pomsakul, who is a member of a community council. "We want a chance to buy our own plots of land here on long-term credit, and we want some services—health and sanitation."

"Even during the dry season," he went on, "the marsh here is up to our chests and the paths are under water. There is every kind of disease here."

Last year, for the first time, they got a school, he said.

Social workers concerned about the proliferating problems of the Bangkok metropolis say that there are at least 200 scattered areas of slums within the city limits and that at least 400,000 of Bangkok's three million people live in them.

Kong Toey by all accounts, is the worst, it is swampland that belongs officially to the Port of Bangkok, which has roughly the same relationship with the city of Bangkok that the Port of New York Authority has with New York City.

To this day many of Klong Toey's residents still earn their living scrabbling through the garbage dump for metal scraps, plastic or other waste that they can sell. Some earn as much as 50 cents a day this way.

John F. C. Turner (1969) cites a United Nations report that estimates that during the 1960s over 200 million people migrated into the Third World cities of

Asia, Africa, and Latin America. "One-and-a-half million people, over one third of the population of Mexico City, live in the 'colonias proletarias'—known originally as 'barrios paradaidaristas' or 'parachutists' neighborhoods; nearly half of Ankara's [Turkey] population of 1,500,000 live in the 'gecekondu'—the squatter settlements whose name describes an over-night house-builder; the area of the 'villes extracoutumiers' of Kinshasa is greater than that of the city itself" (Turner, 1969:507). The housing problem of these newcomers is not unique to the Third World; in France, the *bidonvilles* ("tin-can towns") surrounding Paris house over 100,000 North African and Portuguese migrants in flimsy wood and cement dwellings and in abandoned buses. The world-wide extent of such *bidonvilles* is listed in Table 6.1.

Turner points out that squatter settlements vary greatly in terms of permanency and security of tenure settlement and vary as well in the financial and social resources of its inhabitants. A correlation exists between the conditions of the settlement with the wealth and income levels of a given society's population. The *bustee* settlements of Old Delhi, India, are among the poorest, whereas the cuevas *barriada* of Lima, Peru, has residents whose income approaches that of the average working-class level. Settlements such as those in Peru are seen to be transitory phenomena that will eventually evolve into working-class suburban areas; however, their present state is merely at or a little above the poverty level. William Mangin presents a vivid picture of the *barriadas* around Lima:

> At worst a "barriada" is a crowded, helter-skelter hodge-podge of inadequate straw houses with no water supply and no provision for sewage disposal; parts of many are like this. Most do not have a rough plan, and most inhabitants convert their original houses to more substantial structures as soon as they can. Construction activity usually involving family, neighbors, and friends is a constant feature of "barriada" life and, although water and sewage usually remain critical problems, a livable situation is reached with respect to them.
>
> For most of the migrants the "barriada" represents a definite improvement in terms of housing and general income, and Lima represents an improvement over the semi-feudal life of the Indian, "Cholo," or lower-class mestize. (Mangin, 1960:911–917)

The people who inhabit the barriada are portrayed in the following manner:

> The early stereotype held by most middle and upper class Peruvians of the barriada dwellers as illiterate, nonproductive, lawless, recent communistic Indian migrants is still held by many—but is giving way among young architects, politicians, academics, and anthropologists to an equally false picture. Perhaps as an antidote to the first, it paints them as happy, contented, literate, productive adjusted, politically conservative— forever patriotic citizens. They are, in fact, about like the vast majority of Peruvians, moderately to desperately poor, cynical *and* trusting of politicians, bishops, outside agitators, and their own local leaders. They are alternately hopeful and despairing about

Table 6.1 Extent of Uncontrolled Peripheral Settlements

Country	City	Year	City Population (Thousands)	Total (Thousands)	Uncontrolled Settlement — As Percentage of City Population
Africa					
Senegal	Dakar	1969	500	150	30%
Tanzania	Dar es Salaam	1967	273	98	36
Zambia	Lusaka	1967	194	53	27
Asia					
China (Taiwan)	Taipei	1966	1300	325	25
India	Calcutta	1961	6700	2220	33
Indonesia	Djakarta	1961	2906	725	25
Iraq	Baghdad	1965	1745	500	29
Malaysia	Kuala Lumpur	1961	400	100	25
Pakistan	Karachi	1964	2280	752	33
Republic of Korea	Seoul	1970	440 [a]	137 [a]	30
Singapore	Singapore	1966	1870	980	15
Europe					
Turkey	Ankara	1965	979	460	47
		1970	1250	750	60
	Izmir	1970	640	416	65
Central and South America					
Brazil	Rio de Janeiro	1947	2050	400	20
		1957	2940	650	22
		1961	3326	900	27
	Brasilia	1962	148	60	41
Chile	Santiago	1964	2184	546	25
Colombia	Cali	1964	813	243	30
	Buenaventura	1964	111	88	80
Mexico	Mexico City	1952	2372	330	14
		1966	3287	1500	46
Peru	Lima	1957	1261	114	9
		1961	1716	360	21
		1969	2800	1000	36
Venezuela	Caracas	1961	1330	280	21
		1964	1590	556	35
	Maracaibo	1966	559	280	50

[a] Dwelling units.

Source: Adapted from U.N. General Assembly, *Housing, Building and Planning: Problems and Priorities in Human Settlements*, Report of the Secretary-General, August 1970, Annex III, p. 55. Reprinted by permission. Definitions vary. Additional details are given in the source quoted.

the future of their children and themselves. They love and resent their children and their parents. They are, in short, human beings. (Mangin, 1968:56)

Life in the squatter settlements has been portrayed by two predominant conceptualizations. The first and more prevalent emphasizes the chaotic and socially disorganized aspects of the settlement. Marital breakdowns, anomie, alienation, poverty, and misery are the lot of the migrant population. The second position takes an opposite stance. It argues that the settlement is able to maintain community organization and family continuity and that the residents have the general ability to adjust to the somewhat overwhelming demands of the potentially debilitating consequences of urban poverty.

As we have discussed, the social disorganization approach stems from the intellectual tradition in the social sciences that has developed an ideal type dichotomization of rural and urban life. The ideal typification of rural life stresses the group solidarity and the primacy of personal relationships anchored by familial and kinship bonds. The typification of urban life, on the other hand, sees the development of secondary relationships based on a pragmatic philosophy of looking out for oneself; the absence of viable family and neighborhood relationships, which ultimately lead to social and personal disorganization; the breakdown of personal integration; and crime, delinquency, and individual isolation.

I washed the children, put them to bed, then washed myself and went to bed. I waited until 11:00 for a certain someone. He didn't come. I took an aspirin and laid down again. When I awoke the sun was sliding in space. My daughter Vera Eunice said: "Go get some water, Mother!" *July 16* I got up and obeyed Vera Eunice. I went to get the water. I made coffee. I told the children that I didn't have any bread, that they would have to drink their coffee plain and eat meat with farinha. I was feeling ill and decided to cure myself. I stuck my finger down my throat twice, vomited, and knew I was under the evil eye. The upset feeling left and I went to Senhor Manuel, carrying some cans to sell. Everything that I find in the garbage I sell. He gave me 13 cruzeiros. I kept thinking that I had to buy bread, soap, and milk for Vera Eunice. The 13 cruzeiros wouldn't make it. I returned home, or rather to my shack, nervous and exhausted. I thought of the worrisome life that I led. Carrying paper, always lacking things. Vera doesn't have shoes and she doesn't like to go barefoot. For at least two years I've wanted to buy a meat grinder. And a sewing machine.

I came home and made lunch for the two boys. Rice, beans, and meat, and I'm out to look for paper. I left the children, told them to play in the yard and not go into the street, because the terrible neighbors I have won't leave the boys alone. I was feeling ill and wished I could lie down. But the poor don't rest nor are they permitted the pleasure of relaxation. . . .

Yesterday I ate that macaroni from the garbage with fear of death, because in 1953 I sold scrap over there in Zinho [a section of São Paulo, Brazil]. There was a pretty little black boy. He also went to sell scrap in Zinho. He was young and said that those who should look for paper were the old. One day I was collecting scrap when I stopped at

Bom Jardim Avenue. Someone had thrown meat into the garbage, and he was picking out the pieces. He told me:

"Take some, Carolina. It's still fit to eat."

He gave me some, and so as not to hurt his feelings, I accepted. I tried to convince him not to eat that meat, or the hard bread gnawed by the rats. He told me no, because it was two days since he had eaten. He made a fire and roasted the meat. His hunger was so great that he couldn't wait for the meat to cook. He heated it and ate. So as not to remember that scene, I left thinking: I'm going to pretend I wasn't there. This can't be real in a rich country like mine. I was disgusted with that Social Service that had been created to readjust the maladjusted, but took no notice of we marginal people. I sold the scrap at Zinho and returned to São Paulo's back yard, the favela.

The next day I found that little black boy dead. His toes were spread apart. The space must have been eight inches between them. He had blown up as if made out of rubber. His toes looked like a fan. He had no documents. He was buried like any other "Joe." Nobody tried to find out his name. The marginal people don't have names. . . .

The children eat a lot of bread. They like soft bread but when they don't have it, they eat hard bread.

Hard is the bread that we eat. Hard is the bed on which we sleep. Hard is the life of the *favelade*.

Oh, São Paulo! A queen that vainly shows her skyscrapers that are her crown of gold. All dressed up in velvet and silk but with cheap stocking underneath—the favela. (From *Child of the Dark* by Carolina Maria de Jesus, translated by David St. Clair. Pp. 17–18, 41, 42. © 1962 by E. P. Dutton & Co., Inc. and Souvenir Press, Ltd. (under the title *Beyond All Pity*). Reprinted by permission of the publishers.

The problems of urban life may be seen to fall most heavily on those who do not have the financial resources to cope with the monetary demands of urban life and who do not have the personal contacts to provide them with aid in times of need. The social group that is at the greatest disadvantage is the poverty class. We will examine the poverty classes in this chapter, focusing on the family structure of these people. Following Rodman (1971), we believe that the study of poverty families' behavior and values is important in that they provide information on a people's culture. The family represents the major organizational group in which adaptations are made to poverty conditions, thus it provides a convenient analytical unit in which to examine the ways of life of people living in poverty.

An additional factor that supports our contention of looking at the family in poverty is that the family has been the focal point for much of the intellectual discussion on the consequences of poverty on individuals, and it has also served as the center of social policy programs aimed at helping the poor. A notable and somewhat notorious illustration is the controversy surrounding a policy document of the U.S. Government, *The Negro Family: The Case for National Action* (U.S. Department of Labor, 1965)—known as the Moynihan report. The framework for our discussion is the contemporary social disorganizational position—the culture of poverty—which stresses cultural or subcultural developments in poverty families that prevent them from taking advantage of occupational opportunities—if and when they occur. The opposing position stresses the conditions under poverty to which poor families must adapt and that account for the different behavioral forms such families take in contrast to the more affluent families in society. As we will see, the intellectual stance that is advocated, culture or conditions, has implications not only for the analysis of poverty families but also plays a strong role in determining the nature and extent of governmental policies relating to the poor. We will illustrate our discussion by exploring how these opposing positions have been utilized in the study of the poverty classes and family systems in the United States and in Latin America.

OSCAR LEWIS AND THE CULTURE OF POVERTY

Oscar Lewis's studies of the poor in Mexico, Puerto Rico, and New York have appeared in a series of anthropological monographs that have stimulated a vast amount of interest in both academic and public circles. His biographical analysis and sympathetic portrayal of different families is organized around a conceptual framework that he called the culture of poverty.

In *La Vida: A Puerto Rican Family in the Culture of Poverty–San Juan and New York* Lewis presents a benumbing and almost overwhelming portrayal of three generations of a Puerto Rican family in the slums of San Juan and New York. He portrays through a family biographical framework (much of which is told in the tape recorded words of the subjects themselves), "the life histories of the individuals . . . reveal[ing] a picture of family disruption, violence, brutality, cheapness of life, lack of love, lack of education, lack of medical facilities—in short, a picture of incredible deprivation the effects of which cannot be wiped out in a single generation" (O, Lewis, 1966:xiv). Lewis believes that the study of specific families can best help us understand the relationship between societal institutions and the individual. Through intensive analysis of family systems, the interrelationship between culture and personality becomes meaningful with "whole-family studies bridg[ing] the gap between the conceptual extremes of culture at one pole and the individual at the other" (O. Lewis, 1966:xx).

Lewis contends that people who live in capitalistic societies under the poverty conditions of slums, ghettos, and squatter settlements develop similar family structures, interpersonal relationships, and value systems that transcend national boundaries. The culture of poverty is seen to flourish in societies that have the following characteristics: high rate of unemployment and underemployment, low wages for manual labor, stress on the importance of accumulated wealth and property, and an interpretation that attributes the lack of the accumulation of wealth by the poverty people residing in these societies as a result of their personal inadequacies and inferiorities. In these societies a virtually autonomous subculture exists among the poor, one which is self-perpetuating and self-defeating. Oscar

Lewis sees the culture of poverty developing from families adapting to societal conditions. These adaptations represent an effort to cope with the feelings of hopelessness and despair that arise from their realization that achieving success in terms of the prevailing values and goals is improbable. This hopelessness and despair, this sense of resignation and fatalism involves an inability to put off the satisfaction of immediate desires to plan for the future. A self-perpetuating cycle develops: low educational motivation leads to inadequate job preparation that, in turn, perpetuates unemployment, poverty, and despair:

> The culture of poverty, however, is not only an adaptation to a set of objective conditions of the larger society. Once it comes into existence it tends to perpetuate itself from generation to generation because of its effect on the children. By the time slum children are age six or seven they have usually absorbed the basic values and attitudes of their subculture and are not psychologically geared to take full advantage of changing conditions or increased opportunities which may occur in their lifetime. (Lewis, 1966:xiv)

Oscar Lewis points out that in African towns, where a tribal heritage is still strong and village relationships carry over into the towns, the culture of poverty does not appear. The tribe and ethnic group organizes the social life of the impoverished migrant town dweller. In a similar way the caste and clan system of India provides members of the lower impoverished castes a sense of identity and belonging that integrates them into the larger society. The Jews of Eastern Europe are seen as another exception. Although poor, they escaped from many of the traits of the culture of poverty because of their traditions of literacy and learning and the strong communal solidarity centered around their religion, rabbis, and the proliferation of voluntary associations. The fourth exception is speculative and relates to socialism, particularly in Cuba. Although poverty conditions still exist, Oscar Lewis reports little evidence of the despair, apathy, and hopelessness that are characteristic of urban slum dwellers in capitalistic societies. He attributes this to the people's optimism about a better life in the future, the highly organized structure of the community and a concomitant new sense of power and importance. "They were armed and were given a doctrine which glorified the lower class as the hope of humanity" (O. Lewis, 1966:xlix). A final exception is that of preliterate people living at subsistence levels who suffer from dire poverty and the absence of technology. These people do not exhibit the culture of poverty because of strong communal organization that centers around the tribal band and band chiefs, tribal councils, and local self-government.

Oscar Lewis's (1966) studies identify over 70 traits that characterize the culture of poverty. They are grouped by him into four major categories: the relationship between the subculture and the larger society; the nature of the ghetto, slum, or squatter settlement community; the nature of the family; and the attitudes, values, and character structure of the individual.

1. *The relationship between the subculture and the larger society.* Lewis believes that one of the most crucial characteristics of the culture of poverty is the disengagement and nonintegration of the poor in the major institutions of the larger society. Poverty, segregation and discrimination, fear, suspicion, and apathy are all factors accounting for this lack of effective participation, especially in the larger economic system. Low wages, chronic unemployment, and underemployment lead to low incomes, little savings, the use of the services of exploitative money lenders, the payment of high prices for used furniture and secondhand clothing, and the overpayment for smaller quantities of food staples. There is a low level of literacy and education among the poor that further aggravates the situation.

Although exposed to middle-class values, poor people, on the whole, do not live by them. For example, although many will claim that marriage by law, by the church, or by both is ideal, few will marry. For those with few job prospects, no property, and with little expectation for improvement in the future, a consensual marriage or free union makes good sense and avoids the expense and legal expenses and difficulties involved in marriage and divorce. Women will often turn down marital offers because they feel that it will unnecessarily tie them down to men who are immature, difficult, and generally unreliable. As with the men, the women feel that a consensual union gives them greater freedom and flexibility. By not giving the fathers of their children legal status as husbands, the women have a stronger claim on the children and also maintain exclusive rights to their own property.

2. *The nature of the ghetto, slum, or squatter settlement community.* Poor housing conditions, crowding, and gregariousness characterize the slum community. Most important, however, is the minimum of organization beyond the nuclear and extended family. Oscar Lewis (1966) observes that most preliterate people have achieved a higher level of sociocultural organization than the urban slum dweller.

3. *The nature of the family.* The family in the culture of poverty is characterized by the absence of the middle-class trait that cherishes childhood as a specially prolonged and protected stage in the life cycle. In the culture of poverty there is, for example, an early initiation into sex. Free unions or consensual marriages are common, and there is a relatively high incidence of the abandonment of wives and children by men. With the instability of consensual marriage, the family tends to be mother-centered and tied more closely with the mother's extended family of orientation. The female-centered household is given to authoritarianism. Although there is lip service given to family solidarity, it is rarely achieved because of intense sibling rivalry for the limited supply of goods and maternal affection.

4. *The attitudes, values, and character structure of the individual.* Individuals who grow up in the culture of poverty have strong feelings of fatalism, helplessness, dependence, and inferiority. Oscar Lewis (1966) points out that these characteristics are common among Black Americans who have the additional disadvantage of racial discrimination; they are also prominent in slum dwellers in Mexico City and

San Juan for people who are not segregated or subject to discrimination as distinct ethnic or racial groups. He lists other traits including a high incidence of weak ego structure; confusion of sexual identification, which reflects maternal deprivation; a strong present-time orientation, with relatively little disposition to delay gratification or plan for the future; and a high tolerance for psychological pathology of all kinds. Finally, there is a widespread belief in male superiority and, among men, a strong preoccupation with machismo (masculinity).

CRITIQUE OF THE CULTURE OF POVERTY: THE ANALYSIS OF SQUATTER SETTLEMENTS

The urban anthropologist, William Mangin (1970), reviewing the literature on squatter settlements in Peru, Turkey, Athens, Hong Kong, and Brazil, reports that they are characterized by an absence of the culture of poverty. He further points out that the poor of a given country have more in common with their compatriots in that country than with the poor in other societies. For example, the poor of Mexico and Puerto Rico are seen to have more in common with the general population of their respective countries than they do with the poor of France or Pakistan: ". . . In terms of cultural views of the world, ideal family and kinship patterns, aspirations, values, and even body movements and language habits, the poor of a country have more in common with the rest of their country (or culture) than they have with the poor of another country (or culture)" (Mangin, 1970:xvii).

Oscar Lewis's culture of poverty position is similar to the social disorganization view that sees the impact of urbanization in terms of depersonalization and anomie with the poverty community almost totally devoid of community and associational life. However, as Charles Valentine has pointed out (1968), Lewis himself contradicts this position in his description of La Esmeralda:

> The setting for the story of the Ries family is La Esmeralda, an old and colorful slum in San Juan, built on a steep embankment between the city's ancient fort walls and the sea. Squeezed into an area not more than five city blocks long and a few hundred yards wide are 900 houses inhabited by 3,600 people. . . .
>
> Seen from the walls above, the slum looks almost prosperous. This is because all the houses have roofs of new green tar paper. . . .
>
> Even though La Esmeralda is only ten minutes away from the heart of San Juan, it is physically and socially marginal to the city. The wall above it stands as a kind of symbol separating it from the city. La Esmeralda forms *a little community of its own* [italics added] with a cemetary, a church, a small dispensary and maternity clinic, and one elementary school. There are many small stores, bars and taverns. . . .
>
> To the people of Greater San Juan, La Esmeralda has a bad reputation . . . today the residents of La Esmeralda think of it as a relatively elegant healthful place, with its beautiful view of the sea, its paved streets, its new roofs, the absence of mosquitoes, the low rentals and its nearness to their places of work.

. . . the general mood of the people of La Esmeralda is one of gaiety and exuberance. They seem outgoing, friendly and expressive, with relatively little distrust of outsiders. They live amid constant noise from radios, juke boxes, and television sets, and spend a great deal of time in the stores and bars, where they drink and play dominoes. (O. Lewis, 1966:xxxii−xxxiii)

Among the town dwellers in sub-Saharan African cities, there is the continued presence of traditional networks of social relations, which have facilitated the adoption and assimilation of migrants into city life. The voluntary associations found in African cities combined with the persistence of extended kinship relationships assures the continuity of rural ways in the city and has resulted in the strengthening of tribal consciousness in the new urban environment.

Janet L. Abu-Lughod's (1961) analysis of Cairo, Egypt, and Edward M. Bruner's (1963) study of Medan, Sumatra, Indonesia, contradicted their social disorganization position on the existence of anonymity, alienation, and absence of primary relationships. Bruner's study concluded that the Medan migrants were part of a single kinship community. Every person in the kinship community was bound by multiple ties in a wide-ranging kinship network that once established structures all subsequent interaction including those with the voluntary associations. He concludes that the Batak clan groups of Medan are similar to the clan associations of the overseas Chinese, to the tribal associations of West Africa, and to the *zaibatsu* of industrial Japan. Further, he hypothesizes that future research on peasant communities in societies undergoing rapid cultural change and urbanization will "disclose not only the maintenance of existing kinship ties, but also the development of novel and stable recombinations based upon traditional structural principles" (Bruner, 1963:134).

Charles A. Valentine (1968), who has written a much-cited critique on the culture of poverty, argues that the essence of that position is the comparisons of the lifeways of groups who live by a distinctive poverty culture that consists largely of negative qualities, lacks and absences—group disintegration, personal disintegration, and lack of purposeful action in contrast to that of the more affluent segments of the population, who exhibit positive qualities. It is further argued that the poor maintain a self-perpetuating and self-defeating way of life.

Valentine poses an alternative interpretation by suggesting that the destructive nature of the social life of these poverty level people is determined by the structure of the society as a whole as well as forces beyond the control of poor people. That is, the variations in life styles of the poor are not shaped by a distinct culture. Rather, they are influenced by the actual conditions of life under poverty that is inconsistent with the fulfillment of the cultural design. Mangin (1970) reaches a similar conclusion. He criticizes the view of the cyclical nature of the culture of poverty—the passing down of the patterns from one generation to the next. Mangin believes that it is necessary to emphasize the fact that peasant communities are part of the larger society and that decisions made by the more powerful elements of the society relating to the peasant community are more important in maintaining their economic depression than are any questionable social and personality attributes of the poor. "It is to the advantage of commercial interests and the middle classes, as well as to some peasant leaders and professional leaders of the poor, to maintain social systems with large numbers of peasants and poor people on the bottom rungs" (Mangin, 1970:xxviii).

Valentine (1968) applies this perspective to the family and argues that varieties in family patterns of the poor can be seen as adaptations to the externally imposed conditions of poverty. More specifically, consensual unions and female-centered or mother-centered households may be regarded as flexible adaptations to the uncertainty and fluctuations of economic circumstances. Thus alternative family structures are developed as necessities to cope with poverty conditions and should be seen as positive contributions to the health and well-being of family members. The following family adaptations are viewed by Valentine as responses to economic deprivation:

> Separation by mutual consent, sometimes including considerations of alternative means of support for mother and children.
> Informal and extralegal but effective adoption which shifts dependents to households better able to support them.
> Attenuated affinality, in which kin ties and support sources established through the marital union continue to function in the absence of the husband.
> Reunion, planned or otherwise, after temporary separation.
> Support of fatherless families through other lines of kinship connection. (Valentine, 1968:267)

For children, socialization occurs in a wider network of relatives, adults, and peers rather than being concentrated in the nuclear family. Valentine asserts that this may contribute to healthy early maturity, including development of numerous supportive relationships and sources of emotional security.

In a similar vein, Hyman Rodman states (1965) that it would be more appropriate to interpret the behavior of poverty families (he uses the term, lower class families) as *solutions to problems* they face—owing to life under poverty conditions—than as *problems*. In an insightful illustration, Rodman points out that the characteristics attributed to the poor—*promiscuous* sexual relationships, *illegitimate* children, *desertion* by husbands and fathers, *unmarried* mothers—use middle-class biased terminology and distortions that tend to emphasize a social disorganization model of family behavior. Rodman emphasizes that these italicized concepts are not utilized by the poor and that it is misleading to describe their behavior in this manner. Since such words as *promiscuity, illegitimacy,* and *desertion* have middle-class meanings and judgmental implications, Rodman believes that it is necessary to analyze and describe the family patterns of the poor by paying more attention to the language and description that the poor employ in analyzing their own behavior. By doing this, social scientists can avoid ''the major middle-class conception of lower-class families—viewing certain patterns as problems when in reality, they can easily be viewed as solutions'' (Rodman, 1965:225).

Rodman (1971) completed an ethnographic and explanatory description of lower class family behavior and attitudes in Coconut Village, a small rural village in northeastern Trinidad. He documents how the use of the conceptualizations of the people themselves aids his own sociological analysis. Rodman focuses on lower class family behavior and attitudes and the impact that poverty has on culture and family organization. Of particular interest to us is Rodman's concern with the validity of the culture of poverty theory to explain family patterns.

Rodman finds three types of marital or quasi-marital relationships—friending, living, and married—in Trinidad. The three types vary in the degree of acceptance of marital responsibility, especially on the part of the man. During friending, which involves the least responsibility and which occurs most frequently, the marital pair do not live together in the same household. In this form of relationship the woman is supposed to make herself sexually available to the man at his leisure, and the man is supposed to provide support to the woman and any children they may have. Children ordinarily live with the mother, although they may live with the father if it is more convenient. Rodman reports that most friending relationships eventually dissolve, but a substantial number evolve into a living relationship. During living, the marital pair live together but are not legally married. The living relationship is seen to combine the advantages of common residence characteristic of legal marriage without its legal responsibility but with the limited responsibility of friending.

Rodman reports that the living relationship is more common among the lower classes than marriage and usually precedes marriage when and if it occurs. This marital relationship is socially acceptable and has a reciprocal base with the husband contributing to the household and the wife carrying out the household chores of cooking, cleaning, and washing.

The married relationship, to all extents and purposes, is similar to a living relationship but there is a church wedding and legal ties between the man and woman. The legal advantage of the marital relationship is that the woman is entitled to financial support from her husband. In a living relationship only the man's children are eligible for such support. The marriage relationship occurs less frequently than the living among the lower class and is seen to reflect the reluctance to take on responsibility.

Rodman believes that the reluctance to take on the responsibility of marriage is closely related to the general cautionary attitude of both sexes in placing trust and confidence in the other as well as a shared feeling that any marital relationship is a temporary one. These attitudes reflect the relation of family life to the structure of the larger society, particularly to its economy. The lower class families of Coconut

Village suffer from economic deprivation. The land is poor and the meager crops that are produced are difficult to market because of inadequate transportation systems. Consequently, wage earning is necessary to supplement and in most cases to provide a more reliable income base for the family. Unfortunately, wage earnings are unreliable: the lower class man involved in wage labor finds much unemployment, underemployment, poorly paid employment, and unskilled employment. Since the man's role as wage earner and income provider is central to the family relationship, his status within the family is determined by his economic success. If the man is responsible for the financial support of his wife and children and since the economic circumstances are so precarious, it becomes more understandable why men are reluctant to take on the additional responsibilites of marriage. The consequences for the man when he is unable satisfactorily to complete his duties as a wage earner are the loss of status, esteem, income power, and his position in the community and in the family. It is this economic factor that explains the greater frequency of friending relationships than living relationships, living relationships than marriages. These variations provide the individual with different patterns to permit some semblance of family life in the face of economic uncertainties.

These three forms of marital and quasi-marital relationships are seen by Rodman as being functional for the lower class family since they provide solutions to social, economic, and legal problems. In response to the culture-of-poverty argument, Rodman suggests that members of the lower class stretch the values of the society to fit their circumstances—they do not develop a distinct culture of poverty. They do not abandon the values of legal marriage and legitimate children but stretch these values to allow for other marital systems (e.g., friending and living), which allow for the existence of nonlegal unions and illegitimate children. By not rejecting the general value systems of the society (its culture), the poor are able to add additional value choices to their cultural base, which thus help them to adjust to their deprived circumstances. The following passage summarizes Rodman's perspective:

> The theories we have presented put a new perspective upon lower-class family life and values. As the middle-class critic sees lower-class life it is characterized by "promiscuous" sexual relationships, "illegal" marital unions, "illegitimate" children, "unmarried" mothers, "deserting" husbands and fathers, and "abandoned" children. These are typically viewed in a gross manner as, simply, *problems* of the lower class. According to our perspective it makes better sense to see them as *solutions* of the lower class to problems that they face in the social, economic, and perhaps legal and political spheres of life. This means that the typical member of the lower class is faced with a chronic economic problem that spawns a series of related problems. Part of the solution to these problems is to be found in the nature of lower-class family life and values. By permitting certain practices (e.g., marital shifting and child-shifting) and by developing certain relationships (e.g., *friending, living*) the lower-class person is able to solve some of the problems that he faces because of his deprived position in society. (Rodman, 1971:197)

THE CULTURE OF POVERTY IN THE UNITED STATES: THE MOYNIHAN REPORT

The Moynihan report, *The Negro Family: The Case for National Action,* is a document prepared in 1965 by the Office of Planning and Research of the U.S. Department of Labor under the supervision of the Assistant Secretary of Labor, Daniel Patrick Moynihan. The report is an illustration of the use of the culture-of-poverty position and, as we will see, has important social policy implications. The report is loaded with such terms as *tangle of pathology, broken* families, *illegitimacy,* and *social disorganization,* to describe the family structure of blacks living in poverty. These terms are commonly associated with the culture-of-poverty orientation, which we described previously. The implications of the report are that it is necessary to change the culture of poor black families if the government expects them to improve their economic position. The focus of social policy legislation that follows from this position is concerned with psychiatric treatment, social welfare reforms, dissemination of information relating to birth control and family planning, and other individual-oriented programs. Alternative policy would see the need to create jobs, to train individuals to fill these jobs, and to institute reform designed to reduce the large economic distribution inequalities in the United States. Although the report was published in 1965 and has been severely criticized for its biases and distortions, it still reflects a viewpoint that is held by many laypersons, social scientists, and legislators in the United States. This is especially important in that such a position has led to the wastage of public monies and has diverted maximum effort away from the task at hand—the ending of poverty and its concomitant evils in the United States.

The dominant thesis of the Moynihan report is stated dramatically:

> At the heart of the deterioration of the fabric of Negro society is the deterioration of the Negro family.
>
> It is the fundamental source of the weakness of the Negro community at the present time.
>
> The white family has achieved a high degree of stability and is maintaining that stability. . . .
>
> By *contrast, the family structure of lower class Negroes is highly unstable, and in many urban centers is approaching complete breakdown.* [Printed in boldface.] (U.S. Department of Labor, 1965:5)

Although the Moynihan report discusses discrimination, unemployment, and poverty and sees them as being contributory causes of the difficulties of poverty in black family systems, the report places its primary emphasis on the demographic data culled from census and governmental reports on households—*dissolved* marriages, *broken* families, *illegitimacy,* welfare rates, Aid-to-families-with-dependent-children figures, and delinquency and crime rates. From these sources,

Moynihan develops a social disorganization thesis with a lower class subculture that is characterized by matriarchy, emasculated males, educational failure, delinquency, crime, and drug addiction.

Rainwater and Yancey (1967) note that the report is neither a scholarly article prepared for a professional journal nor a simple governmental position paper. It is a hybrid, presenting certain social science information to advocate a social policy position. This position follows the guidelines of the culture-of-poverty argument and postulates the existence of a self-perpetuating cycle of poverty anchored by the family system. The policy implications follow directly from this position:

> The harsh fact is that as a group, at the present time, in terms of ability to win out in the competitions of American life, they [the Negro people] are not equal to most of those groups with which they will be competing. . . . the circumstances of the Negro American community in recent years has probably been getting *worse, not better.* . . .
>
> The fundamental problem, in which this most clearly is the case, is that of family structure. . . . the Negro family in the urban ghettos is crumbling. . . . for vast numbers of the unskilled, poorly educated city working class the fabric of conventional social relationships has all but disintegrated. . . . So long as this situation persists, the cycle of poverty and disadvantage will continue to repeat itself.
>
> . . . a national effort towards the problems of Negro Americans must be directed towards the question of family structure. The object should be to strengthen the Negro family so as to enable it to raise and support its members as do other families. After that, how this group of Americans chooses to run its affairs, take advantage of its opportunities or fail to do so, is none of the nation's business. (U.S. Department of Labor, 1965: Preface, 47–48)

The controversy surrounding the report lies in its support of the culture-of-poverty position in its stress on the cultural deprivations of the Black family that have impeded it from taking advantage of the opportunities the United States offers. Further, although briefly stating that the socioeconomic system played a role in the deterioration of the Negro community, the Moynihan report emphasizes the dysfunctional characteristics of a black matriarchal family structure. The report argues that female-headed families constitute a problem for the black family:

> In essence, the Negro community has been forced into a matriarchal structure which, because it is so out of line with the rest of the American society, seriously retards the progress of the group as a whole, and imposes a crushing burden on the Negro male and, in consequence, on a great many Negro women as well. (U.S. Department of Labor, 1965:29)

It is vital to consider in detail the basis of the culture-of-poverty criticism of the black matriarchal family structure and its alleged consequences. In addition, it is necessary to determine the extent that black families are headed by women and its implications for the family members. At the onset, a conceptual clarification must be made. The term, matriarchy, refers to a family authority system controlled by females, whereas a female-headed household refers to a household where no male head is present. It does not necessarily follow that a census-defined female-headed household is a matriarchy. Thus it is a gross oversimplification to simply equate the two, which is what Moynihan does without any further basis of information. That is, Moynihan does not justify his use of social statistics as indicators of cultural patterns. Although census figures give us a demographic picture of statistical shape, they tell us nothing directly about either the structure or process in a cultural system or about the variety of cultural designs underlying it:

> Consider, for example, a demographic pattern in which at any time there are many households without an observable resident adult male heading the domestic menage. This picture may reflect a system of plural marriage in which co-wives reside separately and husbands live with one wife at a time, as in the case of polygynous societies in numerous parts of the world. It may reflect a community organization in which all adult males reside together and apart from their wives and children, as in much of the Southwest Pacific. It may be associated with a traditional family form in which male support for the household comes from kinsmen by blood, with no such social position as resident husband, as among the Nayar of South India. It may be found in societies where males are migrant laborers for periods of years while their spouses and offspring remain in the home community, as in many colonial areas. Or it may reflect a variety of systems in which multiple consensual unions involve males in various standardized obligations to women and children, not including cohabitation, as reported from Caribbean societies. *Thus the census taker's finding by itself has no definite cultural significance but may turn out, with further investigation, to have many different meanings.* [Italics added.] (Valentine, 1968:6−7)

In addition to the unwarranted suppositions drawn from the statistical data in regard to cultural patterns, the Moynihan report also distorts that data. The report has been criticized quite heavily on methodological procedures. Rainwater and Yancey (1967) note the following major methodological criticisms:

1. The data was oversimplified. Moynihan failed to include data that tended to contradict his hypothesis and the data that was reported did not lead to such semantically loaded conclusions as "rapid deterioration" and "alarming rate of illegitmacy."
2. The thesis did not consider the effects of economic position and the differences between social classes; controlling for these variables wash out the racial differences. Blacks and whites of the same economic classes virtually have the same type of family structure.
3. The report downplayed the great range and variability in the black family and family behavior, including the great diversity of low-income families.

To illustrate these criticisms, let us look at the third point in more detail. The report states that demographic data indicates that black families are more likely to be characterized as having a female head than white families, 21 percent to 9 percent, respectively. However, the report virtually ignores the fact that the overwhelming majority of black families, over 70 percent, were headed by both a husband and a wife. This point must be stressed: when less than 30% of black families are headed by women, it is erroneous to talk about *the* black family. As Hylan Lewis (1965) points out, when the great diversity, range, and variability of black families is overlooked, "there is danger that the depreciated, and probably more dramatic and threatening, characteristics of a small segment of the population may be imputed to an entire population" (H. Lewis, 1965:315). For another thing, even if there is a greater predominance of female-headed families among blacks, the question remains whether this condition is pathological.

Robert Staples (1971) argues that, regardless of the role of black women in the family, it is necessary to stress that the female role evolved out of the struggle for black survival. The position is similar to that of Rodman (1965; 1971), who views the behavioral adaptations of poverty people as solutions to the problems of economic deprivation. Andrew Billingsley (1969) has shown that many families in the black inner-city ghettos have demonstrated an impressive capacity to adapt to the social, cultural, and economic deprivations fostered on them by the larger society and have developed strong family relationships. Finally, Rainwater (1966) contradicts the notion that female-centered households are dysfunctional; in research of poverty families, Rainwater finds an *adaptive* urban matricentric family form (among others) that successfully copes with the problems of poverty. Carol B. Stack offers additional support to this position.

Carol B. Stack's *All Our Kin* (1974) is an anthropological study of a poor black community, which she called The Flats, that is located in a midwestern city called Jackson Harbor. She examines how families cope with poverty by adapting domestic networks to link people who are not necessarily related. Stack emphasizes that a census-defined female-headed single-parent household does not indicate separatedness or isolation. A cooperative support network exists that is composed of both relatives and fictive kin, who are treated as kin by family members and are given such kinship terms as sister, aunt, and uncle. These people unite for mutual aid and to meet daily needs:

> Black families living in The Flats need a steady source of cooperative support to survive. They share with one another because of the urgency of their needs. Alliances between individuals are created around the clock as kin and friends exchange and give and obligate one another. They trade food stamps, rent money, a TV, hats, dice, a car, a nickel here, a cigarette there, food, milk, grits, and children.
>   . . . Without the help of kin, fluctuations in the meager flow of available goods could easily destroy a family's ability to survive. . . . Kin and close friends who fall into

similar economic crises know that they may share the food, dwelling, and even the few scarce luxuries of those individuals in their kin network. Despite the relatively high cost of rent and food in urban black communities, the collective power within kin-based exchange networks keeps people from going hungry. (Stack, 1974:32–33)

Stack stresses that social scientists who employ such culture-of-poverty terms as *pathology* and *social disorganization* fail to understand the adaptive forms of familial and quasi-familial relationships and structures that have developed in these economically deprived communities. Further, they are not aware how resilient urban black families are to the socioeconomic conditions of poverty, the inexorable unemployment, and the limited access to scarce economic opportunities of single-parent mothers and their children who receive welfare under such programs as Aid to Families with Dependent Children (AFDC). Stack points out that these structural adaptations do not lock people into a cycle of poverty or prevent them from marrying or removing themselves from the networks. But her study does indicate that the very success of these cooperative networks force women to think twice about marriage:

> Forms of social control both within the kin network and in the larger society work against successful marriages in The Flats. In fact, couples rarely chance marriage unless a man has a job; often the job is temporary, low paying, insecure, and the worker gets laid off whenever he is not needed. Women come to realize that welfare benefits and ties within kin networks provide greater security for social mobility. A woman may be immediately cut off the welfare roles when a husband returns home from prison, the army, or if she gets married. Thus, the society's welfare system collaborates in weakening the position of the black male. (Stack, 1974:113)

In summary, Stack's work graphically reveals how viable family structures develop to handle chronic poverty and governmental programs that reinforce welfare dependency and unemployment.

As for the Moynihan report overall, most social scientists conclude that it was more of a polemical document with social policy implications than a scientific one. Gans (1967a) believes that the focus on family problems leads to a clamor for pseudopsychiatric programs as well as to a wave of social and psychiatric solutions that are intended to change the alleged dysfunctional black female-headed family to an alleged functional white middle-class type of family. Gans argues that the knowledge of the black poverty family is relatively weak, whereas there is much greater certainty on the primacy of economic deprivation. He concludes that, "it would thus be tragic if the findings were used to justify demands for Negro self-improvement or the development of a middle-class family structure before further programs to bring about real equality are set up" (Gans, 1967a:456). Gans feels that too much attention is devoted to the disabilities and that insufficient attention is given to the causes. He advocates that instead of psychiatric solutions the following types of programs should be instituted: the establishment of jobs, the development of income miantenance programs, the building of housing outside ghetto areas, and the desegregation of existing housing.

His position is an illustration of the situational approach. This orientation argues that although the behavior of poverty families is different than the middle-class pattern, both groups have a similar culture. The behavior is viewed as an adaptation to poverty conditions. This is a direct rebuke of the culture-of-poverty position. In a different paper, Gans (1967b) views the poor as an economically and politically deprived group whose attitudes and behavior are seen as adaptations, just as the behavior and attitudes of the affluent are adaptations to their social situation. Similarly, Elliot Liebow (1967) in his ethnographic study, *Tally's Corner: A Study of Negro Street Corner Men,* stresses the point that although each generation may provide role models for each succeeding one, of greater importance is that the similarities between generations "do not result from 'cultural transmission' but from the fact that the son goes out and independently experiences the same failures, in the same areas, and for much the same reasons as his father" (Liebow, 1967:000). Liebow in his study of lower class black men in Washington, D.C., found no evidence indicating deviation from white middle-class norms nor did he find that family role deviancy is perpetuated intergenerationally. Liebow concludes that there is a direct relationship between socioeconomic discrimination and family instability.

William Ryan (1971) argues that the culture-of-poverty position and such manifestations of it as the Moynihan report blame the victim for being poor; the reform is still to be of the lower classes, the poor, with some saying that they should reform themselves and others saying that the rich and more affluent classes should help. As Charles A. Valentine (1968) has argued, few say that the more powerful, the influential controlling classes of the culture, should change or that the total social structure needs changing. Instead, they place the burden for reform on the poor and are primarily concerned with doing away with a culture and not with poverty.

Our position is that the culture-of-poverty perspective that focuses on family structure is too narrow. It does not matter whether one evaluates family structure as pathological (a problem) or as a positive functional adjustment (a solution), the real issue is the causes and consequences of racial, economic, political, and social inequality. The following statement by Leonard Reissman (1972), although concerned with the black poverty family can be generalized to all families who live under the wretched conditions of poverty:

> It must certainly be the case that, if blacks did not suffer from inequalities and were economically secure, then the type of family they have would not bother anyone; at the most, the nature of the concern would be of an entirely different order than it is now. By the same reasoning, 1 must assume that the efforts to change the matriarchy, and thus to

cure the pathology, are not likely to make much difference in the conditions of blacks if the causes and consequences of their inequality are left untouched. Rather, I am convinced that if the causes and consequences of inequality are removed, then the structure of the Negro family will become much less important as an issue for reformers. (Reissman, 1972:94)

If the Family Were the Same as the Military . . .

Happy Fernandez

Envision what would happen in the 1980s if President Carter's State of the Union address had been about family policy rather than defense policy as the nation's highest priority. He would have said:

"Our nation's survival in the 1980s and beyond requires that every family unit have the resources it needs to nurture healthy, creative contributors to our society. I, therefore, propose that the Department of Family and Community Development receive a 5 percent real increase in its budget that is over and above inflation.

"I realize that the Department of Family and Community Development already receives the biggest share (42 percent) of the federal budget. But our top priority has been and must continue to be the health of our families. That is the keystone of our nation's strength.

"Our nation is only as strong as our weakest link. Thus, an all-out attack on the causes of birth defects, malnutrition, sub-standard housing, child and spouse abuse, failing schools, juvenile delinquency, and environmental pollution are our top priorities. Forces will be deployed at the neighborhood level to attack these problems, and our most sophisticated electronic systems will be activated at the federal and state levels to find the root causes. In addition, one half of all research funds will be used for this purpose.

"We will sustain this effort. My five-year family and community development program provides real funding increases that average more 4½ percent a year.

"I intend to carry out this program. With careful, and efficient management we should be able to do so within the budget increases I propose. If inflation exceeds the projected rates, I intend to adjust the Family and Community Development Department budget as needed, just as was done in 1980.

"Much of this program will take five years of more to reach fruition. The imbalances it will correct have been caused by more than a decade of disparity and they cannot be remedied overnight, so we must be willing to see this program through. To insure that we do so, I am setting a growth rate for family and community development that will be tolerable over the long haul.

"The most wasteful and self-defeating thing we could do would be to start this necessary program, then alter or cut it back after a year or two when such action might become politically attractive. The family and community development program I am proposing for the next five years will require some sacrifice—but sacrifice we can afford. It will not increase at all the percentage of our Gross National Product devoted to family and human development, which will remain steady at about 5 percent.

"I must also announce that every 18- to 20-year-old must register for the draft. Able-bodied young men and women will be trained for the Family and Community Development Corps and must serve a two-year tour of duty. The corps will assist families and communities to renovate houses, plan urban gardens, build playgrounds and multi-age recreation centers, staff care centers for children and older adults, develop comprehensive health services, clean up rivers and parks, and develop community organizations that enable families to be involved in decision-making in the community.

"You can see how this two-year corps experience will provide training and on the job experience for young people. They will be gaining skills and experience that will equip them for future jobs.

"I prefer investing our federal tax dollars in human services that will continually be reinvested in services for families in this country. A dollar invested in family life will have more than nine lives as it is continuously earned and respent in the economy.

"I have heard some complaints about the so-called 'over-kill' effects of our family policy to date. Yet I must defend our goal of teaching young people to read 100 times faster than may be needed at this moment. In the years 2000 and 2050, our young people will be the adult leaders and voters. They will need these skills.

"Likewise, I intend to maintain our procedures on 'cost-overruns' in the Department of Family and Community Development. If original estimates of the cost of rehabilitating juvenile delinquents, for example, prove to be too low, the cost-overruns will be covered.

"Two additional announcements must be made. We must have a Rapid Deployment Force to achieve energy independence immediately. Solar-Watt Teams commonly known as SWAT Teams will be trained as energy specialists and deployed to assist every family and community to convert to solar energy. My goal is to have 50 percent of our energy needs met by solar power in 1985.

"My commitment to an International Family Policy is reflected in my budget request of $20 billion to assist developing nations with child development, nutrition, health, and solar energy assistance. This is only a 5 percent increase over last year's allocation but my commitment to this priority is clear.

"My priorities are clearly reflected in these budget decisions. My first concern and that of every American President is and must be vitality of our families and communities."

Happy Fernandez in *The Philadelphia Inquirer*, Op-Ed, April 3, 1980. Reprinted by permission.

WHITE FAMILIES IN POVERTY

We believe that it would be instructive to discuss the characteristics of poor *white* families living in poverty. All too frequently, sociology textbooks focus solely on poor black families in America and disregard the plight of their white counterparts. In addition, discussions of the American white family in these textbooks virtually ignore the existence of poor white families and tend implicitly to juxtapose in the reader's mind poverty and social minorities.

Robert Coles (1968) describes the situation of poor white families in Appalachia and notes their adaptation to poverty is similar to the adaptation made by persons living in the racial ghettos of urban American and the squatter settlements of the Third World. He sees the behavior of the poor as symptoms of a dysfunctional cultural system rather than as reasonable responses to poverty conditions. The following statement summarizes Coles' position:

> Appalachia is full of ironies, but nothing is more ironic than the fact that America's oldest ethnic group, its white Anglo-Saxon Protestants, live there in poverty as desperate as that experienced by any other impoverished people. It took courage and enterprise to settle the region—and now the region's people are called inert, apathetic, and unresourceful. The region has experienced the severest kind of unemployment as a result of technological change, and yet side by side one sees an almost primitive economy. If ever there was a section of America that needed planned capital investment, federally sustained—as indeed this country has done in other regions of the world with its money—then indeed Appalachia is that reason.
>
> In my experience the people of Appalachia do not fit the usual sociological and anthropological descriptions applied to them. By that I mean that their apparent inertia and apathy are reasonable responses to a lack of opportunity and a lack of employment. Given jobs, real jobs, jobs that are not substitutes for work, Appalachian men and women work well and hard. They also can be open, friendly, and generous—even to an outsider like me. What they do not want is a kind of patronizing and condescending sympathy. They are proud and stubborn people who want from this country a share of its wealth. Given that, I don't think we would have any "psychological problems" with the region's citizens. (Coles, 1968:27)

An interesting monograph is that of Joseph T. Howell (1973), *Hard Living on Clay Street*. Howell's book concerns his participant observation field study of poor white families living in a blue-collar suburb of Washington, D.C. The families, who lived on Clay Street, were southern migrants who moved to Washington from farms in North Carolina and the mountains of West Virginia. The men had service-oriented jobs: painters, plasterers, plumbers, repairmen, auto mechanics, truck drivers, and so on. Stereotypically, they are called rednecks, lower class, irresponsible, and white trash.

Howell (1973:263−352) distinguishes between two opposing life styles, which represent two ends of a continuum of family life on Clay Street—hard living and settled living—by delineating seven general areas of attitudes and behavior:

1. Heavy drinking. Heavy drinking occurred quite frequently in hard-living families and occurred only occasionally if at all among settled families.
2. Marital Stability. Hard-life families were married more than once, with their current marriages being precarious. Settled families had long-term stable marriages.
3. Toughness. Profanity, talks of violence, and general attitudes of "toughness" were commonplace among both husbands and wives, whereas the settled-living families had a moderate approach to life.
4. Political Alienation. Clay Street's hard-living families rarely voted or held strong political beliefs. This was based on their view that government was unresponsive, corrupt, and irrelevant to their needs. In contrast, despite their feelings of frustration, the settled-living families voted as political conservatives and felt that it was worthwhile to fight for and preserve the society.
5. Rootlessness. The hard-living families were more mobile, they rented their houses, moved frequently, and had a general attitude that they had no roots in the community or anywhere. The settled families lived in the same, owned homes for a period of time and felt ties to the community.
6. Present-Time Orientation. Hard-living families were preoccupied with surviving from day to day and gave little thought to the future. The settled families of Clay Street, by virtue of the fact that they could save a little money, expressed greater concern about the community and their family's future.
7. Individualism. Hard-living families valued independence and self-reliance, calling themselves loners. They had little involvement with or use for clubs or organizations, and they liked to work alone. The settled families, on the other hand, participated in community life and in groups and rarely had the same feelings of individualism.

Howell believes that the degree of marital stability was a key indication of involvement in either of the two life styles. Howell quotes a local police officer to illustrate this:

Well, there are basically two types of folks in this community: middle-class and what you might call lower class. The middle-class folks, the working people, they never cause no trouble—law abiding, upright, quiet. Now the lower class, they are different. We're all the time getting calls when husbands and wives get into fights, husband leaves, wife leaves, that sort of thing. (Howell, 1973:274)

The hard-living families of Clay Street were characterized by family instability. Howell reports that practically every hard-living family member has been married more than once, with many having common-law consensual marriages. A striking characteristic of the Clay Street marriages was the changing nature of the marriage relationship: many marriages were on shaky grounds and obviously stable couples would suddenly break up, their marriage dissolved. The causes of marital dissolution varied—adulterous affairs, drinking, unemployment were the most frequently cited causes. The couples viewed divorce as an eventual consequence of marriage; remarriage was also seen as an integral part of the hard life. Howell quotes a frequent philosophical attitude regarding marriages: "Divorce is simply part of life, that's just the way things are" (Howell, 1973:290). Their ambivalence toward marriage was quoted of a male resident of Clay Street:

Well it's too bad. Sure, I want my marriage to work out. But it didn't. And it doesn't for most folks around here. The way I see it, it's inherited. My grandaddy, he had it. He was married several times. My dad and mom, hell, they had it. And my children, they are going to have it, too. Divorces, separations, broken marriages. Hell, that's just the way life is. It just runs in the family. It's inherited. (Howell, 1973:292)

The frequency of divorces and other forms of marital instability had ramifications not only for the couple but also for their involvement with each of their extended families. Howell reports that the residents of Clay Street rarely saw their relatives, including such close ones as sisters and brothers. Many did not know whether these relatives were alive or not. The absence of ties with relatives is partially explained by the fact that the husbands and wives were themselves from broken homes. Further, the ones who moved from the South or from the Appalachia Mountains to Clay Street described themselves as black sheep compared to the rest of their family. The general pattern, according to Howell, was for the families to scatter, with some remaining on the farm; some settling in the Washington, D.C., area; some going to industrial northern cities or moving out West; or some just disappearing. The result was that although many of the hard-living families of Clay Street had nostalgia for their rural homes, there was no "home" for them to return to and there were very few close relatives who stayed there. The result was a feeling of rootlessness.

Most husbands and wives fought and both tried to maintain an image of toughness and independence. These attitudes reflect the difficult marital experiences of the couple. One hard-living wife experienced an early marriage, divorce, the birth of six children and the death of two of the children, poverty, poor health, and her current husband's alcoholism and violence. She explains her attitudes this way: "Take me, . . . If I wasn't a fighter I'd never of made it, not to say that I've made it now" (Howell, 1973:303). Yet underneath that tough image, Howell reports that most hard-living families of Clay Street were compassionate and sensitive and demonstrated compassion and affection for each other and their children.

Howell concludes that simplistic social psychological and social and cultural causal theories do not provide an adequate explanation of these families. He argues that providing social psychological reasons for a particular individual's behavior—coming from a broken home, alcoholism prevalent, and so on—obscures the structural and cultural forces that influence an individual's and a family's behavior patterns. Howell also condemns sweeping societal generalities to explain the behavior of the poor. He rejects simplistic structural arguments and culture-of-poverty theories that see the main reason for "reckless" and "unstable" behavior as a result of self-perpetuating family instability. In his concluding cautionary statement he argues a point that it is important for all of us to keep in mind in our own personal analysis and depiction of poverty families:

> June [a Clay Streeter] put it better than anyone else: "You can call us what you want to, but folks around here, hell, we're just plain folks. We got problems like everybody else. Maybe the difference is we don't try to shove 'em all into some closet. That's 'cause we ain't too proud to admit we're just folks." Above all else, the people on Clay Street were "just folks," and their humanity expressed itself in every aspect of their lives. (Howell, 1973:359–360)

CONCLUSION

This chapter concludes our discussion of the family in the city. We devoted our attention to poverty families in both industrial and nonindustrial Western societies. Two theoretical orientations dominate the analysis of poverty families, and both have different consequences for social policies affecting the poor.

The cultural position (the culture of poverty) emphasizes the cultural dynamics of poverty and is seen to have long-range effects on individuals' and families' behavior and values. This position argues that although social conditions may be or may have been the underlying cause of poverty, emergent cultural conditions may lead to the development of self-perpetuating cultural patterns that are inimical to movement out of poverty. A self-perpetuating cycle is seen to come into play—broken families and low educational motivation lead to inadequate job preparation, which, in turn, perpetuates poverty, unemployment, despair and broken families.

The second position, the situational approach, hypothesizes that although the behavior of poverty families is different than the middle-class pattern, the values of culture of the poverty group are basically the same. The behavior of poverty families is seen as adaptations and solutions to poverty conditions. The cultural similarity among generations is seen to result from the perpetuation of poverty conditions—no jobs, discrimination, inadequate housing, and so on—rather than the cultural transmission of a poverty culture.

By comparatively examining a diverse number of poverty families representing different races and different societal cultures, we reach a similar position with that of the situationalists. Our position is that the culture of poverty perspective tends to put the blame of poverty on the very victims of poverty—the poverty families themselves. It downplays the societal factors and the debilitating consequences of inequality. We share the viewpoint of men like Leonard Reissman who have argued that the removal of the causes and consequences of inequality will also remove the "tangle of pathology" of poor people: if one wants to change poverty families one must end poverty.

Three

SEX ROLES, COURTSHIP, AND MARITAL RELATIONSHIPS

CHAPTER 7

Premarital Relationships

The social sciences make an important distinction between sex and gender. Sex refers to biologically determined differences between males and females, which is most evident in male genitalia and female genitalia. Maleness and femaleness are determined by biology. Gender refers to social and cultural definitions of masculinity and femininity based on biological differentiation. Gender involves socially learned patterns of behavior and psychological and emotional expression and attitudes that socially distinguish males from females. Ideals about masculinity and femininity are culturally derived and provide the basis for differing self-images and identities of men and women.[1]

Cross-cultural and historical research reveals that societies allocate different tasks and duties to men and women. Among other animals the differentiation is biologically determined, and all the animals within a given species behave in the same way and take on the same tasks. Among humans, however, social and cultural factors account for variations in the roles and attitudes of the two sexes. The relationship between man and woman although influenced by biology is not determined by it. Rather, gender identities acquired through social learning provide guidelines for appropriate behavior and expression.

Biological factors can be seen as having a great influence on sex-role

[1]Given this distinction between sex and gender, the term used to describe social and cultural roles of men and women should be *gender* roles, not *sex* roles. However, we bow to the constraints of popular usage and will also employ the term, sex roles, in this book.

relationships in less technologically developed societies. Physiological factors, periodic childbearing, and the relative physical strength of men and woman play an important part in designating the role allocations within these societies. Clellan S. Ford, the noted anthropologist, argues that for preindustrial peoples "the single most important biological fact in determining how men and women live is the differential part they play in reproduction" (1970:28). The woman's life was characterized by an endless cycle of pregnancy, childbearing, and nursing for periods of up to three years. By the time the child was weaned, the mother was likely to be pregnant again. Not until menopause, which frequently coincided with the end of the woman's life itself, was she free from her reproduction role. In such circumstances, it is not surprising that such activities as hunting, fighting, and building were usually defined as the male's task; the gathering and preparation of grains and vegetables were female activities as was the care of the young.

In an early study, George Murdock (1937) provided data on the division of labor by sex in which 224 preliterate societies divided their labor. Such activities as metal working, weapon making, boat building, wood and stone working, hunting and trapping, house building, and clearing the land for agriculture were tasks performed by men. Women's activities included grinding of grain; the gathering and cooking of herbs, roots, and seeds as well as fruits, berries, and nuts; basket, hat, and pottery making; and the making and repairing of clothing. D'Andrade (1966) after reviewing the cross-cultural literature concluded that a division of labor by sex occurs in all societies. Generally, the male activities are those that involve vigorous physical activity or travel; the female activities are those that are less physically strenuous and require less geographical mobility.

One should not overestimate the importance of biological factors in sex-role relationships. Although physiological factors tend to play a more influential role in sex-role differentiation in preindustrial societies, that is not to say that biology *determines* these allocations. A classic illustration of the diversity of human behavior is Margaret Mead's (1935/1963) study of sex and temperament in three South Pacific societies.

Each society held a different conception of male and female temperament. The Arapesh were characterized as gentle and home loving, with a belief of temperamental equality between men and women. Both adult men and women subordinated their needs to those of the younger or weaker members of the society. The Mundugumor assumed a natural hostility between members of the same sex and slightly less hostility between the sexes. Both sexes were expected to be tough, aggressive, and competitive. The third society, the Tchambuli, believed that the sexes are temperamentally different, but the sex roles were reversed relative to the Western pattern.

> I found . . . in one [society], both men and women act as we expect women to act—in a mild parental responsive way; in the second, both act as we expect men to act—in a

fierce initiative fashion; and in the third, the men act according to our stereotype for women—are catty, wear curls and go shopping, while the women are energetic, managerial, unadorned partners. (Mead, 1963; Preface to the 1950 edition)

Even if one grants the premise that physiological factors are contributing components in the distribution of tasks in preliterate societies, they are not as important in societies that are more technologically developed. That is, as technology develops, one moves further away from cultural patterns where tasks are allocated on the basis of physiological justifications. Yet we continue to find the tasks, roles, and rights of men and women to be different. The justification for these differences have been moral and "sacred" arguments, combined with and stemming from the physiological argument.

In recent years there has been a reexamination of the basis on which tasks and roles are allocated and their concomitant justification. Modernization processes, scientific and technological developments, rapid social change, and the resurrection of such social movements as women's liberation have led to the questioning of traditional sex-role relationship patterns. In an earlier time, one marked by relative stability, little discussion or argument was made on the appropriateness of socially derived gender identifications and societal notions of masculinity and femininity. The "proper" roles, statuses, and attitudes for men and women were taken for granted. This has changed not only in the industrialized West but also in varying degrees throughout the world.

This and the next three chapters will examine the different ways that patriarchy, the main ideological justification for the sexual division of males and females, manifests itself. This chapter will outline the major components of patriarchal ideology. It will also examine premarital sex-role relationships. The next chapter will discuss love and mate-selection processes. It will be followed by two chapters that focus on the sexual division of labor. Chapter 9, provides a cross-cultural view of men and women vis-à-vis their marital relationship and their respective involvements in the world of work and in domestic household and child-care activities. This discussion is followed in Chapter 10 by an historical examination of marital sex-role relationships in Great Britain and the United States.

PATRIARCHAL RULE AND SEX ROLES

Patriarchy has been the basis on which tasks, rights, and roles are allotted to the sexes, usually with the woman's position subjugated and inferior to the man's. Patriarchy also voices the belief that a woman's "proper" place is within the home and her role devoted to domestic activities—housework and the bearing and rearing of children. As societies have developed, industrially and technologically, and have moved further and further away from cultural patterns where tasks are distributed on the basis of physiological factors, patriarchal ideas are increasingly open to challenge. It is necessary to understand the multifaceted nature of patriarchy to understand sex-role relationships.

A patriarchal ideology has two components; the first emphasizes the dominance of males over females, the second the subjugation of younger males by older ones. The first component will be of concern here; the second will be examined in the chapters devoted to generational relationships.

The institution of patriarchy is anchored in an ideology of male supremacy and it is reinforced by traditional socialization practices that implement it in matters of status, role, and temperament. Patriarchy has been deeply entrenched in political, social, and economic institutions. Kate Millett (1970) persuasively argues that patriarchy must be viewed in political terms as the domination of males over females. The term, sexual politics, is used by Millett to emphasize the power-structured basis of the male-female relationship and the arrangements whereby one group of persons, females, is controlled by another, males. This relationship is legitimated through the socialization of both sexes to the patriarchal ideology, for example, temperament, which involves the formation of self-concepts and is stereotyped along sex lines. Aggressiveness, force, intelligence, and efficacy are seen as "masculine" traits; passivity, ignorance, docility, and ineffectuality are "feminine" traits. Sex roles are associated with temperament. Millett observes that "sex role assigns domestic service and attendance upon infants to the female, the rest of human achievement, interest, and ambition to the male" (Millett, 1970:26). Socialization practices are biased towards male superiority and male superior status. Women are viewed as inferior. Millett sees these three facets—status, temperament, and role—in terms of political, psychological, and sociological components. Each are interdependent and, in totality, they serve to support the patriarchal ideology.

The patriarchal ideology has dominated the Greco-Roman, Semitic, Indian, Chinese and Japanese civilizations. It has also been the predominant pattern in Western Christian civilization. The European sociologist, Evelyne Sullerot (1971), believes that the basis for the patriarchal pattern stems from the reproductive function of women, which serves as the justification for women's existence and the reason for their subordination. Sullerot sees patriarchal rule as a coherent system linked by four elements—attitudes toward fertility and adultery, domestic confinement, property, and civic rights. She proceeds to show how these four types of restriction on women are elaborated in patriarchal civilizations.[2]

1. *Fertility and adultery.* Sullerot observes that the primary function of the woman was "as a breeding machine to perpetuate the male line of the husband, the tribe, and the race" (1971:20). The entire rationale for the woman's existence was her ability to produce children, particularly male children. Failure to do so resulted in severe punishment. The Manu code of India states that if a wife had no children

---

[2]The following discussion follows that of Evelyne Sullerot, 1971, pp. 20−28.

after 8 years of marriage, she would be banished; if all her children were dead, she could be dismissed after 10 years; and if she only had produced girls, she could be repudiated after 11 years. Similarly, the Mosaic law of the Biblical Israelites allowed a husband to repudiate his infertile wife and to father children with servants. The story of Abraham and Sarah is illustrative.

Female adultery was prohibited and punishments were extremely severe. Female adultery represented an attack against male dominance and the assertion of female individuality and free will. This was seen as a threat to the patriarchal system. Potentially, it was destructive to the patriarchal based system of property, inheritance, and power. Common to the historical civilizations of Israel, China, India, and Greece was the norm that a husband could put to death his adulterous wife. It was this assault on patriarchy, not simply emotional jealousy, that was the underlying motivation for such extraordinary punishment.

Crimes of Honor Persist in Greece

Though Old Patterns Decline, Violence Can Still Follow
Abandonment of Lovers

Steven V. Roberts

ATHENS, July 12—After Pagona Argyriou and Nicos Iliopoulos became engaged, they started sharing the same bed. When young Nicos, a bus driver here, broke off the engagement before the wedding, Pagona's mother marched into his apartment and stabbed him to death.

"In our part of the world life is not worth living when somebody disgraces you by rejecting your daughter," Spyroula Argyriou told the court that tried her for murder. "It is preferable to kill him or yourself."

The story of the vengeful mother, who received a life sentence, made big headlines here. Many writers treated her as an oddity, or a relic. But her case pointed up the powerful role still played by honor, and disgrace, in Greek life.

As this country of nine million moves toward modernization, traditional rules of behavior are breaking down, leaving many people lost and confused. A domestic worker from the island of Lesbos told a friend that her daughter had been abandoned by her fiance. "If I were back in my village I would know what to do," complained the mother, "but here in Athens, I don't know."

Crimes of honor are not nearly so common as they once were, noted Gregorios Zafiropoulos, a lawyer here for 24 years. "The changes started during the postwar period, when young people started getting good educations," he explained. "Now they believe they are in a position to control their own lives as they wish. The older people who see the things that are going on now just cannot believe their eyes."

Instead of using knives to salvage their honor, more Greeks are using the courts, and an Athens judge recently tried to place a price on a woman's reputation. As the magazine Tachydromos put it, "The case is so typical of Greek habits and mentality."

After four years, a man walked out on the woman he lived with, and the woman sued. Since the man had promised marriage, she explained, they had had sexual relations. "I may be poor but I have my sense of honor," the woman testified. "And I want compensation, as he has dishonored me."

The former lover said that the woman had not been a virgin at the time they met. "When I discovered this," he said, "I told her bluntly: 'You must know that I will not marry a second-hand woman, so don't expect marriage from me.' "

"The defendant," commented the court, "has admitted a common fact: that a 'second-hand woman' has difficulty in getting married." And since the defendant had contributed substantially to her soiled status, the court ruled, he would have to pay her almost $3,000. The woman could then use the money as a dowry to attract a husband.

In rural Greece, some people still take honor into their own hands, and the motive is often sex. A 45-year-old merchant, the press reported recently, "was shot dead by an unknown person while having sexual intercourse with a married woman in a deserted spot in northern Greece."

In Crete, two brothers tried to kill two other brothers after an engagement between the two families was broken off. In Xanthi, Vassilis Tonidis recently received a 15-year sentence for raping the wife of Constantine Petroglu. In defending himself, Mr. Tonidis charged that Mr. Petroglu had recently raped his daughter.

Another cause of violent reprisal involves disputes over property. Efstrafios Paschalis recently stabbed and killed his brother, Apostolos, on the island of Skiathros while their father was dividing up his farm between them. Two families from Crete—where the islanders are known for their sensitivity—fought a gun battle over an old land feud and left five persons seriously wounded.

It is not like the old days, when the residents of the remote Mani region lived in fortified tower houses and pursued vendettas for generations, but a minor affront can still turn into an affair of honor. A 22-year-old student was recently arrested for breaking the arm of a man who lingered over a telephone call in a public booth. A waiter in a nightclub in Egaleo was stabbed during a quarrel over a bill.

In one case 31-year-old Eleftherios Zahariou died of gunshot wounds inflicted by Antonios Velisariou. The two men rooted for different soccer teams, and after Mr. Zahariou's club had won a game betwen them, he started kidding his friend. Mr. Velisariou then grabbed a shotgun and fired four bullets into his tormentor. The murderer later explained that his "soccer honor" had been insulted.

2. *Domestic confinement.* The seclusion and separation of woman was practiced to assure masculine dominance and to prevent the possibility of adultery. The confinement world had both actual and symbolic significance. Such confinement symbolized the inferior status of women. Domestic activities were viewed as less important and subordinate to outside involvements. In traditional India, the Hindu religion conceived of women as strongly erotic and thus a threat to male asceticism and spirituality. Women were physically removed from the outside world. They wore veils and voluminus garments and were never seen by men who were not members of the family. Similar practices existed in China and Japan and in the Moslem Middle East. Only men were allowed access to and involvement with the outside world.

3. *Property.* Stemming from the patriarchal ideology was the practice of excluding women from owning and disposing of property. The prevalent practice in traditional Hindu India was that property acquired by the wife belonged to the husband. Similarly, restrictions on the ownership of property prevailed in Greece, Rome, and in ancient Israel.

4. *Civic rights.* The general pattern was the exclusion of women from civic matters. This included, as is the case in Jewish tradition, the exclusion of women from the majority of religious observations. Islam uses as its justification for the exclusion of women from the city and religion the notion of female impurity and uncleanliness. Oriental religions share a similar philosophy. In ancient China female infanticide was practiced through child neglect. The birth of a daughter was accompanied by a period of mourning. The low status and power of women is summed up in the following passage from the book, *Several Articles Intended for Women,* written in the first century A.D. by a Chinese woman, Pan Hoei Pan:

> Never let us forget that we belong to the lowest form of human life. We must expect only contempt. There will never be disillusionment for a woman so long as she remembers that she will always be made to suffer by those with whom she lives. (Cited in Sullerot, 1971:27–28)

ROMANTIC LOVE AND THE DOUBLE STANDARD

The advent of Christianity in Europe after the fall of Rome witnessed a continuation of the patriarchal ideology. Reacting against the ''corruption of Roman morals'' and the increased freedom of woman in imperial Rome, the Christian Church under the influence of St. Paul developed a very low regard for sexual relations, marriage, and women. Women were hated, feared, and degraded. The following passages from St. Paul illustrate this attitude. The first demonstrates the extent of the depreciation of heterosexual relations; the second enunciates the ideal of sexual abstinence and the subjugation of women.

> To avoid fornication, let every man have his own wife, and let every woman have her own husband. . . . For I would that all men were even as I myself [a bachelor] . . . I say therefore to the unmarried and widows, it is good for them if they abide as I. But if they cannot contain, let them marry; for it is better to marry than to burn. (1 Cor. 7:7–9)
>
> . . . For a man indeed ought not to have his head veiled, forasmuch as he is the image and glory of God: but the woman is the glory of the man. For the man is not of the woman; but the woman of the man: for neither was the man created for the woman but the woman for the man: for this house ought the woman to have a sign of authority on her head. (1 Cor. 11:3–10)

During the Middle Ages Christianity adapted a strong ascetic morality. Sex was inherently evil and shameful. Abstinence was viewed as the ideal with the proper role of sex being limited to procreation. In the fifth century, St. Jerome expressed the limited view of sex in marriage when he said:

> It is disgraceful to love another man's wife at all, or one's own too much. A wise man ought to love his wife with judgment not with passion. Let a man govern his voluptuous impulses, and not rush headlong into intercourse. . . . He who too ardently loves his own wife is an adulterer. (Cited in Hunt, 1959:115)

Tied to the ascetic morality was an ambivalent attitude toward women. At one end of the continuum was the depiction of woman as Evil, the temptress Eve, and at the other end was the depiction of woman as Good, Mary, the Virgin Mother of Christ. Women, as the source of sin, were lesser beings who deserved subordination to men. They were not allowed to own or inherit property. However, certain females, nuns, were respected. They were often permitted to exercise vast authority and power within their convents.

Arising out of this dual conceptualization of women was the pattern of chivalry and of courtly or romantic love among the nobility of the eleventh century. This sentiment flourished in the world of chivalry, of knights and ladies, and was spread by troubadours and poets—finally to become the ideal of the European middle classes. The essence of courtly love was the belief in the distinction between love and lust. Love was seen as a pure and enobling romantic ideal. It was anchored by the belief that one could become obsessed with the beauty and character of another. Romantic or courtly love occurred only outside of marriage. An integral feature was that it was asexual. It idealized a fantasy of unconsummated desire: lovers were allowed to kiss, touch, fondle, and even to lie naked together, but they could not consummate their love. It was thought that to consummate the love was to destroy it.

In contrast to love was the attitude of lust. Lust allowed sexual relations and was confined to marriage. It was viewed as an inferior emotion to romantic love. Morton M. Hunt (1959), who has written a delightful historical account of love in Western society, observes that marriage during the Middle Ages was primarily a business proposition. It involved the joining of lands, loyalties, and the production of heirs and future defenders (Hunt, 1959:137). Romantic love thus offered an alternative to the mundane relationships of marriage. Hunt's presentation of the autobiography of a thirteenth century knight, Ulrich von Lichenstein, dramatically illustrates the dynamics of romantic love.

The Creation of the Romantic Ideal

Morton M. Hunt

When he was a mere lad of five, says Ulrich, he first heard older boys saying that true honor and happiness could come only through serving a noble and lovely woman; he was deeply impressed, and began to shape his childish thoughts in that direction. Even at that tender age it was perfectly clear to him that such service, the keystone of courtly love, could be undertaken only for a woman one could never marry. True love had to be clandestine, bittersweet, and beset by endless difficulties and frustrations; by virtue of all this, it was spiritually uplifting, and made a knight a better man and a greater warrior.

The subject evidently dominated the thoughts of the boy, for by the age of twelve he put away childish things and consciously chose as the lady of his heart a princess. In every way, it was a perfect choice; she was far too highborn for him, considerably older than himself, and, of course, already married. He became a page in her court, and conscientiously cultivated his feelings of love until they commanded his whole being. He adored her in total secrecy, and trembled (inconspicuously) in her presence. When he saw her hands touch the petals of flowers he had secretly placed where she would see them, he was all but in a faint. And when she washed her hands before dinner, young Ulrich would sometimes filch the basin, smuggle it off to his room, and there reverently drink the dirty water.

Five years of this went by; his love affair progressed no further, however, since being totally unworthy of the lady he dared not even tell her of his feelings. At the age of seventeen he therefore took himself off to the court of the Margrave Henry of Austria, to raise his status; there he studied knightly skills for five more years, and at last was made a knight in 1222, during the wedding festival of the Duke of Saxony. By a marvelous coincidence, his ladylove, whom he had not seen but religiously dreamed of during those years, was one of the guests at the wedding, and the very sight of her so moved him that he immediately took a secret vow to devote his newly won knighthood to serving her. This decision filled him with melancholy and with painful longings, a condition which apparently made him very happy.

That summer, feverish and flushed with his infatuation, he roamed the countryside fighting in numerous tourneys and winning many victories, all of which he ascribed to the mighty force of love within him. At last, having compiled an impressive record, and feeling worthy to offer the lady the tribute of his devotion, he persuaded a niece of his to call on her and privately tell her of his desire to be an acknowledged but distant, respectful admirer of hers; he even got his niece to learn and sing for the

Princess a song he had written (Ulrich was already a competent *Minnesinger*—the German equivalent of the troubadour—as were many young noblemen of breeding).

The heartless lady, unmoved by his ten years of silent devotion and his recent feats of valor, sent back a cruel and pointed reply: she considered him presumptuous, was scornfully critical of the high-flown language of his quite inappropriate offer, and for good measure, took the trouble to let him know he was too ugly to be considered even in the role of a very distant admirer. For it seems (and the lady was specific) that the unhappy young knight had a harelip. Undaunted—perhaps even inspired by this obvious proof that she had actually noticed him—Ulrich promptly undertook a journey to a famous surgeon and had his lip repaired. Considering the techniques of medieval surgery, this must have been both excruciatingly painful and quite dangerous; indeed, he lay feverish on a sickbed for six weeks. News of this, plus a new song he wrote for her, softened the lady's heart, and she sent word that he might attend a riding party and enjoy the rare privilege of speaking with her for a moment, if the opportunity should arise. And it did, once, when he had the chance to help her down from her horse, and could have uttered a sentence or two of devotion; unfortunately he was tongue-tied by her nearness and could say nothing. The lovely lady, considerably put out, whispered to him that he was a fraud, and gracefully indicated her displeasure by ripping out a forelock of his hair as she dismounted.

Not in the least angered by this, Ulrich reappeared the next day, this time found his voice, and humbly begged her to permit him to be her secret knight and to allow him to fight for her and love her. She accepted his service, but under the very minimum conditions, granting him no "favor" whatever—neither embrace, kiss, nor word of promise, and not so much as a ribbon to carry in his bosom. Ulrich, nevertheless, was filled with joy and thankfulness for her kindness, and sallied forth, tilting about the countryside with anyone who would break a lance with him, and composing many a song to his ladylove, which his secretary set down for him since writing was not a knightly accomplishment. The messages and letters that passed between him and the Princess at this time conveyed, in the one direction, his endless, burning, worshipful feelings and, in the other direction, her condescension, coldness, and criticism. But this was exactly what was expected of her in the situation, and he found each new blow a delicious pain; it even sounds somewhat as though a part of his pleasure lay in observing his own noble constancy under duress. If so, he must have had a thoroughly agreeable time for the next three years.

At the end of that period, Ulrich petitioned her forthrightly through a go-between to grant him her love, at least verbally, in return for his faithful adoration and service. The Princess not only sharply rebuked the go-between for Ulrich's unseemly persistency, but expressed her scorn that Ulrich had falsely spoken of losing a finger fighting for love of her. Actually, he had suffered a finger wound which healed, but an incorrect report had reached her. When the go-between related her scornful message, Ulrich paled for a moment, then resolutely drew out a sharp knife and ordered his friend to hack off the finger at one blow. This done, the knight had an artisan make a green velvet case in which the finger was held by gold clasps, and sent her the mounted digit as a keepsake, together with a special poem about the matter. Deeply impressed by this evidence of her power over him, she returned word that she would look at the finger every day from thenceforth, a message which, incidentally, he received as he did all other communiques from her—on his knees, with bowed head and folded hands.

Determined now to earn her love by some stupendous feat, Ulrich conceived the scheme of the jousting-trip from Venice to Bohemia in the disguise of Venus. He went to Venice and there had seamstresses make a dozen white gowns to his own measurements; meanwhile he sent off a messenger with the open letter announcing the event. The northward march began on schedule on April 25, and concluded five weeks later, during which time Ulrich shattered an average of eight lances every day, made the notable record already mentioned, and acquired great glory and honor, all in the cause of love and for the sake of the Princess he so faithfully adored.

All this being so, it comes as something of a shock when one reads Ulrich's own statement that in the midst of this triumphal *Venusreise* he stopped off for three days to visit his wife and children. For the fact is that this lovesick Galahad, this kissless wonder, this dauntless knight-errant, had long had a wife to lie with when he had the urge, and a family to live with when he felt lonely. He himself speaks of his affection (but not his love) for his wife; to love her would have been improper and almost unthinkable. Like the other men of his class and time, Ulrich considered marriage a phase of feudal business-management, since it consisted basically of the joining of lands, the cementing of loyalties, and the production of heirs and future defenders. But the purifying, ennobling rapture of love for an ideal woman—what had that to do with details of crops and cattle, fleas and fireplaces, serfs and swamp drainage? Yet, though true love was impossible between husband and wife, without it a man was valueless. Ulrich could therefore unashamedly visit his wife during his grand tour, proud of what he had been doing and certain that if she knew of it, she too was proud, because *Frauendienst* made her husband nobler and finer.*

Having completed his epochal feat of love service, Ulrich waited for his reward, and at long last it came: the Princess sent word that he might visit her. Yet he was to expect no warm welcome; she specified that he must come in the disguise of a leper and take his place among lepers who

---

*Ladies, too, were increased in value by being loved. In a fictional counterpart of Ulrich's relations with his wife, a lady in an old Provencal romance, reproached by her husband for having a lover, proudly replies: "My lord, you have no dishonor on that account, for he is a noble baron, upright and expert in arms, namely, Roland, the nephew of King Charles." (*Gesta Karoli Magni ad Carcassonam et Narbonam*, p. 139).

would be visiting her to beg for alms. But of course this monstrous indignity fazed the faithful Ulrich not in the least; nor did he falter when she knowingly let him, disguised in his rags, spend that night in a ditch in the rain; nor was he outraged when the next night he was finally allowed to climb a rope up the castle wall to her chamber, only to find it lit by a hundred tapers and staffed by eight maids-in-waiting who hovered about her where she lay in bed. Though Ulrich pleaded urgently that they all be sent out, she continued to be coyly proper, and when she began to see that this patient fellow really was getting stubborn at last, she told him that to earn the favor he would have to prove his obedience by wading in a near-by lake. She herself assisted him out the window—and then, bending to kiss him, let loose the rope, tumbling Ulrich to the ground, or perhaps into a stinking moat. (It is worth remembering at this point that this painful incident was not recorded by any enemy or satirist of Ulrich, but by himself, his purpose being to make clear the extent of his suffering for love and his fidelity in the face of trials.)

Even such torments cannot go on forever. The cruel Princess next ordered Ulrich to go on a crusade in her service, but when she learned that he joyfully and obediently received the direct command from her, she suddenly relented, bade him rather stay at home near to her, and finally granted him her love. What an outpouring of thankful verse then! What a spate of shattered lances, dented helmets, broken blades, humbled opponents! For having won her love, Ulrich was puissant, magnificent, impregnable; this was the height of his career as a knight. Regrettably, it is not clear in the *Frauendienst* just which of her favors she so tardily vouchsafed after nearly a decade and a half, but in the light of other contemporary documents concerning the customs of courtly love, one can be fairly sure that she permitted him the kiss and the embrace, and perhaps even the right to caress her, naked, in bed; but if she gave him the final reward at all, it was probably on extremely rare occasions. For sexual outlet was not really the point of all this. Ulrich had not been laboring nearly fifteen years for so ordinary a commodity; his real reward had always been in his suffering, striving, and yearning.

Morton M. Hunt, 1959, *The Natural History of Love*. New York: Knopf, pp. 134–139.

Eventually, the ideal of romantic love with its nonconsummating characteristic was rejected. However, it was of extreme importance in the evolution of sex-role relationships in Western civilization. Prior to its inception, the Middle Ages were distinguished by a pervasive male-dominate/female-subordinate society. Women were treated with hatred and contempt. Hunt (1969) believes that courtly love brought about three major changes in the male-female relationship. First, it introduced tenderness and gentleness into it. It developed an emotional relationship between men and women that eventually played a role in increasing the status of women. Second, it advocated the sexual fidelity of one partner to another, even though marital fidelity developed out of adulterous fidelity. Third, it introduced the revolutionary notion that love must be mutual and must involve respect and admiration. Thus "the adulterous flirtation and illicit infatuations of the Middle Ages were the very instrument that began to enhance woman's status, and hence eventually to alter marriage" (Hunt, 1959:171−172).

Unfortunately, the dichotomization of love and lust and the "good" and "bad" woman, which was part of courtly love, continued to be manifest in the patriarchal ideology of the double standard. The double standard, which has been the dominating pattern of the sex-role relationship, is based on the notion of female inferiority. Women were divided into two categories: "good" women, who were premaritally chaste and thus were eligible marriage partners, and "bad" women, who were available to satisfy men's sexual needs outside of marriage. Men were allowed sexual access to women both in and out of marriage. "Good" women must restrain their sexual activities prior to marriage and in marriage. The double standard had a two-pronged basis: the notion of the lesser sexual interests of women and the idea of women as personal property. The argument was made that a woman was the personal property first of her father and secondly of her husband, and a woman had no right to give herself to another man without their consent.

In addition to the rights and privileges of men in regard to sexual activities, the double standard was extended to other spheres of life, including religion, politics, and economics. In all spheres women had subordinated duties and obligations. Moreover, the placing of women on a pedestal (derived from romantic love ideology) further discriminated against them. Although supposedly protected from the harsh "realities" of the outside world, women were actually placed in a position of subservience and dependency. By viewing women as "delicate flowers" who must be protected and sheltered, men effectively removed women from those spheres in the outside world that would have made the equality of women possible. We will be returning to these themes in later chapters. Here, let us look at the double standard in its affects on premarital dating, courtship, and mate-selection processes.

THE DOUBLE STANDARD AND PREMARITAL RELATIONSHIPS

In the United States, individual motives, particularly love, play an important role in the decision-making process related to whom one should marry. Yet falling in love is usually limited to someone who is socially approved by parents and peers. That is, through informal long-term socialization and through informal pressures, marriage is usually restricted to partners who share similar backgrounds, social class, religion, race, and education. We will now discuss an additional factor that helps explain American dating, courtship, and mate-selection processes—the double standard.

The double standard is usually associated with sexual behavior. It allows greater freedom for men to have premarital and extramarital sexual experiences than for women. It originates in ancient Hebrew, Greek, Roman, and early Christian doctrines. Ira Reiss, who has done extensive analyses of premarital sexual standards and behavior, observes that the basis of the double standard involves the notion of female inferiority. Reiss (1960) argues that the double standard is not solely restricted to sexual behavior. The double standard allows men preferential rights and duties in a variety of roles. By and large, the more challenging, the more satisfying, and the more highly valued positions are awarded to men and not to women. Furthermore,

> It is not just a question of different roles—anyone looking fairly at the division of roles will see that women's roles are given low status as compared to men's roles. The particular role does not matter; whatever a woman does is valued less and whatever a man does is valued more, e.g., if men herd then herding is highly valued—if women herd it is not (Reiss, 1960: 92−93).

In later chapters we will examine in more depth the origins of the double standard and its implications for sex-role relationships in the family and in other spheres. Now we will investigate its impact on mate-selection processes.

The double standard has had a pervasive affect on mate-selection processes. As Willard Waller (1938) has pointed out in his classic study of the family, double-standard-based courtship practices can be analyzed in terms of bargaining and exploitive behavior that denigrates both men and women. The stigma attached to being an unwed nonvirgin combined with the desire for women to marry, partly because of the lack of meaningful alternative options in the work sphere, promoted an atmosphere in courtship that was destructive for both sexes. In return for sexual "favors" women bargained for an ultimate marriage contract. But paradoxically, the loss of virginity lessened her marital desirability and eligibility (a man's wish to marry a virgin). The result was a frustrating relationship where there was a constant give and take revolving around sexual permissiveness and marital commitment. Ira Reiss (1960) has stated that the double standard results in a net of contradictory and unfulfilled desires:

> Many women very strongly resent this contradictory virginity-attitude on the part of men. These women feel it most unfair for a man to date a girl, try to seduce her, and then if he succeeds, condemn her and cross her off his marriage-possibility list. Many girls find themselves upset when they become fond of a particular boy and would like to be more sexually intimate with him, but must keep restricting their advances for fear of losing his respect. . . .
> Many girls who tease are merely playing the man's game. If men are so interested in sex, but dislike girls who "go too far," the logical thing to do, these girls feel, is to play up their sexual attributes to attract men and then restrict sexual behavior. The double-standard male creates his own "enemies"—he makes women use sex as a weapon instead of an expression of affection; in this case, the weapon is in the form of the tease. This sort of situation leads to the anomalous case of a female who, on the surface, seems highly-sexed but who internally may be quite frigid—a sweet "sexy" virgin whose dual nature may well cause her much internal conflict. Such a virgin is

similar to wax fruit—in both cases the appearance may be appetizing but the object is incapable of fulfilling its promise. (Reiss, 1960:106)

Bernard Farber (1964) has observed that mate-selection processes used to be characterized by a series of stages that cumulated in marriage—dating, keeping company, going steady, a private agreement to be married, announcement of the engagement, and finally marriage. This pattern can be seen as a reflection of the double standard, which placed a great deal of emphasis on "approved" sexuality confined to marriage and women's confinement to marriage as the only career possibility. Today this pattern is changing. The increased independence of women and their greater involvement in institutions other than the family, work, politics, religion, and education has provided them with career alternatives. Further, technological developments in controlling impregnation (the pill, the loop) combined with less stringent norms about sexual permissiveness for both sexes has changed the courtship process. Farber points out that such a term as keeping company is no longer in the courtship vocabulary. As for the term, going steady, it now mainly refers to a person with whom one is currently involved. Since Farber wrote his monograph, such terms as dating and courtship have become antiquated. Farber concludes that with the whole system of courtship, which was based on the double standard, there was an ever-narrowing field of eligible spouses. This has given way to a series of personal "involvements," one of which may result in marriage (Farber, 1964:161).

Michal M. McCall (1966) has analyzed this new courtship pattern. Sexual exploitation is not associated with it. In this new relationship there is an emphasis on intimacy and exclusiveness with a personal commitment. This commitment includes sexual intimacy. Most men no longer expect women to be virgins at the time of their first marriage. The relationship is more egalitarian and can be terminated by either partner if it turns out to be dissatisfactory. In this relationship exploitation refers to the possible impregnation of the woman and the failure of the man to marry her. Analogous to the earlier pattern, where there was a legitimate expectation that marriage followed sexual intimacy, today's pattern has a legitimate expectation that marriage follows impregnation. The relationship of the couple is intensely personal. Given the greater equality of women, there is a greater tendency for either the man or woman to break the relationship and seek to form a new one. This is attributed to the fact that the notion of the "one and only love" (a main component of romantic love) is no longer as viable as before. It also helps explain why contemporary premarital relationships are less stable and enduring.

FROM DATING AND RATING TO COHABITATION

We will expand the above discussion by examining changes in premarital relationships in the United States during the past 50 years. We will begin our discussion with Willard Waller's (1937) famous study of the dating and rating complex that existed at Pennsylvania State University in the later 1920s and early 1930s. We will end with an analysis of nonmarital cohabitation.

Waller (1937) distinguished courtship from dating. Dating refers to the pursuit of sexual pleasure as an aim in itself. Courtship involves interaction with a person who is seen as a possible marriage partner. Hedonistic considerations count for less than in dating, and the person's family and class backgrounds count for much more. Waller describes the dating process within the context of the fraternity system then in existence at Penn State. Half the male students lived in fraternities. These students were a homogenous group predominantly from the lower middle class. For these men the dating system was highly competitive and was based on a scale reflecting campus values. Males were rated highest if they were members of the better fraternities, were prominent in activities, had a large supply of spending money, were well dressed, were good dancers, and had access to an automobile. Girls were rated on their appearance, their popularity, their ability to dance well, and who they dated.

An integral aspect of the dating system was the boy's open antagonism toward the girls, the exploitative nature of their relationships, and what Waller calls "thrill seeking." The "thrills" varied by sex; men seeking sexual gratification while women sought to enhance their prestige by going out with the more desirable men and gaining financial benefit, such as free admission to amusements, restaurants, theaters, and the like. This resulted in dating becoming a bargaining relationship with exploitative and antagonistic overtones. Waller illustrates this point by citing a woman student informant:

> A fundamental antagonism exists on this campus between the men and women students. There is an undercurrent of feeling among the men that the school really belongs to them, and that the coed is a sort of legalized transgressor on their territory. A typical procedure of the college man is to give a coed a terrific rush, and then either drop her suddenly without any explanation whatsoever, or tell her that "Mary Jane Whosis, the girl he is engaged to at home, is coming up for Senior Ball," or something of that sort. . . .
>
>   Against this sort of attitude the coeds build up a defense mechanism which usually takes the form of cynicism. "They're out for what they can get? That's fine. So are we." Everything is just one grand, big joke. Many of the girls really fight against liking a boy and try very hard to maintain this cynical attitude. One way in which they do this is the use of ridicule. Many coeds put on an act for their girl-friends after a date, mimicking certain characteristic actions of the boy she has been out with, and making a joke of the things he has said to her. Often the less a girl feels like doing this, the worse she will make it. It is her way of convincing herself that her armor of cynicism is as strong as ever. (Waller, 1938:252−253)

Waller attributes the development of the dating and rating system to the disappearance of community controls over the younger generation. Their loss is seen in the decline of the primary group community and in the reduction of such adult supervised activities as school and church socials. "From the sociological viewpoint, this represented social disorganization, a decay of older forms, a replacement of socially agreed upon definitions of situations by hedonistic, individualistic definitions" (Waller, 1938:223). In short, Waller saw the dating and rating process being dominated by a desire for fun and amusement that was expressed in a system of exploitativeness, antagonism, and bargaining.

Waller saw dating becoming separated from courtship. The implications of Waller's study are that the sex-role antagonisms generated by the dating system are carried over to courtship and lead to undesirable emotional tensions in this relationship and in marriage. Waller developed the conceptualization of the "principle of least interest" to summarize this point. He believed that courtship grew out of dating as one or both partners became emotionally involved. But, unequal emotional involvement could lead to the person with "least interest" to exploit the other, thus repeating the debilitating dating relationship:

> . . . Exploitation of sort usually follows the realization that the other person is more deeply involved than oneself. So much almost any reasonably sophisticated person understands. The clever person, in my observation usually a woman, knows how to go on from that point. A girl may pretend to be extremely involved, to be the person wholly dominated by the relationship; this she does in order to lead the young man to fasten his emotions and to prepare the way for the conventional denouement of marriage, for, in the end, while protesting her love, she makes herself unattainable except in marriage; this is certainly not an unusual feminine tactic and is executed with a subtlety which makes the man's crude attempts at guile seem sophomoric. (1938:276–277)

Waller sees love and marriage emerging out of courtship. Love is depicted as an outgrowth of the initial desire of one partner, to get the other partner emotionally involved in the relationship. However, individuals, without being aware of it, may develop an idealized image of the other that takes on an irrational characteristic and thus they get caught up in an emotional surge that culminates in marriage. The consequences are that the couple must reorient their early stages of marital adjustment to a relationship based on the reality of each other not on their idealizations of each other. For many, this becomes an impossible task, culminating in a marital relationship that is characterized by conflict and in many cases divorce.

Attempts to replicate Waller's finding of the existence of a "rating and dating complex" have not been successful. Christopher Lasch (1977a) in a review of the studies of the 1940s and 1950s finds many flaws in their methodologies, particularly in the way they operationalized Waller's concept of rating and dating. Michael Gordon (1978) and Richard R. Clayton (1979) in their respective reviews of studies done in the 1950s, 1960s, and 1970s report that personality factors may play a more influential role than Waller's rating criteria in dating relationships. Gordon further develops the view that these more recent studies may reflect historical changes that have occurred in the attitudes and values that govern premarital heterosexual relationships as well as to the greater possibility that marriage may take place either during or immediately after college. Another factor that is emerging in the nature of premarital relationships is the dramatic increase in the number of college students who are now cohabitating. Cohabitation represents a significant movement away from the situation in which the dating relationship—which according to Waller was a means to an end—to a relationship that is an end in and of itself and characterized by personal involvements and commitments. Let us now turn our attention to this emerging new trend in premarital relationships.

Researchers [see Gordon (1978) and Leslie (1979) for reviews of these studies] have observed that there is a movement away from pairing off in casual dating patterns to more informal group activities among high school and college students. Exclusive dating begins at a later age and is more clearly associated with greater emotional involvements and commitments. Further, a more innovative development is occurring. This is the increasing number of nonmarried couples beginning to live together in a marriage-like situation. This development, nonmarital cohabitation, is characterized by greater informality, spontaneity, and intimacy outside the parameters of traditional dating and courtship relationships.

The research of Rebecca S. Vreeland (1972a, 1972b) studied dating patterns among Harvard University men college students during the 1960s and early 1970s. She identified four dating patterns among the class of 1964. The *instrumental* pattern most clearly approximated Waller's rating and dating complex. The emphasis was on sexual exploitation and the enhancement of one's social reputation. Harvard men students would take their dates to football games, dances, nightclubs, and so on, where they could be highly visible and "show off." In the second pattern, the *traditional* relationship, dating was ultimately designed to find a suitable wife. Women who ranked high by virtue of their good reputation, sexual inhibition, family background, and social status were the most sought after. In the *companion* pattern, the emphasis was on informal couple activities. A goal was to find someone with whom to share intimacies and engage in private activities. The fourth and last pattern that Vreeland thinks may be more typical of elite colleges was *intellectual* dating. Here, the emphasis was to find a woman who was the man's intellectual equal and with whom he would be able to share discussions and concerns.

Vreeland compared these patterns of the 1964 class with that of their 1970 counterparts. The companion pattern and the intellectual pattern still persisted. The former, while emphasizing friendship, broadened its activities to include more recreational and social involvements. The latter became a defensive mechanism for intellectually gifted but socially inadequate men and more a means to form a mature relationship. The greatest changes occurred in the instrumental and the traditional dating patterns. The instrumental relationship became characterized by less emphasis placed on sexual exploitation and a greater concern placed on political activities, drug taking, and shared love making. Men in the traditional dating pattern were now more concerned with finding women who were ''liberated'' and nonconventional and who shared their rejection of traditional social patterns rather than becoming involved with socially acceptable women. Vreeland believes that these trends indicate that dating has become less formal and less exploitative. ''Students in search of their own humanity, have begun to treat their dates as persons and potential friends rather than as competitors or candidates for marriage'' (Vreeland, 1972a:66).

Vreeland's findings reveal one aspect of the change in heterosexual premarital relationships. The other change, and the more dramatic one, is the movement toward nonmarital heterosexual cohabitation, particularly among college students. Eleanor D. Macklin (1978), after reviewing the abundant research evidence, opens her discussion with the following statement: ''Nonmarital cohabitation is fast becoming a part of the dominant culture in this country and it seems likely that in time to come a majority of persons will experience this lifestyle at some point in their life cycle'' (1978:1). She estimates that about 25 percent of the undergraduate college population have engaged in living together under marriage-like conditions. Before we begin our analysis of this phenomenon in the contemporary American middle class, a brief examination of its historical and cross-cultural existence is appropriate to set the discussion in perspective.

College Sex Rises, Poll Says

Sam W. Pressley

Cassie, an 18-year-old, brown-eyed freshman at Drexel University, likes dorm life. She also likes engaging in sex in her room with her "steady."

Don, 19, a sophomore, who lives in a coeducational dorm in the University of Pennsylvania, recently experienced his first sexual encounter.

Stan, 21, a Penn junior, has "daily" sexual intercourse with his girl friend, a 19-year-old Penn coed. He says they plan to live together next year, off-campus.

The sexual attitudes and behavior of Cassie, Don, and Stan (not their real names) reflect part of a growing campus trend of sexual activity, according to the findings of seven national surveys of residential college students between 1970 and 1977.

But greater sexual freedom during the past decade has led surprisingly to a "deemphasis of sex" among college students as a test of prowess or popularity and has become "a form of self-expression and caring."

So say the surveys conducted by Dr. Joseph Katz, a professor of human development at the State University of New York at Stony Brook, and Denise M. Cronin, a professor of sociology at Queens College, City University of New York.

Between 1970 and 1975, the proportion of undergraduates agreeing that "full sexual relations are permissible before marriage" rose from slightly more than 50 percent to 90 percent.

Between 1970 and 1977, however, the proportion of undergraduates who reported having sexual intercourse rose from about 50 percent for both men and women to 78 percent for men and 72 percent for women. Most of those saying they had had sexual intercourse said they did so by their sophomore year.

During the years the surveys were taken, the average age at which students had their first sexual experienced dropped from 18 to 17.

A higher proportion of women students than men students reported having intercourse five times a month or more—52 percent versus 40 percent. Women also were more apt to describe their sexual experience as highly satisfying—66 percent versus 50 percent earlier.

One disturbing finding, Katz said, is a failure of "a considerable proportion" of students to use contraceptives.

In 1977, one-sixth of all sexually active women students, he said, reported they had undergone an abortion. The recently released surveys made no mention of incidence of venereal diseases.

"It is astonishing to reflect that not long ago women were thought not to enjoy sex," Katz said in a recent telephone interview. "Women were thought to tolerate sex only for the sake of their husbands and for the purpose of procreation."

The seven surveys collected data on questionnaires from 6,098 men and women students living in campus facilities at 13 different colleges and universities. The schools differed in size, location and academic status.

Katz named only two of the participating schools, the State University of New York at Stony Brook and Stanford University, Palo Alto, Calif., where Katz worked with the Institute for the Study of Human Problems.

None of the other schools is in the Philadelphia area, Katz said.

Throughout the years of their surveys, the college professors said they found half of the sexually active students reported having no more than two or three partners over the entire course of their sexual history.

During the 1976–77 school year, for example, ¾ of the coeds and a slightly smaller proportion of the men said they had only one partner. Most of the rest surveyed said they had two relationships.

However, the 1977 survey showed that about 15 percent of the students sampled said they had at least once engaged in "group sex," where three or more persons participated.

Katz said students also indicated that they "frequently" engaged in sex after a relatively short relationship. For these students, he said, there is no guilt or lewdness associated with the act.

Instead, said Katz, sex has come to be regarded as but "one of many facets in achieving closeness and mutual understanding."

Recent interviews with Drexel and Penn dorm students support his claim.

"I'm all for premarital sex," said a Penn medical student and former university undergraduate, who gave his first name as Richard. "I think it's important for two people to get to know each other before marrying. And the sexual act is a good way to establish a relationshhip."

But as this Penn student pointed out, and as the surveys showed, women remain more likely than men to link sex with affection.

Katz said previous surveys showed that many students were "preoccupied with sex."

"Marriage often took place because of unfulfilled obsessive fantasies influenced by sexual inexperience," he said.

But the elimination of "barriers between sexes," Katz said, has made possible "expanded opportunities for acquaintance, friendship, and work between men and women, quite apart from direct sexual expression."

"Future marriages may be based more on knowledge than romantic idealization," Katz contended.

In the mid-1960s, Katz was a major contributor to a national study entitled "Sex and the College Student," which was published by the Group for the Advancement of Psychiatry.

Sam W. Pressley in *The Bulletin,* March 2, 1980. Reprinted by permission of The Bulletin Co., Philadelphia.

COHABITATION: A BRIEF CROSS-CULTURAL VIEW

Cohabitation is not a phenomenon unique to contemporary America. Miriam E. Berger (1971) cites cross-cultural evidence to document its existence in nonWestern societies. Traditionally, among the Peruvian Indians of Vicos in the Andes, cohabitation was an integral form of courtship. The Andese parents made cohabiting arrangements for their children to test the work capabilities of the girl and the couple's compatibility. In modern Vicos the young are free to choose their own partners, with romantic love playing an important role. Yet the men still value the traditional virtues of responsibility, hard work, household skills, and the willingness of the women to help in the fields. Trial marriage is still practiced. It lasts an average of about 15 months and 83 percent of these arrangements are finalized in marriage. M.E. Berger notes that this practice seems to aid in the transition from adolescence to adulthood by virtue of the partners acquiring the social and sexual advantages of adulthood without assuming the full responsibilities of marriage.

Precedent also exists in Western Europe. M.E. Berger discusses the old Teutonic custom of trial rights, which is still practiced in the traditional community of Staphorst, the Netherlands. With parental acknowledgment, a man can spend three nights a week with his girl friend. The hope is that the woman will become pregnant, for no marriage can take place if she is barren.

Jan Trost (1975, 1978) has observed that Germany, Sweden, Norway, Denmark, and Ireland have long traditions of cohabitation. However, attitudes toward cohabitation do undergo modification from time to time and are reflected in the cohabiting rate. Trost observes that the rate of cohabiting is also related to the marriage rate. During the four-year period of 1970 and 1974 the number of lasting nonmarried cohabiting Swedish couples doubled (from 6.5 percent to 12 percent). Concomitantly, the number of marriages decreased steadily from 61,000 marriages in 1966 to 38,125 in 1973. Trost argues that cohabitation is a kind of test or trial marriage to see if the couple are compatible or to be sure that the woman can conceive. He believes, if this view is correct, that the marriage rate in Sweden should eventually increase. Trost also thinks that cohabitation will also have an effect on future divorce rates. ". . . The situation will arise that many marriages between two partners not fitting together will never be formed, those marriages being formed will be happier and thus the divorce rate, ceteris paribus, will be lower" (Trost, 1975:682).

Trost also observed that the incidence of cohabitation is related to political pressure and social policy. Scandinavian countries have liberalized their social policies and societal sanctions against cohabitation. As a result there is less fear of social stigma and a resultant high cohabitation rate. In contrast, Trost cites the situation in Mexico. In 1950, 20 percent of the couples living together were unmarried. Trost believes that this figure may have declined in recent years as a result of governmental pressure to get unmarried couples married officially and legalize their relationship. Through the efforts of a wife of a Mexican president, the Mexican government has sponsored "Wedding Days." These governmental proclamations have been promoted since 1955 and an estimated 240,000 couples have legalized their cohabitation by getting married.

COHABITATION ON AMERICAN COLLEGE CAMPUSES

Nonmarital cohabitation has been a topic of debate through most of the twentieth century in the United States. Miriam E. Berger (1971), in her historical account, mentions the controversy surrounding the beliefs of Ben B. Lindsay in the 1920s in his call for "companionate" marriage and the tumult surrounding the opinions of the philosopher Bertrand Russell. Russell advocated trial marriages for university students and believed that students could more easily combine work and sex "in a quasi-permanent relationship, than in the scramble and excitement of parties and drunken orgies" that prevailed during the 1920s Prohibition Era (Russell cited in M.E. Berger, 1971:39). Russell's beliefs aroused a storm of controversy when he was appointed to a professorship in New York.

In the 1960s Margaret Mead (1966) recommended a two-step marriage. The first step, "individual" marriage, provided for a simplified marriage ceremony, limited economic responsibility of each partner to the other, easy divorce, and no children. "Parental" marriage, the second step, would be undertaken only by those couples who wished to share a lifetime involvement in a marital relationship that would include children. Such a marriage would be more formalized with divorce more difficult to obtain. Mead argued that for too many young people their desire for sexual relationships led them into making premature decisions on marriage and parenthood and often led to unhappiness and divorce. Similar proposals have been voiced and have had wide publicity. These include Vance Packard's (1968) call for a two-year marriage confirmation period, after which the marriage could be finalized or dissolved, and the much-publicized ideas of Robert H. Rimmer (1966) in *The Harrad Experiment*. Rimmer advocated a trial marriage period with group marriage overtones. His novel depicted Harrad as an institution where college-aged couples would live together under the benevolent guidance of a husband and wife team of sociologist and marriage counselor. This couple would require their students to become well versed in the subjects of marriage, love, sex, contraception, moral values, and philosophy. Rimmer's belief was that through a structured, socially approved form of premarital experimentation more viable and stronger marital and parental relationships would ultimately be developed.

These intellectual discourses on the desirability of nonmarital cohabitation reached behavioral fruitation in the experiences of a significant number of college students by the late 1960s and increasing numbers through the 1970s and into the 1980s. Paul C. Glick and Graham B. Spanier (1980), on the basis of national data from the Census Bureau's *Current Population Survey* (1975, 1977, and 1978), report that there has been a profound increased in unmarried cohabitation in the last 20 years. Further, there has been an accelerated rate increase since 1970 as shown in Figure 7:1. Using data derived from the June 1975 *Current Population Survey*, Glick and Spanier report that 1.8 percent of all couples living together then were unmarried. This was approximately 886,000 unmarried couples. In comparison, unpublished data from a survey only three years later showed that an estimated 1.1 million couples, or 2.3 percent, were living in the same household and were not married to each other. Commenting on these and other statistics they observe:

> Rarely does social change occur with such rapidity. Indeed, there have been few developments relating to marriage and family life which have been as dramatic as the rapid increase in unmarried cohabitation. (Glick and Spanier, 1980:20)

These authors believe that the explanation for this increase is that young Americans are finding this emerging life style as most attractive and that their parents are voicing little objection as long as the relationship does not end in childbearing and the couple are economically independent. To support this

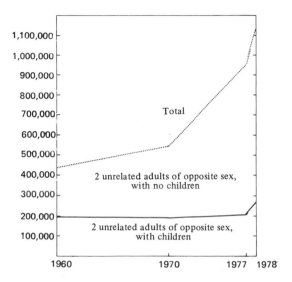

Figure 7.1 Unmarried couples living together in the United States, 1960–1978. *Source:* Paul C. Glick and Graham B. Spanier. 1980. "Married and Unmarried Cohabitation in the United States," *Journal of Marriage and the Family* 42, February, 1980:20. Copyright © 1980 by the National Council on Family Relations. Reprinted by permission.

explanation, Glick and Spanier compared unmarried couples with married couples in which the women were under 35 years of age. One observed difference is that the unmarried partners were more likely to be college educated. Both were also more likely to be in the labor force than their like-aged married counterparts. Further, in the situations where neither the man or woman was employed among the unmarried couples (12 percent), it seemed likely that the couples were either students living on money give them by their parents or young, poor couples living on welfare payments. The authors conclude by speculating on the future:

> The rapid increase in the number of adults who choose to live with an unrelated person of the opposite sex has been showing no signs of diminishing . . . . Increased freedom in adult behavior, less pressure to marry at traditionally normative young ages, and greater acceptance of unmarried cohabitation as a lifestyle are evidently providing a context in which this way of living is becoming increasingly accepted as an alternative to marriage or as a temporary arrangement preceding or following marriage. (Glick and Spanier, 1980:30)

Glick and Spanier working primarily with quantitative data are somewhat limited in their analysis of the qualitative nature of the relationship of the cohabiting couple and the internal dynamics of the relationship and their consequent effects. Eleanor D. Macklin's (1978) review essay complements the work of Glick and Spanier. Macklin was one of the first researchers (1972) to report on the rising incidence of nonmarital cohabitation on college campuses. In her 1978 article, "Nonmarital Heterosexual Cohabitation," she systematically analyzes the growing number of studies about this phenomenon. The balance of our discussion will examine her conclusions.

Macklin argues that it is inaccurate to talk about *the* cohabitation relationship. She asserts that there are at least five types, which significantly vary, and that at this time there is insufficient data to say what proportion of cohabiting couples fall into each category. The five types are:

1. *Temporary casual convenience* . . . where two persons share the same living quarters because it is expedient to do so;
2. *The affectionate dating-going together* type of relationship where the couple stays together because they enjoy being with one another and will continue as long as both prefer to do so;
3. The *trial marriage* type, which includes the "engaged to be engaged" and partners who are consciously testing the relationship before making a permanent commitment;
4. The *temporary alternative to marriage,* where the individuals are committed to staying together, but are waiting until it is more convenient to marry; and
5. The *permanent alternative to marriage,* where couples live together in a long-term committed relationship similar to marriage, but without the traditional religious or legal sanctions. (Macklin, 1978:3)

With that cautionary note, Macklin compares cohabiting and noncohabiting couples in terms of their degree of commitment, division of labor, satisfaction, and sexual exclusivity. Because of the lack of systematic differentiation of the five types of cohabitation listed above, Macklin limits her analysis to a comparison of a composite type of cohabitation with unmarried couples not cohabiting and married couples. Reviewed studies report that nonmarried cohabitants indicate significantly less commitment to continuing the relationship than do married couples. In comparison to engaged couples, the unmarried cohabitants express the same degree of commitment to each other but are less committed to the idea of marriage. Finally, research evidence reveals that the amount of exploitation in the relationship is uncertain. There is some evidence to suggest that women who tend to have a higher degree of commitment to the relationship than their male partners may be more vulnerable to exploitation.

Macklin reports a surprising finding: the division of labor of the cohabiting pair is traditional. Researchers expected that the couple's innovative life style and their relatively liberal attitudes would be evidenced in a shared division of labor. Macklin observes that the cohabiting couple tend to share the same attitudes and behavioral patterns of their more conventional counterparts. Macklin citing one researcher makes the following conjecture: "The many years of subtle socialization and role scripting, and the fact that role adaptation requires constant negotiation and accommodation, serve to maintain more conventional modes of behavior, even in what on the surface would appear to be nontraditional relationships" (1978:5).

The satisfaction with each other of the cohabiting couple did not seem to be sufficiently different from other couples. Finally, most cohabiting couples believe in sexual exclusivity and voluntarily restrict their sexual activities to their partner.

Macklin then discusses the internal dynamics of the cohabiting couple. She states that the decision to cohabit is a gradual one as opposed to a planned, considered decision. Usually, couples tend to drift together over a period of time after sleeping with each other and gradually moving their possessions to one household. In some cases external events, such as the end of the semester, graduation, and housing or other economic needs, become a determining factor. The evidence on the length of the cohabiting relationship or how many relationships end in marriage is incomplete. Longitudinal studies, which would follow cohabiting couples over a period of time, have not been done. We are left with studies that have an atemporal dimension with no systematic follow-up. This limitation also affects the information that we have on how cohabitations end and their resultant effects on the cohabitants. Macklin hypothesizes that their readjustment in the postseparation period may be faster and less traumatic than if they were married and then separated or divorced. She attributes this to two factors; friends and relatives may place less social pressure on them to maintain an unhappy cohabiting relationship and litigation is usually not involved when they break up. The lessened social stigma and reduced visibility of ending their living-together arrangement should result in a lessened feeling of guilt and sense of failure.

One of the popular arguments in favor of cohabitation is that it has positive effects on the participant's personal growth, the quality of later marriage, and serves as an effective screening device that will eventually reduce the society's divorce rate. Macklin examines each of these arguments. She reports that there is no evidence to support the belief that cohabitation leads to enhanced personal growth more than any other form of premarital relationship. The lack of evidence reflects the fact that no studies directly test this belief. However, research findings do reveal that the vast majority of cohabitants indicate that this experience was very positive and that "they would elect to cohabit again if they 'had their lives to live over' and would not wish to marry without having lived with the partner first" (Macklin, 1978:6). There also is a gap in the literature about the opinions of individuals who had unsatisfactory cohabiting experiences and their assessments of it in terms of their personal growth.

In examining the effects of cohabitation on the quality of future marriages, Macklin observes that there is little systematic evidence to prove or disprove the popularly held belief that it leads to successful or different types of marriages.

However, Macklin does speculate that the transition into marriage would most likely result in easier relationships with relatives, less problems with social institutions, and may increase the likelihood of traditional forms of sex-role behavior, possessiveness, and reduced autonomy.

The impact of cohabitation on marriage and divorce rates also receives Macklin's scrutiny. Unlike Jan Trost (1975), who believes that cohabitation has an effect on marriage and divorce rates in the Scandinavian countries, Macklin argues that there should be no substantial decrease in overall marriage rates in the United States owing to the strong social supports for marriage. Rather, cohabitation will remain a part of the courtship phase for most people and will eventually culminate in marriage. The effects of cohabitation on the divorce rate is less certain, according to Macklin. She speculates that with the long life span, changing views of marriage, and yet-to-emerge life style options, it seems doubtful that whether a couple cohabitated or not will have significance on their decision to divorce.

Macklin concludes by examining the implications of nonmarital heterosexual cohabitation for the society. Among her observations she notes the need to change legal statutes and practices that view living together as man and wife without being legally wed a crime (in 20 states in 1976) and having sexual relationships without being married a crime (in 16 states in 1976). Changes also have to be made in the financial obligations of the man and women to each other if and when they decide to separate. The Lee Marvin/Michelle Marvin legal case is illustrative of this problem. In that case the courts examined the question on the legality of agreements between nonmarital partners regarding income and property. (They concluded that such agreements are legal but ignored the issue of whether a partner is entitled to support after separation). Also the rights of children born to unmarried couples have to be clarified as do the respective parental custody rights.

The essay ends with a call for new research to answer the questions suggested by the review. Macklin urges that future research include longitudinal studies on noncollege and older populations. Finally, she sounds a different note: she questions the wisdom of placing too much emphasis on the legal status of heterosexual relationships. Instead, she calls for more emphasis on the study of relationships, regardless of whether the couple is legally wed or not:

> Knowing that an individual is living with someone to whom she/he is not married tells us little about either the relationship or the person. Rather than focus on the specific legal status of a given relationship, investigators should be concerned with how the particular individuals define their own relationship, their degree of commitment to and investment in that relationship, the quality of the interaction, and the emotional maturity and interpersonal skills of the individuals involved. If the focus of research were more on the dynamics of intimate relationships and on the skills needed to function effectively within them, and less on the structural quality of relationships would be more rapid. (Macklin, 1978:11)

CONCLUSION

This chapter introduced the reader to an important theme of this book—patriarchal ideology and its effect on sex-role relationships. Patriarchy legitimates power and authority vested in the hands of men, with the eldest man usually wielding the greatest authority and power. We outlined the major components of patriarchal ideology, emphasizing four types of restrictions for women: attitudes toward fertility and adultery, domestic confinement, property, and civic rights.

The double standard was then studied. We discussed how it became an integral part of the Westernized idea of romantic love. (In Chapter 14 we will discuss the opposite side of romantic love—the belief in witches.) An historical analysis of the origins of romantic love was presented, ending with an examination of contemporary dating relationships. The chapter concluded with a discussion of premarital heterosexual cohabitation and its implications for premarital sex-role relationships.

In the next chapter we will comparatively examine differences in mate-selection processes and how they are influenced by the pervasiveness of patriarchal ideology.

CHAPTER 8

Mate Selection

In earlier chapters we discussed an important structural change occurring in family systems—the movement toward the conjugal family. The conjugal family emphasizes the importance of the marital relationship and the ties of parents with children. In contrast, the consanguineal family stresses the extended kinship relationship based on a common ancestry. In this family form the emphasis is on the reciprocal ties and obligations of individuals with their extended kin. The importance of the conjugal (marital) relationship is deemphasized, whereas the individual's involvement with the consanguineal (blood) family is emphasized.

A most dramatic piece of evidence of the movement toward the conjugal family system is in the area of premarital sex, conceptions of love, and in mate selection. In many societies men and women were not expected to choose the person they would marry; marriages were arranged by their parents and kinsmen. The freedom to choose one's spouse is an emerging phenomenon. In this chapter we will investigate the why's and wherefore's of arranged marriages and nonarranged marriages. We will examine the factors that accounted for the prevalence of arranged marriages and the various forms these marital arrangements took. Of considerable interest is the relationship of modernization processes with marital arrangement patterns and of the contemporary modification of these patterns. Changing conceptualizations regarding premarital sex and love and the relationship of these to marital selection arrangements attracts our attention. Finally, the consequences of the changes in attitudes and behavior regarding sex, love, and marriage for the individual, the family, and the society will be investigated and analyzed.

MATE SELECTION: FREE CHOICE OR ARRANGED?

"Who do people marry?" One way this question can be answered is to look at how spouses are chosen. William N. Stephens (1963) states that, when persons have freedom to choose their spouses, individual motives account for marital decisions. These can include romantic love, sexual desire, loneliness, desire for children, and the feeling of the attainment of adulthood. In some societies individual motives are allowed to be the determinants in selection of spouses. However, the majority of the world's societies chose to have family elders arrange the marriage of the potential couple. Frequently, this occurred without the consent of the prospective marital couple and in some societies, like Hindu India, China, and Japan, the couple did not meet until the marriage day. In these societies individual motives, like romantic love, were not supposed to be factors in mate selection. For example, in Classical China or Tokugawa Japan, love was viewed as a tragedy and at best as irrelevant to the family. The criteria for the selection of a spouse revolved around such matters as the size of the bride price or dowry, the reputation of the respective kin groups, and traditional, customary, and obligatory marital arrangements.

Stephens (1963) (see Table 8.1) is concerned with the frequency, distribution, and forms of mate choice and the factors that account for them. He delineates four forms of social mate choice: (1) arranged marriage, (2) free choice of mate, subject to parental approval, (3) free choice of mate, not subject to parental approval, and (4) societies in which both arranged marriage and free choice of mate is practiced. Stephens compared data from 40 societies. These data were based on interviews with ethnographers familiar with a particular village or other subcommunity in a variety of traditional, feudal, and modern industrial societies. Stephens found that those societies that had extended family systems or unilineal kin groups tended to give the heads of these families either the entire responsibility for arranging the marriage of their children or did not allow children to choose for themselves without reserving the right to veto that choice. Further, those societies that were characterized by a nuclear conjugal family system and bilineal kin groups were exclusive in that they were the only ones that allowed free choice of mate with parental approval not being necessary. Stephens concludes ''. . . the form of mate choice is in part a function of extended kinship: when large kin groups are strong and important, then marriage tends to be a kin-group affair—it is taken out of the hands of the potential bride and groom'' (Stephens, 1963:198).

This strong relationship between types of family organization, extended or nuclear, and the form of mate choice is consistent with our earlier discussion of conjugal and consanguineal family systems. The conjugal family system, which takes the nuclear form, emphasizes strong husband-wife and parent-child ties. As William J. Goode (1963) has noted, the *ideology* of the conjugal family emphasizes the independence of the marital couple from extensive obligatory ties with extended consanguineal kin. It stresses individual choice in mate selection that is guided by romantic love and sexual attraction. Upon marriage the marital couple set up their own independent household (neolocal residence), which symbolically and actually demonstrates their commitment to the development of strong conjugal ties and then desire to sever potentially dominating ties with either kin groups.

The consanguineal family, on the other hand, is a quite different form of family organization. Here the stress is on the maintenance of extended blood relationships. On marriage a couple may move into or near the household of either the husband's or wife's family (patrilocal or matrilocal residence). Children are socialized into the larger extended kinship group. The consequent strong blood ties of unilineal members of the consanguineal family system thus accounts for the greater need and desire to control the mate choice of their members.

Table 8.1 Mate Choice Compared with Presence of Unilineal Kin Groups and Extended Family Households

Form of Mate Choice	Society	Unilineal Kin Groups Present	Extended Family Households the Norm
Free mate choice, parents' approval not necessary	Ifugao	no	no
	Jamaica	no	no
	Kaingang	no	no
	Barranquitas (Puerto Rico)	no	no
	San Pedro la Laguna (Guatemala)	no	?
	United States (modern)	no	no
Free mate choice, parents' approval necessary	Colonial America	no	?
	Hopi	yes	yes
	Iban	no	yes
	Peyrane (France)	no	no
	Samoa	no	yes
	Trobriands	yes	no
Both arranged marriage and free mate choice practiced	Alor	yes	no
	Fiji	yes	yes
	Kaska	yes	no
	Kurtachi	yes	no
	Kwoma	yes	no
	Lepcha	yes	yes

MARRIAGE REGULATIONS

There is a striking increase in the number of societies that now allow individuals to marry through free choice in contrast to their former predominant practice by which family elders arranged the marriage. The choice of eligible mates for their children was governed by two conflicting types of marital regulations. The first, *endogamy,* refers to the requirement that an individual marry someone within a particular group. This group could be a kinship group, a clan, a religious organization, or any other social category. The second, *exogamy,* refers to the requirement that an individual marry someone outside a particular group.

Exogamous rules usually coincide with incest taboos—the prohibition of sexual intercourse between certain blood relations, for example, between father and daughter, mother and son, or brother and sister. Exogamous rules are primarily kinship based and generally prohibit sexual activities and marriage among people who are closely related. Frequently, exogamous rules are extended to apply to larger

Table 8.1   (cont.)

Form of Mate Choice	Society	Unilineal Kin Groups Present	Extended Family Households the Norm
	Murngin	yes	no
	Navaho	yes	no
	Ojibwa	yes	no
	Tikopia	yes	no
	Tepoztlan	no	?
	Wogeo	yes	no
Arranged marriage	Anglo-Saxons	no	?
	Ashanti	yes	no
	Cheyenne	yes	no
	China (Taitou)	yes	yes
	Hindu India (Rajputs)	yes	yes
	Ireland (County Clare)	no	yes
	Hebrews (Old Testament)	yes	?
	Japan	no	yes
	Kipsigis	yes	no
	Muria	yes	?
	Mundugumor	yes	no
	Papago	yes	yes
	Pukapuka	yes	no
	Siwai	yes	no
	Subanum	no	no
	Tibet	yes	yes

Source: William N. Stephens. 1963. *The Family in Cross-Cultural Perspective,* New York: Holt, Rinehart & Winston, p. 199.

social units. In Classical China, a man was not permitted to marry a woman who had the same surname, even though they were not kinship related. Certain societies prohibit the marriage of members of the same village or of the same tribe. Yonina Talmon (1964) reports that children raised in the same peer group on a collective settlement (kibbutz) in Israel are informally pressured against intrakibbutz marriage. She suggests that the excessive familiarity of young people socialized together prevented them from falling in love.

There are numerous theories of incest and exogamy. This is a much-discussed topic in the social sciences with many explanations proposed through the years. The explanations seem to fall into two main categories: first, there are theories that revolve around biologic, genetic, and psychological factors to explain individual motivations; second, there are theories that deal with mate-selection patterns in terms of their effect on intragroup or intergroup solidarity with macrolevel analysis of the society.

Falling into the first category are such theories as: (1) a horror instinct against incest, (2) Freudian psychoanalytical theory, and (3) genetic influences on the incest taboo. The first theory, "horror instinct against incest," postulates that individuals have an instinctive horror of having sexual relations with close kin. To avoid such an occurrence, incest taboos were created to provide further social pressure against the commitment of such a "horror." This theory is somewhat contradictory in that if there was an instinctual dread of incest, there would be no need for the creation of social taboos socializing individuals against it. This theory has been generally discarded.

The Freudian psychological theory in regard to the incest taboo was developed out of Sophocles's tragedy, *Oedipus Rex*. Oedipus, the son, unknowingly slays his father and marries his mother. On becoming aware of his actions, he blinds himself. Freud stressed the universal tendency of children to have a strong sexual attraction to the parent of the opposite sex. Incest taboos arise as a reaction to incestuous wishes and are a rejection of the forbidden and frightening sexual attraction of the opposite-sex parent. The Freudian theory is weak in that it does not explain the extension of incest taboos beyond the immediate family.

The genetic theory postulates that incest taboos were developed to prevent the potentially harmful effects of inbreeding, that is, madness, hemophilia, and so on. The theory emphasizes the real and imagined deleterious effects of inbreeding and ignores the positive ones. For example, the inbreeding of cattle to develop a superior strain of usable beef. Further, although there is some genetic evidence of the negative consequences of inbreeding, the theory assumes a level of biologic sophistication and knowledge that goes beyond that exhibited by most persons in most societies. An extreme example is the Arunta of Australia who were unaware of the role of the father in procreation.

There are several theories that focus on societal factors in regard to the incest taboo. George Murdock (1949) used psychological behavior theory, Freudian psychoanalytic theory, and previously developed theories in anthropology and sociology to construct his theory of the incest taboo. His ideas were enhanced by his use of his own cross-cultural data from 250 societies. He argues that the origins of the incest taboo arise out of the unwillingness of parents and siblings to satisfy personally the child's sexual desire. Further, the family, which provides important societal needs (economic cooperation, reproduction, education, and socialization), wishes to avoid anything that weakens it. It is thought that weakening the family would, in turn, weaken the larger social system. Conflict within the family resulting from sexual competition and jealousy would be highly disruptive. Thus "the reduction of sexual rivalry between parents and children and between siblings consolidates the family as a cooperative social group, promotes the efficiency of its societal services, and thus strengthens the society as a whole'' (Murdock, 1949:295).

Murdock then argued that the extension of the incest taboo to more distant and remote relatives beyond the nuclear family can be explained by the behavioristic psychology concept of stimulus generalization. According to this principle, any response evoked by one stimulus will tend to be elicited by other stimuli in direct proportion to their similarity to the original stimuli. Murdock sees that secondary or remote relatives who resemble a sexually tabooed member of the nuclear family will hvae the avoidance behavior extended to them. His illustration is that of a mother's sister (ego's aunt), who may possess similar features and other physical traits of the mother. This relative will be perceived as similar to the mother and thus will be sexually avoided. He states that there is a prevalence of applying the same kinship term to the two women in many societies (both referred to by the term, mother) and ego exhibits similar patterned behavior towards both.

Murdock does not answer the question on why the marital restrictions and taboos are extended further in many societies. The theory of reciprocity by Claude Levi-Strauss seeks to answer this question. Levi-Struass (1957) believes that the prohibition of incest is one of the rules related to reciprocity. The marriage between individuals belonging to different nuclear families may be viewed as an exchange between two families, one providing the husband, the other the wife. The newly formed nuclear family is conceived of as a social organization that links several families in a chain of reciprocal exchanges. The cultural development of a society is seen to be dependent on the development of a more complex culture than can be developed by any given family. Cultural development is enhanced by the linking of families into wider social organizations through reciprocal social bonds.

To illustrate this, Levi-Strauss utilizes the following model. The prohibition of incest is a rule of reciprocity when it means that a family must give up a daughter or sister if its neighboring family will also do so. Marriage is viewed as an exchange between families in which, at one point in time, a given family gives up a daughter and at another point accepts one. Thus there is a perpetual mutual obligation to supply women in marriage. If one looks at a hypothetical situation in which one family has a monopoly on desirable women, whereas the other family in the group has none available, a potential climate of hostility and tension can arise. Reciprocity thus serves to assure a more balanced state. This illustrative model assumes that women are treated as property and that there is a scarcity of women for marriage. It is based on an assumption of male polygyny and on the greater attractiveness and desirability of certain women. More important, the principle of reciprocity in regard to marriage is seen by Levi-Strauss as assuring the occurrence of social exchange and the establishment of alliances between families. The incest taboo serves as the basis for the development of groups larger than the nuclear family and is a key organizing factor in society. The family, then, is vital to society as it establishes broader social relationships through the patterned exchange of sexual relationships.

Rules of endogamy ran counter to the rules of exogamy, or totem prohibition. To repeat, endogamous rules require a person to marry someone within a given social grouping. These social groups can range from the extended kinship system, the tribe, community, social class, race, or nationality. Linton C. Freeman (1974), following the analysis of Geroge Murdock, sees the basis for endogamous rules stemming from ethnocentrism, or group conceit, which is common to all social groups. Freeman observes that, almost universally, outsiders are suspect; people tend to distrust or to dislike people who are different from themselves. People discriminate on the basis of race, creed, and cultural backgrounds. Conversely, they accept members of their own family and community more readily since they share a common background and heritage. In sex relations and mate selection, ethnocentrism is expressed by prohibiting marriage with outsiders through specified rules of endogamy. In the United States, endogamous rules are exhibited through pressures for individuals to marry someone of the same race, social class, ethnic group, religion, and of the same age.

Together, exogamy and endogamy are seen by Freeman as delineating a "field of eligible mates" (Freeman, 1974:355). This field of eligible or approved marital partners can be large or small, depending on the relative strengths of the two complementary tendencies of endogamy and exogamy. Together, they are seen to make up the rules for preferential mating. In addition to preferential mating, a second principle is seen to underlie the process of mate selection: marriage arrangement. Marriage arrangement is defined by Freeman as referring to the degree to which persons other than the prospective bride and groom participate in the process of selection: for example, whether or not parents are involved in the mate-selection process. Here, again, a wide range of societal patterns exist, ranging from families having little involvement in the selection of a spouse to societies where families select the individual's spouse with little or no involvement by that individual in the decision-making process. Using these two principles—preferential mating and marriage arrangement—Freeman in Table 8.2 goes on to analyze four cultures that vary according to the interplay of these principles.[1]

The Yaruros of Venezuela are a nomadic tribe of fishermen and hunters who inhabit a vast plain southeast of the Andes. They have few material possessions: some baskets and pots and some hunting equipment. There is a strict division of labor in the tribe, with men doing all the hunting and fishing and women gathering plants, herbs, and roots. Young crocodiles are the basic staple in their diet, along with crocodile eggs, turtles, turtle eggs, and various plants and herbs. Clothing is sparse in this hot and dry climate with temperatures climbing well above 100° during the day. Men wear a simple loincloth; women a more elaborate foliated fashioned girdle.

---

[1]The following discussion is based on Linton C. Freeman's (1974) analysis.

Table 8.2   Marital Selection Typology

	Preferential Mating	
Degree of Arrangement of the Marriage	Highly Specified Preferences Leading to Narrow Field of Eligibles	Little Specification of Preferred Mate Leading to Wide Field of Eligibles
High: Parents or others select one's spouse	Yaruros	Feudal Japan
Low: Principal selects own spouse	Hottentots	Middle-class U.S.A.

Source: Linton C. Freeman, 1974. ''Marriage without Love: Mate-selection in non-Western societies.''
Pp. 354–366. In Robert F. Winch and Graham B. Spanier (eds.), *Selected Studies in Marriage and the
Family,* 4th ed. New York: Holt, Rinehart & Winston, p. 366.

Yaruro society is divided into two halves. This division serves as the basis of
kinship, with each tribal member belonging to one or the other moiety. Descent is
matrilineal; one inherits moiety from one's mother. Marriage is both arranged and
highly specified. One must marry into the opposite moiety and, more specifically,
one must marry a cross-cousin, that is, a man must marry the daughter of his
mother's brother or the daughter of his father's sister. An incest taboo exists against
the marriage to his sisters, his mother, his mother's sisters or their daughters. His
mother's sisters are called by the same classificatory term as his own mother. The
taboo also exists for the daughters father's brother since they belong to the same
moiety as he does.

The marriage to an eligible cross-cousin is arranged by the shaman, or religious
leader, on consultation with one of the boy's uncles who, in turn, selects one of his
daughters. The boy then moves into his uncle's household and is obligated to work
and hunt with his uncles. In effect, he takes the place of his uncle's sons who, in
turn when they marry, move into the camp of their father-in-laws. These marriage
practices are seen to be necessary to maintain tribal solidarity.

> Yaruro marriage practices, therefore, typify a procedure which serves to delimit an
> extremely narrow field of eligibles. Taken together, the incest taboos and the attitudes of
> ethnocentrism restrict the field of eligibles for the typical Yaruro man to one of his
> cross-cousins. Such an arrangement solves the problems raised by poor communication
> and sparse population. It affords access to a potential mate in the immediate vicinity but
> requires that the mate be obtained from another camp. This promotes interaction
> between camps and tends to maintain interfamilial solidarity. (Freeman, 1974:360)

The Hottentots of southwest Africa are a group of seminomadic herders who
live in a great grassy plateau. Their economy is based on hunting and herding, with
milk and meat constituting the basic part of their diet. The Hottentots, who number

about 20,000, are divided into 12 tribes. Each tribe is comprised of a number of clans—groups of persons united by a common ancestor. The clan is the organizational unit of Hottentot society; the members of each clan form a single community.

Dwellings in a community are arranged according to age seniority. Like many preliterate societies, the Hottentots place great value on age, and the eldest male member serves as the clan chief. The clan, however, is governed by a council of peers, consisting of the older men of the clan. They direct the clan's activities, settle quarrels, and punish minor offenders.

The Hottentots allow polygyny, but the practice tends to be restricted to those who can afford it; the wealthier men take more than one wife. Each wife lives in a separate dwelling with her children. They own their dwellings and have their own herds of animals. Women control the distribution of household provisions. They are involved in milking the animals, gathering edible plants, cooking, making clothing and pottery, and maintaining the houses. The herds are tended by young boys or servants. Hunting is the primary responsibility of adult males.

Prior to becoming eligible for marriage, Hottentot boys and girls must pass through a series of rites at puberty. Each boy must also demonstrate his proficiency as a hunter by killing some big-game animal. Once eligible for adulthood, the young are allowed considerable sexual freedom. However, like the Yaruros, cross-cousin marriage is required. But, unlike the Yaruros, the Hottentots are free to choose for themselves which cross-cousin to marry.

The process of choosing a marriage partner is set by established ritual. When the male youth has chosen from eligible cross-cousins, he informs his parents, who, in turn, send emissaries to the girl's parents to seek permission for their son to marry her. The tradition dictates that they refuse. The youth then elicits the support of the girl. At night, after everyone is asleep, he goes to her house and lies down beside her. Tradition dictates her actions; she gets up and moves to another side of the house. The next night he returns and if he finds her in the same side as she was originally and she stays, the marriage is consummated.

The couple live with the bride's family for a one-year period or until the first child is born. They then set up permanent residence in the camp of the groom's parents.

For the Hottentots, the field of eligibles is narrowly defined, limited to cross-cousins; but, unlike the Yaruros, the persons are allowed to choose their own spouses. Freeman concludes:

> . . . the field of eligibles for the Hottentots is established on the basis of kinship. Incest prohibitions are strong—they are extended to include every member of a person's clan—everyone in his local encampment. The Hottentots camp in clan groups like the Yaruros, and most interpersonal contacts are with kinsmen. And like the Yaruros, isolation and ethnocentrism force them to seek a spouse from a neighboring encampment. In both cases the person sought is a cross-cousin. But here the resemblance ends.

For while Yaruro custom dictates that the choice among cross-cousins be made by the uncle, the Hottentots allow the persons marrying to make their own choice. (Freeman, 1974:365)

Freeman next looks at feudalistic Japan (Tokugawa Japan) in the eighteenth century. It illustrates a society that permits a wide variety of marital eligibles, but the actual choice is determined by the family, not the marrying person.

Feudal Japan was divided into local small duchies, each ruled by a lord and supported by an army of knights (samurai). Governing the society was a hereditary military leader with the Emperor having little importance. As in most feudal societies, there was a clearly delineated social class system, with each class restricted to designated dwellings, styles of clothing, food, and so on.

The family in feudal Japan was at the heart of an individual's activities. The family was ruled by a patriarch with the assistance of a family council, which included most of the mature males and the old women in the family. The extended family included the patriarch's wife, all his sons and their wives and children, his unmarried daughters, younger brothers and their wives and children, and finally the servants. As head of the family, the patriarch's approval is required for marriages and divorces, for adoptions, and for the expulsion of recalcitrant members. He is responsible for the family's fulfillment of its obligations to the state. Professor Kawishima, a Japanese social scientist, observes:

> As a means of emphasizing through external impressions the mental attitude of filial obedience, the head of a family (generally the father) enjoys markedly privileged treatment in everyday life. The family head does not do with his own hands even trifling things—or rather is prohibited from doing such things because it is thought to compromise his authority. He must be served in everything by his wife, children or others subject to his patriarchal power. For instance, he should get his wife or servant to hand him anything which is right under his nose. The family head must be better fed and must not eat the same things as other members of his family (especially children), for it impairs his authority as such. When entering or leaving his house, he should be treated with special ceremony. In his house the head's room must be one fit for his authority. In all other trifles of everyday life the head of a family should enjoy special treatment becoming his position as absolute ruler. A parent's, especially a father's, position is majestic and supreme. (Kawashima cited in Mace and Mace, 1960:35)

The power of the patriarch was exercised in the name of the preservation and perpetuation of the lineage and the enhancement of family status. The independence of the individual was strongly deemphasized. The stress was on the importance of familial obligations and responsibilities as a member of the family and of the immediate community. Within the family, a rigid hierarchy existed that delineated social roles and responsibilities. David and Vera Mace (1960) illustrate this by noting that a rigid ordering of rank is exhibited in the sequence in which family members take turns in using the bathtub. The sequence reflects the rank order in the family and where the person stands in the official family hierarchy. The father has the first turn, followed by the eldest son and all other sons, according to birth order; then, the mother is followed by the daughters in birth order; finally the servants take their turn.

The practice of subsuming individuality to the family system was most evident in socialization practices and in mate selection. Children were socialized relative to their position in the family hierarchy. Robert N. Bellah (1957) points out that the socialization of sons differed depending on whether they would inherit the property or not. The oldest son, who most likely would inherit, was trained to be responsible and cautious, befitting his prospective responsibilities. Younger sons were encouraged to be more independent and show initiative and cleverness, which would aid them in the outside world. Girls were raised with the expectation that they would marry and join their husband's family. Their training emphasized the fact that they would represent their family in the appropriate manner in their husband's household. Thus children were socialized relative to their social positions in the family hierarchy. An intricate system of duties and obligations were taught, these emphasized an individual's position within the family and the position of the family in the larger society. Individuality was submerged in the family system:

> Ideally, by the time they reached adulthood the Japanese had learned to view each other, not as individuals at all, but almost completely as stereotypes. If two people were members of the same family they treated each other in terms of their relationship. They met neither as personalities nor as persons, but only as representatives of particular relationships. All fathers treated, and were treated by their sons in much the same way. Their interaction was based upon their kinship, not upon personal feelings. (Freeman, 1974:362)

With the great emphasis on family lineage and its perpetuation, it is not surprising to learn that marriages were arranged by the family. The marriage gained its importance in the fact that it established a reciprocal bond between the two families and in that it could enhance the prestige and security of each of the families. The concerns and choices of the young people were inconsequential in light of this feudalistic family model.

Marriages were arranged through the services of a family friend, who acted as a go-between. After consideration and negotiation about the respective worth of the families, the marriage ceremony occurred. As was frequently the case, the young couple did not meet until the wedding ceremony.

The feudalistic Japanese family dominated the mate-selection process. Although there was a wide choice of eligible marriage partners, the children were not consulted nor were they involved in the decision-making process. This pattern is a logical development, given the importance of the extended kinship in Japanese society.

In the United States individual motives play an important role in deciding the question of whom one should marry. The common assumption is that two people marry on the basis of love. However, the determination of eligible love-mates is influenced by the principle of preferential mating. Incest taboos preclude the eligiblity of immediate kin. Frequently, the incest taboos extend to the first-cousin relationship, but there are no clan or other kinship structure restrictions.

Rules of endogamy are expressed in ethnocentric beliefs that define "suitable" marriage partners to people of the same social class, religion, ethnic group, and race. The field of "suitable" partners is further limited to people of the same age group and to people who live nearly in the same neighborhood or community. Until recently, ethnocentric biases were supported by legal statutes in the most dramatic case—racial intermarriage. As late as 1967 almost 20 states still had antimiscegenation statutes with penalties up to 10 years' imprisonment and fines up to $1000. In that year the Supreme Court declared that such laws were unconstitutional.

Although there has been some trend away from ethnocentric restrictions, the general pattern continues to be the marriage of people who share similar backgrounds, values, attitudes, and interests. Informal ethnocentric pressures, which still characterize American mate-selection processes, help account for the fact that marriages outside these norms tend to have greater difficulty and more frequently end in divorce. The result is that although the field of eligibles can be the entire unwed opposite-sex population, it is in fact significantly narrower because of these endogamous practices.

The choosing of one's spouse is ideally depicted as being solely within the province of the individual. Parents, friends, and others are normally not supposed to interfere in the mate-selection process. In addition, it is felt that such interference is not effective and can even backfire. For example, *The Fantasticks,* a long-running contemporary play, uses this normative guideline as the central theme: two fathers scheme to keep their respective children apart in the hope that such interference will have the opposite effect and bring them together. In many cases, parents are not informed or consulted by children about their prospective spouse either prior to or after the wedding.

Although their formal input in the marital decision-making process is diminished, the parents have a strong indirect influence in the mate-selection process. By residing in selected areas and sending their children to selected schools, parents restrict the options of young people in forming friendships. Further, through parties and selective invitation lists and verbalizing their own ethnocentric biases, parents influence their children. By influencing the informal social contacts of their children, the parents indirectly control the mate-selection process. As William J. Goode states, "Since youngsters fall in love with whom they associate, control over informal relationships also controls substantially the focus of affection" (Goode, 1959:46).

The following passage from Peter L. Berger's *Invitation to Sociology: A Humanistic Perspective* nicely summarizes our discussion on American mate-selection processes:

In Western countries, and especially in America, it is assumed that men and women marry because they are in love. There is a broadly based popular mythology about the character of love as a violent, irresistable emotion that strikes where it will, a mystery that is the goal of most young people and often of the not-so-young as well. As soon as one investigates, however, which people actually marry each other, one finds that the lightening-shaft of Cupid seems to be guided rather strongly within very definite channels of class, income, education, racial and religious background. . . . The suspicion begins to dawn on that, most of the time, it is not so much the emotion of love that creates a certain kind of relationship, but that carefully predefined and often planned relationships eventually generate the desired emotion. In other words, when certain conditions are met or have been constructed, one allows oneself "to fall in love." (Berger, 1963:35)

Death Leap of Two Chinese Sisters Over Dating Dispute Stuns Friends

Judith Cummings

A double leap to death Friday night from a six-story tenement roof by two teen-age Chinese sisters—apparently in despair over their father's insistence that they stop seeing non-Chinese boyfriends—left their midtown Manhattan neighbors stunned and hushed yesterday.

The girls, 17-year-old Betty Hwang and her 13-year-old sister Jean, plunged from the roof of 211 East 33rd Street shortly after 8:30 P.M., after an argument in which their father ordered a Puerto Rican boyfriend of Betty's to leave the family's top-floor apartment and reprimanded them for breaking his rule against dating non-Chinese boys.

"The father was very strict," said Elder Leiva, a downstairs neighbor of the Hwangs. "He just didn't want them to date Puerto Rican or black boys. He wanted them to stick to the Chinese ways, but they were friendly to everybody."

Neighbors on the heavily Hispanic block stressed, however, that there was no tension between them and the Hwangs, who have lived on the block for more than eight years. The Hwangs opened a restaurant last year, Hwang's Mandarin Inn, at 235 East 33d, and the whole family—including the mother, Sho Lin, and two other children, Jennifer, 16, and Kenneth, 10, worked long hours there.

Red-eyed and apparently exhausted, the girls' father, Yuh-Lin, who indicated he did not speak English, remained in seclusion in the family's four-room apartment the morning after the incident.

Neighbors described the tragedy as "an old story" of city-raised youngsters clashing with parents struggling to preserve old country traditions. Anthony Elias, an 18-year-old neighbor, told of talking the girls into returning to their apartment after Betty had summoned him to the rooftop. But he said a few minutes later he heard the sounds of women screaming, and then he saw the girls' bodies lying on the sidewalk.

"He didn't trust them," Mr. Elias said of the father. "He didn't believe that such good girls could go out in the street and control themselves, know how to handle themselves. He didn't want them to see what's out there for themselves."

The police said the girls had each left a suicide note, but the contents were withheld.

Betty, a student at Seward Park High School, and Jean, who attended Junior High School 104, made friends widely among the Hispanic youths and the smaller number of black teen-agers in the neighborhood. One of these was a black youth with whom Jean had "gone steady," Mr. Leiva said.

"They were so full of life, always had a smile for everybody," said his wife, Yolanda Leiva. The third sister, Jennifer, was described as shyer and less outgoing than the others.

Witnesses told the police that the incident had occurred after Mr. Hwang had become angry on finding 17-year-old Fernando Lopez, a friend of Betty's, in the apartment, where the sisters were celebrating Jennifer's 16th birthday. Angry, he ordered the youth to leave and severely reprimanded the girls before returning to work.

Apparently upset, Betty and Jean climbed to the roof's edge, where Mr. Elias said they begged him to come up and join them from the sidewalk. He said that he joined them on the roof and then the three left the roof together, but that the two girls apparently doubled back and— ignoring the pleas of Jennifer and Kenneth—perched once more on the ledge.

As a police radio car entered the block, Betty stepped off, followed by Jean. The girls were pronounced dead on arrival at Bellevue Hospital.

Professionals working in communities shared by Hispanic people and Chinese, particularly in lower Manhattan, say a frequent point of contention between the two groups involves the schools, which tend to group Chinese students in the better classes and Puerto Ricans in lower-ranked classes. The stereotyping can sometimes extend beyond the schools to the community at large.

Mr. Elias said that Betty, a good student, had been bent on becoming a physician and had told him her father talked of sending her to his native Taiwan for medical school, regarding American schools as not rigorous enough.

The two Hwang girls complained bitterly about the restrictions their father placed on them, Mr. Leivas said, and "used to say they would kill themselves if their father didn't stop being so strict."

Judith Cummings in the New York Times, November 12, 1978. © 1978 by The New York Times Company. Reprinted by permission.

WHY MARRIAGES ARE ARRANGED: LOVE AND MARRIAGE

We now turn our attention to a more systematic analysis of the factors that account for the widespread prevalence of arranged marriages. Of particular interest is the role of love in the arrangement of marriages.

In his essay, "The Theoretical Importance of Love," William J. Goode (1959) has delineated the reasons why marriages are arranged. Goode argues that allowing individuals the freedom to marry on the basis of individual motives, particularly love, can be potentially disruptive of the larger stratification system. Unless love is controlled and channeled in some nonthreatening manner, it could lead to marriages that ultimately could weaken stratification and lineage patterns. Goode argues that, when marriage involves the linking of two kinship groups and when kinship serves as the basis of societal organization, mate choice has important consequences for the social structure. Thus, when marriage affects the ownership of property and the exercise of influence, the issue of mate selection and love have been considered "too important to be left to the children" (Goode, 1959:43).

Goode states that, "Kinfolk or immediate family can disregard the question of who marries whom, only if a marriage is not seen as a link between kin lines, only if no property, power, lineage honor, totemic relationships, and the like are believed to flow from the kin lines through the spouses to their offspring" (Goode, 1959:42). As we have seen in our discussion of the Yaruro, the Hottentot, and feudalistic Japan, societies that emphasize kinship find it necessary to control marriages. Incidentally, the American upper classes also desire to control marital selection processes as a large amount of wealth is involved.

Goode, then, distinguishes among several methods for controlling the selection of marital partners. First, it is controlled by child marriage, where, as in India, the young bride moves to the household of her husband and the marriage is not consummated until a much later date. This practice precludes the possibility of the child falling in love and also limits the resources for the opposition to the marriage. Second, mate selection is controlled by kinship rules, which define a relatively small number of eligible spouses. The Yaruros and Hottentots illustrate this type of selection by limiting the field of eligibles to cross-cousins. Third, mate selection is controlled by socially and physically isolating young people from potential mates. This makes it easier for parents to arrange the marriage of their children in that there is little likelihood that these children would have developed love attachments to conflict with their parents' wishes. In feudal Japan, the social contacts between members of the opposite sex were limited and were highly ritualized. They were permitted only in the presence of elders. This had the effect of minimizing informal and intimate social interaction. Fourth, love relationships are controlled by strict chaperonage by duennas or close relatives. Here again young people are not permitted to be alone together or in intimate interaction. Finally, although formally allowing individuals to choose their own marriage partners, parents control the field of eligibles through the influence of the informal contacts of young people. As we stated, this is done through living in selective neighborhoods, restricting guest lists to parties and informal gatherings, and making the child aware of their parents' ethnocentric biases relating to race, religion, ethnicity, social class, and so on. This pattern, as we have seen, is characteristic of the United States.

Bernard Farber (1964) takes a different theoretical approach than Goode in his analysis of mate-selection processes. Whereas Goode stresses the restrictions placed on mate selection to maintain the social stratification system, Farber stresses the importance of rules regarding mate selection in terms of preserving family culture. Family culture is seen to have as its constituent elements the norms and values that people hold regarding courtship, marriage, divorce, kinship identity and obligations, socialization of children, residence, and household maintenance. Farber argues that exogamous rules may lead to individuals marrying outside of their family group; potentially the possibility does exist that one will marry someone with different norms and values and opens the family system to external influences that can be damaging to the continuity of the culture of the particular family group. The choice of marriage partner, then, is controlled by the family of orientation to assure transmission of the family culture to future generations.

> Thus, at the point of marriage of the child both parental families are in danger of having their culture interrupted in transmission by the introduction of possibly contradictory values from the other family. Restrictions in the society on mate selection would delimit the direction of change in family cultures from one generation to the next. If certain families will permit marriage only with other families very similar to themselves in norms and values, then a general continuity of the cultures of both families can be expected. (Farber, 1964:63−64)

In summary, where societies emphasize the importance of kinship lineage and its preservation—and support this by establishing strong ties between family interests and economic and social interests—marriages are arranged by the couple's respective consanguineal families. On the other hand, where societies emphasize the importance of the conjugal relationship between husband and wife and deemphasize their obligations and responsibilities to the extended family system, the choice of marriage partners is more or less left up to the individuals involved.

On Java, Divorce Ends Many Child Marriages

Isa Ismael

> JAKARTA, Indonesia—Child marriages are still common among the rice growers and fisherman of Indramayu on the northern coastal plains of Java, but many soon end in divorce.

Indramayu district, 125 miles from Jakarta, has the highest divorce rate in Indonesia, mainly because of the prevalence of child marriages. On one day last month about 100 young couples, many of whom had not even consummated their marriages, lined up before the local religious court for a quick divorce.

The girls and boys were only 10 to 15 years old, and although they had been married for up to two years, most had no idea of what marriage involved.

When Indramayuan children are about 10 years old they are paired off by their parents and married according to local customs.

The weddings are lavish by local standards, costing hundreds of dollars each. The young bride and groom are paraded around the village dressed in colorful new clothes, with flowers and imitation jewelry on their heads and a noisy band following behind.

Afterward, however, the husband and wife separate to their respective parents' homes and resume their play with the neighborhood children.

The people of Indramayu are proud if they can marry their children off early. They are satisfied that their sons and daughters are considered worthy by their fellow villagers.

Child marriage is also spurred by plans for perpetuating family wealth or enlarging it by marrying into wealthier families.

Before 1975, when a national marriage law was enacted to reduce the rate of divorce and cut down the incidence of polygamy, allowed under Islamic law, at least half the 30,000 marriages registered in Indramayu each year ended in divorce.

The divorce figures dropped sharply soon afterward, but by last year had risen to previous levels.

It is not unusual to see young boys and girls sitting on the long benches in front of the local religious court, waiting for their marriages to be ended.

Changed economic circumstances is the reason given in most cases, followed by desertion; others contend that they have been forced to marry a person they do not like.

The Jakarta daily, Kompas, said in a recent article that trying to prevent the large number of child marriages and divorces in Indramayu was "just as difficult as controlling the flooded Cimanuk River that flows in the district during the rainy season."

It carried a photograph of a 55-year-old woman who said she had been married 50 times, 49 of which ended in divorce. Her shortest marriage lasted just 11 days.

Isa Ismael, *The Philadlephia Inquirer,* October 4, 1979. Copyright 1979 by Reuters Ltd. Reprinted by permission.

MODERNIZATION AND ARRANGED MARRIAGES

The concern here is to examine the effect of modernization processes, industrialization, urbanization, and the ideologies of egalitarianism and individualism on traditional contractual marriage-arrangement procedures. One question that we will seek to answer is whether there is an emerging pattern toward romantic love as a prime criterion in the mate-selection process. We will begin our investigation by first examining the findings of George Theodorson (1968) who investigated the impact of Westernizing influences on the attitudes toward romanticism and contractual marriage arrangements in three non-Western societies, Chinese Singapore, Burma, and India. We will then examine, in some detail, changes that are occurring in contemporary Japan. This should provide an interesting comparison with the earlier discussion of marriage in feudal Japan.

Theodorson believes that contemporary attitudes toward romanticism and marriage in non-Western societies can best be analyzed by looking at the relationship between contractualism (arranged marriage) and cultural change. Theodorson observes that the degree of contractualism was different in the three societies of China, Burma, and India. In China and India arranged marriages were commonplace; a high degree of contractualism existed. The criteria for the selection of suitable marriage partners was based on economic and social (e.g., caste in India) considerations. Child marriages and the separation of the bride and groom until the marriage ceremony prevented romantic love from being a factor in mate selection. The prime responsibility and obligations of sons were to their extended families, not to their wives.

By contrast, traditional Burmese culture was characterized by arranged marriages but usually with the child's consent. Romantic love, although not a widespread pattern, did occur and was a factor in the mate-selection process. Unlike India and Japan, Burma allowed its young people some opportunity to meet in supervised social gatherings. Children could initiate the contractual arranged-marriage process by informing their parents of their desire to marry. It must be emphasized that the marriage was contractual and that the contacts between the young were restricted and were supervised. Dowries were paid by the groom's family to the bride's parents.

The second analytical variable is the degree of cultural change. The Burmese were the least changed by Western influences. India experienced major changes in attitudes in regard to divorce, widow remarriage, intercaste marriage, and equality of the sexes. However, the Singapore Chinese experienced the greatest change in traditional patterns regarding the consanguineal family system. Theodorson attributes this change to three factors. First, the Singapore Chinese were immigrants from rural farming Chinese provinces to a highly urbanized society. Second, there was a confusion of dialects, subdialects, and sub-subdialects among the Singapore Chinese, a result of their diverse province backgrounds. And third, the separation from the ancestral home heightened family mobility.

Theodorson developed five indices to test the hypothesis that the impact of industrialization, urbanization, and Western education would lead to the development of a romantic-love orientation toward mate selection. He tested his hypothesis with a large sample of college students from India (1038 men and 202 women), Burma (249 men and 237 women), and Singapore (510 men and 287 women). For comparative purposes he examined the findings from American students (748 men and 576 women) with those of his non-Western groups.

He concludes that "Despite the impact of industrialization, urbanization, and Western education, despite changes in specific traditional family norms and despite the sexual frustration which results from delayed marriage combined with premarital sexual taboos, Indian, Burmese, and Singapore Chinese respondents have maintained a contractualistic value-orientation toward marriage and basically have not accepted the ideals of the romantic orientation" (Theodorson, 1968:130).

However, Theodorson's finding of the differential degrees of contractualism of the three non-Western groups is of considerable importance. The Chinese, who traditionally had elaborate contractual marriage procedures, had the greatest amount of cultural change. The result was that they accepted the ideals of the romantic orientation more so than the Burmese, who have a tradition of acceptance (albeit limited) of the romantic orientation. The Indians, despite many cultural changes, still express the most contractual value orientations. The following conversation between David and Vera Mace and a group of 10 Indian girls illustrates the attitudinal position that makes change to a romantic love ideology difficult.

Who Picks Your Partner

David Mace and Vera Mace

"Tell us," said Kusima, "about the young people in the West. We want to know how *they* get married."

Night was falling at the close of a sultry Indian day. A cool, refreshing breeze playfully caressed the glittering black tresses of the girls' hair and set their gay saris fluttering. All teen-agers, they had been invited along by our host because we had expressed a desire to know what Indian young people thought about love and marriage. The girls, ten of them, were squatting on the veranda floor in a wide circle. Being awkward Westerners who couldn't sit comfortably on folded legs, we had been provided with low stools.

We gave as good an account as we could of how our young people are free to meet each other and have dates; how a boy and girl will fall in love; and how, after a period of going steady, they become engaged and then get married. We knew that young people in the East live a very restricted life, and have their marriages arranged for them by their parents, so we felt a little relieved that they had chosen to question us about our delightful romantic traditions. We didn't want to make them *too* envious, but we naturally were glad to demonstrate our superiority in this matter of finding a mate.

When we had finished, there was a meditative silence. Concluding that they had been impressed, we decided to start a discussion.

"Wouldn't you like to be free to choose your own marriage partners, like the young people do in the West?"

"Oh no!" several voices replied in chorus.

Taken aback, we searched their faces.

"Why not?"

"For one thing," said one of them, "doesn't it put the girl in a very humiliating position?"

"Humiliating? In what way?"

"Well, doesn't it mean that she has to try to look pretty, and call attention to herself, and attract a boy, to be sure she'll get married?"

"Well, perhaps so."

"And if she doesn't want to do that, or if she feels it's undignified, wouldn't that mean she mightn't get a husband?"

"Yes, that's possible."

"So a girl who is shy and doesn't push herself forward might not be able to get married. Does that happen?"

"Sometimes it does."

"Well, surely that's humiliating. It makes getting married a sort of competition in which the girls are fighting each other for the boys. And it encourages a girl to pretend she's better than she really is. She can't relax and be herself. She has to make a good impression to get a boy, and then she has to go on making a good impression to get him to marry her."

Before we could think of an answer to this unexpected line of argument, another girl broke in.

"In our system, you see," she explained, "we girls don't have to worry at all. We *know* we'll get married. When we are old enough, our parents will find a suitable boy, and everything will be arranged. We don't have to go into competition with each other."

"Besides," said a third girl, "how would we be able to judge the character of a boy we met and got friendly with? We are young and inexperienced. Our parents are older and wiser, and they aren't as easily deceived as we would be. I'd far rather have my parents choose for me. It's so important that the man I marry should be the right one. I could so easily make a mistake if I had to find him for myself."

Another girl had her hand stretched out eagerly.

"But *does* the girl really have any choice in the West?" she said. "From what I've read, it seems that the boy does all the choosing. All the girl can do is to say yes or no. She can't go up to a boy and say 'I like you. Will you marry me?' can she?"

We admitted that this was not the done thing.

> "So," she went on eagerly, "when you talk about men and women being equal in the West, it isn't true. When our parents are looking for a husband for us, they don't have to wait until some boy takes it into his head to ask for us. They just find out what families are looking for wives for their sons, and see whether one of the boys would be suitable. Then, if his family agree that it would be a good match, they arrange it together."
>
> David Mace and Vera Mace. *Marriage: East and West.* Garden City, N.Y.: Doubleday, pp. 130–131. Copyright © 1959, 1960 by David and Vera Mace. Reprinted by permission of Doubleday.

MATE SELECTION IN CONTEMPORARY JAPAN

Contemporary Japanese society emerges out of a feudal past that emphasized an elaborate formal hierarchical and authoritarian structure. As we saw earlier, marital arrangements were determined by the respective family heads in the name of the preservation of lineage and the enhancement of family status. The marrying individuals had little or no say in the determination of their prospective marriage partners. Robert O. Blood, Jr. (1967), in a comprehensive analysis of Japanese marital arrangement patterns observes that a revolutionary transition is occurring in contemporary Japan. There is a movement toward greater equality between parents and children and between men and women. This change is reflected in the appearance of a new system of mate selection parallel to the older system. Further, the old system of marriage arrangement is gradually being transformed.

Blood presents the following illustrative case of a Japanese colleague's father on "what marriage was like in the old days" (Blood, 1967:4).

In those days (the 1850's), marriage was a contract between families, not between individuals. My grandparents carefully investigated my mother's family background before choosing her to be my father's wife. They wanted to be sure that her background was of the same rank, was of good financial reputation, and had no hereditary diseases that might be transmitted to later generations of Kondos. After they decided she was suitable, they went around and got the approval of all their close relatives before entering into negotiations with the other family, using a relative as a go-between. The wedding was followed by a series of drinking parties lasting several days, first at the groom's home and then at the bride's home. The women attended these festivities, but only the men did any drinking. Every year after that, the two families got together at every festival occasion.

My father and mother were from villages ten miles apart in an age when sedan chairs were the only means of transportation. They never met until the wedding ceremony. My own marriage was unusual in that my wife and I didn't meet even then. I was away from home at the Imperial University and studying hard for the civil service exam. Since I was the eldest son, my parents were anxious to have me get married. My father's uncle and my mother's uncle were good friends and made the arrangements on behalf of the two families. My wife was 17 years old at the time of the wedding, and I was 27. She had seen my picture, but I had never seen hers—I was too busy to be disturbed. The wedding was unusual becuase I was presented by proxy. After the ceremony, the main relatives on both sides brought my wife to Tokyo to meet her, completed the formalities, and then left us to being living together. In those days, love affairs were unheard of except in the lower class. (Blood, 1967:4)

Blood contrasts two major forms of marriage arrangement in Japan, the love match and the arranged marriage. Since the mid-nineteenth century, arranged marriages were negotiated through the *nakodo* ("go-between"). By using a go-between, families avoided direct dealings with each other and the possibility of losing face in the event that one family would reject the arrangement. It also protected the family who broke off the negotiation from any negative consequences of offending a family that, by virtue of its social status, was important to them.

The *nakodo* had three basic functions: introduce the participants, negotiate the conditions, and perform a ceremonial function at the wedding. The *nakodo*'s task was to assess the compatibility of the respective families in terms of lineage and socioeconomic status. In addition, a woman's physical appearance was important as was the fact of her proper instruction in marital and family affairs. If all proved satisfactory, a *miai* ("formal introductory meeting") was arranged for the prospective partners and their parents. Blood notes that although the meeting attempts to introduce the young people to each other in an informal manner and encourages them to converse, the underlying motive for the meeting makes such interaction difficult. The tension of the situation, a marital eligibility trial, makes conversation stiff and awkward if it occurs at all. He observes that *miais* are standard fare for slackstick movies in Japan. David and Vera Mace discuss the *miai* in the following passage:

> The atmosphere was very formal, and there was much bowing. Politeness forbade any mention being made of the object of the meeting, and the boy and girl had little chance to talk with each other. Even when attempts were made to get them to talk, these were not generally successful. "Some young couples are so shy that they keep silent from beginning to end. The matchmaker tries to make them talk but usually fails. Then when a daughter who has kept her eyes cast down on the tatami throughout the interview is later asked by her family how she likes the man, she says she cannot say because she didn't see him!" (Mace and Mace, 1960:144)

The arranged marriage was made with the sole aim of assuring the continuation of the family line. Although love might be expected to occur over time, the extended family household deemphasized the husband-wife relationship. Households consisted of three generations, with the emphasis on strong ties between mother and son. For the husband, sexual satisfaction and affection were more usually obtained through a concubine or mistress than through the relationship he had with his wife.

Arranged marriage still occurs in contemporary Japan, but its character has changed. Blood states that *miai kekkon* ("interview marriage") is no longer arranged by parents on behalf of unknowing children but rather by matchmakers on the behalf of the participating families. " 'Arrangement' now means primarily the formal introduction of potential marriage partners to each other and secondarily the follow-up message-carrying which cements a promising relationship" (Blood, 1967:12). The prospective husband and wife preview each other through personal and family credentials and photographs provided by the matchmaker. This provides the young people a chance to reject one another prior to the arrangement of a *miai*.

If the impressions after meeting at the *miai* are favorable, the couple are allowed to meet informally in limited contact for a period of up to six months. R. P. Dore (1965), who has written an interesting monograph entitled *City Life in Japan: A Study of a Tokyo Ward,* reports that it is not uncommon for the young couple to go to the cinema after the *miai* and to court each other for some weeks or months afterward. The continued involvement of the courting couple with each other provides the indication that the marriage is acceptable and usually, in less than six months after the *miai,* the marriage takes place within the guidelines of the traditional marriage ceremony and the exchange of betrothal gifts.

Blood (1967) believes that his findings indicate that the main function of the formal introductions was to allow the prospective couple the opportunity to meet and assess their interest in one another. It was not to arrange the marriage. Hardly more than 10 percent of the *miais* led to marriage. Further, this modern version of the marriage arrangement usually occurs among young people who fail to contract a successful love match. They also tend to be confined to the "old-fashioned" (less educated, less emancipated girls) segments of the younger generation.

By contrast, the love match is defined as the falling in love of the man and woman prior to getting engaged. The love match couples do not date much more than the arranged-marriage couples. The difference is that their relationship developed into love. It must be remembered that traditionally Japan has been a sex-segregated society and potentially eligible partners had little opportunity for informal socialization. Blood reports that almost 75 percent of the love-match couples met at work. The scarcity of coeducational colleges and congregational churches and the nonprevalence of using the homes of friends and relatives for informal meetings account for the importance of the place of work for the meeting of eligible singles.

The criteria for the selection of a spouse is different for the love-match couples and the arranged-marriage group. The traditional emphasis in arranged marriages is the wife's ability to fit into the husband's family, provided that the family background and status qualifications are met. In the self-selection process of love-match individuals, the emphasis is on personal qualifications. Those who are introduced through the *miai* stress the husband's income and the wife's health and housekeeping ability. Couples who meet through their own initiative emphasize the importance of love.

Blood (1967) then raises the question: Which of these two patterns of mate selection, the modernized version of arranged marriage or the love match, is superior in terms of the ultimate happiness of the couple and the stability of the marriage? This is a somewhat inappropriate question since where marriages are arranged, the happiness of the spouse is not the primary purpose of the marriage. Yet Blood's answer is interesting. He found that the happiest arranged marriages were those in which the couple dated for an extended period of time after the formal introduction at the *miai*. These couples had the opportunity to get to know each other and to start developing a love relationship. The happiest love-match couples were those whose parents were enthusiastic about the pending marriage. When the parents viewed the love match negatively, the consequent marriage ran into the greatest difficulty. In general Blood believes that those marriages that combined affectional involvement and parental approval tended to be the most successful. The combining of the positive sentiments of both generations, the parents and the children, gave the greatest assurance of the eventual happiness of the marrying couple.

Job Opportunity in Japan: Be a Bar Girl

Leonard Boasberg

"My name is Umeko," she says, sitting beside you.

It means "Plum Child," and she's a hostess in a "naito kurabbu" (nightclub) called The Sisters, in Kyoto, the old capital of Japan.

If you'd been listening to the public address system in the crowded, cavernous room, you'd have heard her summoned—"Umeko, Table 66."

"May I know your name?" she asks the patron at Table 66.

The Sisters is on the Kamo River, which flows through the center of Kyoto.

The club is near the celebrated narrow street called Ponto-Cho. If you're looking for a certain kind of action, that's where it is.

The Sisters, you get conversation. Umeko keeps the drinks flowing (the more you drink, the more she earns). She dances with you, to the music of a Japanese rock band. She fusses over you and tells you how skillfully you speak Japanese even if you speak only a few words. But at ll P.M., when the Sisters closes, she walks to the door with you and, bowing, bids you "sayonara."

Umeko is 23. She was born on a small farm not too far from Kyoto. Until a year or so ago, she worked in an office. Now she earns twice as much, an average of 100,000 yen a month—About $340. Her family, back on the farm, does not know that she works at The Sisters, she says.

"They would be unhappy."

Umeko is not a geisha, that unique Japanese entertainer, trained from childhood in the arts of singing, dancing, and pleasing men. She is not a joro, a prostitute. She is a hostess, one of 60 at The Sisters, and one of an estimated 500,000 in large nightclubs and small bars in Japan today.

Maybe she would have drifted to The Sisters even if it hadn't been for the combination of recession and inflation that currently grips Japan. Maybe not. For many Japanese women, there is not too much choice.

"Of course they are not working willingly," says Hatako Shimizu, the motherly secretary general of Shufuren, the Japanese Housewives Association, a consumer organization.

But with part-time jobs falling off, especially for women, and prices rising, Japanese women can go back to the farm, if that's where they're from, to their homes, or into the bars and nightclubs.

Mrs. Shimizu blames the government for two reasons. One is the long-standing policy of permitting businessmen to deduct the costs of entertaining clients from their taxes.

The other is the economic policies of the Japanese government under the Liberal Democratic Party (which is conservative) now headed by Premier Takeo Miki.

Partly as a result of the four-fold increase in the price of oil, Japan last year ran the highest inflation rate of any industrialized nation—25 percent, more than twice the U.S. rate.

To wring inflation out of the economy, the government has tightened money, curbed spending and encouraged business and industry to resist organized labor's demands for catch-up raises.

The policies have had some success in slackening the rate of inflation—economists predict about 15 percent this year—but at the cost of the first decline in gross national product since World War II, an unprecedented number of small business bankruptcies, and an unprecedented rate of unemployment—about a million jobless out of Japan's work force of 52 million.

But some women, like Umeko, have found work that allows them to cope. Another, Akiko Ishiyama, earns the equivalent of $500 a month working for an airline in customer service. Last year, her salary was increased about 30 percent, along with salaries of other organized workers in Japan. Under the Japanese tradition of "lifetime employment," she will keep her job unless she gets married and decides to stay home and raise children.

Born 26 years ago in Tokyo, she lives there with her parents.

She has her own Toyota, but usually rides to work on Tokyo's clean, quick, efficient subway system. It takes her only half an hour. For most commuters, who work in Tokyo but can't afford to live there, the average commuting time is an hour and ten minutes, each way.

Sitting in a coffee shop in Tokyo's swinging Akasaka district, a Degas print on the wall, melancholy Japanese music alternating in the background with modern folksongs, Akiko talks about life in Tokyo.

> Not a bad place to live, she says. As a matter of fact, though she'd like to travel, she can't see herself living anywhere else. Sure, it's crowded and expensive, but there are things to do—movies, museums, dates with boyfriends.
>
> She likes to read, especially love stories and stories of old Japan. Recently she read Jonathan Livingston Seagull, a popular book in Japan, especially among the young.
>
> Next year, says Akiko Ishiyama, she will get married. Why next year? "Well, I will be 27, and it's time." Her parents already have tried to make arrangements. They've introduced her to three—or was it four?—young men. "But I didn't like them. When I marry, it must be for love."
>
> What does she expect in her husband-to-be?
>
> "First, he must have good prospects. Second, he must have brains. Third, he must have a warm heart."
>
> Leonard Boasberg in *The Philadelphia Inquirer*, April 20, 1975. Reprinted by permission of The Philadelphia Inquirer.

INSTITUTIONAL MATCHMAKERS: A COMPARISON OF CONTEMPORARY JAPAN AND AMERICA

In traditional Japan, the matchmaker (the *nakodo*) provided an invaluable service for families in arranging the marriage of their children. The *nakodo* served as a go-between negotiating the delicate relations between families and providing a face-saving service in case the negotiations failed. Today, the Japanese matchmaker's primary function is to introduce young people formally and give them the opportunity to get to know each other rather than actually to arrange a marriage. Blood (1967) found that almost 90 percent of the formal introductions did not culminate in marriage. Further, despite the pressure of families on young people to marry as soon as possible, the remaining 10 percent who did eventually marry did so only after a considerable period of time and a considerable number of dates.

In a later book, Blood (1972) observes that urbanization and mobility have made it more difficult for Japanese families to find potential partners for their children. This has produced a gradual shift away from the personalized matchmakers toward municipal governmental sponsorship of matchmaking agencies. Marriage consultation centers in urban areas provide an inexpensive public service to individuals in search of marriage partners. He reports that the Tokyo center in the early 1960s arranged 1000 marriages a year through its facilities. One problem was that twice as many women applied as men; the result was that men were more likely to find partners than women. An additional form of matchmaking agency was established by the segregated women's colleges in Japan for their alumnae. The general belief was that such alumnae would become "submissive" wives and this image attracted large numbers of men from the largely segregated men's prestige universities.

Blood (1972) observes that analogous institutional matchmaking agencies are to be found in the United States. Here they take the form of computer matchmaking centers or dating services, singles or date bars, summer resorts, and holiday cruises. Additional mating institutions include matrimonial bureaus, lonely hearts clubs, encounter groups, classified ads, and sexual liberation groups.

The American matchmaking institutions are somewhat different from the Japanese ones. Blood points out that the American pattern emphasizes personal qualities of the prospective partner, a natural consequence of the American system of self-selection. In Japan the emphasis is on objective family background criteria, an outgrowth of traditional kin-selected arranged marriages. In America the couple arrange their own dates through correspondence or by phone; in Japan the agencies set up formal introductory meetings at their establishments that are presided over by a staff counselor. However, as in Japan, more women in America avail themselves of these institutional matchmaking agencies then men. Again, this reflects the double-standard ethos that allows women less initiative than men in personally soliciting dates.

The mass media in America have found that stories on such matchmaking institutions as computer dating services and singles bars sell newspapers, and the tendency is to publicize them beyond their actual importance. Starr and Carns (1973) in an article titled, "Singles in the City," make this point. They report on a sample of 70 never-married male and female college graduates in Chicago. These people did not find singles bars the best place for making friends or for meeting persons of the opposite sex. Singles bars were seen to lack the spontaneity required for making contacts. Further, these people found that apartment dwellings and their neighborhoods were also unsatisfactory in this regard. The home and neighborhood were seen as havens for privacy in which the person either did not have the desire or the time to interact informally with neighbors.

The work setting was most frequently mentioned as the place for developing personal associations. Starr and Carns report that a two-stage process operates in the relationship between work and dating. Most graduates form friendships on the job. But they do not date their work associates since they desire to avoid intimacy with those whom they must interact, regardless of whether their personal relationship succeeds or not. Rather, they use work-friends to arrange dates through a friend-of-a-friend pattern.

The authors conclude that the popular image of the swinging singles developed and nurtured by the media is patently false. Singles bars and their ilk do not attract people looking for meaningful relationships. Further, singles do not lead lives of hedonistic abandonment. "They are people coping with the same problems we all face: finding a place to live, searching for satisfaction from their jobs and seeking friends, dates and ultimately mates in an environment for which they have been ill-prepared and which does not easily lend itself to the formation of stable human relationships" (Starr and Carns, 1973:161). In response to the lack of institutional supports found in the city environment, these people look to the world of work, much as their Japanese counterparts do, to provide them with the opportunities to meet and form friendships.

A final word on the computerized dating service may be of interest. It is a mushrooming business. Individuals fill out lengthy questionnaires dealing with family backgrounds (i.e., religion, race, social class, etc.), interests, and attitudes. Men and women are then matched on the basis of similar backgrounds and likes and dislikes. By and large the computer is a gimmick since matchings can occur by other sorting techniques. Its basic function is a legitimizing one, giving "scientific" credibility to the sorting procedure. The computer simply sorts punched cards, coded with biographical information, and pairs individuals on the basis of "compatible" areas of interests, attitudes, and desires.

The entire procedure rests on the quality of the questionnaire data. In-depth, detailed questionnaires, if properly utilized, can match individuals on common interests, attitudes, and backgrounds. Such match-ups do not necessarily guarantee that the two people will be attracted ot each other:

> The most obvious weakness of the system, however, is its inability to gauge attraction. At its scientific best it can only weigh a certain limited range of psychological and physical factors and conclude that two people are *compatible*. Frequently this means nothing whatsoever in terms of human relationships. How little compatibility may count was shown by this letter addressed to another dating outfit:
>
> "Your computer was right. Mitzi W. and I like all the same things. We like the same food, we both like the opera. Mitzi likes bike riding and so do I. I like dogs, and so does Mitzi. Actually, there was only one thing we didn't like—each other." (Goodwin, 1973:87)

Computer dating services and other formalized introduction agencies can provide a service for those people who cannot or will not find dates or prospective marital partners on their own. Although many find the use of such agencies repugnant and artificial, they can be helpful to others. As they are currently operated, the initiative to develop the relationship rests solely on the participants. Thus the individual decision-making process on the compatibility and attraction of the matched individual still remains a personal matter. Unfortunately, a significant number of these "mating trade" organizations have been guilty of exploitation. The charges against them run from the charging of exorbitant fees to fraudulently based "computer" match-ups. Some have exploited the weaknesses and desires of their clientele. If the abuses of the system can be minimized, perhaps through effective governmental legislation, these agencies can provide a service for those so inclined to use them.

Where Are They, the Dreammates in Singles Land?

Ann Kolson

A Friday night in the city.

At PT's, a popular singles bar on Front Street, the line to get in stretches around the block.

Inside, men in jackets and ties mill about carrying drinks and dropping offhand remarks, such as "a perfect specimen" and "she has a 24-year-old mind and a 19-year-old body." The men know they can leave with a woman.

The women who are the objects of this attention sit in groups of two and three on sofas and at cocktail tables, forcing smiles. They are hoping they will leave with a man. But many will not.

It is just part of the meet market—one stop on the center city singles' circuit in a town where the women outnumber the men by more than 100,000 (by comparison, New York City women outnumber men by 500,000).

Simply, "there are more females to be married and less males to marry," University of Pennsylvania sociologist Frank Furstenberg said. "It's like not having enough storage space."

It is simple economics. Supply and demand. What is in short supply (in this case, men) becomes the valued commodity. What is overly abundant (in this case, women) loses value.

Combine this with the innate feeling that many women still harbor (not without some embarrassment) that they are worth less without a man, and you have an unenviable situation for women.

It's a buyers' market, and some of the sellers are feeling the pinch.

"You get tired of feeling the other person has the advantage, you really do," sighed Jane, a 31-year-old lawyer who has never married.

"Look, it's still a man's world, no matter what," she added, regretfully.

Despite the glorification of singlehood as an ideal state, women are still looking for men and vice versa.

"Women are taught they are nothing without a man," said Debby, a 33-year-old artist who lives in Queen Village. "Even though I know that's a bunch of ——, the feeling is still there."

Some women complain that the men they meet are creeps, losers, bores, cads or babies. "They are unwilling to make any commitment, any effort. They act as if they are doing you a big favor just by spending time with you," said Marianne, 30, a librarian, who is divorced.

All the good men are taken, they say—or gay. "Meet a man where I live?" scoffed Gerri, who lives in center city. "You mean in the Swish Alps?"

So that leaves the bars.

There are half a dozen spots like PT's—mobbed most nights. It is a scene so depressing that many women avoid it, even though they have tried it at least a couple of times.

"It's not my atmosphere," said Marianne. "It's like freshman week at college. And, besides, it's so easy to get hurt, to pick up a liar. Or you'll get an incredible sob story to get your sympathy. I'm not a games-player. You feel like saying, 'If you're screwed up, stay away.' "

Steven, a 31-year-old center city lawyer, hits the bars regularly and has for years. It is fun. He always finds female companionship. But he despairs of finding Ms. Right there. "I've had it," he says. "I spent last Saturday night at the Penn law library." And, by the way, met a third-year law student (female) there.

"Prime" women are hardest to meet, men acknowledge. They've dropped out of the fray.

Sexual revolution or no sexual revolution, to many men the world is still divided into two categories. There are the "good women"—educated, well-dressed, attractive, bright, interesting, independent, sexually knowledgeable—and they are hard to find.

The second category—Steven calls them "friskies"—are flashily dressed and coiffed and are into "euphoria, drugs (downers)" and sexual exploits of all kinds. They may or may not be well-educated or successful. But they do go to bars.

The first kind a man could have a serious relationship with; with the second kind he probably won't.

A frisky, Steven explains, might want a serious relationship with you or even think she's in love, but "you get rid of her on Sunday morning." Then you spend the day with good friends, or alone, reading.

Alone is where many of the women are, too. "A lot of very attractive women just sit at home," said Robert, a very successful ladies' man. "They stay at home and are desperate. They're not about to go out with any Tom, Dick or Harry anymore. But they don't know where they can find a man who's not jaded, unreachable or untouchable."

Women, it seems, have come farther faster then men. Women complain that behind much-spouted feminist rhetoric lies many a 1950s man. The Alan Bates character from the film "An Unmarried Women"—that cuddly, empathetic, loving, playful, attentive, successful man—is a myth.

"Even the men I know, my friends," admitted Jack, 29 and divorced, "are on a par somewhere less than their female counterparts. They're not as interesting. I can readily see the women's complaint."

"Many of my counterparts have the emotional makeup of their dads," he continued, "which is just not acceptable to the woman of today (These men) aren't open, aren't capable of being in touch with their feelings. They will only go so far, then shy away.

"More women are in touch with their emotions, they feel more of a right to demand that from a male. And many males are not equipped to do that. They are not able to achieve intimacy."

"So," Jack concluded, "wanting a relationship and being able to achieve it are two entirely different things."

Everyone wants a relationship, but nobody knows how to get one. Everyone has the same questions: How do you meet the right person? Where do you go?

A lot of men report that they can't avoid meeting women; they're everywhere.

Robert says he meets them in stores, restaurants, on the street, at the dry cleaners. And he also knows that any night he cares to, he can walk out of a bar with a woman.

For men like him, who've "been on the street a long time"—his last serious relationship ended seven years ago—a certain cynicism ("that's part of the stance") sets in.

Women are a dime a dozen. But, that special woman, well, that's something else again. "After years, things become predictable, you become jaded," he said. "But at the same time, you also become more desperate to find that needle in the haystack."

So, despite the disparity in numbers that men may enjoy while they are sampling the goods, when they get serious, the numbers don't seem to help.

Women like Debby, for example, are hard to meet. She and many of her friends have, in a way, given up. They spend time with each other and wait for fate to step in.

They have resolved not to put life on hold waiting for a man.

Debby won't go to bars and hasn't quite figured out how to meet men. She works at home, making jewelry.

But, she says, she's feeling good about herself. "I think I have a real good attitude towards men because I have a real good attitude about myself."

"I've decided that I should be happy by myself and then, if I'm happy by myself, I'll come across somebody," she said with a mixture of certainty and hope.

That is a philosophy endorsed by therapists like Susan Mathes, whose patients are mainly middle-class females.

"Society has programmed everybody to be in a relationship," she said, "so people grow up searching. They don't know that you need to be happy first to find a good relationship.

"Everyone is scared and confused. They are scared they aren't going to get what they want, so they put a lot of energy into second-best relationships. Many are willing to settle."

"People are tired of being isolated, but they don't know how to become un-isolated," Ms. Mathes said.

"I am overwhelmed about the desperation and sadness I see," she added.

There are, however, other ways of fighting the isolation, of fending off the desperation and sadness. It is not uncommon, for example, for single men and women to spend a great deal of time cultivating or creating a support system for themselves—a net under them for the rough times.

"I may not have a man in my life," Marianne said, "but I'll have people in my life whom I love and who love me . . ."

But having good close friends and being madly in love are not the same. The urge for intimacy—for a relationship—is strong.

So the hunt goes on, at P.T.'s and other places. The searchers want one person they can count on, even if they know that the chances of a fairy-tale ending, of everlasting love, are slim.

"All of my friends want the same thjing, yet there are 30 of them home by themselves on a weekend," Jack said.

"Everybody wants the same thing, but somehow it's just not happening."

Ann Kolson in *The Philadelphia Inquirer,* December 31, 1978. Reprinted by permission of The Philadelphia Inquirer.

CONCLUSION

In this chapter we looked at different marital arrangement structures in different societies. We examined the social factors that account for the wide prevalence of arranged marriages in many of these societies and the reasons that a relatively small proportion of societies allow for free choice of spouse. A predominant correlation exists between types of marital arrangements and types of family systems. Generally, where a consanguineal family form exists—one that emphasizes the rights, obligations, and duties of family members to the larger extended family—there is a tendency for such families to control the marriages of their members. On the other hand, where a conjugal family form exists, there is a greater emphasis on individual motivations and, consequently, a greater freedom is allowed family members in choosing their partners.

Of particular interest to us was the effect of modernization on traditional arranged-marriage structures. The emerging pattern is the breaking down of arranged marriages and the development of free-choice systems based in large part on romantic love. We took a longer look at the mate-selection procedures of Japan and the United States. Japan is a society that historically has controlled the marriages of its youth; the United States has emphasized the importance of individual decision making. Our analysis has indicated that both societies are moving along the same path; both are emphasizing the free-choice system.

Finally, we looked at the emerging phenomenon of computer dating services. Arising out of the needs of an increasingly urbanized society, these agencies seek to be the contemporary counterparts of traditional matchmakers. Their limitations are insurmountable to a society that views romance as the cornerstone of marriage; although they can match people's interests, they cannot guarantee that the one ingredient deemed essential for marriage will surface in the relationship—love.

CHAPTER 9

Sex Roles in Changing Societies

In Chapter 7, we pointed out that sex-linked factors based on physiology as well as patriarchal ideology served as the philosophical and moral justification for discriminatory sex-role differentiation. We observed that variations on the patriarchal theme predominated in Greco-Roman, Semitic, Indian, Chinese, Japanese, and Western Christian civilizations. We also mentioned that in recent years there has been a reevaluation of patriarchal ideology. Modernization processes, scientific and technological developments, rapid social change, and ideological revoluations have led to questioning of the ways that tasks and roles are allocated on the basis of sex. Traditional sex-role-relationship patterns and their ideological justification have been undergoing scrutiny and change. In the past societies marked by relative stability, socially derived gender identifications, and role allocations were non-debatable and were taken for granted. In a rapidly changing world this is no longer the case.

We begin now by turning our attention to societies with different economic systems and examine the relationship between patriarchy and values about the sexes in work and in the family. First, we will look at agricultural societies. Some of them are patriarchal, some are not. However, those, in non-western societies, that are not based on patriarchy were forced to adopt such an ideology through the policies of European colonial administrators. These agricultural societies provide interesting illustrations of how patriarchy influences men and women.

Then, we will explore sex-role relationships in highly industrialized societies.

The focus will be on the relationship between the sexes, particularly as it revolves around the areas of work and the family. This relationship is examined by looking at societies that have officially espoused an antipatriarchal ideology: the Soviet Union, Sweden, and Israel. The Soviet Union has a government that uses Marxist principles in its policies regarding the status of the sexes. The major goal of these policies has been to bring about equality of women and men in all spheres of life. Both Sweden and Israel have developed highly elaborate social welfare systems. They, too, share a desire for equality of the sexes. Unlike the Soviet Union, they start from different ideological points of view that stem from their different philosophical positions and their different societal circumstances. Yet they are striving to change the patriarchal ideology and practices still inherent in their societies. Further, since all of these countries have attempted to bring about equality of the sexes, they should provide a useful perspective for looking at future problems and their possible solutions that countries, such as the United States, may face as they seek to change the formal and traditional barriers to women's full participation in society.

SEX ROLES IN MALE AND FEMALE FARMING SYSTEMS

Anthropologists distinguish between two types of agricultural system: shifting agriculture and plowing agriculture. Shifting agriculture is practiced by clearing an area of trees and brush, burning them, and planting seeds. Rainfall waters the growing crops and the ripened foods are harvested. The cleared fields are used for two or three years and, when the soil becomes depleted, they are abandoned and allowed to lie fallow. The people then move on to cultivate a new area that has been cleared and the cycle is repeated. The technology is rather simple: digging sticks serve as the most common agricultural implement.

The second form of agriculture is plow agriculture. It uses either the plow and fertilizers or irrigation works in permanently cultivating the land. Domestic animals are raised on those parts of the land that are not being cultivated. This is a more advanced technological form of agriculture and is the most widespread form of farming found throughout the world today. Shifting agriculture was found most frequently in Africa, the Pacific, and the Americas.

Ester Boserup (1970), a researcher and consultant with the United Nations and other international organizations, refers to shifting agriculture as the female farming system and plow agriculture as the male farming system. Using Africa as an illustration of a shifting agricultural culture, Boserup observes that this farming system dominated the whole of the Congo region, large parts of southeast and East Africa, and parts of West Africa. Men and young boys helped to fell trees and hoe the land in preparation for the planting of the crops. The bulk of the work with the field crops, including sowing, weeding, and harvesting, was done by women. Before European colonization and involvement, the men devoted their time to hunting and warfare.

Closely tied to the female farming system, shifting agriculture, is a widespread pattern of polygamy that is closely related to economic conditions (Boserup, 1970:37 – 51). In such farming communities, the more wives a man has the more land he can cultivate. This adds to his wealth and prestige. In the typical polygamous marriage arrangement, a husband has two or three wives, each residing in a separate household, cultivating her own land and feeding her children. The economic advantage of having multiple wives leads to an increase in the status of women. This is evident in the payment of a bride price to the prospective wife's family by the bridegroom. Women have relatively high status, enjoy considerable freedom, and have some economic independence derived from the sale of some of their own crops.

The ability to sell one's own crops is an important aspect of the female farming system. The regions in Africa where women dominate the food trade of rural and urban markets are usually those regions that are characterized by a tradition of female farming. Such agricultural products as fruits, vegetables, milk, eggs, and poultry are sold by the women. Boserup (1970:93) reports that marketing is done by two-thirds of adult women in the Yoruba region of Nigeria and by 70 percent of adult women in the towns of Ghana. Associations of women traders are formed and wield considerable power. Boserup points out that the cultural tradition of female farming and involvement in traditional market trade accounts more for her relatively high status and placement in the modern trade sector of contemporary independent African states than does the stage of modernization achieved by any given country.

Although shifting cultivation is quite prevalent in Africa, it is not exclusively found there. It also occurs in Latin American communities and in regions of India and Laos. Here, too, agricultural work is solely within the province of women. Boserup notes that the lazy-man label applied to African males by Europeans is also applied to the males of shifting agricultural communities by both Europeans and by the people of the plowing agricultural communities.

> Thus, the Vietnamese find that the Laotians, with shifting cultivation and female farming, are lazy farmers, and the Indians have a similar opinion of the tribes of Manipur (in North-East India) which likewise practice shifting cultivation and female farming. They are said to take it for granted that women should work and it is quite usual to hear that men wile away their time doing nothing very much. (Boserup, 1970:24)

The value judgment implied in such lazy-men labels reflects an ethnocentric bias by those who do not believe or practice this form of agricultural system. The sex-role allocations do not reflect a laziness attitude, but rather, they reflect a distinctive form of economic enterprise.

According to Boserup, in regions that apply plow agriculture, the division of labor between the sexes is quite different than that in shifting agricultural societies. The agricultural labor force is primarily composed of men, with women being almost completely excluded from field work. Most of the techniques associated with plow agriculture, for example, sowing the land by using draft animals, are done by the men. Women are confined to domestic duties and the care of some of the animals. It is for this reason that Boserup labels plow agriculture as the male farming system (1970:16).

Associated with the male farming system is the low status and treatment of women. Whereas, in female farming systems, men pay a bride price to the prospective wife's family, in societies where plow culture predominates, a dowry is usually paid by the girl's family. With the lessened economic importance of women, there is a concomitantly lower number of polygamous marriages. Where polygamy does occur in plowing cultures, particularly in Asia, it is not closely related to economic conditions associated with agriculture. A further factor contributing to the low status of women is their almost complete economic dependence on their husbands.

Women's low status may be seen as a result of their low economic value. In contrast to a shifting cultivation system where women have high status and economic value, in a plowing cultivation system, women's primary status is in their reproductive role—particularly giving birth to sons, who are considered to be more valuable than daughters.

The low economic value of women is attributed to the fact that female births are not welcome. In some extreme cases, China and India being prime illustrations, female infanticide was practiced. In northern Indian communities that practiced plow cultivation and where women did little work in agriculture, parents bemoaned the birth of daughters, who were considered economic burdens and would eventually cost their parents a dowry. It, therefore, became customary to limit the number of surviving daughters through infanticide. Although this practice has virtually disappeared, vestiges of it still remain in a more subtle form: boys are treated better than girls in matters of nutrition, clothing, and medical care. The result is a much higher mortality rate for female children than for male children. Thus, although female infanticide is no longer prevalent, the neglect of female children continues. Boserup illustrates this with a quote from a study done by an Indian social scientist in a district in central India that had a deficit of women:

> The Rajputs always preferred male children. . . . Female infanticide, therefore, was a tolerated practise. . . . Although in the past 80 years the proportion of the females to males has steadily risen yet there was always a shortage of women in the region. . . . When interrogated about the possibility of existence of female infanticide, the villagers emphatically deny its existence. . . . It was admitted on all hands that if a female child fell ill, then the care taken was very cursory and if she died there was little sorrow. In fact, in a nearby village a cultivator had twelve children—six sons and six daughters. All the daughters fell ill from time to time and died. The sons also fell ill but they survived. The villagers know that it was by omissions that these children had died. Perhaps there

has been a transition from violence to non-violence in keeping with the spirit of the times. (K. S. Bhatnagar cited in Boserup, 1970:49).

Not only were women barred from field work in plow agriculture, they were also barred from public life. The loss of economic function was replaced by a rise in the sexual valuableness of women. The result was a practice of guarding women. This was evident in the physical isolation of women from the outside world and their virtual segregation in the household. In Moslem societies the wearing of the veil symbolized this segregation. In northern India Hindus adopted the Moslem practice of female isolation. Their custom, *purdah,* which literally means a curtain, segregated women from all outside contact. Women were locked up out of sight in the *zenana,* or women's private quarters of the household.

> Women were shut away in crowded, airless and isolated rooms at the back of the house, or screened in by shuttered devides through which only faint glimpses could be obtained of the life outside. These rooms were usually overcrowded, poorly lit and ventilated— the barest and ugliest in the whole house. Under such crowded conditions, shut away from all cultural life, with no stimulation from outside, how could women preserve a sense of beauty? It grew to be an envied boast for a Hindu woman to be able to assert that not even the eye of the sun had ever beheld her face. (Freida Hauswirth, cited in Mace and Mace, 1960:68)

David and Vera Mace (1960) report that estimates place the number of women in *purdah* at the close of the eighteenth century as 40 million. As late as 1930 the number of women restricted to their households was estimated at between 11 and 17 million.

Iran's "New" Women Rebel at Returning to the Veil

YOUSSEF M. IBRAHIM

TEHERAN Iran—"I'll never wear a chador. I'll never put on a scarf. No man—not the Shah, not Khomeini, and not anyone else—will ever make me dress as he pleases. The women of Iran have been unveiled for three generations, and we will fight anyone who bars our way."

The words bounced off the walls of Teheran University's faculty of fine arts last week, laced with rage and spoken by Farzaeh Nouri, a lawyer and woman activist. Several hundred women listened in hushed silence. Loudspeakers carried Miss Nouri's voice outside the hall where another couple of thousand women in an equally sour mood, and several hundred men, stood braving Teheran's nastiest snow storm this winter.

It was March 8, International Women's Day, but the gathering was not a celebration. Throughout the city on that day and into the weekend thousands of women—all dressed in skirts and jeans—staged the most vocal protest yet against Ayatollah Ruhollah Khomeini since the Shiite Moslem leader returned to Iran from 15 years of exile. "Death to despotism under any cover," they chanted. "Unity, struggle, victory." Yesterday, one demonstrator said that several women would immolate themselves if their protests were not heeded within two weeks.

Their fury was unleashed on Wednesday when Ayatollah Khomeini declared that the proper dress for a Moslem woman was the hijab—a code that entails covering the woman's hair, arms, and legs, and hiding her "zinaat," or enticing parts. The few million educated, professional and working women of Iran—many of whom took on the chador as a symbol of defiance against the Shah—are finding out that their return to Western dress since the revolution as well as their choice of life style and work are being circumscribed by a strict ethical code that the Ayatollah, and the secretive circle of religious men who surround him, are laying down every day.

In the past month, the Ayatollah has said that he disapproves of the Family Protection Act of 1975 which grants Moslem women the right to seek divorce in court and protects them against arbitrary rejection or polygamy by their husbands. His religious supporters in the Government have decreed that women can no longer serve in the armed forces. The Moslem leader also described coed education, introduced here only a few years ago, as an evil practice that has turned many of Iran's schools into "centers of prostitution."

Following the Ayatollah's admonition against women "who are naked," zealots at various Government offices began to ban from entry women employees who were not clad in chadors or head scarfs. Bands of hoodlums and Moslem moralists walked the streets chanting "Rusari ya tusari" which translates into "Wear a head wrap or get a head rap."

The women employees of Iran Air issued a statement saying that the only veil women need is "a veil of purity which is in their hearts." They were joined by nurses in many Government hospitals, teachers in high schools and most of the women employees of the Ministries of Agriculture and Foreign Affairs who refused to go to work. In a message to Prime Minister Mehdi Bazargan, the Women's Organization of Iran appealed to the Prime Minister "not to abandon us." Prominent leaders of the women's movement said the assault by the religious establishment was now pushing them to reach out for help from more experienced groups outside Iran. American woman activist Kate Millett and France's feminist Claudine Moullard arrived here this month and have participated in the women's demonstrations.

Many well-respected women intellectuals in Iran, who had allied themselves with Ayatollah Khomeini, are beginning to hedge their support. "The Imam has done an incredible feat here when he rid us of the

Shah, and we will always be grateful to him," said Simin Daneshvar, a noted novelist, journalist and lecturer at Teheran University. "But he has an important drawback in the fact that he is isolated in Qum which is overflooded with backward mullahs who want power and who have little to offer to a democratic state," said Dr. Daneshvar, whose late husband, Jalal Al-Ahmed, a prominent writer, was highly respected by the country's religious leadership, including Ayatollah Khomeini.

But the tide is not running in favor of the minority of educated women in Iran. While the women showed up in force in Teheran over the last four days, Ayatollah Khomeini can call millions into the streets to force his way. The women's movement is almost totally confined to the big cities, particularly Teheran. Illiteracy among Iranian women runs at a rate of 75 percent, 25 percent higher than that among men. The number of women doctors, engineers and white-collar workers, who are the natural constituency of the movement, is small and the limits on their ability to fight for their way of life are many. Their only hope would be ride along with all the dissatisfied factions here—Social Democrats, Socialists and Communists—who feel that religious fanatics are stealing the Iranian revolution.

"This is after all a revolution and there is a new atmosphere in Iran where people feel they have rights and they can fight for them," said Dr. Daneshvar. A young woman technician at Iran's radio and television organization put the same thought differently: "They are calling us American dolls because we don't want to wear the chador. They say our moral character is flawed because we wear Western clothes. But we are getting tired of people who cannot tolerate another way of life or another point of view. Khomeini knows that this is why we got rid of the Shah and he is now talking a different tune from what he used to say in Paris. He has betrayed our trust." She paused, then added with a smile: "Besides, doesn't he know that his Islamic women can also fool around under the chador?"

M. Ibrahim in *The New York Times,* March 11, 1979.©1979 by The New York Times Company. Reprinted by permission.

The phenomenon of the seclusion of women from the outside world and the restriction of their appearance in public is associated with plow cultivation and is virtually unknown in regions of shifting cultivation where women are involved in agricultural work (Boserup, 1970:25−27). To illustrate, the seclusion of women was more prevalent among rich families than poor families in northern India. The reason was that poor women were involved in agricultural work and this economic necessity helped to break the custom. Similarly, in Pakistan, a Moslem society, the wearing of the *burqa,* or veil, was and is a more common sight in Pakistani cities than villages. The *burqa* envelops women from head to foot in a cloaklike garment. It even covers the face, leaving only holes or an open mesh through which the women can see. However, in the villages, where 85 percent of the people live, women do not wear the *burqa* or observe *purdah*. The reason for this is that they have to work in the fields. The *burqa* would be too restricting and *purdah* would be economically unfeasible (Aziz-Ahmed, 1967:48).

In general, then, the movement from shifting agriculture to plowing agriculture is accompanied by a rigid sex-role differentiation, with women becoming more isolated and confined to the domestic sphere and more dependent on the male. In shifting cultivation, where women are involved in economic production, they are highly valued as both workers and mothers. In plow cultivation, where women take little part in field work, they are valued less and their value tends to be restricted to their reproductive role of bearing sons.

SEX ROLES, AGRICULTURE, AND MODERNIZATION: AFRICA

The coming of the European colonizers in Africa initially benefited women in societies that were based on shifting agriculture. The foreign powers ended intertribal warfare and built roads. This gave women greater geographical mobility and increased their trading profit. Missionaries and colonial governmental policies alleviated some of the harsher treatment of women—they suppressed the slave trade, reduced the husbands' power of life and death over their wives, and rescued women who were abandoned after giving birth to accursed twins (Van Allen, 1974:61).

As time passed, however, the colonial imposition had detrimental impact on women. Foreign powers did not recognize or approve of the practice of women being primarily responsible for the cultivation of crops. Europeans had little sympathy with the role allocations of shifting agriculture. They came from plow cultivation societies where men were primarily responsible for agricultural cultivation. They viewed men in shifting agriculture societies as lazy and, with the decline in the importance of tree felling and hunting and the prevention of intertribal warfare, there was little work remaining for the men to do. A self-fulfilling prophecy thus operated—men are lazy because they do not do anything, and they do not do anything because the Europeans were instrumental in the decline of the male-role tasks.

A dramatic change in the relative status of men and women occurred through the colonial imposition of modern agricultural techniques. Europeans saw a need to introduce modern commercial agriculture and its accompanying technology. The crops produced were designed for export to European markets. The Europeans were ethnocentrically biased against women's involvement in agricultural work. They believed that cultivation was a job for men and that men could be better farmers than women. This bias led the colonial male technical experts to train only men in the new farming techniques. Female cultivators were neglected and ignored.

As a result of these practices, the women were at a distinct disadvantage. Whereas the men were cultivating crops by applying modern methods and equipment, the women were confined to use the traditional methods of cultivation—hoes and digging sticks. The inevitable result was that cash cropping became a completely male enterprise. The men were able to expand their production; women who produced the food crops for the family had no cash income for improving their farming techniques. The result was an inevitable decline in the status of women and the enhancement of the status of men. Men were involved with modern technology; women with traditional drudgery. "In short, by their discriminatory policy in education and training the Europeans created a productivity gap between male and female farmers, and subsequently this gap seemed to justify their prejudice against female farmers" (Boserup, 1970:57).

Further, the European policy of recruiting men to work, voluntarily or forced, in road building, mining, and other heavy construction work was detrimental to women as well as men. The migration of husbands and sons to cities or plantations or mines increased the agricultural workload of women. Their independence was not increased. Men still retained the rights to land, to cattle, and to the sale of the cash crops that women cultivated. Women were responsible for cultivating their own land and that of their husbands without any personal benefit.

These practices continue in independent African states, like Kenya and Zambia, where Europeans control mining companies and plantations. Judith Van Allen (1974:61) reports that wages to migrant laborers are set too low to support a whole family. The husband, then, treats his wages as his alone and does not, and cannot, spend them for housing and food for his family. Where provisions are made for nearby housing of worker's families, farm plots are provided so that women produce food for the family. In both situations, then, women are primarily responsible for the feeding and housing of their families. The economic pattern is one of exploitation. Wages are kept at a minimum and women's farming subsidizes both the mining company and plantation wages. The companies, in their turn, make exorbitant profits.

> The small wages migrant laborers receive are not enough to provide for the accumulation of capital for agricultural development. The companies themselves, especially the mining companies (which account for almost half of African exports), are not integrated into local economies; the profits they make are taken out of Africa. Yet their high rates of profit would not be possible except for the unpaid labor of the wives of their African workers, who feed, clothe, and care for themselves and their children at no cost whatsoever to the companies. Far from the traditional agricultural sector being a "drag" on the modern sector, then, as it is sometimes claimed, the modern sector is dependent for its profits on the free labor done by women. (Van Allen, 1974:61)

In summary, the loss of women's rights and status can be seen as a result of agricultural land-reform policies of colonial European administrations. The Europeans were against the involvement of women in agricultural work, which they viewed as antithetical to the proper roles of men and women. This discriminatory policy continues in independent African states that are dependent on foreign aid and investment. The result is that for women in Africa "modernization means more dependency" (Van Allen, 1974:60)

Africa's Women

Robin Wright

Nairobi, Kenya. She is an ambassador and a cab driver. She is a noted marine biologist and a paratrooper. She is an ad agency executive and a supreme court judge. Once she served the United Nations as president. And today she is a prime minister.

Yet she is also considered the world's most primitive woman, for in each case "she" is African.

Long stereotyped as black woman naked to the waist, lip plug or scars decorating her face, the African woman has begun to shatter this narrow image. In the Arab north, the black central states, and the white-dominated south, she has emerged as a key to development during Africa's first generation of independence.

"And it's only the beginning, because the momentum is irreversible," according to Fibi Muneme, a young reporter and columnist for Kenya's Daily Nation. "Once exposed to a more modern way, there's no turning back. I couldn't—and I don't think any young African woman could—go back to my mother's way of life.

Miss Muneme's mother, who lives 100 miles from her daughter's modern Nairobi apartment, still grows coffee and tea on a small farm in an area dominated by her tribe.

She has no running water or electricity. She cooks over a charcoal fire. And she spends most of her day in the fields or selling her crops, which she carries on her back two miles to market, even when her daughter's car is available.

"That way of life will phase out of our family with my mother's generation," says the pantsuited reporter, whose sister is a law student and sister-in-law a teacher.

Miss Muneme quickly admits her situation is exceptional. The majority of Africa's women still lead lives of drudgery and subjugation in rural, primitive environments. "But more and more are getting educations, jobs, and speaking out," she said, "even if it's just to keep a husband from marrying a second wife."

Marriage actually may be the area most radically affected thus far. Traditionally it has been a contractual arrangement between families; after the childbearing period, men and women often led separate lives. Today, indications are that there is less polygamy; partners are more selective; and, in some cases women are delaying marriage or even choosing careers over marriage.

Miss Muneme says she has delayed marriage to develop her career. So has Fatima Bihi, a member of Somalia's UN delegation.

"Equality is what we're after," Miss Bihi says. "Women want equal pay, equal benefits, and the chance for promotion in the same time as a man."

Three factors have caused the change for women in Africa:

Polygamy has forced many women to be more independent. As Mrs. Felicia Ademola, owner of a thriving boutique in Ghana, explains, "We started off a polygamous society, and this emphasized the need for women to be financially independent of men.

"If a man has four wives and only £20 [$50] of income, obviously no one is going to get more than £5 [$12]. But if you can make it £10 [$25], it helps. I think the tradition of women working to have their own income now has become sort of habit with us.

"We find that the men after the baby has come don't care very much. It's the woman who is saddled with the house and the child, and she has to go out and feed it and see that it gets an education. This, over the years, has inculcated in the woman this urge to go out and work, no matter what it is."

Along with growing financial independence, women are gaining political power. They played key roles during the fight for independence. From Algeria to Zaire, they served as paratroopers, spies, and arms smugglers alongside the men. Some gained international prominence, like Algeria's Djamila Bouhired, who was sentenced to death by the French during the Algerian conflict, but escaped execution.

After independence, women again played key roles, since they gained the franchise along with the men. From the beginning, they have had a voice in forming the new indigenous governments.

Because of female involvement—both political and military—most men in power felt "women couldn't just be thrown aside," according to Mrs. Famah Josephine Joka-Bangura, an official in Sierra Leone's Ministry of External Affairs. "We were already established. They never had a chance to subjugate us."

Just this month Elizabeth Domitien of the Central African Republic became Africa's first woman Prime Minister.

Manpower shortages and educational systems often favor women. In an increasing number of states, females outnumber males in school, mainly because men are forced to leave at a younger age to get jobs to support a family.

A shortage of trained personnel has also opened the way for women, as in the eastern state of Somalia. As Miss Bihi notes: "When foreign civil servants were pulled out after independence, the government needed anyone who was qualified. There was such a shortage of trained personnel that little attention was paid to [an applicant's] sex."

The growing rejection of traditional roles and values resulting from these factors can be seen mainly in the migration to the cities. In the past 15 years, thousands of young women throughout the continent have left their villages, many never to return. In the Ivory Coast, for example, seven times as many women as men are moving to the cities to take advantage of better opportunities.

Some join the growing student population. But many· also come to work—and not always in the usual female jobs.

In many nations, the African woman holds a position of high status: as Governor in Zaire, tribal chief in Sierra Leone, Cabinet minister in Cameroon, or playwright in Ghana. She is a member of the foreign ministry in Egypt and a television director in the Ivory Coast. And she is a member of Parliament in at least two dozen African nations.

More often she holds lower-level, formerly male-dominated jobs: In Liberia, women drive cabs; in South Africa, one heads a labor union; and in Nigeria several are police officers. In the Ivory Coast women pump gas, and in Somalia they dig ditches and build houses.

In every nation the African woman is most active in a commercial capacity. Ever since many of the warring clans in the sub-Saharan states used only women to do their bartering, "market mammies" have been a formidable force in economics.

"Women really have built up most of the big [local] commercial concerns in this country," says Regina Addae, head of an advertising agency in Ghana. "And now we are branching off into new fields."

Urban women have also become outspoken through a modern addition to the market role—consumer rights. "Getting involved in campaigns against high prices and poor products is the way most Nigerian women first gain the confidence it takes to speak out generally," explained Mrs. Remi Johnson, who produces a children's TV program in Lagos.

Yet it is also economics that prevents more women from getting an education and good jobs. In several nations, the average per capita income is under $200, which often puts training and opportunities beyond reach.

Liberia's Angie Brooks, for example, had to work as scrubwoman, cook, and dishwasher to pay for the education that led her into law, government, and eventually, in 1969, to the presidency of the UN General Assembly. And South Africa's Miriam Makeba was a servant in a white home before she made it as a singer.

Not all by-products of the new female activism are positive. In Nigeria, officials estimate that 70 to 80 percent of all smuggling is done by women. Prostitution has become a chronic problem in some of the larger cities. And in many nations, the divorce rate is skyrocketing. As a Cameroon man at the United Nations explained, "Many men cannot yet accept a working wife. She presents a threat."

Many governments are trying to bypass some of these limitations of poverty by providing education for all children of both sexes, as exemplified by new programs in Somalia and Nigeria. Scholarships for advanced degrees are increasingly available on an equal basis for women and men in a number of states.

Even the traditional dowry is being phased out or modernized. In 1966, the Central African Republic promised to slap a jail term and a fine of up to $200 on any family demanding a dowry. And Tanzania's new marriage code permits a young man to pay the bride price after the wedding on the installment plan.

"When it is given now, it's thought of more as a wedding gift to a young couple who needs financial help," Miss Muneme explained.

Encouragement has also come from many nongovernment sources, such as the various international conferences held in Algeria, Senegal, Ethiopia, Tanzania, and Kenya to discuss and promote participation of women in public life.

And there are a growing number of national women's groups fighting for women's rights, educational opportunities, and new consumer laws. One of the oldest is Kenya's Maendeleo ya Wanawake, which recently called for a woman in Parliament from every Kenyan province.

The press also has been supportive. "Kenya women . . . were in the forefront of the country's struggle for independence. They have also contributed a great deal to the task of turning the country into a thriving, functional democracy," Kenya's Daily Nation has editorialized.

But the biggest boost may have come from Louise Crane, the Zaire-born author of Ms. Africa." "The feminist movement has much to learn from the women of Africa," she writes. "They have been a vital part of independence movements in all the 38 [now 43] nations that have become free of colonial rule since 1950."

SEX ROLES IN INDUSTRIAL SOCIETIES

It is beyond the scope of this book to fully document the entire range of social historical changes in male-female relationships that have accompanied the advent of the Industrial Revolution over the last 200 years. But certain changes have been especially significant in how they affected sex-role relationships. The demographic revolution, the changing nature of economic life, and the changing ideology pertaining to sex-role and family relationships are important factors.

The demographic revolution includes the lengthened life span and the lowered mortality rate of mothers and infants during childbirth. Before industrialization, women were defined primarily in terms of their reproductive and maternal roles. The scientific advances in medicine that accompanied industrialization had a qualitative effect on the conceptualization of women. No longer need they be defined solely in terms of their maternal role. Their life span has increased to the extent that they no longer devote their longest phase of life to maternity. They are now free to pursue additional roles, both in the family and outside it in the economy.

Industrialization has also been a factor in changing sex roles. Children are no longer the economic necessity that they are in nonindustrial agricultural or hunting-and-gathering societies. They are an economic burden since they are unable to participate in the economic sphere until completing a long period of training. This has resulted in the loss of the importance of women's reproductive role as the entire rationale for their existence. Also, the economic value of the housewife has declined; her economic contribution no longer justifies the housewife role. Evelyne Sullerot (1971:79−80) has observed that the increased use of labor-saving and relatively expensive prepared-food items has made the housewife a consumer rather than an earner through her production in the home. The result is that for women who wish to contribute to the economic well-being of their families, it is more efficient to do so by becoming wage earners than by staying housewives.

In addition, the increased economic demand for labor in industrial socieites increases the involvement of women in the economy. Women particularly have found a place in the tertiary sector (office work and service jobs) of the Western industrial economy, they hold jobs in occupations that are clearly related to traditional female sex-role activities and personality traits. Betty Yorburg (1974:68) has observed that there is an overwhelming concentration of women in canning and clothing factories, teaching, nursing, social work, dietetics, and at occupational levels that require little or no organizational leadership or organizational characteris- tics. As we will see, the pattern is somewhat different in the Soviet Union and Eastern Europe.

The third element, the changing ideology pertaining to sex roles and family relationships, intersects with the other two factors in influencing the changes in the relationship between men and women. The lessened economic importance of children as producers has fostered a shift in values regarding children. Children are socialized in a more permissive manner than when they were of high economic value. The increased life span of the husband and wife has also allowed for the development of a more romantic love ideology, the development of a companionate notion of marriage, and the seeking of erotic gratification within the marital relationship. This has been concomitant with the increase in the number of years that the husband and wife can spend with each other in activities other than childbearing and childrearing.

We will be returning to the discussion of the changing ideologies of men and women in the marital relationship in the next chapter. The discussion of the demographic revolution and its impact on parent-child relationships will be themes discussed more fully in later chapters. We will examine the relationship of men and women within the economy of industrial societies. To put the examination of occupations into perspective, we will be reviewing recent developments in the Soviet Union and contrasting them with those in the United States, Sweden, and Israel. These industrial societies, which are based on varying ideological perspectives, have differentially involved men and women in the economy. Yet, there is similarity underlying all of them. These differences and similarities are the concern of the remaining pages of this chapter.

The socialist countries of Eastern Europe along with the Soviet Union have made a strong and conscientious effort to bring women into positions of equality in the economy. They have been ahead of Western industrial societies in this endeavor and thus the problems and solutions that they have experienced can provide guidelines for Western societies in their attempts to bring women into full participation in the occupational world. Two major elements, ideological and economic considerations, have been the forces behind this movement. Let us examine each in turn.

Ideology has been a prime factor influencing the relationship between the sexes in the Soviet Union. The Marxists, and particularly Friedrich Engels in his *The Origin of The Family, Private Property, and the State* (originally published in 1884), saw monogamy as a tool of economic capitalism. The division of labor between men and women in the monogamous household, according to this argument, has as its effect the subjugation of women and children to the capitalistic patriarchal system. The division of labor between the sexes is viewed as the prototype of the class struggle between the men who own the means of production and those who toil in their behalf. Engles conjectured that the socialist revolution would dissolve the monogamous family system. Women would be able to achieve equality by entering the economic system and there would be created public household services and societal centers for the socialization of children.

> At all events, the position of the men thus undergoes considerable change. But that of the women, of *all* women, also undergoes important alteration. With the passage of the means of production into common property, the individual family ceases to be the economic unit of society. Private housekeeping is transformed into a social matter. (Engels, 1884/1972:83)

The Marxists believe that the housewife role is alienating. Work and social interactions outside the household are necessary to realize one's full potential. Housewives who are cut off from such outside contacts are cut off from the creative source and thus can never realize their full capabilities. Ultimately, the family and the society are the losers by this underutilization of women. This philosophy serves as the foundation for the policies of the Soviet Union after the Russian Revolution of 1917. Lenin, echoing Marx and Engels, saw the necessity of removing women from the "slavery" of the household to full participation in the socialist economy:

You all know that even when women have full rights, they still remain downtrodden because all housework is left to them. In most cases, housework is the most unproductive, the most savage and the most arduous work a woman can do. It is exceptionally petty and does not include anything that would in any way promote the development of the woman. . . . To effect her complete emancipation and make her the equal of the man it is necessary for housework to be socialised and for women to participate in common productive labour. Then women will occupy the same position as men. (Lenin, 1919/1966:69)

Following the Russian Revolution, legislation was passed that aimed to achieve the liberation of women from the household and their equality in all spheres of life. Laws regulating family relationships and questions concerning divorce and abortion were designed to aid in this task. Marriage and divorce regulations were simplified. Abortions were legalized in 1920. The goal was to bring women into full participation in the social economy and into government. The means to accomplish this was seen in the transfer of economic and educational functions from separate households to the society as a whole. Barriers to educational institutions were removed for women. Communal household services, kitchens, dining halls, laundries, and repair shops were established. Infant care centers, kindergartens, and educational institutions for older children were expanded.

However, economic considerations and demographic realities caused vicissitudes in Soviet family law and the implementation of many programs. Throughout Soviet history women have constituted a majority of the population. The Soviet Union had over 25 million war deaths in World War II. These were mostly men. This was in addition to the massive losses in World War I, the revolutionary civil war, the famine and epidemics of the 1920s, the industrialization drive, the forced collectivization of agriculture, and the purges of the 1930s—all brought about a most uneven sex ratio. Census reports from the 1920s, 1930s, 1940s, and 1950s show a significantly greater number of women in the population than men. The range is from 51.7 percent of the population in the first census report of 1926 to 57.4 percent more women than men in the postwar census of 1946. This latter figure represents an excess of 25 million women in a total population of 176 million (Field and Flynn, 1970:260).

It must be emphasized that, for the post World War II population, this difference is at its highest in the marriage-age groups. The census of 1959 reflects this: although more than 90 percent of Soviet men between the ages of 30 and 69 were married, only 72 percent of the women between between 35 and 39, only 62 percent of those between 40 and 44, only 54 percent of those between 45 and 50, and less than half of all women in the ages over 50 were married (Field and Flynn, 1970:261). In human terms, the loneliness of Soviet women is reflected in the poem by Vladimir Semenov addressed to a Soviet girl:

You tried to find him everywhere
He must exist
He is someplace.
You asked:
Where is he? Where?
There was no answer.
Your youth is gone.
You paled and withered.
You, whose beauty shone once,
You do not know the verity
That a wife to no one
You long since are
A widow . . .
You do not know that he was killed
in War
Before you met him. (Semenov, 1959, cited in Field And Flynn, 1970:261)

In addition, then, to the ideological factors, the severe shortage of men in the Soviet Union necessitated women's involvement in the economy. This involvement is not as in Western societies where women constitute a reserve labor force, but rather women are integrated into and indispensable to the Soviet labor force. Although the labor shortage encouraged the employment of women, it also required an emphasis on childbearing to replace the decimated population. The stress placed on childbearing modified the application of the Marxist ideology.

In 1936 abortions were once again made illegal, except in exceptional medical circumstances. Divorces were made more difficult and costly. Unregistered marriages lost their validity and equality with registered marriages. In 1944 a decree was passed encouraging large families by establishing the honorific title, heroine mothers. These were women who had more than five children. They received special economic rewards and honors.

At the onset of these changes, child-care facilities proved inadequate. Eventually, they were expanded, particularly in industries that employed a large percentage of married mothers. Since 1953, the end of the Stalinist era, there has been a return to a more ideological implementation of the Marxist principles regarding male and female relationships. But, the general pattern through Soviet history has been one of vacilation in ideological implementation, which has depended on the needs of the Soviet economy.

This discussion gives us some overview of the history of the factors that have influenced the involvement of Soviet women in the labor force. Now, let us look at the type of jobs these women occupy. Data from the Soviet census of 1959 reveals some interesting facts. Slightly more than four-fifths of the women are employed in industry, construction, transportation, agriculture, and so on. Slightly less than one-fifth are employed in such services areas as education, public health, medicine, and science. Mark G. Field and Karin I. Flynn (1970:262−263) also note that women are underrepresented in occupations that entail directive, managerial, and executive functions. They also tend to be overrepresented in subordinate and minor positions as well as menial jobs.

However, if we compare the Soviet figures for professions—including engineering and medicine—with those of Western countries, one is astonished by the greater proportional participation of Soviet women. Sullerot (1971:151−57) examined data gathered in the 1960s on women's participation in the medical, legal, and engineering professions in the Soviet Union and in Western societies. The differences are overwhelming. For example, there are more women surgeons, specialists, and hospital directors in the Soviet Union than in all the Western countries put together. In the engineering profession, there are over 500,000 engineers (37 percent) in the Soviet Union compared to only 6000 (3.7 percent) in France, the country with the next highest percentage.

Despite the great progress that women have made in the Soviet Union, there still remain problems in the achievment of complete equality. As mentioned previously, a greater proportion of women are found in subordinate positions and menial labor. They also tend to be discriminated against in jobs that demand directive, managerial, and executive skills. A recent survey of Soviet women by David K. Shipler (1976) reports that women do not reach the upper echelons of responsibility in occupational institutions, the professions, or in governmental politics. They are overrepresented at the lower ranks where the prestige and pay is less. To illustrate, although some 71 percent of secondary school teachers are

Table 9.1   Percentage of Women in the Professions

	Medical Profession	Barristers	Engineers
USSR	76.0%	38.0%	37.0%
Great Britain	25.0	4.0	0−0.06
France	22.0	19.0	3.7
West Germany	20.0	5.0	1.0
Austria	18.0	7.0	nd
Sweden	13.0	6.7	nd
Denmark	nd	10.0	nd
USA	6.0	3.0	0−0.07

Note: nd = no data.

Source: Adapted from Evelyne Sullerot, 1971. *Woman, Society and Change,* New York/Toronto: McGraw-Hill (World University Library), pp. 151−152. Copyright 1971 by World University Library, McGraw-Hill Book Company. Reprinted by permission.

women, 72 percent of the principals are men. Similarly, in the medical profession, which is composed of 70 percent women, the heads of hospitals and other medical facilities are usually men; women are at best assistant directors. The large number of women in medicine is explained by the relatively low salaries that doctors make. Doctors earn about 100 rubles a month, about $135, which is about three-quarters of the average industrial wage.

Women in Soviet Face a Stark Choice: Career or Children

CRAIG R. WHITNEY

MOSCOW, Aug. 22—Marina N. Ivanova, a scientist at an institute in a large Soviet city, decided three years ago that she wanted a second child, something the Government wishes more women would do.

She had a daughter but was then unable to place her in a day-care center because the baby was frequently ill. Both her mother and her mother-in-law refused to help. So Mrs. Ivanova had to give up her job to take care of her children, and now she has lost most of her professional scientific skills.

Albina D. Antropova is a 45-year-old woman with an unusual career in the Communist Party leadership. In August 1978, the party transferred her to Yakutia, the capital of an economically developing area in eastern Siberia, where she is editor of the most important newspaper. Asked how her husband had adjusted to the move, she replied, "I do not have a husband."

Vasya and Galina Tarasov work at the same consumer goods store in downtown Moscow. They have a comfortable apartment in a housing project at the southern edge of the city. It takes them more than an hour by bus to get to work by 7:30 A.M., five days a week. Before they go home, they stand for hours in shopping lines to buy food and other necessities. They are saving for a car, but that will take years of waiting and more than $10,000.

Galina has no children. She is too tired, she says, and she has no time.

For Soviet women, the choice is stark: a career, or children, but not both, or at least not both without a great deal of difficulty.

And since most Soviet women work—they make up 51 percent of the labor force—there has been a decline in the birth rate, which has resulted in a population growth rate of less than 1 percent. The rate is even lower in some areas of the Russian countryside and in the cities of the European part of the Soviet Union.

The drop in the birth rate is only one of the consequences of the changed place of women in this society.

The collapse of traditional family and social values, "defeminization" of what Russians used to call "the beautiful half," and a loss of dignity by Soviet men are all being laid to the influence of women's drive toward equality.

The low rate of population growth has become a key economic problem. The country is entering a period of severe labor shortage, and the traditional means of making it up, drafting women into the labor force, is already exhausted.

A running debate in the Soviet official press over what can be done about the problem reveals a clash between inherited social and cultural attitudes and some contemporary Soviet policy goals.

To some extent, Soviet social and economic policy has created its own demographic crisis, without satisfying women's demands for equality.

Despite the often-photographed female construction workers, the female doctors who make up 69 percent of the country's physicians and the 1977 Constitution that proclaims full equality of all citizens without regard to sex, women are as far from being "liberated" in the Soviet Union as they are in the West.

Despite the number of female doctors, only half the chief physicians and supervisors in Soviet hospitals are women. Working women are concentrated in the worst-paid jobs, such as retail sales, where they make up 84 percent of the personnel.

Political power in this country is firmly in the grip of men. Women make up only 24.7 percent of the party's membership. In the party's Central Committee, only 8 of the 287 full members are women, and there are no women on the Politburo, the nation's supreme political organ.

In the traditional Soviet family, the power also lies with men. Soviet women have made some inroads in law, but few in practice. The national census taken in January included for the first time a question about who the head of the family was. Many men were incensed; the answer was no longer automatic, and the results have not yet been published.

The sanctity of the family had been discarded as prerevolutionary superstition until the 1930's. Then Stalin restored family values as necessary for population growth. But women were also drafted into the labor force to insure economic growth.

Soviet men now expect their wives to work, but they also expect them to do most of the housework after they come home.

A Leningrad sociologist has calculated that the average load of work at home for a Soviet woman is one and a half times that of a Soviet man. Counting the time a woman spends at a job outside the home, her overall workload is 15 to 20 percent higher than the average man's, according to this calculation.

A social scientist in Moscow explained these facts to a foreign student of his and was surprised to hear the reaction: "How do you manage to live without sexual life?" the student asked. "Exhaustion must be inhibiting."

Sex is not a problem ordinarily discussed in the Soviet press. But recently there has been a rash of articles deploring the loss of femininity, a quality not much prized in brigades of female construction workers.

"Apparently women's realization of social equality with men has not only positive aspects but certain minuses as well," the journal Literaturnaya Gazeta said recently. Alcoholism is rising faster among women than among men, the article said "even though they are censured more for heavy drinking; when drunk, women easily lose their poise and become unrestrained, loose and aggressive."

Stereotyping of sexual roles is still powerful in Soviet culture. A man's place is thought to be neither in the kitchen nor in the nursery. Images of women, even in modern Soviet literature, stress the ideals of sacrifice and selflessness rather than self-fulfillment.

But the traditional family is an institution under threat.

Until recently in most Soviet households, mothers of small children were able to work only because of the "babushka," the grandmother, usually from the father's side, who lived with the family, fed and cared for the children and cooked the evening meal for the weary working parents.

But babushki want liberation too, even in traditionally Moslem areas of the country.

Sonna Anifayevna, principal of an elementary school in Baku in Soviet Azerbaijan, said she could retire and take care of her grandchildren at home. "But as long as I'm on my feet," she said, "I want to keep on working."

Nadezhda V. Sidorova, chief engineer of a factory in the Volgograd area, recently told a Soviet interviewer: "A babushka helped raise my daughter. But kindergartens and day care centers raised my grandson. How could I give up the factory to be a nanny?"

In the interview, published in Sovetskaya Rossiya last fall, Mrs. Sidorova expressed regrets. She thought that there should be "limits" to a woman's career. Hers had cost her most of her friends, she said, and only a woman could make the family a truly happy place. There are only about 4,000 women like her in leading positions in industrial enterprises.

Materialism—the desire for comfortable furniture, expensive food, night life, the freedom that must be sacrificed for children—is one reason many Soviet working women decide against having children.

Another is simply lack of time. Only 15 percent of housework in the Soviet Union is mechanized, compared with 80 percent in the United States, an economist wrote in the magazine Eko. Another economist calculated that $225 billion of productive labor time is lost needlessly every year for that reason, and the Soviet economy can ill afford the loss.

> For years, Soviet law has sought to break restrictive family patterns, get women to join the labor force and promote childbearing, all at the same time.
>
> Women have been encouraged to work by means of such devices as paid maternity leave 56 days before and 56 days after childbirth as well as free day care centers and kindergartens. They have been encouraged to have more children through social security stipends for each child beyond the third and through "hero-mother" awards given to women with 10 or more children.
>
> Divorce has been made so free of stigma that 400 in 1,000 marriages in major Soviet cities end that way.
>
> Today the atmosphere is changing, but the goals remain as contradictory as ever.
>
> "What does it signify, that now women demand not only equality but supremacy?" Tolstoy wrote in 1895. "Only that the family is evolving and that its earlier forms are disintegrating." Few find his words encouraging today.
>
> Craig R. Whitney in *The New York Times,* August 26, 1979. ©1979 by The New York Times Company. Reprinted by permission.

Shipler (1976) reports a similar pattern existing in light industry and factory work. Women are discriminated against in salary, overrepresented in the more tedious jobs, and underrepresented in administrative posts. This is attributed to the underrepresentation of women in politics. Membership in the Communist Party is mandatory for those who hold many key positions in industry and the professions. And, women make up only 24 percent of the total number of Communist Party members. Here, again, men hold the important positions.

The pattern of discrimination continues in the academic world. Women comprise only 13.7 percent of the membership of the Union of Writers and in the prestigious Academy of Sciences just three of the 243 full members are women. More than two and one-half times as many men as women hold the academic degree of candidate to science, which is equivalent to somewhere between the master's and doctorate degree in the American system. At the doctorate level (the equivalent of a "superdoctorate"), men outnumber women by six to one (Shipler, 1976:9)

Thus, although the Soviet Union has advocated a public policy designed to stimulate women's involvement in the economy and although it has pioneered in the development of maternal and child-care services, it still does not have full equality of women in the work sphere. There are a number of reasons to explain this situation. Examination of these reasons may prove instructive to Western countries in their attempts to develop policies and procedures.

First, there is the continuation of patriarchal attitudes. Traditionally, the people of the Soviet Union share the patriarchal ideology that has characterized Western countries. Even today, despite the introduction of Marxist egalitarian principles over 60 years ago, patriarchy still flourishes. The following quotation by a women who had made a career commanding cargo ships reflects the prevalence of sexism in the Soviet Union. She advises women not to become sea captains and endorses the regulation that closed seafaring schools to women in 1944:

> In the previous 20 years probably hundreds of girls studied to become ship commanders, but only four in the whole country made it. So is it worthwhile to continue spending money teaching girls? You cannot fight against life. To command a ship is still a man's business.
>
> Let men go to sea and women remain on shore to raise children, to occupy themselves with things traditionally feminine. (Anna I. Schchetinina cited in Shipler, 1976:9)

Despite the remarkable achievements of women in the Soviet economy, many men and women share patriarchal assumptions of women's intellectual inferiority and emotional frailty. This attitude is most representative in the women's dual role, which demands that they continue to keep a home (without expecting much help from their husbands) and at the same time that they hold down a full-time job. The result is that women work longer hours than their husbands; in addition to their full-time jobs they put in an additional five to six hours a day in household activities. Their task is complicated by the fact that there is little domestic help, there are few labor-saving devices available, and few conveneiences, such as supermarkets and prepackaged food. Traditional sexist attitudes persist in the household. Soviet men view household tasks as "feminine" and refuse to do their fair share in the household. David Shipler observes that "it is common to go into the homes of Moscow intellectuals and discover women professionals with their own careers, who participate fully in conversation and are accustomed to having their views respected. Yet it is rare to see men clearing tables, shopping for food or doing housework" (1976:9).

A second factor is the emerging patterns of marriage in the Soviet Union and the changing ideas regarding childrearing and family roles. The Soviet Union originally conceived of a minimal role for the family and placed higher stress on family members' involvements with outside institutions. This has changed in recent years to a greater emphasis on the closeness and intimacy of the family and its concern with its members' formation and emotional support (Fogarty, Rapoport, and Rapoport, 1971:85). Tied to this conceptualization is the desire for the mother to spend more time with her children, especially the very young. The implications are that the wife should restrict her commitments in outside involvements.

Also occurring is a change in the assessment of institutionalized nursery care and early childhood day care. There has been some discrediting of these institutions in terms of their potentially negative effects on children. The result is a tendency to make less use of them and there also has been considerable popular resistance to them. The result has been a dilemma that still has not been resolved. On the one hand, there is the desire of the state that women should continue to be involved with their jobs during the early childrearing years and, on the other hand, there is the desire of the couple for greater involvement of the wife with her children. Although some congruity of these objectives is now occurring, sentiment has swayed toward a greater emphasis on individual and personal development and on the family as a central agent to it (Fogarty, et al. 1971:84−91).

A third reason for the dilemma between women's work and family roles is the failure of employment agencies to develop recruitment, training, and promotion practices adapted to the life cycle (i.e., maternity) of married women. Michael T. Fogarty et al. (1971) report that this failure is combined with the failure to develop career patterns for women that would assist them in making it to top-echelon positions.

Fogarty et al. (1971) believe that the fourth reason in the uncertain record of women's career achievement is related to the ambiguity regarding feminine identity and its implication for working life. The traditional conceptualization of femininity is still echoed in the Soviet economy. Roles related to sex differences are still prevalent in Eastern Europe and the Soviet Union:

> . . . girls and women tend to be more conscientious and disciplined than boys and men, but less path-breaking; than girls' interests tend to run to the humanities, to "maternal" fields such as teaching or medicine and to menial work, rather than to outdoor work, technology, or mastering nature as such, that women tend to be more emotional, personal, and concerned with detail than men, and less able to deal logically and objectively with broad issues; that they tend towards ancillary rather than leadership roles; that married women tend to defer publicly to their husbands, and to be reluctant to earn more or reach higher than them; and that both women and men tend to accept that a mother, unlike a father, will treat her domestic role as primary (Fogarty, et al., 1971:95)

Extensive attempts have been made to remove these alleged and real sex differences. There have been developments in coeducational curriculums to provide girls with equal opportunities to develop technological skills and to enter into all fields of work. Further, new attitudes are emerging, encouraged by governmental programs, such as the belief that feminine roles can include both career and motherhood. The choice of career should be based on a principle of equal opportunities and the free choice of men and women. But, Fogarty and his coauthors conclude that there still remains uncertainty between the old and new conceputalizations that have not been fully realized. The dilemma is to reach some accommodations in terms of the acceptance of some new criteria relating to sex differences and the achievement of the goals relating to equal opportunity.

In summary, the Soviet Union has to a large extent been in the forefront in the effort to establish equality between the sexes and has made giant steps toward the accomplishment of that goal. Yet, formal and traditional barriers to women's progress still exist. However, in light of the relatively minor advances of Western countries in the quest for sexual equality of opportunity, the achievements of the Soviet Union are notable. Further, its experience provides a useful perspective in which to foresee the development of problems and ultimate solutions of Western countries in their movement toward achieving sexual egalitarianism.

THE WESTERN EXPERIENCE: SWEDEN

For almost half a century, Sweden had been under the influence of the Social Democratic Party. In that time, Sweden has created one of the most progressive social welfare systems in the world. Comprehensive governmental programs and services exist in the fields of health, education, and welfare. Parents receive family allowances for their children. Education is free and universal. Old age pensions and benefits are available to all citizens, regardless of the amount of their prior contributions. Day-care facilities are numerous and are well utilized. Birth control information, contraceptive devices, and abortions are readily available.

Sweden has made great strides in bringing about gradual equality between men and women in politics, education, employment, and the family. To accomplish this goal the Swedes approach the problem through far-reaching policies carefully conceptualized and pragmatically implemented. To illustrate, Sweden during the depression of the 1930s had a dramatically declining birthrate. People could not afford to have children. The Swedish government realized that, if they wished the population to rise, it must implement a comprehensive and supportive social welfare program. This was essential to encourage marriage and childbearing and to protect the lives and health of both the parents and the children. The policy that was developed was multifaceted and included the following elements: "encouragement of sex education and contraception; state-financed housing; a child-allowance benefit for all families; the creation of mother-baby health clinics throughout the country; a commitment to feed every schoolchild every day; and medical services for all'' (Herman, 1974:77).

Although Sweden has been notably successful in its attempt to equalize the relationship between the sexes, vestiges of traditional patriarchal ideology still are manifest. In work, women are predominantly employed as office workers and sales help. They are overrepresented in the lowest civil service grades—81 percent are women—and underrepresented—only 3 percent—in the highest paid grades. According to the 1972 tax tables, women's income was almost half that of men's, 14,600 crowns to 28,600 crowns (Herman, 1974:78). This variation reflects women's lower job status positions and the proportionately greater number of women who are employed part-time. This persistence of part-time employment and lower echelon positions for women reflects the traditional viewpoint that women's place is in the home.

The double burden of the employed wife is as prevalent in Sweden as it is in the Soviet Union and in Eastern European societies. The old idea that women have greater responsibility in the home for both domestic activities and child care still predominates. This has handicapped the drive for the advancement of women in the field of employment, in labor unions, and in political organizations.

The Swedish approach to bringing about changes in these traditional ideas has been to broaden the discussion concerning women's rights and "the problem of women" in relation to the overall problem of sex roles. In 1962, a controversial book was published that has stimulated this debate. This book, *Kvinnors Liv och Arbete (The Life and Work of Women)* (Dahlström, 1962), consists of a series of essays by noted Scandinavian sociologists, social psychologists, and economists who center their attention on the overall problem of sex-role discrimination in society. The book was a major breakthrough in that it placed the discussion about the "women's question" into the larger social context. One of the contributors to this book, Rita Liljestrom, summarizes by alluding to the similarity between sex-role discrimination and racial discrimination:

> If a society shows sexual discrimination in the labor force, if its decision-making bodies, councils, and parliament contain an overwhelming majority of men, if sexual discrimination is practiced in connection with household tasks, it is as unreasonable to talk about 'the problem of women' as to lay the blame for racial prejudice upon the Negro. (Liljestrom, 1970:204)

The placing of "women's problem" into the broader social issue relating to discrimination and civil rights was a significant turning point in changing traditional ideas. The widening of the debate beyond the conventional focus of discussions on the conflict between women's two roles—family and work—to encompass the two roles of men has also had an effect on men. Liljestrom (1970:200−1) notes the use of the expression "men's emancipation," means the rights of husbands and fathers to become involved in child care and domestic activities. Further, the phrase is taken to mean that options for both men and women should be expanded in both economic and in family institutions.

In conclusion, what has been occurring in Sweden can be insightful for other Western industrial countries and the United States. Sweden is far ahead of the United States in achieving the ultimate goal of sex equality. Its government has been progressive and farsighted. It has supported and led meaningful programs and reforms. However, the traditional idea of masculine dominance still persists and hinders the drive for equal opportunity for men and women.

THE WESTERN EXPERIENCE: ISRAEL

Our last societal illustration in this chapter will be that of Israel. We will focus on the kibbutz movement. The kibbutz movement is a prime illustration of communities whose major goal is the emancipation of women and the establishment of complete equality between men and women in all aspects of life. The kibbutz is a collective agricultural settlement comprising betweeen 100 to 2000 inhabitants. There are some 230 kibbutzim (plural of kibbutz) in Israel with a population of about 100,000. This is a little less than 5 percent of Israel's population.

The kibbutz movement originated in the beginning of the 20th century by East European Jews who settled in what was then Palestine. It represented an attempt to implement the ideologies of Zionism (the belief in a Jewish homeland), socialism, and the ideals of Tolstoy and his disciples concerning the virtues of agricultural pursuits and the belief that the greatest happiness is a return to mother earth.

There are a great number of different types of kibbutzim in Israel. Politically, they range from mild social democratic ideologies to extreme left Marxian positions. Generalizations, therefore, must be made cautiously. Most, generally, try to maintain the belief in economic collectivism. Essentially, this principle eliminates private property and the opportunity to accumulate wealth. The common feature of these collective settlements is the common ownership of property and the communal organization of production and consumption. Except for a few personal belongings, all property belongs to the community. All income goes into the common fund. Everything is provided by the community, based on the collective decision of the community. Through a general assembly and an extensive committee system, the member's needs are provided on an equalitarian basis.

A most striking feature of the kibbutzim is their attitudes and practices regarding the family. Kibbutz founders expounded their revolutionary and collectivist ideology toward the family. The kibbutz philosophy demanded the complete commitment and involvement of all its members (kibbutzniks). It was felt that this goal could be best accomplished if family and kinship ties were minimized. The late Israeli sociologist, Yonina Talmon (1965b:146), stated that the kibbutz founders saw the family as an obstruction to the desired collectivist community. Individuals' attachment to the family and their intense emotional involvement with family members were seen to infringe on the loyalties to the kibbutz. They also believed that involvement with family members might impede the ideological and work goals of the kibbutz. Finally, it was felt that "inasmuch as they act as buffers and protect the individual from the direct impact of public opinion, they reduce the effectiveness of informal collective control over members" (Talmon, 1965b:261).

With this antifamilistic ideology, the kibbutz founders rejected the double standard for men and women and the traditional patriarchal structure of the Jewish family. This traditional structure required women and children to be subservient to the husband and father in the family. The division of labor was rigidly segregated in the Jewish family. Women had little involvement with external family matters in the social, cultural, religious, and economic life of the community. Women were confined primarily to the house; their activities revolved around children and domestic chores.

The kibbutz movement seeks to counter the debilitating effects of the family on women and its accompanying double standard through a series of dramatic steps designed to limit drastically the function of the family. Men and women are given jobs based on egalitarian principles. Although husbands and wives are housed in separate household units, their meals are cooked in communal kitchens and taken in the communal dining room. Clothing is purchased, washed, and ironed by assigned kibbutzniks. The community is run as a separate household. From infancy, children are raised in a separate children's house with other children of their own age group. They sleep, eat, and study in these houses. The children are allowed to visit their parents and siblings for several hours daily, but they are raised as a group by community members assigned to this task. Thus many of the tasks traditionally performed by the wife/mother are transformed in the kibbutz into occupational roles requiring trained and professional staffs.

This, then, is the philosophical basis of the kibbutz movement and the implementation of that philosophy. However, in recent years there is evidence that the collectivist system is losing ground to the reemergence of individual values and patriarchal patterns.[1] Manifestations of this change are apparent in the development of discriminatory sex-role differentiation patterns in the work sphere and the reestablishment of family and kinship ties. Talmon (who had done extensive studies on the kibbutz movement before her untimely death) examined (1965a) the developing division of labor between the sexes in both the internal system of the family and the external system of the occupational and leadership areas. She found that whereas the predominant egalitarian ideology is formally applauded, in reality a segregated sex-role division of labor exists.

In the sphere of the family, there has been a gradual increase of family functions. Parents are now taking a more active role in raising their children. This is a partial reversal of the collective's role in the care and socialization of the children. Further, although the differentiation between the mother and the father role is not as segregated as it is in the United States, there is a trend to a division of labor between the parents. Women become more involved in taking care of the children in the home. Women also are becoming more involved in the domestic activities of the home: cleaning, washing clothes, and so on. Men, in turn, have their responsibilities geared to work outside the home—in the yard, on the farm, and in dealing with communal affairs of the kibbutz. The result is that "in the eyes of the growing

---

[1]For an extensive review of contemporary patterns in the kibbutzim, albeit with a different interpretation than that given here, see Lionel Tiger and Joseph Shepher, *Women in the Kibbutz* (1975).

child, the father emerges gradually as the representative of the kibbutz, and its values within the family, while the mother acts primarily as the representative of the family in the kibbutz'' (Talmon, 1965a:147).

Sex-role differentiation is also developing in outside-work assignments and in the involvements of kibbutz committees. Men's work activities are concentrated mainly in agriculture and in the production services: transportation, equipment- and machinery-maintenance shops, and the like. Women are found in extensions of traditional women's occupations. Workers in the communal kitchens, in the clothing shops and stores are almost exclusively women. In education, women are found teaching in the primary grades, men at the high school level.

Talmon found a gradual trend toward growing sex-role differentiation in the participation on committees and in the overall leadership of the community. Generally, men predominate in overall leadership and in the central governing committees. The committees on which women are predominant are those involving education, health, and consumption. Thus, here too, the sex-role division of labor begins to follow traditional patriarchal male-female patterns.

Talmon accounts for the growing sex-role differentiation in the kibbutz to two major reasons. First, there are the vestiges of traditional patriarchal thought that surfaced again in the kibbutzim. Second, there are the factors attributed to pregnancy and lactation. Childbearing necessitates that women become involved with activities that do not jeopardize their child-care role. Tied to pregnancy and childrearing is the overall increase in family function. The family thus regains some of its lost functions and becomes more active in internal activities. In addition, ''the identification with the specifically and typically feminine role of mother undermines the masculine image of the feminine role upheld by the official ideology and weakens the resistance to sex-role differentiations'' (Talmon, 1965a:151).

The role differentiation within the family gradually exerts pressure and influences the work sphere. Lines between appropriate work for men and women become more sharply delineated. The equalitarian basis for the designation of occupations becomes lost. The result is the continued acceleration of sex-role differentiation.

The implication of these findings is that the differentiation of sex roles is ultimately based on physiological factors—the reproductive function of women. The argument is that even when a social group desires to construct a community based on sexual equality, the biologic differences between the sexes have a determining role. Tiger and Shepher (1975), in a polemical study of women in the kibbutz, continue this argument by postulating that biologic reasons may ultimately be the determining causal factor in the allocation of sex-role patterns. It is our opinion that biology, although influential, is not deterministic. That is, although it would be negligent to ignore the influence of biology on human activities, we believe that the pervasive influence of the traditional patriarchal ideology combined with other social factors can best account for the reemergence of discriminatory sex-role differentiation patterns.

Further, it must be emphasized that the kibbutz movement is not an isolated social phenomenon. It occurs in a society that is predominately a Western-oriented capitalistic system. A study by Dorit D. Padan-Eisenstark (1973) found that women have not achieved an appreciably higher degree of equality in Israeli society than their counterparts in other Western industrial societies. More specifically, the findings—based on a secondary analysis of surveys and studies conducted in Israel from 1930 through 1971—reveal that women's employment is concentrated in various service occupations. Almost three-quarters of the women held jobs in teaching and nursing occupations, clerical and service occupations, and the catering industries. Padan-Eisenstark points out that these occupations are those that have been traditionally linked to women and represent the professionalized form of the domestic household tasks. In addition, a large number of women held jobs that had flexible hours and were part-time. This allowed them to be less committed to employment and more involved with family and domestic tasks. Finally, Israeli women are underrepresented in all managerial and high-status professional occupations. Thus the kibbutzim pattern is a reflection of the larger societal patterns.

In conclusion, the kibbutzim are not isolated from the dominanting Israeli society that continues to discriminate against women following patriarchal sexist guidelines. Nor are its members immune to this ideology. The kibbutz movement cannot be studied and treated as if it were a totally autonomous and independent entity. Although the kibbutz movement can be viewed as a noble experiment and although it has not achieved the long-sought goal of sex equality, its failure in this area can be attributed to specific social factors rather than through unproved biologically determined theories of causality.

CONCLUSION

This chapter presents a broad range of topical areas regarding sex-role relationship patterns. We began the chapter with an examination of the arguments that seek to explain the almost universal female subordinate patterns that exist cross-culturally and historically. Two factors, one physiologically based, that is, women's reproductive role and their lesser physical strength, and the second ideologically based, that is, patriarchy, have served as the philosophical and moral justifications for discriminatory sex-role differentiation. These ideologies have held sway in Greco-Roman, Semitic, Indian, Chinese, Japanese, and Western Christian civilizations.

Next, investigation of different economic systems and the accompanying sex-role differentiation patterns was undertaken. We found that in shifting agricultural economies the prevalent pattern was equalitarian. On the other hand, in plow agricultural systems the patriarchal ideology held sway. As a result of imperialistic colonization, many shifting agricultural systems, most notably in Africa, were forcibly transformed to plowing agricultural systems. In addition, the Western patriarchal ideology accompanied this transformation. The result was a decided loss of feminine status and power.

The nature of the male-female division of labor in industrial societies was then investigated. To dramatize the continued impact of patriarchal sexist thought, we looked at societies that have adopted the goal of female liberation and of sexual equality as official policy. European Marxist countries and the Western societies of Sweden and Israel espouse the egalitarian ideology, but they have not achieved total equality. They still are plagued by vestiges of the discriminatory ideology of patriarchy. Although great strides have been taken by women in the occupational economy, they are overrepresented in service occupations and underrepresented in managerial and executive positions. Further, they are burdened by a dual role that expects that in addition to their full-time occupational involvements they must also be involved full-time with home tasks—domestic and chid-care activities. Husbands and fathers, although equally involved in the occupational sphere, continue to be relatively noninvolved in the home sphcre.

The examination of sex-role differentiation patterns occurring in these industrial societies provides Americans with an interesting comparative perspective. The pitfalls, problems, and experiences of these societies, more advanced than we are in sexual equality, can serve as important models in our own drive toward sex-role liberation. By profiting from the experiences of other countries, we may be able to develop alternative strategies in assuring sex equality.

10

Marital Relationships: The World of Work and the World of the Home

This chapter is a continuation of the previous one since many of the same underlying issues that were discussed there are also pertinent here. In the previous chapter we emphasized different types of economic systems and how they are related to the male-female relationship. These underlying conditions, which have influenced the differentiation between the sexes, are notably manifest in the marital relationship. The economic variable framework will allow further exploration and insight into the relationship between the sexes in marriage.

Our orientation in this discussion will be on the activities of males and females in public and private spheres. The differentiation of these spheres of activities has been a factor dominating the expression of marital roles. They are important in determining power, privilege, respect, and deference patterns within the family. We will begin our discussion by looking at this differentiation in preliterate societies, and then we will shift our attention to a social historical examination of marriage in Western Europe and the United States since the Industrial Revolution.

PUBLIC AND PRIVATE SPHERES OF ACTIVITY: NONINDUSTRIAL SOCIETIES

William N. Stephens (1963) in his excellent cross-cultural survey of the family examined three aspects of husband-wife roles: togetherness versus separateness, men's work versus women's work, and power and privilege. Stephens used existing ethnographic data and interviews with ethnographers on family deference customs and power relations. These data comprise the ''ethnographer-interview'' and total 53 cases. Stephens found that traditional barriers curtail the intimacy, sharing, and togetherness of husbands and wives. Many nonindustrial societies practiced avoidance customs in public: the ethnographers interviewed said that these societies did not allow husbands and wives to share affection in public. Only 11 societies allowed this. Further, in over half of the reported cases, husband and wife may not even touch each other in public (Stephens, 1963:275). These avoidance customs were carried over into the private sphere. In the home, traditional barriers ordained that the husband and wife sleep in separate beds, live in separate houses, own separate property, eat separately, and go separately to community gatherings.

Stephens also found that the sexes worked at separate tasks. As we have seen in the previous chapter, this task differentiation was not based on biologic capabilities or limitations of the two sexes. Yet, the women's capacity for bearing and nursing children tends to influence the work allocations of men and women. Stephens uses George P. Murdock's (1937) cross-cultural survey of the division of labor by sex and his own ethnographer-interview data. He finds that men were assigned the following tasks: metal working, stone cutting, lumbering, and killing or herding large animals. They were also given tasks that required geographic mobility: hunting, fishing, warring, and trading away from home. These tasks were allocated to men not so much because of their alleged superior physical strength or ability but because of their exemption from childbearing and child care. This was a chronic condition for women in precontraceptive eras. A wife's work was centered in the home and in nearby locations because she could tend to her babies at the same time she completed other tasks. These tasks were nearly always done by women: cooking, water carrying, and grain grinding as well as housekeeping and care of young children. Stephens also notes that in most preliterate societies women's work was not solely confined to the home; they also were involved in the subsistence work of getting, growing, and processing food. In hunting-and-gathering societies women gather plant food while the men hunt. In agricultural societies, particularly those that practice shifting agriculture, women do a large share of the farm work.

The third aspect of husband-wife roles examined by Stephens was power and privilege. He found that power tends to be controlled by men.

> If there are social inequities between the sexes, women tend to be the ''underprivileged minority group'' in matters of marriage form (polygyny), sex restrictions, marital residence (moving far from home), and access to public gatherings and public office. (Stephens, 1963:305)

Stephens concludes that traditional rules having to do with power relationships tend to be made for men: deference patterns (the ritual expression of cultural expectations of an unequal power relationship) and real power (who dominates and who submits, who makes the family decisions, who commands, who obeys, etc., in the family) are in the majority of cases determined by men. Stephens examines some of the widespread transcultural discrimination against women. The following findings are based on his ethnographer-interview sample:

The Double Standard

In a good many societies, sex restrictions are more severe for women than they are for men. For thirteen sample societies, premarital sex restrictions bear more heavily on girls than on boys. . . . For no society is it reported that premarital sex regulations are stricter for men than for women. Likewise, I know of no society in which restrictions on adultery are more severe for men than for women. On the other hand, in eight cases, husbands are free to practice adultery, but wives are supposed to remain faithful. . . . For two other cases, adultery rules seem to be stricter for wives than for husbands.

Deference

In six societies in my ethnographic notes, a wife must kneel or crouch before her husband. . . . In six societies, the woman is reported to walk behind her husband. . . . For five cases, the husband is said to get the choice food. . . . For no society in my ethnographic notes is there any mention of husband-to-wife deference customs.

Power

In the language of politics, husbands and wives may be viewed as two separate and opposing interest groups. If a husband gains in power, his wife must lose power; if he gains in privilege, his wife loses privileges, and vice versa. Marriage—seen in these terms—is a power struggle. The husband may "win" (and become a dominating patriarch) or "lose" (and be a hen-pecked husband): or they may "tie" (and have an equalitarian marital relationship). One gets the impression that men usually have an initial advantage in this struggle. It looks as if men often make the rules to suit themselves; the deference customs, the jural rights, generally point in the direction of a power advantage for the husband. (Stephens, 1963:290, 294, 302)

Many investigators have asked why there is almost a universal classification of women to secondary status. Sherry Ortner (1974:69), an anthropologist, observes that "everywhere, in every known culture, women are considered in some degree, inferior to men." She provides some answers when she observes the types of criteria particular cultures use to assign women inferior roles. The first type of data are the statements of cultural ideology that explicitly devalue women, their roles, their tasks, and their products. Second, there are the symbolic devices, such as the attribution of defilement, associated with women. Last, there is the exclusion of women from participation in or contact with areas believed to be most powerful in the particular society, whether religious or secular. We will concentrate our discussion on the third element in this analysis.

A recent explanation on the universality of women being alloted secondary status is offered by sociologists and anthropologists who see this stemming from the

Table 10.1 Comparative Data on the Division of Labor by Sex

	Number of Societies in Which Activity is Performed by				
	Men Always	Men Usually	Either Equally	Women Usually	Always
Metal working	78	0	0	0	0
Weapon making	121	1	0	0	0
Pursuit of sea mammals	34	1	0	0	0
Hunting	166	13	0	0	0
Manufacture of musical instruments	45	2	0	0	1
Boat building	91	4	4	0	1
Mining and quarrying	35	1	1	0	1
Work in wood and bark	113	9	5	1	1
Work in stone	68	3	2	0	2
Trapping or catching of small animals	128	13	4	1	2
Work in bone, horn and shell	67	4	3	0	3
Lumbering	104	4	3	1	6
Fishing	98	34	19	3	4
Manufacture of ceremonial objects	37	1	13	0	1
Herding	38	8	4	0	5
House building	86	32	25	3	14
Clearing of land for agriculture	73	22	17	5	13
Net making	44	6	4	2	11
Trade	51	28	20	8	7
Dairy operations	17	4	3	1	13
Manufacture of ornaments	24	3	40	6	18

Agriculture—soil preparation and planting	31	23	33	20	37
Manufacture of leather products	29	3	9	3	32
Body mutilation, e.g., tattooing	16	14	44	22	20
Erection and dismantling of shelter	14	2	5	6	22
Hide preparation	31	2	4	4	49
Tending of fowls and small animals	21	4	8	1	39
Agriculture—crop tending and harvesting	10	15	35	39	44
Gathering of shellfish	9	4	8	7	25
Manufacture of non-textile fabrics	14	0	9	2	32
Fire making and tending	18	6	25	22	62
Burden bearing	12	6	33	20	57
Preparation of drinks and narcotics	20	1	13	8	57
Manufacture of thread and cordage	23	2	11	10	73
Basket making	25	3	10	6	82
Mat making	16	2	6	4	61
Weaving	19	2	2	6	67
Gathering of fruits, berries and nuts	12	3	15	13	63
Fuel gathering	22	1	10	19	89
Pottery making	13	2	6	8	77
Preservation of meat and fish	8	2	10	14	74
Manufacture and repair of clothing	12	3	8	9	95
Gathering of herbs, roots and seeds	8	1	11	7	74
Cooking	5	1	9	28	158
Water carrying	7	0	5	7	119
Grain grinding	2	4	5	13	114

Source: Adapted from George P. Murdock, "Comparative Data on the Division of Labor by Sex," *Social Forces,* 1937. Vol. XV, p. 552. Reprinted by permission of University of North Carolina Press.

relegation of women to the domestic, private domain of the household, whereas men remain in the public sphere of activities. The greater involvement of women with childbearing and childrearing leads to a differentiation of domestic and public spheres of activity. Michelle Zimbalist Rosaldo (1974:36) in her introductory essay to the excellent anthology of cross-cultural writings on women, *Woman, Culture, and Society,* argues that "women's status will be lowest in those societies where there is a firm differentiation between domestic and public spheres of activity and where women are isolated from one another and placed under a single man's authority in the home." Rosaldo believes that the time consuming and emotionally compelling involvement of a mother with her child is unmatched by any single involvement and commitment made by a man. The result is that men are free to form broader associations in the outside world through their involvement in work, politics, and religion. The relative absence of women from this public sphere results in their lack of authority and power. Men's involvements and activities are viewed as important, and cultural systems give authority and value to men's activities and roles. In turn, women's work, especially when it is confined to domestic roles and activities, tends to be oppressive and lacking in value and status. Women are only seen to gain power and a sense of value when they are able to transcend the domestic sphere of activities. Societies that practice sex discrimination are those in which this differentiation is most acute. Those societies in which men value and participate in domestic activities tend to be more egalitarian.

Rosaldo points out that in contemporary America, although giving perfunctory lip service to the idea of sex equality, society, nonetheless, is organized in such a way that it heightens the dichotomy between private and public, domestic and social, female and male. Further, through the restrictions of the conjugal family, women tend to be relegated to the domestic sphere. Yet, when the society places values on men's work and women's work, the tendency is to place greater value and higher priority on the public work associated with men rather than the domestic work associated with women. This is symbolized by the phrase, "only a housewife." This dichotomization is encouraged by the admonitions placed on women to cease work and take almost exclusive care of small children and to sacrifice their career aspirations to those of their husbands. These normative strictures perpetuate the assignment of women to the domestic, private sphere, whereas men are almost exclusively involved in the higher valued and higher status activities of the public sphere.

The question then arises on why this particular state of affairs exists and what are the factors that account for its prevalence. We believe that it would be useful to trace this development in Western civilization since the beginning of the Industrial Age.

A Major Resource Awaiting Development: Women in the Third World

Adrienne Germain

Who does the major part of the work in poor countries? Women do. Yet they are probably the most underrated economic resource in "resource-poor" third world countries.

For them, work is neither a choice nor a right, but a necessity. The majority are producers of food, household implements and other market-able items; they hire out as wage labor. They do not want "liberation" but tools and training. They have usually been denied both because development policies assume men work and women raise children.

Governments and international assistance programs have been virtually oblivious to certain paradoxes.

Women in sub-Saharan Africa provide as much as 80 percent of the labor (often eight to ten hours a day) necessary for food production. But when training, improved seeds and machines are available, they go most often to men.

In Chile, Colombia and Kenya at least 25 per cent of families are headed by women who must work for their families to survive. Even in households headed by men, most women need to work. But, the argument is still made that it is impossible to employ women when male unemployment rates are high.

Ironically, modern technology often throws women as well as men, out of work. Hundreds of thousands of the poorest women in Indonesia and Bangladesh have lost their only source of income (rice-husking) because machines can do the job faster. But, no plans have been made to develop substitute sources of income.

Everywhere in the third world women are tremendously burdened by domestic chores (four to six hours a day to grind corn and fetch water for the family's meals) that consume energy and time that could be used more productively. But, little attention has been paid to developing simple machinery (such as maize mills) to reduce those burdens and make it possible for women to invest time in literacy classes.

Government and international agencies are only beginning to recognize a number of important things:

- People are one of the few abundant development resources most third world countries have; they cannot afford to abuse and under-utilize fully half that resource.
- The solution of the world food problem depends to a large extent on improving the productivity of all workers, especially women.

- Reduction of population growth rates will be facilitated if women's dependence on large numbers of children can be reduced. As long as motherhood is defined as women's main mission in life, women have good reason to continue having large families.
- Achievement of an equitable distribution of national wealth and services depends not only on distribution to different economic groups but also to women and men within each economic group.

Few people have thought much about the issues raised here. No one seems to know what to do about them. There are at least three beliefs that prevent objective discussion.

First, policymakers, at present primarily male, assume the issue is "women's lib" and therefore culturally imperialistic. It is neither. The issue is how to enable all people to be more productive in order to reduce poverty.

Second, policymakers have their own ideal concepts of what women should and should not do, which often contradict the reality of poor women's lives.

Third, it is usually argued that national economic development problems need to be solved before women's lives can be improved. This argument ignores the fact that women's work is part of the solution.

One of the most important messages of the International Women's Year conference in Mexico is that these and other beliefs are mistaken.

There was consensus at the conference on the critical importance of increasing women's economic and decision-making power not just to benefit women but to accelerate the achievement of national development.

The conference may have helped dissipate debate over whether to act, but arguing over what to do and how is likely to continue. In the meantime, women themselves must take the initiative despite handicaps of inexperience, insufficient education, lack of political and economic power.

Governments and international agencies can be helpful, not only by employing more women and putting them in policymaking positions, but by assigning budget and staff members to help implement the world plan of action agreed on in Mexico.

Specifically, they should support women's organizations as a focal point for work, a source of credit, training, information and community power; develop and distribute work-saving devices (such as wheelbarrows) to lighten the burden of work, and organize training programs in simple accounting, for example, to increase women's productivity.

They should also generate data and analysis on women's actual and potential economic contributions in order to influence policymakers; and change the images of women in the news media, textbooks and other educational materials.

These proposals are necessary steps in the solution of an immense problem. They focus on women's strengths and potential. They recognize that women are producers, as well as mothers, and that they are key actors in the development process, not merely its beneficiaries. Existing welfare-oriented development programs that do reach women—family planning, health, nutrition—are important but insufficient.

PUBLIC AND PRIVATE SPHERES OF ACTIVITY: PREINDUSTRIAL SOCIETIES

When we switch our attention to the impact of industrialization on the family, we find a heightened dichotomization between private, noneconomically productive domestic work and the public world of finance, industry, commerce, and wage-earning work. It would be instructive to contrast the preindustrial world of Western Europe at the advent of industrialization and in our contemporary era.

Philippe Ariès, a French social historian, has written a seminal work in the analysis of the historical evolution of the Western family. Ariès's *Centuries of Childhood: A Social History of Family Life* (1962) traces the developments in the conceptualization of the family from the Middle Ages to the present. His data sources include paintings and diaries, the history of games and pastimes, and the development of schools and their curricula. Ariès's basic thesis is that the contemporary conceptualization of family life and the modern image of the nature of children are recent phenomena. He argues that the concept of the family did not emerge until the 17th century. He does not deny the existence of the family prior to that time but makes a critical distinction between the family as a *reality* and the *idea* of the family, which is sensitive to change. Ariès states that the physical existence of the family is not in question: fathers and mothers and children exist in all societies. But, the point is that the ideas entertained about family relations can be radically dissimilar over lengthy periods of time.

> . . . it would be vain to deny the existence of a family life in the Middle Ages. But the family existed in silence: it did not awaken feelings strong enough to inspire poet or artist. We must recognize the importance of this silence: not much value was placed on the family. (Ariès, 1962:364)

The low valuation placed on the family in preindustrial Europe occurred because of the individual's almost total involvement with the community. People lived in their communities; they worked in them, played and prayed in them. The communities monopolized all their time and their minds. They had very little time for their families. The gathering point for the community was the "big house." These houses contained up to 25 people, including families, children, and servants. They fulfilled a public function by serving as places for business and sociability. Here friends, clients, and relatives met and talked. The rooms of the house were multi-functional: they were used for domestic activities as well as for professional purposes. People ate, slept, danced, worked, and received visitors in them.

They ate in them, but not at special tables: the "dining table" did not exist, and at mealtimes people set up folding trestle-tables, covering them with a cloth. . . . It is easy to imagine the promiscuity which reigned in these rooms where nobody could be alone, which one had to cross to reach any of the communicating rooms, where several couples and several groups of boys or girls slept together (not to speak of the servants, of whom at least some must have slept beside their masters, setting up beds which were still collapsible in the room or just outside the door), in which people foregathered to have their meals, to receive their friends or clients, and sometimes to give alms to beggers. (Ariès, 1963:394−395)

The general situation was one in which most activities were public and one where people were never left alone. The density of social life made isolation virtually impossible. Families were part and parcel of the society and were intertwined with relatives, friends, clients, proteges, debtors, and so on. Ariès argues that the lack of privacy attributed to this overwhelming community sociability hindered the formation of the concept of the family. The concept of the family developed as other specialized institutions relieved the home from its multifaceted functions. The growth of the tavern, cafés, and clubs provided alternative outlets for sociability. The establishment of geographically distinct business and occupational places freed the family from its business functions. The strengthening of the family was to be seen in the increased privacy for family life and a growing intimacy among family members. Gradually, the family cut itself off from the outside world and a separate and distinct family life emerged. As we will see, this isolation has had critical implications for women and children.

Edward Shorter in a provocative book, *The Making of the Modern Family* (1975), continues the general theme of Philippe Ariès. He sees the family tied integrally with the community. Shorter states that ordinary families in western and central Europe from 1500 to the end of the 18th century were "held firmly in the matrix of the larger social order" (Shorter, 1975:3). The family was secured to the community by two ties: one was the intricate web of extended kin, including uncles, aunts, and cousins; the other was to the wider community. The family had no sense of privacy or separation from the community. The marital roles were not viewed as independently important. Marriage was frequently arranged on the basis of advancing the extended family's economic interests.

Shorter's central argument is that the history of the family can be seen in the shift in the relationship between the nuclear family and the surrounding community. During the preindustrial period, the physical matrix discouraged privacy and intimacy within which the traditional family found itself. However, unlike Ariès—who presents a rather rosy, idealized depiction of preindustrial life, where all peoples of different ages, sexes, and classes intermingled in a Bruegelesque scene—Shorter stresses the negative characteristics of marital and family life. Shorter argues that family life was characterized by emotional coldness between husband and wife and an emotional isolation through a strict division of work assignments and sex roles. The emotional detachment of the marital pair and their demarcation of tasks are seen to be revealed in the following French regional Proverbs:

—"Mort de femme et view de cheval font l'homme riche." (Brittany) (Rich is the man whose wife is dead and horse alive.)

—"Deuil de femme morte dure jusqu'a a la porte." (Gascony) (Your late wife you so deplore until you enter your front door.)

—"L'homme a deux beaux jours sur terre: lorsqu'il prend femme et lorsqu'il l'enterre." (Anjou) (The two sweetest days of a fellow in life are the marriage and burial of his wife.)

—"Les femmes a la maison, comme les chiens, les hommes a la rue, comme les chants." (Gascony) (Women belong at home, like the dogs; men belong in the streets, like the cats.)

—"Femme fenestriere et courriere n'est en rien bonne menagere." (Gascony) (If you hang out the window or run around, you'll have the sorriest home in town.)

—"Jamais femme ni cochon ne doivent quitter las maison." (Dauphine) (Never let go out the doors either the women or the boars.)

Unlike other social historians—who stress the importance of women in domestic industry in preindustrial England—Shorter sees the life of women in preindustrial continental Europe as being relatively removed from economic enterprises and confined to having children and doing household tasks. The significance of this is spelled out in the considerable inequality between working men and domestically confined women. This finding is a notable contrast to the status and treatment of working women in England.

Shorter finds women having considerable power within the household but "women's control over certain domestic spheres, which were isolated from the economy as a whole, did not free them from subordinate social rules" (Shorter, 1975:66−67). Women's roles were subservient and she was expected to be the inferior. Three specifically feminine roles are delineated: passivity of women in external relations and with men in general, self-abnegation and personal sacrifice for the family, and finally "women's work was found in sex and reproduction: sleeping with husbands on demand and producing babies to the limits set by community norms" (Shorter, 1975:75).

Both Ariès and Shorter, then, observe that the preindustrial family was one which was characterized by a lack of privacy and intimacy. However, Ariès emphasizes the positive qualities of preindustrial community life, which compensated for the lack of marital "togetherness." Shorter, on the other hand, decries the lack of emotional involvement as being detrimental to the individual well-being of men and women; he does not regard community involvement positively. For our purposes a more rounded picture of the nature of husband-and-wife relationships can be seen when we examine the couple's lives in terms of their involvement in work and in the home and the impact of their marital relationship on the power and status of women.

In the preindustrial period the family was the unit of production. There was relatively little role differentiation among men, women, or children working together in the home and in the fields. Life was characterized by an interweaving of the husband's and wife's involvement with domestic life and with a productive work life. Women were involved in both the care of the home and the children as well as being a participant in the family basic economic productive system. Family industry was common. The food or goods produced did not yield much more than a bare subsistence. The family was the unit of production, with its members tied together in economic partnership. With the husband working in the home as well as the wife and children, there existed an integration of the public and private spheres of activities.

Alice Clark, in 1919, wrote an important work entitled, *The Working Life of Women in the Seventeenth Centry*. She examined women's work in agriculture, textiles, and the woolen trade in England during this period. All these activities were performed under a system of family industry. All goods and services produced by the family were intended for either family consumption or for sale or trade. Work, then, was not distinguished between that for domestic consumption or that for sale or trade. Cotton production illustrates this. The home was set up like a miniature factory; the entire process of cotton production from raw material to finished cloth was contained within the home. Men and women worked side by side. Both were actively involved in all aspects of the work. Clark summarizes her observations on the role of women in the preindustrial economy in the following manner:

> Under modern conditions, the ordinary domestic occupations of English women consist in tending babies and young children . . . in preparing household meals, and in keeping the house clean. . . . In the seventeenth centry [the domestic role] embraced a much wider range of production; for brewing, dairy work, the care of poultry and pigs, the production of vegetables and fruit, spinning flax and wool, nursing and doctoring, all formed part of domestic industry. (Clark cited in Oakley, 1974:15)

Ann Oakley (1974), who has written a valuable work of the social history of the housewife, observes that women at the time of marriage were expected to be economically productive, whether in agriculture or in the handicraft trades. The notion of women's economic dependence was foreign to the family system. Men were not viewed as the economic supporters of women. To demonstrate, Oakley (1974:22) examined the list of the occupations of married couples taken from the Sessions Papers of the Old Bailey. These were couples who were either witnesses, prosecutors, or prisoners of the court. She found that only 1 out of 86 married women did not have an occupation of her own. The remaining 85 women's occupations ranged from plumber to poultry dealer to seller of old clothes.

Traditionally, the husband was seen as the head of the household. He presided over the division of labor in various work and domestic tasks. Michael Young and Peter Willmott (1973) argue that the doctrine of St Paul—''Wives submit yourself unto your own husbands, as it is fit in the Lord''—was still the canon in the 17th century. The husband's power was tempered by the importance of the wife's economic contribution and also that of the children. Thus, although most wives were in fact beaten (some beaten severely), it was not to the husband's economic advantage to antagonize his wife too much. ''Her economic value was her saving, especially if she not only worked herself but also produced for her employer other workers, so putting him in the state recognized in the words of the Psalm—'Happy is the man who hath his quiver full of children' '' (Young and Willmott, 1973:67).

In summary, traditional life in preindustrial Europe can be seen as being characterized by a much greater involvement of the family with the surrounding community. The relationship between husband and wife was not as intimate or private as it is in today's contemporary industrial societies. In addition, the status and treatment of women can be seen to vary with their involvement in economically productive work. When a woman contributed, she had more power and control over her own life. When she did not, her life was that of a domestically confined slave; servile and subservient to her master—her husband.

PUBLIC AND PRIVATE SPHERES OF ACTIVITY: EARLY INDUSTRIAL SOCIETY

The Industrial Revolution shattered the domestic economy centered in the household. Looking at mid-18th-century England, we are best able to observe its impact. England was primarily rural with men and women largely engaged in some form of domestic industry. This activity occurred within the home. In the cities, women as well as men were involved in some form of trade, frequently serving as partners in joint work activities. The agrarian revolution at the end of the 18th century saw the lessening of the necessity for productive work at home. Industrial development deprived them of their involvement in the older domestic industries and trades:

If you go into a loom-shop, where there's three or four pairs of looms,
They all are standing empty, encumbrances of the rooms;
And if you ask the reason why, the older mother will tell you plain
My daughters have forsaken them, and gone to weave by steam. (J. Harland, *Ballads and Songs of Lancashire*, 1865. Cited in Thompson, 1963:308)

Family members were absorbed into the new economy as wage earners. This led to the differentiation between work and the home. E. P. Thompson, the English historian, in his *The Making of the English Working Class* (1963) comprehensively examines the changes occurring in people's ways of life between 1780 and 1832. In the following passage he contrasts the differences between two economies:

> Women became more dependent upon the employer or the labour market, and they looked back to a ''golden'' period in which home earnings from spinning, poultry and the like, could be gained around their own door. In good times the domestic economy, supported a way of life centred upon the home, in which inner whims and compulsions were more obvious than external discipline. Each stage in industrial differentiation and specialisation struck also at the family economy, disturbing customary relations between man and wife, parents and children, and differentiating more sharply between ''work'' and ''life.'' It was to be a full hundred years before this differentiation was to bring returns, in the form of labour-saving devices, back into the working woman's home. Meanwhile, the family was roughly torn apart each morning by the factory bell. (Thompson, 1963:416)

During this period, the family lost its productive function to industry. Work was now separated from the family. The differentiation of the family from the economy necessitated by the new industrial economy was accompanied by the differentiation of roles within the family. For men it meant involvement in the outside world and in the expanding occupational marketplace; for women, it increasingly meant the confinement into the home. ''The women became the non-employed, economically dependent housewife, and the man became the sole wage or salary earner, supporting by his labour his wife—the housewife—and her children'' (Oakley, 1974:34).

At the outset, women gained by the transference of economic production from the home to the workplace. It was instrumental in improving domestic conditions. The grime, filth, and industrial wastages associated with industrial production were now being removed from the home. Ivy Pinchbeck (1930), another English historian, observed that with the home no longer a workshop, women for the first time in the history of the industrial age were now able to turn their attention to homemaking and the care of children.

Shorter (1975) also is impressed by the positive consequences of industrialization. Shorter believes that the family underwent some major changes with the advent of market capitalism. By market capitalism Shorter is referring to the development of the modern marketplace economy with the linking of local markets with regional and national ones. The effect was that local tradesmen, artisans, craftsmen, and small shopowners developed a lesser parochial orientation. For the family this translates into a more cosmopolitan attitude with a lessening of importance given to local lineage concerns. Further, market capitalism contributed to the growth of the philosophy of individualism and freedom. The wish to be free emerges in sex-role relationships as romantic love and conjugal marriage.

Shorter is concerned with the changes in the relations between husbands and wives and parents and children since 1750. He believes that there was a great onrush of emotions and sentiment in family life and he examines changes in three areas: courtship, the mother-child relationship, and the relationship of the family with the community.

In courtship, he notes the emergence of sentiments of affection and friendship and the romantic love ideology. The result was that marriage became more and more a matter of free choice rather than an arranged concern determined by the parents on the basis of economic and social considerations.

The second area, mother-child relationships, is depicted as of secondary importance to the needs of domestic work and activities in the traditional preindustrial era. Shorter presents a shocking picture of a mother neglect and disinterest in their children. The result is an all too frequent occurrence of unattended children burning to death or eaten by the pigs or succumbing to the indifference of wet nurses. The absence of bereavement at the death of the infant or child supports Shorter's belief that mother-child relationships were unimportant. Although his description of events is parallel, in some respects, to Ariès's social history of childhood, it is embroidered with horrific analysis and commentary.

Shorter downplays the importance of economic factors. He deemphasizes both the fact that "ordinary" families were living under bare subsistence conditions as well as the lack of medical sophistication needed to combat the epidemic diseases rampant throughout Europe. Instead, he stresses the prevalance of an ideology of maternal neglect and indifference.

> The high rate of infant loss is not a sufficient explanation for the traditional lack of maternal love *because precisely this lack of care was responsible for the high mortality.*
> . . . It came about as a result of circumstances over which the parents had considerable influence: infant diet, age at weaning, cleanliness of bed linen, and the general hygienic circumstances that surrounded the child—to say nothing of less tangible factors in mothering, such as picking up the infant, talking and singing to it, giving it the feeling of being loved in a secure little universe. . . . The point is that these mothers did not *care,* and that is why their children vanished in the ghastly slaughter of the innocents that was traditional child-rearing. (Shorter, 1975:203;204)

Shorter believes that attitudes toward children began to change in the 19th century. New sentiments of affection and love emerged and neglect and indifference became less common. The result was an increase in the growth of maternal care, defined in terms of maternal breast feeding and the development of a more loving attitude toward children by their mothers.

The relationship of the family to the community is seen to have undergone dramatic changes with these shifting sentiments. The family became more of an emotional unit rather than a mainly productive and reproductive one. The affectional and caring sentiments tied the husband-wife relationship tighter. It began to replace lineage, property, and economic considerations as the foundation of the marriage. Simultaneously, there was a lessening of the couples' involvement with the community. Peer-group pressures lessened and with it the ending of community controls on young couple. The emphasis was on a value system that exalted personal happiness and self-development as opposed to the value system that emphasized generational allegiances and responsibility to the community.

These new sentiments manifested themselves in the rise of the companionate family and domesticity. The companionate family is one in which the husband and wife become friends rather than superordinate and subordinate, and equally share tasks and affection. Domesticity, which Shorter (1975:227) defines as "the family's awareness of itself as a precious emotional unit that must be protected with privacy and isolation from outside intrusion," is a central feature of the companionate family. Domesticity serves to sever the involvement of the family from the surrounding community. Thus two processes are at work: the first is the couple's almost complete withdrawal from the community; the second is the corresponding strength of the ties of the couple with each other and with their children and close relatives.

Shorter has been criticized on both methodological and theoretical grounds. Reviewers, notably Richard T. Vann (1976), have criticized the inadequacies and inconsistencies of Shorter's analysis of admittedly impressionistic data culled from contemporary accounts by physicians, priests, local magistrates, and family members. For our purposes the criticisms of Shorter on theoretical grounds (Gordon, 1977; Plumb, 1975; Vann, 1976) are more relevant. These critics question the theoretical conclusion on the relationship among sentiment, the family, and industrialization. A basic viewpoint is that Shorter overemphasized the importance of the "sentimental revolution." He tends to overlook the enormous impact the loss of women's economic involvement and their confinement to the home have for their power and status. Let us look at another perspective on the relationship between early industrialization and the family. This orientation differs from Shorter's in two ways. It stresses the negative consequences of both the industrial revolution and the Victorian patriarchal ideology, which sought to fight the evils of industrial labor practices with a highly protective philosophy that secluded and confined women and children to the household.

We have discussed the fact that the family ceased to be a productive unit in society. The world of work was separated from the family household, and there was an increased differentiation of roles between husband and wife. These changes had dramatic effects on the family. The separatedness of workplace and home meant that husbands and wives were also physically separated during working hours, which were quite long. Husbands' work became isolated from family contact. The wife no longer knew what the husband was doing nor how much he was earning. The lack of occupational visibility also meant that children could not be socialized into their father's profession by their father. People no longer worked as a family;

now men were employed as individuals for a wage. If the wages were good the husband could support his family; unfortunately, too often, they were low and inadequate to provide for the family.

Young and Willmott (1973) observe that this new economic system had disastrous consequences for the family. They cite 19th-century sources in England to argue their case. They note that the husband as the prime breadwinner controlled the economic resources of the family. All too frequently this was much to the family's detriment. There was an extraordinarily high consumption rate of spending on such items as betting, tobacco, and liquor. The quantity and quality of food purchased for the home was also disproportionately distributed, the husband getting the most and the choicest. Physical abuse of the wife and children, which was held in check by their economic contribution in the preindustrial family-oriented economy, now occurred with greater frequency and duration. The husband's actions become more understandable if one takes into consideration the relatively low wages that these men were paid. Employees were not paid according to the number of dependents that they had. The inadequate income of these men combined with the low status and power of women and children led to the last two being a convenient scapegoat for the former.

The subjugation and subordination of women during the 19th century was a central concern of the great English humanists of the Victorian era: Henry Mayhew, John Stuart Mill, and Friedrich Engels. Mayhew, in his investigations of the poor in London, reported on the great prevalence of wife beatings in his classic work, *London Labour and the London Poor:*

> They can understand that it is the duty of the woman to contribute to the happiness of the man, but cannot feel that there is a reciprocal duty from the man to the woman. The wife is considered as an inexpensive servant and the disobedience of a wish is punished with blows. She must work early and late, and to the husband must be given the proceeds of her labour. Often when the man is in one of his drunken fits—which sometimes last two or three days continuously—she must by her sole exertion find food for herself and him too. To live in peace with him there must be no murmuring, no tiring under work, no fancied cause for jealousy—for if there be, she is either beaten into submission or cast adrift to begin life again—as another's leavings. (Mayhew cited in Young and Willmott, 1973:76)

John Stuart Mill (1869/1966), in his essay, "The Subjection of Women," attacks the condition of legal bondage, debilitating education, and the oppressive ethic of "wifely subjection." Mill views the home as the center of a system of domestic slavery, the wife a bondservant within marriage. He observes that under Victorian law women have less rights than slaves. Women and children are owned absolutely by the husband-father. Unlike slaves, who were sometimes spared coercion into sexual intimacy, wives could not be entitled to any household items and, if the husband so desired, could be compelled by the courts to return to him.

There was little legal opportunity for women's freedom through divorce. Mills also observed the prevalence of physical brutality in marriage, it being the logical conclusion of women's subjection.

> And how many thousands are there among the lowest classes in every country, who without being in a legal sense malefactors in every other respect, because in every other quarter their aggressions meet with resistance, indulge the utmost habitual excesses of bodily violence toward the unhappy wife, who alone, at least of grown persons, can neither repel nor escape from their brutality; and toward whom the excess of dependence inspires their mean and savage natures, not with generous forbearance and a point of honor to behave well to one whose lot in life is trusted entirely to their kindness, but on the contrary with a notion that the law has delivered her to them as their thing, to be used at their pleasure, and that they are not expected to practice the consideration towards her which is required from them towards everybody else. (Mill, 1966:467–468)

Mill advocated legal change—suffrage and a just property law—to alleviate the debilitating conditions of women. He also saw the need for women to enter the labor market and the professions and urged the right of women to work.

Friedrich Engels, as you recall, took a more radical approach. He argued that the monogamous family system was created by the industrial capitalist economy to enslave women and use them as a cheap source of domestic labor. He felt that the attainment of legal equality for women was not enough unless it was also accompanied with total social and economic equality. Further, it was necessary to broaden the opportunities of women to assure personal fulfillment in productive work. The dependent status of women was seen as antithetical to equality. And, equality can only be assured with the end of masculine dominance over economic production and the entrance of women into the economic world on a parallel level.

Contributing to the lowly position of women during the Victorian industrial period was the development of an ideology whose explicit goal was to assure the safety and well-being of women but that implicitly added to her political and social demise—the ideology of domestic confinement. A central tenet of this philosophy was the belief in women's natural domesticity. This belief prevented and restricted the employment of women outside the home. It advocated the economic dependence of married women on their husbands and their sole involvement with household tasks and child care. This ideology was in direct contrast to the practices of the preindustrial era when women were a part of domestic industry. It can be seen as the Victorian answer to the harshness and severity of early industrial labor practices.

Numerous laws were passed that restricted or prevented female and child labor in mining, factories, and the textile industries. This protective legislation led to the creation of the modern housewife role that has become the prime source of feminine subservience. It is ironic that this legislation passed by "chivalrous" Victorian gentlemen to alter the brutality of industrial work had as its ultimate effect the substitution of a different form of subjugation.

Ann Oakley (1974) investigated contemporary Victorian documents to find the rationale for the confinement of the women to the household and their restriction or prevention from outside employment. Four main reasons are delineated: "female employment was condemned on moral grounds, on grounds of damage to physical health, on grounds of neglect of home and family, and lastly, simply on the grounds that it contravened the 'natural' division of labour between the sexes" (Oakley, 1974:45).

Oakley reports that over the period from 1841 to 1914, housewifery increasingly became the sole occupation of women. She cites figures from England to show that 1 of 4 married women were working in 1851 compaired to only 1 in 10 by 1911. The ideology of women's confinement to the home originated in the middle and upper classes. A woman's idleness was seen as a mark of prosperity. The leisured lady at home was the idea. The development and elaboration of society and rules of etiquette became the epitome of the latter Victorian era. For the working classes the doctrine of female domesticity began to crystallize in the last quarter of the 19th century. It ran counter to the economic needs of the family but, yet, became prevalent. For the working classes, too, "the idea that work outside the home for married women was a 'misfortune and a disgrace' became acceptable" (Oakley, 1974:50). A closer look at Victorian society and its accompanying etiquette rules can be enlightening. For it was etiquette rules established by the emerging bourgeoise upper class that proved to be influential in affecting sex-role relationships not only for that class but also for the entire society.

Sexual Politics in Victorian Etiquette[1]

In an insightful monograph, Leonore Davidoff (1975) examined the significance of manuals of etiquette within the larger context of Victorian England "society." Davidoff observed that during the 19th century England saw a radical transformation of its ruling classes. As newly rich families began to gain eminence, these families through individual achievement in industry and commerce were supplanting the traditional rich whose positions were based on hereditary and family connections. To govern the social mobility of these new personnel, an elaborated formalized society developed. The rules of etiquette set down in housekeeping books, etiquette manuals, and the advice columns in magazines were most relevant for highly structured social gatherings. Presentations at Court, country and city house parties, and the round of afternoon calls regulated the behavior of all participants.

The rules of "society" were created to control entrance and involvement

---

[1]The discussion that follows is based on Pearl W. Bartelt and Mark Hutter, *Symbolic interaction perspective on the sexual politics of etiquette books.* Paper presented at the meeting of the American Sociological Association, Chicago, September 1977.

within social classes. This was viewed as necessary since Victorian "society" was undergoing unprecedented social change; rigid rules of social acceptance provided a haven of stability. The elaborated code of etiquette created barriers to social entry. Ceremonial behavior can be seen as rites of passage, especially during certain important events as births, marriages, and deaths. The introduction of new individuals and families into group membership and activities was also a sensitive area and it, too, was marked by etiquette rules. Introductions, visitation calls, and dining patterns became formalized and vastly elaborate.

The home became increasingly an important area for social gatherings. It served to control and regulate the contacts that the "ins" wished to have with their equals and the new people seeking entrance into their group. The private clubs served a similar function. The "society" can be seen as controlling access to and involvement with those of the upper classes. For the newcomer it necessitated the abandonment of old allegiances, family and nonfamily, for this new prestigious social group (Davidoff, 1975:27).

The role of women was paradoxical. Influenced by the male-dominating patriarchal ideology, Victorian "society" was elaborated by its women. Women were exhorted to act as guardians of the home; men were exhorted to leave the home for the struggles of the business world, the Army, the church, or politics. Women's duties were to regulate and control social gatherings and thus keep order in the ever-changing social scene. However, their sequestration in the home and the confinement of their activities to domestic and "society" matters, occurred at the same time that men were expanding their influence and involvement in the new industrial world. This, ultimately, proved disastrous for women's independence and autonomy.

Socialization practices reinforced this dichotomy. Men were being socialized to operate in the ever-changing and complex world of industry, finance, and commerce. Women were socialized into the complexities of etiquette and the running of the home with its hierarchy of servants. Dress was a sign of social position and achievement. It serves as a good illustration of the extent to which etiquette rules were elaborated:

> Every cap, bow streamer, ruffle, fringe, bustle, glove and other elaboration symbolised some status category for the female wearer; mourning dress being the quintessence of this demarcation. A footman, with long experience in upper-class households, said "jewelry was a badge that women wore like a sergeant major's stripes or field-marshall's baton, it showed achievement, rank, position." It is not surprising, then, that girls and women of all classes were preoccupied with dress. (Davidoff, 1975:95)

The rules governing sexual behavior for women were also paradoxical. The emphasis was on respectability through control of sexual behavior and desire. Victorian women gained status by denying their own sexuality and treating the

Victorian masculine sex drive as sinful. Purity beliefs and the elaborate etiquette norms, which stressed modesty, prudishness, and cleanliness, as well as the rules governing demeanor and appearance served to provide a sense of order, stability, and status in the everyday world. However, it also served to be psychologically stultifying. Further, the placing of women on a virginal pedestal and limiting their involvement to the home and excluding them from the economic sphere served to reinforce the patriarchal ideology. Through idolatry subservience emerged.

PUBLIC AND PRIVATE SPHERES OF ACTIVITY: INDUSTRIAL SOCIETY

Industrialization and a patriarchal ideology led to the development of a conjugal family system with a clear delineation of roles between husband and wife. The breakdown of larger community involvements was supposed to be compensated for by an increased intimacy and emotionality between family members. Unfortunately, many husbands, burdened by inadequate wages to support their families and finding themselves isolated from domestic everyday activities, did not provide the necessary emotional as well as economic supports for their wives and children. An all too frequent occurrence was family neglect and physical abuse. Thus the breakdown of community involvement with the family and the disintegration of the traditional extended family, which characterized preindustrial rural life and domestic industry, led to an intolerable situation for women and children. They were dependent both economically and emotionally on the whims of detached, autocratic, and often despotic husbands.

Young and Willmott (1973), in their astute history of the family in England, developed the thesis that women—after acclimating themselves to industrial-based city life—eventually developed a family organization based on mother-daughter maternal bonds. They did this to protect themselves and their children from the unreliability and indifference of their husbands. With the husband absent from the household and working elsewhere, daughters developed strong ties with their mothers. They lived near them and mothers served as an oasis of security for both married daughters and grandchildren. In addition, mothers could provide day-care services if their daughters got jobs, and they were also able to pass on gifts and money during periods of need.

We have discussed this family system earlier in our analysis of working-class communities and families in England and the United States. Young and Willmott base their thesis on the working class community of Bethnel Green in London.[2] As

---

[2]In addition to Young and Willmott's *Family and Kinship in East London,* (1957) the following monographs are pertinent: Willmott and Young's *Family and Class in a London Suburb* (1960); Peter Townsend's *The Family Life of Old People,* (1957), and Peter Marris's *Widows and Their Families* (1958).

you may recall, these communities were labeled closed communities by John Mogey (1964) and urban villages by Herbert Gans (1962a). These communities were depicted as ones in which intense interfamilial cooperation exists, are cohesive and homogeneous in cultural values, and are closed to nonmembers. In our discussion of working-class family life in Bethnel Green, we saw that husbands and wives performed a separate set of household tasks. In times of emergency, aid for either the husband or wife is provided by other husbands and wives in the area. Frequently, these are same-sexed relatives. Under these conditions, a strict role segregation of tasks is maintained. Leisure-time activities are similarly segregated. Within segregated role-pattern families, mother-daughter relations tend to be stronger than father-son relations. This is particularly the case when the married couple take up residence in close proximity to the wife-mother. Intimate, emotional and isolated conjugal families did not live in these communities.

When we examine these internal family structures in more detail, we find the opposite of the conjugal family form. Elizabeth Bott (1957), in an interesting typology, focuses on the husbands' and wives' involvement with social networks comprised of kin, friends, and neighbors in the community as well as their relationship and involvement with each other. Bott found that if neither family members maintained ties with a network of friends, neighbors, and relatives who knew one another and interacted, husband-wife ties would be minimal. Husbands and wives who are members of such close-knit networks when they marry and continue to maintain such relationships during their marriage have a marital-role organization based on a clear differentiation of tasks with few shared interests or activities. If either needs assistance, whether economic or emotional, they do not ask their spouse but rather seek help from network members. The result is that the husband-wife relationship is not close. The couple live in relatively separate worlds with different involvements and activities.

The picture presented is quite different from that drawn by Edward Shorter (1975) of families emotionally and intimately involved with each other. It is a family that has weak marital ties and strong lineage ties. It is an industrial-age version of the community dominating the family pattern, which was characteristic of preindustrial society. This developed out of the felt need of economically and emotionally dependent women and their children to assure some stability and continuity in their lives. Young and Willmott (1973) observe that this family system becomes self-perpetuating. Once the female-centered system developed, it served to exclude men from the intimacies of domestic family life and to seek other ways to satisfy their needs:

> This sort of structure—weak on the family of marriage, strong on the family of origin—tended to perpetuate itself. Husbands were often squeezed out of the warmth of the female circle, and took to the pub as their defence against the defence. They had to put up with mothers-in-law who were constantly interferring, as the man might see it, with the arrangements in his own home. His wife could seem more her daughter than his

wife, and both of them belonged to a group which did not award men a high place in its order of values. He could find himself undermined, in a hundred ways, subtle and unsubtle. He could be pushed into becoming an absentee father, so bringing on the insecurity which the extended family in this form was established to counter. (Young and Willmott, 1973:92)

In this section we have seen that the Industrial Revolution had important and long-lasting effects on the family. It meant the separation of men and women into two isolated worlds—the world of work and the world of the household. This had the effect of setting apart the life of the husbands from the intimacies of everyday domestic activities and estranging them from their wives and children. Women found themselves outside of the work force and involved solely in housework and childcare. Economic factors coincided with a misguided Victorian patriarchialism that saw economic employment as a threat to womanly virtue and bad for her from both a physical and emotional standpoint. Not, incidentally, that a woman working for wages was seen as an indication of her husband's failure to earn sufficiently to support her and his family. The increased sentiments, emotions, and intimacies of the newly emerged conjugal family did not compensate for women's economic dependence on their husbands and their resultant decline in social status. Particularly, this became a problem as it occurred at the same time that the ties with extended kin and with the surrounding community diminished. Thus the emotional supports of these "outsiders" collapsed, and the increased emotional dependency of the marital couple with each other—heretofore called on far too infrequently—occurred. To help compensate for their loss, working-class women in England developed an alternative family system that emphasized mother-daughter ties and deemphasized the ties between husband and wife.

However, the predominant idology was focusing more and more on the belief in the primacy of the conjugal family with its accent on intimacy and emotionalism between husband and wife. At the same time an integral aspect of the ideology of the conjugal family, female domesticity, worked against it. Thus the conjugal family system found itself in a dilemma. Its advocacy of differentiated spheres of activity—masculine public life and feminine private life—was antithetical to the very intimacy it sought. That is, female dependency ran counter to conjugal intimacy. It is now time to examine the contemporary conjugal family system and see how it attempts to resolve this issue.

PUBLIC AND PRIVATE SPHERES OF ACTIVITY: THE FAMILY IN CONTEMPORARY INDUSTRIAL SOCIETY

The theme running through this chapter has been the distinction between public and private spheres of activity and their respective implications for male and female marital relationships. The trend has been gradual, from a more public family system with high community involvement to a more private closed family system. The public family was one in which there was little distinction made between work and the home and where community played a major role in shaping and determining family relationships. Community control and scrutiny was primarily responsible for the limitations on family intimacy and privacy. Women in the preindustrial period were actively involved in work. In fact, the distinction between work and domesticity hardly existed. The ideology of the private family emerged during the Industrial Revolution. Work was separated from the household and there was a greater differentiation and specialization of the roles of husband and wife. Coinciding with industrialization was the development of an ideology that stressed the importance of sentiments regarding emotionality, intimacy, and privacy among conjugal family members. However, through much of the history of industrialization, the reality of the private family was relatively uncommon since it was restricted to the more affluent middle classes of the society. The upper classes, desiring to maintain and control their family wealth and power, continued to maintain a family system that placed great importance on extended kinship lines. For the working classes, especially in the city, maternal-centered, three-generational family systems developed to compensate for the emotional unwillingness and the too-frequent economic unfeasibility of the conjugal family form.

Certain conditions have become prevalent in contemporary industrial society that have had great significance for family relations. Demographic changes, the lengthened life span, the decline in infant and child mortality rates, the decline in maternal deaths in childbirth, lower birth rates, the dissociation of reproductive from sexual activities, and the decline in the period of life devoted to maternity in relation to the total life expectation have contributed to attitudinal and behavioral changes in the family. For example, the typical couple now spend a great number of years together outside of parental concerns. This has helped foster the emergence of the conjugal role ideology. The emphasis on love, emotional support, friendship and companionship, and erotic and sexual gratification can transform the marital relationship into the ideal conjugal family.

Feminism has also been influential in the reshaping of the family. Through the 20th century women have been gaining in legal equality. Areas of legal change include the right of suffrage, rights of separation and divorce, and rights of equal employment and opportunity. Although equality has not been fully realized, as the struggle over the Equal Rights Amendment (ERA) can testify, there has been marked improvement of the power and status of women compared to life in the 19th century. The result has been a growth of female independence.

The higher standard of living for ordinary families and the migration of families from rural to urban and from urban to suburban residences has contributed to these changes. As we saw in our earlier discussion on suburban families, the emphasis became more and more focused on conjugal family ties at the expense of the extended family. The acquisition of better homes has made the household a more attractive place in which to spend time and on which to spend money.

Husbands are devoting more time to their families, and there is a diminishing of the segregation of marital couples that characterized working-class couples of the earlier industrial period.

Observing these changes in England, Young and Willmott (1973) have postulated the emergence of a new family form that epitomizes the ideals of the conjugal family but with some notable differences. This is the symmetrical family. The symmetrical family is seen as one in which there is recognition for the continued differences in the work opportunities and ways of life of husbands and wives but in which there is marked equalitarianism between the sexes. Young and Willmott note a similarity between this family form and the family of domestic industry. Both families emphasize the relationship among husband, wife, and children. However, unlike the domestic industrial family, which functioned as a productive entity, the symmetrical family functions as a unit of consumption:

> When husband, wife, and children worked together on a farm or in handicrafts the family was *the* productive unit even if it did not yield much more than a bare subsistence to its members. When individual wage-employment became almost universal (except for housewives) the family had to give way to a wider division of labor. But in the course of time the family has re-established a new kind of primacy, not as the unit of production so much as the unit of consumption. (Young and Willmott, 1973:xxi)

Couples, particularly husbands, see themselves as no longer having to devote as much time in earning a living and providing for a family. They are now able to spend more time with their families in leisure and home-centered activities. The new equalitarianism is realized in the assumption of joint responsibility in the planning of children and the increased tendency for greater husband involvement in the rearing of the children. Feminism is evinced in the symmetrical family as the belief that there should be no monopolies for either husband or wife in any sphere of activity. Women, then, are entitled to the same rights as men to become involved in work outside the home as in it. The result has been a movement of women back to the labor force, the usual pattern being the wife staying at home during the early years of childrearing, then taking first a part-time job, and later a full-time job as the children grow older.

Young and Willmott (1973) believe that the traditional pattern of the husband being the primary wage earner will continue.

> The devotion of a husband to a career, if it goes with scant sympathy for a partner who does not have one, may drive his wife to espouse the values as himself and follow him, out. But that is exceptional. (Young and Willmott, 1973:276)

These authors observe a similar phenomenon to the one that we discussed in our analysis of the Soviet Union, where the wife has become responsible both for her outside work and for all domestic tasks. This dual role or double burden for women is practiced among the London families interviewed by Young and Willmott.

Notably, Young and Willmott see positive gains in the strength of the feminist movement. They believe that just as the worlds of work and leisure are merging so too will the worlds of men and women merge. The result will be an eventual sharing of the tasks by men and women in both domestic and outside work. They recognize the strains that will have to be overcome: the caring of children as well as arrangement of work and leisure schedules so that the family can spend time together. Generally, they are optimistic for the future: technology and family wants can both be fulfilled.

This hopeful and sanguine portrait of family life is not shared by many contemporary sociologists. They see the various social movements that have become manifest in recent years—the youth counterculture; the women's liberation movement; the rise in experimental forms of family life, particularly swinging, communal marriage, and so on—as reflections of the dissatisfactions with the dichotomization of public and private worlds and the growing privatization of the family. Barbara Laslett (1973), in an intriguing article, observes that the private family—manifested to an advanced degree in the United States—is a central feature of contemporary life. Its development is a consequence of the separation of work and family activities. The privatization of the family results in less community and social control over how family members behave toward each other as well as providing less social support for family members. Barbara Laslett speculates that the experimentation with alternative family styles, such as communal living, group marriages, and single-parent families, has been one adaptation to the strains of nuclear family living. This view sees the final blooming of the intimate private conjugal family as not achieving the long-sought needs of individualism and equalitarianism. Instead, the private conjugal family is seen as mired with problems. Let us look at this position in some detail.

The above arguments by the critics of the conjugal family bear a striking similarity to those of Peter L. Berger et al. in *The Homeless Mind: Modernization and Consciousness* (1974). By integrating Berger's analysis with those of the scholars we discussed, we may be better able to grasp the dynamics of contemporary marital dynamics.

In Chapter 3, we saw that *The Homeless Mind* is concerned with the consequences of modernization and the privatization of the family. The authors argue that modernization was supposed to free the individual but has, instead, increased feelings of helplessness, frustration, and alienation and has beset individuals with threats of meaninglessness. Berger et al. develop the argument that technology's primary consequence has resulted in the separation of work from private life. Further, work is characterized by anonymous impersonal relations, individuals interact with each other in terms of the functions they perform in their jobs. There is no need to be aware of each other's uniqueness as individuals. To combat this situation, private institutions like the family are developed. In them, individuals can express their subjective identities and the individualism that is denied them in the work situation.

Berger et al. argue that the reality of the world is sustained through interaction with significant others and an individual who is deprived of relationships with significant others will feel a sense of anomie and alienation. This is the case of the individual at work. However, the marriage relationship is designed to provide a nomos versus an anomic situation. Here intimacy can occur and a meaningful world can be constructed. Marriage is viewed as a "dramatic" act in which the two participants come together and redefine themselves through the unfolding of the marital relationship and the involvement they have with others.

The contemporary character of middle-class marriage, then, has its origins in the development of a private sphere of existence that is separated and segregated from the controls of such public institutions as politics and economics. It is designed to be a haven of security and order. It is a world in which the husband and wife can create their own social reality and social order. This is seen to be of crucial importance to wage earners—it provides them with an environment in which they can gain a sense of control in contrast to their jobs, which are often viewed in terms of powerlessness and unfulfillment, or to politics, which is viewed cynically.

It is important to note that in an earlier work Peter L. Berger in collaboration with Hansfred Kellner (1964) saw marriage as accomplishing these outlined objectives. In that work, "Marriage and the Construction of Reality," the marital relationship is viewed as a nomos institution that helps establish a meaningful reality that is sustained through the interaction of the marriage partners. However, Berger and Kellner's view of the positive nature of marriage is seen from the man's perspective. They virtually ignore women in their analysis. Although noting how the family serves as a refuge for men from the debilitating reality of the workplace, they do not address themselves to the problems of domestically confined housewives who have no refuge from the mundane and repetitive household chores or from the unceasing demands of their children. Further, they overlook the fact of the greater demand placed on women to satisfy the demands and morale of their husbands than the reverse.

In *The Homeless Mind* Berger and his associates come to the realization that marriage is insufficient to satisfy the demands of all family members, including the husband. In this book, they also come to the implicit recognition that the *ideology* of marriage as a nomos institution is one thing and that *reality* is another. That is, marriage, which was seen as providing a meaningful world for the participants, is in fact unable to overcome the modern condition of "homelessness," which results from the separation of work and the family. This "pluralization of life-worlds," which is distinguished by the dichotomy of private and public spheres of activities, fosters both a world of work that is insufficient to give people a feeling of worth and a world of marriage that is unable to provide ample satisfactions in people's private lives.

Berger et al. conclude that the modern private family is in trouble. Evidence of this is the development of processes of demodernization that manifest themselves in various forms of rebellious movements, such as the youth counterculture and the women's liberation movement. Further evidence is apparent in the dramatic rise in the divorce rate, which reflects the desire of individuals to seek more satisfactory private meanings and relationships than those that exist within the marriage.

CONCLUSION

This chapter concludes our four-chapter analysis of the effects of patriarchy on male-female premarital and marital relationships. It is a continuation of the previous analysis that emphasized the interrelationship of patriarchy and economic systems and how they influence the division of labor of husbands and wives.

We demonstrated how the differentiation of activities of males and females in public and private spheres has been a dominating factor in establishing marital roles and responsibilities. The differential involvement of men and women in the worlds of work and in the household are important in determining the power, privilege, respect, and deference patterns within the family. Comparatively, we examined cross-cultural and Western historical evidence to develop our thesis. We concurred with the views of a significant number of social scientists that the greater and exclusive involvement of women in the domestic sphere, devoting their time to household tasks and childrearing, then, the less freedom, authority, and power women have in relation to men. Concomitantly, the more exclusive involvement of men in the outside world of work, politics, and religion, the greater is their authority and power over women.

A large segment of this chapter is devoted to an historical analysis of the effects of the Western industrial revolution on male-female relationships. We discussed the relationship of modernization processes and the privatization of the family (referring back to our opening chapters) and saw striking parallels in the conclusions reached by social scientists coming from different subdisciplines. The common thrust of our presentation was on the negative consequences of the dichotimization of private and public spheres of activities and the privatization of the family. Finally, we argued that such developments as the women's movements, the young counterculture movements, and the new family form (perhaps idealized)—the symmetrical family—represent reactions against the privatized family.

In part four we examine the generational family relationships. These represent a different expression of patriarchal ideology, authority, and power differentiation.

Four

GENERATIONAL
RELATIONSHIPS

11

Fertility Patterns and Parenthood

An inescapable fact of contemporary life is the overwhelming increase of the world's population. Today's population is increasing at a rate faster than ever before in history. It is taking less and less time for the world's population to double. During the Stone Age when man was hunting and foraging for subsistence, the total world population is estimated to have been about 10 million. By the beginning of the Christian era, the world population was about 250 million people. If it took about 35,000 years for the first quarter-billion people to appear, it took only about 1650 years for the population to double to half-a-billion. But, in a mere 200 years (A.D. 1850), it doubled again. Then, in a time span of only 80 years—from 1850 to 1930—the population increased to 2 billion. By 1975, 45 years later, the population again doubled to approximately 4 billion people. Demographers predict that by the end of this century the human population will have again doubled to 8 billion people. This change is depicted graphically in Figure 11.1.

Rapid population growth and the size of the contemporary world population is one of the most urgent concerns of the 20th century. Its consequences for the quality of life and for the future are subject to extensive analyses, discussions, and speculations. Population-control programs have been implemented throughout the world. Within the contexts of modernization and the family, our analysis will examine some of the elements that account for this phenomenon. In addition to examining the broad demographic trends, we will discuss changing attitudes and values regarding parental roles and the transition to parenthood period of Americans.

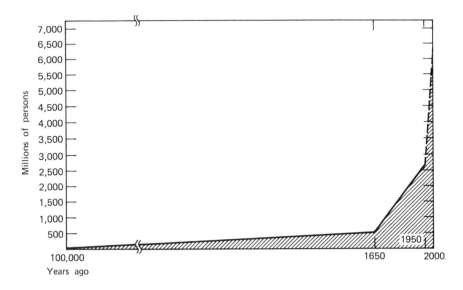

Figure 11.1 A schematic representation of the increase in the human species. (Adapted from William Petersen, *Population,* Third Ed. (New York: Macmillan, 1975, Figure 1-1.) Copyright © by William Petersen. Reprinted with permission of Macmillan Publishing Co.

FERTILITY PATTERNS IN PREINDUSTRIAL FAMILY LIFE

Earlier, we have noted a distinction between mating and marriage. Mating refers to a biologic phenomenon, whereas marriage, as a sociologic concept, refers to a social institution. Marriage controls sexual activity and reproduction. Throughout the world, we find copulation and reproduction reinforced by cultural norms. William Petersen, the noted demographer, has observed that ''a society's demographic and cultural persistence depends on the fact that the physical care, socialization, and social placement of its young are not left to the sometimes haphazard dictates of sexuality alone'' (Petersen, 1975:202). Reproduction, which is vital to a society's continuation, is always controlled by cultural norms about family size and such related matters as marriage, frequency of intercourse, and abortion. It is never a matter left up to the individual couple alone.

There are notable differences in fertility rates for underdeveloped preindustrial societies and more developed industrial societies. Demographers (Freedman, 1963:68; Davis, 1955) have observed that, generally, underdeveloped societies have higher fertility levels. These fertility levels are related to various factors found in these societies. Ronald Freedman (1963/68) presents two very general explanations. High fertility can be seen as an adjustment to high mortality and to the centrality of kinship and family structures to community life. Let us examine each factor in more detail.

High infant and child mortality along with a relatively short and precarious life expectancy require a high fertility rate to assure a society's perpetuation. Calvin Goldscheider (1971) observes that many families have "extra" children as a hedge against infant and child death and the probable early death of one of the parents. He cautions against making an unwarranted assumption that high birthrates are necessarily associated with large family-size norms. The high birthrates he observed occurred in conjunction with the high mortality of infants and children. Thus families may have had a large number of children so that some of them would survive.

In support of this notion, Freedman (1963/68) finds that a number of studies in contemporary underdeveloped areas reveal a discrepancy between the number of children desired, usually three or four, and the actual number of children that a couple has, frequently six or more. Freedman interprets this finding as a result of the decline in infant and child mortality rates. It is not seen as reflecting a new attitudinal preference for a smaller family size. It reflects previous historical circumstances when, owing to high mortality, six or more children were required if three or four children were to survive. Freedman reports on data from India where social scientists are surprised that surveyed families express a desire for three or four children yet practice little or no birth control.

> However, wanting three or four living children in a high-mortality country is quite consistent with the much higher average number of births. Even if mortality is declining, the peasant who has learned from his culture to depend on his children for labor on the farm, for old-age security, and for other essentials cannot be expected to extrapolate declining mortality with the demographer and to calculate a long-range need for fewer children (Freedman, 1963/1968:164).

Significantly, however, families that have three or four surviving children are more inclined to have favorable attitudes toward family-planning information and supplies. This is consistent with their belief that birth control practices are irrelevant until the essential minimum number of children exist (Freedman, 1963/68).

The second element that accounts for the high-fertility rate in preindustrial countries is the dominance of kinship and family groupings. Prior to modernization, a wide range of activities involved interdependence with kinfolk, especially children. Economic production and consumption along with leisure activities and assistance to the elderly and the infirm occurred largely within family and kinship structures. Freedman (1963/68) states that large numbers of children are desired when the society is based on and its values are achieved through kinship and family ties rather than through other social institutions. Under high-mortality conditions, high birthrates become desirous to assure the survival of the kinship groupings.

Goldscheider (1971), in a comprehensive review of the demographic literature, reaches a similar conclusion. He finds that in kinship-dominated societies pronatalist sentiments are prevalent. Children are a source of protection and prestige. The social strength of a given kinship unit is dependent on its size. Tied to this attitude is the domination of the kinship group over the individual. Kinship ascription provides an occupation for a man and his placement in the society is determined by the family or kin group to which he belongs. Children enable families and the kin group to achieve socially desired goals.

In such instances high value is placed on large families. Further, the viability of extended kinship involvements diminishes the personal responsibilities of the couple in the care and maintenance of their children. The burdens of a large family, economic and social costs, and social and personal care are shared and controlled by the larger kinship-family structure: "Parents not only had personal rewards for having large families but they could escape from direct responsibilities of their many children" (Goldscheider, 1971:142).

The sex-role segregation that predominates in these kinship-based societies is another important facet in encouraging a large family. The role and status of women is clearly linked with their childbearing function. Prestige and other social and economic rewards and benefits can only be obtained through motherhood. The production and survival of healthy offspring for the continuation of kinship lines provide the chief source for rationalizing a woman's existence.

The familial-based economic system found children to be important productive assets. Children were an integral part of the labor force. Thus the more offspring, the more workers within the family. Further, the larger the number of offspring, the greater the chances of their providing for their parents when they got old. Children, then, represented one type of old age insurance (Goldscheider, 1971:153). The lack of geographic and social mobility combined with the lack of personal aspirations also increased the desirability for large families.

Taken altogether, the kinship-based society was dependent on high fertility for the perpetuation of its social system. Demographic, social, familial, and economic conditions resulted in the institutionalization of high fertility. The entire society—its values and goals as well as the various aspects of its cultural and religious life—were organized around high-fertility values and behavior.

Turning our attention to the industrialized nations of the world, we find that the rate of population growth has decreased after an earlier rapid increase. Demographers have referred to this phenomenon as the demographic transition. Simply put, the demographic transition refers to the movement from high-fertility and high-mortality rates to low-fertility and low-mortality rates. Demographers have traced the historical sequence of population growth in the Western world over the last 200 years. They observed three broad stages of population dynamics.

During the preindustrial period, birth and death rates were high, variations occurring during periods of famine and epidemics. Population size was relatively stable. Industrialization ushered in the second stage. It was accompanied by improvements in sanitation and sewage systems, better transportation systems for shipping foods, and more productive family techniques. Improvements in these conditions led to a reduction in the death rate. Although the death rate was reduced, there was no commensurate reduction in birthrates. This resulted in a period of rapid population growth. By the end of the 19th century, through the 20th century, and continuing until today the high birthrate has been reduced. The disparity that existed between birthrates and deathrates, which was characteristic of the second stage, is reduced in this, the third stage. Today the industrialized nations of the world have a low, steady deathrate and a low, but somewhat fluctuating birthrate.

How can we explain this dramatic decline in the rate of population growth in contemporary industrial societies? Goldscheider (1971) has developed an argument that is similar to that articulated by William J. Goode (1963) in his *World Revolution and Family Patterns*. Goldscheider (1971:148–151) believes that there are three key social processes that can account for the transition from high to low fertility and family size. First, there is the shift from kinship dominance to the conjugal family unit. He sees the breakdown of the dominance and centrality of the kinship-based consanguineal family as one of the significant features of modernization. The extended family system can no longer dictate the number of children that a given nuclear family should have. Individual couples emphasize their family of procreation rather than their family of orientation. They have their own economic and social responsibilities and the welfare of their children is primarily in their hands. The break with the extended family system allowed for the development of new behavioral and value patterns. It coincided with the processes of migration, urbanization, and social mobility.

Second, there is a marked improvement in living standards accompanied by increased economic opportunities. These contribute to rising aspirations for social mobility. This aspiration is frequently in conflict with the desire for a large family. These social and economic changes are seen to have exerted direct pressures toward fertility control and reduction. The decline in family-based agricultural and preindustrial enterprises diminished the importance of children. Children are no longer productive assets. The decline in fertility is accentuated by the rapid urbanization that accompanied industrialization. Urban conditions contribute to the decline of the traditional classical extended family system. It frees the conjugal family from the socioeconomic controls of the extended family system. Further, urban life styles, living standards, and aspirations all run counter to the traditional values that encouraged large family size and high fertility.

The third and last factor is the development of new values and attitudes that stress individualism, secularism, and rationalism. These values all share a common belief in the desirability of limiting family size. Values in favor of smaller families are also shared by the emerging value of achievement versus ascription. Together, these three processes greatly affect the decline in fertility and family size in industrialized societies. Let us examine how these factors operate by looking at India as a case study.

Why the Poorest Nations Have So Many Babies

BERNARD WEINRAUB

The 20th Century began with a population of a little over 1.5 billion. It will end with about 7 billion, of whom 1 billion will be Indians. Today, the world's population is around 4 billion. Population has already outstripped food supplies. It is estimated that as many as half the world's people are chronically undernourished, and that more than 10,000 people die of starvation weekly. Famine last year was severe in Bangladesh and parts of Africa and India.

NEW DELHI—The most obvious and pointed question arising from the population-food crisis is why do impoverished people have six or seven children when they can barely afford to feed themselves and when they know that several of the children will die of disease or starvation?

"I have two sons and three daughters and we're all half-starved," said Anwara Khalam, a widow, crouching beside a charcoal fire in a Calcutta *bustee,* a slum of mud huts and shacks. As she broiled vegetables in a tin pot, a visitor asked if she ever wanted fewer children.

She shrugged and laughed. "It's God's will," she said. "Children come and children go."

It is evident now that in India and other nations, couples who have numerous children are unwilling to adhere to what seems like simple logic: that more children in the family means less food for everyone. Why, then, is the global population increasing at 2 per cent a year?

The answer seems rooted in illiteracy, a valid fear that parents will be left homeless and without support in old age unless they have several sons, the failure of governments to commit money and energy to birth-control measures, and the realization among poor people that some of their children will die and that an extra mouth or two to feed will hardly alter the family's plight.

"Look, if I were a poor man in India there's no reason on earth why I should limit my family," said one foreign family-planning specialist here. "You want to have a son to look after you in old age, and you want a couple of them just to make sure. In event of any disaster, like being unemployed or getting old or sick, you fall back on the family. If you don't have a family, you just die. No one else is going to take care of you."

At this point, the population explosion seems too abstract and too overworked a phrase—at least in the West—to comprehend. After all, numerous nations in Europe as well as Taiwan, Korea, Japan, the United States and probably China have shown that population growth can be checked.

But in South Asia, Africa and parts of Latin America, the population explosion is a real danger. A European diplomat, sitting in his home in Dacca, said that the population growth was woven into the conflicts of recent years: the Nigerian civil war between 1967–70, the Bangladesh war in 1971, the massacres in Burundi in 1972–73, the question of Palestinian refugees.

Currently, for every birth in the developed countries, there are five in the underdeveloped countries. As a result, the worsening world food situation, and the inability of the rich to keep feeding the poor, has evoked a sense of urgency in the West.

Norman Borlaug, the Nobel prize winner for his contribution to the "Green Revolution", the agricultural breakthrough involving the scientific use of fertilizer, pesticides, irrigation and improved seeds to boost food production, has said: "By the Green Revolution we have only delayed the world food crisis for another 30 years. If the world population continues increase at the same rate, we will destroy the species."

Western nations seem more alarmed about the population spiral than many impoverished countries. Government commitments to family planning vary; in Bangladesh, the most overcrowded nation in the world, Sheik Mujibur Rahman, the Prime Minister, has yet to say anything forceful about birth control and a program has not taken shape.

United Nations population experts believe that there is growing resistance in black Africa to include population policies in official government-sponsored programs. With the exception of Egypt and Tunisia, African and Middle East nations avoid birth control programs for several reasons: the issue is not popular, politically or culturally; space and density are not problems and Africans look around them and see open land; there is an element of pride in having large populations.

Bernard Weinraub in *The New York Times,* February 2, 1975. © 1975 by The New York Times Company. Reprinted by permission.

INDIA: A CASE STUDY

India is one of the world's largest nations. It is also one of its poorest. Second only to the People's Republic of China in population size, at mid-1975 India had a population of 608.5 million (Population Reference Bureau, 1976). In a land area one-third the size of the United States, India has three times as many people. India's population represents one-eighth of the entire world's population. Demographers predict that unless the current growth rate is substantially reduced, India will have a population of well over 1 billion by the end of the 20th century.

The Indian government has viewed its population growth as a major deterrent to economic and social development. Initially, however, Mahatma Gandhi, Jawaharlal Nehru, and other government leaders were ambivalent on the need to reduce fertility, but eventually family-planning programs became more and more important, culminating in the coercive sterilization policies of Indira Gandhi and the Congress Party during the "emergency" of 1976–1977. The general position held is that the economic development of the country is dependent on the investment of the national income. However, a rapidly increasing birthrate diverts income to food consumption, housing, education, and other social needs. A lower birthrate would allow for greater modernization, economic development, and increased total production. Population, then, is seen as being a crucial variable in the complex interrelationships of economy, social structure, and culture. In the transition to a modern industrial state, the population growth of the society must be regulated through governmentally sponsored population-planning programs. Since independence in 1948, India has been developing programs to slow its population growth. The result is that the birthrate has dropped from 42 per 1000 in 1951−1961 to 35 per 1000 by 1974 (Population Reference Bureau, 1976). However, the decline in the birthrate has been partially offset by lower mortality rates. Life expectancy in India has risen to about 50 years today. This reflects the great strides India has made in industry, agriculture, education, and public health. However, India's population today is increasing at a rate of 2 to 2.5 percent. At this rate of growth, *every five years* India's population will grow by an additional number that equals the combined population of East and West Germany or more than the population of Australia and New Zealand together (Petersen, 1975). At this rate, its population will double in approximately 35 years.

In 1952, India became the first country to adopt an official family-planning program. At the outset, the program was poorly funded. This reflected the ambivalence of Indian officials to reduce fertility. During the first five-year plan (1951−1956), 147 clinics were established in all of India, 126 in the cities and 21 in rural areas. During the succeeding five-year period, 1956−1961, over 4000 clinics were established. Contraceptives were distributed at subsidized rates or were given out free. Petersen observes that by 1960 only 1.4 million families of the 75 to 80 million families in India were given family-planning advice (Petersen, 1975:652).

The slow rate of growth of the population programs reflects the initial hesitation of the central government to family planning. Nehru in 1956 asserted that family planning was being assisted ''not in a major way but in experimentation'' with emphasis on medical reasons to promote the ''health and happiness'' of the family (Nehru cited in Petersen, 1975:651). The program also reflected the inefficiencies and inaccessibility of the clinics to the vast majority of the Indian population.

The census of 1961 provided a major impetus for the government to develop population-control programs. The continued rapid growth of the population was seen as having detrimental economic and social consequences. The third plan, 1962−1967, saw the beginning of a heightened commitment to population-control programs. The family-planning program was decentralized with federal allocations now dispersed through state projects. The principal means of contraception advocated in the earlier plans, the rhythm method and *coitus interruptus*, were now seen as being ineffectual. Diaphragms and spermicides were also viewed as being inappropriate. Oral contraceptives, ''the pill,'' were too expensive and the general feeling was that women would forget to take them daily. In 1965 two new techniques were introduced: male sterilization (vasectomy) and the intrauterine device (IUD).

Shortly after its introduction, the IUD fell into disfavor. William Petersen (1975) summaries a number of Indian studies that found that whereas less than 1 percent of the women who had IUDs inserted became pregnant, almost one-tenth of the users automatically expelled the devices and as many as one-third of the women had them removed. These women either experienced excessive bleeding, pain, or discomfort, or had them removed because of the fear generated by the failures of others. In all about 800,000 IUDs were inserted during the first year (1965−1966), but only about 790,000 (or 19 percent) of the target population of 6 million were reached during the following year.

Increasingly, male sterilization was gaining favor by government officials. During 1965−1966, 600,000 men had vasectomies. Through various cash incentive payments, the number rose in the following year but started to decline toward the end of the 1960s and the early 1970s. The low vasectomy rates did not approach the governmental goals. Further, most of the men who underwent the operation had already fathered as many children as they wanted.

The failure of the vasectomy program paralleled the failure of the other population-control programs. India's programs have been continually hampered by bureaucratic inefficiency, inadequate funds, poor planning, and the monumental size of the task. Further, India has never been able to convince its people on the necessity for population limitation. As previously noted, although the birthrate has dropped somewhat since the implementation of these programs, the population is still increasing by a rate of 57,000 new births every day. In 1974 a panel of Indian social scientists predicted that by the year 2000 half the Indian population would be homeless and the country would be stripped bare of its resources for fuel and food (McKee and Robertson, 1975:45).

To combat this trend, the Indian National Congress, the ruling party of India since independence, accelerated its family-planning programs. A multitude of programs were implemented. IUDs, condoms, and other contraceptive devices were distributed free. The oral birth control pill was available only through pilot projects and distribution had begun in rural and urban family-planning centers. The mainstay of the program was sterilization.

During the authoritarian "state of emergency" of Indira Gandhi and the Congress Party, a mass sterilization campaign vasectomized millions of Indian males. At the time the program was initiated, Karen Singh, the Health Minister, described the problem this way:

> We are facing a population explosion of crisis dimensions, which has largely diluted the fruits of the remarkable economic progress that we have made. The time factor is so pressing, and the population growth so formidable, that we have to get out of the vicious circle through a direct assault upon this problem, as a national commitment. (Karen Singh cited in Borders, 1977).

Although ostensibly a voluntary program, the government pressured, cajoled, and forced people to undergo sterilization. The national campaign set a target of 4.3 million sterilizations. Over 7.8 million sterilizations were actually performed in the "emergency" between April 1976 and January 1977. The excessiveness of the aggressive birth control program led to a high number of forcible operations.

The sterilization issue was one of the major factors contributing to the dramatic defeat of the ruling Congress Party and of Indira Gandhi in the elections of March 1977. In the so-called vasectomy belt, the populous states of of north and central India, which felt the full brunt of the aggressive family-planning campaign, the Congress Party suffered overwhelming defeat. This was particularly the case in the constituencies of Indira Gandhi and her son Sanjay. After the election, an Indian diplomat provided the following explanation for the startling and unpredicted election results:

> The emergency would never have filtered down to the villages if all that was involved was press censorship and random jailings. But when you corral people without explaining that sterilization is not castration, when you take away their capacity to produce children to care for them in their old age and when you ignore the fact that Hindu philosophy has glorified fertility for 2,000 years, you've got to lose in the end. (Jensen in *Newsweek*, 1977:42).

Soon after the election, Raj Narain, who became the Minister of Health and Family Planning, ended the government sponsorship of sterilization and the cash incentive payments to individuals who underwent sterilization operations. He called for a considerable modification in the birth control program and the elimination of all elements of compulsion. He said that the new program would concentrate on increasing the number of condoms and birth control pills distributed, and it would also encourage other methods of preventing conception, including self-control or abstinence. The immediate result was a dramatic curtailment in sterilization operations: "In the northern state of Haryana, where sterilization was perhaps the single most important campaign issue—and where the Congress Party lost every single seat—20,000 operations were performed last December; the number per-formed in March was less than 20" (Borders, 1977).

The success or failure of population-planning programs can best be understood when examined in the contexts of people's lives. Demographic statistical patterns are, of course, meaningful, but, to get a more in-depth understanding of why they occur it is necessary to look at real people and real families. A study by Mahmood Mamdani, *The Myth of Population Control: Family, Caste and Class in an Indian Village* (1972) does just that. Mamdani is concerned with why the birth control movement was such a dismal failure in a small northern Indian village, Manupur. He looks at the structure of village life, at its caste and class structure, and at its families to determine why the population-planning program was so unsuccessful.

Before we look at Mamdani's study let us provide some additional information on the joint-family system and the village-based caste system. The joint family coupled with the village-based caste system are the main core units of traditional Hindu life. The Indian family is based on an extended or joint-family system. The family in turn is centered around the village, which is and still remains the most significant geographical entity for the vast majority of the contemporary Indian population.

Irawati Karve, an Indian social scientist, provides a precise definition of the traditional joint family: "A joint family is a group of people who generally live under one roof, who eat food cooked at one hearth, who hold property in common and who participate in common family worship and are related to each other as some particular type of kindred" (Karve cited in Ross, 1961:9). The head of the joint family is the oldest male member. His family, his younger brothers, his sons and their wives and children, and his grandchildren reside in the family compound. Relationships of family members are regulated by interlocking patterns of mutual dependence and assistance in times of need, mutuality of interests, and strong primary-group controls. In general, the younger generation is controlled by the elders. Individuality is subordinated to the collective. The marital relationship has little structural importance in the Hindu joint family. Traditionally, all marriages were arranged, and this procedure is only slowly disappearing. Marriage serves as a reaffirmation of a network of caste alliances and hierarchical gradations: "For the ancient sages declare that a bride is given to the family of her husband, and not to the husband alone" (Āpastamba cited in Lannoy, 1971:102).[1]

The joint family is supported and reinforced by the caste system. The numerous castes and subcastes are arranged in a vertical hierarchical pattern. In the Indian census of 1901, the last one to tabulate the many different Indian castes, there were 2378 "main" castes (Ross, 1961). They ranged in size from those that had several million people to others that had only a few. The caste system evolved out of a desire by ruling groups to provide an effective and stable division of labor. Each caste became identified with a particular occupation. Mamdani (1972), for example, discusses such "low" castes as the *Jheevar* who are water carriers and the *Marasi* who are drum beaters. Both, incidentally, have been rendered obsolete as a result of technological change; the water carriers were replaced by the water pump and the drum beaters no longer needed as the *Gurudwaras* (Sikh houses of worship) have become equipped with loudspeakers. Each caste member is assigned a given position, and all are fully aware of their standing and those of their superiors and inferiors.

Together, the joint family and the caste system serve to promote the stability of the social order. Kingsley Davis (1951) has outlined how they have helped to retard social change and the industrialization of Indian society. The joint family coupled with the village-based caste system lowers social mobility and serves to minimize competition.

---

[1]Āpastamba lived about the fourth century B.C.

> [The family system]. . . strongly limits social mobility and social change because it binds the individual to others on the basis of birth, forces him to contribute to the support of a large group independently of their ability, introduces nepotism into both business and politics, and assures control of the younger generation by the elders. (Davis, 1951:216)

The ascription-based caste system rejects qualification by achievement and "introduces unusual rigidities into the social order" (Davis, 1951:216). The caste system "is an effective brake on geographical mobility, ready contact with strangers, and the formation of large-scale business organizations" (Davis, 1951:216).

In modern times, the joint family remains a crucial factor in influencing individuals' lives. Aileen D. Ross (1961) cites a number of studies that provide evidence of the continued viability of the joint family even when family members move to the city. The emerging pattern is for the maintenance of connections with extended kin. The village continues to be the primary source of an individual's family identity. Authority remains vested in the family patriarch who still is the arbitrator of family matters. Family members return "home" on special occasions, such as festivals and marriages. Men who go into the cities to work send money back to their families and seek to return to the village after they have made money in the city, which enables them to buy land or live more comfortably in their village. Karve reports on this pattern:

> . . . instead of founding independent families in the towns where they are employed they tend to keep their ties with the family at home. They send money to the impoverished farmers at home, send their wives home for child-birth and go themselves for an occasional holiday or in times of need. The urge to visit the family for certain festivities and at sowing and harvesting times is so great that there is seasonal migration of mill-labourers in all industry towns. Even if a man earns good wages it is difficult for him to find a bride from a decent house if he has no family with some land in some village. (Karve cited in Ross, 1961:22)

The continued viability of the joint-family system and the caste system in contemporary India have been instrumental factors in explaining the dismal failures and problems of India's population-planning programs. Mahmood Mamdani (1972) examines the family, caste, and class in an Indian village in the Punjab and demonstrates its influence on a big birth-reduction campaign.

Under the sponsorship of the Indian government and the Rockefeller Foundation, the *Khanna Study* was the first major field study in birth control in India. The field study was from 1954 to 1960 and the follow-up study occurred in the summer of 1969. This birth control program was conducted in seven villages with a total population of 8000 people at a study cost of approximately $1 million.

Mahmood Mamdani believes that the primary reason for the failure of the *Khanna Study* was its deep-rooted political conservatism and its inability to understand the realities of village life. The family-planning program implicitly was considered as a substitute for structural and institutional change. The population controllers sought to bring about population control without any fundamental changes in the underlying relationships of the villagers. He argues that to be successful population-planning programs must understand individuals within the given social structure. It is foolhardy to believe that the simple dissemination of birth control information is sufficient to change people's behavior. Such a policy completely ignores the inequalities inherent within the caste and class structure.

Mamdani convincingly demonstrates that poor families will not restrict their family size because large families are economically viable. The only hope that the poor have in raising their status and economic position is to have a large family of sons. They can either work land for their parents and so help them accumulate savings so that they can buy land or they can emigrate to the cities and send back monetary remittances. To overcome poverty, large families are needed. The land can be worked with the manpower available within the family. One farmer puts it this way: "Why pay 2500 rupees for an extra hand? Why not have a son? . . . Instead of land fragmentation more sons increase your land" (Mamdani, 1972:77).

Mamdani points out that in a society that has a low level of technology, large families have high value among agricultural laborers. Under such conditions economic competition is determined by numbers, and the more laborers you have the better off you are. For these people, family planning means voluntarily reducing the family labor source. This would mean economic suicide and would be extremely irrational behavior. For the overwhelming majority (nearly 95 percent) of the people who participate in the agricultural economy, a large family is a necessity. For the small minority, the wealthy, civil servants, teachers, and others who live under radically different material conditions the importance of children is significantly less. Attitudes and perceptions of the villagers toward birth control varied according to their relationship to the economy.

> The majority in Manupur found it difficult to believe that the Khanna Study had actually come to introduce contraceptive practices. Even though the Khanna Study was a reality obvious to all, even though the whole enterprise "must have cost an incredible amount of money," the majority of the villagers never understood why so much money and effort were being spent on family planning when "surely everybody knows that children are a necessity in life." (Mamdani, 1972:144)

The failure of the birth control program does not stem from either the illiteracy or the ignorance of the people. Nor would the demographic education of the villagers change their behavior. It would only change when it becomes economically viable for families to restrict their numbers. And that can only occur when the caste and class system are changed and when technological development economically warrants such a move. Mamdani quotes a low caste water carrier who, mistaking him for a *Khanna Study* worker, proudly exclaims:

You were trying to convince me in 1960 that I shouldn't have any more sons. Now, you see, I have six sons and two daughters and I sit at home in leisure. They are grown up and they bring me money. One even works outside the village as a laborer. You told me I was a poor man and couldn't support a large family. Now, you see, because of my large family, I am a rich man. (Mamdani, 1972:109)

This examination of population dynamics in India reveals that it is interrelated with family conceptualizations and dynamics along with social, political, and economic factors. In the next section we will see how the interrelationship of these factors is manifested in Western societies, particularly in the United States. Our focus of concern centers on the conceptualization of parenthood and its influence on marital and parental relationships.

Two Exploding Populations—Two Different Approaches

MICHAEL T. KAUFMAN and FOX BUTTERFIELD
The two most populous nations in the world, India with 630 million and China with 960 million, are each undergoing radical changes in their population programs—both for political reasons but in opposite directions. In China, where social cohesiveness has been the law of life for centuries, political directives seem easily perceived by the people as identical with their own will. India, divided geographically by language and horizontally by caste, remains recalcitrant. What is at stake in both nations is a world population that may reach 6.35 billion by the end of the century. At present, every fourth person on earth is Chinese. Of the remainder, one out of five is an Indian.

Abandoned Effort After the Gandhi Era*
NEW DELHI—At a gas station near this city's Embassy Row, officials from the Health Ministry a short while ago unveiled the country's first automatic condom dispenser with a statement that such machines are to be placed in a number of locations and that they may encourage the use of contraceptives by Indian men who have been too shy to purchase them from shopclerks.

The most remarkable thing about the ceremony was that the sorry little machine and the sorry little press release that accompanied it represented the single new initiative in family planning since the forced sterilizations carried out during the rule of Indira Gandhi brought family planning almost to a standstill. In view of the enormity of population pressures in India, the condom machine is like a black joke evoking such similes as using a sieve to bail in a tempest or firing bullets at a locust swarm.

It is more than two years since Mrs. Gandhi fell, but family planning is still such an explosive issue in India that it requires unusual political courage to even mention the words. In fact, under the Government of Morarji R. Desai which was toppled this summer, the Ministry of Health and Family Planning was renamed the Ministry of Health and Family Welfare. An election campaign is now starting, but the issue of birth control has not been raised. Recently, when a gathering of Indian feminists met to draw up a list of women's demands for submission to political parties, a move to include a strong family planning program was defeated by a wide margin. In the kind of political shorthand that determines voting patterns, birth control has become linked with authoritarianism.

For the country's planners and demographic experts, the legacy of the overzealous birth control program of three years ago has been tragic. "We've suffered about a five-year setback," said Dr. Pai Panandikar, chairman of the National Population Policy Group on India's Central Planning Commission. Others say this evaluation may be too optimistic. "A meaningful program can be developed again only if there is strong political backing," said one planner working in birth control. "There is no one around who has either the political strength or commitment to push a renewed program along."

Just how badly the birth control campaign has been hurt by the now-discredited coercive policies is evident in the tables of Government statisticians. In the final year of Mrs. Gandhi's rule, when her controversial son, Sanjay, was cheering the Government program to its most aggressive phase, just under one million vasectomies were being performed monthly. Immediately after Mrs. Gandhi's election defeat—a loss that many feel was brought about largely by widespread disgust at the sterilization program—the number of vasectomies dropped to fewer than 20,000 a month. The program is still in extremis but the number of surgical sterilizations of men and women now stands at about 70,000 a month.

Surgical sterilizations have traditionally been the most common form of birth control used in India. When, under Mrs. Gandhi, population control had high priority, the publicly stated target for the program was to bring the country's annual birthrate down to 30 per 1,000 of population by 1983.

Under the impact of the weakened family planning program, Government planners first recast the goal as 31 births per thousand, and then revised the figure again to 32 births per thousand by 1983. Meanwhile, the rate of population increase, which stood at 33 per 1000 at the end of Mrs. Gandhi's "emergency" rule, has moved upward to 34 per thousand. In order to reach even the revised target, Government planners concede that at least 4 million sterilizations would have to be conducted annually, far more than the number carried out now or likely to be carried out in the near future. All these projections are cast against the background of Malthusian gloom rendered in nearly astronomical numbers. There are now 630 million Indians. Each day there is a net increase of some 35,000. Forty percent of the present population is under 15 years of age with their procreative years ahead of them.

On the momentarily positive side, India has made giant strides in increasing food production and industrial growth. Aided by four successive good monsoons, the country has more than fed itself and has built up a food surplus. There are those, however, who believe that a period of relative prosperity works against population control.

At any rate, Government planners are still clinging to the hope that through education and the pressures of urbanization, the replacement rate of about 2.3 children per family will be achieved by the end of the century. Given current projections, the Indian population should then be around 900 million. Even so, it will still be expanding and even the most optimistic demographers do not see stabilization taking place until the middle of the next century when the population will be between 1.1 and 1.2 billion.

One interesting aspect of the birth control controversy has been the inability of any agency to determine just how widespread were the abuses of the coercive program. That some men were rounded up and subjected to vasectomies through the use of force and intimidation is certain. It is also clear that instances of duress took place more often in India's more populated northern regions than in the south where typically the figures for vasectomies were fraudulently inflated to meet Government quotas. There is now a fairly common view that the perception of forcible sterilizations was more pervasive than the actual violations.

Whether or not this is true, the fact remains that in the countryside family planning has been discredited, not only in regard to sterilization but also in reference to interuterine devices and and birth control pills. Introduction of these means of contraception continues to lag behind levels achieved during Mrs. Gandhi's tenure.

Although population control—which most development experts believe to be the most critical issue facing India—has not surfaced in the political battling that has gripped India since the summer, it may well be raised before parliamentary elections in January. After a period of ostracism, Mrs. Gandhi and her son appear to be returning once again to the center of things. Certainly her opponents will use the reports of forced sterilizations against her. It will be interesting to see if she tries to duck these challenges or whether she takes them on, pointing out the collapse of the family planning program under the governments that have succeeded her.

Popular expressions of concern about continuing unchecked population growth are rare in Indian newspapers and magazines. Not so reticent was a Nepalese craftsman who sells bamboo dolls which are inside each other.

His come-on to tourists is nearly perfect. "Here family planning family," he says, extending a baby doll resting inside a child doll which rests inside a mother doll which is inside the father doll. "Very happy modern family, only two children, not ten children," says the craftsman. The line captivates tourist sensibilities, but the Nepalese does not bother trying it on the Indians.

*Michael T. Kaufman in *The New York Times,* November 11, 1979. ©1979 by The New York Times Company. Reprinted by permission.

In the New China, 1 + 1 Can = 4 — No more[†]

PEKING—Two decades ago, China's most prominent economist, a man named Ma Yinchu, daringly warned that the country's population was expanding too fast and would interfere with economic development plans. For his temerity in going against a Marxist belief that more people mean more production, Mr. Ma was attacked and purged from his job as President of Peking University.

But recently, at the age of 98, Mr. Ma was rehabilitated and named honorary President of the school again. For China's leaders now agree he was right all along.

Indeed, over the past few months Peking has inaugurated what may be its most important campaign, to reduce China's population growth rate to zero by the year 2000. To achieve this, it has introduced new regulations to limit families to one, or at most two children. Those that comply will receive bonuses and preferential treatment in housing and education for their offspring. Those that do not will have their salaries docked and be promoted more slowly.

Given China's vast size, the strong traditional preference for large families and the still overwhelmingly rural makeup of the population—80 percent work on farms—zero population growth is an extraordinarily ambitious target. It is also a critical one. In 1949, when Mao Zedong proclaimed the founding of the People's Republic, China had 540 million people. Today it has 960 million. That is an increase of over 400 million in 30 years, almost double the population of the United States.

As a result of this enormous jump, though China's agriculture has made remarkable advances, most Chinese today get no more to eat than they did in the mid-1950s. There is a severe housing shortage (the average allotment is less than four square yards per person in the cities). Perhaps 20 million people are unemployed. At the same time less than half of all young people can go to senior high school and only 3 or 4 percent to college.

All of these problems are likely to be magnified over the next few years because the children born in the baby boom of the 1950's and 60's are just now coming of age. Half the population is under 21.

Nevertheless, the Government appears confident its new measures will be effective in stopping the increase. The immediate goal is to reduce the growth rate from 1.2 percent in 1978 to 1 percent this year, and then to 0.5 percent by 1985. There are several reasons for the Government's optimism. Peking introduced its first significant population restrictions in 1971, after the end of the Cultural Revolution, when the Government began to grasp the dimensions of its population boom. Since then, the growth rate has already been cut from a high of 2.3 percent a year.

This success was achieved by several measures: men in the cities were required to wait until they were 27 years old to get married, women until 25. Free contraceptives, abortions and sterilization operations were provided.

It is not uncommon in factories or offices to see charts proclaiming the method of birth control being practiced by each worker, with a red star opposite the name of those sterilized. In some factories, women are assigned to monitor the menstrual cycles of their fellow employees, and if a woman who is not supposed to have a child at that time misses her period, she is asked to have an abortion. Americans would be embarrassed to have their friends know such information. But in China, public scrutiny can serve as a weapon.

Peking demonstrated its growing confidence on the population question last summer when for the first time since the 1950's it issued what appears to be a relatively accurate count of its people (the actual figure was 975.23 million, which includes 17 million people on Taiwan). The Government did not say what the figure was based on—there has been no public reference to a new census—but Chinese demographers have privately disclosed further data on birth and death rates to foreign specialists, suggesting Peking does have some basis for its estimate.

The tough new policy of trying to limit families to one child, or at most two, now provides the Government with a further way to curb the growth rate. In Peking, a couple that pledges to have only one child will receive a certificate entitling their offspring to preference in everything from entering nursery school, to better medical care, admittance to high school and college and later to getting a job.

A one-child family will also get an annual bonus equivalent to $40, equal to a month's salary for an average Chinese worker. From now on, it was announced last week, all families in Peking will be allocated housing space as if they had two children, giving single-child families an advantage and penalizing those with more than two.

Conversely, parents who have more than two children will be taxed 10 percent of their salary, to make them share the state's cost of bringing up their offspring. They will also not be eligible for promotion till the extra child is over 14 years old.

The real test of this new policy will come in the countryside, where the birth rate has remained higher. To counter the old economic imperative that more children means more hands and more income, the

Government will grant families with one child a private plot equal in size to that of families with two children. Whether that will really compensate rural families for the lack of more children remains to be seen.

Traditions die hard. Remote Guizhou Province in the Southwest reported in September that a country Communist Party secretary had his promotion cancelled after his wife gave birth to a sixth child. In Jiangxi Province, a barefoot doctor, or paramedic, was sentenced to two years imprisonment for helping 15 women remove their intrauterine devices.

Whatever the outcome of Peking's new program, the neglect of the past three decades has already left its mark. It took only from 1949 to 1979 for China's population to grow by over 400 million people. But it took until 1840 to reach the first 400 million.

[†] Fox Butterfield in *The New York Times,* November 11, 1979. ©1979 by The New York Times Company. Reprinted by permission.

FERTILITY PATTERNS IN THE WEST: PARENTHOOD AND IDEOLOGIES

Paradoxically, although the emerging industrial system propagated ideologies that fostered low fertility and small family size, there were opposing ideologies gaining ascendancy that advocated domesticity and motherhood. That is, doctrines placing high value on the domestic confinement of women and their exclusive involvement with housework and childrearing were being set forth at the same time forces were motivating couples to want fewer births and to restrict their family size. Thus women's entire functions were being defined in terms of motherhood at the same time the societal demands for children were diminishing. This situation was of course inherently unstable. The women's movements, the delay in marriage and childbearing and the increased participation of women in the labor force can all be seen as protests to the untenable position of women in industrial society. We have discussed some of these ideologies and the conditions underlying them in chapter 10. A brief review would be beneficial to help put this discussion of fertility and parenthood in perspective.

The rise of industrialization in the mid-19th century saw a vast migration of people from rural areas to the factories and bureaucracies of a modern urban society. Work became more and more removed from the family setting. Men took jobs away from the home. They became increasingly independent of the previous prevailing domestic economy. With work becoming independent of the home, so did men. These processes had an opposite effect on women and children. They became more economically dependent on the financial contributions of husbands and fathers. Domestic constraints, household tasks, and the care of children became solely the province of women. They were prevented from participation in extrafamilial occupations. Increasingly, they became cut off from the outside world of work. The resultant picture was that women and children were now economic liabilities who were almost totally dependent on the economic viability of men. Ann Oakley (1974:59) summarizes three lasting consequences associated with industrialization: "... the separation of the man from the intimate daily routines of domestic life; the economic dependence of women and children on men; the isolation of housework and childcare from other work."

We have discussed the patriarchal ideology, which advocates the domestic confinement of women. Its basis was the desire of Victorian men to shield the family from the evils of industrialization and urbanization. The isolated home was to provide a safe shelter and protection for the wife and the children. In this cloistered home the mother was to shield and protect the man's children. It was each man's castle and sanctuary. The home and women took on a sacred quality; it became the repository of goodness in a world of evil. John Ruskin has made the classic statement on the nature of the domestic scene as the province of mothers in his essay "Of Queen's Gardens" first published in 1865:

> This is the true nature of home—it is the place of Peace; the shelter, not only from all injury, but from all terror, doubt, and division. In so far as it is not this, it is not home; so far as the anxieties of the outer life penetrate into it, and the inconsistently-minded, unknown, unloved, or hostile society of the outer world is allowed by either husband or wife to cross the threshold it ceases to be home; it is then only a part of the outer world which you have roofed over and lighted fire in. But so far as it is a sacred place, a vestal temple, a temple of the hearth watched over by Household Gods . . . so far as it is this, and the roof and the fire are types only of a nobler shade and light, shade as of the rock in a weary land, and the light as of Pharos in the stormy sea—so far it vindicates the name and fulfills the praise of home. (Ruskin, 1865/n.d.: 151−152)

The Victorian model, then, depicted women as the repository of virtue. The home was seen as the sanctuary protecting women and children from the evils of the outside world. The home was the working man's castle; his refuge from "the jungle out there."

The Victorian idealization of motherhood continues to linger in contemporary society. Betty Rollin talks of " 'The Motherhood Myth'—the idea that having babies is something that all normal women instinctively want and need and will enjoy doing—they just think they do" (Rollin, 1971:346). The motherhood myth is seen to have emerged after World War II. The economic prosperity and growth of post-war America was in striking contrast to the years of want and sacrifice during the Great Depression and the uncertainties of the war years. Rollin cites Betty Freiden who in *The Feminine Mystique,* saw the late 1940s and 1950s as a period when the production of babies became the norm and motherhood turned into a cult.

Psychoanalysis was influential in the development of the mystique surrounding parenthood. Psychoanalysis placed undue emphasis on the mother-child relation-ship. It oversentimentalized it. It argued that only the biologic mother was capable of providing the emotional satisfaction and stimulation necessary for the healthy development of the infant. For the individuals involved, parenthood represented a necessary step on the road to maturation and personality development. For women, parenthood was necessary for them to achieve normality and avoid neuroticism. Freudian psychology insisted that the reproductive potential, that is, childbearing, must be actualized if women were to achieve mental health. Motherhood represented the realization of women's basic psychologic and biologic needs.

Rochelle Paul Wortis (1977) critically reexamined the concept of the maternal role as expressed in psychoanalytic theory. She concluded that the evidence used in psychological studies for the importance of the mother-child relationship was based on scientifically inadequate assumptions. The overemphasis on parenthood and, particularly, on motherhood encouraged "the domestication and subordination of females in society" (Wortis, 1977:361).

Wortis observed that the psychologic studies centering around the mother-infant bond reflected the provincialism of Western psychology and psychiatry. She argues that they turned a cultural phenomenon into a biologic one. Wortis notes that there are diversified ways in which children around the world are raised. Our society is relatively unique in insisting that child development lies solely within the province and responsibility of the mother. Wortis augments her argument by citing from the work of Margaret Mead:

> At present, the specific biological situation of the continuing relationship of the child to its biological mother and its need for care by human beings are being hopelessly confused in the growing insistence that child and biological mother, or mother surrogate, must never be separated, that all separation, even for a few days, is inevitably damaging, and that if long enough it does irreversible damage. This . . . is a new and subtle form of antifeminism in which men—are tying women more tightly to their children than has been thought necessary since the invention of bottle feeding and baby carriages. Actually, anthropological evidence gives no support at present to the value of such an accentuation of the tie between mother and child. . . . On the contrary, cross-cultural studies suggest that adjustment is most facilitated if the child is cared for by many warm friendly people. (Mead, 1954, cited in Wortis, 1977:366)

Additional cross-cultural evidence on the variability of childrearing patterns is provided in a study of six cultures by Minturn and Lambert (1964). The researchers found that only in the New England suburb of Orchardtown were there isolated households and exclusive mother-infant childrearing. In the five more "primitive" societies, there was a greater involvement by other kin and outsiders in the raising of the child. Thus among the Nyansongo of Kenya the child is cared for by an older sibling when the mother is working in nearby fields. Among the Rajputs of India, a caretaker, either an older sister or a cousin, cares for the child. Old men and, eventually, other male relatives—fathers, uncles, or grandfathers—assist in the child's care. Similar shared involvements characterize the Taira in Okinawa, the Mixteans of Mexico, and the Tarong of the Philippines. It is only in our society that women solely have this task.

Judith Blake, a world-famous demographer, argues that in contemporary Western society motherhood is actualized in "coercive pronatalism" (1972). Blake believes that motherhood rather than being a voluntary option for women is, in fact, a mandatory directive. This directive assures that women will bear children. Two pronatalist coercions characterize modern American society. The first is the prescribed primacy of parenthood in the definition of sex roles. The second is the prescribed congruence of personality traits with the demands of the sex roles as defined. Adult sex roles are defined in terms of parenthood. Americans socialize girls and boys to become the proper kinds of people they say that mothers and fathers should be.

Blake believes that the emphasis on the primacy of parenthood limits the accessibility of alternative roles. This is particularly the case for women. Nonfamilial roles are seen as deviant and pathological. Challenges to the role of motherhood arouse widespread opposition since they are viewed as threats to the sex-role expectations relegating women to domesticity and parenthood. Female labor-force participation, higher education for women, and feminism are viewed negatively by society as they run counter to the desired goal of motherhood. Motherhood is seen to represent the fulfillment of a woman's destiny and is the ultimate end.

Myths about motherhood provide the supportive ideology for the above viewpoint. Motherhood is seen to provide a woman with her most rewarding status. Fatherhood demonstrates the masculinity of the man. E. E. Le Masters (1977) has outlined several folk beliefs about parenthood that have been popular in American culture. (A folk belief is one that is widely held but that is not supported by facts.) Here are some of Le Master's examples of these beliefs.:

1. Rearing children is fun.
2. Children are sweet and cute.
3. Children will turn out well if they have "good" parents.
4. Children will improve marriage.
5. Childless couples are frustrated and unhappy.
6. Parents are adults.

Le Masters believes that these myths have been disproved by scientific evidence. However, they still serve to promote parenthood. Further, they downplay the problems associated with the transition to parenthood. Indeed, the transition to parenthood is a period often marked by crisis and marital disruption. Alice S. Rossi (1968), in an enlightening article, argues that the tensions and problems accompanying parenthood can be seen as an outgrowth of the isolation of the nuclear family and the almost exclusive involvement of the mother with infant and child care. An examination of the transition to the parenthood period is revealing in that it highlights the nature of parental roles in our modern industrial society.

For the French, Day Care Centers Have Become a Necessity

OLIVE EVANS

PARIS—A few minutes walk from Pigalle there is a building, dating to the time of Louis XIV, that since 1889 has sheltered very young children. Toward the eastern end of the city, in a middle-class section where there has been much demolition and construction, is another crèche, or day care center, that opened in 1971 in a bright new building in the Rue de Pyrenées.

They are two of approximately 1,000 crèches throughout France, of which about 80 are in Paris. At least 51,000 children are now in some type of day care center in France. The demand for day care, long an established fact of life in France, is becoming urgent, as more and more families realize that to move into the middle class—or even to stay in it—they must have two salaries, and as more mothers choose to work whether they need to or not.

"The crèche is becoming á la mode," said Anne Mariel, who inspects half the crèches in Paris for the Government's Organization for Protection of Mothers and Children.

Mornings spent at the two contrasting public crèches gave an impression that there is a concerted effort to provide more than custodial care for the children, many of whom aged from two months to three years, spend up to 12 hours a day in this communal environment.

A typical day starts at 7 o'clock when the first of 60 children arrive. Each mother or father (there is an increasing effort to involve fathers) on arrival undresses the child, and places the clothes in a tiny individual locker. The children don brightly colored rompers that are far from institutional looking.

The removal of personal garments is part of a pattern of egalitarianism in the crèches.

"Dressed alike there is no way of distinguishing the child of an engineer from that of a chambermaid," explained Yvonne Luor, director of the crèche near Pigalle.

Marianne, 2 years old, was a newcomer at the modern crèche. It was her fifth day, and in the play area she was clutching firmly in her arms one of her just-removed shoes.

After a few minutes of standing apart from the bustling activity in the gaily decorated room, Marianne was taken gently by the hand by a teacher who, with a kiss and a hug, started to show her some picture books.

"Her mother was permitted to stay here all day with her the first two days," said Simone Beinenfeld, director of the modern center.

"There are problems of adjustment when the child joins the crèche later," she added. "We prefer to have them from infancy because then the separation from the mother is not so traumatic, and the crèche becomes the child's normal life. However, even for newcomers, usually after about a month, tout s'arrange."

If things do not work out, Marianne will be seen by a psychologist who visits the crèche periodically.

Mrs. Mariel said that although the incidence of psychological problems is not high, there are indications that children raised in creches learn to talk later.

"There is not the intense relationship of mother to child that stimulates verbalization," she said. These children, however, often do better in school, because they are used to working in groups and taking direction, she pointed out. France has pioneered in early childhood education, and it is normal for French children to enter nursery school when they are 3 years old.

At the newer crèche there appeared to be an innovative approach, with emphasis on intellectual stimulation. Children were not divided according to age, as is usual. In one room the "moyens" or toddlers of 14 months to 2 years were playing with blocks on the floor, while several babies watched, fascinated, from their glass-enclosed cribs.

"This is an experiment," Mrs. Beinenfeld said. "We feel that in mixing the ages we are approximating more nearly the atmosphere of a family." Children were free to wander from one area to another, to choose toys from open shelves. Older infants, barefooted, were crawling and exploring.

There appeared to be a fairly relaxed attitude toward germs, although a nurse was taking the temperature of a child who she thought was acting feverish. Meanwhile children were playing barelegged on the terrace on a blustery day that would have brought American children out in snowsuits.

It is not colds but accidents that are the crèche director's nightmare. Despite heroic measures to avoid them, they happen. Great care was taken to avoid falls, while the children were doing gymnastics, which seem to be stressed even for young babies. A 6-month-old was being rolled around on a huge, plastic red and white balloon, to his great delight. Not far away, toddlers, bracing their legs firmly, were pulled across the room on small felt mats.

"It's good for the legs and develops a sense of balance," Mrs. Beinenfeld explained. "And all these things give the personnel a chance to be involved with the children, to observe them."

Health problems are referred to a physician who visits the crèche twice a week, and vaccinations are done at appropriate ages.

These services cost money, and while private doctors and hospitalization are largely paid for by Social Security in France, all parents must pay to enroll their children in a crèche. Rates are on a sliding scale, based on parents' income, rent and the number of persons in the family; they range from 6 francs a day ($1.25) to 29 francs ($6). The cost to the crèche, however, is about 45 to 50 francs a day, with the French Government paying the balance.

Although the crèche near Pigalle seemed to be more traditional in its approach, the director, Mrs. Luo, who is about 60, seemed strongly maternal, and the children ran to her to be picked up and kissed when she entered a playroom.

As in the newer crèche, the nurseries and play areas were brightly painted and decorated with comic mobiles, gay posters, cut-out animals and paintings done by the children.

"We are trying to be more human than in the past," Mrs. Luo said. "There is more holding, touching, tendresse. We pick the tout-petits up when they cry."

With four infants being fed and six waiting, three of whom were crying vigorously and hungrily, one had the feeling that the nursery could have done with more nurses. The law requires one employe for every five children who do not walk and one for every eight who do.

Recruitment of personnel is a problem, Mrs. Mariel said. "We need people who are motivated as well as qualified." And salaries could be improved.

After lunch, individual folding cots were taken out of the closet, arranged across the playroom, and the children slipped beneath pink gingham coverlets. Soon a hush fell on the room.

There are long waiting lists for admission to the crèches, Mrs. Mariel said. "Pompidou," she said, referring to Georges Pompidou, the late President, "Pompidou promised 2,000 more crèches." Mr. Pompidou's successor, has also promised action.

What may be the long-term effect of this type of child-rearing on the traditional, tightly knit French family?

"One can't ask if it's good or bad," Mrs. Mariel said. "It exists. One has to adapt to necessity. The family today is different from the past, and it may be necessary to organize it in an even different way in the future. Life has changed. Life is changing. But perhaps it is true that—in spite of all we try to do—the child is a little bit the victim of this transformation of society."

Mrs. Mariel has 8-year-old twins, a boy and a girl. They have been in a crèche from the age of two months.

"I was the first woman of my family to work after becoming a mother," she said. "I had to put them in a crèche. The kids didn't suffer—they were fine. It was I who suffered."

THE TRANSITION TO PARENTHOOD

Only in recent years have sociologists recognized that parenthood, rather than marriage, may be the crucial role transition for men and women. Parenthood necessitates the reorganization of economic patterns of earning and spending the family income. It demands the reallocation of space, time, and attention. It necessitates the reorganization of marital decision making and the reorganization of occupation-role commitments, particularly for the wife. It calls for the reworking of relationships with extended family, friends, and neighbors. Finally, it demands the reestablishment of marital adjustment and intimacy, which have been disrupted by the period of transition to parenthood.

Despite the importance of this transition, little research effort has been directed to this concern. The behavioral sciences have almost exclusively confined their attention to the child when studying the husband-wife-child relationships. Thus a vast body of data has been accumulated in the field of child development. There is a great deal of literature concerned with the effect parents have on their children. The corresponding issue—the effects children have on their parents—has received relatively little attention. This reflects the parenthood myth that having children is an enriching and maturing experience. The myth says parenthood enhances personality growth, solidifies the marriage, and indicates the achievement of adult status and community stability. With such positive attributes, the impact of parenthood on the parents was not seen as problematic and was, therefore, not defined as a subject worth studying. The handful of existing studies, although exploratory and having methodological weaknesses, nonetheless reveal that parenthood is not always positive.

In a widely cited article, "Parenthood as Crisis," E. E. LeMasters (1957) found that 83 percent of the 46 couples interviewed experienced extensive or severe crisis in adjusting to the birth of their first child. Some of the problems of adjustment most frequently mentioned by mothers were chronic tiredness, extensive confinement to the home with resulting curtailment of social contacts, and the relinquishing of satisfactions associated with outside employment. Women felt guilt about not being better mothers. Fathers mentioned decline in sexual response of the wife, economic pressures resulting from the wife's retirement, additional expenditures necessary for the child, and a general disenchantment with the parental role.

The amount of crisis experienced by these couples was found to be unrelated to the planning of children, to prior marital adjustment, or to the personality adjustment of the couples. Couples seemed to experience crisis even when they actively wanted the child and had a good marriage. The only variable that LeMasters found to distinguish crisis from noncrisis reactions was professional employment of the mother. All eight mothers with extensive professional work experience suffered severe crisis. LeMasters concludes that parenthood is the real "romantic complex" in our culture and that this romanticizing of parenthood and the attendant lack of training for the role are crucial determinants of problems.

Everet D. Dyer (1963) studied 32 middle-class couples who had their first child within the 2 years before the study. Among these couples, 53 percent experienced extensive or severe crisis, 38 percent experienced moderate crisis, and the remaining 9 percent reported slight adjustment problems. These crises often lasted for several months and involved the reorganization of preexisting role relationships. Difficulties reported by these new mothers were similar to those reported by LeMasters: tiredness, feelings of uncertainty, and curtailment of outside activities and interests. New fathers reported the same problems as their wives and added those of adjusting to one income and getting used to new demands and routines. Overall, the findings from Dyer's study tend to support the contention that the addition of the first child constitutes a crisis event for middle-class couples and those who undergo the severest crises have the most difficulty recovering.

Some studies, however, have found that beginning parenthood should be seen as a transitional period rather than a crisis one. Notably, the studies by Daniel F. Hobbs (1965, 1968) and that of Hobbs and Sue Peck Cole (1976) found only slight amounts of difficulty among parents adjusting to the first child. However, they did find that mothers reported significantly greater amounts of difficulty than did fathers. The Hobbs and Cole study differed from Hobbs's two earlier studies in that his samples were not limited to middle-class couples and the couples were contacted much sooner after the birth of their child. Hobbs speculates that the low proportion of couples experiencing crisis at this early period may be due to a "baby honeymoon." This is a period of early elation over parenthood but, after 4 to 6 weeks, crisis occurs. Another factor, that the samples contained lower-class couples, may indicate variations among the classes in their reaction to parenthood. Let us look at class variations in more detail.

Arthur P. Jacoby (1969), in a reassessment of the transition to parenthood literature, developed hypotheses to explain why his findings and those of LeMasters and Dyer found greater role transition problems for their middle-class samples than for Hobbs's working-class samples. The following key elements were suggested to explain the higher middle-class parenthood-crisis rate:

1. Middle-class standards may be higher. (Middle-class families are seen to have greater expectations in terms of childbearing practices and personal advancement).
2. The working-class woman places a greater intrinsic value on having children.
3. The principal sources of gratification for the working-class woman are located within the family rather than outside it.
4. Parenthood is far more likely to interfere with career aspirations for middle-class mothers.
5. Middle-class mothers are less experienced in the care of children.
6. The middle-class husband-and-wife relationship is more strongly established as affectively positive at the time of birth of a child. (Research on

lower class marriages indicates a weaker and less affectionate conjugal tie than in the middle class. The arrival of a child represents less of a threat to the marital relationship because there is less to threaten.)

Let us build on Jacoby's speculations by analyzing the transition to parenthood within different class groups focusing on the effect of the transition period on three major areas: (1) the marital relationship, (2) the satisfactions of the husband and wife with their marital roles and their lives, and (3) social and career aspirations, interests, and acitivites of the husband and wife. By comparing husbands and wives of different social classes in these three areas we will be able to pinpoint their attitudinal and behavioral differences regarding parenthood.

Marital Interaction

Several studies (Blood and Wolfe, 1960; Campbell, 1970; Renne, 1970; Reiss, 1971) report that after childbirth marital communication is disrupted and marital satisfaction drops for middle-class couples. Harold Feldman (1974) found that in companionate marital relationships the level of marital satisfaction decreased when a couple had a child. It was more apt to increase in differentiated marital relationships. Here, the previously nonexistent closeness between the parents was changed by the new, shared interest in the infant. This may support Jacoby's (1969) proposition that the birth of a child can easily disrupt emotional and affectional middle-class family ties.

Wives involved in household and family responsibilities may resent their husbands' nonfamilial involvements. Reuban Hill and Joan Aldous (1968) believe that this resentment may become manifest in their resistance to husbands' demands for intimacies. Peter Pineo (1961) presents evidence indicating that parenthood may have a disproportionately negative effect on women. Disenchantment with marriage is seen to result from parenthood for them, whereas occupational commitments are seen to be the major factor accounting for male disenchantment.

Working-class couples have been characterized by weak and less affectionate ties and thus a child may not represent a threat to the marital relationship. Mirra Komarovsky (1964) and Lee Rainwater (1965) found that there is a segregated pattern of decision making and task division with working-class couples as well as less expectation that husbands and wives will be companions. This is felt to aid them and better prepare them to interact as father and mother than as conjugal partners. It would seem that a key variable underlying the differences between the classes is the different types of marital relationships that existed before parenthood. Middle-class companionate relationships characterized by joint decision making and task differentiation tends to become more disrupted at parenthood than working-class noncompanionate relationships.

However, Hannah Gavron (1966) reports that for some middle-class couples with an egalitarian relationship there is a tendency for parents to establish some barriers between themselves and their children. But, during the period immediately following the birth of the child, there still is some degree of temporary segregation of spousal responsibilities. Rossi (1968) suggests that, with the strengthening of the egalitarian relationship, there may develop a greater recognition of the wife's need for autonomy and the husband's role in the routines of home and childrearing. In fact, Rossi sees such a movement becoming institutionalized through natural childbirth and prenatal courses for the husband. These developments are seen as a consequence of greater egalitarianism between husband and wife, especially when both work and jointly maintain the household before the onset of the child. If this is a coming trend, then, the disruption of marital communication and marital satisfaction for middle-class parents should diminish.

Marital Roles and Life Satisfactions

The sexual relationship is disrupted and frequently discontinued during the 8 weeks prior to birth and up to 2 months after birth. This allows the woman's tissues to heal. Further, the involvement of the woman with the infant often leads to a disinterest toward sex or frequent disruptions by its cries. The fear of immediate pregnancy after the birth of a child can also be a factor. Studies of working-class families by Rainwater (1960) and Komarovsky (1962) discuss the wife's dilemma: her self-interest in avoiding another pregnancy versus her desire for sexual pleasure to gratify herself and her husband. This is of crucial importance to women who have recently given birth and who do not communicate with their husbands on sexual matters. These studies and many others report that the lack of communication in this area is more characteristic of the working class than the middle class. If this is the case, then we would suspect that middle-class couples may find postpartum sexual adjustments easier than blue-collar couples. However, the revolution in the general technology of contraception, especially the birth control pill, has the potential to alter this factor dramatically. Unfortunately, there is virtually no systematic investigation on the extent that this occurs.

A second factor that affects sexual and marital satisfactions and adjustments after childbirth is the degree of segregation of marital-role tasks. Earlier, we reported on Hill and Aldous's (1968) contention that wives who are tied down by domestic household and child-care duties resent their husbands' external involvements. This resentment becomes evident in their resistance to their husbands' demands for conjugal intimacies. Based on this finding, one may conclude that segregated-task allocations, especially in terms of the wife's involvement with domestic and child-care tasks, will be positively related to poor sexual adjustment and potentially poor marital adjustment. Since role segregation is more prevalent in the working class, one would expect the working class to have the greater frequency of poorly adjusted marital and sexual relationships. However, confounding this expectation is one important fact: the nonfamilial career and social interests, involvements, and aspirations of the wife. This factor, discussed in the next section, is inversely related to class. That is, middle-class wives have greater conflicts with work and family roles than working-class wives. Thus they may resent their relatively total involvement with domestic and child-care duties to a greater extent than their working-class counterparts.

Nonfamilial Career and Social Interests, Involvements, and Aspirations

Bernard Farber (1964) defines the family as a set of mutually contingent careers. Farber's approach sensitizes one to the multiple roles of men and women other than husband and wife. Other roles, such as father and mother and occupational and career roles for men and women, occur over time and make the attainment of marital satisfaction somewhat problematic. Further, Farber's orientation sensitizes one to the fact that marital satisfaction and family satisfaction are not the same. Men and women place differential importance on marital and parental roles as well as on occupational and career roles. Farber has suggested that we classify families as child centered versus parent centered to highlight this variation.

Herbert Gans (1962a) has made a similar observation in his masterful work on Italian-American residents of an urban village in Boston, Massachusetts. He sees more than one set of definitions concerning the behavioral expectations of the parental role. He makes the distinction between adult-centered, child-centered, and adult-directed families and proposes that each type of family is prevalent in different class levels. In each family type, the role of the parents and the children are manifested differently.

The working-class family is characterized as adult centered. Here, the husband and wife live sexually segregated roles. They have separate family roles and engage in little of the companionship typically found in the middle class. The husband is predominantly the wage earner and the enforcer of child discipline. The wife's activities are confined to household tasks and the rearing of children. Children are expected to follow adult rules and are required to act "grown up." They are disciplined when they act as children. Family life is centered around the desires and interests of the adults and does not cater to the demands of the children. Husbands and wives are frequently involved with extended kin and with neighbors and friends, albeit different ones for each.

Husbands and wives of the lower middle class have a more companionate relationship. There are less sexually segregated roles than in the working class. The home and the family are the common interest points. The family is child centered with the home being run both for adults and children. The children are allowed to be themselves and to act as children. The lower middle class family is a conjugal one consisting of only parents and children. The couple tend to share activities, and their social life tends to be informal and primarily involves friends and neighbors.

The upper middle class family is depicted by Gans as being adult directed. Predominately college educated, this family type is interested in and participates in the activities of the larger world. Unlike the preceding two types, it does not confine its activities to the local community. Family and the home are less important to them than to the other classes. Frequently, the wife is pursuing a career prior to having children and is either working or has aspirations to work as the children are growing. Domestic activities are alleviated to some extent through the employment of service help or to the sharing of activities by the husband. Children serve as a common focal point of interest and concern. The upper middle class couple are concerned with the intellectual and social development of their children. They are highly motivated to provide direction for the lives of their children. So that family life is child-centered as well as adult directed.

These variations in social-class family types have differential effects on the importance of parenthood for males and females. Thus, although males in our society derive their primary status and identification from their occupational role and women gain theirs from their familial roles, there are significant degrees of variation between the working class and the more upper middle class. This is particularly the case for upper middle class women. For them, there has been a notable movement to get away from the ascribed roles of wife and mother and to incorporate additional or alternative roles in the occupational sphere. As of now, this movement has had its primary influence on the more educated and affluent women of the upper middle classes. By and large, working-class women still perceive their primary role in terms of marriage and motherhood.

Studies of working-class families have concluded that the parental role maintains a dominant position in a woman's life (Gans, 1962a; Komarovsky, 1962; Rainwater, 1965). Robert Bell (1964, 1965, 1971), in studies of married lower income black women in Philadelphia, found that motherhood was more highly valued than wifehood. Similarly, Rainwater (1960), in a study of sex, contraception, and family planning in a white working-class population, found that motherhood gives a woman her major rationale for existence. He reports that the experience of pregnancy and childbirth aids working-class women in establishing self-validity. It has higher significance for working-class women than for middle-class women, who may place higher value on outside interests. He also found, as did J. Mayone Stycos (1955), that impregnating a woman is a sign of masculine potency and is highly valued by working-class husbands. However, children, outside of being the proof of masculinity, have little significance for the husband in his everyday world. For the wife, on the other hand, the child provides the chief source for her psychic gratification and she defines herself mainly in her mother-hood role. Rainwater (1965) makes the following observation:

> To the working class mother caring for children represents the central activity of her life. She defines herself mainly as a mother and seeks to find gratification in life principally

through this function. The children are considered mainly her property and responsibility and it is through them that she expects to fulfill herself and her potentialities. . . . (Rainwater, 1965:86)

The extent to which the ideologies of egalitarianism and individualism have infiltrated the working class remains open for investigation. Yet, although somewhat stereotypical, the above quotation draws attention to the emphasis placed on segregated role relationships of husbands and wives and the wives' main involvement is defined in terms of the home and children.

In contrast, the upper middle class woman is caught in a dilemma. On the one hand, she has achieved a relatively high degree of educational attainment and frequently is involved in an occupation that she values and to which she has made a considerable commitment. Yet, she is faced with cultural pressures to assume the maternal role. For many, the pressure is so great that they have children in the absence of any genuine desire for them or the ability to care for them.

Alice S. Rossi (1968) points out that parental roles differ dramatically from marriage and work. With the widespread availability of effective contraceptives, parenthood can be postponed indefinitely. Before the technological advancement in contraceptive devices, pregnancy was likely to follow shortly after marriage. Then marriage was the major transition in a woman's life. Couples can now postpone having children until they are ready to have them. Today, many couples have children after they have had the opportunity to establish a workable marital relationship and have acquired sufficient capital and household furnishings to support a child financially. Occupational roles are also something that is learned over a period of time. The attainment of both roles, occupational and marital, can be seen as gradual transitional processes. However, parenthood is an immediate occurrence. All too frequently there is an almost complete absence of training for the role. Most women facing the birth of their first child have had little preparation for the maternal role other than some sporadic babysitting, or occasionally taking care of younger siblings. Suddenly, the inexperienced woman is confronted with the reality of a 24-hour job of infant care. Further, in contrast with other role commitments, parenthood is irrevocable. Rossi notes that we can have ex-spouses and ex-jobs but not ex-children.

The point may be raised that if women insist on maintaining their occupational role in addition to their maternal role the family may become more egalitarian with the husband assuming more of the responsibility for child care. This would alleviate some of the burden of the parental role incurred by a woman's double-role involvements. Earlier, we suggested that there seems to be a growing trend, especially among middle-class couples, for greater egalitarianism. Rossi states that an egalitarian base to the marital relationship may result in a tendency for parents to establish some barriers between themselves and their children. A resultant marital defense against the institution of parenthood. If this occurs, it may be a positive factor mitigating against the development of the crisis of parenthood for middle-class couples, especially for women. Jacoby (1969) concluded that middle-class women place a lower evaluation on having children than working-class women and that parenthood is far more likely to interfere with their career aspirations. Thus, if a coalition of support occurs between husband and wife the crisis may not occur.

Undoubtedly, many couples develop patterns to offset the debilitating aspects of parenthood, yet for most couples, particularly wives, parenthood can be a crisis period. All too frequently, the wife is faced with what we have described as the double burden. The woman is expected to hold down her occupational position and at the same time continue to be primarily involved in domestic tasks, including childrearing. This, of course, is an untenable position.

In summary, we believe that the dissatisfactions and problems associated with parenthood, particularly for the middle class, ultimately stems from the very nature of the conjugal family system. In middle-class American society, the family is relatively isolated from the supports of extended kin and the surrounding community. They are not available to assist in the care of infants and young children. This is quite different from conditions in our historical past or in other societies.

Historically, the family was a part of the community. Philippe Ariès (1962) has observed that the contemporary family has withdrawn into the home. It has become a private place of residence for family members. The former extended family group, who lived in common residence, is gone. The family is segregated from the rest of the world, and the home is isolated from external involvements. This has had profound effects on the wife/mother who has been relegated to domestic tasks and childbearing. She has the major responsibility for the well-being of the child. Fathers are not required to be involved in child care. The community provides minimal institutional supports and assistance. The result has been the increased dissatisfaction with parenthood and particularly motherhood.

This has been the traditional pattern. But, as we have noted, there are movements of change. Increasingly, husbands are becoming involved in domestic activities, including relationships with their children. Another is the increased demands for child-care facilities outside the home. This would allow both the husband and wife to pursue outside family careers. As of this writing, child-care facilities are still woefully inadequate. Finally, and most dramatically, there is the development of ideological arguments for increased options for women. The motherhood myth is less acceptable to many. This should result in a more satisfying and productive parenthood and childhood. Our thoughts echo those of Betty Rollin:

> When motherhood is no longer culturally compulsory, there will, certainly, be less of it. Women are now beginning to think and do more about development of self, of their individual resources. Far from being selfish, such development is probably our only hope. That means more alternatives for women. And more alternatives mean more selective, better, happier, motherhood—and childhood and husbandhood (or manhood)

and peoplehood. It is not a question of whether or not children are sweet and marvelous to have and rear; the question is, even if that's so, whether or not one wants to pay the price for it. It doesn't make any sense any more to pretend that women need babies, when what they really need is themselves. If God were still speaking to us in a voice we could hear, even He would probably say, "Be fruitful. Don't multiply." (Rollin, 1970:17)

CONCLUSION

This chapter sought to integrate demographic analysis to our sociological perspective on social change and the family. We opened with a discussion of fertility and family size, comparing extended family systems, which emphasize kinship ties, with the conjugal family, which emphasizes the marital and parental relationships. We observed that kinship-dominated societies were dependent on high fertility and large family size for the perpetuation of their social system. In contrast, in industrial societies, where conjugal family units prevail, there is an appreciable lower fertility rate and family size.

We then applied our sociologic perspective to understand population dynamics in India. The high birthrate was seen to be detrimental to Indian modernization, economic development, and increased total industrial, commercial, and agricultural production. The failure of family-planning programs reflected governmental policies that ran counter to the economic viability of large family size for the joint-family system and the village-based caste system. It was emphasized that demographic changes could only occur when the class and caste systems are changed and when technological development makes it economically feasible for these families to limit their family size. This examination of population dynamics revealed that it was interrelated with family conceptualizations and dynamics along with social, political, and economic factors.

We then turned our attention to an examination of fertility patterns in the West. Ideologies relating to parenthood and particularly motherhood concerned us. We pointed out that contradictory demands were placed on women. On the one hand, doctrines placed high value on their confinement to the home and their exclusive involvement in household tasks and childrearing; on the other hand, doctrines were being propounded that encouraged families to restrict their family size.

Coercive pronatalism, a term coined by the demographer, Judith Blake, was introduced to point out how social institutions forced women to assume exclusively the everyday parental role. Discriminatory practices in education and in work reinforced by the myth of motherhood relegated women to the wife and mother roles. We pointed out how supportive parental ideologies contributed to the obscuring of the possibility that the transition to parenthood can be problematic.

Our concluding topic in this chapter was the transition to parenthood. This transition necessitates the rearrangement and reorganization of marital roles, relationships with kin, friends, and neighbors, economic patterns, and the reallocation of space, time, and attention. The implications of this transition for families received comparably little attention from sociologists until recent years. We reviewed this literature and compared the research findings on working-class and middle-class families. We indicated some of the problematic areas of concern and pointed out that changes are beginning to take place in the nature of motherhood and fatherhood and on society's responsibilities.

In the next two chapters we continue our investigation of generational relationships. Chapter 12 will be concerned with childhood and adolescence; chapter 13 will focus on the role of the aged.

CHAPTER 12

The Family and Childhood and Adolescence

All human societies are differentiated on the basis of age and sex. Throughout history, the social roles of men and women have differed, as have the roles of children, adults, and the aged. Always, these differences have been linked to status differences in power, privilege, and prestige. In the previous chapters of this book we examined sex differentiation. A power dimension was seen to be inherent in the differentiation between the sexes. Generations are part of the permanent nature of social existence. And, likewise, conflict between generations has been a perennial force in the history of humanity.

In our earlier discussions, the family was viewed as the primary form of social organization that stratified people according to sex. It can also be seen as the basic form of social organization that stratifies people according to age. Basically, families are hierarchical social structures in which older generations or older siblings hold positions of power, authority, and prestige over their younger counterparts. There are different degrees of stratification by age. But, the universal tendency is for the elders to exercise control over younger family members.

The degree of generational control also varies by the tempo of social change in given societies. Generally, in societies that are relatively stable, patterns of generation control become traditionalized. In societies undergoing patterns of rapid social change, the normal relationship between generations is disrupted and can be destroyed.

In this and the next chapter of the book, we will examine different forms of family systems and the relationships between family members of different ages. We are particularly interested in the manifestation of the power dimension that underlies the age hierarchy. We will be looking at children, adolescents, and the aged within different forms of family life. Of noted concern is the role of social change on age differentiation within the family and its influence on generational controls.

SOCIAL CHANGE AND GENERATIONAL CONTROL

Ann Foner (1978) discusses what she has labeled as an age-stratification perspective and applies it to an historical examination of 19th- and 20th-century American families. This approach emphasizes that age must be conceived as a social process as well as a biologic one. Age is seen as a key component in social structure and social change. This age-stratification perspective incorporates both structural and dynamic elements that have implications at both the individual and societal levels for the analysis of the family.

Structurally, age affects how people of different ages relate to each other and influences individual's attitudes and behavior. People of different age groupings are stratified into different role complexes with differential rewards, duties, and obligations. Dynamically, individuals pass through the different age strata as they move through the life cycle. The transition through stages in the life cycle and the transitions of a particular age cohort are historically unique. Thus the age-stratification structure of the population is constantly subject to change.

The family is composed of members of different ages who are differentially related. The dominant perspective in sociology, structure functionalism, has stressed that the age differentiation of family members enhances the solidarity of its members. The interdependence of family members fosters emotional attachments, structural solidarity, and family cohesion. However, as Foner points out, family conflict is also a basic component of family life. Inherent in the differential age structure of family members is the potential for conflict and tension:

> For the family is itself stratified—not merely differentiated—by age. Not only do family members of different ages have diverse functions, but they also receive unequal rewards. . . . There are age differences in power, privilege, and prestige in the family. And these inequalities can generate age—related dissension—for example, resentment about the exercise of power or the way family resources are distributed—in the family unit. . . . (Foner, 1978:S347).

The nature and rate of social change has been associated with the nature and type of generational control parents have over their children. Robert Redfield (1947), in his classic work, "The Folk Society," contrasts the slow changing of rural folk society with the dynamic tempo or urban industrial societies. The tempo of change is associated with the attitudes and behavior patterns between the generations. It has also been observed that the authority and power of parents is correlated with the societal pattern that emphasizes the maintenance of tradition. S. N. Eisenstadt (1971) points out that societies that emphasize traditional practices are characterized by strong intergenerational bonds. These societies are also characterized by a strong central authority.

These tradition-oriented societies have been characterized by the rule of the old. The 19th-century and early 20th century British anthropologist, Sir James George Frazer, called these societies gerontocracies. Using the Australian aborigines as the case in point, Frazer described the authority structure of that culture as

> . . . an oligarchy of old and influential men, who meet in council and decide on all measures of importance, to the practical exclusion of the younger men. Their deliberate assembly answers to the senate of later times: if we had to coin a word for such a government of elders we might call it a "gerontocracy." (Frazer, 1922/1960: 96).

In contrast, in societies that are undergoing rapid social change, generational continuity is deemphasized. Concomitantly, the older generation has less control over the younger one. Indeed, some social observers argue that the pattern in contemporary Western society is characterized by such an appreciable loss of parental control that the family has become largely irrelevant in influencing the behavior and attitudes of children and adolescents. At the same time, and somewhat paradoxically, the argument is also being made that the family is a detrimental force that acts to frustrate and deny the fulfillment of the needs of the younger generation. Margaret Mead's *Culture and Commitment: A Study of the Generation Gap* (1970b) reflects the former position. Later, after we examine this work, we will look at the latter position, which derives from the contemporary conceptualization of the family, childhood, and adolescence.

Margaret Mead in her essay monograph, *Culture and Commitment* (1970b), comparatively examines the generation gap in contemporary societies. She presents an historical explanation on why the elders of preliterate societies exert such powers. She calls these societies postfigurative. In postfigurative cultures children are socialized by their forebears. The children are raised so that the life of the parent and grandparent postfigures the course of their own.

Postfigurative societies are small religious and ideological enclaves. They derive their authority from the past. Their culture are conservative and resist change. There is a sense of timelessness and all-prevailing custom. Continuity with the past is a basic premise underlying the social order. The sacredness of custom and the lack of a written history makes the elders the repositories of societal wisdom and knowledge. The elders have high status because they know best the traditions of the past. Generational turmoil is rare. Adolescent and youth rebellion is almost entirely absent.

In postfigurative cultures the emphasis is on generational continuity. The experiences of the young repeats the experiences of the old. Events that have occurred and that question the traditional order are redefined and reinterpreted to deny changes. To preserve the sense of continuity and identification with the past occurrences that have caused change are culturally blurred and innovations are assimilated into the traditional past. Mead provides some illustrations of elders who edit the version of the culture that is passed to the young. They mythologize or deny change:

> A people who have lived for only three or four generations in tepees on the great American plains, who have borrowed the tepee style from other tribes, may tell how their ancestors learned to make a tepee by imitating the shape of a curled leaf. In Samoa the elders listened politely to a description of the long voyages of Polynesian ancestors by Te Rangi Hiroa, a Polynesian visitor from New Zealand, whose people had preserved a sacrosanct list of the early voyages which was memorized by each generation. His hosts then replied firmly, "Very interesting, but the *Samoans* originated here in Fitiuta." The visitor, himself half-Polynesian and half-European, and a highly educated man, finally took refuge, in great irritation, in asking them whether or not they were now Christians and believed in the Garden of Eden. (Mead, 1970b:18)

The postfigurative society socializes the young so that they behave in accordance with the mores and values of the older generation. They do not question the way things are or the way things were. Indeed, they have a lack of consciousness of alternative ways of life. This sociocultural quality explains the great stability of postfigurative society. It also accounts for the minimal internal change from one generation ot the next.

Mead emphasizes the importance of three-generational households in the socialization of children. In such households, parents raise their children under the eyes of their parents. This arrangement emphasizes cultural continuity and strengthens the power of the older generation. Robert O. Blood, Jr., (1972) has observed that the power of the aged was institutionalized in the extended family system. The high priority and status of the aged gave rise to the extended family system and is, in turn, supported by this form of family structure.

In societies undergoing social change there is a break in generational continuity. The experiences of the younger generation are significantly different from those of their parents and grandparents. Mead characterizes these cultures as cofigurative. The recent past of American society is a prime illustration. Cofigurative cultures can be brought about by rapid technological development; migration to a new country and separation from the elders; military conquest and the subsequent forced acculturation of the captured society to the language and ways of the conquerer; religious conversion, where the younger generation is socialized into a new religious world view; and planned revolutionary changes in the life styles of the young. The consequent differential experiences of the younger generation necessitates the development of different attitudes and behavior. The elder generation can not provide the necessary emulating models and the younger generation must find these models among their generational peers.

One illustration that Mead provides on how these changes have affected family relationships is of particular interest to us. In an earlier discussion in this book we examined the Western urban family and suggested that the diminished importance of extended kinship of city families may have resulted from the differential socialization processes experienced by different-generation family members. Those who were raised in rural areas of European societies and who migrated to the United States will have had a quite different upbringing than their urban Americanized children and grandchildren.

Mead points out that the immigration situation is typified by the concentration on the nuclear family, with grandparents either absent or having very little influence. Grandparents are no longer the models for their grandchildren; parents have little control over grown children's marriages or careers. Characteristic of cofigurative American culture is the relinquishing of responsibility for the elderly. This is associated with the breakdown of sanctions exercised by the elderly over the second and third generations.

In its simplest form Mead sees cofigurative culture as one in which grandparents are absent. The result is the loss of the individual's links with the past. The future is not anticipated through the traditional past but by the contemporary present. The result is that parents and grandparents no longer serve as dominating socialization agents. Formalized educational institutions take over this task. Concomitantly, the elders are no longer authority figures or models for youth's future behavioral and attitudinal patterns.

However, Mead emphasizes that in cofigurative cultures the break is never complete. Elders still have influence to the extent that they set the style and set the limits within which cofiguration is expressed in the behavior of the young. Thus to a certain extent the elders along with youths' generational peers develop a new style that will serve as the model for others of their generation.

Writing at the height of the social unrest of the late 1960s and particularly being influenced by the extensiveness of youth counterculture movements, Mead saw an emerging pattern that made both the postfigurative and cofigurative cultural models inadequate. In this newly emerging era of extreme rapid rates of change, Mead saw the development of a prefigurative culture. In prefigurative society the future is so unknown that change within an elder-controlled and parental-modeled cofigurative culture, which also includes postfigurative elements, is inadequate:

> I call this new style *prefigurative,* because in this new culture it will be the child—and not the parent and grandparent—that represents what is to come. Instead of the erect, white-haired elder who, in postfigurative cultures, stood for the past and the future in all

their grandeur and continuity, the unborn child, already conceived but still in the womb, must become the symbol of what life will be like. (Mead, 1970b:68)

Mead's analysis of permanence and social change demonstrates how it affects different cultures and their respective generational dynamics. The conceptualizations that exist to define the nature of particular age groups also play a significant role in the manifestations of generational attitudes and behavior. A careful examination of the different conceptualizations of young people and the family will now prove instructive.

CONCEPTUALIZATION OF CHILDHOOD AND ADOLESCENCE

As we have observed here and in the previous chapter, societies define sets of people according to age. These age categories influence people's relations to one another. Expectations differ on what involvements, activities, and accomplishments are expected for each age grouping. Societies differ in the age distinctions they make. For example, among the Kikuyu of Kenya age distinctions are prominently defined and explicit, and elaborate ties of passage mark the transition periods that carry the individual from one age category to the next. Age differentiation also has consequent implications for the conceptualization of persons placed in particular age groupings. Further, we must realize that the conceptualization of childhood and adolescence is a reflection of the conceptualization of the family, and together they must be seen in a crosscultural and in a social-historical context.

Anthropologists have long observed the cultural relativity of age roles. They have noted that the conceptualization of childhood and adolescence varies crosscul-turally. Probably the most famous research study in this area was done by Margaret Mead in her *Coming of Age in Samoa* (1928). Mead was concerned with the relationships between adolescents and culture. She contrasted the development of girls in the United States with patterns in Samoa. She was particularly concerned with whether the psychological disturbances and the emotional crises characteristic of Western adolescents was due to the nature of adolescence itself or to the culture. She wanted to ascertain if these disturbances were due to physiological changes occurring at puberty or were largely brought about by social and cultural conditions.

To test the universality of developmental psychologic stages of childhood and adolescence, Mead went to the South Pacific and lived for 9 months in Samoa, where she studied 50 adolescent girls. Among the adolescents of Samoa, she found no period comparable to the storm and stress that characterizes their American counterparts. Samoan adolescence was not characterized by tension, emotional conflict, or rebellion. Indeed, Samoan culture did not even recognize the developmental stage of adolescence, it had no concept of adolescence. Mead concluded that the source of such characteristics in American youth stemmed from the social institutions and traditions found in the United States.

Anthropologists have also compared societies in regard to the conceptualization of childhood. Mead (1949), herself, examined societies that viewed the child as a small adult with responsibilities similar to those of an adult versus societies, like the United States, where the child is thought to be qualitatively different. Ruth Benedict (1938/1973) in her classic study, "Continuities and Discontinuities in Cultural Conditioning," has argued that there is less continuity in treatment and development from childhood and adolescence to adulthood in societies such as the United States then there is in those societies that employ the little-adult conceptualization.

Benedict sees as a distinctive feature of American culture the dichotomization of value patterns between those applicable to the child and those applicable to the adult. "The child is sexless, the adult estimates his virility by his sexual activities; the child must be protected from the ugly facts of life, the adult must meet them without psychic catastrophe; the child must obey, the adult must command this obedience" (Benedict, 1938/1973:100). Benedict points out that the more discrete and isolated the status of the child is from the status of the adult, the more difficult and ambiguous is the transition from one age group to the other. Further, this dichotomous pattern intensifies the status discontinuity experienced by the adolescent.

She argues that children are segregated from the adult world. This is especially the case for work and sex. The children's world is organized around play; little attention is given to the adult world of work. Similarly, strong taboos exist regarding sexual repression and children are required to be submissive to adult authority. As adults, they are expected to work, to be sexually mature, and to be assertive and autonomous. This disjunction between the role of the child and the one he or she is expected to perform as an adult makes the transition painful, awkward, and traumatic.

In contrast, Benedict reports that in nonliterate societies the cultural discontinuities that characterize American society do not exist. For example, in contrasting cultural variations regarding responsibility and nonresponsibility, she finds that preliterate societies encourage children to engage in adult activities and responsibilities as soon as possible. Among the Ojibwa Indians of Canada, boys accompany fathers on hunting trips and girls share the responsibility in preparing the meat and skins trapped by their brothers and fathers in much the same manner as their mothers. Ojibwan children are consistently taught to rely on themselves and to see the world of the adult as not much different from the world of the young.

Similarly, among the Papago of Arizona, children are trained from infancy and are continuously conditioned to responsible social participation while, at the same time, the tasks that are expected of them are adapted to their capabilities. To illustrate, Benedict cites an observer who tells of sitting with a group of Papago elders when the man of the house turned to his little three-year-old granddaughter and asked her to close the door.

The door was heavy and hard to shut. The child tried, but it did not move. Several times the grandfather repeated, "Yes, close the door." No one jumped to the child's assistance. No one took the responsibility away from her. On the other hand there was no impatience, for after all the child was small. They sat gravely waiting till the child succeeded and her grandfather gravely thanked her. It was assumed that the task would not be asked of her unless she could perform it and having been asked the responsibility was hers alone just as if she were a grown woman. (Benedict, 1938/1973:102)

Benedict sees American culture as viewing the adult-child or, specifically, the parent-child relationship in terms of a dominance-submission arrangement. In contrast, many American Indian tribes explicitly reject the ideal of a child's submissive or obedient behavior. To illustrate, Benedict reports on the child-training practices among the Mohave Indians that are strikingly nonauthoritarian:

The child's mother was white and protested to its father (a Mohave Indian) that he must take action when the child disobeyed and struck him. "But why?" the father said, "he is little. He cannot possibly injure me." He did not know of any dichotomy according to which an adult expects obedience and a child must accord it. If his child had been docile he would simply have judged that it would become a docile adult—an eventuality of which he would not have approved. (Benedict, 1938/1973:104)

Benedict then contrasts how children are socialized into sexual awareness in different societies. She notes that in virtually all societies the norms concerning sexual conduct are not identical for children and adults. This is explained by the relatively late onset of puberty and physiologic maturation in human beings. Benedict defines continuity in sexual expression as meaning that the child is taught nothing it must unlearn later. Societies can, therefore, be classified in terms of whether they facilitate continuity or impose discontinuity regarding sexual matters. Adults among the Dakota Indians, for example, observe great privacy in sex acts and in no way stimulate or encourage children's sexual activities. Yet there is no discontinuity since the child is not indoctrianted in ways it has to unlearn later. The Zuni in New Mexico regard premature sex experimentation by children as being wicked. The sexual activity of adults is associated solely with reproduction. Our society, in contrast, associates the wickedness of a child's sex experimentation with *sex itself* rather than as wickedness because it is sex at a child's age. The result is that adults in our culture must unlearn the belief taught them as children that sex is wicked or dangerous.

In concluding her analysis, Benedict examines age-grade societies that, as we have pointed out, demand different behavior of the individual at different times during the life cycle. Persons of the same age-grade are grouped into a society whose activities are oriented toward the appropriate behavior desired at that age. Although there is discontinuous conditioning, Benedict believes that cultural institutions provide sufficient supports to persons as they progress through the age-grade life stages. In striking contrast, Benedict argues that Anglo-American culture contains discontinuous cultural institutions and dogmas that exert considerable strain on both the interpersonal process and the personality system of young individuals.

> It is clear that if we were to look at our social arrangements as an outsider, we should infer directly from our family institutions and habits of child training that many individuals would not ''put off childish things''; we should have to say that our adult activity demands traits that are interdicted in children, and that far from redoubling efforts to help children bridge this gap, adults in our culture put all the blame on the child when he fails to manifest spontaneously the new behavior or, overstepping the mark, manifests it with untoward belligerence. (1938/1973: 108)

The result is that American adolescents face serious problems during this transition period; problems of readjustment and ambiguity are experienced in activities, responsibilities, and the allocation of power: ''. . . The adolescent period of *Sturm und Drang* with which we are so familiar becomes intelligible in terms of our discontinuous cultural institutions and dogmas rather than in terms of physiological necessity'' (1938/1973:108)

Ruth Benedict's thesis anticipated the arguments advanced by the social historian, Philippe Ariès, in *Centuries of Childhood: A Social History of Family Life* (1962). In this classic study, Ariès applied a similar kind of analysis to medieval European society and its evolution to the present. He sought to document how in medieval life the child was integrated into the community and how it was not until the development of bourgeois society that the segregation of children occurred. Implicit within his discussion is a condemnation of the consequences of this segregation.

The theme of *Centuries of Childhood* is how the Western ideas about childhood and family life have changed and developed from the Middle Ages to modern times. Ariès examines the paintings and diaries of four centuries; he documents the history and evolution of children's dress, games, and pastimes; and analyzes the development of schools and their curricula. This leads him to conclude that the discovery of childhood as a distinct stage in the life cycle is a rather recent development, as is the conceptualization of the private family.

He argues that in the Middle Ages children were treated as small adults. As soon as were capable of being without their mothers, children interacted in the adult world. They shared the same world of work and play. By the age of 7 or 8, they were treated as if they had the same mental capacities for understanding and feeling as their adult counterparts and peers. In a particularly notable use of historical resources, Ariès points out that medieval painters portrayed children as ''miniaturized'' adults. Children were depicted in adult clothes and looked like adults, but on a reduced scale. The failure of the artists to draw children as we know them was not due to their incompetence or lack of artistic skill but rather to the lack of a conceptualization of the notion of childhood:

> In medieval society the idea of childhood did not exist; this is not to suggest that children were neglected, forsaken or despised. The idea of childhood is not to be confused with affection for children; it corresponds to an awareness of the particular nature of childhood, that particular nature which distinguishes the child from the adult, even the young adult. In medieval society this awareness was lacking. That is why, as soon as the child could live without the constant solicitude of his mother, his nanny or his craddle-rocker, he belonged to adult society. (Ariès, 1962:128)

The lack of awareness of the particular nature of childhood and the full participation of children in adult life is associated with the nature of the family and the community. Ariès pictures medieval community life as intense; no one was left alone. The high density of social life made isolation virtually impossible. Life was lived in public. The "sociability" of medieval life was lived on the public streets. The private home was virtually nonexistent. The street was the setting of work and social relations. This sociability hindered the formation of the concept of the private family. The medieval family was embedded in a web of relatives, friends, workmates, and neighbors all living in close proximity and in public. The distinct sense of privacy so characteristic of modern-day families was absent. In the following passage, Ariès dramatically provides an illustration of this point:

> The traditional ceremonies which accompanied marriage and which were regarded as more important than the religious ceremonies (which for a long time were entirely lacking in solemnity), the blessing of the marriage bed; the visit paid by the guests to the newly-married pair when they were already in bed; the rowdyism during the wedding night, and so on—afford further proof of society's rights over the privacy of the couple. What objection could there be when in fact privacy scarcely ever existed, when people lived on top of one another, masters and servants, children and adults, in houses open at all hours to the indiscretions of callers? The density of society left no room for the family. Not that the family did not exist as a reality: it would be paradoxical to deny that it did. But it did not exist as a concept. (1962:405–406)

The transition to the modern conceptualization of the child began to emerge during the 17th century. There was a revival of interest in education. This, in turn, introduced the idea that a period of special preparation was necessary before individuals could assume their place as adults. Childhood became defined as a period in which to train children. Children began to be treated differently, they were expected to behave differently, and their nature was viewed as being different. Children were now coddled and a greater interest and concern for their moral welfare and development became common.

Although Ariès recognizes that this change reflects declines in mortality rates and the growing division of labor in the society, he believes that this concept of childhood developed and was given expression in the emergence of the bourgeois family. He argues that from a relatively insignificant institution during the Middle Ages, there developed a growing belief in the virtue of the intimate and private nuclear family. The rise of the private family and the growth of the sentimental bonds among its members came about at the expense of the public community:

> The more man lived in the street or in communities dedicated to work, pleasure or prayer, the more these communities monopolized not only his time but his mind. If, on the other hand, his relations with fellowworkers, neighbors and relatives did not weigh so heavily on him, then the concept of family feeling took the place of the other concepts of loyalty and service and became predominant or even exclusive. The progress of the concept of the family followed the progress of private life, of domesticity. (Ariès, 1962:375)

The continued inward development of the family and its creation of a private sphere of life removed from the outside world was intertwined with the increased importance given to children. The outside community became to be viewed with suspicion and indifference. Proceeding into the industrial era, the family began to withdraw its nonproductive members, women and children, from involvement with the surrounding community. The increased division of labor of family members and the consequent isolation of women and children within the home was the result.

Ariès ends on a pessimistic note. He is highly critical of the contemporary private family. He believes that it has stifled children's autonomy and independence. He views medieval childhood as a period of free expression and spontaneity. The separation of the child from the larger community leads to the development of youth who are deprived of much experience in the outside world. They are increasingly dependent on their parents. The result is the ultimate loss of their individuality:

> The evolution of the last few centuries has often been presented as the triumph of individualism over social constraints, with the family counted among the latter. But where is the individualism in these modern lives, in which all the energy of the couple is directed to serving the interests of a deliberately restricted posterity? Was there not greater individualism in the gay indifference of the prolific fathers of the ancient regime? . . . It is not individualism which has triumphed, but the family. (Ariès, 1962:406)

Similar historical analyses on the changing conceptualization of adolescence have been made by F. Musgrove (1964) and Joseph Kett (1977). Musgrove traces the historical changes in the status of adolescents from the mid-17th century, when adolescence was "invented," to the present. England provides his case in point. Kett examines how youth have viewed themselves and how these views have coincided or clashed with adult expectations in America from 1790 to the present.

Musgrove believes that increasingly youth are segregated from the adult world. This has diminished rather than enhanced their social status. He develops an argument that is similar to the one developed by Ruth Benedict. Musgrove sees the inconsistency and discontinuity of training youth for adulthood by excluding them from the world of adult concerns and of training youth for the exercise of responsibility by the denial of responsibility. The result is the development of compliant, accommodating, and conservative security-conscious adults. He attributes this changing status to economic developments, demographic changes, and to psychological theories on the nature of adolescence that have helped to justify it.

Musgrove attributes the idea of adolescence—a special stage of development that intervenes between childhood and adulthood—to the 18th century French philosopher, Jean-Jacques Rousseau. Adolescence began to be seen as a period during which the individual's movement toward adult maturity should be retarded. The belief developed that the rights, obligations, and responsibilities of adulthood should be delayed by an intervening period of schooling, albeit for the more affluent and privileged segments of the society. Young people were deemed unfit to undertake serious concerns relating to work and politics. A protracted period of preparation for adulthood was deemed necessary. Further, this preparation was to be undertaken in segregated and congregate institutions of formal training that are set apart from the adult world.

Musgrove believes that the changing composition of the population has also helped bring about these changes. He emphasizes the demographic fact that more adolescents have been able to survive childhood and that more people are reaching adulthood and old age. The result is that positions of responsibility and leadership are more likely to be occupied by the older segments of the population and thus youth have reduced opportunities to assume such positions. This demographic fact is readily apparent in the economic sphere. Here, those already in the labor force have a vested interest in maintaining their economic viability as long as possible. The result is the belief that the young should be kept out of the labor force as long as possible.

The demands of a technologically complex and sophisticated society requires skills. The relatively untrained labor skills of the young are not needed. Further, with the increased "professionalization" of occupations, there is an increased demand for the attainment of educational qualifications in terms of specialized courses and degrees before admittance is granted. Finally, labor unions in their desire to maintain the security and well-being of their senior members, have successfully kept young recruits from gaining unrestricted access to skilled and semiskilled positions. They have effectively controlled the flow of the young into the labor force.

Together, all these factors are seen to hold back youth. Together, demographic circumstances, economic conditions, educational strategy and provision, and the institutionalized power of adults make it unlikely that any dramatic changes will occur in the treatment of youth in Western societies. One tangential observation may be of interest here. Musgrove wrote his book in 1964, before the development of the counterculture movements of the late 1960s. From the perspective of the late 1970s, the note of despair that echoes throughout Musgrove's book still seems to be an accurate appraisal of contemporary conditions.

Kett (1977), in his historical study of adolescence in America, observes that the economic and social relationships between youth and adolescents has significantly changed since 1790. Today's youth are characterized as being consumers rather than producers. They have been largely removed from the work force, spend most of their time in school, and tend to be segregated from adult society. The causes of these changes are traced to urbanization, industrialization, demographic changes, and childrearing practices. It is his concern with the moral values associated with childrearing practices that attracts his and our attention.

Kett places particular attention to the period between 1890 and 1920, when the society came to classify the age between 14 and 18 years as a distinct period of youth and labeled it adolescence. Kett seeks to demonstrate that the moral values associated with this conceptualization was subsumed under supposedly universal psychological laws and determined by a biologic process of maturation. These laws provided the basis for the subsequent development of a number of adolescent "helpers," such as educators, youth workers, parent counselors, and scout leaders. Through their efforts, they gave shape to the contemporary concept of adolescence, which necessitated the massive reclassification of young people as adolescents: "During these critical decades young people, particularly teenage boys ceased to be viewed as troublesome, rash, and heedless, the qualities traditionally associated with youth; instead they increasingly were viewed as vulnerable, passive and awkward, qualities that previously had been associated with girls" (Kett, 1977:6).

Kett observes that the most influential study on the nature of adolescence written during this period was by G. Stanley Hall (1904). Hall was profoundly influenced by the theories of Sigmund Freud and sought to link Freud's theory with that of Darwinian evolutionary theory. Hall developed a psychological theory of adolescence that emphasized the significance of hereditary determinants of personality. His theory of the socialization of adolescents was based on the principles of recapitulation theory, which held that every individual repeated the history of the species in his or her own development. That is, Hall took the viewpoint that children passed through the various stages of development from savagery to civilization that had already been traced by their race.

Hall postulated a "storm and stress" (*sturm und drang*) interpretation of adolescence. Although anthropological studies, like Margaret Mead's *Coming of Age in Samoa* (1928), strongly suggested that adolescence need not be a period of turmoil and psychological disruption, Hall's viewpoint combined with changes in industrialization, urbanization, and the developed intimacy and privatization of the nuclear family led to the basic forms of today's concept of adolescence and to the treatment of adolescents in society.

Kett examines three dominating moral values that have continued to be influential in society's response to youth. The first is the belief that youth should be segregated according to their own age, both in school and in work. No longer were mixed age groups of younger and older children to be allowed in the same classroom. Similarly, children were segregated out of the labor force. Increasingly, their work was restricted to part-time or summer employment. The second belief was the characterization of youth by passivity. The view was that adolescents should be easily moldable by grownups into the grownup's definition of adulthood. A third belief was the necessity for adult-directed activities for adolescents. Kett cites August de B. Hollingshead in his landmark sociologic study of adolescence, *Elmtown's Youth: The Impact of Social Class on Adolescents* (1949), on why the discontinuity in the socialization of youth can be so devastating:

> By segregating people into special institutions, such as the school, Sunday School, and later into youth organizations such as Boy Scouts and Girl Scouts for a few hours each week, adults apparently hope that the adolescent will be spared the shock of learning the contradictions in the culture. At the same time, they believe that these institutions are building a mysterious something variously called "citizenship," "leadership," or "character," which will keep the boy or girl from being "tempted" by the "pleasures" of life. Thus the youth-training institutions provided by the culture are essentially negative in their objectives, for they segregate adolescents from the real world that adults know and function in. By trying to keep the maturing child ignorant of this world of conflict and contradictions, adults think they are keeping him "pure." (Hollingshead, 1949:149)

We are struck by the parallel conclusions and opinions reached by such anthropologists as Margaret Mead and Ruth Benedict and sociologists like August Hollingshead—also shared by the social historian, Joseph Kett—on the negative consequences of this conceptualization of adolescence. It remains for us now to fully delineate how these conclusions and opinions on the contemporary definition and treatment of adolescents fits into our conceptual orientation on the nature of social change and the family.

CONTEMPORARY IMPLICATIONS OF THE WESTERN CONCEPTUALIZATION OF CHILDHOOD AND ADOLESCENCE

To assess properly the contemporary condition of childhood and adolescence in the family and the society, it is necessary to re-present a brief historical sketch on the changes that have occurred. Preindustrial societies were characterized by a minimal differentiation of age groupings. Childhood and adolescence were not separated out as separate and distinct chronological stages. Rather, children were conceptualized as miniature adults. As they proceeded through childhood, they increasingly took on more and more adult responsibilities. There was no psychological conceptualization that prescribed an extended moratorium period where adolescents would be segregated and not allowed to take on responsibilities. Life from childhood through adulthood to old age proceeded in a continuous process without cultural and institutionalized disruptions. The "adult" roles of parenthood and work participation were a culminating occurrence that flowed out of this nondifferentiated conceptualization of childhood and adolescence.

Demographic changes, industrialization, urbanization, and the changing conceptualizations of the family and of childhood and adolescence combined to produce the differentiation into the stages of life that characterize today's population. Let us now be more explicit in our delineation of the contemporary condition of young people. We will also observe how social scientists, coming out of different ideological persuasions, develop different assessments on what effect these changes have had. By necessity, we will be referring to previous arguments on the nature of the marital relationship in this discussion. By so doing, we hope to present a more developed analysis.

Industrialization meant the loss of economic participation by young people in the labor force. They, who once assumed economically viable positions in the family, now became economic dependents. In the 18th and 19th centuries the American family acted as a self-sufficient economic unit. Boys and girls were involved in work activities on the farm and in the home. They participated in the growing and harvesting of crops, the storing and cooking of foods, and the caring of domestic animals as well as the making of clothes. In short, the children were an economic asset contributing to the economic well-being of the family. By the end of the 19th century, the family economy was disappearing, giving way to a cash industrial economy. Kenneth Keniston and The Carnegie Council on Children (1977) report that today children are an economic liability with a cost of about $35,000 required to support them from birth just through high school. Further, whereas in the preindustrial period children were not only able to pay their own way by working but also were expected to be the chief source of their parents' support when they got older. There was no government old-age assistance or social security. Today, children can no longer be counted on to provide such an economic resource.

THE CONCEPTUALIZATIONS OF STRUCTURE FUNCTIONALISM

Through what structure functionalists have called the process of structural differentiation, the family has lost a number of functions to outside agencies. These agencies include the schools, the industrial sector, the political parties, and the judicial courts. The structure functionalists, notably Talcott Parsons, have long argued that the increased privatism of the contemporary family has led it to retain and even expand on two functions. These are the maintenance and stabilization of adult personalities and the socialization of children:

. . . what has recently been happening to the American family constitutes part of one of these stages of a process of differentiation. This process has involved a further step in the reduction of the importance in our society of kinship units other than the nuclear family. It has also resulted in the transfer of a variety of functions from the nuclear family to other structures of the society, notable the occupationally organized sectors of it. This means that the family has become a *more specialized agency than before*, probably more specialized than it has been in any previously known society.

. . . We therefore suggest that the basic and irreducable functions of the family are two; first the primary socialization of children so that they can truly become members of the society into which they have been born; second, the stabilization of the adult personalities of the population of the society. (Parsons and Bales, 1955:9, 15).

Structure functionalism has developed an analytical schema for the study of the interrelationships of husband—wife—parents—children in the contemporary family. Although the functionalists, particularly its leading spokesperson, Talcott Parsons, do not discuss the dichotomization of the public and private spheres of work and the household directly, they do analyze and support this dichotomization in the conceptualization of role differentiation. Role differentiation in this context refers to the process where economic production and activities are removed from the kinship household. Further, it postulates that a division of labor between husband and wife is necessary for the optimum functioning of the family system within an industrial economic-social order. The analysis of husband-wife relationships stresses the necessity for the husband to be involved with the outside world, whereas the wife's world is restricted to the home. The segregation of activities is also carried over to interpersonal relationships. The wife's role must be as an affectional and emotional support to her husband and her children. Her interests must be subordinated to those of her husband. The husband as wage earner provides the instrumental leadership that permits the family to function in its dealings with the outside world.

A most influential work in the sociology of the family that has presented this position is the structure functionalist monograph by Talcott Parson and Robert Bales (written in collaboration with James Olds, Morris Zelditch, Jr., and Philip E. Slater). *Family, Socialization and Interaction Process* (1955). This book attempts to analyze the structure and function of the American family by conceptualizing the family as a small group and maintaining that the family can be viewed as a social system with the constituent parts—husband, wife, and children—bound together by cooperative interaction and interdependence. The roles of the family are seen to be differentiated on the basis of age and sex, which correspond to two theoretical axes differentiated by the degree of power and the salience of instrumental-expressive behavior. This is presented schematically in Figure 12.1.

The two axes of differentiation result in four basic role positions, a high power-instrumental leader (father), a high power-expressive leader (mother), a low power-instrumental follower (son), and a low power-expressive follower (daughter).

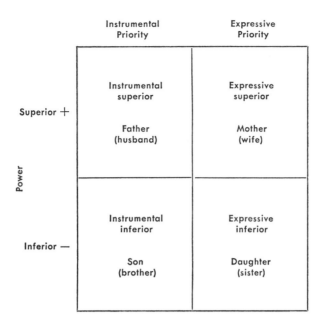

Figure 12.1 Talcott Parsons's basic role structure of the nuclear family. Talcott Parsons and Robert F. Bales, *Family, Socialization and Interaction Process.* New York: The Free Press, 1955, p. 46. © 1955 by The Press Press, a Corporation. Reprinted with permission of Macmillan Publishing Co.

''The great advantage of the family is that these four roles are filled, on the average, by people whose ages and sexes fit especially well the functional requirements of a small group. Hence, the family is a stronger, longer-lasting, and more efficient small group than any other'' (Zelditch, 1964:63).

Instrumental activity is primarily oriented toward maintaining the relations of the system with those outside the system: external activities that emphasize occupational, educational, and political behavior. Although each member of the family can participate in these activities, the primary responsibility for instrumental activities lie in the male role. Expressive functions are concerned with the internal affairs of the system—oriented toward maintaining relationships and activities within the system itself. Activities include the bearing and socializing of children and the caring for the religious concerns of the family members. The family system is seen as striving to maintain an equilibriated balance between these two types of activity.

Parsons and Bales (1955) believe that the basis for this role differentiation and allocation lies in the bearing and early nursing of the child by the mother, which establishes a strong relationship between them. The fundamental importance of this relationship leads Zelditch to state that ''the mother's expressive role in the family is largely not problematical'' (Zelditch in Parsons and Bales, 1955:314). The father unable to compete with the mother for this type of relationship with the child turns instead to instrumental activities. Zelditch argues that the two parents are not only necessary to provide food and shelter for their children but also eventually to loosen the dependency tie between mother and child. This is accomplished through the necessary allocation of disciplinary authority as well as relatively neutral, nonexpressive judgments to the husband-father.

Parsons and Bales believe that the primary importance of the occupational instrumental role of the male is a boundary role, one in which the society unequivocally designates the husband-father as the instrumental leader of the family system; the status of the family and the life style it leads is largely dependent on the level of job and subsequent income the husband-father earns (Parsons and Bales, 1955:13). The roles played with the family structure are seen to be complementary: the wife's role anchored in the internal affairs of the family, as wife, mother, and manager of the household; the husband's role anchored in the external affairs of the family, as income-earner in the job market, which also provides the status for the family with the outside world.

CRITICS OF STRUCTURE FUNCTIONALISM'S CONCEPTUALIZATIONS

Critics of the contemporary family take issue with the structure-functionalist belief that it is the optimum family system for solving the needs for intimacy, individualism, and equalitarianism. Such critics as Arlene S. and Jerome H. Skolnick (1971/1977) believe that supporters of the conjugal family have overlooked problems inherent within the family because of the limitations of structure functionalist based modernization theory. They argue that modernization theory tends to view industrial society as a static entity, representing the final stage in industrial history. The critics believe that the sociologic study of the family in industrial society can be strengthened by extending the line of inquiry to a new stage of development—postindustrial or postmodern society. They see that a better understanding of the conjugal family can be accomplished by studying it as a social problem, viewing the problems of the conjugal family as arising out of its very nature and structure.

Skolnick and Skolnick (1971/1977) and Skolnick (1973/1978) observe that Talcott Parsons and that William J. Goode in his *World Revolution and Family Patterns* (1963) do recognize that tensions and points of strains in the conjugal family system can have negative effects on family members. However, they believe that Goode's structure functionalist orientation tends to prevent him giving full systematic treatment to the implications of these tensions and strains. They assert that the structure functionalist perspective sees society as being in a state of balanced equilibrium, with indiviuals being integrated into society through various social roles and with the family serving as the basis of this integration. What structure functionalism does not see is that these tensions and points of strain may be much more serious in nature and represent fatal flaws and contradictions that question the viability of modern family arrangements and the supportive social system (Skolnick, 1973:125–126).

Critics of the conjugal family condemn the emphasis on privatization and female domesticity. One such critic, Michael Gordon (1972), states that although industrialization has created the possibility of the emancipation of women from the larger extended family, it has substituted the increased domestic burdens inherent in the conjugal family system. Gordon emphasizes what Goode suggests: the division of labor necessitated by the economic system has subjugated women to the household and its domestic-task drudgeries. The reality, then, has not been emancipation but continued subservience. Gordon argues that economic analysis would suggest the greater efficiency of communal work as opposed to the duplicated individuated work of such tasks as child care, meal preparation, and clothes washing, as one structural improvement over the conjugal family system.

Skolnick (1973/1978) amplifies on Goode's observation that strains in the male role result in an industrial system that is based on competition and achievement. This results in great psychological tension and thus men have not totally benefited from the freedom of kinship occupational succession, which was characteristic of traditional society. The demand for excellence in the modern technological system places great psychological demands on the individual in that it demands an unremitting discipline. Lower skilled jobs are psychologically burdensome because they provide little pleasure; higher skilled jobs—professional, managerial, and creative positions—demand standards of excellence in areas where the standards of excellence are high and that in many cases are unspecified and result in pressures to perform to standards that are unattainable.

Kenneth Keniston (1965) has observed that the family is the primary area in which feelings can be fully expressed; it is the individual's emotional center. Men find the world of work demands highly cognitive, unemotional, and analytical behavior. The home-centered family provides the opportunity for them to express sentiment, tenderness, and emotionality. Life is thus compartmentalized: "the feeling, support, sensitivity, expressiveness, and exclusive love of the family contrast with impersonality, neutrality, cognition, achievement and accomplishment of work" (Keniston, 1965:279). A tension can develop—or, at best, a delicate balance may exist—between the man's occupational and domestic commitments, and he can often find himself solely deriving satisfaction from his work (careerism) or his home (familism).

The privacy and domesticity of women leaves them solely responsible for the raising of children. Although this allows a certain independence, it also cuts them off from outside help and supports. The woman's life is cut off from outside involvements and activities. It is only through the accomplishments of her husband or children that the housewife can vicariously derive satisfactions from the world of work.

A common theme running through the criticisms of the conjugal family revolves around the belief that its privatization and isolation has prevented it from achieving for its members the very intimacy and psychological gratification that it was designed to foster. In two widely read and influential books, *The Uncommited: Alienated Youth in American Society* (1965) and *Young Radicals: Notes on Committed Youth* (1968), Kenneth Keniston develops the argument that the isolation of the family fosters childhood dependency and handicaps the development of autonomy and maturity: "Our middle-class families, despite their goodness of fit with many aspects of American society, involve inherent conflicts in the roles of mother and father, and produce deep discontinuities between childhood and adulthood" (Kenniston, 1965:309).

Philip Slater, who was strongly influenced by structure functionalism, breaks with that perspective in his provocative analysis of American culture in *The Pursuit of Loneliness* (1970). This book, written at the height of the antiwar period and of the youth counterculture movement, is highly critical of privatization and the separation of home and work. He sees the emotional dependency of the young on their middle-class suburban parents as leading to their alienation and the inability for affective emotional expressiveness.

These arguments parallel those of the radical psychologists such as David Cooper and R. D. Laing. Cooper in his *The Death of the Family* (1970) states that "The family form of -social existence that characterizes all our institutions essentially destroys autonomous initiative by its defining nonrecognition of what I have called the proper dialectic of solitude and being with other people" (1970:140). Laing (1969) emphasized the repressive nature of the private family and its denial of internal conflicts to itself and to its neighbors:

> So we are a happy family and we have no
> secrets from one another.
> *If* we are unhappy/we have to keep it a secret/
> and we are unhappy that we have to keep it a secret
> and unhappy *that* we have to keep secret/the fact/that we
> *have* to keep it a secret
> and that we *are* keeping all that secret.
> But since we are a happy family you can see
> this difficulty does not arise. (Laing, 1969:100)

Skolnick and Skolnick (1971) examine the dysfunctionality of the conjugal family for children and youth in their discussion of the "politics of child rearing." They emphasize the complete subjugation of children not only in terms of their political rights but also in how they can be psychologically emulsified by their total dependence on the conjugal family. To illustrate, they report on a number of recent theories regarding childhood schizophrenia. The structural organization of the conjugal family, where the child is relatively isolated from other personal and emotional contacts, may be a conducive setting for driving children crazy:

In the isolation of the nuclear family, the parent can easily deny some aspect of reality, usually the parents' behavior or motives, thus causing the child to doubt his own perceptions. For example, the parent may act very angry or sexy, yet deny he or she is doing so. (Skolnick and Skolnick, 1971:306)

Richard Sennett (1974) contrasts the theoretical position of Talcott Parsons with the conservative position of Philippe Ariès on how "private and intense" family life relates to the socialization of children and their preparation for adulthood. Ariès is seen as deploring the division of labor within the family since it isolates the family from the larger society. The result is the children's loss of needed experience with the outside adult world. This leads to subsequent difficulties in functioning in that world and in becoming responsible adults.

In contrast, according to Sennett, the specialization of the family as seen by Parsons is a necessary consequence of the increased specialization of the entire society. Parsons favors the division of labor and role fragmentation within the family as preparing children for the division and fragmentation that they will experience in their adult activities. Sennett reports that Parsons views the socialization of children as requiring a long period of learning about themselves as fragmented beings. This belief develops out of Parsons's integration of the psychoanalytic description of child development and the structural analysis of society. Together these perspectives, as integrated by Parsons, argue that it is the "essence of ego formation to learn the proper limits and spheres of action" (Sennett, 1974:67). Sennett compares Ariès and Parsons in the following statement:

The vices of the modern nuclear family for Ariès are, to a great extent, its virtues for Parsons. Where Ariès sees the specialization of the family as a limitation on human capacities to grow, Parsons sees this specialization as both a necessary consequence of the increased specialization of the whole society, and as a means of leading the child step by step into a position where he could act alone as a adult in a complex industrial world. For Parsons, the fact that the child in an isolated nuclear family would have "farther to go," as he puts it, in becoming an adult than children in another historical era is not an indictment of the family form, but an indicator of the increased complexity of the industrial society, in which the family plays a specialized role. (Sennett, 1974:66)

CONCEPTUALIZATIONS OF STRUCTURE FUNCTIONALISM AND ITS CRITICS: AN ASSESSMENT

In assessing the position of the structure functionalists as compared to that of the critics of the contemporary private family, it is apparent that ideological biases distort the respective analyses. The structure functionalists working off an equilibrium and organismic model tend to view society as an organism that strains toward maintaining itself in some form of balance. The various parts of the system, in this case the members of the family, are seen to act in a cooperative and coordinating fashion. Stability and order are implicitly viewed as being natural and normal.

The critics of the contemporary family—be they conservatives like Ariès, who abhors modernity and its consequences for the family and the child, or the radicals, such as Laing and Cooper, who take an essentially negative view of psychological dynamics and processes in the family—also let their biases distort their analyses. Both groups see the loss of autonomy and individuality as inherently being a loss for young people in the private family. One group, the conservatives, call for the reestablishment of some traditional order, the other group calls for the establishment of a new form of intimate public community without private families.

Essentially, in evaluating all these perspectives, we become cognizant of a 20th-century replay of the ideological positions and arguments put forth by the Social Darwinists, the Conservatives, and the Radicals. In our earlier discussions of 19th-century theories of social change and the family, we examined the moral valuations inherent in these orientations. Structure functionalism can be seen as the 20th-century offshoot of Social Darwinsim; the theories of Philippe Ariès and Carle C. Zimmerman (whom we discussed in that earlier presentation) echo those of conservatives like Frédéric Le Play, whereas the radical positions set forth by the psychologists R. D. Laing, David Cooper, and, to a certain extent, by the sociologists, Jerome H. and Arlene S. Skolnick and the later Philip Slater share a similar perspective to that put forth by Marx and Engels.

In recent years, however, the analysis centering around the implications of the privatized family for children has taken a new turn. There is a growing realization that the private family is not as free and autonomous as has been believed. Arguments have been raised that to study the family without taking into consideration the influence of the larger society leads to serious limitations in properly assessing the impact of the family on children. In particular, critics, such as Christopher Lasch (1977a), argue that not only are educational, political, and economic functions of the family now performed by the state and supporting institutions but increasingly so also are the medical, social, and psychological functions performed by the helping professions. Lasch believes that there has been a progressive reduction in family functions to the extent that there is a growing intervention into the private life of the family. The services provided by the state and professionals are most graphically seen in compulsory education, but increasingly occur in the forms of medical practitioners, social workers, psychiatrists, childrearing experts, and juvenile courts. The increased dependence of the family on these "experts" has ultimately led to the loss of their autonomy.

Christopher Lasch in his stimulating book, *Haven in a Heartless World* (1977a), is highly critical of structure functionalism *and* of what he labels as "revisionist" and "radical" sociology. He asserts that critics of structure functionalism, which include Arlene S. and Jerome H. Skolnick; Kenneth Keniston in *The Uncommitted* (1965), Philip Slater; and R. D. Laing "conjure up a fantastic picture of the isolated nuclear family as a miniature despotism in which parents enjoy nearly absolute power" (Lasch, 1977a:147). Lasch accuses them of over-romanticizing an alternative family model that echoes the medieval village and the extended family system described by Philippe Ariès. And, most important, Lasch says, they fail to see how the private family system itself has been usurped by government social policies and social agencies. He asserts that the ideological shortcomings of structure functionalist sociology is

> . . . because it took for granted the separation of private life and work, leisure and labor; assumed the alienation of labor as an inevitable by-product of material progress; gave scholarly support to the delusion that private life offers the only relief from deprivations suffered at work; and ignored the invasion of private life itself by the forces of organized domination. Revisionist sociology takes all this for granted too, and is equally oblivious to the erosion of the private realm. (Lasch, 1977a:149)

In the concluding section of this chapter, we will examine this argument by examining the development of the child welfare movement. By so doing, we will draw attention to the dilemma faced by children: the desire for the development of personal freedom and autonomy in the face of dependency situations, both in the home and in social institutions.

THE FAMILY AND CHILD WELFARE INSTITUTIONS

In previous discussions we showed that there has been a systematic movement among the bourgeoise middle class, begun several hundred years ago, to segregate and remove children from adult life. It was based on a belief that children and adolescents did not have the psychological capacities, intellectual abilities, and the requisite maturity to participate on an equal footing in adult affairs. Coinciding with this conceptualization was the development of the notion of the private family system.

This conceptualization was fostered by the emergence of the new industrialized urban society, which was viewed as threatening and unpredictable by the emerging middle class. For them, the same ideological currents that saw fit to protect women—by removing them from active participation in the outside world and sequestering them within the home—was carried over to the younger generation. Ostensibly, the desire was to protect both women and children from abhorrent labor conditions and their abuse by industry. In effect, however, this resulted in the subordination and dependence of both women and children. Before we examine its effect on the middle class, we can best understand how it came about by examining the child welfare movement, which developed out of concern for the conditions of poor children of the 19th century. For it was then that social policies regarding children developed and were carried over the contemporary era.

Child labor and the abuse of children in industry was a common occurrence in the burgeoning factories of the late 18th and 19th centuries of England. The prospering middle classes, aghast at the treatment of women and children in these factories, removed their own families from these harsh and brutal work conditions. Unfortunately, the children of the poor, the destitute, and the abandoned children were not as fortunate. Economic and political realities resulted in their being victims of social injustice and forced unemployment in work situations that were inhumane and barbarous:

> With the coming of the machine age . . . mere babies were subjected to terrible inhumanity by the factory systems. . . . Children from five years of age upward were worked sixteen hours at a time, sometimes with irons riveted around their ankles to keep them from running away. They were starved, beaten, and in many other ways maltreated. Many succumbed to occupational diseases, and some committed suicide; few survived for any length of time. (Helfer and Kempe, 1968:11)

To illustrate, poor city children in England employed as chimney sweeps worked day and night. Death from cancer of the scrotum was frequent and pulmonary consumption was so common that it became known as the chimney sweep's disease.

The children who worked under these oppressive conditions were from the poorer classes. They were the young paupers from the workhouse, children without parents to protect them, many as young as 4 and 5 years of age. They also included the children of poor families who could not support them and reluctantly allowed their children to work in the mills and factories. Piven and Cloward (1971), writing on the societal functions of public welfare, note that pauper children relegated to parish poorhouses became an ideal labor source for the English textile industry. Parishes and orphanages supplied children to factories as cheap labor. They were motivated both by greed and the self-serving moral belief that idle children would grow up to be shiftless idle adults. The manufacturers negotiated with them for lots of 50 or more children at a time. These children provided a very stable labor force for they were obligated to work until they fulfilled the terms of their indentures. For many, the terms of their indentures did not expire until the age of 21 and many children did not survive until that age.

In the beginning of the 19th century, the child-labor reform movement started in England with the passage of the First Factory Act in 1802. The act broke up the factory pauper-apprentice system. But, it did not interfere with traditional parental rights over children. It did not apply to children whose parents were living and who allowed them or sent them involuntarily to work. Throughout the 19th century, the laws that were passed to curb the abuses of child labor in industry did not infringe on the Victorian premise that the family was a private and sacred institution into which outsiders had little right to intrude. It was not until the end of that century and the beginning of the 20th that social-reform legislation was passed to protect children of the poor who did not pass the moralistic muster of the moralistic middle-class reformers. An examination of events in the United States during this period will prove instructive.

In the last quarter of the 19th century increased attention was given to the ways in which children were being abused. The first American legal action for child abuse was not broughout about until 1874. Laws, in fact, were enacted to protect animals before there were laws to protect children. Indeed, the first child-abuse case was actually handled by the New York Society for the Prevention of Cruelty of Animals. In this first case the child was treated under the rubric (legal rule) concerning a small animal.

By the turn of the century, a basic philosophy was developed on how best to handle abused and neglected children. These tenets have affected the way we look at abuse and neglect today and so deserve our attention. Muckracking journalists and social reformers argued that these children could best be "rehabilitated" by placing them under the jurisdiction of state industrial schools, reform schools, and the juvenile court systems. Through their influence, such special judicial and correctional institutions were created for the labeling, processing, and managing "troublesome and destitute" youth. An interesting twist is observed in this philoosphy. The victimized child has in effect become the victimizer who must be incarcerated and rehabilitated. It is a 19th- and early-20th-century version of "blaming the victim."

Anthony Platt (1969) has written a fascinating account of the child-welfare movement and the development of the conceptualization of abused children as delinquents. The social reformers, as as he calls them, the child savers, believed that children who were brought up improperly by negligent parents were bound for lives of crime unless taken out of the parents' hands at a very early age. The child savers succeeded in the creation of rehabilitation institutions that were designed to prevent the development of criminal and deviant tendencies.

These reformers were influenced by the prevailing antiurban bias prevalent during that period and by their own middle-class Protestant morality. They reacted against the perceived "social disorganization" of the city. The city became the symbol of all the evils of modern industrial life. It was depicted as the main breeding ground of criminals. The children of the European peasant immigrants were seen as the victims of culture conflict and technological revolution.

The social reformers extolled the virtues of the rural community and placed high valuc on religion, home, work and the family. Parental discipline and woman's domesticity was advocated to control children. The hope for children living in the city slums, who were described as "intellectual dwarfs" and "physical and moral wrecks," was to remove them from these debilitating surroundings (Platt, 1969). Platt cites a 19th-century reformer who reports to the National Prison Association in 1898 that philanthropic organizations all over the country were

> making efforts to get the children out of the slums, even if only once a week, into the radiance of better lives. Seeing the beauties of a better existence, these children may be led to choose the good rather than the evil. Good has been done by taking these children into places where they see ladies well dressed, and with their hands and faces clean, and

it is only by leading the child out of sin and debauchery, in which it has lived, into a circle of life that is a repudiation of things that it sees in its daily life, that it can be influenced. (Platt, 1969:40–41)

The child savers were middle-class moralists who emphasized the values of home and family as the basic institutions of American society. They defined the problems of neglect as attributable to faulty hygiene and lax morality. They minimized or ignored the economic and political-power realities of the urban poor. By extolling such values, they fostered the movement of children out of the homes of the poorer classes that did not meet their standards. Middle-class families, of course, were by and large not affected by their zeal.

Unfortunately, the rehabilitation institutions did not function in the manner intended. They were overcrowded punitive institutions that physically punished boys and girls and that often had them working for industries contracted by their custodians. Platt describes the "educational" program of the Illinois State Reform School, which consisted of boys laboring 7 hours a day for a shoe firm, a brush manufacturer, and a cane-chair manufacturer. He argues that what was purported to be benevolent institutions for the intervention and prevention of crime became themselves abusive, punitive, and authoritarian, breeding their own abusive patterns. He summarizes his view by making four points (1969:176):

1. The reforms of the child-saving movement did not usher in a new system of justice, but rather it reaffirmed and expedited traditional policies.
2. A "natural" dependence of adolescence was promulgated. The creation of a juvenile court imposed sanctions on "premature" indulgence and behavior "unbecoming" a youth.
3. Paternalistic and romantic attitudes were developed but were anchored by authoritarian force. No conflict of interests were perceived between the vested interests of agencies of social control and those of "delinquents."
4. Correctional programs were implemented that required long terms of forced imprisonment, involuntary labor and militaristic discipline. Middle-class values and lower class skills were inculcated.

The child-saving movement resulted in the forced incarceration of many urban poor children. Platt points out that the programs, which were rhetorically concerned with protecting children from the physical and moral changes of increasingly industrialized urban society, diminished the children's freedom and independence. Rather than provide remedies, they aggravated the problem. Platt makes an interesting observation on the relationship of this reform movement and Philippe Ariès's analysis of European historical family life that is worth repeating. It nicely summarizes a major point of this discussion—that ideological and moral biases often have a detrimental effect on the people they are designed to benefit:

The child-saving movement had its most direct consequences on the children of the urban poor. The fact that "troublesome" adolescents were depicted as "sick" or "pathological" were imprisoned "for their own good," and were addressed in a paternalistic vocabulary, and exempted from criminal law processes, did not alter the subjective experience of control, restraint, and punishment. As Philippe Ariès observed in his historical study of European family life, it is ironic that the obsessive solicitude of family, church, moralists, and administrators for child welfare served to deprive children of the freedoms that they had previously shared with adults and to deny their capacity for initiative, responsibility, and autonomy. The "invention" of delinquency consolidated the inferior social status and dependency of lower-class youth. (Platt, 1969:177)

The child-saving movement, in summary, was based on the assumption that physical abuse and neglect were associated almost exclusively with poverty, slums, industrial exploitation and the cultural deprivation of the poor and immigrant populations. As the physical conditions associated with abuse and neglect began to improve by the second decade of the 20th century, the attention began to shift to concerns of the emotional neglect and abuse of children.

The 1920s and 1930s were a period in which the child-welfare movement increasingly turned its attention to the implementation of the new ideas of Freudian psychoanalysis and psychiatry. The emphasis shifted to the advocacy of the utilization of various forms of social services, either voluntary or by judicial intervention, in the hope of assuring the emotional well-being of children. This increasingly led to difficulties as the acceptable legal definition of emotional neglect and abuse was and is more difficult to define or prove than is its physical counterpart. The result was the development of an antagonism between affected families and social institutions that continues today. An examination of the works of Kenneth Kensiton, Christopher Lasch, and Mary Jo Bane will center on this problem.

In *All Our Children: The American Family Under Pressure* (1977), the Carnegie Council on Children, headed by Kenneth Keniston, the psychologist known for his study of youth in the 1960s, reports on a five-year examination on the way children grow up in America. The Council debunks the myth that the family is self-sufficient and self-sustaining as well as the widely held belief that parents alone are responsible for what becomes of their children.

The researchers believe that this myth developed in the 19th century out of the economic doctrine of laissez-faire capitalism and was built on images of the independent farmer and entrepreneur. The authors pick up on a theme, which we have reported in this book, on how the family defined itself as a refuge that guarded women and children from the incursions of an increasingly alien and hostile urban environment. In the preceeding preindustrial era of the 17th and 18th centuries, the family was defined by the Puritan conceptualization of the "little commonwealth." The family was viewed as essentially similar to the surrounding community and governed by the same standards of piety and respect. With the emergence of an industrialized and urbanized society in the 19th century, the belief developed among the more affluent and privileged classes that the home must serve as a refuge protecting its frailer members, women and children, from the temptations and moral corruptions of a threatening outside world. "No longer simply a microcosm of the rest of society, the ideal family became a womb-like "inside" to be defended against a corrupting "outside." (Keniston and The Carnegie Council on Children, 1977:11).

The Council points out that, in reality, this family system was an ideal one that was perhaps realized by only a small segment of the upper middle class segment of the population. Poor families, immigrants, slaves, Indians, and growing numbers of factory workers rarely achieved this ideal of self-sufficiency and independence. Today, it is even less real for all segments of the population. Yet, the myth still persists. It fails to see that the family has been deeply influenced by broad social and economic forces over which it has little control. The Council argues that the family's authority and influence is constantly eroding and dwindling as that of outside institutions' increases. Economic and social pressures of parents' jobs, the cost of raising children, the increased involvement of institutionalized health-care services and of schools, and the entire social ecology—from television programming to the packaging of foods—define and limit parents' autonomy and independence:

> Today's parents have little authority over those others with whom they share the task of raising their children. On the contrary, most parents deal with those others from a position of inferiority or helplessness. Teachers, doctors, social workers, or television producers possess more status than most parents. Armed with special credentials and a jargon most parents cannot understand, the experts are usually entrenched in their professions and have far more power in their institutions than do the parents who are their clients. To be sure, professionals would often *like* to treat each child in accordance with his or her unique needs, and professional codes of conduct urge that they do so, but professionals who really listen to parents or who are really able to model their behavior in response to what parents tell them are still few and far between. (Keniston and The Carnegie Council on Children, 1977:18).

The Council concludes that the family is changing, but it is not collapsing: 98 percent of American children still live with one or both of their parents. They believe that "families"—and the circumstances of their lives—will remain the most crucial factors in determining children's fate" (Keniston and The Carnegie Council on Children, 1977:xiv). But to do this, there is a need to remedy the greatest enemy of the family—poverty. The researchers find that one child out of four has the deck stacked against it by economic conditions. They cite a 1974 study that found that 33 percent of children born into the top-tenth income level would stay there, whereas only 0.4 percent of those born into the bottom-tenth income level would ever rise to the top.

To remedy this poverty, the Council recommends a major overhauling of America's economic structure and sweeping reforms in social policies, work practices, laws, and services. Their proposals are designed to return to parents the authority they should have with the ability to raise their children under better circumstances than now exist. Among their specific recommendations is a guaranteed family income that is no lower than one-half the national median, full employment, income supports for the working poor, and a national health insurance plan.

Christopher Lasch (1977a, 1977b, 1979) is also concerned about the usurpation of family authority by professional social agencies. Lasch, an historian at the University of Rochester, believes that works such as The Carnegie Institute's *All Our Children* reflect the growing disillusionment with the public institutes and welfare agencies that have taken over the functions of the family—the school, the hospital, the mental hospital, the juvenile courts, and rehabilitation institutes. But, he argues, Keniston and his colleagues do not go far enough in their critique of professionalism. He sees a contradiction in Keniston's advocating governmental expansion of services to the family, which includes a federal guarantee of full employment, improved protection of legal rights of children, and a vastly expanded program of health care, while also proposing to strengthen the family by its participation in these programs. He argues that the helping professions have systematically expropriated parental authority by demeaning the capabilities of parents, by arguing that only they have the scientific expertise to know what is best for the child, and by their piecemeal allowance to parents decisions that only serve to perpetuate feelings of inadequacy and dependence:

> . . . the "helping professions," by persuading the family to rely on scientific technology and the advice of scientifically trained experts, undermined the family's capacity to provide for itself and thereby justified the continuing expansion of health, education, and welfare services. Having monopolized or claimed to monopolize most of the knowledge necessary to bring up children, the agencies of socialized reproduction handed it back in the form of "parent education," "consumer education," and other devices intended to enable the citizen to shop more efficiently among proliferating professional services. . . . Having first declared parents incompetent to raise their offspring without professional assistance, social pathologists "gave back" the knowledge they had appropriated—gave it back in a mystifying fashion that rendered parents more helpless than ever, more abject in their dependence on expert opinion. (Lasch, 1977b).

Lasch develops his argument through a social-historical analysis of the family and helping agencies. He asserts that the privatization of the family in the 19th century was short lived. The bourgeois family did try to establish itself as a refuge, a private retreat, where it could become the center of a new form of emotional intensity between parents and children. Following the lines of previous historians, Lasch sees the 19th-century middle-class family developing a cult of the home, where the woman cared for her husband and sheltered her children from the perceived corrupting influences of the outside world. But, and this is the crux of his argument, at the same time that the glorification of private life and the family was occurring, there was developed a realization that the family was inadequate to provide for its own needs without expert intervention. This led to the development of the helping professions.

Lasch states that the helping professions of the 19th and early-20th centuries played on bourgeois fears by inventing and defining social needs only they could satisfy. He is particularly concerned to demonstrate how these professional social agencies condemned and expropriated parental authority and competence:

> . . . public policy, sometimes conceived quite deliberately not as a defense of the family at all but as an invasion of it, contributed to the deterioration of domestic life. The family did not simply evolve in response to social and economic influences; it was deliberately transformed by the intervention of planners and policymakers. Educators and social reformers saw that the family, especially the immigrant family, stood as an obstacle to what they conceived as social progress—in other words, to homogenization and "Americanization." The family preserved separatist religious traditions, alien languages and dialects, local lore, and other traditions that retarded the growth of the political community and the national state. Accordingly, reformers sought to remove children from the influence of their families, which they also blamed for exploiting child labor, and to place the young under the benign influence of state and school. (Lasch, 1977a:13).

He discusses how the schools and social welfare services expanded under the justification that the family could no longer provide for the needs of its children. Likewise, children's aid societies, juvenile courts, and visits to families by social workers became commonplace as the result of this belief that the family was not prepared to take care of the physical, mental, and social training of the child. Lasch believes that the result of these forces has been the usurpation of the family by outside professionals, doctors, social workers, the helping professions, and the schools.

Lasch is particularly critical of contemporary social scientists—sociologists, anthropologists, neo-Freudian psychoanalysts, and most of all of Talcott Parsons and his school of functionalism. He believes their theoretical framework is responsible for the decline of the family. This occurred through their advocacy of "the family's indispensability while at the same time providing a rationale for the continued invasion of the family by experts in the art of social and psychic healing" (Lasch, 1977a:115–116). He maintains that Parsonian theory, although arguing the sociologic justification of the family's importance because of the intensification of the emotional climate of the family, nevertheless undercuts this importance with another line of argument that sees the family creating strains that only the helping professions' experts know how to handle.

Lasch sees this development as undermining the family with severe recpercussions for its children. He reasons that, with the rise of the helping professions, parents become reluctant to exercise authority or to assure responsibility for their children's development. This, in turn, results in the weakening of the child's ability to develop an autonomous personality and prevents the development of moral values. In another work, *The Culture of Narcissism* (1979), he asserts that these developments have undermined American values and that the young are being socialized into a fake world of easy-going, low-keyed encounters. This culture of narcissism represents the decadence of American individualism and the end of the Protestant virtues of hard work, thrift, and capital accumulation. Today, the concern is with personal survival and hedonism.

In summary, both The Carnegie Council on Children report and Christopher Lasch's analysis provide a welcome shift away from the emphasis of debates on the family's psychological structure to the impact of society on the family and children. The policies advocated by the Council are designed to develop a comprehensive and universally accessible public services to support and strengthen, but not to replace, families in the rearing of their children. However, to accomplish this, a fine balance must be achieved between the family's desire for autonomy and privacy and the public policies that seek to help and protect the child. Far too frequently, as Lasch emphasizes, the government acts not as a helping agency but as an opponent that seeks to legislate the family out of existence and to undermine its independence and autonomy. This tension also dominates the analysis of the family and social policy of Mary Jo Bane.

In her study, *Here to Stay: American Families in the Twentieth Century* (1976), Mary Jo Bane—an assistant professor of education at Wellesley College and associate director of the school's Center for Research on Women—after careful statistical analysis concluded that the contemporary American family is still quite viable and persists in its commitment to its children. She takes issue with the widely held notion that the American family of the past was an extended one. She supports the conclusions we reported, namely, that the nuclear family has been the predominant family form.

She opposes the belief that the declining birthrate reflects disintegration within the family. Rather, she observes that it indicates decreasing size of individual families and not the collective decision of the population to stop having children. As for divorce, she views it as a safety valve for families; it assures that only those who desire to stay together do so. Ultimately, it improves the quality of American marriages. Further, although the divorce rate has risen dramatically, most people remarry. Those that do not, tend to keep their children with them. Compared to a century ago, the loss of a parent is less disruptive on the family today.

The major thrust of Bane's study centers around the tension between public social policies designed for the protection of individuals, including children, and the desire for family privacy. She presents a detailed examination of such issues as mandatory day care for all, the Equal Rights Amendment, and Aid to Families with Dependent Children. She is particularly concerned that the rights of minors be protected from abusive and negligent adults and that the rights of children to economic sufficiency does not impinge on and destroy the family's right to privacy and its viability. The argument is made that the tensions between family privacy and values pronounced in social policies can be resolvable by a public stance that emphasizes the rights of individuals and assures the working out of family roles within the privacy of the family.

In conclusion, Bane argues for the view that Americans persist in their deep commitment to the family. Family ties continue to remain as persistent manifestations of human needs for stability, continuity, and nonconditional affection. Paradoxically, the greatest danger to the American family may lie in social policies that reflect the erroneous belief that the American family is dying. Consequently, those who hold that belief may advocate programs that, rather than attempting to supply helpful choices, may actually contribute to the family's decline and demise:

> Family ties and family feelings are integral to the lives of most Americans. The ethic that governs relationships between people who love and care for each other inevitably intrudes into public life, coloring people's perceptions of what they and others ought to do. Policies that ignore this ethic—that imply that public facilities can replace parental care or that the public welfare system is responsible for supporting children—will almost surely be either widely resented or essentially disregarded. Even when family service programs respond to real needs, they are often perceived as undermining the fabric of society. Until such programs are designed to incorporate the very real and very strong values that underlie family life in America, and until they are perceived as doing so, they are doomed to failure. (Bane, 1976:142–143)

Taking Children away from Parents

Ellen Goodman

BOSTON—They were not exactly your everyday, middle-class, happy family. But then they rarely are in cases when the state intervenes to take the children away forever.

For one thing, the parents were half-brother and half-sister. For another thing, the father was once charged with sexual assault against one of the children, found not guilty of that, but guilty of the offense of "touching."

But when the Supreme Court decided to hear the case of Doe vs. Delaware last week, it wasn't to judge the parents. It was to judge the laws which split this family . . . and many others.

The five Doe children were removed, you see, under one of the state statutes that allows the court to permanently end this most basic and primal relationship if parents are "not fitted."

Once upon a time, children were literally the possessions of their parents. It was only gradually that we came to see children as separate human beings with rights of their own—rights that could even conflict with those of their parents.

Since the 1960s, when the states "discovered" child abuse, we have become more and more willing to admit that parents are not always best for their children. One by one, we have passed laws which give social workers and judges the right to intervene in the family and take the kids for "their own good."

But, as Justice Brandeis once warned, "Experience should teach us to be most on our guard to protect liberty when the government's purposes are beneficent."

With good intentions, the system helped remove children from their homes and put them in foster care, or institutions. We worried more about where they were coming from than where they were going.

Today, in "the best interests of the child," parents in many states have fewer legal rights than a common criminal. We often separate family members from each other forever with less due process than we separate a thief from his liberty for 30 days.

The Does are not paragons of parental virtue. But the language of the Delaware law that severs their rights to the children they conceived is so vague that it could include any parent as "not fitted."

In Pennsylvania, where another test case is working its way through the system (Lehman vs. the Lycoming County Children's Services), the language is so broad that the state can take a child away from any parent "who has caused the child to be without essential parental care, control or subsistence."

At some time, any one of us could fill that definition. But it is, of course, mostly the poor who are found "unfitted."

"You have a bunch of poor people, very poor people, on welfare, coming to the attention of the state and losing their children," says Fred Kessler, who worked on these cases at the community legal aide services for five years in Delaware. "Somebody needs to speak for the parents."

Martin Guggenheim, director of NYU Law School's Juvenile Rights Clinic, agrees. "We keep the parents poor and then we take away their children. We have really entered the worst of all worlds when we allow people to move other people's children around under their sense of where the children would be better off. The state only has the right to protect children from death and disfigurement."

Guggenheim is one of those writing new and much narrower

standards for parental termination laws for the American Bar Association. "Before we end this relationship, we should require the state to show that the child would be harmed in a significant manner, and tie the standard very closely to the child and very specifically."

No one denies that there are sometimes urgent reasons to remove children. No one wants to go back to the days when parents could legally and mercilessly abuse their children. But at the moment the courts and social service agencies have too much unchecked power over parents and children. It is this system which is "not fitted."

Ellen Goodman in the *Philadelphia Inquirer,* April 7, 1980. Copyright 1980, Boston Globe Newspaper Company/Washington Post Company. Reprinted by permission.

CONCLUSION

The relationship between family members of different ages captures our attention in this chapter as it will in the following one. Here we were intended in seeing how a power dimension was seen to be inherent in the differential relationships among family members of different ages. Children and adolescents were examined within an age-stratification perspective.

We showed that the nature and rate of social change has been associated with the nature and type of generational control parents have over their children. Margaret Mead's *Culture and Commitment* (1970b) was analyzed for its cross-cultural contribution to the understanding of what has been popularly labeled as the generation gap. Mead's work led us to examine how conceptualizations of childhood and adolescence are an important factor in the way generational attitudes and behavior become manifest.

Our comparative analysis drew on research in anthropology (Margaret Mead and Ruth Benedict) and social history (Philippe Ariès, Frank Musgrove, and Joseph F. Kett). It stressed the commonalities in these research studies and this led to the conclusion that the contemporary Western conceptualization of childhood and adolescence emphasizes the removal of the younger family member from the outside world into the private family.

A digression followed to re-present the conceptualizations of structure functionalism. This time, we focused on functionalism's microlevel analysis of marital, parental, and childrens' roles. We sought to demonstrate how structure functionalist conceptualizations reflected and reinforced the prevailing Western viewpoint. The implications of these conceptualizations for children and adolescents was discussed in the section on family- and child-welfare institutions. The idea of juvenile delinquency developed by child-saving professionals was analyzed.

The chapter concluded with a discussion of the ideas of Kenneth Keniston and The Carnegie Council on Children, Christopher Lasch, and Mary Jo Bane. These researchers asserted that the belief that the family is self-sufficient and self-sustaining is a myth. Public institutions and welfare agencies have had a strong impact on family autonomy and its authority over family members. Christopher Lasch, the most vocal opponent of the helping professions, is highly critical of structure functionalism and neo-Freudianism as forces that are undermining the family. Mary Jo Bane concludes our analysis by emphasizing the tensions that exist between public social policies designed for the protection of individuals, including children, and the desire for family privacy.

This tension also becomes apparent in the relationship between older family members and their adult children. We will be examining this in the next chapter. The theme is also picked up in chapter 14 when we analyze family violence.

Five

FAMILIES IN CRISIS
AND CHANGE

13

THE FAMILY AND THE ELDERLY

In the previous chapter we examined relationships within the family, with particular focus on the relationship between children, adolescents, and their parents. In this chapter we will extend the analysis of age differentiation and age stratification by looking at the relationship between elders and their married children. Here again, our concern lies with the structure of family status and authority patterns within the context of social change.

We will focus our investigation by examining age differentiation in preliterate societies and contrasting it with the contemporary Western pattern. To highlight the differences in the conceptualizations on age, we begin with an analysis of those preliterate societies that use age groupings rather than kinship as a basis for organizing social relationships. We will then seek to demonstrate how age conceptualizations influence generational involvements in preliterate societies that do not employ age-set groupings. We will conclude with an in-depth examination of contemporary Western European and American societies to show how these conceptualizations have implications not only for family relationships but also for government-based social policies that affect these relationships.

AGE DIFFERENTIATION AND AGE-SET SOCIETIES

Age differences are biologically based. They are universally recognized. Age categories help shape people's relations to one another. Expectations vary, depending on the age of the person in question. Yet the categorization of childhood,

369

adolescence, youth, adulthood, and old age are social categories. They are not a mere product of biology. The social roles of child, adult, and the aged, for example, have varied from society to society and within given societies historically.

Yet one consistent pattern exists throughout the world. In all family systems the superiority of parents to children is striking. Authority is vested in the parents, and children legitimate that authority. Thus, although parents treat their children " 'like children,' . . . children treat their parents with respect." (Blood, 1972:457).

Robert O. Blood, Jr., (1972) lists three general reasons for the superiority of parents. First is the biological dependence of infants on their parents. This subsequently is transformed into social dependence, which continues indefinitely. Next, parents have had more experience and, concomitantly, they are wiser than their children by virtue of having lived longer. This especially holds true in nonliterate societies that depend on memory for the transmission of cultural knowledge about the proper ways of doing things. The third reason is that age gives parents a head start in achieving positions of power in the outside world. This, in turn, increases the resources that they can bring to the family. Together, these factors strengthen the power that parents have over their children.

There is a great deal of variability on the relative importance of age in a given society and on the degree to which age forms the basis of a separated social group. The importance of age as the determining factor in social relations varies with the total degree of differentiation in a given society. The extent of age differentiation varies by societal complexity and amount of industrialization. Generally, the more complexly differentiated societies, especially industrial societies, place less emphasis on age. Differences in work, socioeconomic status, ethnicity, religion, and the like are the more important determinants of group membership. In contrast, simpler societies with nontechnologically based economies tend to place primary emphasis on kinship, sex, and age. Kinship, sex, and age serve as the social organizational basis of the society and provide the societal framework for the differentiation of relationships.

AGE SETS IN PRELITERATE SOCIETIES

Usually, age groupings are structurally and functionally subordinated to kinship as a basis for organizing people's relationships in groups. Age groupings are most frequently found as supports for kinship structures. They serve as a basis for the extension of kinship ties. Rarely do they substitute for them. However, in some societies, age does form the basis of corporate social groupings in which the major criterion of membership is chronological age. These societies have formed age sets. Age sets are "social groups based on the principle of recruitment of persons of the same age, without regard to their kinship relations" (Williams, 1972:179). Age sets should not be confused with the mere categorizing of people who are recognized by a culture to be at the same stage of the life cycle (children, adolescent, old men).

This is termed age grade. Age grades are comprised of collectivities of people who have no real social identity or corporate functions.

George Murdock (1957) in his world ethnographic sample of 547 cultures found that less than 5 percent of the cultures (23) formed corporate, nonkin, exclusive social groups based solely on age. Approximately three-quarters of these cultures are located in Africa. It should be emphasized that the age-set system, which serves as a primary base of society-wide integration, is found in only 15 percent of all African cultures. Such age-set systems are most common among East African cultures, such as the Nandi, Kipsigi, Masai, Kamba, Kikuyu, and Meru. In these cultures associations based on age are central to the organization of community life and to the structure and function of the political system. A brief digression to examine one of these cultures will prove instructive.

Jomo Kenyatta (1938), in his classic account of his Gikuyu tribe (his preferred spelling of Kikuyu) *Facing Mt. Kenya,* discusses the importance of age groupings. Upon undergoing an initiation or circumcision ceremony, individuals automatically become members of one age-set, irrespective of their family or kinship group or the geographic district to which they belong. This rite of passage marks the commencement of participation in various governing groups in the Gikuyu tribal administration. The tribal organization is stabilized by the activities of the various age groups. Together the different age groups provide the organizational basis for the political, social, religious, and economic life of the Gikuyu.

Kenyatta observes that Gikuyu society is graded by age and the differential prestige that accompanies a status is age grouped. Social obligations are arranged and differentiated according to this system of age groupings. Within age groups, men have equal standing. Among the age groups, they are differentiated into social grades of junior and senior, inferior and superior:

> When an uncircumcised youth is travelling in the same company as a circumcized youth, he may not drink water until his superior has drunk, nor bathe in the river above the spot where the latter is bathing. So in the distribution of food the order of precedence is observed. What is true of uncircumcised and circumcised is true as between the various circumcised groups. The older group takes precedence over the younger and has rights to service and courtesy which the younger must acknowledge. (Kenyatta, 1938:112)

Kenyatta points out the extent of the importance of the system of age groupings by emphasizing how it affects lesser as well as more important matters. "It determines the different salutations used, the different tasks in homestead or garden; it rules habits of dress or demeanor in the community; and it explains the rights of different people in judging cases, in exercising authority in the clan or family, in ceremonial or religious proceedings" (Kenyatta, 1938:103).

The relationship between males and females is also affected by the age groupings. Gikuyu society allows for polygynous marriage. Women are assigned to domestic roles. In the family, especially when there is more than one wife, the mother is the immediate head of her family set. The family set is made up of her children, her own hut, her personal ornaments and household utensils. She also cultivates her own fields and has her own granary for her crops. In turn, each wife shares in taking care of the common husband: cleaning his hut, supplying him with firewood, water, food, and so on. Each wife is materially independent of each other. The head wife has no superior authority over the rest but is shown deference and respect by virtue of her age seniority.

Wives are expected to give special attention and treatment to members of their husband's age group. Kenyatta discusses what transpires when a visitor who has come from far away desires to spend the night in the homestead. Accommodations are made according to the rules and customs governing the social affairs of the given age group. A form of polyandry comes into play. This ultimately is seen to help reinforce the solidarity among the members of the age group.

> On these occasions the wives exercise their freedom, which amounts to something like polyandry. Each wife is free to choose anyone among the age-group and give him accommodation for the night. This is looked upon as purely social intercourse, and no feeling of jealousy or evil is attached to it on the part of the husband or wife. And, having all been brought up and educated in the idea of sharing, especially at the time when they indulged in "ngweko" (lovemaking), their hearts are saturated with ideas of collective enjoyment, without which there could not be strong unity among the members of the age group. (Kenyatta, 1938:174−175)

The age group composed of the elders has the greatest authority. The elders are treated with respect by virtue of their wisdom. They control economic affairs and political affairs for a period of 20 to 30 years, then, they abdicate their power to the next generation. During this period, the men take on leadership roles and responsibilities. Even after they relinquish their power, they are treated with respect and deference. Simone de Beauvoir, in her massive work on the old, summarizes the attitudes of the Gikuyu toward the elders:

> The elders are looked upon as pious beings, holy men, serene and detached from the world. Their influence depends upon their abilities and upon their wealth. Generally speaking, they are regarded as being wise. The Kikuyu have a saying, "An old goat does not spit without a reason," and again, "Old people do not tell lies." The old women are much respected when they have no teeth left; they are thought to be "filled with intelligence," and their bodies are buried with great ceremony instead of being left to the hyenas. (de Beauvoir, 1973:107)

What places age-set societies like the Gikuyu apart is the paramount importance of age in defining and regulating social integration, ritual activities, government, and military organization. The age-grade system is integrated with the kinship system, but it cuts across lineage membership. It serves as the major integration mechanism for the society. Although most of the world's societies are not organized solely around age sets, age does play an important role in determining societal interactional patterns. Let us now look at this in greater detail.

THE AGED IN PRELITERATE SOCIETIES

The general explanation given by social scientists for age grading follows on the nature of what Robert Redfield (1947) has termed folk societies. Folk societies are slow-changing and emphasize tradition and cermonialism. They tend to be conservative and resist change. Continuity with the past is a basic premise underlying the social order. There is a sense of timelessness and all-prevailing custom. The sacredness of custom and the lack of a written history makes the elders the repositories of societal wisdom and knowledge. The elders have high status because they know best the traditions of the past.

In folk societies the population clusters in small homogeneous communities. The community structure is fairly explicit, and it is anchored by stable values that are sacred rather than secular. The relationships among different age groups tend to be governed by explicitly delineated roles. These relationships are face to face and personal. Relationships among group members are multifaceted; they interact in different contexts, including work, home, and religious settings.

However, Leo W. Simmons (1945), who was one of the first anthropologists to attempt a large-scale cross-cultural study of aging, cautions us to be aware of the wide range of differences in attitudes toward and adaptations made to the problems and opportunities of aging. In a later article, Simmons (1960) observes that there is great diversity in cultural norms in terms of neglect and abandonment of old people on the one hand, and for their succor, support, and even glorification in death on the other. He finds that the influence and security of the elderly varied with the stability of the given society. Generally, the establishment of permanent residence, the achievement of a stable food supply, the rise of herding, the cultivation of the soil, and the increase of closely knit family relationships are all positively associated with the status and treatment of the old.

The status of the old tends to be inversely related to their numbers in the population. Simmons (1960:67−68) states that it is rare to find more than 3 percent of a primitive people 65 years of age and over. He also observes that in more primitive and rudimentary forms of human association there are fewer old people. Further, old age is attributed to these peoples at an earlier chronological date than in modern industrial societies. To illustrute, he cites a 1905 monograph on the Bontoc Igorot in the Philippines:

a woman reaches "her prime" at 23, at 30 she was "getting old," before 45 she was "old," and by 50 if she was so fortunate to live that long, she had become a "mass of wrinkles from foot to forehead. . . . Probably not more than one or two in a hundred lived to be 70 (Simmons, 1960:67).

Further, even though the number was small for those who did attain old age in some societies, the aging years came to be regarded as the best part of life. In fact, some preliterate peoples try to appear and to be regarded as older than they are. The anthropologist Leslie Milne[1] reports that the Palaung in North Burman is one such society where privilege and honor is given to the old:

> The older a person becomes, the greater is the respect that is paid her. The young women are expected to do a great deal of hard work along with the girls, such as bringing wood and water to the village before any festival; so married women are a little inclined to make out that they are older than they really are, in order that they may evade the extra work. (Leslie Milne cited in Simmons, 1960:68)[1]

Simmons hypothesizes that when the old can participate and fulfill themselves in the society, they tend to be treated with respect and deference. He examines their roles in the economic system, in government, and in the family to test his belief. He finds that when the aged have accumulated experience and familiarity with special skills, they retain directive roles in labor. For example, in the arts and crafts of basketry, pottery, housebuilding, boat construction, and the manufacture of cloth, tools, weapons, and other implements the old take on leadership roles based on their expertise. They are also highly valued for their roles of magician, healer, shaman, and priest. Midwifery is a prime illustration of a speciality associated with older women.

When they do not take on leadership roles, they can still find positions of usefulness. These usually involve engaging in secondary economic activities in field, camp, shop, and household. The underlying philosophy is the belief that all members of the society should participate in the society as long as they are physically and mentally able. By such activities, no matter how menial, the aged retain a sense of place and purpose in the society. The Hopi, a herding and farming people in northeastern Arizona, illustrate this principle:

> Old men tend their flocks until feeble and nearly blind. When they can no longer follow the herd, they work on in their fields and orchards, frequently lying down on the ground to rest. They also make shorter and shorter trips to gather herbs, roots, and fuel. When unable to go to the fields any longer, they sit in the house or kiva where they card and spin, knit, weave blankets, carve wood, or make sandals. Some continue to spin when they are blind or unable to walk, and it is a common saying that "an old man can spin to the end of his life." Cornshelling is woman's work, but men will do it, especially in their dotage. Old women will cultivate their garden patches until very feeble and "carry

---

[1]Leslie Milne. 1924. *The Home of an Eastern Clan.* Oxford: Clarendon Press.

wood and water as long as they are able to move their legs.'' They prepare milling stones, weave baskets and plaques out of rabbit weed, make pots and bowls from clay, grind corn, darn old clothes, care for children, and guard the house; and, when there is nothing else to do, they will sit out in the sun and watch the dying fruit. The old frequently express the desire to "keep on working" until they die. (Simmons, 1960:73)

Property rights is an important area for prolonged and effective participation. The ownership or control of property on which younger people are dependent helps maintain the independence of the aged. Property rights also permit the aged to govern the opportunities of the young. Simmons, then, sees property rights as providing benefits to the old when they become sedentary and are not involved in direct economic production.

The high priority and, high status of the aged are supported by the extended family system. It is central to the social structure. The extended family is the basic social group providing economic security for the aged. The obligations to the aged are institutionalized as formal rights; they are not simply generous benefactions of the young. In patriarchal societies, the eldest male has possessed rank and authority. He had absolute authority over his wife (wives) and children. He determined what they should do and whom they should marry. Disobedience meant disinheritance or even death.

The role and treatment of elderly women could be diametrically opposite that for elderly men. Simmons (1960) provides a vivid illustration of this in his discussion of the Ainu of Japan. The Ainu were a technologically primitive society before they were influenced by Japanese civilization. They lived in a very cold coastal area where they subsisted largely on raw fish. Fathers possessed great authority. They could divorce their wives or disinherit their children. The elder fathers received filial reverence and obedience to their dying days. Women throughout their lives were treated as outcasts and their fate grew harsher with advancing age. A. H. S. Landor[2] relates his visit to a hut in 1893 in which he found a feeble old woman crouched in a dark corner:

As I got closer, I discovered a mass of white hair and two claws, almost like thin human feet with long hooked nails. A few fish bones were scattered on the ground and a lot of filth was massed together in that corner. . . . I could hear someone breathing under that mass of white hair, but I could not make out the shape of a human body. I touched the hair, I pulled it, and with a groan, two thin bony arms suddenly stretched out and clasped my hand. . . . Her limbs were merely skin and bones, and her long hair and long nails gave her a ghastly appearance. . . . Nature could not have afflicted more evils on that wretched creature. She was nearly blind, deaf, dumb; she was apparently suffering from rheumatism, which had doubled up her body and stiffened her bony arms and legs; and moreover, she showed many symptoms of leprosy. . . . She was neither ill-treated, nor

[2]A.H.S. Landor. 1893. *Alone With the Hairy Ainu*. London: J. Murray.

taken care of by the village or by her son, who lived in the same hut; but she was regarded as a worthless object and treated accordingly. A fish was occasionally flung to her. (Landor cited in Simmons, 1960:81−82)

Simmons (1960) states that one tactic used by the old men to maintain their advantages in the family was to marry younger women. By so doing, they assured the continuation of their power. The following passage written by the anthropologist W. C. Holden[3] in 1871 describes the position of an aged Xosa or Kafir in Africa:

The man is then supported in Kafir pomp and plenty; he can eat, drink and be merry, bask in the sun, sing, and dance at pleasure, spear bucks, plot mischief, or make bargains for his daughters; to care and toil he can say farewell, and go on to the end of life. As age advances he takes another young wife, or concubine, and then another, to keep up eternal youth, for he is never supposed to grow old as long as he can obtain a youthful bride; she by proxy imparts her freshness to his withered frame and throws her bloom over his withered brow. (Holden cited in Simmons, 1960:80)

The fate of the aged in preliterate societies was ultimately determined by the balance between their contribution to the society and their dependence upon it. As long as the productivity of the old exceeded their consumption, they found places for themselves. However, for those who were regarded as a living liability—the overaged; those at the useless stage; those in sleeping period, the age-grade of the dying; and the already dead—actual neglect or even abandonment was rather common. In Simmons (1945) cross-cultural investigation of 39 tribes in which definite information was available, neglect and abandonment were customary in 18 tribes. He reports that among the Omaha, a nomadic North American Indian tribe, the very feeble were customarily left at a campsite provided with shelter, food, and a fire. Similar practices occurred among the Hopi, the Creek, the Crow and the Bushmen of South Africa (de Beauvoir, 1973). The Eskimo persuaded the old to lie in the snow and wait for death or put them on an ice flow and abandoned them when the tribe was out fishing or shut them up in an igloo to die of the cold.

Yet, the abandonment, exposure, or killing of the aged was not necessarily disrespectful. It occurred out of dire necessity rather than from personal whims. It was the hardness of preliterate life, not the hardness of the preliterate heart that was the basic reason. Environmental necessity forced the rather drastic deaths of the few helplessly aged persons (Simmons, 1960). Simone de Beauvoir in her comprehensive study, *"The Coming of Age,"* cites anthropologist Paul-Emile Victor's dramatic example of a sick Amassalik Eskimo man in Greenland who was unable to get into his kayak. The man asked to be thrown into the sea, drowning being the quickest way to the other world. His children did as he asked. But, buoyed up by his

---

[3]W.C. Holden. 1871. *The Past and Future of the Kaffir Races.* London: the author.

clothing the man floated over the freezing water. A beloved daughter called out to him tenderly, ''Father, push your head under. The road will be shorter'' (cited in de Beauvoir, 1973:77−78).

Our final illustration from Simmons will serve to conclude this discussion. Simmons indicates that the abandonment of the sick and very old was a reciprocal process with the ''victim'' actively participating in the process without harboring feelings of ill will toward the young. He quotes from J. A. Friis's[4] 1888 monograph on the Lapps of Finland:

> To carry the sick and disabled persons such a long journey is impossible, and so there is no choice but that he or she, whoever it may be, perhaps one's own father or mother, must be left behind, provided with food, in some miserable hut on the mountain, with the alternative of following later or else fo dying entirely alone. . . . But a father or mother does not think this being left alone on the mountain a sign of cruelty or ingratitude on the part of their children. It is a sad necessity and a fate that perhaps had befallen their parents before them. (Friis cited in Simmons, 1960:85−86)

Simmons (1960:88) concludes by outlining five universal interests of aging people:

1. To live as long as possible.
2. To hoard waning energies.
3. To keep on sharing in the affairs of life.
4. To safeguard any seniority rights.
5. To have an easy and honorable release from life if possible.

These five wishes are seen to be shared by people living in the most primitive societies and the most complex. Simmons believes, however, that the ability to obtain these wishes becomes more problematic with social change. He argues that in stable preliterate societies a pattern of participation becomes relatively fixed for the aged. A structured framework for participation is developed in which statuses and roles are defined, sex-typed, aptitude-rated, and age-graded. With permanence, the pattern solidifies and the aged are able to intrench themselves. However, all becomes upset with social change:

> In the long and steady strides of the social order, the aging get themselves fixed and favored in positions, power, and performance. They have what we call seniority rights. But, when social conditions become unstable and the rate of change reaches a galloping pace, the aged are riding for an early fall, and the more youthful associates take their seats in the saddles. Change is the crux of the problem of aging we well as its challenge. (Simmons, 1960;88).

---

[4]J.A. Friis. 1888. *Jajla: A Tale of Finmark*. London: G.P. Putnam's Sons.

We will now investigate the impact of social change on the aged by looking at a type of society that differs radically from the so-called primitive societies—Western industrial societies.

Soviet Centenarians Say It's Diet, Work and Family—Not Yogurt

CHRISTOPHER S. WREN

KIEV, U.S.S.R.—A few years ago, a grizzled patriarch in Soviet Aberbaijan looking forward to his 167th birthday was asked how he had managed to live so long.

"I am never in a hurry," Shirali Mislimov replied. "So don't be in a hurry to live, this is the main thing. The one must observe a regular daily regimen, of course. I have been doing physical work for about 150 years."

Despite some current American television commercials, it is not yogurt that has promoted longevity in the Soviet Union, specialists say, but a combination of more subtle factors that make up an active yet uncomplicated life.

The onslaught of modern times is reflected in a statistical drop of Soviet centenarians, from 21,708 in 1959 to 19,304 in 1970, as of last reported count, though this is also partly explained by more accurate records.

Now, with the Soviet Union's birth rate declining and a potential labor shortage ahead, there is growing official interest in prolonging the useful years of average citizens. At Kiev's Institute of Gerontology, a branch of the Soviet Academy of Medical Sciences, researchers have been probing the secrets of long life. Some of their conclusions sound deceptively simple.

Those who live longest have had a simple, low-fat diet and passed up cigarettes and liquor, but not wine. They started working young, usually outdoors, and continued into old age. And they have been made to feel socially useful, both as a productive member of a closely knit society and a respected head of an extended family.

"The life span of any biological species is programmed. For instance, a crow can life 150 years and a horse only 30 years," said Nikita B. Mankovsky, deputy director of the Kiev institute. "We consider that the average human life span should be about 100 or 110 years. We also believe that this life span should be socially active."

"Nowadays, citizens of the United States and Soviet Union live 30 to 50 years less than their biological system can provide," continued Dr. Mankovsky, a vigorous white-haired gerontologist. "We have a number of social and environmental factors today that limit the average human life span. We can very easily shorten this life span. But it is very hard to make it longer."

There have already been attempts to prolong life artificially. L.V. Komarov, a biologist at the Institute of General Genetics, says he extended the life span of common houseflies form 86 to 130 days by feeding them magnetized sugar. At the Institute of Chemical Physics, two scientists prolonged the lives of experimental mice by 10 months with compounds similar to vitamin B6. Vladimir V. Frolkis, a prominent specialist in Kiev, used antibiotics to retard metabolic changes that cause aging.

Dr. Mankovsky, developing a theory pioneered by Dr. Frolkis, said that "the aging process is not a gradual decline of physical functions. We think that process of aging embraces different organs and systems at different times. The aging rates of the heart, liver and brain are quite different." These can be accelerated by outside influences like stress, he said, "The factors that limit our lives today are primarily social ones."

Soviet centenarians have been clustered not only in the mountainous Caucasus, where they are most celebrated, but also in other rural areas like Yakutia in Siberia or the Poltava district of the Ukraine. Invariably, they worked outdoors, whether as shepherds, beekeepers, gardeners or carpenters. The institute at Kiev found that they also ate more products and vegetables and less meat than Russians in the cities.

"When I was in the United States, I was treated to a gin and tonic," Dr. Mankovsky wryly noted. "This is something that no doubt shortens life." But he added that happily those living longest often drank dry wine. "I think that the wine contains organisms, vitamins and microelements that stimulate the system," he said.

Such persons were also found surrounded by large families, which Dr. Mankovsky called "very important, because they enjoy the respect of others." But he said, "the most interesting thing was that these long living people began work at 10 or 12 years old, and kept working until retirement at 130 years old."

Recently, the Communit Party newspaper Pravda reported that medical checkups given 40,000 Soviet citizens had disclosed that the centenarians among them kept working until an advanced age. "We should note that physical activity that began at 10 years old was connected with positive emotions," Dr. Mankovsky said. "The person made things and he was happy."

One result has been a new look at the Soviet pension system, which permits men to retire at 60 years and women at 55. The readjustment from work to retirement has sometimes produced what Soviet physicians call "pension illness." Zoya G. Revutskaya, another gerontologist at the institute in Kiev, concluded that "the need to be engaged in some sort of activity is well-pronounced in the elderly."

Dr. Revutskaya pointed to a number of programs to keep pensioners active, including handicraft industries and volunteer jobs. In Kiev, a supervised exercise program was organized three times a week at a local football stadium. Senior citizens who joined in subsequently visited the doctor less and had fewer chronic ailments.

Responding to criticism that not enough was being done to promote longevity, the Soviet Academy of Medical Sciences has passed a resolution creating a committee under Dr. Komarov that will coordinate the research of at least 40 institutes on the subject.

And in the face of a labor squeeze, some workers may eventually be encouraged to stay on the job longer. Dr. Mankovsky noted that the life span of Russians had more than doubled to an everage 70 years since the turn of the century. "There are at least 34 million people over 60 and they have accumulated vast professional experience," he said. "Therefore, the state is concerned with preserving these people, to pass their experience on to younger ones."

Christopher S. Wren in *The New York Times,* September 9, 1977. ©1977 by The New York Times Company. Reprinted by permission.

THE AGED IN THE WEST

Irving Rosow, a contemporary American social scientist, has written persuasively and elegantly on the status of the old in the industrial United States. In a thoughtful article, Rosow (1973) contrasted the role of the aged in preindustrial societies with their role in America. He wished to explain the societal variations in the welfare of the aged. He outlined seven contributing factors: property ownership, strategic knowledge, religious links, kinship and extended family, community life, productivity, and mutual dependence. All seven involve the resources that old people command, the functions they perform, and the state of social organization. We will use them as the organizational framework for our discussion. In the following pages we will point out how social changes relating to these factors have affected the role of the elderly in Western industrial societies.

Property Rights

Preindustrial agrarian Western societies were characterized by the elders' ownership, control, and direct operation of the principal form of productive property—the farm. In such circumstances, the aged maintained their independence at the same time that their offspring were dependent on them.

Conrad M. Arensberg's *The Irish Countryman* (1937/1959) and his *Family and Community in Ireland* written with Solon T. Kimball (1959) are the classic works on the family in a farming economy. They are concerned with rural Irish communities of the 1930s consisting of families with small farms. The family's total existence is centered around the keeping and maintenance of the family farm. "Keeping the name on the land" is the central value that governs the family. The Irish farm is too small for feasible economic subdivision. Family continuity demands that the farm pass to the next generation intact. Economic necessity means that the inheritance of the farm can only be passed to one child, usually one of the eldest sons. All the other sons "must travel" and seek their fortunes elsewhere. Likewise, daughters who are not provided with dowries must leave the farm.

Until the time when the father dies or retires and gives one of his sons the family farm, he controls the life of his children. Even though his sons do the major work on the farm, he mandates the direction of farm work and the distribution of the farm's income. The farm bears his name in the community and his sons are spoken of as his "boys." The subordinating of sons can continue even to the ages of 45 and 50. As long as the old couple have not given over the farm, the sons remain "boys" both in farm work and in the rural vocabulary:

> In 1933, a deputy to the Dail raised considerable laughter in the sophisticated Dublin papers when he inadvertently used the country idiom in expressing country realities. He pleaded for special treatment in land division for "boys of forty-five and older"—boys who have nothing in prospect but to wait for their father's farm. For "boyhood" in this instance is a social status rather than a physiological state. A countryman complained to me in words which tell the whole story. "You can be a boy forever," he said, "as long as the old fellow is alive." (Arensberg, 1937/1959:39)

The change in the "boy's" status occurs when he marries and inherits the farm. Country marriages are called "match-making" and involve parental negotiations and a dowry. Marriage symbolizes the transfer of economic control and the attainment of adult status. The marriage and the transfer of land to the son accomplishes a drastic transformation in the relationships of household members. The sons and daughters must be provided for elsewhere. They feel themselves entitled to some form of inheritance, either in the form of dowries to marry into another farm or of soem other form of aid to help establish themselves. Typically, they must leave the farm.

The "old people" must abandon their power and move into a new status of old age. They relinquish the farm and their economic direction of the family properly passes to the young people. For the old man, it means the abandonment of the farm ownership; for the old mother, it means that she is no longer woman of the house.

Marriage is a central focus of rural life. It represents a universal turning oint in individual histories. Marriage coincides with the transfer of economic control and land ownership. It means the reformation of family ties, advance in family and community status, and entrance into adult procreative sex life (Arensberg and Kimball, 1968). For this reason, we can understand why Ireland had the highest rate of late marriage of all record-keeping societies in the 1930s. When Arensberg first reported on his research in 1937, 62 percent of all men between the ages fo 30 to 35 were still unmarried, as were 42 percent of the women in this same age group. Late marriage can be assocaited with the reluctance of the old couple to renounce their leadership.

In many instances a smooth transition occurs when father and son continue to work together. This occurs when the son shows deference and respect to the accumulated knowledge of the parent. One such family is described by a neighbor who observed the old man working by the side of his son, "Look at the Careys; old Johnny gives his boy a hand in everything. You wouldn't know which one has the land" (Arensberg, 1937/1959:86). The old woman can also be of help in assisting the son's wife with domestic chores and the raising of the children.

In cases where there are disagreements between the old couple and the new farm-couple owners, it is the old people who must leave. It is only in this way that the family continuity, the giving their "name to the land," can be continued. "For the pattern of family and land must continue in the persons of the new man and woman and their children" (Arensberg, 1937/1959:88). In summary, rural Irish family life maximizes the importance and the power of the aged. The Irish rural community can be viewed as a virtual gerontocracy.

In comparison to the control of property by the elders in an agrarian society, property ownership by the elderly is not typically found in industrial American society. Irving Rosow (1973) argues that property ownership has spread broadly through the American population. Further, capital ownership and management is not centered in the hands of elderly people. The expanded industrial economy has created new jobs occupied by younger people. Higher education also provides further opportunities for the young.

Together, these developments have increased the opportunities and reduced the young's dependence on the old. Rosow concludes, "While an old property owner may be financially independent, he no longer has significant control over the life chances of the young; and they have less need to defer to him" (Rosow, 1973:230).

Strategic Knowledge and Religious Links

In our examination of the role of the elderly in traditional societies, we saw that the elderly are viewed as the repositories of societal wisdom and knowledge. They have full understanding and knowledge of occupational skills and techniques. They have a virtual monopoly of strategic knowledge regarding healing, religion, warfare, cultural lore, and the arts.

Now things are vastly different. The proliferation of new occupations and newer knowledge diminishes and minimizes the elders' control of strategic knowledge. Different universes of discourse are created between the generations. This, in turn, lessens the communication between the generations. For whom among the young wants to hear from the old and their "old-fashioned" and "out-of-date" ideas and opinions.

Formal education has taken on the job of teaching the young occupational and other skills. The popular media teach the new attitudes and values of the society. The peer group, not the elderly, socialize the young. The result is that the elderly are no longer considered "strategic agents of instruction nor founts of wisdom" (Rosow, 1973:230).

In the past the aged were seen as the links to the past and were venerated. In tradition-oriented societies, classical China being the prime example, old age was honorific and the aged were religiously revered. Ancestor worship of the dead parents was the norm.

The movement from the sacred order of the traditional society to the secular one of contemporary industrial society sees no corresponding role for the elderly. In practice, the old are not venerated by religious tradition nor are they venerated as links to ancestors, gods, or the hallowed past.

Kinship and the Extended Family

As we have noted, in the past, the extended family was a more highly integrated economic unit. The aged parents were at its head. The obligations of the young to the old were institutionalized as formal rights, not simply generous benefactions. In recent years social historians have been reaching the conclusion that, in the last 200 years, the extended family in Western industrial society was not as predominant as social scientists had earlier assumed. However, Tamara Hareven (1976), a prominent social historian of the family, believes that this does not alter the nature of the elders' involvements in the family. Even when the elderly lived apart from their adult children, they maintained active family roles. Reciprocal support relationships and the exchange of services characterized integenerational relationships. These ties were reinforced by a societal value and normative system that governed children's obligations. These reciprocal relationships allowed the elderly to maintain their autonomy in a period when programs of social security and other forms of public old-age assistance were relatively nonexistent.

The reader may note a similarity between Hareven's description of the 19th-century family and Eugene Litwak's conceptualization of the modified extended family of the mid-20th century. As you recall from our earlier discussion on families in the city, Litwak was one of a number of social scientists in the post World War II period to criticize theoretically and to test empirically the prevalent notion of what Talcott Parson's labeled the "isolated" nuclear family. These writers held that it was an oversimplification to believe that the American family was organized on a conjugal basis with no involvement with extended kin. In their collective research, they found ample evidence for the existence of linkages of conjugal families joined together on an equalitarian basis for mutual aid. Further, residential propinquity, occupational solidarity, and authoritarian control by the family did not characterize their family life.

On the surface it would seem that the "modification" of the extended family system is not a recent phenomenon but a process that has been occurring for a rather long time. We are acutely aware that the lot of today's elderly is not as satisfactory in most aspects of their lives as it was in the early 20th and in the 19th centuries. The reason lies not so much in changes in family structure or residential arrangements but in ideological changes that have transformed and redefined family functions. Tamara Hareven (1976) believes that the erosion of instrumental values and the ascendancy of intimacy and sentimentality as the foundation of the family has led to the weakening of the role and function of extended family members. This change has been particularly felt by older couples.

She develops her thesis by noting that the emphasis in the 20th century has been on domesticity and childrearing as the sole role expectation for women. This, combined with the insulation of the conjugal family and its removal and detachment from aging parents and other relatives, results in the loss of power and influence by the old people in the family.

Harven then uses a recurring theme in family sociology—the development of the ideology of family privacy. Family privacy results in the separation of the family from the community. It also leads to the lessening of social supports to friends, neighbors, and kin. The household becomes a self-contained unit. The family develops a self-initiated isolation. This development particularly affects older parents who are no longer needed for the handling of everyday family concerns, nor is their advice solicited. For example, childrearing "bibles" like Dr. Spock's are preferred to the guidance and advice of the grandparents. The accumulated result is the increased segregation of different age groups in the society and the elimination of older people from viable family roles.

The distinct conjugal family has shifted its responsibilities to its own members well-being—the father, mother, and children. Although token attention is given to aged parents, the major responsibilities for old people has shifted to governmental programs, like social security and social welfare. Hareven points out that unfortunately the welfare system is grossly inadequate. The result is that the elderly have been caught in the middle with neither families nor the government providing the necessary resources to assure a financially secure life for the elderly. We will continue discussion of this aspect later in this chapter.

Community Rights

Irving Rosow (1973) makes the following general observations. He notes that in traditional societies the population clustered in relatively small stable communities. The community structure clearly delineated formal age gradings and definite roles, linking different ages. The interaction of community members was multifaceted; they came together in all spheres of life—home, work, and the church. In contrast, the urbanized society has less community stability. Changing neighborhoods, residential mobility, and urban impersonality are all seen to undermine the stable community. The result is that the urban community has been unable to accommodate older people.

Rosow's analysis echoes our viewpoint on the changing nature of communities and family relations. We have noted that the preindustrial family was intertwined in community life. Philippe Ariès (1962) found that in preindustrial France the lives of the people were totally absorbed in community functions. The family played a secondary role. The family itself was caught in a web of interconnection to the small community. The public nature of the family predominated. The marital couple was prevented from living a life of intimacy and separateness. The intensity of the collective life prevented this occurrence. Community pressures and involvements assured the openness of the nuclear family. Intergenerational households with the older generation controlling individual family members also assured this outcome. From the arrangement of marriages to the control of property, the elders held sway over the individual and prevented the development of autonomous family units.

The development of the ideologies of individualism and nuclear family privatism and domesticity intersected with the rise of the new industrial order and contributed to the breakdown of community control and the power and control of the older generation. Gerrit A. Kooy, a Dutch sociologist, has done a number of empirical studies of family life in the Netherlands. In one of his studies, Kooy (1963) examines the rural agrarian population of Achterhoek, one of the sandy districts of eastern Holland. His description of traditional Achterhoek is very similar to Arensberg's description of the rural Irish countryside. Similar to the situation in Ireland, the large majority of farms in Achterhoek are small. The labor is provided entirely by the farmer and his immediate family.

Before 1875, Achterhoek was a relatively isolated regional community. Loyalty and identification was restricted to neighborhoods located within the district. The community was homogeneous with intensive social controls. The population was stable. Individuals were born there, were raised there, were married there, and worked on the land there until their death. The church, the neighborhood, and the family influenced every aspect of an individual's life.

The church was influential in religious concerns. In addition, it played an important role in the social life of the community. It kept the population informed on who was selling livestock. Before and after services, it gave the people an opportunity to meet and exchange bits of news and gossip. For the young, it gave them a chance to see each other, a rare occurrence in a life geared to isolated farm work. The moral standards of the people were not solely determined by the church. Rather, morality was defined within the broader rubric of proper social behavior that was set by the community's normative structure.

The extended family had a great deal of power over the individial. This included such issues as deciding on whether a child should marry and whom. Marriage was defined primarily in economic terms with young couples remaining subordinate to the parental generation even after marriage. "In this type of communal situation, each marriage has a tremendous influence on every member of both families of an engaged couple, causing significant changes in the personal relations of many relatives who customarily cooperate economically and socially" (Kooy, 1963:47–48). Grandchildren, too, were strongly influenced by their grandparents. In sum, the extended family with its generations and relatives controlled the education and dominated the behavior of the family members. It was not the parent-child unit.

The family system was interlocked with the neighborhood. Neighborliness was not social in nature nor was it based solely on friendship. Common law mandated mutual duties among neighbors. These duties included "assisting at births, weddings, or funerals in a neighbor's household; helping in difficult situations; or visiting and receiving neighbors in winter. If the need arose, neighbors would not hesitate to discipline the child of someone else within the group" (Kooy, 1963:48).

The traditional neighborhood in Achterhook began to change around 1876. Improvements in transportation and communication systems opened the district to outside influence. New farming methods and the development of educational facilities fostered the district's integration into the larger Dutch society. The result was the gradual loss of control by the neighborhood. Neighborhood stability became undermined. Today, although the tradition of the neighborhood still persists, its group loyalty is weakening. Younger members of the community view "neighborliness as a communal burden rather than as a duty. Personal interest and the development of professional services are replacing community cooperation in a wide range of activities including the arranging of weddings to the plowing of fields" (Kooy, 1963:48–50).

Kooy then examines how these changes have affected the position of the aged and the nuclear family. As mentioned, in the traditional neighborhood, the elders held influential positions relating to all aspects of life. The elders were the embodiment of customs and traditions. Economically, they controlled the extended family system. Socially, they held sway not only over their own children but over their grandchildren as well. They were integrally connected to all facets of communal life.

Today, although still influential, their previous all-encompassing power and high status is eroding. Kooy sees the rise of the power of the individualized nuclear family as a major contributing factor to the decline of the importance of the aged. Traditionally, the nuclear family was incorporated into the all-embracing extended family, which, in turn, was closely integrated with the neighborhood and church. A new ideology has now arisen that emphasizes the independence of the nuclear family and the opposition to the extended family role. This sentiment is expressed in the following statement of farmers and countrywomen between the ages of 25 and 45:

> Father does not trust anything beyond his hands, and the other generation never gets a chance. Such a life does not have any advantage.
>
> Marriage can be fully enjoyed only when husband and wife are together.
>
> Living with relatives is entirely wrong because a young women feels like a maidservant. Previously she accepted this, but the younger generation does not.
>
> In the households I know the atmosphere shows that these people should not live together. The person who has married into this extended family suffers the most. The older people do not give up their authority. The younger ones are (treated) no better than servants.
>
> A woman taken into an extended family loses her personality. Very often she cannot lead her own life because of the domination of her in-laws, especially her mother-in-law. The loss of personality is common.
>
> In my opinion only a mother and father should have authority over their children. (Kooy, 1963:52–53)

The breakdown of the local community and the increased importance of the nuclear family has resulted in the loss of status and the decline in institutional-role participation by the elderly. Instead of old age meaning higher rank in the community it now signifies the loss of rank. Further, other persons are becoming defined as outsiders in community affairs. The loss of traditional supports has affected the elderly's need of self-maintenance and self-development. Kooy concludes that as modern ideas continue to become predominant, older people's feelings of frustration and uncertainty will increase.

Productivity

In preindustrial societies, especially those living at a bare subsistence level, the elderly play a significant role in economic productivity. In such societies—which have a minimal division of labor and low technological development—each individual, regardless of age, can be of value as long as he or she is able to contribute to the small gross product. Every little bit helps. This fact explains Rosow's somewhat paradoxical finding that, "the greater the poverty and the struggle to survive, the *relatively* better off old people are by the standards of their group" (Rosow, 1973:229–230).

When we turn our attention to highly developed and technologically advanced societies, we find a minimal productive role for the elderly. The increased emphasis in these societies is to retire people who are defined as having little value in the labor market. An examination of the historical development of the conceptualization and implementation of retirement highlights the relationship of old people to productivity.

Industrial development in the West has seen a transformation in the age makeup of the work population. During the 18th and 19th centuries in America, individuals worked throughout their lives. Work involvement only ceased with illness or death. With increased specialization, the demand heightened for productive efficiency. The emerging belief in the late 19th century was that old people were not as productive as the young. This was in fact the case for many physically demanding jobs. In these cases, the growing practice was to shift older workers into less demanding and less productive work. The automotive industry with its notorious assembly line was a prime illustration. Its workers were relegated to nonproductive positions as soon as they were thought to be unable to keep up with the pace of the assembly line. Ely Chinoy, in his study of automobile workers, quotes a worker who complained bitterly of this practice:

> You see the fellows who have been there for years who are now sweeping. That's why most of the fellows want to get out. Like you take Jim, he's been there for thirty years and now he's sweeping. When you aren't any good any more, they discard you like an old glove.'' (Chinoy, 1955:84)

Soon, however, even this practice gave way to the retirement of the older worker, bowing to the demands of industrial efficiency.

The swift growth in technological knowledge also contributed to the dislodgment of old people's involvement in the economy. The emergence of many new specialized occupations with new knowledge requirements proved disadvantageous to the old. The young benefited with educational improvements; the elderly fell behind. The exposure of the younger generation to new educational, technological, and industrial ideas heightened the inequality between the generations. New jobs and new occupations had higher status than the old ones. The younger generation filled them. As people got older, they became more and more confined to the older, less prestigious, and, sometimes, obsolete occupations.

Accompanying the notion of elderly nonproductivity was the emerging belief in the cult of youth. No longer were older people venerated and exalted. The growing disparity between generations in occupational skills helped account for this change. So did the loss of the strategic knowledge of the elders. Stemming from the Protestant work ethic—with its emphasis on efficiency, productivity, and progress—the society increasingly placed emphasis on the virtues of modern youth as opposed to the old-fashioned ways of the elderly. The result was disparagement of the elderly. Increasingly, the older individual was being defined as useless and a drain on the social and economic well-being of the society.

The cumulative result was that by the end of the 19th century age-related standards of usefulness and productivity began to be implemented. And, by the beginning of the 20th century, retirement at a specific age became commonplace. Thus, paradoxically, although men found themselves living longer than ever before, they also found themselves being forcibly retired to a stigmatized status at an earlier age than ever before.

Older women were not directly affected by the growth of the retirement movement since relatively few women were actively involved in the work force. Yet, they, too, were affected by the demographic social and economic changes of the 19th century. This resulted in what best can be described as maternal retirement (Fischer, 1977:146). the great demographic changes in fertility and mortality rates of the 19th century had a profound effect on women's lives. More and more women began to survive childbirth and the childbearing years. Earlier, women had had a life expectancy of about 45 years. Their life span coincided with the period when they were raising their children. As the life span of women increased, a proportionately greater number of years were spent outside the maternal period. For example, a woman today with a life expectancy of approximately 75 years can look forward to a period of about 25 years after her youngest child leaves home.

Women whose lives had been defined almost exclusively by their maternal role were now faced with a stage in the life cycle where no explicit norms or rules existed to govern their behavior and to provide meaningful direction for their lives. The postparental period, coinciding with the physiological changes of menopause, proved to be a period characterized by depression and alienation. Trained solely for domestic activities and childrearing roles, women suddenly found themselves "retired" at a much earlier age than their spouses. Thus, although men were being retired in their late 50s and 60s, women were confronted with the fact that their last child left home before they were 50.

For many older Americans, mandatory retirement is a blessing in disguise. It frees them from boring and tedious jobs. It provides them with the opportunity to pursue leisure activities, travel, and hobbies that they could not pursue when they were employed. But, too many old people find themselves more a victim than a beneficiary of mandatory retirement. A recent committee report of the American Medical Association states that the mental and physical health of many people are seriously hurt by the loss of status, lack of meaningful activity, fear of becoming dependent, and the isolation that may accompany involuntary retirement. And, it noted that suicides reached a peak in upper age brackets, 70 years and over, after retirement normally occurs (Flaste 1979:62).

In recent years, to combat the debilitating effect of compulsory retirement, the aged in America have begun to organize into pressure groups, such as the Gray Panthers, the National Council on the Aging, the National Association of Retired Federal Employees, and the National Council of Senior Citizens. They have sought the passage of social legislation to either extend or bar mandatory retirement ages. Congressman Claude Pepper, who was born in 1901, is a leading proponent of this type of legislation to halt discrimination by age. He argues:

Ageism is as odious as racism and sexism. Mandatory retirement arbitrarily severs productive persons from their livelihood, squanders their talent, scars their health, strains an already overburdened Social Security system and drives many elderly persons into poverty and despair'' (*Time,* August 8, 1977:67).

However, modifications and even the banning of compulsory retirement may have profound implications for the society. Many businesses are alarmed at the prospect of changes in compulsory retirement practices. They are concerned that promotion opportunities for hired younger workers will be severely limited—the longer older people hold their jobs, the slower the job advancement for younger people. They also believe that, despite a few exceptions, a significant number of older workers may just be deadwood. These proposed changes would hinder the productivity and progress of their businesses.

In education, for example, the extension of the mandatory retirement age coupled with the tenure system will result in schools and colleges being increasingly staffed by older faculties. Younger generations of scholars will be frozen out of academic positions. It will also hamper efforts of universities and colleges to comply with affirmative action programs for hiring women and minorities. the result will be a continued and increased predominance of older white men on the nation's academic faculties.

To counter this argument, critics of involuntary retirement argue as follows: everyone should be judged on ability and no one should be refused work because of an arbitrary age limit. Such an age barrier is discriminatory and should be rejected, just as it is for sex and race. Old people need work, too, just like everybody else.

Ironically, changes in the mandatory retirement age is gaining some support from younger people. They are concerned with the rise in the elderly population in America as a result of demographic changes and its impact on the Social Security system. Younger workers, whose taxes support those who are retired under Social Security, have seen a constant rise in the money needed to provide benefits. A raising of the retirement age at which people can claim benefits will serve to cut down on the monthly deductions of younger workers. This economic fact may persuade many that it is costing too much to discriminate against older workers.

The extensive debate on the issue of mandatory retirement in the United States is also beginning to occur in Western Europe with some interesting variations (Kandell, 1977). Although the United States is moving to extend the retirement age beyond age 65, in Western Europe there is a movement to lower it. In West Germany, the Netherlands, Spain, and most of Scandinavia retirement takes place at the age of 65 or earlier, and plans are underway in all these countries to lower it even further. France has recently passed legislation to permit employees to retire at age 60. Italy, which already has reduced the retirement age to 60, is witnessing its labor unions striving to lower the age to 55.

Although aged workers are in favor of lowering the age, provided that their retirement income remains adequate, the main thrust behind this movement occurs because of the plight of a high percentage of unemployed young people. This problem has taken on political overtones. Ruling governments, opposition parties, and labor unions, bowing to the political pressure from the young, are all trying to outdo each other to gain their political support. The early retirement programs being instituted in Belgium, for example, require employers to replace those who are being retired with unemployed workers under the age of 30; they are prohibited from hiring pensioners.

Economists are weary of the long-term effects of these policies. They point out that the increase in the inactive retired is outpacing the growth of the labor force. This will ultimately put an expensive burden on most European economies. A recent study by the Organization for Economic Cooperation and Development, which consists of the Western developed countries and Japan, argued this point:

> There may be a slowing down in the trend toward lowering retirement age over the next few years because of unfavorable demographic conditions. . . . If the fertility rate continues to drop as it has done over the last 10 years, the financial burden for pensions will be spread over a smaller number of working people and it will become more an more difficult to increase the number of those drawing pensions by systematically lowering the pensionable age. (Kandell, 1977).

The economic and social problems of the aged are also a concern of some social scientists. The aged in Europe are still counting on their families to support them during the retirement years. But, like the United States, owing to the greater mobility of the population, the long-held values that emphasize obligatory involvement with the old by the community and the family is gradually disappearing. A spokesperson of the Institute for an Active Retirement in France, one of the largest nonpofit organizations for retired people, addresses himself to this point:

> People still have an idyllic image that they can retire to their birthplace in the countryside and find friends and family members. But they often find that friends and family are no longer there. The wife may not know how to drive. The closest pharmacy may be a mile away. And the children do not visit often enough. (Seguin cited in Kandell, 1977).

Eventually, then, the same demographic, social, and economic factors that are operating in the United States will be occurring in Western Europe. Indeed, they may have already started. Although there is still no active militancy among retired and elderly people in Western Europe, aging Europeans are beginning to press their economic demands through unions and white-collar employees' associations. These people have also voiced their dissatisfaction with their social conditions. They believe that they have been discarded by society. And, outside of their involvement with their immediate family, they are upset with their forced lack of participation in the community. Ultimately, the battle between the old generations and the young will be accelerated in Europe and in the United States over these issues.

Mutual Dependency

The development of retirement as a new stage of the life cycle has necessitated a major readjustment for men and women in our society. Unlike other transitional periods that occur throughout the life cycle, the retirement stage is one that lacks a clearly defined social position in the structure of society. In a society that places its strongest emphasis on the necessity of work for the establishment of a man's sense of identity, retirement is almost antithetical. For a woman, the maternal role has served as a primary source of self-conceptualization. As she gets older, this role is no longer viable.

In addition to these social concerns, retirement is problematic because of financial uncertainties and of increasing health concerns. In earlier times, children were obligated to care for their aging parents. Since the new ideology of nuclear family privatization and independence emerged in the 19th century, this obligation has receded in importance. The result has been that the government is becoming more and more involved in providing financial aid and health-care facilities for the elderly. Unfortunately, governmental programs have been woefully insufficient in providing adequate help to these people. Further, the welfare programs developed by the government have not proved to be viable alternatives to the involvements, obligations, and satisfactions that were inherent in the kinship ties that the elderly had with their children and other relatives in the preindustrial period.

Irving Rosow (1973) has pointed out that in preindustrial societies there was a high mutual dependence between age groups. This great interdependence promoted the mutual aid and reciprocity between the generations. In contemporary industrial society, the relative economic affluence of the population and the rise in living standards have undermined this mutual dependence. The result has been a growth in individuality and independence at the expense of solidarity and reciprocity.

Tamera K. Hareven (1976) takes a somewhat different approach to explain the decline of mutual dependency. She believes that the transformation and redefinition of family functions has been instrumental in the growing isolation of older people in our society. The privatization of the middle-class family with its emphasis on internal sentimentality and intimacy precludes the involvement of extended kin, including aged parents. The modern family has also withdrawn from community involvements. The result has been an intensification of the segregation of different age groups within the family and the community and the elimination of older people from viable family roles.

Suburbanization has also contributed to the geographic segregation of older people. As you recall from our discussion of families in the city, after World War II there was a marked increase in the number of conjugal families that migrated into new suburban communities. These middle-class families emphasized privatism and independence from both community and extended kinship involvements. John

Mogey's (1964) distinction between closed communities and open communities provides us with a framework to discuss these variations and the relationships that exist between the generations. A closed community is characterized as one where scenes of intense interfamilial cooperation exists. The involved relationships between mother and married daughter in the English working-class community of Bethnel Green is a prime example. Open communities are those where families have selective attachments to a variety of associations or secondary groups. These families interact with individuals and extended kin in other areas as well as in their own area. Yet, these relationships do not share the same degree of intimacy or involvement as that characterized by the families of the closed community.

Open communities and conjugal family privatism have resulted in the increased geographic segregation of old people. Two groups of old people will be discussed to demonstrate the impact of the loss of mutual dependency. The first group are old people who Herbert Gans (1962b) referred to as the trapped. These are less affluent old people who have been forced to remain in former homogenous working-class communities that have become dilapidated and into which poorer families of different ethnic or racial backgrounds have moved. The second group of old people are the more affluent elderly who reside in age-segregated retirement communities.

The plight of the first group was dramatically conveyed in a series of criminal incidents that occurred in the Bronx, New York City, in 1976 (Klemesrud, 1976:00). Criminals, many as young as 12 and 13, terrorized old people. Unable to defend themselves and afraid to go to court because they feared retaliation, the old fell unwitting prey to a vicious cycle of muggings, beatings, rape, and murder. At the time that the newspaper article was written, 20 old people had been reported murdered in the Bronx (the Manhattan and Brooklyn figures were 34 and 25 murders, respectively.) The headlines tell the story best: "Youth Held in Murder of Bronx Man Locked in Closet Three Days," "Grandmother Is Raped and Robbed by a Burglar in Her Bronx Home," "Elderly Bronx Couple, Recently Robbed, Take Their Own Lives, Citing Fear," "Two More of the Aged Killed in the Bronx," and "Many Elderly in the Bronx Spend Their Lives in Terror of Crime."

The sections of the Bronx that were the scenes of these horrible occurrences were once almost exclusively white. Today their population is about 80 percent black and Hispanic and 20 percent white. The blacks and Hispanics tend to be a mixture of working-class people and welfare families with few elderly members. The whites tend to be elderly Jews living on Social Security payments. They have remained in the area because they cannot afford to move or for sentimental reasons. The racial pattern of crime against old people varies through the city depending on the makeup of the neighborhood. Elderly blacks and Hispanics have also been victimized. It is apparent that these elderly people symbolize the worse consequences befalling the elderly as the result of community and familial abandonment.

The rapid rise in the number of retirement communities in the last several decades reflects on the situation of elderly people in our society. As early as 1942, Talcott Parsons reflected on the circumstances that brought this phenomenon about:

> In view of the very great significance of occupational status and its psychological correlates, retirement leaves the older man in a peculiarly functionless situation, cut off from participation in the most important interests and activities of the society. . . . Not only status in the community but actual place of residence is to a very high degree a function of the specific job held. Retirement not only cuts the ties to the job but also greatly loosens those to the community of residence. Perhaps in no other society is there observable a phenomenon corresponding to the accumulation of retired elderly people in such areas as Florida and Southern California in the winter. It may be surmised that this structural isolation from kinship, occupational and community ties is the fundamental basis of the recent political agitation for help to the old. It is suggested that it is far less the financial hardship of the position of elderly people than their social isolation which makes old age a problem. (Parsons, 1942:616)

Retirement communities were developed out of a felt need by the aged for more satisfactory community involvement. They also sought to provide residents with meaningful interpersonal relationships, which the aged were not experiencing with their former nonelderly neighbors and extended kin. The most prominently visible retirement communities are located in warmer regions of the country and have such names as "Leisure Village" and "Retirement World." These communities restrict residency to those in their retirement years, about 55 or older. In the more affluent communities, residents tend to be white, middle-class to upper class persons with professional backgrounds. The goal of these communities is to provide its members with sufficient opportunities to become participants with "people like themselves" in a number of leisure and social activities.

In addition to the more affluent communities, residential housing projects and urban apartments have been set up to provide a supportive social environment for older people. In a number of studies on age-segregated residential communities of all types (see the readings in Part V of Kart and Manard, 1976), researchers have found high morale and social involvement of residents. Critics, however, view them as too homogeneous and confining. They feel that life in an retirement environment is artificial, boring, and that residents have few meaningful involvements and activities.

One such critic is Jerry Jacobs. Jacobs (1976) studied a planned retirement community of approximately 6000 affluent residents over the age of 50. This community, "Fun City," is located 90 miles from a large metropolitan area on the west coast. The sterility of everyday life is revealed in the following interview that Jacobs had with one of the residents:

> *Mr. N:* Well, for me a typical day is—I get up at 6:00 a.m. in the morning, generally, get the newspaper. I look at the financial statement and see what my stocks

have done. I generally fix my own breakfast because my wife has, can eat different than I do. So I have my own breakfast—maybe some cornflakes with soy milk in it—milk made out of soybeans that they sell in the health food store. And uh, then at 8:00 a.m. my wife gets up. The dog sleeps with her all night. And uh, she feeds the dog. Then the dog wants me to go out and sit on the patio—get the sun and watch the birds and stuff in our backyard and have quite a few rabbits back in there. And I finish my paper there. And then she sits and she looks at me. She'll bark a little bit. And uh, then she'll go to my wife, stand by my wife and bark at her. She wants me to go back to bed. So I have to go back to bed with her. So about 8:30 I go back to bed again with my dog for about an hour. And then I get up and I read.

And then I walk up around here and I go over to oh, the supermarket and sit there and talk to people. We go over to the bank. They have a stockroom over there, for people that own stock. We discuss stocks and events of the day. And then I come home and maybe have lunch if I want to or not—it doesn't make any difference. *In fact, down here it doesn't make any difference when you eat or when you sleep because you're not going any place. You're not doing anything. And uh, if I'm up all night reading and sleep all day, what's the difference.* [Emphasis added.] But then, I'll sit around and read and maybe a neighbor will come over or I'll go over to a neighbor's and sit down and talk about something. And then, lots of times, we go over to a neighbor's and play cards 'til about 5:00 p.m. and then we come home and have our dinner. And the evening is . . . we are generally glued to the television until bedtime comes. And that's our day.

Dr. Jacobs: Is that more or less what your friends and neighbors do?

Mr. N: Some of them do. Some of them don't do that much. (Jacobs, 1976:389–390)

Jacobs argues that retirement communities can be false paradises. His example, "Fun City," had little employment opportunities and few gainfully employed persons. It was geographically isolated with no intercity or intracity public transportation and no police department. Inpatient and outpatient health-care facilities were inadequate. The failure lies ultimately in the residential community's denial of the individuality of the residents and the lack of meaningful activities and events.

On a more optimistic note, Arlie Russell Hochschild (1973) reported on an old-age community in a small apartment building that had a viable communal life. There were active involvements among the residents. Friendships and neighboring and social-sibling bonds were prevalent. There was little feeling of alienation or isolation. Hochschild believes that the community life found here counters societal disaffiliation. It fosters a "we" feeling among the residents and an emerging old-age consciousness. Generalizing from this community, Hochschild summarizes the major virtues of retirement communities:

communal solidarity can renew the social contact the old have with life. For old roles that are gone, new ones are available. If the world watches them less for being old, they watch one another more. Lacking responsibilities to the young, the old take on responsibilities to one another. Moreover, in a society that raises an eyebrow at those who do not "act their age," the subculture encourages the old to dance, to sing, to flirt, and to joke. They talk frankly about death in a way less common between the old and young. They show one another how to be, and trade solutions to problems they have not faced before. (Hochschild, 1976:383–384)

CONCLUSION

Our analysis of age stratification focused on the role of elders in the family. We opened with an examination of age-set, a system of age groupings in which paramount importance is given to age in defining and regulating social, political, economic, and family and kinship relationships.

The main emphasis of the chapter was to compare the statuses and roles of elders in preliterate societies with their Western industrial society counterparts. Following the approach of Irving Rosow, we identified seven contributing factors that influence the position of older people in given societies. These factors are property ownership, strategic knowledge, religious links, kinship and extended family, community life, productivity, and mutual dependence.

The effects of family privatization once again proved to be a key factor in the generational relationships of the elderly with other family members. The elderly have little importance in an industrial society that emphasizes individual welfare, social and economic progress and change, and that is opposed to the ideology of family continuity and tradition. The elders of an industrial society—in contrast to elders of a nonindustrial society that views its elders as the embodiment of the societal customs and traditions—are too often treated as unwanted and unknowledgable representatives of a by-gone era who have little functionality in contemporary society. The deemphasis of the role of the elderly, both in the family and in the society, has led to the general erosion of normative patterns of conduct and behavior between generations. The result has been the creation of a sense of futility and uselessness by the elderly and is typified by the development of institutions catering to the elderly. These range from old-age homes with minimal social and medical facilities for the poor to the segregated "leisure towns" for the elderly rich to lead atemporal and often purposeless lives.

CHAPTER 14

Family Violence

A major aim of this book is to demonstrate that the concept of power and stratification are crucial in explaining familial relationships. In our discussion of marital sex roles and generational differentiation patterns, we have sought to demonstrate that those who had higher status, power, and authority often used these to dominate and control relationships. Thus in regard to sex-role relationships, a patriarchal ideology supported by economic, social, political, and religious institutions enables men to have the upper hand in most aspects of the marital relationship. This is particularly manifested in their control of the public world of work, politics, and religion. Women are relegated to the less powerful and less prestigious private world of the household and of childrearing. Similarly, the domination of the older can be seen in age-stratification patterns in political, economic, and religious organizations.

In this chapter and the next, we will be examining two topics that focus on some of the negative consequences of family life. The first deals with the ultimate abuse of stratification and power differentials—family violence. Our analysis of family violence will include two predominant patterns, wife battering and child abuse. In recent years sociologists and the lay public alike have become increasingly aware of the frequency of family violence. We will be studying why it has so recently been discovered when all apparent evidence indicates that it has prevailed for centuries. We will examine the factors that account for its prevalence.

The second topic of concern is divorce. Divorce is a major form of marital dissolution. It represents an ultimate manifestation of marital and familial instability. Divorce has been viewed by some as an indicator of the breakdown of the American family and as a reflection of societal decline. Conversely, others see it as the outcome of a positive individual act, ultimately beneficial to all family members and as such, therefore, as a sign of societal strength. A comparative analysis of divorce will be undertaken. We will be looking at divorce patterns and processes in the United States and in Islamic Egypt. Moslem divorce patterns and processes were selected as the comparative illustration because they are a prime example of a Western stereotype—the patriarchal wish-fullfillment for simplicity in divorce (Rosen, 1973). By debunking this stereotype, we hope to gain a better understanding of this phenomenon.

VIOLENCE IN THE FAMILY: COMPARATIVE AND THEORETICAL PERSPECTIVES

Throughout this book we have examined different theoretical orientations that have been applied to the study of the family in change. We have noted how certain perspectives, such as structure functionalism, have tended to view family conflict and disruptions as somewhat deviant phenomena. Other perspectives, notably conflict theory, have seen such disturbances as natural outgrowths of family dynamics. Until recently conceptualizations that viewed family consensus and cooperation as the ''natural'' state predominated in sociology. In a ground-breaking article published in 1971 in the most prestigious sociological journal devoted solely to the study of the family, *Journal of Marriage and the Family,* John E. O'Brien pointed out that from its inception in 1939 through 1969, not a single title in this journal contained the term, violence (O'Brien, 1971). He argued that this absence may reflect a desire by sociologists to avoid an issue that may be too touchy or may be thought of as too idiosyncratic a feature of ''normal'' families.

The entire issue of the *Journal of Marriage and the Family* containing O'Brien's article was organized around the common theme of ''Violence and the Family.'' It was an outgrowth of the 1970 meeting of the National Council on Family Relations, which was also oriented around this theme. In the years since that conference, social scientists have become increasingly involved in the study of the phenomenon of family violence. It is part of the more general realization that those orientations that view family disorganization as peculiar, abnormal, or as a strange deviation are limited. Instead, violence appears to be an expectable event and process and, therefore, has some legitimacy for study. The popular media also has turned its attention to this concern with particular emphasis on the most dramatic forms of family disorganization: violence between husbands and wives and between parents and children. In this section, these concerns will also be ours.

Prior to the 1970s, the social sciences had given relatively little attention to the extent that violence occurs within the family. Suzanne K. Steinmetz and Murray A.

Straus (1974) surveyed the literature on violence and the family. They compiled a bibliography of over 400 sources and found little material on everyday domestic violence between husbands and wives, which includes fights, slaps, or the throwing of things. The most extensive and accurate data avilable was on more extreme forms of violence, murder and child abuse.

The avoidance of this topic is shared by anthropology. The prominent anthropologist, Paul Bohannan suggested two possible reasons for this neglect: middle-class anthropologists share the middle-class horror of violence, and— possible more significantly—people in cultures under colonial situations did not conduct their family quarrels in the anthropologist's presence; nor did they discuss the violent episodes that might characterize their private lives for fear of governmental-agency intervention (cited in Steinmetz and Straus, 1974:v).

Although relatively little data had accumulated on the prevalence and extent of intrafamily violence, within the last 10 years there has been a notable increase in the scholarly attention given to this concern. One of the pioneer and most active scholars on family violence, Murray A. Straus, has reviewed most of this literature and has presented certain tentative formulations to account for its cross-cultural prevalence. Straus (1977) believes that aggression and violence of all types are so widespread that they can almost be labeled as a cross-cultural universal.

Straus examined the cross-cultural evidence on the most dramatic form of conjugal violence, murder. He found that for many societies a high proportion of homicides occurs within the family. Further, other less drastic forms of aggression are quite common. Straus conjectures that high rates of conjugal violence occur in urban-industrial, agrarian, and nonliterate societies. But, the highest rates of conjugal violence occur in societies that have high violence rates in other institutional spheres. He develops this supposition by examining six factors that provide some explanations for the ubiquity of intrafamily violence.

The first three factors regarding family violence are the extent of time involvements of family members with each other, the number of overlapping activities and interests that the members share, and the intensity of their involvement and attachment. The development of the private conjugal family, particularly in Western industrial societies, can thus be seen as latently contributing to the increased occurrence of intrafamily violence. Because the traditional nuclear family is more involved in community and consanguineal extended family activities, aggressive incidents can less frequently be attributed to these factors.

The fourth factor is sexual inequality. Straus observes the linkage between male dominance and wife beating. He attributes this to the high conflict potential built into a system that ascribes a superior position to the husband and the likely possibility that not all husbands may be able to achieve leadership roles or have wives who will be submissive and subordinate. Sex-role segregation contributes to this problem by further aggravating and heightening the antagonixm between the sexes. Straus presents the argument, which we have discussed elsewhere, regarding the detrimental effects of such segregation, showing how it leads to the inability of women to escape from a violent husband, particularly in Euroamerican societies:

> Such societies throw the full burden of childrearing on women, deny them equal job opportunities even when they can make alternative child-care arrangements, inculcate a negative self image in roles other than that of wife and mother, and reinforce the dependency of women on their husbands by emphasizing the idea that divorce is bad for children. Finally, in most societies, there is a male-oriented legal and judicial system, which makes it extremely difficult for women to secure legal protection from assault by their husbands except under the most extreme circumstances. (Straus, 1977:723)

Straus (1977) illustrates this point by describing a pattern of male behavior labeled as protest masculinity, which has been examined in the machismo pattern of Latin American males. Joseph P. Fitzpatrick (1971) states that machismo, literally maleness, refers to a combination of qualities associated with masculinity. It professes a style of personal bravado by which one faces challenges, danger, and threat with calmness. Through machismo, the individual seeks to develop a personal magnetism that attracts and influences others. It is associated with sexual prowess and power over women. This, in turn, is reflected in vigorous romanticism and jealousy of lover or wife, and it fosters premarital and extramarital sexual relationships.

Mexico: Machismo Thrives in a Matriarchy

MEXICO CITY, Sept. 18—"When I see a pretty girl walking toward me, I sort of block her path and say, 'How lovely you are, you please me,' " Roberto Gomez explained shyly. "Sometimes she smiles and stops to chat. Other times, she swings at me with her handbag."

Roberto Gomez is a 17-year-old student and already he is a budding macho. Despite the growth of feminism north of the border, Mexico today remains a stronghold of machismo, with new generations of men emerging with the same unwavering chauvinism as their fathers.

"I like girls, but they're different from us," Roberto Gomez went on. "They're always trying to get something in exchange. So I have lots of girlfriends, but I wouldn't have just one."

Behind the bluff exterior of machismo, though, the Mexican's attitude toward women remains a complex mixture of indifference and obsession, suspicion and dependence.

In recent years, some of the acutest manifestations of machismo have begun to disappear. A new Government family-planning program has persuaded many middle- and upper-class Mexicans to have smaller families, while the authorities have clamped down on men who in the past felt "undressed" without a gun in their belt.

But a new study by a Mexican sexologist, Dr. Osvaldo A. Quijada, entitled "Sexual Behavior in Mexico," indicated that the basic precepts of machismo are as strong as ever today. "There is a generalized conviction of male superiority," it noted. "Expressions of machismo are notorious. The woman is seen as an object."

After interviewing more than 1,000 men and women, Dr. Quijada, who is a gynecologist, also concluded that, despite their infidelity and their strong need to "conquer" women, Mexican men are unimaginative, insecure and unsatisfied lovers.

The psychological and even sociological reasons for machismo are more complicated, stemming largely from the Mexican male's reaction to what historically has been a matriarchal society. Reinforcing this, according to analysis, is the powerful Catholic veneration of the Virgin Mary, which in Mexico takes the form of worship of the "Indian" Virgin of Guadaloupe.

"Isn't it possible that behind the gross and grotesque caricature of male domination, there should be real female domination?" Dr. Quijada asked in his study. "The man who shouts out his masculinity is often guided and controlled by a woman. His shout is only that: reaffirmation of something he has lost."

But female domination only comes through the figure of the mother, who is seen as a saintly person uncontaminated by eroticism. The traditional disregard for or even ill-treatment of the mother by her husband then creates resentment toward the father figure, even though his behavior is eventually aped by his son.

The mother naturally becomes the model for a wife, who must be a virgin, have a respectable reputation and be inclined to sacrifice. But since the wife can never match the mother's perfection in the eyes of most Mexican men, she can be "punished" through ill-treatment and unfaithfulness.

According to some observers of machismo, most Mexican men have their first sexual experience with either prostitutes or maids and then, after marriage, they graduate to mistresses with whom they may also have numerous children. But all women—except the mother—are considered inferior and unworthy of respect.

The crudest examples of machismo in the home can be found among the country's poorly educated peasants and slum-dwellers, where family planning is still unheard of and wife beating is widespread. But even among the middle and upper classes, it appears, albeit in more disguised forms—anxiety to have a first-born son or the need to boast about new female "conquests." On a day-to-day basis, for example, it is considered macho to make comments, often vulgar, to women on the street or to blow the horn of the car at good-looking passers-by, while in the evening in downtown Mexico City it is "normal" for men of all ages to cruise in the slow lane in the hope of picking up girls waiting for buses.

Foreign women are often shocked by the sexual aggression and overt machismo of Mexican men. Foreigners, however, are viewed as conquests of special significance, and maximum macho points are earned by Mexicans seen walking arm-in-arm with blond, American women.

During the Government of President Luis Echeverria Alvarez, who left office last December, indirect efforts were made to combat machismo. A new birth-control policy, pointedly called "responsible parenthood," was adopted while the then First Lady, Maria Ester Zuno de Echeverria, sponsored numerous programs to bolster the family unit and support women.

Encouraged by that conference, Mexican feminist groups launched a war on machismo. But, while they have achieved minor legislative victories, they have changed few attitudes.

Under the new Government of President José López Portillo, the official family-planning program is being intensified, but for broader developmental reasons and not in order to fight machismo. The unspoken view of the new regime might be typified by a leading official who arrived late for an afternoon meeting with the apology, "Ah, señores, it is so difficult to get up from a warm bed."

Machismo fathers may have little importance or saliency in mother-child households or when the father may be physically present but not psychologically relevant. This often occurs in the extreme sex-role differentiation of the urban lower class. It is a pattern that is often associated with frequency wife beating and the glorification of physical aggression (Straus, 1977).

The privacy of the family is listed as the fifth factor to help account for family violence. The private family insulates the family members from the social control of neighbors and the extended family. Here again, the conjugal family found in Western industrial societies would be the family type most affected by this factor. The strength of the communal norm regarding the sanctity of family privacy is such that even when neighbors overhear family arguments and see the physical results of family aggression they try to ignore such evidence. More than likely they will not contact appropriate public agencies or make personal inquiries of the abused family member on the circumstances of the injury. Nor will they offer assistance.

The sanctity of family privacy is an important variable in Murray A. Straus's analysis of family life. He argues that cultural norms often legitimize the use of violence between family members, even if such aggression is illegal or a serious breach of normative proscriptions in non-familial circumstances. "In Euroamerican societies, to this day, there is a strong, though largely unverbalized, norm that makes the marriage license also a hitting license'' (Straus, 1977:720).

Straus then builds on the relationship between family violence and aggression and various societal patterns. Citing cross-cultural research, Straus argues that the more pervasive the existence of societal violence, the higher is the level of family violence. More than this, Straus postulates the existence of a reciprocal relationship between the aggression and violence in the society and the level of violence within the family: "As societal violence increases, there is a tendency for intrafamily violence to increase; and as intrafamily violence increases, there is a tendency for intrafamily violence to increase; and as intrafamily violence increases, there is a tendency for societal violence to increase'' (Straus, 1977:725).

One final point that we wish to emphasize in this summary of Straus's work is his assertion that there is a strong link berween violence in one family role with violence in other family roles. Thus, in families where violence between husband and wife are prevalent, there is more likely to be violence of parents toward their children. Further, battered or abused children often become parents who batter and abuse their children.

We will conclude this discussion of intrafamily violence by examining one extreme manifestation of violence that occurred both within the family and outside it. We are referring to the destruction of a large part of the female population of the later Middle Ages who were labeled witches. We wish to draw the reader's attention to one pervasive element that is related to all the factors discussed above, that is misogyny—the hatred of women. Misogyny is one outcome, albeit extreme, of the sexist patriarchal view that asserts the superiority of men over women in all spheres of life. In previous discussions we have seen how this ideology was evidenced in marital-role relationships and the sexual division of labor, both in the home and in the workplace. First, we will discuss the persecution of witches, a most dramatic form of patriarchy that is associated with familial and nonfamilial violence.

VIOLENCE TOWARD WOMEN: THE CASE OF WITCHES

Probably the most extreme example of the violence toward women was the persecution of women during the later Middle Ages for allegedly being witches. In our earlier discussion of courtly love during the medieval period, we considered the dichotomy that existed in the conceptualization of women. On the one hand, they were seen as the embodiment of the virtues of goodness reflected by the Virgin Mary; on the other, they were seen as evil incarnate, the temptress Eve, who formed pacts with the devil, Satan. At the same time that the ideology of courtly love was developing, there was a counter movement based on the inherent evilness of women that grew from the 11th to the 14th century and reached its violent peak in the Renaissance belief in witchcraft.

To counter the threat of "evil" women, the church sanctioned the absolute subjection of women to their husbands. The supremacy of the husband was espoused and the physical punishment of nonobedient and nonsubmissive wives was condoned. A wife's loyalty to her husband was likened to the fidelity of dog to master; all the husband's orders—whether just or unjust, important or trivial, reasonable or unreasonable—must be obeyed (Powers, 1975:16). Implicit obedience was part of the ideal of marriage. Disobedient wives could be brought to compliance by force. Canon law specifically allowed wife beating. Divorce was impossible; even obtaining a separation from a brutal and violent husband was extremely difficult. Elizabeth Gould Davis (1971), in her book *The First Sex,* asserts that noblemen and squires beat their wives with such regularity that a 15th century priest, Bernard of Siena, took pity on the lot of wives and urged his men parishoners to exercise a little restraint and treat them with as much mercy as they would their hens and pigs. However, to encourage women to win their husband's good will, the church urged that they be submissive, devote, and obedient.

By the later Middle Ages and the Renaissance, the violent treatment of women reached its most extreme form in the belief in witchcraft and the resultant persecution and execution of witches. A manual of witchcraft written near the close of the 15th century at the request of the reigning Pope reached the following conclusions:

> A woman is beautiful to look upon, contaminating to the touch, and deadly to keep . . . a foe to friendships . . . a necessary evil, a natural temptation . . . a domestic danger . . . a evil of nature, painted with fair colors . . . a liar by nature . . . [She] seethes with anger and impatience in her whole soul. . . . There is no wrath above the wrath of a woman. . . .Since [women] are feebler both in mind and body, it is not surprising that they should come under the spell of witchcraft [more than men]. . . . A woman is more carnal than a man. . . . All witchcraft comes from carnal lust, which is in women insatiable. (*Malleus Maleficarum* cited in Hunt, 1959:177)

The cited document, *Malleus Maleficarum* (The Witches' Hammer) [i.e., a hammer with which to strike witches] was very influential for the next two centuries. It professed to document actual testimony of witnesses and confessed witches on the evil doings of women, ranging from summoning plagues of locusts to causing sexual problems (including infertility, impotence, frigidity, painful coitus, nymphomania, and satyriasis) and to drying up a mother's milk. Witches allegedly were able to fly at night, could turn themselves into beasts of burden, and would kidnap, roast, and eat children (Hunt, 1959:195).

The belief in witchcraft was the clumination of the ideology of the evilness of women. Witchcraft was seen as a women's crime, and the ratio of women to men executed has been variously estimated at 20 to 1 and 100 to 1 (Dworkin, 1974:130). In her discussion of witchcraft, Andrea Dworkin (1974) estimates that the number of executions that may have occurred during this period may easily have reached as high as 1 million. E. William Monter (1977) sets the figure at a much lower number, 100,000. In any case, although the exact number of victims of the witchcraft mania is incomplete, judicial records for particular towns and areas provide some statistical indicators of its prevalence:

> In almost every province of Germany the persecution raged with increasing intensity. Six hundred were said to have been burned by a single bishop in Bamberg, where the special witch jail was kept fully packed. Nine hundred were destroyed in a single year in the bishopric of Wurzberg, and in Nuremberg and other great cities there were one or two hundred burnings a year. So there were in France and in Switzerland. A thousand people were put to death in one year in the district of Como. Remigus, one of the Inquisitors, who was author of *Daemonolativa,* and a judge at Nancy boasted of having personally caused the burning of nine hundred persons in the course of fifteen years. Delrio says that five hundred were executed in Geneva in three terrified months in 1515. The Inquisition at Toulouse destroyed four hundred persons in a single execution, and there were fifty at Douai in a single year. In Paris, executions were continuous. In the Pyrenees, a wolf country, the popular form was that of the loup-garou, and De L'Ancre at Labout burned two hundred. (Hughes, 1971:63)

Women were declared witches and burned at the stake for many reasons. Davis recounts the many pretexts: "for threatening their husbands, for talking back to or refusing a priest, for stealing, for prostitution, for adultery, for bearing a child out of wedlock, for permitting sodomy, even though the priest or husband who committed it was forgiven, for masturbating, for Lesbianism, for child neglect, for scolding and nagging, and even for *miscarrying,* even though the miscarriage was caused by a kick or a blow from the husband" (1971:252).

The significance of witchcraft for the history of women lies in the fact that it is attributable to the long history of misogyny in European religion and law. Misogyny, the hatred of women, has taken many historical forms. Although the witchcraft mania was unique in providing a legal method for killing thousands of women, it was one culmination, albeit extreme, of this misogynistic heritage.

It is ironic that the medieval period, which saw the development of the ideology of romantic love, also witnessed the most terrible persecution of women. Yet, this has been women's fate in Western culture. The medieval historian, E. William Monter makes the final summary observation:

> Although both courtly love and witchcraft were created by medieval European patriarchy, their historical consequences were grotesquely different. The sad truth is that, in women's "real" social history, the pedestal is almost impossible to find, but the stake is everywhere. (1977:135)

CONJUGAL VIOLENCE

Steinmetz and Straus (1974) attribute the avoidance of the examination of intrafamily violence to an idealized concept of the family: by definition the family is nonviolent and a center of love and gentleness. Conflict and violence are perceived as abnormalities that only occur in abnormal families, that is, among "sick" people. Steinmetz (1977) later points out that this belief leads families to fail to acknowledge family conflict or to exhibit what Richard Sennett has labeled the guilt-over-conflict syndrome:

> to most people it appears that good families, upright families, ought to be happy, and it also appears that happy families ought to be tranquil, internally in harmony. . . . For many people, the emergence of conflict in their family lives seems to indicate some kind of moral failure; the family, and by reflection the individual, must be tarnished and no good. (Sennett, 1973:86)

Richard Gelles (1972), in his study of violence in the home, suggests that the societally shared definition of the family as nonviolent and the belief that violence within the home is pathologic leads family members to reconstruct and redefine instances in which physical force is employed into something other than "violence." This prevailing viewpoint is shared by the theoretical orientation that has dominated American sociology, structure functionalism. Structure functionalism is a consensus and integration perspective that labels violence, abrupt change, and tension as deviant or abnormal. It advocates the avoidance of conflict and tension because they are seen as detrimental to group cohesiveness. This is especially the case for groups, such as the family, where great importance is attached to its maintenance and continuation. Steinmetz and Straus (1974) rightly point out that frequently the conflict and tension are not eliminated but are merely covered up, glossed over, or ignored until they reach uncontrollable proportions.

Steinmetz and Straus as well as an increasing number of family sociologists find a conflict-theory perspective on the family more useful in understanding family structure and dynamics. The conflict-theory perspective challenges structure functionalism by viewing such struggles as natural occurrences between subordinate and superordinate individuals. This is not to say that the conflict perspective approves of family violence, but rather it sees the potential for family violence as fundamental as the potential for affection and love. This view stresses that family violence does occur and is a regular part of family life. As such, it needs to be studied. Unfortunately, the idealized portrayal of family life that dominates structure functionalism blinds the investigator to family violence.

A question remains regarding the prevalence of force and violence in the family. Steinmetz and Straus insist that it is a fundamental feature of family life:

it would be hard to find a group or institution in American society in which violence is more of an everyday occurrence than it is within the family. . . . Underneath the surface is a vast amount of conflict and violence—including bitter feelings, anger, hatred, much physical punishment of children, pokes and slaps of husbands and wives, and not altogether rare pitched battles between family members (1974:3,6).

They also report that a survey of the National Commission on the Causes and Prevention of Crime and Violence estimated that between one-fourth and one-fifth of all adult Americans believe that it is acceptable for spouses to hit one another under certain circumstances. In the surveys large representative sample, it was found that about one-third of the population had been spanked frequently (and almost all at least once) as children. Further, one-fifth of the husbands felt that it was alright to slap a wife's face.

In a survey of 385 college students, Murray A. Straus (1974) found that 16 percent reported that their parents used physical force to resolve marital conflicts during a recent 1-year period. These were couples who had been married for many years and who would, the respondents claimed, if at all possible, keep their domestic struggles from their children. Richard J. Gelles (1972), after interviewing 80 families, reported that 55 percent of them had had at least one incident of physical violence. John E. O'Brien (1971), in his study of divorce applicants, noted that more than one-third of the wives complained of the use of physical force by their husbands and almost one-fourth also complained of verbal abuse.

Suzanne K. Steinmetz (1972), in an exploratory study of 78 students at a large urban university, found that about 30 percent of their families had marital conflicts and that, in about 70 percent of cases of parent-child and sibling conflicts, physical aggression was used to resolve intrafamily conflicts. She classified four types of problem solvers. Screaming sluggers, the first type, were characterized as couples who both physically and verbally abused each other. Silent attackers, the second type, sought to avoid quarreling, but, when it became unmanageable, released their frustration through physical assaults. The third type, threateners, were verbally abusive and although they threatened physical violence did not resort to it. Finally, some families were able to resolve their problems without resorting to either physical violence or verbal abuse. They were labeled pacifists.

The accumulated research reported by Steinmetz and Straus (1974) in their anthology reveals that violence in the family is indeed widespread. Actually, this research may have only uncovered the tip of the iceberg of family violence. Gelles (1972), in his study of physical aggression between husbands and wives, also emphasizes that violence may be more widespread and severe than previously thought:

taking into account the figures on the extent of conjugal violence . . . we estimate that violence is indeed common in American families. Furthermore, these incidents of violence are not isolated attacks nor are they just pushes and shoves. In many families, violence is patterned and regular and often results in broken bones and sutured cuts (Gelles, 1972:192).

He argues that the extent of conjugal violence and its intensity indicate that violence between family members is a social problem of major proportions. Further, he points out that marital violence, even if frequent and severe, may not lead to divorce or separation. The reasons why marriages continue are complex. Steinmetz (1977) observes that the physically violent are also more likely to be highly demonstrative in affection, engaging in a great deal of kissing, hugging and embracing.

A Shocking Survey on Wife Abuse

ELSA GOSS

LEXINGTON, Ky.—Wife abuse is a problem that no one likes to talk about and many people like to deny.

But no matter how much we try to pretend that it doesn't exist, wife abuse doesn't go away.

That much has been evident all along to those who cared enough to consider the gruesome figures. In 1972, for instance, 4,900 cases of wife abuse were reported in Detroit. In New York State in 1973, close to 15,000 cases of wife abuse were heard before the Family Court. In Boston in 1974, police responded to 11,081 family disturbance calls. In Washington, D.C., 10,000 cases of wife abuse are reported each year.

And in 1975, the Philadelphia Police Department received 25,000 calls reporting wife abuse.

Despite all the evidence, however, there have been those who have shrugged their shoulders and refused to believe that wife-beating is a nationwide disgrace.

Some, like an elected official here in Lexington, have insisted that it happens only in lower income families. Others, like the lady who at last report was New Hampshire's Commissioner on the Status of Women, have dismissed wife-beating as a natural outgrowth of the women's movement.

When asked some time ago why she had rejected a plan to help battered women, the commissioner explained, "Those women's libbers irritate the hell out of their husbands."

No matter that wife-beating occurs in families from every socio-economic level. No matter that wife abuse existed long before feminism was even a part of our national vocabulary.

No matter that it's been estimated that over half of all married women —or some 28 million American women—suffer physical abuse at the hands of their husbands. It's just been more comfortable to ignore the whole brutal thing.

But it's hard to be comfortable with the results of a Louis Harris survey just released by the Kentucky Commission on Women.

The survey—the first of its kind in the nation—was based on interviews conducted with Kentucky women themselves and not simply on police reports. That's significant because social workers have long maintained that wife abuse is one of this country's most under-reported crimes, along with rape.

In other words, they've insisted, the numbers of battered women are far greater than the figures that appear on police blotters. If the women themselves could be confidentially asked without fear of reprisals, they've gone on, the thesis could be proved as fact.

That's what the Harris survey in this state did, interviewing women by telephone last April. And as the social workers predicted, the findings are staggering.

According to the survey, you see, over 80,000 Kentucky women were abused by their husbands in the past year alone. Put another way, that's close to 220 cases of wife abuse a day in this state during 1978. Yet when asked if they had *ever* been abused during their marriages, the women sent the figures even higher.

Over 21 percent, which translates into 169,000 women, said they had.

Moreover, although the most frequent form of abuse involved wives being pushed, grabbed, shoved or slapped, an alarming number of women suffered greater violence. Over 4.1 percent of the women surveyed said they had been kicked, bitten, hit with their husbands' fists, beaten up, threatened with a knife or gun or actually knifed or shot.

That works out to some 33,000 women who had been severely abused—a figure, by the way, that is greater than the population of the state capital.

But the survey doesn't just show that wife abuse is pervasive. It also refutes any argument that abused women are found only in the urban ghettoes or rural shanties. The victims of wife abuse in this study came from all walks of life, all economic levels and all races.

The only difference between poor women and wealthy ones, in fact, was that when they were beaten up so badly by their husbands that they required medical help, the women with money went to private physicians instead of public hospitals.

That's a pretty ugly picture, but it's a picture that experts think is duplicated in every state in the country. Sadly, it's also a picture that is bound to get worse: Domestic violence always increases in times of economic turbulence.

As inflation rages and recession looms large, the number of women getting knocked around will grow not only in Kentucky but all over the nation.

Of course, we can still pretend that it's not happening. We can tune the problem out and turn on reruns of "The Honeymooners." We can sit back and laugh as Ralph Kramden shouts at his long-suffering wife, "One of these days, Alice, pow, right in the kisser!"

But while we do, millions of real-life Alices will be taking it right on the chin. Whether we choose to believe it or not.

Elsa Goss in the *Philadelphia Inquirer,* July 15, 1979. Reprinted by permission of The Philadelphia Inquirer.

Del Martin (1976) suggests that fear may account for battered wives staying married. The predominant reason may be fear. Fear may immobilize them and rule their actions, their decisions, and their very lives. Martin illustrates with this dramatic account:

"When he hit me, of course I was afraid. Anybody would be if somebody larger than you decided to take out their anger on you. I really couldn't do anything about it. I felt as if I was completely helpless." (Martin, 1976:76)

The fear of reprisal also prevents the abused wife from seeking help. She may be afraid of endangering her children or any neighbors that may become involved. She sees only one alternative—sacrificing herself.

Martin (1976) also sees the contemporary definition of the woman's role in our society as being highly influential in the decision to stay married. A woman assumes that she is accountable for the failure of the marriage, even if she is the one being beaten. The failure of the marriage represents her failure as a woman. Probably even more importantly than the loss of a woman's self-respect is the fact that more often than not she is economically dependent on her husband. Even in those circumstances where the wife is working, she frequently is forced to surrender her paycheck to her husband. Martin argues that although women's roles are changing and women are increasingly establishing new values for living on their own, the changes are not occurring fast enough for many women who have long ago given up hope: "Only by bringing the buried problems of wife-beating and financial exploitation into the open can we begin to inspire the imaginations of those women who silently wait out their time as scapegoats in violent marriages" (Martin, 1976:86).

The prevalence and severity of family violence is particularly acute in our society because of the ideology that stresses the privacy of the family. Throughout this book, we have observed that the rise of the private family is one of the major characteristics of contemporary times. Increasingly, the family has withdrawn from community and extended kinship involvements. Granted that this withdrawal is not absolute and that viable relationships do exist for most families with relatives, friends, and neighbors, nonetheless, the privacy and sanctity of the household is normative and usually nonviolated. The result is that violent outbursts usually occur in private and outside witnesses are rare. Del Martin (1976) refers to the book, *Scream Quietly or the Neighbors Will Hear,* written by Erin Pizzey (1974), to illustrate this point:

> people try to ignore violence inside the home and within the family. Many abused wives who came to Chiswick Center told Pizzey that their neighbors knew very well what was going on but went to great lengths to pretend ignorance. They would cross the street to avoid witnessing an incident of domestic violence. Some would even turn up the television to block out the shouts, screams, and sobs coming from next door (Martin, 1976:16−17).

Richard J. Gelles (1973) observes that the sociologist Erving Goffman's concept of "backstage" is quite relevant in understanding domestic violence. It is in the home, away from the prying eyes of the community, that violent family members find a place where they can fight in private, "Protected by the privacy of one's own walls there is no need to maintain this presentation of family life as harmonious, loving, and conflict-free" (Gelles, 1973:96). Gelles finds three rooms in the house as centers of family violence: the kitchen, the living room, and the bedroom. The first two rooms are focal points of family activity and as such are scenes of much nonlethal violence. It is the bedroom, where most homicides occur and where much nonlethal violence also is prevalent: conflicts regarding sex and intimacy are frequent; it is a room, used at night, from which many undressed victims find it difficult to leave. For where are they to go? It is the bathroom, the most private room for family members, that has relatively little violent episodes.

Family violence also occurs during particular periods of time of the day and the week. Gelles (1972) found that aggression usually occurs in the evening or late evening during the weekend. He accounts for this by observing that it is at these times that the family is usually alone and when the abused family member feels that there is no one to turn to. It is an inconvenient time to disturb neighbors, friends, or relatives with one's domestic quarrels. All too frequently the only alternative is the police, and most are reluctant to take this step.

Wife Beaters: Few of Them Ever Appear Before a Court of Law

J. C. BARDEN

When Maria G. asked her husband what time he wanted to eat after he returned home one evening from his job as a presser in a clothing factory, he punched her in the eye, then in the nose and the mouth, leaving her bruised and bleeding.

It wasn't the first time that her husband had beaten her during their seven-year marriage, but for the first time Maria was angry enough to call the police. She wanted him arrested. Instead, the police convinced Maria that she and her husband should try to settle their differences amicably. The couple have three children, ages 3 to 7, all of whom had witnessed the beating.

After the officers left, Maria's husband beat her again, this time for calling the police, and he told her if she called them again he would strangle her. The next morning Maria went to the South Brooklyn Legal Service Corporation, a Federally funded legal service for people who can't afford lawyers, and asked for help in obtaining a divorce.

Because of the threat on Maria's life, the corporation's one lawyer who handles divorce cases, Marjorie Fields, made it one of her five emergency cases for the week. She saw to it that Maria, with the aid of the Welfare Department, got a new apartment, and Miss Fields obtained the divorce for her in five months.

During the period, Miss Fields said, as she told of the case, Maria's husband entered her new apartment forceably five times and beat her in front of the children each time. On the fifth occasion, the police arrested the husband. The assault charges against him were dropped after he agreed in court not to bother his former wife again. So far he hasn't, Miss Fields said.

The apparent reluctance of the police to take punitive action—they waited, in Maria's case, until several reported beatings had taken place—seems to support the charges made by many wives and lawyers. They say the police in trying to find a mediated solution are not sufficiently trained to recognize the cases where mediation simply will not work and where firmer action is necessary. The result can be repeated beatings.

Another problem seen by some in the field is that the stereotype of the "wife-beater" is misleading. The evidence is growing that there is not a typical offender," that wife-beaters in fact range all along the social scale.

Recent cases here involved a doctor, a college professor and a government investigator—and a study concluded this month in Norwalk,

Conn., indicated that police in that city of 85,000 with its wide socio-economic range received roughly the same number of wife-abuse complaints as police in a Harlem precinct of the same size—which was four or five a week.

Also, court figures show that there were 17,277 family offenses—those in which violence occurred—handled in Family Court throughout the state during the 1972—73 judicial year with the wife the plaintiff in 82 per cent of them. That was about 7,000 more than in the 1963—64 judicial year, the first one after the Family Court law was enacted.

But these figures hardly indicate how widespread wife-abuse is because so few cases get to court, according to Emily Jane Goodman, a lawyer who has handled divorces for many women who have been the target of their husbands' fists.

The police are not even called in many cases, Miss Goodman said, because the women involved are either ashamed to admit what has happened or they are afraid they will get a worse beating if they do, or they know that the police "will do everything possible to discourage them from filing complaints."

"There are cases in which policemen really identify with the perpetrator," Miss Goodman said, "and they feel that the wife is the property of the husband and if he needs to punch her around a little bit to teach her a lesson he's entitled to do it."

Psychologists who have done work in the field of wife-abuse say that most of the husbands involved have no police record. They are often men who are so unhappy with their stations in life that they take out their rage on their wives, as did Maria's husband, the psychologists say, or they are men such as the doctor who began abusing his wife after he came under a great deal of pressure in a new professional position.

"The police simply do not understand the total terror you're in," said the former wife of the doctor, "and they will do nothing. If you have a husband of stature they feel that his reputation is more important than your health."

Even after she moved into her own apartment, the woman said, it was months before she could shake the fear of a possible assault by her husband, even though he never bothered her there.

The beatings leave many wives emotional wrecks, psychologists say, because the women feel they have done something to deserve them, as some rape victims feel they did something to incite their attackers.

While the police have begun to recognize the emotional damage to rape victims, and the New York City Police have special units to deal with such cases, family disputes are handled by all city patrolmen, only a fraction of whom have received any formal training in how to settle them.

Yet, Federal Bureau of Investigation figures show that in 1973 there were 4,764 rapes reported to police in New York State, while there were about 14,000 wife-abuse complaints that go to Family Court during a year of roughly the same period.

For the wife who has been the victim of a husband's assault, there does not seem to be a single agency in the city—public or private—where she can go for temporary protection. Unless she has a close friend or the money and the inclination to spend the night in a hotel or motel, she is stuck at home with an angry husband.

The wives who are the repeated victims of their husbands' assaults are most often those who are trapped in a relationship emotionally or economically, psychologists say. They are so afraid of being alone that they endure the beatings, or do so in the mistaken belief that keeping the family together is always best for the children, or they are totally dependent on the husband for money.

For some of them, sticking it out can result in death. Police have cases on record of wives slain by husbands who had previously beaten them.

As for the children, in addition to the emotional scars that the wife-beating leaves on them, psychologists say there is the distant possibility that the children will grow up modeling themselves after their parents, the girl expecting to be beaten, the boy expecting to do the beating.

For the police, breaking up family fights can be a dangerous business. A nationwide study a few years ago showed that intervening in family disputes accounted for 22 per cent of the policemen killed in the line of duty and about 40 percent of those injured.

The reason, said Dr. Morton Bard, a psychologist and a former policeman, who conducted the comparative study in Harlem and Norwalk, was that police were not trained for the role of family mediator and often behaved in such a way that they brought on violence rather than placated the participants.

Dr. Bard disagrees with those who argue for firm punitive action on the part of the police. He says that most appeals to the police during family disputes "are in the nature of requests for authority and objectivity in the resolution of conflict and not for the enforcement of the law."

Dr. Bard believes that "proper handling" of the cases can result in "peaceful solutions," either through on-the-spot mediation or referral to Family Court or social agencies for counseling.

He believes that the best means of handling family disputes in cities with large police departments is with the creation of specially trained police units that would handle normal duties as well.

Miss Fields, the legal services lawyer, endorses the idea, but to make it effective she strongly believes such a unit should include a woman because, she said, "I just don't believe a woman officer is going to be prone to the same inaction as a male officer when she sees a wife bloody and bruised and with a couple of teeth missing."

J. C. Barden in *The New York Times*, October 21, 1974. ©1974 by The New York Times Company. Reprinted by permission.

The pattern that emerges is that violence is often associated with the presence or absence of other people. The more alone the couple, the more likely violence will occur. The violent family member is often reluctant to abuse his spouse in the presence of others. Further, neighbors not wanting to intrude or become involved in domestic arguments, actively seek noninvolvement in what we define as the private affairs of others.

Gelles (1972) also found that the isolation of the family from the community is a contributory factor in family violence. He contrasts his respondents who had viable neighborhood ties with those who had few friends in the community and rarely visited with neighbors or friends. He found that violent families tended to be those isolated from their neighbors: nonviolent families had viable neighborhood ties and had many friends in the neighborhood. The result was that the victims of a violent family member had minimal social supports and resources in the community to which they could turn for help when they encountered family problems. To highlight the affect of neighborhood involvements on family violence, Gelles compares two neighbors—Mrs. (44) and Mrs. (45). Mrs. (44) owns her own home and has never hit nor been hit by her husband. Mrs. (45) lives across the street and has been involved in some serious knockdown, drag-out physical brawls with her husband. Mrs. (44) discusses her neighbors:

> *Mrs. (44):* I like the neighborhood quite well, surprisingly well for just having moved here two years ago. They have been quite friendly and hospitable. The woman next door is my close friend. She is quite a bit older and has children who are married and are my age. But she has been a very good friend. It's a friendly neighborhood.

In contrast, Mrs. (45) knows few neighbors, has few friends, and does not socialize much with her neighbors:

> *Mrs. (45):* I don't bother with them and they don't bother with me. I don't mean it that way . . . we say hello or they might wave. I'm not the type that goes from one house to the next. I'm not that type of social gatherer anyway. We help them, they help us, things that are needed. They are good neighbors.

Mrs. (45) thinks that they are good neighbors, but does not know the first thing about them. Mrs. (44), however, was able to inventory the family problems in many of her neighbors' families (Gelles, 1972:133–134).

One final series of factors associated with family violence stems from sexist patriarchal ideology. A number of investigators—Goode (1971), O'Brien (1971), and Gelles (1972)—report that the role people play outside the family is important in understanding family violence. Husbands who have not achieved the societal definition of success in their occupational roles frequently take out their frustration on their wives. The investigators' explanation for this occurrence is that although patriarchy asserts that husbands should have a superior position in the household, that position must be legitimated by the husbands' achievements in the outside world of work. In situations where the husband has failed to achieve the necessary societal criteria of success, this can precipitate a conflict situation within the home.

Goode (1971) theorized that fmily violence is likely to occur in situations where the husband fails to possess the achieved statuses, skills, and material objecives necessary to support his ascribed superior status within the household. John E. O'Brien's (1971) research investigation supported this hypothesis. Likewise, Gelles (1972) found in his study of physical aggression between husbands and wives that it is most likely to occur when husbands have lower educational and occupational statuses than their wives. Gelles believes that in such circumstances the husband's inability to measure up to his and his wife's expectations are compounded with the husband's frustration over his inability to provide adequately for his family and thus lead to outbreaks of aggressive hehavior.

In summary, we have investigated some of the dominating factors that are associated with conjugal violence. It is beyond the scope of our discussion to include such additional elements as socialization processes; psychological factors, and societal stress factors, which include unemployment and financial and health problems. We have emphasized those factors that have governed our attention throughout this book. They include sex-role relationships influenced by patriarchal ideology and the family's relationship and involvement in the community. Continuing with this same orientation we turn our attention to child abuse.

CHILD ABUSE IN CROSS-CULTURAL PERSPECTIVE

The abuse of children denotes a situation ranging from the deprivation of food, clothing, shelter, and love to incidences of physical wounding and torture, to selling and abandonment, to outright murder. Although it has received an unusual amount of attention in recent years, violence toward children is as old as humankind. Historically, parents have had the prerogative to wield absolute power over their children's life and death.

Spanking Ban Riles Swedes

DICK SODERLUND

STOCKHOLM—A new law that forbids parents to beat, spank, cuff or otherwise harm their children takes effect in Sweden in July, and some parents are not happy about it.

One father said he thought spanking was good for children, and a spokesman for the small Maranata religious sect said frankly: "We will go underground if we have to, but we will continue to exercise our natural rights."

Sweden will become the first nation with such a law, adopting it in the International Year of the Child. The law is a new step in a long process aimed at protecting children's rights here. A children's ombudsman and an emergency phone watch for youngsters already exist.

When the minority Liberal government introduced the bill to ban parents from spanking in March, Justice Minister Sven Romanus said it meant that "our society has taken an increasingly negative view of beating or spanking as a means of bringing up children."

There has been no organized opposition to the law, but reactions from jurists, lawmakers, and parents have been mixed. Said one annoyed father of three:

"Spanking and spanking . . . there's a difference between deliberate spanking and what I would call an outburst of temper. I never spanked my kids in cold blood, only on the spur of the moment. I am sure it does not hurt them but help them."

Most critical of the law were spokesmen for the Maranata sect, a group of about 300 persons who split from the Pentecostal Church in the 1960s. It sees physical chastisement by parents as a natural means of correction and an "ethical, moral and religious right."

The sect operates its own "pilgrim" schools in protest against the public school system, and Hans Brynte, principal of one Maranata school, said:

"If the authorities try to stop us, we will go underground and fight on. They are suddenly outlawing an old cultural tradition and parents are declared idiots incapable of rearing their children. People in other countries will laugh at this and a whole generation will be criminalized because some sociologists shall have their way."

When the new law was debated in parliament, Conservative Tore Nilsson protested it. Quoting the Bible, ancient Icelandic life rules of the book Havamal and a centuries-old Swedish legal document, he said, "The law against spanking conflicts with our cultural tradition, with parents' rights and personal integrity and with Western humanism."

Justice Minister Romanus took a different view. "This development reflects the now-dominant view that the child is an independent individual who can demand full respect for his person, integrity and own value," he said.

The new law prohibits "any act which, for the purpose of punishing, causes the child physical injury or pain, even if the disturbance is mild and passing." It is meant to include psychological punishment, but legal experts have criticized the wording on this as too vague.

Many child psychiatrists, psychologists, sociologists and doctors have welcomed the new law as necessary to protect children.

"This law is long overdue because so-called spanking has in effect been a legalized, milder form of assault and battery or could lead to worse abuse," said Gunnel Linde, who belongs to a children's rights organization and has written a book on child-beating.

And one welfare officer said: "In my work, I often become amazed at how little parents know about their children. They don't have to be bad to beat them, just ignorant, teaching the kids only the most primitive and ineffective way to solve conflicts—through violence against someone weaker."

Grade school children aged 8 to 10 polled at a recreational center were definitely against being spanked—not surprisingly—though they found it natural to occasionally beat a brother or sister themselves.

Peter, 10, noted, "My sister is always riling me. Then I hit her but that's OK because we are evenly matched. If my dad would hit me, or mom, it would not be fair but I would hit back too . . .

Legal medical officer Sven-Olof Lidholm took a stern view of parents who beat their children. Criticizing authorities for laxness in caring for maltreated youngsters, he said he received more than 600 reports of child beatings annually, about 10 of them fatal. And he believes there are perhaps 5,000 other children who are beaten regularly without it being reported.

The new ban does not carry any specific punishment. However, ordinary criminal law allows sentences of up to 10 years for serious cases and up to two years in milder ones.

Protecting children from bodily harm has been a long process in Sweden. Flogging in schools was partly banned in 1918, but as late as 1958 teachers in lower-grade schools were still allowed to use some physical punishment on students.

Dick Soderlund in *The Philadelphia Inquirer,* May 27, 1979. Reprinted by permission of The Associated Press and by The Philadelphia Inquirer, May 27, 1979.

Violence against children is not a recent phenomenon: it is the term, abuse, that is relatively new. Abortion, abandonment, and infanticide—the willful killing of children, usually infants—have been practiced in varying degrees throughout history and in most of the world's societies. One scholar argues that infanticide "has been responsible for more child deaths than any other single cause in history other than possibly the bubonic plague" (Solomon, 1973).

The most extreme form of child violence, infanticide, was usually related to beliefs concerning religion and superstition. But throughout human history, a more prevalent reason for infanticide has been population control or maintenance of a physically healthy population. William Graham Sumner, in his classic work, *Folkways,* describes the common solution to overpopulation:

> It is certain that at a very early time in the history of human society the burden of bearing and rearing children, and the evils of overpopulation, were perceived as facts, and policies were instinctively adopted to protect the adults. The facts caused pain, and the acts resolved upon avoiding it were very summary, and were adopted with very little reasoning. Abortion and infanticide protected the society, unless its situation with

respect to neighbors was such that war and pestilence kept down the numbers and made children valuable for war. (Sumner, 1906:308).

Sumner also observes the differential treatment given to boys or girls depending on their importance for the family. Where girls were valuable and could bring a bride price to the father they were treated well. In circumstances where they were economic burdens they might be put to death. Another common practice was to kill newborn babies with congenital weaknesses and deformities. Sumner reasons that this occured "in obedience to a great tribal interest to have able-bodied men, and to spend no strength or capital in rearing others" (1906:313).

Class variations also played a determining role in infanticide decisions. David Bakan (1971) in his *Slaughter of the Innocents,* discusses the ubiquity of infanticide and abortion. He cites the observations of Reverend J. M. Orsmond who visited Tahiti in the late 1820s. Orsmond noted the relationship between infanticide and social class. The members of the higher social class were not obligated to kill their children, whereas the lower caste were obligated to kill their babies after the first or second. Failure to do so brought shame and disgrace: "More than two-thirds of the children were destroyed 'generally before seeing the light of day. Sometimes in drawing their first breath they were throttled to death, being called tamari'i hia (children throttled)' " (Bakan, 1971:31).

A common reason for infanticide was to avoid shame and ostracism by unmarried mothers. Up to the dawn of the industrial era about 200 years ago, the killing of illegitimate children was extremely common in Europe. The unmarried woman was confronted with two negative options. If her maternity was discovered, she was excommunicated and lived as a social outcast. Nathaniel Hawthorne, in his American classic, *The Scarlet Letter,* novelizes this situation in his account of Hester Prynne in colonial Salem, Massachusetts.

Bakan reports that in 18th century Germany the most common punishment for infanticide was sacking. The mother was put in a sack and thrown into a river accompanied by a live animal or two to make the death more painful. Frederick the Great, the king of Prussia, in 1740, felt that this practice was too inhumane and substituted decapitation as a more acceptable alternative.

Women who committed infanticide were often tried and prosecuted as witches. In the 17th century, Benjamin Carpoz was credited with the execution of over 20,000 women for witchcraft, a large number having committed infanticide. The manner of execution ranged from sacking to burning, to burying alive, to impalement (Bakan, 1971). Bakan cites a very popular English ballad, "The Cruel Mother," which appeared in B. H. Bronson's (1959)[1] definitive work on child ballads, that illustrates the relationship between illegitimacy and infanticide:

---

[1]B. H. Bronson, 1959, *The Traditional Tunes of the Child Ballads, Vol. 1.* Princeton, N.J.: Princeton University Press.

1. There was a lady came from York
   All alone, alone and aloney
   She fell in love with her father's clerk
   Down by the greenwood siding.
2. When nine months was gone and past
   Then she had two pretty babes born.
3. She leaned herself against a thorn
   There she had two pretty babes born.
4. Then she cut her topknot from her head
   and tied those babies' hands and legs.
5. She took her penknife keen and sharp
   and pierced those babies' tender hearts.
6. She buried them under a marble stone
   And then she said she would go home.
7. As she was (going through) (a-going in) her father's hall
   She spied those babes a-playing at a ball.
8. "Oh babes, oh babes if (you were) (thou wast) mine
   I would dress you up in silks so fine."
9. "Oh mother dear when we were thine
   You did not dress us up in silks so fine,
10. "You took your topknot from your head
    And tied us babies' hands and legs.
11. "Then you took your penknife (long) (keen) and sharp
    And pierced us babies' tender hearts.
12. "Its seven years to roll a stone
    And seven years to toll a bell.
13. "It's mother dear oh we can't tell
    Whether your portion is heaven or hell. (Bronson cited in Bakan 1971:39).

Phyllis Palgi (1973), in her report of a case of infanticide in contemporary Yemen, demonstrates the continued prevalence of this theme in patriarchal societies. In Islamic Yemen, premarital pregnancy is viewed as a horrible, shameful tragedy that disgraces the entire family. A young woman who was able to hide her pregnancy up to the birth of the baby killed the just-born infant at the prodding of her mother. The baby was then wrapped in a bundle and was given to the young woman's brother and uncle, who were not told the contents of the package. They were told to bury the bundle. They did not carry out their task, and the next day the infant's body was discovered and the mother was arrested:

The [young woman's] father first threatened to kill himself and his daughter, and then he fell ill. Later he said he could not understand what had happened: perhaps something supernatural caused the pregnancy. If not, it was rape by design—this other family, the family of the baby's father, wished to have revenge upon him. Furthermore, he stated categorically that a child produced from rape is *dirt*, a sinful object, and must be destroyed. In Yemen the authorities would have no problem in understanding this, he claimed. The mother remained bitter and angry, although she agreed that it would have been impossible for her daughter to tell what had happened that night. She felt cheated that she had always managed her family, and life in general, so successfully and new events had been stronger than she. It appears as if the family held council and it was decided that the mother would change her evidence. It was not her idea to kill the baby, she now maintained; the daughter was solely responsible. The daughter apparently obligingly changed her evidence accordingly. The rationale was simple: the mother was needed at home to look after her husband and small children. And in any case it was only Sara who really felt guilty. She told how she had sat opposite the baby, not seeing it until it sneezed. Suddenly she was confronted with the concrete evidence of her sin which she had denied for nine months and so blindly plunged with knife to destroy it and, perhaps, all her bad thoughts as well. (Palgi, 1973)

The child was killed to avoid a family scandal. In this patriarchal society, the killing of the child was a less onerous task than to bear the child and suffer the shame and ostracism that would inevitably occur not only to the unmarried woman but also to her entire family.

Infanticide continues to prevail in contemporary industrial societies, such as Japan, despite the prevalence and acceptability of abortion. It can be seen as one consequence of modernization and the breakdown of the traditional extended family system. Naomi Feigelson Chase (1975) reports that the Japanese have practiced infanticide for over 1000 years. During the feudal era, the 17th through the 19th centuries, infanticide served as a means of population control. The scarcity of resources and the economic burden of a large number of children caused farmers to kill their second and third sons at birth. Many females were spared because they could be sold into prostitution, servitude, or—for the more fortunate—they could become geishas. This practice, *Mabiki,* an agriculatural term that means thinning out, accounted for the death of 60,000 to 70,000 infants each year for a period of over 250 years (from about 1600 to the 1850s) in northern Japan alone. The practice was prohibited with the onset of industrialization. The national policy encouraged population growth for industry and the army.

After World War II, infanticide reappeared briefly, reaching a peak of 399 cases in 1948, but it then dropped for the next 10 years. In 1958 the incidence of infanticide began to rise. By 1973 more than 100 deaths were reported and an additional 110 children were found abandoned in Tokyo alone. Chase believes that the rise of infanticide and abandonment, despite the existence of a liberal abortion law and the widespread availability of contraceptives, is attributable to rapid urbanization and the shift from the traditional extended family to the more segmentalized nuclear family. Most cases of infanticide occur in nuclear families. A second factor is the belief that the young mother lacks the confidence to raise her children without the supports of the extended family. Infanticide in Japan is not due to promiscuity (illegitimacy) or cruel stepmothers. Chase observes that it is likely in families where the mother spends a lot of time alone with the baby. Chase cites another study that suggests that infanticide or abandonment may be one way of coping with unwanted children by unprepared Japanese mothers. In comparison, their American counterparts are more prone to child abuse.

In summary, infanticide may be seen as an extreme reaction to the stress of having children. It has been the basic practice for the handling of overpopulation. Sumner provides an apt concluding remark on the inherent conflicting relationship beween parents and children:

> Children add to the weight of the struggle for existence of their parents. The relations of parent to child is one of sacrifice. The interests of children and parents are antagonistic. The fact that there are, or may be, compensations does not affect the primary relation between the two. It may well be believed that, if procreation had not been put under the dominion of a great passion, it would have been caused to cease by the burdens it entails. Abortion and infanticide are especially interesting because they show how early in the history of civilization the burden of children became so heavy that parents began to shirk it. (1906:309 – 10)

The considerable attention spent on examining infanticide should not perplex the reader. For infanticide is logically related to child abuse. As David Bakan (1971) observed that there is a similar underlying motivation for both. The largest category of abused children are the very young. Abused children also suffer from systematic neglect. The result is that, over time, the injurious treatment of the child has a cumulative effect with a high proportion of abused children dying as a result of their injuries:

> Thus, the most parsimonious explanation of child abuse is that the parents are trying to kill the child. However, in our culture murder of children is a serious criminal offense. The method of cumulative trauma allows infanticide to take place with relative immunity from detection, prosectution, and conviction. (Bakan, 1971:56)

CHILD ABUSE IN AMERICA

The ideology that argues for the sanctity and privacy of the family household not only hides the extent of domestic violence between spouses but also prevents the full examination of the prevalencc of child abuse. In 1972 only 60,000 childabuse incidents were brought to the attention of governmental agencies. Five years later, the number passed the 500,000 figure. In 1977 the Nationl Center on Child Abuse and Neglect projected that between 100,000 and 200,000 children are regularly abused and assaulted by their parents. Compounding the problem of the reporting of incidents of child abuse is the fact that agents of social institutions—physicians, nurses, social workers, teachers, police, and judges—tend to report actual cases differentially. Particular statistics from given agencies and institutions may be typical only for them or for their geographic locality and may not be an accurate representation of the national rate.

Richard J. Gelles, in a recent study of child abuse, estimates that almost 4 percent of children under the age of 17 are subjected to abuse (Schumacher, 1978). This extrapolates to nearly 2 million children who are stabbed,kicked, bitten, punched, shot, or sexually molested by their own parents. This figure is double that estimated earlier by the Federal National Center on Child Abuse and Neglect. The growing awareness of child abuse and the resultant publicity has undoubtedly encouraged people increasingly to report incidents. The earlier figures compared to the later ones probably reflect our ignorance about the frequency of occurrence rather than indicating a startling new rise in the rate of child violence.

Child Abuse Is Twice as Common as Estimated Earlier, Study Finds

EDWARD SCHUMACHER

Nearly two million American children are stabbed, shot, kicked, bitten, punched or hit with an object each year—by one of their own parents.

The extent of the child-abuse problem in the United States was reported in a study, commissioned by the National Institute of Mental Health, that is to be made public today at a conference at the University of Pennsylvania.

"If we had two million children suffering from a communicable disease, it would be considered a major national epidemic, and people would be committing major resources," Richard J. Gelles, who directed the study, said. "Two million . . . That's twice the population of Rhode Island."

The study found that almost 4 percent of children under age 17 were subjected to abuse. The estimate is double what had been estimated previously by the federal government's National Center on Child Abuse and Neglect.

The center's estimates have been based, however, solely on the number of incidents of child abuse reported to authorities.

The estimate contained in the survey conducted by Gelles, a sociologist at the University of Rhode Island, was derived from interviews of members of more than 1,100 families in a national opinion sample drawn up by Response Analysis Co. of Princeton.

One of the most disturbing findings, Gelles said, is that parents under 30 years of age are 62 percent more likely to beat a child than are parents between the ages of 31 and 50.

"Our findings may indicate an increase in family violence," Gelles said in the study. "It is quite possible that our study has uncovered a violent generation under 30 years of age. This generation was the first to grow up in an age when the majority of all American families watched television and its nightly dose of violence."

Moreover, he said, the trend is likely to perpetuate itself, because when children who have been beaten become parents, they tend to beat their children.

The Gelles study provides the first comprehensive national profile of the type of parents most likely to beat a child, and it differs significantly from many earlier studies of smaller scope.

According to the Gelles survey:

- Black parents and white parents are equally likely to beat their children. Beatings by black parents, however, are more likely to be reported to authorities.
- The South, although it leads the country in homicide and gun ownership, has the lowest incidence of child abuse. The Midwest has the highest.
- Poor parents are much more likely to beat their children than middle-income or wealthy parents, contrary to earlier reports that family income has no relationship to child abuse.

Gelles cautioned that merely because parents may fit his national demographic profile, they should not be assumed to be child abusers. The vast majority of parents who share the characteristics he described do not beat their children, he said.

Concerning race, the study found that 14 percent of white parents interviewed had beaten a child hard enough to cause injuries at least once in the last year, compared with 15 percent of black parents.

"Although blacks experience economic and social oppression, which would lead one to expect high rates of abusive violence, they receive aid and support, especially in the care of children, from extended family and kinship ties," Gelles said.

Gelles said that he was surprised by the finding that there is more child abuse in the Midwest. He could offer no explanation.

According to the study, 19 percent of the families in the Midwest had incidence of child abuse, compared with 10 percent in the South. The percentages for the East and West were in between.

Parents in large cities tended to abuse children more than parents elsewhere. Nineteen percent of parents interviewed in large cities had abused their children, compared with 12 to 14 percent of parents who lived in small cities, suburbs and rural areas.

As for family income, the study found that 22 percent of parents with incomes of less than $6,000 abused children, double the percentage for parents with incomes of more than $20,000.

"Parents of all income levels use severe and abusive violence towards their children," Gelles said. "But the myth of classlessness does not hold up in light of our evidence."

The study found also that blue-collar parents were 45 percent more likely to abuse children than white-collar parents. Unemployed parents were 62 percent more likely to abuse children than employed parents.

Parents who were high school graduates had higher percentages of abuse—18 percent—than did either parents who were college graduates or parents who never had advanced beyond the eighth grade. Both of the latter groups had an 11 percent abuse rate.

Only 6 percent of Jewish parents surveyed had abused children, compared with almost 15 percent of Catholics and Protestants.

The study found virtually no difference between men and women. It did find, however, that families that were heavily dominated by either the mother or father tended more toward child abuse than families that were more democratic.

The two-day conference at Penn is sponsored jointly by Penn's Annenberg School of Communications and the Bush Center in Child Development and Social Policy at Yale University. More than 300 invited representatives from the federal government, the news media and the national academic community are expected to attend.

Edward Schumacher, *The Philadelphia Inquirer,* November 20, 1978. Reprinted by permission of The Philadelphia Inquirer.

Studies of abused children and their parents find it difficult to identify conclusively the traits of the abusive parent. Such parents come from the complete range of socioeconomic classes. Many potential child abusers are ''normal'' parents who overreact to the normal frustrations of being a parent:

Is there any mother or father who has not been ''provoked'' almost to the breaking point by the crying, wheedling, whining child? How many parents have not had moments of concern and self-recrimination about having, in anger, hit their own child much harder than they had expected they would? How many such incidents make a ''child abuser'' out of a normal parent? (Zalba, 1974:412−413)

Steele and Pollack (1968), in one of the early studies of what they termed the battered-child syndrome, found no particular psychopathologic or abnormal character types among the parents. What differentiated the abusive parent was an exaggeration of the contemporary pattern of childrearing:

There seems to be an unbroken spectrum of parental action towards children ranging from the breaking of bones and the fracturing of skulls through severe bruising, through severe spanking and on to mild ''reminder'' pats on the bottom. To be aware of this, one has only to look at the families of one's friends and neighbors, to look and listen to the parent-child interactions at the playground and the supermarket, or even to recall how one raised one's own children or how one was raised oneself. The amount of yelling, scolding, slapping, punching, hitting, and yanking acted out by parents on very small children is almost shocking. Hence we have felt that in dealing with the abused child we are not observing an isolated, unique phenomenon, but only the extreme form of what we would call a pattern or style of childrearing quite prevalent in our culture. (Steele and Pollack, 1968:104)

The realization of the extensity of this social problem reflects our increased realization that the contemporary private conjugal American family is not as conflict-free as previously idealized. Thus, although the privatization of the nuclear family has maximized emotional intensity, it has also made it problematic and difficult.

As we discussed earlier, the battered-child syndrome is not a new problem; it existed historically and it exists cross-culturally. What is new is the attempt to control child abuse legally. And, as we described previously in our analysis of the child-welfare movement, it has its drawbacks and deficiencies. An examination of the law regarding child abuse also reveals similar problems.

In the 19th century, the law supported the premise that the family is a private and sacred institution in which outsiders have little rights to intrude. As mentioned in Chapter 12, the first American legal action for child abuse was not brought about until 1874. Laws, in fact, were enacted to protect animals before there were laws to protect children. Indeed, the first child-abuse case was actually handled by the Society for the Prevention of Cruelty to Animals. In this first case, the child was treated under the rubric (legal rule) concerning a small animal. At about this time, problems of child abuse were handled loosely by various voluntary agencies. When court action was deemed necessary, the child was treated as a ''neglected'' or ''dependent'' child under the juvenile court laws.

Despite the recent existence of laws to protect the legal rights of children, the child-abuse statutes do not protect children adequately. There is great reluctance on the part of governmental agencies to prosecute parents or to remove the child from the home. Further, there is a natural queasiness by social agencies and by doctors and medical institutions to report cases: it is exceedingly difficult to accuse a parent who brings in a child for treatment. This is especially the case in incidents of child abuse among the middle class, where the parents may have the legal clout to contest the issue.

Most of the reported cases arise out of hospital admissions. Generally, these are clinic cases, where the parent or foster parent (of the poorer class) rushes a badly injured child to a hospital. Pediatricians in private practice are reluctant to report child-abuse cases. For example, in 1976 in Westchester County, New York (an affluent suburb of New York City), private physicians reported only 6 of the 891 cases of child abuse investigated by the local child-protective-services agency (Feron, 1977). David C. Honigs the director of the county's Child Protective Services Program questions whether private doctors even ask questions on how the child's injury occurred. One possible motive is the physician's desire to avoid the possibility of spending time in testifying in family courts. Further, they share the prevalent viewpoint of family court judges that public placement for the child may be far worse than returning the abused children to their parents.

Aggravating the problem is the lack of a unifying policy. This reflects the prevalent belief that deemphasizing the extent of child abuse and the reluctance to handle this problem. Social welfare people argue for joint planning and cooperative arrangements between government and private sectors, between agencies and voluntary groups. There is also a need on both the administrative and case level for parent training and self-help for abusing parents.

But, we are reluctant to invade the privacy and sanctity of the home. If and when we do, we have become increasingly aware that the prosecution of negligent and abusive parents does not solve the problem of the victimized children or their parents. Programs designed to treat these parents to maintain the structural integrity of the family are woefully inadequate. In addition, the removal of children from their homes and placement in foster homes or other placement facilities may have negative consequences.

Related to the issue of parental versus social control is the extent to which our society is willing to make investments in broad-based social services that are supportive of the family structure and protective of children. Unfortunately, caught in the dilemma of values supporting parental privacy, control, and autonomy and the desire to avoid overzealous intervention by social agencies, all too frequently the child is victimized.

Although while it is beyond the scope of this discussion to present comprehensive solutions to the problem of child abuse, the following passage written by Serapio R. Zalba may provide some initial guidelines:

> What, then, is to be done about child abuse? We cannot wait for all men and women to become angels to their children. One sensible, concrete proposal has been made to offer preventive mental and social hygiene services at the most obvious points of stress in the family. One such point is reached when a child is born and introduced into the family. This may be especially true for the first child, when husband and wife must now take on the additional roles of father and mother. Assistance for men and women who seem under unusual strain because of this role might lead to fewer incidents of child abuse. More effective remedial efforts will await our willingness to spend greater sums of money on community-based health and welfare services. Protective services are under-staffed for the number of cases requiring their help and surveillance. And, the additional child care resources—whether they are institutions or paid individual or group foster homes—require additional sources if they are to be adequate either in terms of the number of children they can handle or in the quality of personnel. (Zalba, 1974:408)

In summary, what complicates the treatment of child abuse is the prevailing tension between the rights of parents and the intervention of social agencies. Since the privatization of the family, parental rights regarding the rearing of children have been of paramount importance. However, as we have been indicating, there has been a gradual encroachment of helping agencies, which provide "expert" advice and which ultimately subvert the autonomy of the family. In cases of child abuse, society finds itself in a dilemma. It is reluctant to interfere with parental perrogatives and often leaves the child in the family and subject to further neglect and abuse. Taking the child from the home, on the other hand, often means subjecting the child to inadequate foster-care programs and institutional facilities.

CONCLUSION

This chapter was concerned with two manifestations of family violence—wife battering and child abuse. Both were depicted as irrational outgrowths of the excesses of patriarchal ideology. In the first case, wife battering, we sought to demonstrate that the legitimation of male perrogatives, privilege, authority, and power can be abused, and too often it is. This results in the severe mistreatment of women. Both cross-cultural and historical evidence was sighted. However, our predominant concern was to study contemporary American society and its recent "discovery" of the prevalence of marital abuse. We indicated that structural conditions inherent in the private conjugal factor play a contributory role. Further, the belief that "normal" conjugal marriages are happy and well adjusted and that violence is an aberration has led to the underestimation of such abuse and to the treatment of it erroneously as a psychologically determined pathology and not as a social phenomenon.

The second topic covered was child abuse. In many ways this discussion can be seen as a continuation of our previous analysis of childhood and adolescence. We stressed that the conceptualization of children and adolescence as essentially inferior and subordinate human beings makes them particularly vulnerable to child abuse. Here again, structural characteristics of the conjugal family plays an important contributory role. Governmental policies and the underlying assumptions of the helping professions too often work against the best interests of children.

15

Divorce, Single Parenthood, and Remarriage

There are many internal and external situations, events, and activities that require major readjustments on the part of the family. These include death and physical disabilities and illnesses; social and psychological maladjustments, such as mental illness, alcoholism, and drug abuse; marital infidelity, separations, desertions, and divorce; and family violence. External factors that also play a role in family instability include war, unemployment, poverty, and such catastrophes as floods and earthquakes. All of these require changing conceptualizations by family members of their marital and family-role definitions. For example, the women's movement has necessitated the rethinking of family roles for all members of the family as has new-role conceptualizations regarding the aged, children, and youth. In this section we will focus on divorce and see how divorce processes and outcomes are responded to by different family systems.

The "Widows" of Italy Whose Husbands Emigrate and Return Only as Visitors

CHRISTINE LORD

GRAVINA DI PUGLIA, Italy—After a short visit home, Ferdinando Aliano decided to postpone his departure a day, to have more time with his family. The next morning, he boarded an overcrowded train for a 15-hour journey to Stuttgart, Germany. He stood in the aisle the whole way. On arrival, because of the extra day spent at home, he went straight from the railroad to his job as a miner.

His wife, Rafaella, lives here with their children, now 17, 15 and 12 years old. The two youngest have never seen their father for more than a month at a time twice a year. After four years of marriage, he left to seek work in Germany. That was more than 15 years ago.

Mrs. Aliano, 42 years old, is one of the women known in the Italian south as "white widows." They are the women left behind when their husbands emigrated to north Europe or northern Italy.

Like widows, these women bear alone the burden of raising the children, making decisions and keeping a family together, often working outside the home as well. Unlike real widows, they are not free to look for a husband because they are already married.

Since the end of World War II, an estimated six million Italians, mostly men, have emigrated abroad in search of jobs. Still others have gone to the industrialized north of the country to work in plants such as the Fiat auto company in Turin. It is estimated that one out of eight families in Italy lives off the earnings of emigrants and that there are one million white widows, the majority illiterate.

White widows speak knowledgeably about Italy's balance of payments deficit, which is narrowed appreciably by the money their husbands send back into Italy from abroad. They feel bitterness about what they see as the nation seeking to assuage its bad economic situation at their husbands' expense.

Last Easter, Ferdinando was home for five days. For the second-class train fare, he spent nearly $100 out of a paycheck that rarely exceeds $450 a month.

With poignant pride, Mrs. Aliano told a visitor recently how her husband washes his own clothes and cooks his own meals in his shabby room in Stuttgart, to be able to send as much money home to the family as possible. She herself works as hired help in the fields around Gravina, a town 40 miles inland from Bari.

"The first years were much sadder," said Mrs. Aliano. "But we have managed. We had to. We had no choice because there were no jobs here."

"Still," she reflected, "the kids feel the lack of a father. They don't eat so well when he's not here."

Not unexpectedly, the children are the most vulnerable. "The role of the father is one of the fundamental things a southern boy has to deal with," said a southerner living in Rome. "The mother can be a figure of authority as long as he's young, but once he's reached adolescence he needs a father figure. Instead, these boys are often without guidance, or else have to fill in themselves as head of the family to the younger children without ever having really known their own father."

Mrs. Aliano and her husband are deeply attached. She has managed to pass on to the children an image of their father that has remained real to them despite his infrequent visits home. They look forward twice a year to the day he will arrive, and when he is home there is a festive air about the house.

It would never occur to Mrs. Aliano not to feel that she is Ferdinando's wife. The idea that she might be tempted to take up with another man seems foreign to her.

The dramatic cases of emigrants who, after years abroad, marry a local woman and end up with two wives and two sets of children, are almost impossible to document but appear to be less common than is generally thought. But it is almost taken for granted that most emigrants establish some unofficial second relationship to help relieve the unmitigated grind of their daily existence.

These second relationships, however, do not necessarily mean the breakup of a marriage.

"No one wants to say it, but often the wife alone has a companion the same way the emigrant has a girlfriend," said Graziella Praturlon, a Rome social worker. "Such relationships may help keep the family stable temporarily, but they really are just a palliative," she said.

The children of Angelo Lo Russo have long grown accustomed to not having a father.

"When they were little, they used to ask when he'd come home. Now they don't bother to ask. They're almost indifferent," their mother said, sitting in the family's roomy kitchen.

Her husband left Gravina 19 years ago for Germany, after just two years of marriage. He would like to come back, but so far has not found any possibility of work in his native town.

Mrs. Lo Russo, who lives with her three children and her husband's aging mother, sees her husband about four times a year.

"As soon as he arrives, I start dreading the day he'll have to leave," she said. Her face is worn. "When you're alone you always worry whether you're doing the right thing with decisions about the children, how to spend what money there is. Sometimes I don't know where to turn."

Francesco Compagna, a 53-year-old Neapolitan who is minister for the south in the present government, suggests that emigration "may be the lesser of two evils" compared to unemployment.

"The emigrant acquires reverence and respect from his family, because he sends money home so the family can live," he said in an interview recently. "These are not just men who run off; they're men who write home from some lonely rooming house or shack because they are concerned with providing for their family."

Christine Lord in *The New York Times,* August 20, 1979. ©1979 by The New York Times Company. Reprinted by permission.

Greater attention is given to divorce than other forms of marital dissolution because it often represents the culmination of other types of family disruption. In this, we follow the example of William J. Goode (1976)—one of the few structure functionalists who has given extensive attention to family disorganization—who reasons that differential consideration should be given to the study of divorce ''because so many other types of family disorganization are likely to end in divorce sooner or later, because it is the focus of so much moral and personal concern, and because changes in the divorce rate are usually an index of changes in other elements in the family patterns of any society'' (Goode, 1976:517).

The United States has the highest divorce rate among industrialized societies. The noted demographer, Paul C. Glick (1975), reports that other societies with high divorce rates include the USSR, Hungary, and Cuba. Other societies that have had high divorce rates in the recent past include Japan (1887–1919) and Egypt (1935–1954). In Table 15:1 comparative divorce rates are presented to illustrate some of these trends. In this discussion we will first examine divorce in the United States and why it has risen in the 20th century. Then, we will look at the situation in Japan and Egypt and try to explain why the divorce rate has declined in these societies.

Our attention will also de drawn to the common opinion that the high frequency of divorce is associated with the decline of marriage and threatens the very existence of the family. Tied to this belief is the feeling that contemporary marriages are less harmonious and gratifying than ''traditional'' marriages. Further, the argument follows that a lowering of the divorce rate would enhance the stability of the family. We will examine the assumptions underlying these beliefs and will test their validity by looking at the implications of divorce for the individual, the family, and the society.

Table 15.1   Divorces per 1000 Marriages in Selected Countries, 1890–1974

Country	1890	1900	1910	1920	1930	1940	1950	1971–1974
United States	55.6	75.3	87.4	133.3	173.9	165.3	231.7	424.0[c]
Germany[a]		17.6	29.9	40.7	72.4	125.7	145.8	186.0[d]
England and Wales				8.0	11.1	16.5	86.1	279.0[e]
France	24.3	26.1	46.3	49.4	68.6	80.4	106.9	117.0[f]
Sweden		12.9	18.4	30.5	50.6	65.1	147.7	380.0[g]
Egypt					269.0[b]	273.0	273.0	204.0[h]
Japan	335.0	184.0	131.0	100.0	98.0	76.0	100.0	98.0[i]

Sources: Adapted from William J. Goode. 1976. ''Family Disorganization.'' In Robert K. Merton and Robert Nisbet (eds.), *Contemporary Social Problems* (4th ed.). New York: Harcourt Brace Jovanovich, p. 526. Reprinted by permission of the publisher. All figures calculated from governmental sources and from United Nations. 1974. *Demographic Yearbook,* New York: United Nations.

Note: A better measure of divorce frequency is the number of divorces per 1000 existing marriages, but the latter figure is not often available. The above rate compares marriages in a given year, with divorces occurring to marriages from *previous* years. However, changes from one year to another or differences among countries may be seen just as clearly by this procedure.

[a] 1950–1971, West Germany.
[b] 1935.
[c] 1974.
[d] 1971.
[e] 1972.
[f] 1971.
[g] 1972.
[h] 1971.
[i] 1972.

We will conclude by analyzing changes in divorce laws that reflect changes in traditional concepts of marriage and the family. Coming under scrutiny will be the consequences of divorce for the resultant single-parent family. Our analysis ends with a discussion of family structures and the dynamics of remarriage.

DIVORCE IN NON-WESTERN SOCIETIES

We will begin our analysis by looking at divorce in preliterate societies. George Murdock (1950) has compiled systematic cross-cultural descriptive data on divorce in 40 small and preliterate societies in Asia, Africa, Oceania, and North and South America. In all but one society (the Incas), institutionalized provisions existed for dissolving marriages; in three-fourths of these societies both sexes had equal rights to initiate divorce. Murdock estimates that divorce rates in about 60 percent of all preliterate societies are higher than in the United States. On the basis of these findings, he concluded that: ''Despite the widespread alarm about increasing 'family disorganization' in our society, the comparative evidence makes it clear that we shall remain with the limits which human experience has shown that societies can tolerate with safety'' (Murdock, 1950:197).

The higher divorce rates in preliterate societies does not mean that divorce is associated with social disorganization. The society reintegrates the divorced person into the family and that person is not stigmatized and can remarry. Further, a variety of devices are employed to preserve the stability of marital relationships. These include prohibitions against incest, dowries and bride prices, and parental influence and supports. A most important stabilizing practice is the custom of vesting parents with the right to arrange the marriage for their sons and daughters. In societies where marriages are arranged, marriage is usually not defined by characteristics associated with Western romantic love. These marriages do not exhibit the same degree of intimacy and emotionality as their Western counterpart for they are not based on the personal attraction between the persons getting married. Their solidarity derives from the obligations, duties, and rights of members of consanguineally related extended families.

High divorce rates can, and often are, associated with stable extended family systems. When divorce does occur, there are clear norms that specify what will happen to family members after the separation. Many societies have provisions for the reintegration of the divorced husband and divorced wife back into their respective kinship group. The children usually remain within the prevailing unilineage's locality. Further, high divorce rates do not necessarily mean that the family system is being undermined nor is it necessarily associated with societal disorganization. High divorce rates may not reflect family breakdown; in fact, they may reflect culturally prescribed ways of eliminating disruptive influences.

Family sociologists have found it useful to distinguish between the instability of the family unit and the instability of the family system in a given society. William J. Goode (1966) points out that both types of instability must be distinguished from social change and family disorganization. He observes that high divorce rates have been common in many Arab Islamic societies for centuries, and they did not reflect, until recently—when the divorce rate declined—changes in the family system. The high divorce rate remained unchanged for many generations and the essential structure of the Arab family created it and has coped with it.

Goode further observes that the direction of change in the divorce rate of a given family system depends on the characteristics of the system prior to the onset of change. For example, the divorce rate in Arabic Islam and in Japan were decreasing rather than increasing when the reverse pattern was occurring in the West. Thus, he reaches the somewhat paradoxical conclusion that social change, rather than bringing about disorganization, may actually reduce the rates of occurrence of such disorganization phenomena as divorce:

> With respect to change, it is evident that if the rates of occurrence of major family happenings, such as the percentage eventually marrying, percentage married at certain

ages, divorce rates, fertility, patterns and so on, are changing, then it may be that the family system is also changing and that at least some parts of it are dissolving or undergoing disorganization. On the other hand, some of these changes may actually reduce the rates of occurrence of such phenomena classically called "disorganization," such as divorce, separation, illegitimacy or desertion. Thus, for example, the rate of desertion has been dropping in the United States. In Latin American countries in the process of industrialization, with all its predictable *anomie,* the rate of illegitimacy has been dropping. Japan's family system has been undergoing great changes over the past generation and thus by definition certain parts of it must have been "dissolving," but the divorce rate has steadily dropped. Finally, even though the old family patterns may be dissolving, they may be replaced by new ones which control as determinately as the old. (Goode, 1962/1966:388).

These conclusions bring us to our next concern: Why are divorce rates changing in contemporary societies? Goode (1963), in his influential *World Revolution and Family Patterns,* attributes the relatively high divorce rates in the West to the emergence of the conjugal family system and the decline of the consanguineal extended family system. The large kin groups associated with unilineage systems in Non-western societies subordinate their younger members and arrange their marriages. Love as a basis for marriage is discouraged as the affectional ties between the couple may undermine their loyalty to the extended family. Nothing is permitted to conflict with the obligations and loyalties one has to the larger kin group. The development of the conjugal family leads to the assumption that greater emotional ties between husband and wife will be present. The diminished importance of the larger family group removes the alternative source for emotional sustenance and gratification. The conjugal relationship now becomes all important. The consequent mutual dependence of spouses on one another for support combined with the comparative isolation of the conjugal unit from kin fosters a relatively more unstable relationship with a concomitant rise in the divorce rate.

Thus the emotions within this unit are likely to be intense, and the relationship between husband and wife may well be intrinsically unstable, depending as it does on affection. Consequently, the divorce rate is likely to be high. (Goode, 1963:9)

Goode cites the experiences of Japan and Arabic Islam to provide the illustrative cases of cultures whose high divorce rates have declined in the 20th century. He attributes this decline to the development of the independent conjugal family. A brief examination of Japan and a somewhat more detailed look at Islamic Egypt will demonstrate some of the dynamics operating in the lowering of the divorce rate.

Divorce Around the World: Even When Easy, It Carries a Stigma

NAN ROBERTSON

PARIS—Last May's referendum on divorce, Italian style, reached heights of passion topped by the absurd. In Sicily, Amintore Fanfani, a former Premier who dominates the powerful Christian Democratic party, warned darkly that unless the divorce legislation were repealed, Italian wives would desert their men en masse to flee with lesbians.

The divorce reform—one of the most conservative in Europe—passed anyway.

Curiously, the most drastic recent push for equalizing the rights of women, including the right to divorce, came in Italy's former colony of Somalia, a Moslem nation gone Socialist. There, 10 local sheikhs who opposed women's lib were executed last January.

Reports from New York Times' correspondents around the world tend to show that neither is opinion as traditionalist on the issue of divorce as in Italy nor are governments as radically egalitarian as in Somalia.

Divorce is easiest in India and Japan, but it brings social stigma and loss of face. It is most difficult in Latin America—unless one is rich. Thus, Antinor Patiño, the tin multimillionaire, once paid Bolivia $5 million to pass a law applying only to him that untied his nuptial knot with a Bourbon princess.

A divorce law is around the corner in Brazil, the world's biggest Roman Catholic country, with 100 million persons, including a lot of sinners.

Scandinavia, Switzerland and Germany have liberal divorce statutes. So now does Britain. In both Britain and France, controversies endure about what makes a valid motive for divorce. The French Parliament has been debating a Government proposal that attempts to abolish the worst anomalies and injustices.

Divorce was voted by Italy's Parliament on Dec. 1, 1970 after a bitter controversy between supporters of the Roman Catholic Church and the Vatican—unswervingly against divorce—and the so-called "lay forces," which maintained that matters such as divorce should be left to individual conscience.

After the law passed, those opposing divorce—spearheaded by conservatives in the Christian Democratic party—immediately called for a national referendum to repeal it. Almost three times as many as the necessary half-million signatures asking for a referendum were collected.

The referendum was finally held on Mother's Day last May. The date was amply exploited by divorce opponents.

They lost, but the upheld divorce law can hardly be placed in the vanguard of liberal social thinking. Divorce now can be granted after a de facto, legal separation of five years.

To the surprise of nearly everybody, the rate of divorce since has been rather low in Italy: fewer than 100,000 to date in a nation of 55 million people. An overwhelming majority of the Italians to whom divorces have been granted had already been separated from their spouses for more than 20 years.

Moslem Nations

The bloody enforcement of sexual equality in the "scientific Socialist" nation of Somalia overturned custom. In this and other Moslem countries a man could cast off his wife simply by saying: "I divorce you" three times.

The new Somalia decree allows divorce on grounds similar to those in Western nations, such as incompatibility, desertion and cruelty. Either the husband or wife can initiate action in court and either party may contest or agree to the divorce.

In most Arab Moslem countries, marriage as well as divorce is religious rather than civil. But in states such as Syria, Algeria, Tunisia and Iraq, Moslem courts will now also have to agree before a divorce becomes legal.

India

In many tribal communities in India, divorce means just walking across to another woman or man, as the case may be. Despite greatly relaxed divorce statutes passed 20 years ago, social stigmas still apply to the divorce and remarriage of Hindu women.

Japan

Legally speaking, getting a divorce in Japan is simple. If the couple agrees on the divorce (and 90 per cent of them do) they just march down to their local ward office and submit a form that has been signed by two adult witnesses. The cost is nominal. In the agreement must be a decision of who takes custody of any children they have.

In the few cases where a divorce is contested, either party can ask for one on any of five grounds—conjugal infidelity, abandonment with malicious intent, the whereabouts of a spouse unknown for more than three years, a spouse with an incurable and serious mental disease, and other grave reasons that make continuing the marriage difficult.

Breaking up a marriage involves many more people than just the husband and wife. And . . . for allowing their differences to come out in public and for admitting defeat, the two of them lose face, an important consideration in that part of the world. More important—and the source of great social pressure to stay together—are the parents on each side, the marriage go-between, the families and anyone else involved in the marriage in the first place. All lose face.

That doesn't mean that divorced persons are outcasts in Japan. The Governor of Tokyo, Ryokichi Minobe, who is 70, was divorced about 20 years ago and later remarried and yet has had a successful political career. Indeed, much of his support comes from upper middle-class women who are drawn to his refined manners and gentle ways. Divorced women can also make their way in Japanese society. But it's very difficult and is thus liable to discourage all but the most unhappily married or the strongest in character.

Latin America

In Latin America, roadblocks to divorce are no problem for the well-to-do, as the case of Bolivia's Patiño dramatically illustrates. (In the end, before the special law granting him his divorce went into force, the impatient Patiño got a quick decree in Mexico.)

The vast majority of South Americans are not so lucky. With the exception of Uruguay, Spanish-speaking Latin America still is frozen in restrictive divorce legislation.

ARGENTINA

The late Argentinian President, Juan Domingo Perón, rammed through a divorce law during his first era in power in December, 1954. He did it probably in a fit of pique at the Catholic church and succeeded in antagonizing it further—which proved an important factor in his downfall.

The military government that took over after Perón's fall in 1955 immediately suspended the divorce law. Attempts to restore it or pass a new one have repeatedly failed, although recent opinion polls indicate that two-thirds of Argentine Catholics favor some sort of change in divorce laws.

URUGUAY

Uruguay's legislation dates back to the beginning of the century and has attracted disgruntled middle-class and wealthy couples from nearby countries. The principal grounds usually cited for divorce are "incompatibility of character, disputes and arguments."

Foreigners are required to establish permanent residence in Uruguay to obtain divorce papers, but in practice this can usually be accomplished through a "broker" who steers the couple through the bureaucratic red tape. Other couples establish residence by spending the summer months—January and February—at the Punta del Este, a chic Atlantic beach resort.

BRAZIL

In Brazil, a bill to amend the Constitution to permit divorces to couples who have been separated legally for five years or in fact for seven has finally been presented before the Legislature.

Brazil does have an institution called "desquite," a form of legal separation that splits residences and other property. But that is the end of the road. It does not permit remarriage, so more people separate without legal formalities than those who take the legal steps.

Maritza Osorio, the widow of a prominent businessman in Rio de Janeiro, said: "Without divorce, people get together and separate with the greatest of ease. I have a hundred friends who do not have the slightest embarrassment in introducing a new woman every year. A new marriage would give them more responsibility."

And Helo Amado, a society woman commented: "The question should be, are you in favor of marriage? The need for divorce is so obviously necessary that it is silly to have to explain why. It is to legalize a situation that exists in fact."

SOVIET UNION

Divorce in the Soviet Union of the Stalin years was difficult, time-consuming and tedious and could cost a worker up to five months' pay. Changes in 1965 made it relatively simple; the cost is now about $140 or less.

Local courts handle cases of mutual consent within a few months. The rate of divorce has been climbing since the change. In 1974 there were 28 divorces for every 100 marriages. The public attitude is generally sophisticated. Judges make some effort to persuade couples to get back together, but despite the Government's desire for a population increase there has been no campaign for people to stay married.

SWEDEN

In Sweden, a new divorce law went into effect last year. Each spouse has an unconditional right to a divorce. It is now legally of no importance what motive he or she might have for wanting to end a marriage, nor is the court, as before, required to examine the reasons.

A six-month period of "reconsideration" applies when one of the couple has custody of a child under 16. This need not be observed when the parents have lived apart for two years.

No question of blame affects the decision of which parent shall have custody, if both are equally suitable. The court is charged to hand down the ruling from the "standpoint of the child's best interests only."

WEST GERMANY

In West Germany a change in divorce court procedures that will greatly speed up judgments seems certain to pass the Parliament by the end of this year. A bill now in committee would allow divorce merely on grounds of a "broken marriage" rather than overt guilty actions by the partners. Alimony would become purely a question of economic need.

SWITZERLAND

The grounds for divorce set forth in the Swiss civil code are so broad that any couple can obtain a divorce without difficulty. If both partners agree—and with only slightly more trouble even if one is opposed.

They include adultery, threats of physical violence, insanity, "grave insults" and a catch-all provision that says divorce should be granted if the bonds of marriage have been so distended that life together has become "insupportable."

FRANCE

Divorce in France is often an orchestrated masquerade in which the two principal parties, the lawyers and the judge must collaborate in order to circumvent the existing law. This includes writing false, abusive letters. Under the 171-year-old Napoleonic civil code, the guilt of one of the spouses must be determined even if they fully agree beforehand that they wish to end the marriage.

The Government has just drafted a bill allowing divorce by mutual consent, as well as for other reasons long accepted in the United States and other Western democracies. The French Parliament will debate the proposals this spring.

BRITAIN

Britain's existing legislation on divorce went into force in 1971. The main purpose of the act was to make the "irretrievable breakdown" of a marriage a criterion of divorce. The definition of cruelty was broadened to include incompatibility.

The Times of London complained that "the familiar matrimonial offenses" also remained as grounds for divorce. "It is quite wrong," The Times said, "to assume that one isolated instance of adultery is evidence that a marriage is finished."

Sir Neville Faulks, a judge of the family division of the High Court, put this objection in more down-to-earth terms during a divorce case last fall.

"All you have to do," he said, "is fill your wife with gin, giver her a complaisant lodger and file your petition next day . . . or a husband might just say he found it intolerable to live with his wife because she wears pink knickers or nothing at all."

The new law, apart from effectively broadening the definition of cruelty, allows divorce after a couple has lived apart for two years with the consent of both parties; or after five years against the will of one spouse.

One illustration of the British law in action: the case of a wife who, after 20 years of marriage, recently filed for divorce on the ground that her husband had behaved in such a way that it was unreasonable to expect her to live with him.

The wife complained that her husband, a do-it-yourself enthusiast, tore up the floorboards of their home and that two years later the floorboards were still up. Not only that—the husband had taken to mixing cement in the living room.

A county court judge dismissed the wife's petition, quoting from the marriage ceremony the words, "for better or for worse."

An appeals court judge finally allowed her a divorce. He ruled that "such matters are to be judged not by the language of the prayer book, but the language of the statute."

DIVORCE IN JAPAN

Goode (1963:321−365) reports that in the early Meiji period of the late 1860s and 1870s as well as for many prior generations, Japan had a high divorce rate in a very stable society. Marital instability did not affect the stability of the family system nor did it undermine Japanese social structure.

The Japanese conception of marriage and divorce differed from that of the West. They were neither sacramental affairs nor a concern of the state. Marriage was arranged by extended families through go-betweens. The typical pattern after marriage was for the wife to move into her husband's family's household. This was especially true for the wealthier families. But, regardless of wealth, the wife was expected to accommodate herself to her in-laws. This included showing deference, respect, and obeying them by performing all the assigned tasks. Failure to comply or meet the approval of in-laws would result in the termination and repudication of the marriage. This was done without regard to the relationship between the woman and her spouse.

This system permitted rather free divorce and the divorce rate was higher in the lower social strata than in the upper strata. Goode attribuges this to a system that allowed noblemen to obtain concubines if marital problems existed. If a wife got along with her in-laws and if she bore sons, the marriage continued. For the purpose of marriage was not for the emotional gratification of the couple but rather for the development of the extended family alliances. Divorce could be too disruptive and could cause unnecessary conflict between the two families.

In a later work, Goode (1976) presents statistical data (see Table 15:1) that reveals that the Japanese divorce rate has declined since 1890. He sees this decline as related to the increased proportion of marriages that are based on personal choice or preference and only then approved by the respective parents. The result is that the relationship between spouses has increased in importance as the influence of the extended family has declined in importance.

DIVORCE IN EGYPT

Table 15.1 also documents that the divorce rate has declined in Egypt, an Arab Islamic society. Goode attributes this lowering of the divorce rate to the loss of the absolute right of a man to repudiate and divorce his wife. ". . . Where the union under the earlier system was fragile because of the elders, as in Japan, or dependent on the whim of the man, as in Arab countries, the new system, with its greater independence of the young couple, more intense emotional ties of husband and wife with one another, and the increased bargaining power of the woman may mean a somewhat greater stability of the family unit'' (Goode, 1976:528).

Islam derived its origins in seventh century Arabia. It reflected a combination of the seminomadic tribal and the feudal conditions present at that time. Prior to the rise of Islam, women had no rights and were viewed as qualitatively different and inferior to men. With Islam, the position of women greatly improved. Women were freed from the domination of the male. This social revolution included the right to education, the right to buy and sell property, and the right to hold a job and go into a business. Islam gave women legal rights and protections that were incorporated into the Koran as a series of permissions and prohibitions that have continued to be influential to this day. Islam, then, as an integral religion formulated a total pattern of living rather than focusing primarily on theology.

From the perspective of pre-Islamic Arab society, Islam appeared as a great social revolution in the history of women's rights. Unfortunately, as the centuries proceeded, the advances of Islam stagnated and reversed. Influenced by pre-Islamic culture, a strong tradition developed that led to the exclusion of Arab women totally from the world of public affairs. We have observed how the veil and the gradual exclusion of women from the public world has lowered the general status of women, has reduced their awareness of the subjugation of their rights, and has robbed them of the opportunity to exercise those rights. Eventually, men gained dominance over women. This dominance included not only power over women's involvement in public matters, including business, wealth, and education, but also in private matters regarding marriage, the family, and in personal decisions regarding their own destiny. Islam has come to emphasize patriarchal authority of the husband-father along with the corresponding subservience of women and children. The marriage bond is subsumed under patriarchal authority and polygyny and easy divorce are permitted.

The situation has begun to change with the liberating and social revolutionary movements of recent times. In the Arab countries today, there is a recognition that to develop and achieve national identities and goals, the equality of women must be achieved. The more Westernized segment of the Arab population have been in the forefront of the movement to achieve and regain women's rights. But this view is held by only a small, rather limited group. Even in those Arab countries that have sought to reestablish women's legal rights there is a large segment of the population that has been fighting a successful battle to deny these rights. The situation in Egypt is a good case in point. Although a new constitution has been written that is very strong in securing equality for women in public matters, it is weak in terms of achieving equality in personal matters within the family structure. Aminah al-Sa'id, a leading Egyptian feminist, voices the opinion that:

> If we look at the new Egyptian constitution which in my opinion is one of the leading documents in terms of women's emancipation, we find it rich in laws designed to assure equality between men and women *except* in matters relating to personal status. These laws (The *Shari'ah*, or canon, laws governing the family, divorce, inheritance, marriage) were established in the time of ignorance and are based on faulty interpretations which are no longer suitable for the needs and the spirit of our institution within the nation, that is, the family, the fact that they are still in operation leads to the biggest contradictions to be found in our new life. It is hard for the mind to connect these two situations: the home and family situation, in which the Arab woman's position is very weak, and the public and social situation, in which she has achieved so many victories—victories which hae placed her in important cabinet posts, in positions as deputy ministers in the government, as judges in the courts, and as representatives in important economic and political conferences (al-Sa'id, 1977:385).

An examination of Egyptian marriage and family conditions today provide the necessary evidence to support her sentiments.

The pre-Islamic inhabitants of the Arabian Peninsula had no limitations on the number of wives a man was allowed. The Koran, although permitting a man to have as many as four wives, signifies a rise in the status of women. Further, it restricts the men to provide equal treatment, both sexually and in the matter of support. Indeed, it was this Koranic provision that justified the legal prohibition against polygyny in 1955 in Tunisia. The view taken was that it was an obvious impossibility for wives to be treated equally, and thus polygyny was specifically disapproved; few Islamic men ever managed to obtain more than one wife at a time (Goode, 1963). Informal forces against polygyny are strong and its economic advantages are minimal.

Divorce has been the alternative method for having more than one wife during the course of one's life. Divorce in Islam is the unlimited right of the man, provided he follows the proscribed forms. Women do not have the same rights of divorce as men. According to Islamic law, a husband is allowed to divorce his wife by simply saying, "I divorce thee," three times before two witnesses. The husband need have no ground for divorce. However, it is rarely used. The more typical pattern is for a final and terminal divorce to go through three stages. During the first two stages a man may remarry the same woman. But should he divorce her a third time, he is forbidden to remarry her unless in the meantime she has been married and divorced by another man. Forbidding remarriage to a thrice-divorced couple follows the logic that they have not and probably will not be able to get along in the future. The pronouncement "I divorce thee," three times on the same occasion counts as a triple divorce and remarriage must follow this same rule. Therefore, it is rarely used.

Goode (1963) asserts that this procedure disproves the popularly supposed belief held by non-Moslems that the male perogative of divorce is unqualified under Islam: "The Koranic tradition did not evaluate divorce very highly: 'Of all that he has permitted, God detests nothing more than divorce' " (Goode, 1963:155). Koranic tradition assumed that a man would not express the formula, "I divorce thee," three times at a single conflict. Rather, ethical injunctions held that only after three successive trials would a man finally and irrevocably divorce a woman. The usual pattern was that, after the first conflict, a husband could reverse the divorce process merely by living together with her again within a three-month period, the *'iddah:*

> The *'iddah* is a period during which the woman cannot marry another man. Its main purpose is to make sure that, if the woman is carrying a child fathered by the husband, there will be no conflict regarding paternity. If the husband does not take back his wife during the *'iddah* period, he cannot thereafter do so without a new contract. The divorce in the latter case is called *ba'in,* or absolute, in contrast to the *rag'i,* or temporary divorce during the *'iddah* period. If the husband exercises his right of absolute divorce three times, he cannot remarry his wife unless the latter is married first to another man, or *muhallal,* and then divorced by him. (Mohsen, 1974:41)

The emphasis in Koranic tradition, therefore, is placed not on the simplicity of the verbal formula, but on the necessity of the three stages before the dissolution is completed. However, although Islamic strictures hold divorce seriously, the extraordinarily high rate of divorce leads one to conclude that the religious tradition is not strictly followed. One explanation is that divorce is not viewed with the same stigma and negative consequences for women as it is in most Western Christian societies. Goode (1963) observes that, under the Arab institutional structure, the wife's family does not pressure an unhappy wife to remain in an unsatisfactory marriage. If her divorce is irrevocable, when she returns to her family they can obtain another bride price for her.

Smock and Youseff (1977), in their study of women's roles and statuses in Egyptian society, found that the proportion of adult women reported in a census count as "currently divorced" was only 2 percent in 1960 and 1.7 percent in 1966. They attribute this low figure to the fact that most divorced women are young and remarry quickly. Further, the woman's extended family has moral and financial obligations to provide her status placement and economic support. Children, if any, are not a problem because the legal code and religious family statutes assign guardianship of young children to either the maternal or paternal grandparents. The slight social stigma attached to divorce allows the divorced woman to be placed back on the marriage market and to compete with single girls: "All these factors produce a situation in which the divorced woman is thought of as an 'expectant wife' and as such is often subjected to the same family restrictions and controls imposed on the single girls so as to secure a remarriage that will reflect favorably on her own standing and that of her family" (Smock and Youseff, 1977:46).

Of particular interest to us is the effect of modernization processes on the traditional Islamic way of life. Egypt, which has been in the forefront of social change, makes an interesting case study on how Westernization has affected Islamic divorce practices. Mohsen (1974) observes that there have been legal changes that aim at achieving the equality of women. However, "despite the appearance of modernity, the attitude toward the role of women in public life—as well as in private—still remains a fairly conservative one" (Mohsen, 1974:38). Mohsen's analysis concentrates on practices and attitudes relative to the role of those women who have been most immediately affected by Western ideas—urban middle-class and upper middle class women.

The divorce laws in Egypt have been changed to make it easier for a woman to obtain a divorce. Yet, economic factors are an important deterrant, preventing unhappily married women from resorting to divorce. This is especially true for women who have no independent financial resources and who must rely on their parents. If children are involved, even more pressure is placed on the woman to remain with her husband. Her family does not wish to assume the responsibility of child support. Unlike the traditional situation, where little significant social stigma is attached to divorce, these "modern" women, even if they have independent sources of income, experience enough social stigma that they think twice before divorcing their husbands. Mohsen cites an article written by Aminal al-Sa'id (1977) on the plight of these women: in this article, al-Sa'id reports that letters received from divorced women describe how friends avoid them and that men colleagues in their places of work view them as easy sexual prey and make sexual advances. These women discuss their loneliness and the difficulty of finding suitable second husbands. Available men turn out to be much older than they are and the men are socially and economically less desirable than their first husbands.

Mohsen (1974) argues that the desire for a new conception of the role of women based on equal participation and rewards can only come about through changing and conservative cultural practices and attitudes of men and women. It is not enough simply to change the laws of personal status and family relations:

> Men's conservatism stems from the need to maintain the status quo, which is to their advantage. Women's conservative attitude stems partly from the fear of having to compete in areas for which they have not been culturally trained. The home for the woman is the domain of her authority and the source of her security. Some women view equality (especially if it entails cooperation between husband and wife in domestic activities) as a sacrifice of the woman's only stronghold. It will take more than legislation to change some of these attitudes. It might take a few generations for women to achieve the self-conficence needed to compete in the man's world. But until this happens, any attempt to change the role of women by mere legislation is bound to effect minimal results (Mohsen, 1974:58).

In summary, what we discover is that in the traditional Islamic family there are structured safeguards for women in the form of extended kinship institutions. The relative ease with which a man can gain a divorce is compensated by various forms of social and familial supports for both women and children. Obviously, the Islamic sanctioning of polygyny, the unilateral power of the husband in divorce, and other religious-legal sanctions and prohibitions against women mitigate against their achieving equality. Yet, modernization in the form of legal reforms in Egypt have not led to the achievement of an equitable position for married and divorced Egyptian Islamic women. This can only be achieved when the cultural attitudes and practices of Egyptian society are changed to accommodate the equalitarian elements of Islam with those of modernization.

Egyptians Back Women's Divorce

HENRY TANNER

CAIRO, March 6—A draft law giving an Egyptian woman, for the first time, the right to sue for divorce if her husband takes a second wife has been sent to the Ministry of Justice by a commission including the powerful head of Al Azhar, the conservative Islamic university, and other Moslem leaders.

Politically, the most significant aspect of the draft law is that the Moslem sheiks, or dignitaries, who represent the religious leadership in the country, are backing a move to give more rights to women.

The Commission on Islamic Studies that wrote the text of the bill was headed by Sheik Abdel Halim Mahmoud, the head of Al Azhar University and as such the most powerful religious personality in the country. Islamic leaders have opposed liberalization of divorce laws in the past.

Since it has the backing of the religious authorities, the draft law is certain to be enacted.

A first attempt to liberalize divorce laws was made over a year ago by Aisha Rateb, the Minister of Social Affairs and the only woman in the Government. But when her draft proposal became known about a hundred students from Al Azhar demonstrated in front of Parliament and the bill was quietly shelved.

Jihan Sadat, the wife of President Anwar el-Sadat, is thought to have been instrumental in reviving the reform proposal. She has come out strongly in public and in private in favor of greater rights for women.

Mrs. Sadat and Mrs. Rateb are understood to hope that the draft law will further discourage the practice of polygamy in Egypt, although it does not directly affect a Moslem husband's right to have up to four wives.

About 2 percent of Egyptian husbands have more than one wife, according to official estimates, and the practice is declining. Most enlightened Egyptians would like to see it vanish altogether.

At present, Egyptian women have the right to initiate divorce proceedings for such reasons as adultery, sexual abuse and desertion but not for polygamy, legal experts said today.

The draft law also gives women protection against quick automatic divorce. If a husband wants a divorce and his wife objects, he will have to go through lengthy court and reconciliation proceedings.

The draft law also gives divorced wives more financial protection than they had in the past. It stipulates that the court may impose immediate temporary support duties on the husband pending a final ruling. At present, divorced women often remain without financial support for years as the final ruling is delayed.

Another important provision says that in the case of divorce, custody over the children shall pass from the mother to the father at the age of 13 for girls and 11 for boys. Under the present law, girls come under the father's custody at 9 and boys at 7.

The change has economic as well as personal and sentimental implications because children often help support the family.

"The draft law is an important step for us but we are still far from equality," a professional woman interested in women's rights said.

If a woman initiates divorce proceedings and the husband objects, the prescribed procedures through which she has to go are so long and complicated that it would take an extraordinarily determined and well educated woman to see it through, experts here say.

Few women are apt to be so resourceful. Illiteracy among Egyptian women is far higher than among men. Moreover, tradition demands that the woman defer to the man in almost all aspects of life and this has become second nature to all but a small urban élite, according to sociologists.

The meshing of civil and Islamic law is a subject of permanent debate in Egypt as in all other Moslem countries.

A committee of Parliament is now debating proposals to make Islamic law the basic tenet of national legislation. Islamic law includes such punishment as cutting off the hand of a thief and stoning an adulterer.

But an expert on Islamic law said that such debates in Moslem countries are misunderstood by non-Moslems.

Islamic law, he said, must take in all the teachings of the Koran, including for instance a rule that the state must provide for the needs of all its citizens. Under this, a man who steals because he is poor is not committing a crime and cannot be punished.

DIVORCE IN THE UNITED STATES

Paul H. Jacobsen (1959), in his much-cited work on American divorce patterns from 1860 to 1956, reports that, at about the time of the Civil War (1860–1864), the divorce rate per 1000 of existing marriages was 1.2 percent. By the turn of the century (1900–1904) the rate had risen to 4.2 percent and 25 years later (1925–1929) the rate climbed to 7.6 percent. Through the depression years of the 1930s, the rate stayed relatively stable; but, near the end of World War II and the postwar 1940s, the rate hit a high of 13.7 percent, which was not reached again until the 1970s. The high rates reached during the 1940s can be seen as an aftermath of a stressful period when many marriages deteriorated. The divorce rate declined steadily through the 1950s until the end of that decade, at which time the rate (9.4 percent) reached approximately the same level as that for 1940. However, since the beginning of the 1960s, the divorce rate has dramatically risen (Carter and Glick, 1976). It more than doubled between 1960 and the mid-1970s. Carter and Glick (1976) predict that at least one-third of the first marriages of couples about 30 years of age would eventually end in divorce.

The rise in the divorce rate in the United States can best be seen by relating it to other family and social changes. Probably the most important change is the relation of the family to the economic process. In earlier times, the family had greater economic self-sufficiency. Both men and women were involved in the economic process. Men worked in an agricultural and hunting setting to produce food, clothing materials, and other economic necessities. Women's work was interdependent with that of the men. In addition to domestic household and childrearing activities, women processed the food, made the clothing, and assisted the men whenever needed. In situations where domestic industry prevailed, the home served as a production unit, with all family members involved in labor participation. The result was an economic interdependence that often translated into an emotional interdependence as well.

With technological development, all this has changed. Domestic activities, once exclusively the provence of women, were taken over by outside institutions. The manufacturing of clothing and many aspects of food processing and production moved outside the home to commercial establishments. The husband became a wage earner, and work became separated from domestic activities. The family became more a center of consumption than of production.

A second major change that has affected marital relationships has been the urbanization and increased geographic mobility of the American population. This has effectively diminished the controls and sanctions of the community and religious institutions over family members and their treatment of each other. As we have observed, the family was once integrally tied to the community. The community exerted pressure and control over family members. The family's openness to community scrutiny assured the conformity of the family to community standards. Community influence was enhanced by religious institutions that, through church religious and secular activities for all members of the family, tied the family even more tightly to the community. The church served as a reinforcer of the parental-authority structure and imposed prescribed attitude and role patterns to govern the relationship between husband and wife and between parents and children. Collective religious ritual and family religious and secular devotions and rituals reinforced the ideology on the sanctity of marriage and the abhorrence of divorce. In essence, then, there may be some truth to the adage that "the family that prays together stays together."

These changes interacted with the changes occurring in family ideology—that is, the new emphasis on the independence and the privatization of the nuclear family. New marital orientations and expectations developed that sought maximum and almost exclusive personal and emotional involvements within the nuclear family. The husband and the wife became dependent on each other for their emotional gratification and allowed little external sources of additional support— unlike the earlier period when marital solidarity and interdependence was tied to an interdependent familial economy. However, the new economic system does not foster such interdependence. The development of specialized services in an industrialized economy permits one to purchase many domestic goods and services, such as clothing, laundry, prepared foods, and housing. The wife finds increased opportunities to enter the labor force and thus has obtained self-supporting economic options.

The increasing economic independence of women allows them greater opportunity to dissolve unsatisfactory marriages. Ross and Sawhill (1975) observed that as the wife's earnings increased, so does the likelihood that her marriage will end in divorce. One may interpret this finding to mean that occupational involvement takes too much time away from a woman's domestic and marital life or that the woman sought employment in preparation for divorce. A more likely and plausible explanation, however, is that financial security gives her the options to pursue more satisfactory possibilities than remaining in an unhappy marriage. We would argue, then, that part of the explanation for the lower divorce rates of several decades ago was that the great majority of women were financially dependent on their husbands and thus did not have the financial independence to leave them. Their increased involvement in the labor force has led to the removal of this economic barrier to divorce.

Taken together, all the above-mentioned factors lead to a highly unstable situation. Unrealistic or hard-to-satisfy expectations are placed on the marital relationship. Marriage is expected to lead to the exclusive attainment and fulfillment of an individual's affectional, personal, and communal needs. When it proves incapable of meeting those needs, marital unhappiness and often divorce occur. The increased independence of men and women combined with the lessened stigma attached to divorce and the possibilities of remarriage help account for the rise in the divorce rate. In sum, the rising divorce rate is an indication that, for an increasing number of people, divorce with all its future unknown uncertainties is a preferable option to continuing in a marriage relationship that has proved debilitating and unsatisfactory.

We will now make a more detailed examination of the implications of marital, family, and social changes on American divorce and remarriage structures and processes. We will begin by looking at how these changes are reflected in American divorce laws. Our attention centers on an analysis of no-fault divorce laws and the adjudication of child custody. An examination of the single-parent household and the effects of divorce on children follow. We will conclude with a discussion of remarriage.

LEGAL ASPECTS OF AMERICAN DIVORCE: NO-FAULT

Weitzman and Dixon (1980), in an excellent analysis of the implications of no-fault divorce, emphasize that the laws governing divorce reflect the society's definition of marriage, provide the parameters for appropriate marriage behavior, and point out the reciprocal rights and obligations of marriage partners. Further, divorce laws are also seen to define the continued obligations that the formally married couple have to each other after divorce: "One can generally examine the way a society defines marriage by examining its provisions for divorce, for it is at the point of divorce that a society has the opportunity to reward the marital behavior it approves of, and to punish spouses who have violated its norms" (Weitzman and Dixon, 1980:355). Given this viewpoint, the authors assert that a study of changing divorce laws will reflect social changes in family patterns. For this reason, they chose to examine no-fault divorce laws to demonstrate how "this new legislation seeks to alter the definition of marriage, the relationship between husbands and wives, and the economic and social obligations of former spouses to each other and to their children after divorce" (1980:354).

Prior to no-fault divorce in America, divorce laws followed Anglo-American legal tradition. Divorce was cast in the traditional common-law model of an adversary procedure. The plaintiff's success depended on proving defendant's fault. Both parties were assumed to be antagonists and were expected to be at odds and were expected to bring forth all the relevant facts to be assessed by the judge in reaching his or her verdict. No-fault divorce laws are based on a new concept of marital dissolution. The first such law in the United States, The Family Law Act, was passed in 1970 by the California legislature. The suggested procedure begins with a neutral petition—"In re the marriage of John and Jane Doe" rather than *"Doe* v. *Doe"*—requesting the family court to inquire into the continuance of the marriage.

The California law abolished completely any requirement of fault as the basis to dissolve the marriage. One spouse is not required to bring charges against the other nor is the evidence needed of misconduct. Under traditional divorce laws, the division of property and the allocation of alimony payments are determined under the concept of fault. Property and support are given to the judged "innocent party" as a reward extracted from the "guilty party" as punishment. The non-fault law gives legal recognition to "marital breakdown" as a sufficient justification for divorce. Indeed, the Californian legislation eliminated the term, divorce, replacing it with the phrase, "dissolution of marriage." The dissolution is granted on the basis of "irreconcilable differences" that have caused the irremediable breakdown of the marriage. Under the no-fault law, property is substantially divided equally, and alimony is based on the duration of the marriage, the needs of each party, and their respective earning ability.

By 1977 provisions for no-fault divorce existed in all but three states. Its popularity reflects the increased recognition that the cause for the marital dissolution is usually a result of a number of factors and is shared by both partners. Carter and Glick (1976) point out the positive aspects of no-fault divorce laws:

> No fault divorce procedures avoid exploring and assessing blame and concentrate on dissolving the marriage and tidying up the inevitable problems—responsibility for the care of the children (there still are children involved in the majority of divorce cases despite the decline in the birth rate), financial support of children, division of jointly owned property, and spousal support (alimony) if this seems indicated. The moment it is established that the question of blame is irrelevant to settlement of the case, some of the bitterness (but by no means all of it) goes out of the divorce proceedings. (Carter and Glick, 1976:458)

Weitzman and Dixon argue that non-fault divorce reflects changes in the traditional view of legal marriage. By eliminating the fault-based grounds for divorce and the adversary process, the new law recognizes the more contemporary view that frequently both parties are responsible for the breakdown of the marriage.

Further, the law recognizes that the divorce procedure often aggravated the situation by forcing the potentially amicable individuals to become antagonists.

No-fault divorce laws advocate that the financial aspects of marital dissolution are to be based on equity, equality, and economic need rather than on fault- or sex-based role assignments. Alimoney is also to be based on the respective spouses economic circumstances and on the principle of social equality, not on the basis of guilt or innocence. No longer can alimony be awarded to the "injured party," regardless of that person's financial needs. The new law seeks to refelct the changing circumstances of women and to their increased participation in the labor force. By so doing, it encourages women to become self-supporting and removes the expectation that husbands have to continue support of wives throughout their lives. Although it considers custodial care for children, the thrust of the law is on financial criteria. California judges are directed to consider the following in setting alimony: "the circumstances of the respective parties, including the duration of the marriage, and the ability of the supported spouse to engage in gainful employment without interfering with the interests of the children of the parties in the custody of each spouse" (California Civil Code 4801 cited in Weitzman and Dixon, 1980:363).

Weitzman and Dixon (1980) see the overall impact of no-fault legislation as its redefinition of the traditional marital responsibilities of men and women by instituting a new norm of equality between the sexes. No longer are husbands to be designated as the head of the household and solely responsible for support nor are wives alone obligated to domestic household activities and childrearing. Sex-neutral obligations, which fall equally on husband and wife, are institutionalized. These changes are reflected in the new considerations for alimony allocation. In addition, the division of property is to be done on an equal basis. Finally, child-support expectations and the standards for child custody reflect the new equality criteria of no-fault divorce legislation. Both father and mother are equally responsible for financial support of their children after divorce. Mothers are no longer automatically given custody of the child; rather, a sex-neutral standard instructs judges to award custody in the "best interests of the child."

In conclusion, Weitzman and Dixon (1980), while praising the changes in divorce legislation raise one important caveat. They see the law as reflecting idealized gains for women in social, occupation, and economic areas, gains toward equality that may, in fact, not reflect women's actual conditions and circumstances. This can have extremely detrimental effects on women's ability for self-sufficiency after divorce:

> Thus, while the aims of the no-fault laws, i.e., equality and ex-neutrality are laudable, the laws may be instituting equality in a society in which women are not fully prepared (and/or permitted) to assume equal responsibility for their own and their children's support after divorce. Public policy then becomes a choice between temporary protection and safeguards for the transitional woman (and for the older housewife in the

traditional generation) to minimize the hardships incurred by the new expectations, versus current enforcement of the new equality, with the hope of speeding the transition, despite the hardships this may cause for current divorces. (Weitzman and Dixon, 1980:365)

LEGAL ASPECTS OF AMERICAN DIVORCE: CHILD CUSTODY

Another legal change regarding divorce involves decisions of which parent should be given custody of children. Robert S. Weiss (1979b) reports that mothers are currently awarded legal custody of children in about 90 percent of American divorce cases. However, in recent years there has been an increased recognition of fathers' rights regarding custody. It reflects a recognition of the changing role of American fathers. This change has been popularized in the 1980 Oscar-award-winning motion picture, *Kramer vs. Kramer*. In addition, courts are now beginning to view joint custody as another legal option. To understand the basis for custody adjudication decisions, a brief review of the historical changes in parental roles and their relationship to the judicial principle of ''best interest'' is necessary.

Weiss points out that historically courts have been governed by the ''best interests'' principle in awarding custody of children. Judges are supposed to treat as irrelevant the issue of which parent was at ''fault'' in the divorce. Rather, their sole concern was to ascertain which parent would best serve to maximize the children's future well-being and welfare. Prior to the mid-19th century, fathers were judged as the best parent who could take care and educate the child. Women were thought to be too dependent on men, whether it was their fathers, husbands, or related kin. Since they too needed the protection of men, the courts judged them as not being the best parent able to provide for the children.

Beginning in the mid-19th century, there was a change in judicial decisions in custody awards, which became almost standard by the end of the century. Mothers came to be seen as better able to serve the child's ''best interests.'' This change reflected the changing popular belief about the aims of the family and the raising of children. With increased industrialization, fathers withdrew from taking an active role in domestic matters, including child care, and they devoted more of their attention to earning a living outside the home. This movement away from domestic-oriented economic involvements to commerce and factories also affected children. They were gradually removed from the work force and were no longer economic assets. The family household began to be viewed in Christopher Lasch's eloquence as a ''haven in a heartless world'' (1977a). The home was designed to protect the child from the incursions of a changing and threatening outside world. The family was viewed as a place where children should be nurtured and protected, and, increasingly, it was the mother who was considered the preferred parent to do this.

In the 20th century this pattern continued. It reached its culmination in the post-World War II period of the 1950s and 1960s. The affluence and materialism of this era, embodied in the development of middle-class suburbia, heightened the division between husband/father and wife/mother. The feminine mystique and the motherhood myth dominated—only the mother was deemed as the appropriate parent and was thus given almost complete responsibility for childrearing. The total responsibility for child care carries over to divorce. The legal assumption regarding the mother's natural superiority in parenting is reflected in custodial dispositions. As mentioned earlier, women are awarded custody in over 90 percent of divorce cases.

Leonore Weitzman (1977) has made some interesting observations on the implications of courts automatically granting custody to the mother. Although it is true that most divorcing women want custody of their children, this practice also tends to reinforce the women's social role as housewife and mother. It also frequently reinforces women's dependency on their husbands for support. Further, this judicial preference may coerce women to accept custody even if they do not wish to do so. They may bow to social pressures and be subject to feelings of deviancy and guilt.

Fathers are also subjected to discrimination by this practice. They are often legally advised of the futility of contesting custody, particularly in the case of young children. The burden of proof is on them, either to document the unfitness of the mother or to show that they could do a qualitatively better job of parenting. In those cases where the father could be the better parent, both his interests and the "best interests" of the child are denied.

In recent years the increased recognition of the changing role of fathers is beginning to influence the judicial decision-making process of custodial award. In addition, inherent contradictions in the principle of "best interest" has also led to a reevaluation of the practice to giving mothers custody of the children automatically. Let us look at each of these changes in turn.

With the end of the period of prosperity of the 1950s and 1960s, there was a growing disenchantment with family-role segregation, which extended from the end of the 1960s on through the 1970s. The feminist movement began to articulate fully women's dissatisfaction with their confinement to the home and exclusive parenthood. In addition, fathers were reevaluating their role involvements. An increasing number of them began to express doubts about lives characterized by an almost total involvement in occupational careers and almost complete withdrawal from family matters, including the raising of children. Kelin E. Gersick (1979) expresses these changes this way:

> In recent years . . . the role of the American father has been enjoying a resurgence. Several factors may be involved: a decrease in the average man's working hours and resulting increase in leisure time; the woman's dissatisfaction with her role limitations and movement toward greater economic and social flexibility; and the spreading disenchantment with material acquisition as the exclusive measure of the good life, along with the espousal of close relationships as a principal measure of happiness. Whatever the reasons, there appears to be a recent upswing in father's involvement in their families. (Gersick, 1979:307)

Additional factors particularly apparent as we enter the 1980s include the change in the economic fortunes of Americans now that inflation and recession have become a way of life. This has increased the economic necessity for women to work. The transition of women into the labor force has been made smoother as a result of the women's movement, which has persuaded most men and women of the legitimacy of women's work. This has led to the growth of dual-income families with more and more household's composed of working parents who are also sharing domestic involvements and childcare. These changes have played a contributory role in the reassessment by judicial court systems on the adjudication of custody of children when parents separate.

Robert S. Weiss (1979a) observes that criticism of the legal presumption in favor of the mother began to appear in the 1960s and by the early 1970s some state statutes that had required mothers be preferred had been repealed. In 1973 the bellwether state of California, repealed such a statute and replaced it with the "best interests" principle. The growing sensitivity to sexual discrimination has also played a contributing role in these changes. One way that this has been shown is in the increased debunking of the belief in the natural superiority of women in parenting. It is now argued in several states that a presumption in favor of the mother constitutes unfair discrimination owing to sex and deprives the father of his right to equal protection by the law (Weiss, 1979a:327). Weiss mentions a second element contributing to this change, which ties in with the arguments against job discrimination because of sex. He says that "defenders of fathers' " rights pointed out that if men are to have no advantage over women in the competition for jobs, and if most single mothers can be expected to work, then women should not be seen as having more right to the children: 'A man can hire a babysitter as well as a woman' " (Weiss, 1979a:327).

An additional issue, which we wish to draw to the reader's attention, is the way the idea of children's rights is tied to the "best interests" principle. Weiss observes that many key states have adopted the custody statute proposed by the American Bar Association that "direct[s] judges to consider the wishes of the child's parents and of the child, the relationship of the child and the parents, the child's adjustment to home, school, and community, and the mental and physical health of all involved" (1979b:330). Further, in some states judges are required to take into consideration the economic potential of each parent, their cultural background, and a catchall other-relevant-factors clause. Increasingly, judges have turned to investigations by members of the helping professions, including social workers, probation officers, and psychiatrists, to help them in their decision making on which parent is to be awarded custody so that the best interests of the child can be maximized.

Tied to this concern over children's rights, the courts are focusing attention on the pros and cons of whether children should be consulted during the judicial process. Weiss states that although there are obvious reasons why the child should be consulted, there are also pitfalls including the child's immaturity. Weiss questions whether some children might make decisions on the basis of one parent's leniency regarding homework, chores, and discipline. Further, after divorce, the parent not chosen may become spiteful and voice resentment, which could endanger their future relationship with the child.

One final issue concerns Weiss. It is the inherent contradiction of awarding custody to one parent and allowing visitation rights to the other. The problem is to what extent does the visitation parent have custody rights when the child is in that parent's care. Two solutions have been offered. One would place visitation rights solely at the option of the custodial parent. By so doing, it would increase that parent's authority and would strengthen their dealing with the other parent, who may be viewed as a disruptive or dangerous influence on the child. Weiss objects, he uses recent research to demonstrate that children desire free access to the noncustodial parent and rarely is it disruptive to their development.

The second solution, more to Weiss's liking, requires joint custody with both parents having custodial rights and responsibilities. Children would be under the custodial care of the parent with whom they were living at a given time. Weiss indicates that preliminary studies, which are somewhat impressionistic, indicate that such a solution may work. However, he cautions that this favorable outcome may be restricted to situations where both parents are in agreement and when the parting was amicable. More evidence is required before an adequate assessment can be made.

In summary, as Weiss (1979b) points out, the full implications for children and their parents of these different procedures and approaches are still not known. The courts, in their deliberation on custody and visitation, are well advised to keep abreast of the empirical evidence, which seeks to determine the consequences of various arrangements after parents separate and divorce.

THE EFFECTS OF DIVORCE ON CHILDREN

'' 'What will happen to me if anything goes wrong, if Mommy dies or Daddy dies, if Daddy leaves Mommy or Mommy leaves Daddy?' '' (Mead, 1970a:113). This question has particular meaning to American children since our society stresses the importance of parents in raising children. Father's kin or mother's kin, including the respective grandparents, have no legal responsibility to children as long as the parents are alive. Further, cultural norms emphasize parental independence and freedom from extended-family involvements in childrearing. In contrast, the larger extended family, or clan, which still exists in many societies, has formally defined rights, duties, and obligations over each member of the family grouping, including children. For such children, the question of death, divorce, or separation of their own parents is less problematic than in the American situation. Extensive kinship ties provide sufficient sources of intergeneration involvement so that marital disruption or dissolution has relatively minimal impact on children's psychological well-being. In the contemporary United States these wider kinship networks are lacking at a time when many families are dissolving because of divorce. This fact is complicated by the lack of sufficient preparation or the development of alternatives for the child's psychological dependence on his or her parents. Margaret Mead addresses herself to this anomaly:

> We have constructed a family system which depends upon fidelity, lifelong monogamy, and the survival of both parents. But we have never made adequate social provision for the security and identity of the children if that marriage is broken, as it so often was in the past by death or desertion, and as it so often is in the present by death or divorce. We have . . . saddled ourselves with a system that won't work. (Mead, 1970a:115)

Mary Jo Bane (1979) observes that since 1900 the proportion of children affected by marital disruption has been between 25 and 30 percent of the total population of children under the age of 18. There has been a change, however, in the dominant cause of the disruption. At the turn of the century, the ratio of disruption by death was much higher than disruption by divorce and long-term separation. By 1980 the ratio was reversed; divorce is now affecting more children, particularly at an earlier age, than is the death of a parent. The number of children involved in divorces has risen sharply since the 1950s. In 1955, 347,000 children under 18 years of age were involved in divorce cases (National Center for Health Statistics, 1977, 1978). The figure almost doubled by 1965 to 630,000. In 1972, for the first time, more than 1 million children were annually affected by divorce. This figure has remained relatively stable through the 1970s. Bane (1979) estimates that about 30 percent of the current generation of children will witness the breakup of their parents' marriage. There are currently 12 million children under the age of 18 whose parents are divorced.

Bane goes on to discuss the economic effects of marital disruption. She projects that two-fifths of children born in the 1980s are likely to experience parental divorce. These children will be living in a single-parent household for an average of 5 years. During these years, financial resources will be limited. This results from the following causes: the greater prevalence of divorce among low-income families; irregular and low levels of alimony, child support, and public assistance; fewer adult wage earners in the family; fewer opportunities for females heading the household to find employment; and the lower wages paid women as compared to men (Bane, 1979:283).

Bane is concerned with the effect of family poverty on the physical well-being of the children of divorced parents. She also believes that economic deprivation could result in psychological stress, tension, and frustration. She calls for the development of governmental programs, such as a guaranteed maintenance allowance, to improve the situation for separated, divorced, and widowed mothers who share the brunt of the responsibility in raising children. Bane observes that in many European countries programs exist to meet the needs of single-parent families. Sweden is the cited example. It provides all families with children both housing and child allowances. Widows receive pensions. Divorced and separated women receive a major part of their income in the form of guaranteed maintenance allowance regardless of a husband's ability or willingness to pay for support or alimony. It is the government's responsibility to recover the allowance from the husband. Bane provides the following statement on why such an allowance policy is needed in the United States:

> A guaranteed maintenance allowance, or something like it, could dramatically improve the situation of single-parent families in the United States. It would take from women the burden of collecting alimony and child support and ensure that payments were steady and adequate. It would take most single-parent families off welfare, and if designed correctly would provide strong incentive to work. (Bane, 1977:285)

The recitation of statistics and the delineation of the economic difficulties accompanying divorce cannot reveal the potentially negative effects on children's psychological well-being. For the parents involved, divorce often produces anger and a sense of failure. For children it raises issues of conflicting loyalties and it necessitates their readjustment from a two-parent family to a single-parent household. The popular impression is that divorce contributes to the development of children's psychological disorganization and has other ill effects. Recent evidence, however, indicates that this view is an oversimplification of what actually occurs. It is worth examining some of the research on this issue.

Early research by the criminologists Sheldon and Eleanor Glueck (1951) and others seem to support the belief that children from broken homes are more likely than others to be psychologically disturbed, low achievers, and delinquents. However, critical analyses of these studies by Lawrence Rosen (1970) and Karen Wilkinson (1974) disprove these conclusions. Separately, these reviewers argue that the earlier studies lacked adequate controls and asked wrong and biased questions. Rosen's analysis of 11 of these studies demonstrates that there is no significant relationship between broken homes and juvenile delinquency. Wilkinson reaches a similar conclusion: ideological biases distort this relationship.

Studies by Lee G. Burchinal (1964) and Judson T. Landis (1962) provide evidence that unhappy, unbroken homes may have more detrimental effects on children than do broken homes. Burchinal's findings reveal either few differences or that the children from broken homes have better personality development and demonstrate less stress and deviancy than children living with parents.

His findings are based on a comparison of seventh and eighth graders in Cedar Rapids, Iowa, who were grouped into five categories: unbroken families, those living only with their mothers, and those from three types of reconstituted families—mothers and stepfathers, both parents remarried, fathers and stepmothers. Burchinal concludes that his findings "require the revision of widely held beliefs about the detrimental effects of divorce upon children" (1964:50).

In an earlier study, Landis (1960) studied 295 university students whose parents divorced when they were children. He concludes that divorce of parents affects children in various ways depending on such factors as the age of the child at the time of divorce and the children's evaluations of their parents' marriage and their own feelings of security. Those who viewed their homes as happy prior to the divorce experienced more trauma than those who perceived the home as being unhappy and characterized by parental conflict. This latter group often felt relief that their parents' troubled relationship ended.

In a systematic review of the literature Cynthia Longfellow (1979) concluded that the emotional impact of divorce on chldren relates to the family relationship, the single mother's mental state, and the child's own viewpoint. In support of Landis's and Burchinal's studies, Longfellow reports that a body of research finds that a child who experiences parents' marital discord is likely to face great psychiatric risk. The child's stress may, in fact, be reduced if the parents separate or divorce. However, if the conflict persists after the marriage is dissolved, through each parent demanding exclusive loyalty from the child or by conflict over other issues, the child may experience adjustment problems.

Longfellow also examined the extensive research that has been accumulating on the effect of divorce on different age categories of children. She reports that young children are more adversely affected and experience greater stress than older children. Preschoolers are found to be cognitively less able to cope with divorce. This inability is also associated with the fact that single-parent mothers with young children are the most vulnerable to economic instability and are among the most highly stressed group of women:

> Age, then, appears to be an important mediator of the effects of divorce on children. In two contexts, it is the younger child who is more adversely affected: preschoolers create a greater psychological strain on their divorced parents and at the same time seem cognitively less able to cope with the divorce. . . . A family with young children is also often at the point in its life cycle when job and financial pressures are the greatest. Therefore, we might expect that a divorce at this time simply overtaxes the family, placing both mothers and children at greater psychiatric risk. (Longfellow, 1979:305)

Longfellow ends her review by briefly mentioning some of the factors that may help mitigate the impact of divorce on children. These include the beneficial effects of a good parent-child relationship, a supportive network of friends and relatives, and an ex-husband who continues to be supportive toward his family. Her concluding remarks lead us to our next area of examination, the single-parent household.

SINGLE PARENTHOOD

Single parenthood is becoming more common in our society. Paul C. Glick and Arthur J. Norton (1979), in their review of governmental statistics, report that the proportion of children living with one parent has more than doubled from 1960 to 1978. By 1978, a little more than 5.5 million American families with children were headed by a single adult. This represents 19 percent of the 30 million families with children in the United States.

Alvin L. Schorr and Phyllis Moen (1980), citing early 1970s statistics, observe that the popular image of the conventional family—husband, wife, and children—is, in fact, a minority family form in the United States. Single parenthood, couples without children, and reconstituted families (remarrieds with and without children) represent 55 percent of American families; the conventional form accounts for only 45 percent of American families.

Mary Jo Bane (1979) estimates that nearly 30 percent of the children born around 1970 will experience parental divorce by the time they are 18. An additional 15 to 20 percent may live in a one-parent household because of death, long-term separation, or birth to an unmarried mother. Together, then, 45 to 50 percent of the children born around 1970 will live for a period of time with a single parent. Further, as Robert S. Weiss notes, ''among all children who now live with either their mothers or their fathers alone, 93 percent live with their mothers'' (1979a). As pointed out earlier, mothers currently become the custodians of children in over 90 percent of all American divorces.

Variations in the single-parent experience depends on the circumstances that resulted in the single parent raising children alone. It can occur because of marital separation or divorce, death of one parent, or bearing children out of wedlock. Weiss (1979a), citing governmental statistics, states that 70 percent of single-parent households are created by separation and divorce. The remaining 30 percent result from death (14 percent), unwed parents (10 percent), and those who define themselves as being temporarily alone (most typically women whose husbands are in the armed forces (6 percent). Collectively, these demographic realities dictate that the main part of our discussion focus on legally separated and divorced mothers. First, however, we would like to examine variations in the single-parent circumstance. Also, we will conclude with an analysis of the growing phenomena of single-parent households headed by fathers.

One common characteristic shared by all female-headed single-parent families is poverty. The mother, in the vast majority of cases, must provide for the child's care as well as being the principal and, in the case of no employable older children, the only wage earner in the family. Often this proves an impossible task with an appreciable number of such families falling into the poverty class. A 1976 U.S. Department of Labor report showed that only 28 percent of female-headed households had incomes in excess of $10,000, whereas about 40 percent of such households had incomes of less than $5,000. The comparable figures for families headed by a man were 70 percent with incomes above $10,000 and only 10 percent with incomes of less than $5,000. Ross and Sawhill, in their study of the problems of female-headed households, provide the following explanation for this situation:

> The inadequate incomes of most female-headed families stem from the loss of a male earner, the mother's continuing responsibility for the care of young children, and the

inability of most women to earn enough to support a family. However, the loss of a male earner within the household need not mean the loss of all of the father's income. Alimony and child-support payments as well as more informal gifts of money and other items help to maintain women and children living on their own. But indications are that the flow of those private transfers is somewhat smaller than is commonly believed. They are certainly inadequate to the task of keeping many women and children out of poverty. (Ross and Sawhill, 1975:175)

Variations in the Single-Parent Experience: A Brief Sketch

Separated or divorced single parents, the widow or widower now raising children alone, and the unwed mother or father will have different attitudes and experiences toward single parenthood. Weiss (1979a) finds many divorced and separated parents have feelings of wariness and self-doubt. Another result of an unhappy marriage is that the divorced often have disparaging, critical, and untrustworthy images of each other. In contrast, single parenthood brought about by death often results in an idealization of the marital relationship and reinterprets it, emphasizing only the happier moments. The widow or widower also display greater commitment to their former marriage; they begin to date later and do not contemplate new attachments as early as divorced parents.

Weiss contrasts divorced parents, widows and widowers in terms of their involvement with their children and the larger community. Widows or widowers often turn to their children for solace and comfort. The divorced parent finds it difficult to talk about his or her marriage to the children; their marital difficulties are seen as a private matter. The larger community is more sympathetic to widows and widowers; the divorced are often stigmatized. Weiss also makes the following distinction between the separated and divorced from widows and widowers in regard to the role of the other parent in their lives:

> There are many ways in which a separated parent's relationship with the other parent may develop, yet almost always that relationship has aspects of discomfort. The other parent almost always continues to have rights and responsibilities to the children that the separated parent must acknowledge. The other parent can be regularly intrusive, telephoning or appearing at unexpected times. Furthermore, the children of separated and divorced parents are likely to be loyal to both their antagonistic parents and to search for some method by which they can preserve their identifications with both parents despite the parents' criticisms of each other. Insofar as the children attempt to defend their relationships with the absent parent, they may enter into conflict with the parent with whom they live. (Weiss, 1979a:9)

The role of kin and the financial situation can also vary between these two groups. For the widow and widower as well as the separated or divorced, kinship bonds can be of immeasurable importance. A supportive atmosphere is almost automatic for the widows and widowers. However, it can be somewhat problematic with the divorced. This depends on the circumstances surrounding the marital breakdown. Parents and other relatives of the single parent as well as the deceased spouse's family may and often do provide various forms of aid. With the separated and divorced, the spouse's family may not be as willing to help, particularly when they feel that their son or daughter was not at fault. Further, continuation of aid may be longer for the living spouse, in that family members may feel greater obligations.

Unwed single parent's circumstances differ from the others. Although it is beyond the scope of this discussion to deal with this matter in great detail, a few points will be mentioned. Weiss (1979a) observes that for the majority, although the pregnancy is often unwanted, the child is wanted. Weiss distinguishes between the younger and older unwed mother. Older women tend to be more realistic and more self-reliant than younger women. The younger mother's adjustment is often associated with her parents' willingness to have the child raised in their home, their assistance in child care, and their financial help.

The children of never-married mothers are particularly vulnerable to abuse and neglect. In contrast to the widowed mother—who can blame fate, medicine, or God for her circumstances—and to the separated or divorced—who can blame their failings on their spouse—the unwed mother can only blame herself or her child (Weiss, 1979a). Based on data gathered from a national sample conducted by Nicholas Zill, Weiss (1979a) states that 30 percent of never-married mothers say that, if they had to do it again, they would not have children. This compares to the 20 percent of separated mothers, 15 percent of divorced mothers, and 10 percent of widowed mothers. More disturbingly, the never-married group are more likely to abuse their children physically. The study found that 27 percent of never-married mothers are more likely to admit that at some point in their relationship with their children they lost control and may have hurt them. The figure for the separated or divorced is 15 percent and for widowed mothers it is 5 percent.

Female-Headed Single-Parent Families

The female-headed single-parent family can be studied best within the larger context of the "proper" roles of the husband/father and wife/mother and the importance of the intact, or unbroken, family. Social scientists (see Brandwein, Brown, and Fox, 1974, and Schorr and Moen, 1980) have pointed out that our society is dominated by the assumption that families headed by a single parent, particularly when that parent is a woman, are deviant and pathologic. Such families are characterized as broken, disorganized, or disintegrated, rather than being recognized as a viable alternative family form. Rather than being seen as a solution to circumstances and examined in terms of their strengths, they are viewed negatively with emphasis on their alleged weaknesses and problems.

Similar to the simplifications and distortions of poverty families taken by culture-of-poverty advocates, depicting the single-parent family in these terms denies the realities of this family form and misrepresents it. This has led to biased governmental, employment, and social policies that have proved detrimental to single-parent families. Further, many separated and divorced women reacting to their stigmatized status have often incorporated the negative images into their own conceptualizations. This can prove particularly disabling in their attempts to readjust their lives after separation and divorce. Thus taken together, a self-fulfilling prophecy can come into effect and thus limit the capabilities of the single-parent family. Let us see how this operates in more detail.

Our society has believed that men should be primarily involved in outside-the-home matters. Through such activities they dominate the economic resources of the family and are legitimated as the head and brains of the family. This situation forces women to be dependent on husbands, particularly when they are parents and society dictates that their appropriate roles are housewives and mothers. This dependency situation becomes even more problematic and acute if a woman is granted custody of the children after divorce. Far too often she does not have access to comparable resources as her husband. Janet A. Kohen, Carol A. Brown, and Roslyn Feldberg (1979) make the following observations on this situation:

> If a couple divorces, the woman loses most of her right to the man's resources, but she also loses her personal dependence and obligations of service. She now stands in direct relationship to society as the head of her family. But male-dominated society neither recognizes a divorced woman's right to head a family nor makes available to her, as a woman, the necessary resources. The divorced mother has exchanged direct dependence on one man for general dependence on a male-dominated society. Employers, welfare officials, lawyers, judges, politicans, school authorities, doctors, even male relatives and neighbors, set the parameters of her ability to take on successfully the role of family head (1979:229).

Economic discrimination particularly affects divorced mothers. The traditional view that the proper role for women is housework and child care has fostered the opinion that women are marginal workers and should be given only marginal jobs, which pay less, have less status, and are less secure than those given to men. The result is that women, regardless of marital status, do not earn the same salaries as men in comparable jobs. They also are found in more dead-end jobs that have little or no possibilities for promotion. The jobs are more likely to be nonmanagerial and nonadministrative. These biases and discriminations make it extremely difficult for women raising their children alone to support a family.

Inadequate, unreliable, and, when available, expensive child-care facilities complicate the divorced mother's situation. The scarcity of child-care facilities reflects society's values—that the only acceptable setting for the care of children is in the home and by the mother. Child-care facilities are viewed negatively; they can only hinder the psychological development of the child and thus they are deemed undesirable and unnecessary. Unfortunately, for the single parent the absence of alternative child care prevents their full involvement in the labor force and limits them to marginal, part-time, and seasonal jobs. Such women often suffer severe economic hardships because far too frequently their insufficient earnings are not offset by other forms of child support. The child support payments from the ex-husband are often inadequate, irregular, or nonexistent, as is welfare and assistance from governmental programs and social agencies. Ironically, then, the parent least able to support the family is often left with the major economic responsibility. The effects of this downward income mobility can be severe:

> Lowered income means not only a drop in consumption within the home, but often a change in housing to poorer accomodations in a poorer neighborhood. . . . Moving is itself a stress . . . in this case often compounded by problems of reduced personal safety, higher delinquency rates, and poorer schools. A rapid change in socioeconomic status is associated with anomie . . . , adding to the problems of emotional support. . . . Some of the correlation between multi-problem families and divorced parents has been explained in terms of lowered SES and poorer housing (Brandwein, Brown, and Fox, 1974)

In our society men are commonly depcited as the household member with the power and authority to command respect within the family and as the one who can act on behalf of the family in its dealings with outside social agencies and institutions. The divorced mother may legally be the head of the family, but her family group is considered deviant because she and not a man heads it. Kohen, Brown, and Feldberg, in their study of 30 mothers who were divorced or separated from 1 to 5 years, report that intrusions that did not occur when these mothers were married, now occur in their new status. These intrustions included "schools and hospitals ignoring their requests for their children, men attempting to break into the house, landlords refusing to rent to them, [and] their own parents interfering in their lives" (Kohen, Brown, and Feldberg, 1979:236). These researchers believe that such incidents provide indications of the lack of social legitimacy to females heading families. Additional evidence is the disproportionate number of divorced mothers who are confronted with discrimination by businesses, credit-granting institutions, and mortgage banks who, in effect, deny these women their head-of-household status.

The divorced mother's authority within the home can also be undermined by these patriarchal ideas. This is a difficult task because of the lack of external social institutions to provide such services. We have already described this factor in our discussion of child-care facilities. The same holds true for other institutions, such as schools and businesses, that, in their independent demands on single-parent mother, often require her to be in two places at the same time. In addition, the cultural denial of the legitimacy of the female-headed family can affect both the women herself and her children. She is now required to assume both the mother and father roles within the family. Both she and her children may not be ready to accept this amalgamation. However, research reported by Brandwein, Brown, and Fox

(1974) show that women's ability to overcome this difficulty should not be underestimated. Likewise, Kohen, Brown, and Feldberg (1979) point out that their sample of divorced and separated mothers report that they developed increased feelings of mastery over their relationships with their children. They were also able to take on new responsibilities and perform unfamiliar tasks around the household and outside it—tasks that were exclusively in the province of the husband/father before the separation or divorce. Finally, they developed more positive self-images and stronger self-concepts.

The future for female-headed single-parent families can improve if and when governmental and social policies provide adequate financial supports—either directly or by enforcing spouses' child-support agreements—as well as such services as child care and crisis intervention when needed. Finally, societal attitudes toward women must change to allow them to gain employment oppportunities that would provide them with the financial security to take care of themselves and their families.

Father-Headed Single-Parent Families

It is an unusual development for a father to assume custody of his children after divorce. As discussed previously, in over 90 percent of the cases women are granted custody. Kelin E. Gersick (1979) points out that this results not solely because of court-mandated decisions but also because a very high percentage of divorcing couples have reached pre-court agreement that the wife will have custody. This agreement primarily reflects the role allocation of the couple during their marriage and their anticipation of the postdivorce roles as well as their assumption that the court will award custody to the mother if the custodial issue is contested. Gersick explains:

> Men have been more likely to be employed full time, to be making the larger income, to have higher status jobs, and to be in a career progression. Following the divorce, it has usually been easier for the father to continue his occupation than for a non-working mother to leave the home and start a new career. Regardless of the man's emotional attachment to his children, the couple's pre-divorce division of labor was most likely to have assigned the primary childcare role to the mother. This not only increased her childcare skills and the dependence of the children on her, but also established patterns of many years' standing which would take great effort to reverse, and at best would require a major adjustment for all the family members. In addition, the social pressure on mothers to take custody has been overwhelming. (Gersick, 1979:308)

The beginnings of the breakdown in parental roles and postdivorce parental roles has begun to affect custodial outcomes of divorce. Concomitantly, a small but growing number of fathers are now taking custody of their children. Gersick (1979) reports on his exploratory study of 20 single-parent fathers awarded custody of their children and a comparable group of noncustodial fathers. He observes that four complex variables appear to play the determining role on whether the father would consider gaining custody. The first variable is that the custodial fathers reacted against their own families' relationships with them when they were children. In particular, they wished to overcome in their own relationship with their children the emotional detachment they had experienced with their own fathers. This was not an important consideration for the noncustodial fathers.

The second factor was the feelings concerning the departing wife. Most of the men who sought custody believed that their wives betrayed them and their children through their involvements with another man. Their concern for the future well-being of the children was combined with a desire to punish their wives. A third and possibly the determining factor related to fathers getting custody of the children was that, in 18 of the 20 cases, the wives gave pretrial consent. The last factor was their respective attitudes toward their attorneys. In the control group of fathers who did not receive custody, a dominant belief was that their attorney's reluctance to contest the issue played a decisive role in their decision to agree on giving custody to the wife. The fact that so many of the custodial fathers had their wives give pretrial consent made this a nonfactor for them.

In summary, the issue of a father's custody is tied explicitly to the underlying premises of the proper roles of fathers and mothers after divorce and on the "best interest" principle concerning children. These premises are reflected in the court's orientation. Gersick's description of the 20 father-headed single-parent families can serve as a fitting summing up of this little-researched phenomenon:

> In addition to *caring* deeply about their children, the fathers in the custody sample also felt that *raising* them was important enough to be worth sacrifices in other areas; in some instances, particularly regarding their careers, sacrifices did have to be made. It is interesting to note that many of the difficulties the men faced as a result of taking custody were exactly the same as those widely experienced by single-parent mothers. Money was tight. Childcare became a problem, which made work more difficult. Visits by the mother were often anticipated with wariness and anxiety. In addition, for some of the men the strain of the divorce, combined with the emotional demands of parenthood, made the development of a new life very difficult. Yet none of these fathers said he regretted his decision to take custody. (Gersick, 1979:322–323)

REMARRIAGE AFTER DIVORCE

Even with today's liberalizing attitudes toward divorce, individuals report varying degrees of loneliness, confusion, and depression after divorce (see Goode, 1956b; Bohannan, 1971; and S. Gordon, 1976). Many find that they are not able to confide in their friends and relatives. The failure of the society to provide clear-cut normative standards to guide the divorced individual aggravate the situation.

Further, the societal ideologies that stress individualism and separation from extended kinship structures often prevent divorced persons from seeking aid or involvements with their families. The individual's ties and interpersonal relationships with married friends are also often shattered by divorce. The somewhat stigmatized identity combined with the necessity to change old relationships often proves difficult to resolve.

Combined, all these factors often result in the desire of the divorced person to remarry. Indeed, a society that provides few alternate emotional resources outside of marriage limits the institutionalized options of the divorced person. The ideology that stresses the marital relationship as the most beneficial institution for the realization of individual emotional gratification and happiness almost mandates that the individual seek a new marital partner. The result is that remarriage is increasingly becoming more predominant. Almost one out of five currently married people were married previously; one out of four marriages is a remarriage for one of the spouses. Furthermore, the divorced are remarrying sooner after their divorce.

William J. Goode (1956) in his seminal study, *After Divorce,* argues that high divorce rates do not imply social disorganization. The high remarriage rate provides corroborating evidence. It leads us to reconsider divorce as a temporary state rather than a permanent one for many people committed to marriage:

> Indeed, the divorce system then becomes in effect part of the courtship and marriage system: that is, it is part of the "sifting out" process, analogous to the adolescent dating pattern. Individuals marry, but there is a free market both in getting a first spouse, and in getting a second spouse should the individual not be able to create a harmonious life with the first one. Indeed, to the extent that marriage becomes a personal bond between husband and wife, and they marry after they are formed psychologically, there would seem to be at least some ideological arguments for their being free to shift about in order to find someone who fits better (Goode, 1962/1966:387).

Remarriage After Divorce: The American Experience

Remarriages have always been common in the United States. During the colonial period and through the 19th century the death of a spouse was almost always followed quickly by remarriage. The harshness of life demanded that a single parent obtain a spouse to help care and provide for children. Although remarriage after the death of a spouse has been an accepted institution, our society rejected the remarriage of divorced individuals. Duberman (1977) states that the American clergy were disinclined to remarry divorced individuals. State laws also existed to discourage this practice.

However, after World War I, the divorce rate in the United States began to rise. This gradually affected the attitudes and rates of remarriage of divorced people. Jacobson (1959) estimates that into the 1920s there were still more remarriages after the death of a spouse than after divorce. But, beginning in the

1930s, this pattern changed. Arthur J. Norton and Paul C. Glick (1976), reporting on remarriage patterns, have observed that at the present time the overwhelming majority of remarriages occur as a result of the divorce of one or both of the new partners.

The proportion of remarriage to all marriages occuring is steadily increasing. At the turn of the century, about nine-tenths of all marriages were first marriages; most of the remaining one-tenth involved widows or widowers. Jacobson (1959) calculates that only about 3 percent of all brides were previously married in 1900. The figure increases three-fold to 9 percent by 1930. The current estimate is that about one-fourth (25 percent) of all brides are divorced (Carter and Glick, 1976).

Concurrent to the rise of divorced persons who remarry is the increasing presence of children found in these remarriages. Andrew Cherlin (1980), citing U.S. Bureau of the Census figures, reports that nearly 9 million children lived in two-parent families where one or both parents had been previously divorced. He conjectures that a significant number of the children were from previous marriages. Given the acceleration of these figures, we would estimate that an even larger number of children are involved in these families of remarried divorced people today. The existence of such large numbers of remarried families necessitates an in-depth examination of the adjustments that these family members have to make after remarriage occurs.

The Adjustment of Members of Remarried Families After Divorce

There is a myth surrounding remarriage that says that the second marriage is more successful than the first. In popular parlance "love is better the second time around." The explanations given include the belief that remarried individuals are now older, wiser, and more mature. Also, it is assumed that divorced persons who remarry will work harder to assure a more successful second marriage. Yet, the divorce rate for persons who remarry after divorce is higher than for persons who marry for the first time (Cherlin, 1980). Paul C. Glick, the senior demographer of the Bureau of the Census, estimated that in 1975 about 36 percent of all first marriages may end in divorce, whereas about 40 percent of remarriages after divorce may also dissolve (cited in Westoff, 1977).

An apparent contradiction is noted by William J. Goode who cautions against viewing the divorced remarrieds as divorce-prone. Instead of comparing divorce rates, he suggests that one should ask all those who have remarried to compare their second marriages with their first. He reasons:

> Granted that the divorced who remarry are somewhat more prone to divorce than those who marry for the first time; nevertheless, the only comparison that makes sense to those divorced people is between their second marriage and *their own first marriage*. Our divorcees are not, after all, asserting that their second marriages are better than

marriages of *others* who are first married. They are only claiming that their second marriages are "happier" than their *own first* marriages. (Goode, 1956:334−335)

Andrew Cherlin (1980), however, argues that the divorce rate *is* the best indication of the differences in the unity between families of remarriages after divorce that include children from previous marriages and those of first-marriage families. Cherlin contends that there are insufficient institutional supports and guidelines to assure optimal success of these remarriages. He observes that family members of such remarriages face unique problems that do not exist in first-marriage families. He believes that the origins of these problems lie in the complex structure of remarried families and the normative inadequacies to define these familial roles and relationships:

> These families are expanded in the number of social roles and relationships they possess and also are expanded in space over more than one household. The additional social roles included stepparents, stepchildren, stepsiblings, and the new spouses of noncustodial parents, among others. And the links between the household are the children of previous marriages. These children are commonly in the custody of one parent—usually the mother—but they normally visit the noncustodial parent regularly. Thus they promote communication among the divorced parents, the new stepparent, and the noncustodial parent's new spouse. (Cherlin, 1980:375)

Cherlin is of the opinion that our society's overemphasis on first marriages provides little guidance for the handling of the potential problems of remarriages stemming from these complexities. To support this contention, he refers to the study of Paul Bohannan (1971) that calls attention to the inadequacies of our kinship terminology. Bohannan states that the term, stepparent, originally meant the individual who the surviving parent married to replace a parent who had died. A stepparent after divorce is an additional parent not a replacement. Our society has not developed norms on how to handle this situation. We do not have norms to govern our behavior and expectation, nor do we have norms to show the differences between parent and stepparent. The difficulties in what we call these stepparents highlights this problem. If a noncustodial biological parent is still alive and maintains contact with his or her child, does the the child also call the stepparent "Mom" or "Dad?" Cherlin points out that the lack of appropriate terms also exists for the new complex of extended relationships, including uncles, aunts, and grandparents. The significance of these absent terms is stated by Cherlin:

> Where no adequate terms exist for an important social role, the institutional support for this role is deficient, and general acceptance of the role as a legitimate pattern of activity is questionable. . . . These linguistic inadequacies correspond to the absence of widely accepted definitions form many of the roles and relationships in families of remarriage. The absence of proper terms is both a symptom and a cause of some of the problems of remarried life. (Cherlin, 1980:376, 377)

Legal and social difficulties also confront the families of the persons who remarry after divorce. The social and financial obligations of former spouses who have also remarried as well as the obligation incurred as the result of subsequent divorces and remarriages further complicates matters. Bohannan (1971) indicates that there are a whole series of social groups that emerge with remarriage. He refers to them as quasi-kinship groups as a result of the chain of relationships that are formed among spouses and their ex-spouses. These "divorce chains also result from complications which exist within the household which contains stepparents, stepsiblings, and half-siblings and by the ways that these household members behave in relation to ex-spouses and *their* families" (Bohannan, 1971:128−129).

Margaret Mead (1971) has identified the legal regulations regarding incest and consanguineal marriages that become problematic for remarried family members. She argues that incest taboos allow children to develop affection for and identification with other family members without risk of sexual exploitation. But incest prohibitions are drawn to blood or genetic relationships rather than to domestic relationships among household members. This failure in incest taboos can lead to inadequate security and protection of children. In more dramatic situations, it can lead to the sexual abuse and exploitation of individuals by their stepparents or stepsiblings. In ordinary circumstances, it can lead to psychological confusion and inability to develop adult relationships.

> As the number of divorces increases, there are more and more households in which minor children live with stepparents and stepsiblings, but where the inevitable domestic familiarity and intimacy are not counterbalanced by protective, deeply felt taboos. At the very least, this situation produces confusion in the minds of growing children; the stepfather, who is seen daily but is not a taboo object, is contrasted with the biological father, who is seen occasionally and so is endowed with a deeper aura of romance. The multiplication of such situations may be expected to magnify the difficulties young people experience in forming permanent-mating relationships, as well as in forming viable relationships with older people. (Mead, 1971:120)

Indeed, most customs and conventions of family life are not applicable to remarried families after divorce. These include such everyday activities as discipline of children—how much authority should stepparents have—the relationships of individuals with their spouse's ex-spouse, and the relationship among siblings and stepsiblings resulting from the various combinations that could come about when individuals remarry, divorce, and remarry. In all, the everyday nature of family life can be seen as problematic to these remarried family members.

The necessity for a critical examination of remarriage after divorce, especially when children are involved, is vitally needed. Such empirical research and analysis not only will increase our understanding of these family structures and processes but can also be of immeasurable aid in understanding the nature of the institutional relationship between the family and society in the transmission of social norms governing individuals. This point is the central concern of Andrew Cherlin and captures our attention:

> We need to know what the institutional links are between family and society which transmit social norms about everyday behavior. That is, we need to know exactly how patterns of family behavior come to be accepted and how proper solutions for family problems come to be taken for granted. And the recent rise in the number of remarriages after divorce may provide us with a natural laboratory for observing this process of institutionalization. As remarriage after divorce becomes more common, remarried parents and their children probably will generate standards of conduct in conjunction with the larger society. By observing these developments, we can improve our understanding of the sources of unity in married—and remarried—life. (Cherlin, 1980:380–381)

CONCLUSION

All societies permit divorce or the dissolution of marriage. In our cross-cultural examination of divorce we saw that there is no necessary association between divorce rates and societal breakdown or disorganization. Indeed, for many preliterate societies high divorce rates often serve to stabilize extended family systems. In our study of divorce in Japan and Egypt we observed that their respective rates of divorce have declined in the 20th century, whereas the rates in the United States have risen. Yet, as William J. Goode (1963) has observed, these changes in the divorce rates although going in opposite directions reflect a similar pattern—a growing tendency for both women and men to have equal rights of divorce.

Our attention then turned to an in-depth examination of divorce in the United States. The steady climb in the American divorce rate was shown to be related to social and familial changes closely associated with the family's relationship to economic processes. Changes in family ideology reflecting an emphasis on the independence and the privatization of the nuclear family has also played an important role in changes in the divorce rate. Of particular interest is the relationship of working wives and their increased economic independence and the possibility that their marriages may end in divorce.

Change in law regarding divorce and child custody were shown not only to reflect changes in familial roles but also to serve as an impetus to bringing about changes in the definition of marriage and the responsibilities of husbands and wives with each other and with their children. Further, divorce laws and custody decisions also define the continued obligations that the formerly married couple have to each other and to their children after divorce.

What happens to the wives, husbands, and children following a divorce and how familial roles change with the dissolution of the marriage was the next topic of concern. The effects of divorce on children was seen to be associated with the child's conceptualization of the parent's marriage. It is also associated with the child's age. We emphasized the need for more systematic research in this area and cautioned against imputing solely negative consequences of divorce on children. The readjustments, problems, and solutions of single parents raising children alone was then investigated. In the case of female-headed single-parent households we saw the interrelated affects of government and social policies regarding financial support—either direct or by enforcing spouse's child-support agreements—social services—such as child care and crisis intervention—and societal attitudes toward divorced women, especially in terms of employment opportunities and their ability to cope with circumstances.

Our final discussion was on remarriage. Remarriage rates, divorce rates of remarrieds, and the problems confronted by reconstituted families were analyzed. Here, again, we saw the necessity for more systematic investigation of remarriage.

16

Epilogue: The Family in China

This concluding chapter differs from summaries generally found in other texts. We apply the themes discussed in previous chapters to an analysis of a family system that we have only briefly discussed previously—the Chinese family. Thus the utility of the conceptual frameworks introduced earlier in this book can be tested by looking at changes in the Chinese family system. Our analysis will use modernization processes, the family's relationship with the wider kinship networks and surrounding communities, premarital and marital relationships, and age-and-sex differentiation and stratification patterns. In the pages that follow we will trace the changes that the traditional Chinese family system has undergone in the 20th century.

China is a vast country with almost 1 billion people. Its urban population, 200 million, is probably the largest urban population in the world. Yet, almost 80 percent of the population lives in the rural countryside. In the 20th century many changes have occurred. It has moved from a semifeudal country to a world force. It has undergone major political and social revolutions that have shaken the world. It has fundamentally transformed traditional agricultural and industrial ownership, production, and distribution. Its traditional family system with its emphasis on the needs of the collective rather than the individual has been influential in the development of a modern family form that differs fundamentally from the Western private conjugal family.

A brief footnote on the English spelling of Chinese names and places used in this chapter may be appropriate. The reproduction of Chinese sounds in written English is, at best, an approximation. The Chinese spellings in this chapter are drawn from the Wade-Giles system named for two nineteenth century British linguists. This is the familiar system for Chinese personal and place names that has long been in use. But in 1979, China officially adopted another system, known as Pinyon (phonetic spelling). In the same year, the United States government began to use Pinyin exclusively for Chinese names and places. While some of the printed media have also adopted the new system, others have not. This has complicated the translation period from Wade-Giles to Pinyon. With Pinyon, "Mao Tse-tung" is transformed into "Mao Zedong," "Hua Kuo-feng" becomes "Hua Guofeng," and "Teng Hsiao-ping" turns into "Deng Xiaoping." The spelling of China's capital changes from "Peking" to "Beijing." "Hong Kong" becomes "Xianggong." Indeed, if there wasn't a concession by the Chinese government "China," itself, would become known as "Zhonggo." To minimize confusion and given the historical emphasis of this chapter the author has decided to utilize the more familiar Wade-Giles system that already is well known to readers.

An understanding of these changes and the underlying issues involved is of immeasurable value not only in the understanding of the Chinese experience but also in understanding much of the sweeping social, political, and economic changes occurring in the contemporary world. Such an understanding will serve to illuminate much of our concern with the nature of social change and the family.

MODERNIZATION PROCESSES AND THE CHINESE EXPERIENCE: THE SETTING

In chapter 3 we discussed some of the implications of modernization processes on the individual, the family, and the society. The themes developed by Szymon Chodak (1973) and Peter L. Berger, Brigette Berger, and Hansfield Kellner (1973) helped us to examine modernization processes in Third World societies. Chodak referred to two types of modernization—accultural and induced. Both types were characterized by the absence of industrialization and were aimed at creating favorable conditions for future industrialization.

Accultural modernization, which was typical of the African colonial systems, emerged from direct confrontation and the superimposition of European colonial culture on the traditional culture. This frequently led to a phenomenon called detribalization. Detribalization is a process in which there was substitution of traditional positions and roles by a new system of positions and roles based on the Western model. Chodak sees the acculturative process as leading to alienation: the individual becomes marginal to both his traditional and modern worlds.

Berger and his associates (1973) voice similar conclusions. They observe that detribalization is a process of radical social reclassification. Not only is the world redefined but also the social relationships are reclassified and the individual's sense of identity is undermined: "At this point, all of reality becomes uncertain and threatened with meaninglessness—precisely the condition that sociologists commonly call anomie" (Berger, Berger, and Kellner, 1973:153). A condition that, they say, leads to the development of the "homeless mind."

In contrast, induced modernization, as described by Chodak, is a process of nation building and the generation of national identities. Its primary purpose is to transform the society into a new, national entity by integrating significant parts of the traditional culture into the new social order.

Berger's group examines modernization processes and its effect on traditional ways of life, kinship patterns, and "social constructions of reality." Although these authors do not explicitly make the distinction between acculturated and induced modernization, they reach a conclusion similar to Chodak in his discussion of induced modernization. They view this phenomenon as representing a later stage of the modernization process occurring in the Third World. With political independence and with the installation of revolutionary socialist governments, the state itself becomes the agent for development. The basic goal is to relate the ideologies of nationalism to socialism and to combine the benefits of modernity with the traditional tribal community that offers the individual meaning and solidarity. The aim is to prevent the alienating, fragmenting, and disintegrating processes relating to the destruction of tribal and communal solidarities.

This task is extremely difficult because modernization brings with it reclassification of social relationships based on economic status, occupation, and national relationships rather than having social relationships based on tribal and kinship criteria. Berger, Berger, and Kellner see modernization as both liberating and oppressing. Modernization liberates individuals from colonization and from the controls of family, clan, and tribe. It oppresses individuals in the quest for the development of technological and bureaucratic institutions. The tensions of the processes at work in induced modernization are dramatically presented in China after the revolution of 1949.

William Hinton (1966) titles his vivid account of revolutionary change in a rural Chinese village, *fanshen. Fanshen* is a Chinese word meaning a complete turnabout in the nature of the social world:

> Every revolution creates new words. The Chinese Revolution created a whole new vocabulary. A most important word in this vocabulary was *fanshen*. It means "to turn the body," or "to turn over." To China's hundreds of millions of landless and land-poor peasants it meant to stand up, to throw off the landlord yoke, to gain land, stock, implements, and houses. But it meant much more than this. It meant to throw off superstition and study science, to abolish "word blindness" and learn to read, to cease considering women as chattels and establish equality between the sexes, to do away with appointed village magistrates and replace them with elected councils. It meant to enter a new world. (Hinton, 1966:vii. Copyright © 1966 by William Hinton. Reprinted by permission of Monthly Review Press.)

The Communist Revolution was a total revolution. Not only was there a change of the political and economic system but also of the social system. The fundamental social relationships among individual, family, and community were dramatically transformed. This chapter is devoted to an examination of that transformation.

THE TRADITIONAL CHINESE FAMILY

The traditional extended Chinese family persisted without substantial structural change for almost 2000 years. There had been a general pattern of continuity and gradual assimilation of some changes into basic Chinese society. This long period without major social changes is partially accounted for by a deeply rooted tradition of paternalistic authority and control. Michael Gasster (1972) points out that the relationships between leaders and followers is central to all societies, but in China these relationships, especially the questions concerning duties, social obligations, and conflicting loyalties, were a primary concern of China's philosophers and statesmen throughout its history.

To ensure stability, an elaborate code developed that was anchored on fundamental family relationships. A rigid structural hierarchy became dominant and dictated proper attitudes and behaviors among people of different social statuses. The hierarchy of submission and dominance, which so characterized the family, was reflected in the larger semifeudal economic system. By the 19th century China was divided into two groups: a very small, privileged group, the gentry, and the vast majority group, the peasantry. The gentry claimed the position akin to the father's position in the family. Their claim was based on tradition and built on the foundation of family life. To fully understand the traditional family system, it is vitally necessary to see how it operated in this larger context. China's struggle to achieve modernization can best be studied by focusing on this relationship.

Marion J. Levy, Jr. (1949) characterizes the gentry as having the following characteristics:

1. Their primary source of income was from land, which they did not cultivate themselves, as well as income from government offices.
2. They held most of, if not all, the intellectual and academic positions.
3. They controlled the administrative, judicial, and legislative systems of the state.
4. They controlled the economy by absentee land tenure. As China moved into the 20th century, the gentry also became involved in industry and commerce—as owners and managers—and in banking. The gentry composed less than one-fifth of the population.

China was basically agricultural, and the peasantry, which accounted for more than 80 percent of the population, was predominant. The peasantry cultivated the land of the gentry. The peasantry did contain members who cultivated their own land, but, generally, they were tenants or hired nonlandowning agricultural laborers. Those groups that fall outside the status dichotomy are the handicraftsmen, the merchants, the servants, the soldiers, the domestic industry workers, the factory workers, and a miscellaneous group containing priests and entertainers. These later groups, according to Levy, were relatively unimportant in the social structure and generally followed the social patterns of the peasantry.

Levy claims that the picture of the gentry has been taken as representative of the entire population. He points out that the confusion is due to the fact that gentry family patterns were considered ideal patterns by almost the entire society. Western observers, therefore, have had great difficulty separating the ideal from the empirically valid descriptions of Chinese society. But, given this caveat, one should realize that the influence of the gentry can not be overemphasized. Their ways were the ideal patterns and served as the standards for the entire country.

The Chinese peasantry was faced with a dual system of oppression based on a hierarchy of domination and subservience that was enforced with brutality and violence. Oppression came from a semifeudal economic system and from the traditional family. Traditional family and village life was characterized by omnipresent exploitation. William Hinton describes it in his study of Long Bow, a rural village, during the transition period to Communist rule in the mid-1940s:

> Violence was chronic at all levels of human relationship, husbands beat their wives, mothers-in-law beat their daughters-in-law, peasants beat their children, landlords beat their tenants, and the Peace Preservation Corps beat anyone who got in their way. The only living creatures that could hope to avoid beatings, it seemed, were adult male gentry and draft animals—the donkeys, mules, horses, oxen, and cows that were the basis of Long Bow's agriculture. (Hinton, 1966:51)

In his graphic presentation of prerevolutionary family and village life, Hinton sees the entire system as being characterized by barbarity, terror, and cruelty. The system originated in the division of the society into the two classes of gentry and peasantry and extended this ideology to age and sex relationships. Two of the tales told to Hinton provide some indication of the pervasiveness of this everyday torment:

> There were three famine years in a row. The whole family went out to beg things to eat. In Chinchang City conditions were very bad. Many mothers threw newborn children into the river. Many children wandered about on the streets and couldn't find their parents. We had to sell our eldest daughter. She was then already 14. Better to move than to die, we thought. We sold what few things we had. We took our patched quilt on a carrying pole and set out for Changchin with the little boy in the basket on the other end. He cried all the way from hunger. We rested before a gate. Because the boy wept so bitterly a woman came out. We stayed there for three days. On the fourth morning the woman said she wanted to buy the boy. We put him on the *K'ang*. He fell asleep. In the next room we were paid five silver dollars. Then they drove us out. They were afraid when the boy woke up he would cry for his mother. My heart was so bitter. To sell one's own child was such a painful thing. We wept all day on the road. (Hinton, 1966:42−43).

The family life of both peasants and gentry was dominated by a rigid authoritarian hierarchy based on age and sex. The family strongly influenced every aspect of an individual's life. Three interlocking factors—generation, age, and proximity of kinship—resulted in the placement of each person into a fixed kinship group that determined one's ascribed status and determined one's obligations, rights, and privileges. These factors, particularly age hierarchy, laid the foundation for the hierarchy of status and authority of the family organization and the clan.

The oldest man had the highest status and unquestionable control of all important family decision making. Women's status was lower than that of all men, but increased with age and with the birth of male offspring. A great emphasis was placed on respect for age differences. Just as the wishes of the woman was subjugated to those of the man, the wishes of the young were subjugated to those of the old. There was dominance by parents and stratification of status and distribution of functions by sex and age. C. K. Yang observes that the Confucian canon of the kinship relation of Mencius (372−289 B.C.)[1] was followed: "between father and son there should be solidarity and affection; . . . between husband and wife, attention to their separate functions; between old and young, a proper order" (Yang, 1959:6−7). The relationship between father and son was held to be of primary importance.

The familial hierarchy of status and authority was anchored on the dual principles of filial piety and veneration of age. C. K. Yang[2] states that "filial piety demanded absolute obedience and complete devotion to the parents, thus establishing the generational subordination of the children" (Yang, 1959:89). Ideally, filial piety benefited both parents and children. Filial piety did not operate solely through coercion; it also included an emphasis on mutual interdependence, parental affection, and the child's moral obligation to repay parental care and affection. This is reflected in the Chinese proverb that says, "Men rear sons to provide for old age; they plant trees for shade" (Chao, 1977:123). Thus Paul Chao observes that filial piety can be related to group insurance.

Filial piety, the devotion of sons to their parents, was considered to be a vital necessity of family stability and order. It served as a major force of formal and informal social control. It was extended and institutionalized in the tradition of ancestor worship (the worship of dead male ancestors from the patrilineal group).

The veneration of age was the second pillar of social control. The elderly, the closest living contacts with ancestors, received deference, respect, and obedience. They were depicted as the repositories of wisdom. They held important positions both in the family and the community. They were considered the models of skill and knowledge in all areas, ranging from handicrafts to farming. Yang provides the following personal experience to emphasize the position of importance and prestige the elderly held in traditional China:

> In 1949 the writer tried to introduce into a village an improved weeder which worked much more effectively than hand weeding or hoeing. The younger peasants tried it and liked it very much, but a few days later nobody wanted to use the new instrument because "the old people concluded that it will hurt the root system of the plant." The writer challenged the younger peasants to experiment with the instrument by offering to pay for any damage resulting from it, but to no avail. Confucius' advice of learning to farm from an "old farmer" still stood firm. (Yang, 1959:92)

Yang attributes the long stability of the traditional family institution to the strength of filial piety and the veneration of age. However, he is quick to point out

---

[1]Mencius, born a century after Confucius' death, is generally regarded as one of the great developers of Confucian thought.

[2]C. K. Yang, *Chinese Communist Society: The Family and the Village*. Reprinted by permission of The MIT Press, Cambridge, Mass. © 1959 by the Massachusetts Institute of Technology.

that this great stability was achieved at the price of strenuous repression of the young and their almost complete lack of equality and freedom. Parents had absolute authority over their children including the right to put them to death:

> The proverb "The son must die if so demanded by the father" was a means of compelling obedience from the young in traditional China, especially in rural communities, although the carrying out of the threat was extremely rare. A childhood that passed without frequent physical punishment was an exception rather than the rule. When a child reached his mid-teens, his increased physical strength and his ability to run away bolstered his security, but the requirement of filial piety kept a tight rein on him. The necessity of observing this moral code was not merely impressed upon him in the operation of the family institution and group pressure of the community; it was also enforced by formal law. In the Ch'ing period sons were flogged or banished by the court merely on the charge of disobedience brought by the father. (Yang, 1959:93)

Together, filial piety and the veneration of age assured the preservation of a status system dominated by a hierarchy of age for the operation of family authority and control. In effect it was a system designed for the perpetuation of the traditional family institution and the rule of the old over the young.

Mate Selection

The domination of the elders over the young can be readily illustrated through an examination of mate-selection processes. Marriages were arranged by the families and were considered to be too important to be left to the whims and desires of the young. Since marriage served to draw two families together, it took precedence over the fact that it also brought together two individuals. In this and in other situations, the needs of the family took precedence over the needs of the individual. Of utmost importance was the desire to arrange a marriage that would produce a male offspring and thus assure continued ancestor worship.

Traditionally, there was little emotional involvement between the selected prospective marriage partners. Further, such involvement among eligible marriage partners was frowned on and was seen as a potential threat to the extended family. When emotional involvement was perceived by the elders, another suitable marriage was arranged. The disruption of such relationships provided a popular theme in Chinese literature. But, it should be emphasized, rarely did children disobey the wishes of their parents.

Arranged marriages were particularly difficult for the women. With marriage, the bride moved into her husband's family residence. Marriage often meant a complete uprooting of the wife from her family, friends, and community. Katie Curtin (1975) cites a study of a Chinese village in the 1920s that found that although almost 97 percent of the farm operators were born in the village and 94 percent of their fathers, only 6.6 percent of their wives had been.

The husband's parents sought a prospective bride who would be submissive to her new relatives, particularly her mother-in-law. The relationship between a new bride and her mother-in-law was frequently quite antagonistic. The daughter-in-law had to be resocialized and integrated into her new household and coercion was the popular mode to accomplish this.

Burgess and Locke (1945)—in their now classic textbook, *The Family from Institution to Companionship*—provide us with a document secured in 1932 from a Chinese student in Burgess's class at the University of Chicago. It records an interview with an aged woman in Chicago's Chinatown. Burgess and Locke point out that this document is of particular interest in that it depicts the traditional conception of the roles of mother-in-law and daughter-in-law in the context of the changing conceptualization of these roles. This is revealed by the younger woman's inner rebellion against the traditional power and authority of the older woman:

Mother-in-law was deeply religious, a faithful follower of Buddhism. My husband and I were Christians. Before I was married friends frankly warned me that it is impossible for a Christian to marry into a pagan family without domestic troubles. Some told me that mother-in-law was cruel. Accordingly, the double image of the tender Buddha and devilish mother-in-law constantly appeared in my mind. But I had to sacrifice my own happiness for the sake of my beloved husband.

A part of the marriage ceremony involves the giving of presents between the mother-in-law and daughter-in-law. Mother-in-law gave me a gold bracelet and I gave her the customary present of a skirt made by my mother. This signified the resignation of family duties by the mother-in-law. According to the old idea a full-dress was inconvenient for work; and hence the removal of a skirt signified taking on the duties of work. I thought this signified that the wife was to be the successor of the mother-in-law in carrying on family duties. My mother-in-law, however, interpreted it in a very restricted sense. Family duties to her were but the hard labor and the rest of the duties she kept for herself. Family policies were devised and executed by her, as a queen sitting on the throne of her kingdom.

Every morning, while the sun was still lying behind the morning dews, I went quickly to prepare morning tea for mother-in-law. Afterward I came back to my room to comb my hair, and then, I put on my formal dress. The skirt was indispensable for a full dress.

Going to her bedroom, I found that she was still asleep. I stood beside her bed for an hour waiting to attend her. At last she awoke. I bowed to her humbly; then I gave her my arm in support until she reached her armchair. I went to the kitchen and took a basin of hot water to her bedroom and helped her wash her face. Then I presented her a cup of hot and fragrant tea with all the eastern virtue and politeness I could command.

It was nine now; I had to prepare breakfast. We had servants, but did they help me do anything at all? No. My own status was lower than any of them. I had no experience in cooking. The criticisms of my cooking were hardly bearable. Such criticisms as "It is too salty." "It is tasteless," etc. prevented me from being calm; my tears flowed like an inexhaustable fountain. I came back to my private room, crying and crying.

At night I had to take care of her bed. I had to hang down her mosquito net in order to keep mosquitoes out. Besides, I had to say good night while leaving.

I disliked two things particularly. The prohibition against having a private talk with my husband destroyed the best part of my marriage life. Occasionally we talked in our private room. As soon as she discovered it she would call me out with a scornful voice. In her own philosophy private talks were undesirable at home since everything in the home was opened to every individual. There was no privacy at all.

Second, I was not permitted to visit my mother's home often. I was permitted to go to her home once a year, though she was living near by. Once when I went to my mother's home for five days, I suddenly found out that a carriage was waiting outside for my return. Mother-in-law tried to cut me off from both my husband and my mother. (Burgess and Locke, 1945:46−47).

From *The Family: From Institution to Companionship,* by Ernest W. Burgess and Harvey J. Locke. Copyright 1945 by American Book Company. Fourth Edition by Ernest W. Burgess, Harvey J. Locke, and Mary M. Thomes. © 1971 by Little Educational Publishing, Inc. Reprinted by permission of D. Van Nostrand Company.)

Marriages generally occurred when girls were between the ages of 15 to 17 and boys were between the ages of 16 to 18. Child marriages of girls was a frequent occurrence. The young bride became the property of her husband's family and was discouraged from having any contact with her own family. Symbolizing her new life was a new name, which reflected her position in her new household. Her wishes and desires were subordinated to that of her new family. Thus she had no alternative means of financial support. She was in effect in bondage to her husband and his family. And, since she was separated from her own kin, she had no external kin supports.

Divorce

Divorce occurred infrequently in the traditional family system of China. It was discouraged and uncommon although the husband had the right to divorce his wife on several grounds, these included disobeying the husband's parents, failing to have children, acquiring a loathsome disease, committing adultery, displaying jealousy, or being overly talkative and stealing (Leslie, 1979:119). But husbands rarely resorted to this measure. The poor could not afford it; the wealthy found it stigmatizing. Further, the structural reality of the extended family mitigated against it.

Husbands also had alternatives to divorce that were quite acceptable. They could find relief from an unhappy marriage through prostitutes or by obtaining a concubine. Concubines, although not legally wed, could become members of the man's household. For women, however, there was no emotional or sexual institutionalized outlet outside of marriage. Marion J. Levy, Jr. (1949), in his discussion of divorce, observes that a distraught daughter-in-law had only two options, either to run away or to commit suicide. Divorce was not a viable alternative. Its occurrence was viewed as a tragedy for women. Her repudiation by her mother-in-law or by her husband necessitated that she return to her own family in shame. She was no longer deemed suitable for marriage. She had minimal rights within her parents' household, and she was denied the opportunity of becoming wife, mother, and mother-in-law, her only source of status, prestige, and power.

In extremely unbearable situations, unhappy wives saw suicide as the only way out from the rigidities of the marital bond. William J. Goode (1963), in his examination of suicide statistics in China during the pre-Communist 20th century, argues that the prevalence of suicide may have been exaggerated by romantic legend. He further states that the young bride, realizing that suicide was her only alternative, reduced her motivation to struggle against her mother-in-law. He also declares that, "Conversely, since suicide was a great disgrace for the family that caused it, it is likely that most families *reduced* their pressures on the daughter-in-law when she showed any such intention" (Goode, 1963:312).

C. K. Yang (1959), on the other hand, provides us with some evidence—vivid testimony of the difficulties and "solutions" encountered by wives in domestic situations that proved to be irresolvable—that may be indicative of a prevailing pattern:

> In sixteen counties in southern Shansi, from July to September of 1949, there were twenty-five women who died of inhuman treatment by their husbands or their fathers- or mothers-in-law. In Hotsin and Wanchuan counties of the same province, in the second half of 1949, twenty-nine women committed or attempted suicide by hanging themselves or jumping into the well for the same reason. In the months of July to September in Wenshui county and in November in Taiku county there were twenty-four legal cases involving the loss of human lives; among these fourteen were women who met death for the same reason. In Pingyao county the wife of Chao Ping-sheng demanded a divorce and Chao killed her. In Lingchuen county, Li Shao-hai, a young married woman, commited suicide on account of maltreatment by her husband and mother-in-law. (Communist report cited in Yang, 1959:66)

Women's Status

Women were considered inferior in traditional China although their status increased with age, the bearing of male heirs, and the ascending to the head of domestic household in older age. In the prerevolution years female babies were considered an economic liability and throughout their lives females were downtrodden and suffered.

> How sad it is to be a woman!
> Nothing on earth is held so cheap.
> Boys stand leaning at the door.
> Like Gods fallen out of heaven.

Their hearts brave the Four Oceans,
The wind and dust of a thousand miles.
No one is glad when a girl is born;
By her the family sets no store.

(Fu Hsuan cited in Curtin, 1975:13)

The practice of female infanticide was common, particularly in time of famine, drought, high taxes, and other economic catastrophes (Levy, 1949:99). Although the actual killing of a female child at birth may not have occurred with great frequency, the child frequently suffered neglect with a resultant higher death rate among female children than among their male counterparts. The selling of female children into slavery occurred frequently among the peasantry. The neglect and maltreatment of female children was tied to the oppressive feudal economic system. William Hinton (1966), in his analysis of rural village life, presents the following case study on the integral relationship of child neglect and economic conditions:

In Chingtsun one old woman said, "I sold four daughters because I had to pay back a landlord debt. I wept the whole night, and the tears burned my eyes. Now I am blind. Poverty forced me to sell my own daughters. Every mother loves her child." Others said, "In the old society no one loved a daughter because you brought them up and they left the house. Many parents drowned their little daughters. In the old society feet were bound with cloth. Small feet were thought to be one of the best qualities of women. But to bind a woman's feet is to tie her body and soul. Small feet are a symbol of the old society." (Hinton, 1966:397−398)

A heartrendering illustration of the abuse of females was the prevalent practice of foot binding. Young girls between the ages of 5 and 7 had their feet bound. This practice, which was introduced into China in the 10th century, continued well into the 1940s, although it was officially banned in 1911. Ostensibly, the bound foot was romanticized as a mark of femininity and beauty; in actuality it became a symbol of the subordinate role of women in China. An old Chinese proverb states its essential purpose: "Feet are bound, not to make them beautiful as a curved bow, but to restrain women when they go out of doors" (Curtin, 1975:10). The binding process, which was excruciatingly painful, required the flexing and pressing of four toes over the sole of the foot. The feet were then bound in bandages, and the girl was forced to walk in shoes that became progressively smaller until, after a two- or three-year period, the feet were reduced to three or four inches in length from heel to toe.

The inferior position of women was actualized within the marriage structure and in their seclusion and lack of education. C. K. Yang (1959) observes that the seclusion of women was not only to prevent them from contact with men outside the family, thus forestalling romantic love as a basis of marriage, but also to prevent them access to opportunities for independence in political, economic, and social activities. The following passage illustrates how the traditional ways still survived in the early years of Communist rule:

> Restricting and interfering with women's participation in social activities is a form of mistreatment. After the victory of the Chinese people's revolution, due to the growth of political awakening, the broad masses of women have begun to participate in social activities, but they face a great deal of resistance. Some women who participated in the women's association, in literacy classes, or in newspaper-reading groups, have come home to confront the long faces of a husband and mother-in-law. Some women have returned from a meeting and the family would not give them food to eat, and some have even been locked out of the house. Some husbands and mothers-in-law summarily forbid women from participating in any social activity. Still other women are beaten up or even tortured to death by their husbands and mothers-in-law because of participation in social activities. Such conditions occur not only among peasants and workers, but also among urban bourgeoisie, and even among the intelligentsia. (Yang, 1959:112)

In summary, the rigidity of the class lines that separated the gentry from the peasantry provided for the strength and stability of the traditional family system. But such stability was achieved at the price of immeasurable repression and suffering. Within the rigidity of the family hierarchy, women and the young were subjected to harassment and punishment by men and the old. The subjugation of individual rights and the rights of women and the young were traditionally justified as practices that preserved and strengthened the family. Ultimately, the traditional age and sex hierarchy and the system of family status and authority facilitated its very downfall. To document the changes in the family, we now turn to an examination of the historical processes and forces both before and after the Communist revolution.

THE COMMUNIST REVOLUTION AND THE FAMILY

Prior to the founding of the People's Republic of China in 1949, the traditional social order was already undergoing changes. Beginning in the mid-19th century, the eastern seaboard and inland river ports were industrializing and open to Western trade. Improved means of transportation and the development of new economic opportunities brought many peasants and intellectuals into the emerging cities. Western ideas, norms, and material goods introduced through religious missions, trade, education, and political intervention led to the rapid disintegration of the traditional family among the intellectuals. They demanded a less authoritarian family structure, equality of women, free choice in marriage selection, greater freedom for the young, and the end of footbinding, concubinage, and female slavery.

The traditional family system, with its rigid hierarchy and institutionalized subjugation of women, the young, and the individual, was challenged by the intellectuals and by the oppressed age and sex groups. In 1911, with the overthrow of the

Ch'ing Dynasty and the rise to power of Sun Yat-sen, these groups demanded a new family system. Despite the intensive and extensive resistance of traditionalists, modern changes were gradually legitimated through a series of legal statutes that stressed equality of the sexes and individual rights over those of the kinship group. Through the 1910s, 1920s, and 1930s, a series of civil codes were formulated that sought to change the family system into a more equalitarian one. However, the movement had its greatest impact on the already liberalized higher status intellectual groups located in the urban centers. It had relatively little impact on the vast agricultural region that contained more than three-quarters of the population. Further, there is very little evidence that the Nationalist government enforced any of these codes, and it is relatively certain that there was minimal change when the Communists gained political control of the country in 1949.

The Chinese Communist Party (CCP) from its inception in the early 1920s realized that the traditional family system was dependent on the traditional ideological, political, and class systems as well as the semifeudalistic agricultural economy. Its persistence through 2000 years without major substantive changes was attributed to the fact that it was thoroughly integrated with the traditional system and, indeed, served as the center of all social activities. From its beginning the CCP desired to replace the Confucian-based virtues and ethics of the family with a new family system based on Marxist ideology. The family was conceived as the institution basic to providing the necessary link to the building of the new socialist individual and the socialist society. Reflecting the views of Marx, Engels, and Lenin, the CCP attacked the old family system for its maltreatment and oppression of women. Mao Tse-tung's report to the Executive Committee published at the Second National Congress of Representatives of the Soviets held in March 1934 demonstrated the Communist emphasis on the liberation of women from the tyranny of the family:

> This democratic marriage system destroys the feudal shackles which have fettered humanity and in particular the women and it establishes new norms in accordance with human nature. It is one of the greatest victories in human history, however this victory depends on the victory of democratic dictatorship. Only when, after the overthrow of the dictatorship of the landlords and capitalists, the toiling masses of men and women—in particular women—have acquired political freedom in the first place, and economic freedom in the second, can freedom of marriage obtain its final guarantee. (Mao Tse-tung cited in Chao, 1977:126–127)

This historical concern of the CCP formed the basis of the Marriage Law of 1950. It was the first civil code announced by the CCP after the establishment of the People's Republic of China. According to Teng Ying-chao, vice-president of the All-China Democratic Women's Federation and the wife of Chou En-lai, the purpose of the law was "to ensure to people the full freedom of marriage, and to deal a death blow to the old marriage system" (cited in Curtin, 1975:35).

The Marriage Law of 1950 is based on the equality of the sexes. It excludes the influence of extended family members in the selection of marital partners and abolishes arranged marriages. It outlaws polygamy, concubinage, child marriage, and the practice of paying a price in money or gifts for a wife. The new law, which actually is a moral code for the regulation of many aspects of family life, also prescribes new methods of contracting marriages, defines the rights and duties of the husband and wife, redefines the relations of parents and children, and protects the rights of children. The articles on divorce allow for divorce by mutual consent or on the insistence of either spouse. It describes the obligations of divorced parents to their children and defines the division of property after divorce.

The Marriage Law of the People's Republic of China

CHAPTER I: GENERAL PRINCIPLES

Article 1

The feudal marriage system based on arbitrary and compulsory arrangements and the supremacy of man over woman, and in disregard of the interests of the children, is abolished.

The New-Democratic marriage system, which is based on the free choice of partners, on monogamy, on equal rights for both sexes, and on the protection of the lawful interests of women and children, is put into effect.

Article 2

Bigamy, concubinage, child betrothal, interference in the re-marriage fo widows, and the exaction of money or gifts in connection with marriage, are prohibited.

CHAPTER II: THE MARRIAGE CONTRACT

Article 3

Marriage is based upon the complete willingness of the two parties. Neither party shall use compulsion and no third party is allowed to interfere.

Article 4

A marriage can be contracted only after the man has reached 20 years of age and the woman 18 years of age.

Article 5

No man or woman is allowed to marry in any of the following instances:

a) Where the man and woman are lineal relatives by blood or where the man and woman are brother and sister born of the same parents or where the man and woman are half-brother and half-sister.

b) Where one party, because of certain physical defects, is sexually impotent.

c) Where one party is suffering from venereal disease, mental disorder, leprosy or any other disease which is regarded by medical science as rendering a person unfit for marriage.

Article 6

In order to contract a marriage, both the man and the woman should register in person with the people's government of the district or township in which they reside. If the proposed marriage is found to be in conformity with the provisions of this Law, the local people's government should, without delay, issue marriage certificates.

If the proposed marriage is not found to be in conformity with the provisions of this Law, registration should not be granted.

CHAPTER III: RIGHTS AND DUTIES OF HUSBAND AND WIFE

Article 7

Husband and wife are companions living together and enjoy equal status in the home.

Article 8

Husband and wife are in duty bound to love, respect, assist and look after each other to live in harmony, to engage in productive work, to care for their chidren and to strive jointly for the welfare of the family and for the building up of the new society.

Article 9

Both husband and wife have the right to free choice of occupation and free participation in work or in social activities.

Article 10

Husband and wife have equal rights in the possession and management of family property.

Article 11

Husband and wife have the right to use his or her own family name.

Article 12

Husband and wife have the right to inherit each other's property.

CHAPTER IV: RELATIONS BETWEEN PARENTS AND CHILDREN

Article 13

Parents have the duty to rear and to educate their children; the children have the duty to support and to assist their parents. Neither the parents nor the children shall maltreat or desert one another.

The foregoing provision also applies to foster-parents and foster-children.

Infanticide by drowning or similar criminal acts is strictly prohibited.

Article 14

Parents and children have the right to inherit one another's property.

Article 15

Children born out of wedlock enjoy the same rights as children born in lawful wedlock. No person is allowed to harm them or discriminate against them.

Where the paternity of a child born out of wedlock is legally established by the mother of the child or by other witnesses or material evidence, the identified father must bear the whole or part of the cost of maintenance and education of the child until the age of 18.

With the consent of the mother, the natural father may have custody of the child.

With regard to the maintenance of a child born out of wedlock, if its mother marries, the provisions of Article 22 apply.

Article 16

Neither husband nor wife may maltreat or discriminate against children born of a previous marriage by either party and in that party's custody.

CHAPTER V: DIVORCE

Article 17

Divorce is granted when husband and wife both desire it. In the event of either the husband or wife alone insisting upon divorce, it may be granted only when mediation by the district people's government and the judicial organ has failed to bring about a reconciliation.

In cases where divorce is desired by both husband and wife, both parties should register with the district people's government in order to obtain divorce certificates. The district people's government, after establishing that divorce is desired by both parties and that appropriate measures have been taken for the care of children and property, should issue the divorce certificates without delay.

When one party insists on divorce, the district people's government may try to effect a reconciliation. If such mediation fails, it should, without delay, refer the case to the county or municipal people's court for decision. The district people's government should not attempt to prevent or to obstruct either party from appealing to the country or municipal people's court.

After divorce, if both husband and wife desire the resumption of marriage relations, they should apply to the district people's government for a registration of re-marriage. The district people's government should accept such a registration and issue certificates of re-marriage.

Article 18

The husband is not allowed to apply for a divorce when his wife is pregnant, and may apply for divorce only one year after the birth of the child.

Article 19

In the case of a member of the revolutionary army on active service who maintains correspondence with his or her family, that army member's consent must be obtained before his or her spouse can apply for divorce.

Divorce may be granted to the spouse of a member of the revolutionary army who does not correspond with his or her family for a period of two years subsequent to the date of the promulgation of this law.

CHAPTER VI: MAINTENANCE AND EDUCATION OF CHILDREN AFTER DIVORCE

Article 20

The blood ties between parents and children are not ended by the divorce of the parents. No matter whether the father or the mother has the custody of the children, they remain the children of both parties.

After divorce, both parents continue to have the duty to support and educate their children.

After divorce, the guiding principle is to allow the mother to have the custody of a breast-fed infant. After the weaning of the child, if a dispute arises between the two parties over the guardianship and an agreement cannot be reached, the people's court should render a decision in accordance with the interests of the child.

Article 21

If, after divorce, the mother is given custody of a child, the father is responsible for the whole or part of the necessary cost of the maintenance and education of the child. Both parties should reach an agreement regarding the amount and the duration of such maintenance and education. Lacking such an agreement, the people's court should render a decision.

Payment may be made in cash, in kind or by tilling land allocated to the child.

An agreement reached between parents or a decision rendered by the people's court in connection with the maintenance and education of a child does not obstruct the child from requesting either parent to increase the amount decided upon by agreement or by judicial decision.

Article 22

In the case where a divorced woman re-marries and her husband is willing to pay the whole or part of the cost of maintaining and educating the child or children by her former husband, the father of the child or children is entitled to have such cost of maintenance and education reduced or to be exempted from bearing such cost in accordance with the circumstances.

CHAPTER VII: PROPERTY AND MAINTENANCE AFTER DIVORCE

Article 23

In case of divorce, the wife retains such property as belonging to her prior to her marriage. The disposal of other family property is subject to agreement between the two parties. In cases where agreement cannot be reached, the people's court should render a decision.

In cases where the property allocated to the wife and her child or children is sufficient for the maintenance and education of the child or children, the husband may be exempted from bearing further maintenance and education costs.

Article 24

In case of divorce, debts incurred jointly by husband and wife during the period of their married life should be paid out of the property jointly acquired by them during this period. In cases where no such property has been acquired or in cases where such property is insufficient to pay off such debts, the husband is held responsible for paying them. Debts incurred separately by the husband or wife should be paid off by the party responsible.

Article 25

After divorce, if one party has not re-married and has maintenance difficulties, the other party should render assistance. Both parties should work out an agreement with regard to the method and duration of such assistance.

CHAPTER VIII: BY-LAWS

Article 26

Persons violating this Law will be punished in accordance with law. In cases where interference with the freedom of marriage has caused death or injury to one or both parties, persons guilty of such interference will bear responsibility for the crime before the law.

Article 27

This Law comes into force from the date of its promulgation.

In regions inhabited by minority nationalities in compact communities, the people's government (or the Military and Administrative Committee) of the Greater Administrative Area or the provincial people's government may enact certain modifications or supplementary articles in conformity with the actual conditions prevailing among minority nationalities in regard to marriage.

Adopted by the Central People's Government Council at its 7th Meeting on April 13, 1950. Promulgate on May 1, 1950 by order of the Chairman of the Central People's Government on April 30, 1950.

To destroy the authority base of the traditional family system, a multifaceted attack was launched in the form of land reform, economic innovation, class struggle, class consciousness, and thought reform. It was deemed necessary to destroy the authority structure of the gentry, which was based on land ownership and the power of the *tsu* (clan).

The CCP viewed the traditional family, the clan organization, and the landlord system as interlocking agents of the old feudal system and, therefore, as obstacles that must be removed for the society to modernize. The *tsu*, in particular, came under attack. The *tsu*, which was the largest corporate kin group, included all persons with a common ancestor. The *tsu* could be composed of thousands of people and could include both gentry and peasantry. It varied in importance from one section of the country to another, but it could often include all the inhabitants of a village. In such cases, it served as the judicial and enforcement authority, and it acted as a governmental agency in the collection of taxes. The educational system was controlled by the *tsu*. It ultimately had control over individual families and served as the final mediator in their disputes. It maintained ancestral graves and the extensive *tsu* property.

The interrelationships among families of the same *tsu*, who often have the same surname, are depicted in the following document written in the pre-Communist era:

> Every family in X village where I live bears the surname "Chu." These families are all descended from Ting Ling Chu who moved from a village twenty miles away to X about three hundred years ago. The X village is one of six villages which make up the Chang River clan of Chus with fifteen villages. Our family has intimate relations with the group of Chu families in the village. The village has an ancestral hall which is the center of social and religious life of the Chu families in X. When some extraordinary thing happens to some one family, other families are willing to help. Therefore, there is no need of any philanthropic institution. When a person of the village dies a tablet made of wood bearing his or her title and name is put in the shrine of the ancestral hall and the ceremony of ancestor worship is conducted there.
>
> The families of the village are well organized. A board of elders consisting of the oldest member of each family is in charge of the village affairs. At regular meetings the birth of every male child and every marriage are recorded. The board of elders also has judicial power. When there is a dispute between two families, they refer the matter to the board for decision. The board of elders then calls a meeting in which not only the elders of the board but all influential members of the village are present. The two parties present their claims and arguments and after discussion, persuasion, and compromise, a certain agreement is brought about.
>
> The Chu county clan has no definite organization. All Chu families of the same county have good will toward each other and under some extraordinary circumstances they may combine. About fifty years ago a member of a family in a Chu village was mistreated by the magistrate of a neighboring county. He presented his case to the members of the Chang River Chu and they decided to take revenge. Chus from two districts of the county joined the crusade. About a thousand people marched to the neighboring county and caught the magistrate. They brought him to the office of the prefect and demanded that he be dismissed from office. The prefect consented.
> This incident reflects how members are protected by family organizations in China.
> (Burgess and Locke, 1945:39–40)

Land-reform practices sought to attack the *tsu* at its base. Traditionally, the family farm was viewed as a family enterprise, as were other kinship-based industries. Even the farming equipment was the joint property of the extended family. All deeds and contracts were signed in the family name. The CCP acted through an atomizing land reform. They proceeded to redistribute land regardless of the two bastions of traditionalism, age and sex. It was presumed that, by undermining the traditional economic base, the traditional social structure would also be undermined. Confiscation of land and subsequent redistribution to the peasantry was to create a new social base, tear down the class structure, and, in turn, help reorder the state.

Social classes were reclassified. Village social life was no longer centered on the *tsu*. Only approved social meetings took place under party scrutiny. All informational sources were placed under party control. The educational system underwent drastic revisions. The CCP recognized the importance of education and sought to implement a new system that would nullify and destroy the old ways. Education became available to all, especially women, who were systematically excluded under the traditional system.

In *China Shakes the World,* Jack Belden gives a vivid illustration of the major changes that took place in the lives of peasant women as Mao's Eight Route Army was liberating areas of the country from Japanese control during the years 1938–45. The CCP was committed to the equality of women. When they gained control of large areas, they initiated land reform and won the support of the peasants. They found that women were an important ally. The CCP adopted a radical social program to mobilize the population in the continued fight against the Japanese and the Chinese Nationalists:

> In the women of China the Communists possessed, almost ready made, one of the greatest masses of disinherited human beings the world has ever seen. And because they found the key to the heart of these women, they also found one of the keys to victory over Chiang Kai-shek. (Belden, 1970:275)

One of the first acts was to organize a women's association. A cadre (political worker) would get some women together and would encourage them to talk about their lives. The cadre would tell them that they no longer were in bondage to men, that they had the right to equality, the right to eat well, and should not be beaten by their husbands or in-laws. At first, the women were reluctant to speak of their bitterness and misery. But slowly, they began to speak up. And so was born the Speak Bitterness sessions.

The Speak Bitterness sessions can be compared to the consciousness-raising groups of contemporary American women. In these meetings groups of women would gather in the village and publicly recount the brutality of the old system. Women soon realized that their personal torments were not unique but rather reflected social conditions under which they had all been living. Their individual concerns were transformed into a collective force against the oppressive system. It led to their unification.

Belden dramatically describes this process in ''Gold Flower's Story'' (Belden, 1970:275–307). Gold Flower gave her account of her problems and received the encouragement of other women to change her unhappy situation. She returned to her in-laws home and attempted to force them and her husband to alter their brutal treatment of her and consider her as an equal. When her wife-beating husband did not comply, the women's association took collective action and vented their fury and anger:

> The crowd fell on him, howling, knocked him to the ground, then jumped on him with their feet. . . . Those in the rear leaped in, tore at his clothing, then seized his bare flesh in their hands and began twisting and squeezing till his blood flowed form many scratches. . . . Chang let out an anguished howl. "Don't hurt me anymore." Under the blows of the women, his cries were soon stilled. The women backed off. Gold Flower peered down at her husband. He lay there motionless on the ground, like a dead dog, his mouth full of mud, his clothes in tatters and blood coming in a slow trickle from his nose. "That's how it was with me in the past." Gold Flower thought. Unable to restrain a feeling of happiness, she turned to the other women. "Many thanks, comrade sisters, for your kindness. If it had not been for you, I would not have been able to get my revenge." (Belden, 1970:302)

The tensions and conflicts were not simply between the wife and husband. There was also an inherent problem between women of different generations that surfaced. Mothers-in-law saw the drive for female equality as a real threat to their status and interest, with a resultant loss in their economic and social security in old age. Equality, they perceived, would mean that they no longer would be able to control their sons' wives and force them to assume their workload. William Hinton (1966) illustrates this conflict in his account of a man who was criticized for favoring his wife over his mother and thus was not fulfilling his filial piety.

In the three decades since the revolution of 1949, China has experienced four major campaigns all directed in part to assure the emancipation of women and the destruction of the traditional patriarchal family system. The first thrust was the passage of the Marriage law of 1950, which sought to free the individual from the old traditional feudal system. The second, the Great Leap Forward of 1958, was intended to achieve greater productivity in agriculture and independence in industrial development. Through the establishment of communes, it sought to achieve women's equality by circumventing traditional male perogatives in the family and household. The third campaign was the Great Proletarian Cultural Revolution, which began in 1965. With the death of Mao Tse-tung in 1976 and the ascendancy to power of Teng Tsaio-ping, China can be seen to have entered into the present phase of social and family change. Our account will continue by examining events after the passage of the Marriage Law of 1959, which culminated in the Great Leap Forward Campaign of 1958.

Although the Marriage Law of 1950 made important inroads toward the achievement of women's equality and the destruction of the patriarchal family, significant problems were encountered. National priorities after land reform focused on increasing production, nationalization, and the collectivization of agriculture. Lower priorities were given to the struggle against the traditional family institution. These economic and political factors resulted in the downplaying of women's rights and increased emphasis was placed on mobilizing women while admonishing them to perform traditional family duties as well.

This, in turn, led to a revival of traditional family practices in rural areas. Aline K. Wong (1974) examined Chinese documents that revealed that the practice of early marriage, arranged marriage, and the payment of exorbitant bride prices still prevailed well into the second half of the 1950s. For example, Inger Hellstrom (1963) reports that, in 1953 in two rural counties, 90 percent of all marriages were arranged. He also cites a study undertaken in 1953 to investigate enforcement of the Marriage Law of 1950, which concludes that:

> The law was only partially effective in the Central-South and East China, and hardly at all observed in Northwest and Southern China, where parents still arranged marriages, reared daughters-in-law for their sons, and married off their children too young; even female slavery and concubinage were still practiced. (Hellstrom, 1963:272)

THE GREAT LEAP FORWARD AND THE CULTURAL REVOLUTION

The period 1953 through 1958 was designated as the "transition to socialism" period and was governed by policies of the first Five Year Plan. This period was marked by unbalanced production: industry experienced enormous growth, but agriculture proceeded at a much slower pace, barely keeping up with the increase in production. The dissatisfaction with the unbalanced production and countrywide economic problems led the CCP to adopt a new policy, the Great Leap Forward, which would stress more balanced economic growth in agriculture as well as in heavy and light industry. This plan also desired to achieve a more efficient balance between centralized planning and local initiative. The result was the development of the communal system in rural and urban areas. This was essentially a major reworking of provincial political boundaries and a new administrative system. The primary thrust was to get communes located in the countryside to combine all fucntions from industry and agriculture to education and self-policing. The Second Five Year Plan began in 1958 and was to initiate "the construction of socialism." An allied objective of the Great Leap Forward was to bring women into full economic partnership with men.

The Chinese Communists following in the intellectual position of Marx, Engels, and Lenin believed that women could not achieve a full position of equality in the society if they were confined to household tasks. Tied to this belief was the allied idea that as long as production centered on the family unit women would be restricted to the home. If the family continued as the unit or production, women would be solely involved in the care of the children and of housework. The solution to this problem was seen in the collectivization of the land and with everyone, women and men alike, working it:

In the old society, women were generally regarded as men's dependents, no matter how hard they worked at home. The profession of housewife did not pay. Apart from political and social discrimination against women, the economic dependence of women was the source of men's superiority complex and their undisputed authority as head of the family. Under such circumstances, notwithstanding all talk to the contrary, inequality between men and women existed in fact so long as women had to depend on men for their support. . . .

Liberation brought political and social discrimination against women to an end [sic]. But the problem of economic dependence of women took a long time to solve, with the result that women were usually at a disadvantage in public life. This unfortunate state of affairs changes rapidly when women stand on their own feet economically and become equal partners with men in supporting the family. In this way the status of women is raised. . . . Thus women acquire an increasing sense of their economic independence and the old practice of the male head of the family bossing around the home is on the way out. (cited in Johnson, 1976:300)[3]

The CCPs introduction of the system of the commune in 1958 was claimed to represent a stage in the development of the ultimate Communist form of common ownership and equal distribution according to need. A major objective of the communes was to facilitate the destruction of the clan and its replacement by the commune itself. It sought to replace the preexisting pattern of familism with communalism. It developed out of the traditional family values that stressed the extended family over the individual. Individualism continued to be submerged within the newly emergent unit—the commune.

Ancestral graves were converted into farmlands, and economic life fell under the domination of the commune not the clan. The political control exercised by the clan was surrendered. Rural populations were resettled—to break up the local village ties, which often were under the domination of the *tsu*. The *tsu* was attacked as the embodiment of the old feudal system, which served to perpetuate the corrupt Nationalist Government. It was also seen as the basis for the dominance of both the older generation and males. In general, the aim was to replace the *tsu* with the commune and its own network of authority and loyalty.

By the end of 1958 the government had taken ownership of almost all heavy industry. It established some 26,000 rural communes, each averaging 5000 households and about 2400 acres of land. The commune became the administrative standard of rural community organization. It sought to be self-sufficient by manufacturing its own tools, fertilizers, and clothing, as well as its food.

To get women into the labor force, many household tasks were collectivized. As part of the program, the rural communes set up communal dining rooms, kitchens, nurseries, and child-care centers, and kindergartens and schools. Additional services, developed to reduce further the need for individual women's work

---

[3]The quotation is from Yang Kan Ling—in "Family Life—The New Way," *Peking Review,* November 18, 1950) pp. 9–10.

within the family, included laundries, weaving and sewing cooperatives, barber shops, and shoe-making and repair shops.

William J. Goode (1963) astutely points out that the establishment of the communal system and its accompanying collective domestic services can be seen as one way of radically revamping sex-role relationships without insisting that men get involved in traditionally female-defined tasks. Further, this collectivization had as its primary aim not so much the destruction of sexually designed division of labor but rather the socialization of women's work so that they could enter the labor force and get out of the home:

> In certain respects, the development of communal dining halls, nurseries and kindergartens, laundry services, and so on may be more acceptable to the Chinese male than would be any serious attempt to force him to conform to egalitarian values that would direct him to share the household tasks equally or to give up the services which were traditionally his male right. Under the communal system, he may still obtain these services, even though they are not so individualized as they would be in his own household; at least he does not have to take part in such "women's activities," himself. . . . after many generations of ideological debate in the West, men have not yet conceded egalitarianism in the home or in the economic life. How much less, then, would Chinese men have accepted such a move. To this degree, then, the communal solution bypasses the still strong insistence on male prerogatives among Chinese men. (Goode, 1963:302)

The communes brought about a massive introduction of women into the labor force. In 1959, 90 percent of the total female labor force worked in the rural communes. Johnson (1976) cites figures that report that men worked an average of 249 days in rural areas before the Great Leap Forward; in 1959 their work load had increased to 300 days. For women, the figures almost double: 166 days in the precommune year and 250 days at the height of the commune movement. Most of the jobs women obtained were not in heavy industry—these still remained male-defined occupations—but were in such new industries as water conservancy, afforestation, construction projects, as well as in increased sideline jobs in fisheries and animal husbandry. Several hundred million women were employed in these newly created labor markets. Thus, in these occupational areas as well as in the collectivization of such domestic services as food preparation and child care, the CCP was careful to avoid generating hostility among men: "The Great Leap policies, it seems, did not attack norms that operated against women's participation in certain types of work so much as it created new jobs in areas that women could enter more easily" (Johnson, 1976:301).

However, soon after the implementation of the policies of the Great Leap Forward, China experienced great economic difficulties. In 1959 almost half of the cultivated land was affected by heavy floods or serious drought. The following year more drought, typhoons, floods, and insect pests seriously affected almost three-quarters of the cultivated land. Soon after the creation of teh communes, a rift developed between the Soviet Union and China, which led to the withdrawal of Soviet economic aid in 1960. This caused critical problems in heavy industry and was a severe setback to China's industrial progress.

In addition to these difficulties, organizational problems in the communes compelled a slowdown in the rate of economic growth and expansion. This centered around the anger of the peasants to communal administrative policies. Katie Curtin (1975) points out that the reasons for the failure of the Great Leap Forward were not directly related to its reforms of family life. Rather, the difficulties stemmed in part from the attempt to radically reorganize traditional villages under a central commune administration. This centralism changed the work pattern by drastically lengthening the workday and by transferring a large part of the harvest out of the hands of the peasants for distribution to the cities and for industrial uses.

William Gasster describes the failures of the Great Leap Forward in the following summarization of the analysis by Ta-Chung Liu:

> The Great Leap Forward was based on a sound diagnosis of the basic weakness of the mainland economy but a serious misconception of the proper way to deal with it. The poorly conceived treatment included excessive regimentation in rural life, impossibly long working hours, removal of incentives (such as family plots), unworkable farming and water control techniques, excessive pressure on industrial enterprises to expand production, and total miscalculation of technical possibilities in introducing the backyard furnaces." . . . "The whole economy suffered a serious leap backward from 1958 to 1961." (Gasster, 1972:122).

During the 1960s, almost immediately after the implementation of the Great Leap Forward in 1958, the massive economic difficulties experienced in China led to a reversal in the policy concerning the mobilization of women into the labor force. In 1959 and 1960 the Great Leap Foward began to be abandoned. The communes were radically altered. Gasster (1972) reports that the 26,000 large communes were divided into about 74,000 smaller ones—a three-fold increase. This approximated the number of townships that existed before 1958. The organizational structure of a given commune was also reduced in size. Families were given small private plots. Land that they farmed collectively with other families coincided with the land that they had always farmed. The communes still controlled a variety of functions, including birth, death, and marriage registry, regulation of civic disputes, and management of schools and hospitals. They were still viable administrative entities.

For women, the collapse of the Great Leap Forward meant a retrenchment in their drive for equality. Nurseries, dining halls, and other collective domestic services were scaled down or abolished. The many special industrial and agricultural projects that had been newly created and that employed a high percentage of women were consolidated or shut down. The result was that a large number of women who had just entered the labor force found themselves laid off or unemployed. The CCP, although recognizing that this retarded the achievement of women's equality and prevented the redressing of serious inequities, felt that first priority was overcoming the economic reversals:

> Concerning the status of women, marital status and family relationships, survivals of old ideas and viewpoints still remain.
>
> On top of this, the extent of women's participation in social labor, viewed either from the number of persons employed or from the role they have played, still suffers a certain limitation although it is the correct proportion in relation to the present stage of development of our national economy. As a result of this limitation, there is still a difference in fact though not in law for women in the enjoyment of equal rights with men both in society and in the home. This difference will gradually disappear following the further development of production. That is to say, to do away completely with the old survivals in marriage and family relationships, it is necessary to create the more mature socio-economic and ideological conditions this requies. (cited in Johnson, 1976:301−302)[4]

China underwent political and economic turmoil throughout the 1960s. In the years from 1961 through 1966, China experienced a retrenchment in many of the radical political, economic, and social policies advocated by Mso Tse-tung. During this period Mao was replaced as head of state by Liu Shao-ch'i. Liu's primary concern was to proceed with economic development and saw no necessity to insist on the rigorous following of Maoist policies. Western models or those of the Soviet Union could be adopted if they would increase industrial and technological developments.

Liu emphasized material incentives, private plots were encouraged, and free markets flourished. His policies relaxed Mao's demand for political indoctrination and party discipline. Liu also desired to strengthen the family to help establish higher production outputs. The result of these policies was an increase in the standard of living and a relaxation of the miltary-style aspects of everyday life, but it also led to the increased power of the family.

Liu's policies meant a return of women to domestic life and a reaffirmation of traditional family roles albeit with a Communist twist. Ai-li S. Chin (1969), in a content analysis of Chinese fiction from 1962 to 1966, reports that it stressed the solidarity of the nuclear family, the renewal of wider kinship ties, and a respect for elders in general and the father in particular. Chin observes that the stories that emphasize family unity have as a common theme the partial return to the old pattern

---

*The quotation is from Yang Liu—in ''Reform of Marriage and Family Systems in China, *Peking Review*, March 18, 1964, p. 19.

of paternal authority and filial piety. They emphasize the solidarity of the father-son tie and the reassertion of younger generation subordination. Father relationships with daughters includes strictness with an element of affection, a pattern that repeats the traditional practice of fathers disciplining their daughters less severely than their sons. Interestingly, Chin finds ambivalence in the stories dealing with the proper roles of women. Two rival ideologies are present: the first emphasizes the authority of elders; the second concerns the basic doctrine of individual responsibilities. Further, the stories reflect a dilemma on the correct position for liberated women: Should she be independent or demure? Should her place be with her family and the household or as a full participant in the labor force in the building of the socialist state?

In 1966 Mao wrestled political control away from Liu and his supporters through his brilliant use of the Red Guard and the subsequent launching of the Great Proletarian Cultural Revolution. The objective was to wipe out the "four olds"— old ideas, old culture, old customs, old habits. According to a Maoist document of the period, the aim was to "use the new ideas, culture, customs and habits of the proletariat to change the mental outlook of the whole of society" and to "touch people to their very souls" (cited in Gasster, 1972:130). Integral to this view was Mao's desire to prevent the development of a Soviet-style bureaucratic ruling class.

Handwritten posters were pasted on walls, posts, and kiosks throughout the country. The Red Guards, consisting primarily of the young, attacked the Liu-led leadership and their followers as well as the intellectuals and the bureaucrats who in their view had lost sight of the needs of the masses and who no longer followed the objectives of the revolution. There was a wholesale purge of party members at all levels. Liu Shao-ch'i was disgraced and purged.

The years 1966 through 1969 were marked by turbulence. The remnants of traditional society were violently attacked and suppressed. Traditional artifacts, such as old art objects, were smashed and old books were burned. It was as if all visual evidence of the past had to be destroyed.

The Red Guard entered peoples homes and shattered family altars that denoted allegiances to the Confucian reverence for ancestors. Churches, mosques, and temples still serving religious functions were closed and put to secular use. This included the great Buddhist, Lama, and Taoist temples of Peking, which had been allowed to remain open partially because of tourists. All religious statues, altars, and other religious artifacts were removed.

Tillman Durdin (1971), writing for the *New York Times*, vividly described the effects of these policies based on his observations of a three-week visit to the vast coastline of China. He reported that not a single home that he visited had any family altar; nor were there tablets to ancestors or any representation of the old gods worshipped by the Chinese masses—which would still be found in family homes in Hong Kong. Women no longer wore the traditional sheath dresses, nor did they use cosmetics. They wore the same garments as men, frumpy blue or gray trousers and jackets. The traditional large Chinese family was not visible. Indeed, housing could only accommodate a husband, wife, and one to three children. He observed the absence of traditional art, music, and literature, which had been replaced by Maoist equivalents. He concludes:

> In the Chinese People's Republic there is no "mysterious East" any more, just worka-day people following workaday routines that seem essentially familiar and ordinary to the Westerner, even though they operate within a Marxist totalitarian framework . . . . A new generation has appeared and though much of the old China is too indelible to erase as yet, a new China with ways quite different from the old is in existence. (Durdin, 1971:125–126)

It can be seen that the ultimate aim of the Cultural Revolution was to revive and expand many of the goals of the Great Leap Forward. Mao hoped that this would enable China to overcome the "Three Great Differences—the differences (or contradictions) between town and country, industry and agriculture, and mental and manual labor" (Gasster, 1972:130). Mao believed that to build a proletarian society it was necessary to have a viable commune system:

> In Mao's view, the ultimate solution to problems of political unity, social change, and economic development continues to be the commune system, in which a relatively high degree of administrative decentralization encourages the people's sense of participation, releases their energies and productive capacities, and avoids excessive bureaucratization; and ideological solidarity, which means common allegiance to Mao's thoughts, provides national unity. Indeed, it sometimes seems that ideological solidarity, which means common allegiance to Mao's thoughts, provides national unity. Indeed, it sometimes seems that ideological unity is intended as a substitute for political and economic centralization. If so, Mao's China bears a certain resemblance to traditional China. But Mao believes that only the commune system can permanently eliminate the Three Great Differences. (Gasster, 1972:134)

The implementation of the policies of the Cultural Revolution had a significant impact on the family and on women's roles. Once again, emphasis was placed on the need for women to engage in the collective economy to achieve fully equality. Women, including working women and housewives, were politically mobilized. They were encouraged to criticize and question the power structure, whether it be in the home, at work, or in the community. The authoritarian structure of the family came under attack:

> Over thousands of years our family relations have been that son obeys what his father says and wife obeys what her husband says. Now we must rebel against this idea. . . . We should make a complete change in this . . . . It should no longer be a matter of who is supposed to speak and who is supposed to obey in a family but a matter of whose words are in line with Mao Tse-tung's thought (Johnson, 1976:310).

However, despite some additional gains, the pendulum once again swung toward conservative norms and values. By 1972 the revolutionary zeal subsided and the concern for women's political mobilization, equal education, and full involvement in the collective economy once again died down. Kay Ann Johnson (1976) makes the following points in her concluding remarks on the women of China, which presents, in succinct form, an overall assessment of the Cultural Revolution:

> However, the Cultural Revolution may have accelerated the creation of a new generation of young women leaders. These women, without personal knowledge of the wretched female oppression of the past, may be more conscious of the persistence of serious discrimination of the present. Like the Red Guards who, taking their elder's socialist ideal seriously, became critically aware of the elitist nature of established institutions before their elders in authority, young educated women may be more likely to take the propagated ideals of sex equality to demand more complete equality in politics, family life, and work. What is certain is that the struggle to make families, jobs, and opportunities equal has only begun. Liberation will be won only through protracted struggles—struggles that persistently raise issues of sex inequality to the level of political saliency and that overcome the ever present tendency to shelve these issues and mask continued inegalitarian practices and values. (Johnson, 1976:315−316)

CHINA AFTER MAO

New policies about social change were revised dramatically in China during the 1970s. The Cultural Revolution of 1966−1972 weakened the economy. In addition, the excesses of revolutionary zeal among radical Maoists curtailed the development of education, science, and technological knowledge. In 1971 the U.S. Secretary of State, Henry Kissinger, and in 1972 President Richard M. Nixon visited China. In addition to the broader perspective of global politics, the process of diplomatic normalization can be seen as a desire by the Chinese to obtain scientific and technological know-how.

In 1974 two years before their deaths, Chairman Mao and Premier Chou put forward the Four Modernizations Program. It was not until after their deaths and the ascendancy to power of Teng Hsaio-p'ing that the ambitious plan calling for the complete modernization of China by the year 2000 began to be implemented. This plan calls for four modernizations—in farming, industry, science and technology, and defense. Its primary aim is to accelerate scientific, technological, and industrial development to increase economic growth.

The Four Modernizations Program has three phases. The first, covering the years 1978−1980, is aimed at the nationwide mechanization of agriculture and the consolidation and restructuring of existing industry. Phase two covers the next five years, 1980−1985. It calls for major developments in factory production. The final stage, 1985 to the year 2000, seeks further expansion of production by including more sophisticated consumer goods and such advanced technological items as electronics and computers. All indications of military modernization are given lower priority in the creation of a technological and industrial base (*Newsweek,* 1979).

To improve planning, make administration more efficient, and raise productivity, greater stress is being put on material incentives, adopting relatively elitist policies to foster the development of needed talent and using market forces to spur competition and foster development. Teng Hsaio-p'ing has reversed Mao's view of human nature. Mao argued that individuals are motivated to work their hardest for the common good, whereas Teng takes the view that individuals are primarily motivated by material encouragements. The range of material incentives introduced by Teng include bonuses for productive factory workers, bigger incomes, increased private plots, and the lowering of the costs for agricultural equipment for hardworking agricultural workers. Students with the highest grades are given preferential treatment in entering colleges and studying abroad.

In January 1979, in an attempt to take advantage of the unused talents of the prerevolutionary capitalists, landowners, and other members of the gentry still residing in China (whose power and influence were stripped during the Cultural Revolution), China restored their citizens rights. In announcing these policy changes, the CCP began a blistering attack leveled against those who were instrumental in the programs, implementations, and practices of the Cultural Revolution. Coming under attack was Lin Piao, the former Defense Minister, and Mao's leftist associates, known as the Gang of Four. By October 1979 Mao himself was criticized, and the Cultural Revolution was described as appalling and leading to catastrophe.

The implications of these changes for the Chinese family are beginning to be felt. An integral aspect of the Four Modernizations Program is the desire for stability and unity. This means a reinforcement of family values over individual concerns. It has led to a hardening of attitudes regarding divorce. Divorce is now viewed as "going against the feeling for social harmony and economic efficiency" (Butterfield, 1979). The reading on a divorce trial illustrates this change.

U. S. Senators In China View Divorce Trial

FOX BUTTERFIELD

SHANGHAI, April 18—It could almost have been a tale out of an old Chinese novel. The irate woman, angered by her husband's filial devotion to his parents rather than to her and by her mother-in-law's scorn when she failed to give birth to a son, sued for divorce.

Under a liberal divorce law decreed by the Communists to lessen what they view as the oppression of traditional family life, she was entitled to the divorce, because her husband's family, which she had been forced to live with, was guilty of what the Communists term feudal thinking. But in practice, as Wei Jinfeng, 35 years old, found out in a protracted court mediation session here that was opened to visitng American legislators, asking for a divorce can be asking for trouble. It goes against the feeling for social harmony and economic efficiency and it exposes a married cou;e to the full force of community pressure.

After a two-and-a-half-hour debate involving Mrs. Wei, her husband, a judge, two assessors, or jurors, and half a dozen representatives from the couple's work places and neighborhood, Mrs. Wei agreed to a reconciliation. Only she had argued for the divorce.

"At present our country is carrying out the four modernizations," the judge told her, referring to the Government's economic development program in agriculture, science and technology, defense and industry. "Our country needs stability and unity, so families must practice stability and unity also."

"Our duty is to educate people, not to attack them," he counseled both Mrs. Wei and her husband, Hung Sungdao, a 39-year-old clerk in an import-export office. Their names differ because in China a woman does not adopt the husband's name.

The judge and the others who urged the couple to get back together did not use the term love, which is officially regarded as a suspiciously decadent Western bourgeois conceit.

Instead, a co-worker of Mrs. Wei's at the Shanghai Meterological Instrument Factory advised, what they needed was to base their marriage "on a good political understanding," such as she had with her husband. The remark elicited a titter from the spectators.

The proceedings, held in a compound belonging to the local district committee, were witnessed by a delegation of the United States Senate Foreign Relations Committee, headed by Frank Church, Democrat of Idaho, its chairman. The group, which included Senator Jacob K. Javits of New York, the ranking Republican member, was on a six-day tour of China.

Foreigners are seldom permitted to witness court cases, so the hearing offered an unusual insight into features of life under the Communists: the strength of peer pressure, the persistence of such traditional values as filial piety and the ready resort to Communist phraseology in everyday life.

Mrs. Wei, who held her 5-year-old daughter on her lap during much of the session, applied for a divorce in August. If both partners agree, "there is freedom of divorce," the judge Li Haiqing, explained. Divorce can also be granted, he said, in cases of adultery or if the couple did not have a chance to get to know each other well before marrying or when one partner is discriminated against because of the lingering "poison of feudal thinking," as in Mr. Wei's instance. The law calls for attempts at reconciliation before a divorce is approved.

As Mrs. Wei described her situation, their "contradiction," the Maoist term for troubles, began when she gave birth to a daughter instead of a son. Male offspring have traditionally been more treasured because they can earn more and stay with their parents after marriage. A daughter is like spilled water, according to an old saying, because she moves to her in-laws after marriage.

When Mrs. Wei came home from the maternity hospital, she told the court, her mother-in-law greeted her by holding up a male infant, a sign designed to insure that she would have a boy next time. Later the two women quarreled over how much Mrs. Wei ate, and the contradiction sharpened when she secretly had an abortion, fearing the consequences of another daughter.

Mrs. Wei then moved out, taking a small room for herself and her child, and demanded that her husband give her their share of the family's ration cards for the many essentials that are strictly rationed.

Her husband recalled the story differently, testifying that she showed no respect for his parents, smashed much of the furniture in anger, ripped his clothes one day when they met on the street and went to his office over 140 times to complain about his behavior. Still, he did not want a divorce.

After husband and wife finished testifying, some of the people they work with and live with took turns urging them to make up. "You should carry out more ideological work with your mother to correct her feudal thinking," a man told the husband. "In our society women can be airplane pilots, like men, so girls are not less good than boys."

What finally seemed to sway Mrs. Wei was concern for her daughter, who, she said, blamed her for the troubles. When she related this she began to sob, producing tears from several of the witnesses.

It is difficult to gauge how widespread is the old-fashioned thinking encountered by Mrs. Wei. A woman interpreting the case for Senator Church commented: "I didn't have the same problem. My child is a boy, and my mother-in-law can't bear to be separated from him."

Fox Butterfield, in *The New York Times*, April 22, 1979. © 1979 by The New York Times Company. Reprinted by permission.

The Four Modernizations campaign has led to a change in Chinese population policies. The CCP believes that a high growth rate could wipe out most of the anticipated development gains. "The rapid growth of the population has brought a lot of difficulties to the national economy, the people's livelihood and employment, creating a roadblock for socialist construction. Fast population growth has hampered the four modernizations and the raising of the people's living standards." (Chinese official cited in Sterba, 1979). This is a radical change from the earlier philosophy that population growth is beneficial to the national interest.

China has launched an extensive birth control educational campaign, using radio, television, newspapers, commune reading rooms, and exhortative songs at concerts to spread the new policy about population size. Birth control devices are readily available and are distributed without cost. Sterilization operations for both men and women are encouraged. Abortions are largely free and given on request. Abortion does not carry the same emotional overtones that it does in the United States, and it never has been a political issue. The operations last about an hour and are either acupuncture abortions or Western-style procedures. Unless there are complications, women are expected to return to work the next day. In addition to birth control and abortions, the Chinese are encouraging later marriages, usually not before 28 for men and 25 for women. Legally, women cannot register for marriage until age 23. The marriage age for men is 26 in urban areas and 25 in rural areas. This modifies the Marriage Law of 1950 which prescribed the marriage age of men at 20 years and women at 18 years of age.

Economic incentives are used to curb population. Economic rewards are given families who have the required number of children (two or one) and those families who accede that number (three or more) are punished economically. In Sichuan province—with 90 million people, it is more populous than all but seven countries in the entire world—cash subsidies and other incentives are provided to families who have only one child, and 10 percent bonus in monthly income is offered. Such families are also eligible for the same amount of housing as larger families. Their child would also receive preferential treatment in admission to schools and in job assignments. In other provinces, salaries of those who have a third child are reduced 10 percent until that child reaches the age of 14. The child will also be denied free education and medical care.

China's approach to population control includes using group pressures. Factory managers and commune leaders maintain records on the number of children each woman has borne as well as the type of contraceptive she uses. Women's groups reach communal decisions on which family will be allowed to have a baby. Decisions are reached by checking with the provincial family planning committee on the factory or agricultural production team's birth quota. In addition, women's groups monitor the menstrual cycles of the female employees to check compliance. In this way, they hope that the unit's productivity will not be adversely affected by having too many women out on maternity leave (Butterfield, 1979).

Men are not exempt from social pressures. Publicly kept birth control charts report on the techniques used by men to control their family size, and the charts are open to scrutiny by all members of the production unit. Butterfield (1979) reports that on one wall of the clinic of a production brigade there is a listing of the 29 officials and how they are complying with the birth control campaign. Of the 27 men named (2 are women), the chart shows the 10 who have had vasectomies and the 14 whose wives are using the pill or the interuterine loop. Of the remaining 5, 2 of the men are married but are not practicing family planning and 3 others are too young to marry under China's strict policy of delaying wedlock until the prescribed age.

Recent newspaper dispatches have reported changes in Chinese attitudes toward heterosexual relationships. Under headlines with such titles as "Love Blooms Again"[5], "Chinese Discover Love and other Feelings"[6], and "First Cautious Steps: Dancing in a Changing China,"[7] these news stories report a loosening up of the strict moral codes covering relationships between men and women. Noticeable increases in the number of young men sporting mustaches and longer hair are being seen on Peking's streets. The young are increasingly shedding their Mao tunics and are wearing such fashions as tweed coats and leather jackets. These changes indicate that there is less pressure for social conformity. Finally, romance itself is making a comeback, or at least a Western version of romance. Western observers report that there are now young persons holding hands or sitting on public benches and gazing into each other's eyes. We must caution the reader to be weary of misreading these events as evidence that certain Chinese customs are emerging as Oriental versions of Western courtship, marriage, and family patterns and values. That is far from the case.

Westerners in their assessments of Chinese culture frequently fail to acknowledge one of the most significant differences in their culture and that of the Chinese: the differential value placed on individual rights versus group values. Westerners place primary emphasis on individual rights, whereas the Chinese favor the role of the individual in the group. Ross Terrill (1979), one of the most astute Western authorities on China, observes that all rights and duties flow from "self fulfillment of the person" and "shared values among the people." Occidentals favor the former, Chinese the latter. The group emphasis stems from the Confucious tradition and the Communist ideology. The contemporary social structure of Chinese society is based on the need for self-sacrifice in the building of an advanced industrialized nation. The imposition of Western values have led Americans, in particular, to misjudge and misunderstand developments in Chinese policy regarding modernization and the family.

Since the Communist Revolution, China has been influenced by two goals that sometimes coincide, sometimes conflict with each other. One is the desire to create antiauthoritarian social relationships within a collectivist social organization. The other is to develop heavy industry and reach economic and development parity with the Soviet Union and the United States. After the 1949 revolution, China embarked on a policy that stressed heavy technological development and rural modernization. The development of an elitist class of managerial experts and the potential for the creation of a managerial and bureaucratic new class led to the Great Leap Forward and the establishment of the communes in 1958. Emphasis was placed on more egalitarian social relationships and on women's equality and involvement in the labor force. The failure to develop medium and light industry in the rural coun-

[5]*Newsweek*, February 5, 1979, pp. 51, 53.
[6]*Philadelphia Inquirer*, March 12, 1978.
[7]Fox Butterfield in the *New York Times*, December 31, 1978.

tryside led to a retrenchment in the drive for equalitarian social relationships.

From 1962 to 1966 China was governed by the conservative policies of Liu Shao-ch'i. The emphasis was on the development of heavy industry and a hierarchical division of labor, greater stress was placed on material incentives and market-capitalism considerations. The issue of women's liberation and the development of a more egalitarian family system was ignored. The Cultural Revolution of 1966 through 1972 was a return to a concern for the development of labor-intensive industry and more egalitarian social relationships. Technological-intensive heavy industry and its inherent hierarchical division of labor fell into disfavor.

The post-Mao period, under the leadership of Teng Hsaio-p'ing, once again called for technological and heavy industrial development. That is the essence of the Four Modernizations program. In the past, similar programs have meant the reemergence of autocratic social relationships, including the domination of the individual by the family system. It remains to be seen what the future holds for the individual and the family in China.

The Chinese Rock

Tom Lee

Thirty years ago, on the docks of Shanghai, my parents said goodbye to their families. They had married a few days before, and were sailing for America, where my father was to study engineering. No one spoke of adventure or opportunity that day. Instead, most of the relatives wept over the separation, and begged them to return in one year rather than two. But just before departure, my grandfather took my father aside and told him that turmoil was coming to China, that he might have to remain in America indefinitely, and that they probably would never see each other again.

My father didn't believe him; if he had, I doubt that he would have left. Such was the power of the Chinese family. But my grandfather was right—my parents' American honeymoon became a generation. And my grandfather never saw his son again or met his American grandchildren.

I like to think he would have been pleased that so much of the family that had said goodbye to my parents that hot day in 1948 had gathered again to greet me when I arrived in China earlier this year. One aunt rode the train 44 hours to reach Peking on time. I understood at once that my family had come through the revolution intact. Only later did I realize that the institution of the Chinese family itself had survived too. It had changed to serve the revolution, as has practically everything, but it remains an asset to the new China.

Ironically, revolutionary ideology poses less of a threat to the

Chinese family than the sociological consequences of industrialization, which are all too familiar in the United States. Until recently, the opposite seemed true. The Chinese family was, after all, the basic unit of Confucian society. Bloodlines were virtual chains of command, and filial piety superceded all other allegiances—to friends, neighbors, even country.

In contrast, the heart of the Chinese revolution is a passion for community: The awareness among individuals that their lives are intertwined, that united they are—as Chairman Mao said—history's greatest motive force. Culturally, all of the saying of Confucius on traditional loyalties have given way to the simple slogan, "Serve the people."

How has the rise of the communal spirit changed the Chinese family?

In the 1950s, China experimented with collectives where traditional roles were abolished; cooking, eating and child-rearing were all communal. Most of these experiments failed, and for a good reason. "People didn't like them," one veteran told me.

Nevertheless, families have been forced to bear other equally painful stresses. For example, "serving the revolution" has required many couples to separate from each other or their children when their skills were needed in different provinces. Attempts have been made to romanticize these sacrifices' I read in one child's English-lesson book, "My father is a worker. He lives in another province. We see him once or twice a year. We are very proud of him . . ." Such separations are less common now that many "ultraleft" policies have been rejected along with the so-called Gang of Four—unhappy workers are, after all, unproductive workers.

Of greater social impact are enormous efforts to integrate family life and work, such as the superb day-care centers at most factories, where parents can visit and even nurse children during work breaks.

In rural China, though, children still tend to be reared in the traditional way—by grandparents. Many homes are three-generational, as the oldest son usually stays with the parents after marriage. If a family has no sons, one of the daughters and her husband remain at home. (Now that the revolution has raised women's status, such arrangements bring no shame.)

Thus, families include grandparents far more often than in the United States, with obvious benefits. The elderly rear the children while the parents work. Children learn to respect and be comfortable with their elders, so old age carries little or no stigma. More importantly, the elderly remain fully integrated in family and society. They take their responsibility for the next generation as a sacred trust. One woman in her 70's told me, "Rearing my granddaughter is hard work, but very important."

This traditional system is consistent with basic themes of the new Chinese society: Everyone has a role, everyone can make a contribution, everyone has a place in the world. It also echoes Chairman Mao's teaching to take what can serve China from the old and the foreign, and discard only the bad.

A far greater danger to the three-generation nuclear family lies in the social changes reminiscent of recent United States trends—trends that have contributed to serious problems in American life.

China is still a backward nation, but it is industrializing rapidly. Huge factories have spawned cities and suburbs, and the new homes are usually small two-room apartments. The families that fill them often can no longer find room in their homes or lives for grandparents. Thus a few institutions have sprouted, similar to American nursing homes for the victims of progress—dormitories for old folks with nowhere else to go.

Still, China remains 80 percent rural, geographically and culturally. For Chinese youths to leave their families for either work or adventure— as my parents did 30 years ago—is still unusual and a minor tragedy.

These values are reflected in the Chinese view of the West, parts of which emerged recently when I asked three Chinese college students what they wondered about America. Their questions: "Why do American children leave their parents?" "Who takes care of the parents when they are old if the children are not there?" "What happens when the old people get sick?" "Don't the children feel guilty?" "Is it true that when parents visit their children in America, they have to pay a bill at the end of their stay?"

These questions came from students who themselves had left home to attend Nanking University. They are a key part of China's current "long march" for modernization, a push that involves learning from and even imitating the West.

What worries me is the possibility that American misfortunes must be repeated, that the Chinese family will be a casualty of the pursuit of progress just as in America, and that the Chinese won't realize it until too late.

Following Chairman Mao's advice to take only what serves China and discard the rest may, in the end, be impossible.

CONCLUSION

Winston Churchill once described the Soviet Union as "a riddle wrapped in a mystery inside an enigma." For many, this description is even more fitting in describing China. We chose to study the Chinese family extensively in the concluding chapter of this book for a number of reasons. In its own right, the permanence and change of the Chinese family is unique. In the 20th century, there has occurred an accelerated development of the Chinese family sysem that, although strongly influenced by Western technology and ideologies, remains fundamentally Chinese. We pointed out how the traditional family system with its emphasis on the needs of the collective—family, clan, village, and China—rather than the individual continues to be reflected in the development of a modern family form that differs fundamentally from the Western private conjugal family.

However, the themes raised in this book—modernization and social change, consanguineal and conjugal family forms, the family's relationship to the community and the society, premarital and marital relationships, parent-child relationships, and age- and sex-differentiation and stratification patterns—can be better understood through an examination of the modern Chinese family system, which is in change. We examined these topics historically through an analysis of the convoluting changes of the Chinese revolutions of the 20th century. The tensions existing between different ideological positions—first between the Nationalists and the imperial Manchu dynasty, next between the Communists and the Nationalists, and finally between the radical Maoist wing of the Communist party and the more pragmatic wing, represented today by Teng Hsaio-p'ing—was investigated. This investigation was not directed at world political implications but rather at the implications for the Chinese people and their family system.

In conclusion, we remind the reader that the revolution in 20th-century China was a total revolution. The political, economic, social, and family revolution occurring in China during this period was unique in its totality and its fundamental effects on the individual. The social relationships between the individual, the family, and the community are being transformed radically. Yet, it is this acceleration of change that has made the study of the Chinese family so fascinating and useful. It highlights, in a most dramatic fashion, the themes relating to social change and the family. In sum, we trust that our examination of the Chinese family experience will increase the reader's knowledge and understanding not only of China but also of much of the sweeping social, political, and economic changes occurring in today's world and how they affect families and their members.

References

Abu-Lughod, Janet L. 1961. "Migration adjustments to city life: The Egyptian case." *American Journal of Sociology* 67:22–32.

Adams, Bert N. 1975. *The Family: A Sociological Interpretation*. 2nd ed. Chicago: Rand McNally.

Aldous, Joan. 1968. "Urbanization, the extended family, and kinship ties in West Africa." Pp. 297–305 in Sylvia Fleis Fava (ed.), *Urbanism in World Perspective: A Reader*. New York: Thomas Y. Crowell.

al-Sa'id, Aminah. 1977. "The Arab woman and the challenge of society." Pp. 373–390 in Elizabeth Warnock Fernea and Basina Qatan Bizirgan (eds.), *Middle Eastern Women Speak*. Austin: University of Texas Press.

Anderson, Nels. 1923. *The Hobo*. Chicago: University of Chicago Press.

Applebaum, Richard P. 1970. *Theories of Social Change*. Chicago: Markham.

Arensberg, Conrad M. 1937. *The Irish Countryman*. Gloucester, Mass.: Peter Smith. (Reprinted 1959.)

Arensberg, Conrad M., and Solon T. Kimball. 1968. *Family and Community in Ireland,* 2nd ed. Cambridge: Harvard University Press.

Ariès, Philippe. 1962. *Centuries of Childhood: A Social History of Family Life*. Robert Baldick (trans.). New York: Knopf.

Axelred, Morris. 1956. "Urban structure and social participation." *American Sociological Review* 21:13–18.

Aziz-Ahmed, Shereen. 1967. "Pakistan." Pp. 42–58 in Raphael Patai (ed.), *Women in the Modern World*. New York: The Free Press.

Bachofen, J.J. 1948. *Das Mutterecht*. Basel: Beno Schwabe. (Originally published, 1861.)

Bakan, David. 1971. *Slaughter of the Innocents*. Boston: Beacon Press.

Bane, Mary Jo. 1976. *Here to Stay: American Families in the Twentieth Century*. New York: Basic Books.

———. 1979. "Marital disruption and the lives of children." Pp. 276–286 in George Levinger and Oliver C. Moles (eds.), *Divorce and Separation: Context, Causes, and Consequences*. New York: Basic Books.

Bardos, Panos D. 1964. "Family forms and variations historically considered." Pp. 403–461 in Harold T. Christensen (ed.), *Handbook of Marriage and the Family*. Chicago: Rand McNally.

Bartelt, Pearl W., and Mark Hutter. 1977. "Symbolic interaction perspective on the sexual politics of etiquette books." Paper presented at the meeting of the American Sociological Association, Chicago, Ill. September 1977.

Bascom, William. 1968. "The urban African and his world." Pp. 81–93 in Sylvia Fleis Fava (ed.), *Urbanism in World Perspective: A Reader*. New York: Thomas Y. Crowell.

Belden, Jack. 1970. *China Shakes the World*. New York: Monthly Review Press.

Bell, Robert R. 1964. "The lower-class Negro mother and her children." *Integrated Education*, December.

———. 1965. "Lower-class negro mother's aspirations for their children." *Social Forces* 44:483–500.

———.1971. "The related importance of mother-wife roles among lower class black women." Pp. 248–245 in Robert Staples (ed.), *The Black Family*. New York: Wadsworth.

Bell, Wendell. 1958. "Social choice, life styles and suburban residence." Pp. 225–247 in William Dobriner (ed.), *The Suburban Community*. New York: G.P. Putnam's Sons.

Bell, Wendell, and Marion D. Boat. 1957. "Urban neighborhood and informal social behavior." *American Journal of Sociology* 62:391–398.

Bellah, Robert N. 1957. *Tokugawa Religion: The Values of Preindustrial Japan*. New York: Macmillan.

Bendix, Reinhard. 1967. "Tradition and modernity reconsidered." *Comparative Studies in Society and History* 9:292–346.

Benedict, Ruth. 1973. "Continuities and discontinuities in cultural conditioning." Pp. 100–108 in Harry Silverstein (ed.), *The Sociology of Youth: Evolution of Revolution*. New York: Macmillan. Originally published in *Psychiatry* 1:161–167, 1938.

Berger, Brigitte. 1971. *Societies in Change*. New York: Basic Books.

Berger, Miriam E. 1971. "Trial marriage: Harnessing the trend constructively." *The Family Coordinator* 20:38–43.

Berger, Peter L., 1963. *Invitation to Sociology: A Humanistic Perspective*. Garden City, N.Y.: Doubleday (Anchor Books).

Berger, Peter L., Brigitte Berger, and Hansfried Kellner. 1973. *The Homeless Mind: Modernization and Consciousness*. New York: Random House.

Berger, Peter L., and Hansfred Kellner. 1964. "Marriage and the construction of reality." *Diogenes* 46:1–25.

Berger, Peter L., and Thomas Luckmann. 1966. *The Social Construction of Reality*. Garden City, N.Y.: Doubleday.

Berkner, Lutz K. 1975. "The use and misuse of census data for the historical analysis of family structure." *Journal of Interdisciplinary History* 4:721–738.

Bernard, Jesse. 1975. *The Future of Motherhood*. New York: Penguin Books.

Berry, Brian J. L. 1973. *The Human Consequences of Urbanization: Divergent Paths in the Urban Experience of the Twentieth Century*. New York: St. Martin's Press.

Billingsley, Andrew. 1969. "Family functioning in the low income black community." *Social Casework* 50:563–572.

Blake, Judith. 1972. *Coercive Pronatalism and American Population Policy*. (Preliminary paper no. 2 on results of current research in demography). Pp. 17–22 in *International Population and Urban Research*. Berkeley: International Populattion and Urban Research, University of California.

Blood, Robert O., Jr. 1967. *Love Match and Arranged Marriage: A Tokyo–Detroit Comparison*. New York: The Free Press.

———. 1972. *The Family*. New York: The Free Press.

Blood, Robert O., Jr., and Donald M. Wolfe. 1960. *Husbands and Wives*. New York: The Free Press.

Blumberg, Leonard, and Robert R. Bell. 1959. "Urban migration and kinship ties." *Social Problems* 6:328–333.

Bohannan, Paul. 1971. "The six stations of divorce." Pp. 33–62 in Paul Bohannan (ed.), *Divorce and After*. Garden City, N.Y.: Doubleday Anchor.

Borders, William. 1977. "India will moderate birth-curb program." *New York Times*, April 3, 1977.

Boserup, Ester. 1970. *Woman's Role in Economic Development*. London: Allen & Unwin.

Bott, Elizabeth. 1957. Family and Social Network. London: Tavistock Publications.

Brandwein, Ruth A., Carol A. Brown, and Elizabeth Maury Fox. 1974. "Women and children last: The social situation of divorced mothers and their families." *Journal of Marriage and the Family* 36:498–514.

Bruner, Edward M. 1963. "Medan: The role of kinship in an Indonesian city." Pp. 1–12 in Alexander Spoehr (ed.), *Pacific Port Towns and Cities*. Honolulu: Bishop Mussua Press. Reprinted pp. 122–134 in William Mangin (ed.), 1970, *Peasants in Cities: Readings in the Anthropology of Urbanization*. Boston: Houghton-Mifflin.

Burchinal, Lee G. 1964. "Characteristics of adolescents from unbroken, broken, and reconstituted families." *Journal of Marriage and the Family* 26:44–51.

Burgess, Ernest W., and Harvey J. Locke. 1945. *The Family from Institution to Companionship*. New York: American Book.

Butterfield, Fox. 1979. "As population nears a billion, China stresses curbs." *New York Times*, April 24, 1979.

Campbell, F. L. 1970. "Family growth and variation in family role structure." *Journal of Marriage and the Family* 32:45–53.

Carter, Hugh, and Paul C. Glick. 1976. *Marriage and Divorce: A Social and Economic Study*, rev. ed. Cambridge: Harvard University Press.

Chao, Paul. 1977. *Women Under Communism*. Bayside, N.Y.: General Hall.

Chase, Naomi Feigelson. 1975. *A Child Is Being Beaten*. New York: McGraw-Hill.

Cherlin, Andrew. 1980. "Remarriage as an incomplete institution." Pp. 368–382 in Arlene S. Skolnick and Jerome H. Skolnick (eds.), *Family in Transition: Rethinking Marriage, Sexuality, Child Rearing, and Family Organization*, 3rd ed. Boston: Little Brown. Reprinted from *American Journal of Sociology* 1978, 84:634–650.

Chin, Ai-li S. 1970. "Family relations in modern Chinese fiction." Pp. 87−120 in Maurice Freedman (ed.), *Family and Kinship in Chinese Society.* Stanford, Calif.: Stanford University Press.

Chinoy, Ely. 1955. *Automobile Workers and the American Dream.* Garden City, N.Y.: Doubleday.

Chodak, Szymon. 1973. *Societal Development: Five Approaches with Conclusions from Comparative Analysis.* New York: Oxford University Press.

Christensen, Harold T., (ed.). 1964. *Handbook of Marriage and the Family.* Chicago: Rand McNally.

Clark, Alice. 1919. *The Working Life of Women in the Seventeenth Century.* London: G. Routledge & Sons. (Reissued by Frank Cass, 1968).

Clayton, Richard R. 1979. *The Family, Marriage, and Social Change,* 2nd ed. Lexington, Mass: D.C. Heath.

Coles, Robert. 1968. "Life in Appalachia—the case of Hugh Mc Caslin." *Transaction* June:22−33.

Cooper, David. 1970. *The Death of the Family.* New York: Random House (Vintage Books).

Curtin, Katie. 1975. *Women in China.* New York: Pathfinder Press.

Dahlström, Edmund (ed.). 1962. *Kvinnors Liv och Arbete* (The Life and Work of Women). Stockholm: Studieförbundet Näringsliv & Samhälle.

———. 1971. *The Changing Roles of Men and Women.* Boston: Beacon Press.

D'Andrade, Roy G. 1966. "Sex Differences and cultural institutions." Pp. 174−204 in E.E. Maccoby (ed.), *The Development of Sex Differences.* Stanford: Stanford University Press.

Darwin, Charles. *Origin of Species.* New York: Random House, Modern Library. (Originally published, 1859).

Davidoff, Leonore. 1975. *The Best Circles: Women and Society in Victorian England.* Totowa, N. J.: Rowman & Littlefield.

Davis, Elizabeth Gould. 1971. *The First Sex.* New York: G.P. Putnam's Sons.

Davis, Kingsley. 1951. The population of India and Pakistan. Princeton, N.J.: Princeton University Press.

———. 1955. "Institutional patterns favoring high fertility in underdeveloped areas." *Eugenics Quarterly* 2:33−39.

de Beauvoir, Simone. 1973. *The Coming of Age.* New York: Warner Books (Warner Paperback Library).

de Jesus, Carolina Maria. 1962. *Child of the Dark: The Diary of Carolina Maria de Jesus.* David St. Clair (trans.). New York: E.P. Dutton.

Demos, John. 1970. *A Little Commonwealth.* New York: Oxford University Press.

Dore, R.P. 1965. *City Life in Japan: A Study of A Tokyo Ward.* Berkeley/Los Angeles: University of California Press.

Duberman, Lucile. 1977. *Marriage and Other Alternatives,* 2nd ed. New York: Praeger.

Durdin, Tillman. 1971. "Elimination of 'Four Olds' Transform China." Pp. 123−126 in the *New York Times* (ed.) *Report from Red China.* New York: Avon Books.

Durkheim, Emile. 1915. *The Elementary Forms of the Religious Life.* Joseph Ward Swain (trans.). London: Allen & Unwin. (Originally published 1912.)

———. 1933. *The Division of Labor in Society.* George Simpson,(trans.). New York: Macmillan (Originally published, 1893).

————. 1951. *Suicide: A Study in Sociology.* John A. Spaulding and George Simpson, (trans.). New York: The Free Press of Glencoe. (Originally published, 1897.)

————. 1964. The Division of Labor in Society. George Simpson. (trans.). New York: The Free Press. (Originally published, 1893.)

Dworkin, Andrea. 1974. *Women Hating.* New York: E.P. Dutton.

Dyer, Everett D. 1963. "Parenthood as crisis: A restudy." *Marriage and Family Living* 25:196–201.

Eisenstadt, S. N. 1971. *From Generation to Generation.* New York: The Free Press.

Engels, Friedrich. 1972. *The Origin of the Family, Private Property, and the State.* New York: Pathfinder Press. (Originally published, 1884).

Epstein, A. L. 1969. "Urbanization and social change in Africa." Pp. 246–287 in Gerald Breese (ed.), *The City in Newly Developing Countries: Readings on Urbanism and Urbanization.* Englewood Cliffs, N.J.: Prentice-Hall.

Eshleman, J. Ross. 1978. *The Family: An Introduction,* 2nd ed. Boston: Allyn & Bacon.

Fanon, Frantz. 1965. *The Wretched of the Earth* (Preface by Jean Paul Sartre). Constance Farrington (trans.). New York: Grove Press.

————. 1967. *Black Skin White Masks.* Charles Lam Markmann (trans.). New York: Grove Press.

Farber, Bernard. 1964. *Family: Organization and Interaction.* San Francisco: Chandler.

Feldman, Harold. 1974. *Development of the husband—wife relationship* (research report). Mimeographed, Ithaca, N.Y.: Cornell University.

Feron, James. 1977. "Suburban child abuse: Its subtle forms hinder identification." *New York Times,* April 11, 1977.

Feuer, Lewis S. 1969. *The Conflict of Generations: The Character and Significance of Student Movements.* New York: Basic Books.

Field, Mark G., and Karin I. Flynn. 1970. "Worker, mother housewife: Society woman today." Pp. 257–284 in Georgene H. Seward and Robert C. Williamson (eds.), *Sex Roles in Changing Society.* New York: Random House.

Firestone, Shulamith. 1970. *The Dialectic of Sex: The Case for Feminist Revolution.* New York: William Morrow.

Fischer, David Hackett. 1977. *Growing Old in America.* New York: Oxford University Press.

Fitzpatrick, Joseph P. 1971. *Puerto Rican Americans: The Meaning of Migration to the Mainland.* Englewood Cliffs, N.J.: Prentice-Hall.

Flaste, Richard. 1979. "Research begins to focus on suicide among the aged." *New York Times,* January 2, 1979:C2.

Fogarty, Michael P., Rhona Rapoport, and Robert N. Rapoport. 1971. *Sex, Career and Family.* Beverly Hills, Calif.: Sage.

Foner, Ann. 1978. "Age stratification and the changing family." Pp. S340–S365 in John Demos and Sarane Spence Boocock (eds.), *Turning Points: Historical and Sociological Essays on the Family. American Journal of Sociology* 89(suppl).

Ford, Clellan S. 1970. "Some primitive societies." Pp. 25–43 in Georgene H. Seward and Robert C. Williamson (eds.), *Sex Roles in Changing Society.* New York: Random House.

Frazer, Sir James George. 1960. *The Golden Bough: A Study in Magic and Religion.* One volume, abridged edition. New York: The Macmillan Company. (Originally published, 1922.)

Freedman, Ronald. 1963. "Norms for family size in underdeveloped areas." Proceedings of the Rural Society, B 159: 220–245. Reprinted pp. 157–180 in David M. Heer, (ed.), 1968, *Readings on Population.* Englewood Cliffs. N.J.: Prentice-Hall.

Freeman, Linton C. 1974. "Marriage without love: Mate-selection in non-Western societies." Pp. 354–366 in Robert F. Winch and Graham B. Spanier (eds.), *Selected Studies in Marriage and the Family,* 4th ed. New York: Holt, Rinehart & Winston.

Gans, Herbert. 1962a. *The Urban Villagers: Group and Class in the Life of Italian-Americans.* New York: The Free Press.

———. 1962b. "Urbanism and suburbanism as ways of life: A reevaluation of definitions." Pp. 624–648 in Arnold Rose (ed.), *Human Behavior and Social Process.* Boston: Houghton-Mifflin.

———. 1967a. "The Negro family: Reflections on the Moynihan Report." Pp. 445–457 in Lee Rainwater and William B. Yancey (eds.), *The Moynihan Report and the Politics of Controversy.* Cambridge: M.I.T. Press.

———. 1967b. "Culture and class in the study of poverty: An approach to anti-poverty research." Pp. 201–228 in Daniel P. Moynihan (ed.), *On Understanding Poverty.* New York: Basic Books.

Garvon, Hannah. 1966. *The Captive Wife.* London: Routledge & Kegan Paul.

Gasster, Michael. 1972. *China's Struggle to Modernize.* New York: Knopf.

Gelles, Richard J. 1972. *The Violent Home.* Beverly Hills, Calif.: Sage.

Gersick, Kelin E. 1979. "Fathers by choice: Divorced men who receive custody of their children." Pp. 307–323 in George Levinger and Oliver C. Moles (eds.), *Divorce and Separation: Context, Causes, and Consequences.* New York: Basic Books.

Gil, David G. 1971. "Violence against children." *Journal of Marriage and the Family* 33:637–648.

Gist, Noel P., and Sylvia Fleis Fava. 1974. *Urban Society,* 6th ed. New York: Thomas Y. Crowell.

Glick, Paul C. 1975. "A demographer looks at American families." *Journal of Marriage and the Family* 37.

Glick, Paul C., and Arthur J. Norton. 1979. "Marrying, divorcing, and living together in the U.S. today." Population Bulletin, vol. 32, no. 5. Washington, D.C.: Population Reference Bureau.

Glick, Paul C., and Graham B. Spanier. 1980. "Married and unmarried cohabitation in the United States." *Journal of Marriage and the Family* 42:19–30.

Glueck, Sheldon, and Eleanor Glueck. 1951. *Unraveling Juvenile Delinquency.* New York: The Commonwealth Fund.

Goldscheider, Calvin. 1971. *Population, Modernization and Social Structure.* Boston: Little, Brown.

Goode, William J. 1956. *After Divorce.* Glencoe, Ill.: The Free Press.

———. 1959. "The theoretical importance of love." *American Sociological Review* 24:38–47.

———. 1962. "Marital satisfaction and instability: A cross-cultural analysis of divorce rates." Pp. 377–387 in Reinhard Bendix and Seymour M. Lipset (eds.), *Class, Status, and Power,* 2nd ed. New York: The Free Press. (Reprinted 1966.)

———. 1963. *World Revolution and Family Patterns.* New York: The Free Press.

———. 1964. *The Family.* Englewood Cliffs, N.J.: Prentice-Hall.

————. 1971. "Force and violence in the family." *Journal of Marriage and the Family* 33: 624–636.

————. 1976. "Family disorganization." Pp. 511–554 in Robert K. Merton and Robert Nisbet (eds.), *Contemporary Social Problems*, 4th ed. New York: Harcourt Brace Jovanovich.

Goodwin, John. 1973. *The Mating Trade.* Garden City, N.Y.: Doubleday.

Gordon, Suzanne. 1976. *Lonely in America.* New York: Simon & Schuster (Touchstone Books.)

Gordon, Michael. 1977. Review of *The Making of the Modern Family*, by E. Shorter. *Contemporary Sociology*, 169–171.

————. 1978. *The American Family: Past, Present, and Future.* New York: Random House.

Gordon, Michael (ed.). 1972. *The Nuclear Family in Crisis: The Search for an Alternative.* New York: Harper & Row.

Greer, Scott. 1957. "Urbanism reconsidered: A comparative study of local areas in a metropolis." *American Sociological Review* 21:19–25.

Greven, Philip J., Jr. 1970. *Four Generations.* Ithaca, N.Y.: Cornell University Press.

Gusfield, Joseph R. 1967. "Tradition and modernity: Misplaced polarities in the study of social change." *American Journal of Sociology* 72:351–362.

Gutkind, Peter C. W. 1969. "African urban family life and the urban system." Pp. 215–223 in Paul Meadows and Ephraim H. Mizruchi (eds.), *Urbanism, Urbanization, and Change: Comparative Perspectives.* Reading, Mass.: Addison-Wesley.

Hall, G. Stanley. 1904. *Adolescence: Its Psychology and Its Relation to Physiology, Anthropology, Sociology, Sex Crime, Religion and Education.* New York: Appleton.

Hance, William A. 1970. *Population, Migration, and Urbanization in Africa.* New York: Columbia University Press.

Haraven, Tamara K. 1971. "The history of the family as an interdisciplinary field." Pp. 211–226 in Theodore K. Rabb and Robert I. Rotberg (eds.), *The Family in History: Interdisciplinary Essays.* New York: Harper (Torchbooks).

————. 1975. "Family time and industrial time: Family and work in a planned corporation town, 1900–1924." *Journal of Urban History* 1:365–389.

————. 1976. "The last stage: Historical adulthood and old age." *Daedalus:* 105:13–27. (Fall issue titled, "American Civilization: New Perspectives.")

Harris, Marvin. 1968. *The Rise of Anthropological Theory: A History of Theories of Culture.* New York: Thomas Y. Crowell.

Heesterman, J. C. 1973. "India and the inner conflict of tradition." *Daedalus* 192:97–114. (Winter issue titled, "Post-Traditional Societies.")

Helfer, Ray E., and C. Henry Kempe (eds.). 1968. *The Battered Child.* Chicago: University of Chicago Press.

Hellstrom, Inger. 1963. "The Chinese family in the Communist Revolution: Aspects of the changes brought about by the Communist Government." *Acta Sociologica* 6:256–277.

Henretta, James A. 1971. "The morphology of New England society in the colonial period." Pp. 191–210 in Theodore K. Rabb and Robert I. Rotberg (eds.), *The Family in History: Interdisciplinary Essays.* New York: Harper (Torchbooks).

Herman, Sondra R. 1974. "The liberated women of Sweden," *The Center Magazine*, 7:76–78.

Hill, Reuban, and Joan Aldous. 1969. "Socialization for marriage and parenthood." Pp. 885–950 in David A. Goslin (ed.), *Handbook of Socialization Theory and Research.* Chicago: Rand McNally.

Hinton, William. 1966. *Fanshen: A Documentary of Revolution in a Chinese Village.* New York: Random House (Vintage).

Hobbs, Daniel F. 1965. "Parenthood as crisis: A third study." *Journal of Marriage and the Family* 27:367–372.

———. 1968. "Transition to parenthood: A replication and an extension." *Journal of Marriage and the Family* 30:413–417.

Hobbs, Daniel F., Jr., and Sue Peck Cole. 1976. "Transition to parenthood: A decade replication." *Journal of Marriage and the Family* 38:723–731.

Hochschild, Arlie Russell. 1976. "Communal life systems for the old." Pp. 367–384 in Cary S. Kart and Barbara B. Manard (eds.), *Aging in America: Readings in Social Gerontology.* Port Washington, N. Y.: Alfred Publishing. (Reprinted from: *Society* 10, 1973.)

Hollingshead, August de B. 1949. *Elmtown's Youth: The Impact of Social Class on Adolescents.* New York: John Wiley & Sons.

Howell, Joseph T. 1973. *Hard Living on Clay Street.* Garden City, N. Y.: Doubleday (Anchor Books.)

Hughes, Pennethorne. 1971. *Witchcraft.* Harmondsworth, Eng.: Penguin Books.

Hunt, Morton M. 1959. *The Natural History of Love.* New York: Knopf.

Hutter, Mark. 1970. "Transformation of identity, social mobility and kinship solidarity." *Journal of Marriage and the Family.* 32:133–137.

Jacobs, Jerry. 1976. "An ethnographic study of a retirement setting." Pp. 385–394 in Cary S. Kart and Barbara B. Manard (eds.), *Aging in America: Readings in Social Gerontology.* Port Washington, N.Y.: Alfred Publishing Co. (Reprinted from: *Gerontologist* 14: 483–487, 1974.)

Jacobson, Paul H. 1959. *American Marriage and Divorce.* New York: Rinehart.

Jacoby, Arthur P. 1969. "Transition to parenthood: A reassessment." *Journal of Marriage and the Family* 31:720–727.

Jensen, H. 1977. "Cobblers tale." *Newsweek* 89 (April 4): 42.

Johnson, Kay Ann. 1976. "Women in China: Problems of sex inequality and socioeconomic change." Pp. 286–319 in Jean I. Roberts (ed.), *Beyond Intellectual Sexism.* New York: David McKay.

Kart, Cary S., and Barbara B. Manard (eds.). 1976. *Aging in America: Readings in Social Gerontology.* Port Washington, N.Y.: Alfred Publishing Co.

Kendell, Jonathan. 1977. "Retirement age falling in Europe." *New York Times,* December 4, 1977.

Keniston, Kenneth. 1965. *The Uncommitted: Aliented Youth in American Society.* New York: Harcourt, Brace and World.

———. 1968. *Young Radicals: Notes on Committed Youth.* New York: Harcourt, Brace and World.

Keniston, Kenneth, and The Carnegie Council on Children. 1977. *All Our Children: The American Family Under Pressure.* New York: Harcourt Brace Jovanovich.

Kenkel, William F. 1977. *The Family in Perspective,* 4th ed. Santa Monica, Calif.: Goodyear.

Kenyatta, Jomo. 1938. *Facing Mt. Kenya.* New York: Random House (Vintage Books).

Kett, Joseph F. 1977. *Rites of Passage: Adolescence in America 1790 to the Present.* New York: Basic Books.

Key, William H. 1961. "Rural urban differences and the family." *Sociological Quarterly* 2:49−56.

Klemesrud, Judy. 1976. "Many elderly in the Bronx spend their lives in terror of crime." *New York Times,* November 22, 1976.

Kohen, Janet A., Carol A. Brown, and Roslyn Feldberg. 1979. "Divorced mothers: The cost and benefits of female control." Pp. 228−245 in George Levinger and Oliver C. Moles (eds.), *Divorce and Separation: Context, Causes, and Consequences.* New York: Basic Books.

Komarovsky, Mirra. 1962. *Blue Collar Marriage.* New York: Random House.

Kooy, Gerrit A. 1963. "Social system and the problem of aging." Pp. 45−60 in Richard H. Williams, Clark Tibbits, and Wilma Donahue (eds.), *Processes of Aging: Social and Psychological Perspectives* (Vol. 2). New York: Atherton Press.

Laing, R.D. 1969. *Self and Others.* Baltimore: Penguin Books.

Landis, Judson T. 1962. "A comparison of children from divorced and nondivorced unhappy marriages." *Family Life Coordinator* 11: 61−65.

———. 1960. "The trauma of children when parents divorce." *Marriage and Family Living* 22: 7−13.

Lannoy, Richard. 1971. The Speaking Tree: A Study of Indian Culture and Society. New York: Oxford University Press.

Lasch, Christopher. 1975a. "The emotions of family life." *New York Review of Books,* November 27.

———. 1975b. "The family and history." *New York Review of Books,* November 13.

———. 1975c. "What the doctor ordered." *New York Review of Books,* December 11.

———. 1977a. *Haven in a Heartless World: The Family.* New York: Basic Books.

———. 1977b. "The siege of the family." *New York Review,* November, 24.

———. 1979. *The Culture of Narcissism.* New York: W. W. Norton.

Laslett, Barbara. 1973. "The family as a public and private institution: An historical perspective." *Journal of Marriage and the Famly* 35:480−492.

Laslett, Peter. 1965. *The World We Have Lost: England Before the Industrial Revolution.* New York: Charles Scribner's Sons.

Laslett, Peter, (ed.). 1972. *Household and Family in Past Time.* Cambridge: At the University Press.

Le Masters, E. E. 1957. "Parenthood as crisis." *Marriage and Family Living* 19:352−355.

———. 1977. *Parents in Modern America.* Homewood, Ill.: Dorsey.

Lenin, V.I. 1966. "The tasks of the working women's movement in the Soviet republic." (Speech delivered at the fourth Moscow City conference of nonparty working women, September 23, 1919.) Pp. 66−72 in *The Emancipation of Women: From the Writings of V.I. Lenin* (Preface by Nadezhda K. Krupskaya). New York: International Publishers.

Le Play, Frédéric. 1855. *Les Ouvriers Européens.* Paris: Imprimerie Royale.

Lerner, Daniel. 1958. *The Passing of Traditional Society: Modernizing the Middle East.* Glencoe, Ill.: The Free Press of Glencoe.

Leslie, Gerald R. 1979. *The Family in Social Context,* 4th ed. New York: Oxford University Press.

Leslie, J. A. K. 1963. *A Social Survey of Dar es Salaam*. London: Oxford University Press.

Levi-Strauss, Claude. 1957. "The principle of reciprocity." Pp. 84—94 in Lewis A. Coser and Bernard Rosenberg (eds.), *Sociological Theory: A Book of Readings*. New York: Macmillan.

————. 1971. "The family." Pp. 333—357 in H. L. Shapiro (ed.), *Man, Culture and Society*. New York: Oxford University Press.

Levy, Marion J., Jr. 1949. *The Family Revolution in Modern China*. Cambridge: Harvard University Press.

————. 1966. *Modernization and the Structure of Societies*. Princeton, N.J.: Princeton University Press.

Lewis, Hylan. 1965. "Agenda Paper No. 5: The family: Resources for change—Planning session for the White House Conference to fulfill these rights." November 16—18, 1975. Pp. 314—343 in Lee Rainwater and William B. Yancey (eds.), *The Moynihan Report and the Politics of Controversy*. Cambridge: M.I.T. Press.

Lewis, Oscar. 1966. *La Vida: A Puerto Rican Family in the Culture of Poverty–San Juan and New York*. New York: Random House.

Liebow, Elliot. 1967. *Tally's Corner: A Study of Negro Street Corner Men*. Boston: Little, Brown.

Light, Richard J. 1974. "Abused and neglected children in America: A study of alternative policies." *Harvard Educational Review* 43:556—598.

Liljestrom. Rita. 1970. "The Swedish model." Pp. 200—219 in Georgene H. Seward and Robert C. Williamson (eds.), *Sex Roles in Changing Society*. New York: Random House.

Little, Kenneth. 1965. *West African Urbanization: A Study of Voluntary Associations in Social Change*. Cambridge: Cambridge University Press.

————. 1973. *African Women in Towns: An Aspect of Africa's Social Revolution*. London: Cambridge University Press.

Litwak, Eugene. 1959—1960. "The use of extended family groups in the achievement of social goals." *Social Problems* 7:177—188.

————. 1960a. "Geographical mobility and extended family cohesion." *American Sociological Review* 25: 385—394.

————. 1960b. "Occupational mobility and extended family cohesion." *American Sociological Review* 25:385—394.

Lloyd, Peter Cutt. 1969. *Africa in Social Change: Changing Traditional Societies in the Modern World*. Baltimore: Penguin Books.

Longfellow, Cynthia. 1979. "Divorce in context: Its impact on children." Pp. 287—306 in George Levinger and Oliver C. Moles (eds.), *Divorce and Separation: Context, Causes, and Consequences*. New York: Basic Books.

Lowie, Robert H. 1937. *The History of Ethnological Theory*. New York: Holt, Rinehart & Winston.

Mace, David, and Vera Mace. 1960. *Marriage: East and West*. Garden City, N.Y.: Doubleday.

Macklin, Eleanor D. 1972. "Heterosexual cohabitation among unmarried college students." *The Family Coordinator* 21:463—472.

————. 1978. "Nonmarital heterosexual cohabitation." *Marriage and Family Review* 1:1—12.

Maine, Henry Sumner. 1960. *Ancient Law*. London: J.M. Dent & Sons. (Originally published, 1861.)

Mamdani, Mahmood. 1972. The Myth of Population Control: Family, Caste and Class in an Indian Village. New York: Monthly Review Press.

Mangin. William. 1960. "Mental health and migration to cities." *Annals of the New York Academy of Sciences* 84:911−917.

———. 1968. "Tales from the barriadas." *Nickle Review,* September 25−October 8, 1968. Reprinted pp. 55−61 in William Mangin (ed.), 1970, *Peasants in Cities: Readings in the Anthropology of Urbanization.* Boston: Houghton-Mifflin.

Mangin, William (ed.). 1970. *Peasants in Cities: Readings in the Anthropology of Urbanization.* Boston: Houghton-Mifflin.

Marris, Peter. 1958. *Widows and Their Families.* London: Routledge & Kegan Paul.

———. 1961. *Family and Social Change in an African City: A Study of Rehousing in Lagos.* Evanston, Ill.: Northwestern University Press.

Marsh, Robert. 1967. *Comparative Sociology.* New York: Harcourt, Brace and World.

Martin, Del. 1976. *Battered Wives.* San Francisco: Glide Publications.

Martindale, Don. 1960. *The Nature and Types of Sociological Theory.* Cambridge, Mass.: Houghton-Mifflin.

1962. Social Life and Cultural Change. Princeton, N.J.: Van Nostrand.

Mbate, Robert Muema. 1969, Nairobi. "Identity." *Bursara* 2, no. 3:31−34.

McCall, Michael M. 1966. "Courtship as social exchange: Some historical comparison." Pp. 190−200 in Bernard Farber (ed.), *Kinship and Family Organization.* New York: John Wiley & Sons.

McKee, Michael, and Ian Robertson. 1975. *Social Problems.* New York: Random House.

Mead, Margaret. 1928. *Coming of Age in Samoa.* New York: William Morrow.

———. 1949. *Male and Female: A Study of the Sexes in a Changing World.* New York: William Morrow.

———. 1954. "Some theoretical considerations on the problems of mother-child separation." *American Journal of Orthopsychiatry* 24:471−483.

———. 1963. *Sex and Temperament in Three Primitive Societies.* New York: William Morrow. (Originally published, 1935; Reprinted in 1950.)

———. 1966. "Marriage in two steps." *Redbook* 127:48−49.

———. 1970a. "Anomolies in American postdivorce relationships." Pp. 107−125 in Paul Bohannan (ed.), *Divorce and After.* Garden City, N.Y.: Doubleday (Anchor Books.)

———. 1970b. *Culture and Commitment: A Study of the Generation Gap.* New York: Natural History Press/Doubleday.

———. 1975. *Blackberry Winter: My Earlier Years.* New York: Pocket Books.

Mill, John Stuart. 1966. *On Liberty, Representative Government, The Subjection of Women. Three Essays.* London: Oxford University Press (The World Classics). (*The Subjection of Women* was originally published in 1869.)

Millett, Kate. 1970. *Sexual Politics.* Garden City, N. Y.: Doubleday.

Minturn, Leigh, and William W. Lambert. 1964. *Mothers of Six Cultures: Antecedent of Child Rearing.* New York: John Wiley & Sons.

Mogey. John. 1964. "Family and community in urban-industrial societies." Pp. 501−534 in Harold T. Christensen (ed.), *Handbook of Marriage and the Family.* Chicago: Rand McNally.

Mohsen, Safia K. 1974. "The Egyptian women: Between modernity and tradition." Pp. 37–58 in Carolyn J. Matthiasson (ed.), *Many Sisters: Women in Cross-Cultural Perspective.* New York: The Free Press.

Monter, E. William. 1977. "The pedestal and the stake: Courtly love and witchcraft." Pp. 119–136 in Renate Bridenthal and Claudia Koonz (eds.), *Becoming Visible Women in European History.* Boston: Houghton-Mifflin.

Moore, Wilbert E. 1964. "Social aspects of economic development." Pp. 882–911 in Robert E. L. Faris (ed.), *Handbook of Modern Sociology.* Chicago: Rand McNally.

Morgan, Lewis Henry. 1963. *Ancient Society.* Edited with and introduction and annotations by Eleanor B. Leacock. New York: World (Meridian Books). (Originally published, 1870).

Murdock, George. 1937. "Comparative data on the division of labor by sex." *Social Forces* 15: 551–553.

———. 1949. *Social Structure.* New York: Macmillan.

———. 1950. "Family stability in non-European cultures." *Annals of the American Academy of Political and Social Science* 272:195–201.

———. 1957. "World ethnographic sample." *American Anthropologist* 59:664–687.

Musgrove, Frank. 1964. *Youth and the Social Order.* Bloomington: Indiana University Press.

National Center for Health Statistics. 1977. "Marriage and divorce." *Vital Statistics of the United States 1973, III* Washington, D.C.: U.S. Government Printing Office.

———. 1978. "Births, Marriages, Divorces and Deaths for 1977." Monthly Vital Statistics Report, vol 26, no. 12. Washington D.C.: U.S. Government Printing Office.

Newsweek. 1979. "Special report: The new China." February 5:32–59.

Nisbet, Robert A. 1966. *The Sociological Tradition.* New York: Basic Books.

Norton, Arthur J., and Paul C. Glick. 1976. "Marital instability: Past, present, and future." *Journal of Social Issues* 32:5–20.

O'Brien, John E. 1971. "Violence in divorce-prone families." *Journal of Marriage and the Family* 33:692–698.

Oakley, Ann. 1974. *Woman's Work: The Housewife, Past and Present.* New York: Pantheon Books.

Ogburn, William F. 1922. *Social Change.* New York: Viking Press.

Ogburn, William F., and Meyer F. Nimkoff. 1955. *Technology and the Changing Family.* Boston: Houghton-Mifflin.

Ortner, Sherry. 1974. "Is female to male as nature is to culture?" Pp. 67–87 in Michelle Zimbalist Rosaldo and Louise Lamphere (eds.), *Woman, Culture and Society.* Stanford, Calif.: Stanford University Press.

Pace, Eric. 1975. "A changing Iran wonders whether the gain will exceed the loss." *New York Times,* January 16, 1975.

Packard, Vance. 1966. *The Sexual Wilderness.* New York: David McKay.

Padan-Eisenstark, Dorit D. 1973. "Are Israeli women really equal? Trends and patterns of Israeli women's labor force participation: A comparative analysis." *Journal of Marriage and the Family* 35:538–545.

Palen, John J. 1975. *The Urban World.* New York: McGraw-Hill.

Palgi, Phyllis. 1973. "Discontinuity in the female role within the traditional family in modern society: A case of infanticide." Included in E. James Anthony and Cyrille Koupernik (eds.), *The Child in His Family: The Impact of Disease and Death* (Vol. 2). New York: John Wiley & Sons.

Park, Robert E., and Ernest W. Burgess. 1925. *The City*. Chicago: University of Chicago Press.

Parsons, Talcott. 1942. "Age and sex in the social structure of the United States." *American Sociological Review* 7:604−616.

————. 1943. "The kinship system of the contemporary United States." *American Anthropologist* 45:22−38.

————. 1949. Essays in Sociological Theory, Pure and Applied. Glencoe, Ill.: The Free Press.

————. 1955. "The American family: Its relation to personality and to the social structure." Pp. 3−33 in Talcott Parsons and Robert F. Bales (eds.), *Family, Socialization and Interaction Process*. New York: The Free Press.

Parsons, Talcott, Robert F. Bales, James Olds, Morris Zelditch, Jr. and Philip E. Slater. 1955. *Family: Socialization and Interaction Process*. New York: The Free Press.

Peterson, William. 1975. *Population,* 3rd ed. New York: Macmillan.

Pinchbeck, Ivy. 1930. *Women Workers and the Industrial Revolution 1750−1850*. London: Routledge & Kegan Paul. (Reissued by Frank Cass, 1969; reissued by Augustus M. Kelley, New York, 1971).

Pineo, Peter. 1961. "Disenchantment in the later years of marriage." *Marriage and Family Living* 23:3−11.

Pitt-Rivers, A. Lane-Fox. 1916. *The Evolution of Culture and Other Essays*. Oxford: Oxford University Press.

Piven, Frances Fox, and Richard Cloward. 1971. *Regulating the Poor*. New York: Vintage Books.

Pizzey, Erin. 1974. *Scream Quietly or the Neighbors Will Hear*. London: IF Books.

Platt, Anthony M. 1969. *The Child Savers: The Invention of Delinquency*. Chicago: University of Chicago Press.

Population Reference Bureau. 1976. *World Population Growth and Response*. Washington, D.C.: Population Reference Bureau.

Power, Eileen. 1975. *Medieval Women*. Cambridge: Cambridge University Press.

Rabin, A.I. 1970. "The sexes: Ideology and reality in the Israeli kibbutz." Pp. 285−307 in Georgene H. Seward and Robert C. Williamson (eds.), *Sex Roles in Changing Society*. New York: Random House.

Rainwater, Lee. 1960. *And the Poor Get Children*. Chicago: Quadrangle.

————. 1965. *Family Design*. Chicago: Aldine.

————. 1966. "Crucible of identity." *Daedalus* 95:172−216.

Rainwater, Lee, and William B. Yancey (eds.). 1967. *The Moynihan Report and the Politics of Controversy*. Cambridge: M.I.T. Press.

Redfield, Robert. 1941. *The Folk Culture of Yucatan*. Chicago: University of Chicago Press.

————. 1947. "The Folk Society." *The American Journal of Sociology* 52:293−308. Reprinted in pp. 180−205 in Richard Sennett, (ed.), 1969, *Classic Essays on the Culture of Cities*. New York: Appleton-Century-Crofts.

————. 1953. *The Primitive World and Its Transformations*. Chicago: University of Chicago Press.

————. 1955. *The Little Community*. Chicago: University of Chicago Press.

Reiss, Ira. 1960. *Premarital Sexual Standards in America*. New York: The Free Press.

————. 1971. *The Family System in America*. New York: Holt, Rinehart & Winston.

Reiss, Paul J. 1965. "The extended kinship system: Correlates of and attitudes on the frequency of interaction." *Marriage and Family Living* 24:333−339.

Reissman, Leonard. 1972. *Inequality in American Society: Social Stratification.* Glenview, Ill.: Scott, Foresman.

Renne, K. S. 1970. "Correlate of dissatisfaction in marriage." *Journal of Marriage and the Family* 32:54−68.

Rimmer, Robert H. 1966. *The Harrad Experiment.* Los Angeles, Sherbourne Press.

Rodman, Hyman. 1965. "Middle-class misconceptions about lower-class families." Pp. 219−230 in Hyman Rodman (ed.), *Marriage, Family, and Society: A Reader.* New York: Random House. Originally published in Arthur B. Shostak and William Gomberg (eds.), 1974, *Blue-Collar World: Studies of the American Worker.* Englewood Cliffs, N. J.: Prentice-Hall.

———. 1971. *Lower-Class Families: The Culture of Poverty in Negro Trinidad.* New York: Oxford University Press.

Rollin, Betty. 1970. "Motherhood: Who needs it?" *Look,* September 22, 1970, pp. 15−17. Reprinted pp. 346−356 in Arlene S. Skolnick and Jerome H. Skolnick (eds.), 1971, *Family in Transition: Rethinking Marriage, Sexuality, Child Rearing, and Family Organization.* Boston: Little, Brown.

Rosaldo, Michelle Zimbalist. 1974. "Woman, culture and society: A theoretical overview." Pp. 17−42 in Michelle Zimbalist Rosaldo and Louise Lamphere (eds.), *Woman, Culture and Society.* Stanford, Calif.: Stanford University Press.

Rosen, Lawrence. 1970. "The broken home and male delinquency." Pp. 489−495 in Marvin Wolfgang, Norman Johnson, and Leonard Savitz (eds.), *Sociology of Crime and Delinquency.* New York: John Wiley & Sons.

Rosen, Lawrence. 1973. "I divorce thee." Pp. 39−43 in Helena Z. Lopata (ed.), *Marriages and Families.* New York: Van Nostrand.

Rosow, Irving. 1973. "And then we were old." Pp. 229−234 in Helena Z. Lopata (ed.), *Marriages and Families.* New York: Van Nostrand.

Ross, Aileen D. 1961. *The Hindu Family in its Urban Setting.* Toronto: University of Toronto Press.

Ross, Heather L., and Isabel V. Sawhill. 1975. *Time of Transition: The Growth of Families Headed by Women.* Washington, D.C.: The Urban Institute.

Rossi, Alice S. 1968. "Transition to parenthood." *Journal of Marriage and the Family* 30:26−39.

Rothman, David J. 1971. "Documents in search of a historian: Toward a history of children and youth in America." Pp. 179−190 in Theodore K. Rabb and Robert I. Rotberg (eds.), *The Family in History: Interdisciplinary Essays.* New York: Harper (Torchbooks).

Ruskin, John. *Sesame and Lilies: Three Lectures.* New York: Chatterton-Peck Company. (Originally published, 1865.)

Ryan, William. 1971. *Blaming the Victim.* New York: Random House (Vintage Books).

Safilios-Rothschild, Constantina. 1970. "Toward a cross-cultural conceptualization of family modernity." *Journal of Comparative Family Studies* 1:17−25.

Schorr, Alvin L., and Phyllis Moen. 1980. "The single parent and public policy." Pp. 554−566 in Arlene S. Skolnick and Jerome H. Skolnick (eds.), *Family in Transition: Rethinking Marriage, Sexuality, Child Rearing, and Family Organization,* Boston: Little, Brown.

Schumacher, Edward. 1978. "Child abuse is twice as common as estimated earlier study finds." *Philadelphia Inquirer,* November 20, 1978.

Scott, Marvin. 1970. "Functional analysis: A statement of problems." Pp. 21–28 in Gregory P. Stone and Harvey A. Farberman (eds.), *Social Psychology Through Symbolic Interaction.* Waltham, Mass.: Ginn-Blaisdell.

Seeley, John R., Alexander Sim, and E.W. Loosley, 1956. *Crestwood Heights: A Study of the Culture of Suburban Life.* Toronto: University of Toronto Press.

Sennett, Richard. 1973. "The brutality of modern families." Pp. 81–90 in Helena Z. Lopata (ed.), *Marriage and Families.* New York: Van Nostrand.

———. 1974. *Families Against the City: Middle Class Homes of Industrial Chicago.* New York: Random House (Vintage Books).

Shipler, David K. 1976. "Life for Soviet woman all work, little status." *New York Times,* August 9, 1976.

Shorter, Edward. 1975. *The Making of the Modern Family.* New York: Basic Books.

Simmons, Leo W. 1945. *The Role of the Aged in Primative Society.* New Haven: Yale University Press.

———. "The aging in preindustrial societies." Pp. 62–91 in Clark Tibbitts (ed.), *Handbook of Social Gerontology: Societal Aspects of Aging.* Chicago/London: University of Chicago Press.

Sirjamki, John. 1964. "The institutional approach." Pp. 33–50 in H. T. Christensen (ed.), *Handbook of Marriage and the Family.* Chicago: Rand McNally.

Skolnick, Arlene S. 1973. *The Intimate Environment: Exploring Marriage and the Family.* Boston: Little, Brown. (Revised, 1978.)

Skolnick, Arlene S., and Jerome H. Skolnick. 1971. *Family in Transition: Rethinking Marriage, Sexuality, Child Rearing, and Family Organization.* Boston: Little, Brown. (Revised 1977, 1980.)

Slater, Philip. 1970. *The Pursuit of Loneliness.* Boston: Beacon Press.

Smelser, Neil J. 1959. *Social Change in the Industrial Revolution.* Chicago: University of Chicago Press.

———. 1973. "Processes of social change." Pp. 709–761 in Neil J. Smelser (ed.), *Sociology: An Introduction,* 2nd ed. New York: John Wiley & Sons.

Smith, Joel, William H. Forn, and Gregory P. Stone. 1954. "Local intimacy in a middle-sized city." *American Journal of Sociology* 60:276–283.

Smock, Audrey Chapman, and Nadia Haggag Youseff. 1977. "Egypt: From seclusion to limited participation." Pp. 33–79 in Janet Zollinger Giele and Audrey Chapman Smock (eds.), *Women: Roles and Status in Eight Countries.* New York: Wiley-Interscience.

Solomon, Theodore. 1973. "History and demography of child abuse." *Pediaatrics* Part 2, 51, No. 4:773–776.

Southall, Aidan. 1961. "Introductory Summary." Pp. 1–66 in Aidan Southall (ed.), *Social Change in Modern Africa.* London: Oxford University Press.

Spencer, Herbert. 1897. *The Principles of Sociology* (3 vols.). New York: Appleton.

Stack, Carol B. 1974. *All Our Kin.* New York: Harper & Row.

Staples, Robert. 1971. "Towards a sociology of the black family: A theoretical and methodological assessment." *Journal of Marriage and the Family* 33:119–138.

Starr, Joyce R., and Donald E. Carns. 1973. "Singles in the city." Pp. 154–161 in Helena Z. Lopata (ed.), *Marriages and Families.* New York: Van Nostrand.

Steele, Brandt F., and Carl B. Pollock. 1968. "A psychiatric study of parents who abuse infants and small children." Pp. 103–113 in R.E. Helfer and C. H. Kempe (eds.), *The Battered Child*. Chicago: University of Chicago Press.

Stein, Maurice. 1964. *The Eclipse of Community*. New York: Harper (Torchbooks).

Steinmetz, Suzanne K. 1977. *The Cycle of Violence: Assertive, Aggressive and Abusive Family Interaction*. New York: Praeger.

Steinmetz, Suzanne K., and Murry A. Strauss (eds.). 1974. *Violence in the Family*. New York: Dodd, Mead.

Stephens, William N. 1963. *The Family in Cross-Cultural Perspective*. New York: Holt, Rinehart & Winston.

Sterba, James P. 1979. "Chinese Will Try to Halt Growth of Population by end of Century." *New York Times*, August 13, 1979.

Stone, Gregory P. 1954. "City shoppers and urban identification: Observations on the social psychology of city life." *American Journal of Sociology* 60:36–45.

Straus, Murray A. 1974. "Leveling, civility, and violence in the family." *Journal of Marriage and the Family* 36:13–29.

———. 1977. "Societal morphogenesis and intrafamily violence in cross-cultural perspective." *Annals of the New York Academy of Sciences* 285:719–730.

Stycos, J. Mayone. 1955. *Family and Fertility in Puerto Rico*. New York: Columbia University Press.

Sullerot, Evelyne. 1971. *Woman, Society and Change*. New York: World (University Library).

Sumner, William Graham. 1906. *Folkways*. Boston: Ginn.

Sussman, Marvin B. 1953. "The help pattern in the middle class family." *American Sociological Review* 18:22–28.

———. 1959. "The isolated nuclear family 1959: Fact or Fiction?" *Social Problems* 6:333–340.

Sussman, Marvin B., and Lee Burchinal. 1962. "Kin family network: Unheralded structure in current conceptualizations of family functioning." *Marriage and Family Living* 24:231–240.

Tallman, Irving. 1969. "Working-class wives in suburbia: Fulfillment or crisis." *Journal of Marriage and the Family* 31:65–72.

Tallman, Irving, and Romona Morgner. 1970. "Life style differences among urban and suburban blue collar families." *Social Forces* March:334–348.

Talmon, Yonina. 1964. "Mate selection in collective settlement." *American Sociological Review* 29:468–508.

———. 1965a. "The family in a revolutionary movement—the case of the kibbutz in Israel." Pp. 259–286 in Meyer Nimkoff (ed.), *Comparative Family Systems*. Boston: Houghton-Mifflin.

———. 1965b. "Sex-role differentiation in an equalitarian society." Pp. 144–155 in Thomas E. Lasswell, John H. Burma, and Sidney H. Aronson (eds.), *Life in Society*. Chicago: Scott, Foresman.

Tambiah, S. J. 1973. "The persistence and transformation of tradition in Southeast Asia, with special reference to Thailand." *Daedalus* 102:55–84. (Winter issue titled, "Post-Traditional Societies.")

Terrill, Ross. 1979. *The China Difference*. New York: Harper & Row.

Theodorson, George A. 1968. "Cross-national variations in eagerness to marry." Pp. 119–134 in H. Kent Geiger (ed.), *Comparative Perspectives in Marriage and the Family*. Boston: Little, Brown.

Thompson, E. P. 1963. *The Making of the English Working Class*. London: Gollancz.

Thrasher, Frederic M. 1927. *The Gang*. Chicago: University of Chicago Press.

Tiger, Lionel, and Joseph Shepher. 1975. *Women in the Kibbutz*. New York: Harcourt Brace Jovanovich.

Time. 1977. "Jobs: Challenging the 65 barrier." August 8: 67–68.

Tönnies, Ferdinand. 1963. *Community and Society [Gemeinschaft und Gesellschaft]*. Charles P. Loomis (trans. and ed.). New York: Harper (Torchbooks). Originally published, 1887; original translation, 1957.

Townsend, Peter. 1957. *The Family Life of Old People*. London: Routledge & Kegal Paul.

Trost, Jan. 1975. "Married and unmarried cohabitation: A case of Sweden, with some comparisons." *Journal of Marriage and the Family* 37: 677–682.

———. 1978. "A renewed social institution: Non-marital cohabitation." *Acta Sociologica* 21:303–315.

Turnbull, Colin M. 1962. *The Lonely African*. New York: Simon & Schuster.

Turner, John F.C. 1969. "Uncontrolled urban settlement: Problems and policies." Pp. 507–534 in Gerald Breese (ed.), *The City in Newly Developing Countries: Readings on Urbanism and Urbanization*. Englewood Cliffs, N.J.: Prentice-Hall.

———. 1970. "Barriers and channels for housing development in modernizing countries." Pp. 1–19 in William Mangin (ed.), *Peasants in Cities: Readings in the Anthropology of Urbanization*. Boston: Houghton-Mifflin.

U.S. Department of Labor. 1965. *The Negro Family: The Case for National Action*. U.S. Department of Labor, Office of Policy Planning and Research. Washington, D.C.: U.S. Government Printing Office.

Valentine, Charles. 1968. *Culture and Poverty: Critique and Counter-Proposals*. Chicago: University of Chicago Press.

Van Allen, Judith. 1974. "Modernization means more dependency: Women in Africa." *The Center Magazine* 7:60–67.

Vann, Richard T. 1978. Review of *The Making of the Modern Family* by E. Shorter. *Journal of Family History* 3:106–117.

Vreeland. Rebecca S. 1972a. "Is it true what they say about Harvard boys." *Psychology Today* 5:65–68.

———. 1972b. "Sex at Harvard." *Sexual Behavior:* 3–10.

Waller, Willard. 1937. "The rating dating complex." *American Sociological Review* 2:727–734.

———. 1938. *The Family: A Dynamic Interpretation*. New York: Dryden.

Weber, Max. 1949. The Methodology of the Social Sciences. Edward H. Shils and Henry A. Finch (trans. and eds.). New York: The Free Press.

Weiner, Myron, (ed.). 1966. *Modernization: The Dynamics of Growth*. New York: Basic Books.

Weiss, Robert S. 1979a. *Going It Alone: The Family Life and Social Situation of the Single Parent*. New York: Basic Books.

———. 1979b. "Issues in the adjudication of custody when parents separate." Pp. 324–336 in George Levinger and Oliver C. Moles (eds.), *Divorce and Separation: Context, Causes, and Consequences*. New York: Basic Books.

Weitzman, Lenore J. 1977. "To love, honor and obey." Pp. 288–313 in Arlene S. Skolnick and Jerome H. Skolnick (eds.), *Family in Transition: Rethinking Marriage, Sexuality, Child Rearing, and Family Organization*, 2nd ed. Boston: Little, Brown.

Weitzman, Lenore J., and Ruth B. Dixon. 1980. "The transformation of legal marriage through no-fault divorce." Pp. 354–367 in Arlene Skolnick and Jerome H. Skolnick (eds.), *Family in Transition: Rethinking Marriage, Sexuality, Child Rearing, and Family Organization*, 3rd ed. Boston: Little, Brown.

Westermarck, Edward A. 1905. *The History of Human Marriage*, 5th ed. (3 vols.). New York: MacMillan. (Originally published, 1891.)

Westoff, Leslie Aldridge. 1977. *The Second Time Around: Remarriage in America*. New York: Penguin Books.

White, Morton, and Lucia White. 1962. *The Intellectual Versus the City*. Cambridge: Harvard University Press/M.I.T. Press.

Wilkinson, Karen. 1974. "The broken family and juvenile delinquency: Scientific explanation of ideology?" *Social Problems* 21:726–773.

Williams, Tomas Rhys. 1972. *Introduction to Socialization: Human Culture Transmitted*. St. Louis: C. V. Mosby.

Willmott, Peter, and Michael Young. 1960. *Family and Class in a London Suburb*. London: Routledge & Kegan Paul.

Wirth, Louis. 1938a. *The Ghetto*. Chicago: University of Chicago Press.

———. 1938b. "Urbanism as a way of life." *American Journal of Sociology* 44:1–24.

Wong, Aline K. 1974. "Women in China: Past and present." Pp. 229–259 in Carolyn J. Matthiason (ed.), *Many Sisters: Women in Cross-Cultural Perspective*. New York: The Free Press.

Wortis, Rochelle Paul. 1977. "The acceptance of the concept of the mortal role by behavioral scientists: Its effects on women." *The American Journal of Orthopsychiatry* 41:733–746. Reprinted pp. 362–378 in Arlene S. Skolnick and Jerhome H. Skolnick, (eds.), *Family in Transition: Rethinking Marriage, Sexuality, Child Rearing, and Family Organization*, 2nd ed. Boston: Little, Brown.

Yang, C. K. 1959. *The Chinese Family in the Communist Revolution*. Cambridge: M.I.T. Press.

Yorburg, Betty. 1974. *Sexual Identity: Sex Roles and Social Change*. New York: John Wiley & Sons.

Young, Michael, and Peter Willmott. 1957. *Family and Kinship in East London*. Baltimore: Penguin Books. (Rev. ed., 1963.)

———. 1973. *The Symmetrical Family*. New York: Pantheon Books.

Zalba, Serapio R. 1974. "Battered children." Pp. 407–415 in Arlene S. Skolnick and Jerome H. Skolnick (eds.), *Intimacy, Family, and Society*. Boston: Little, Brown.

Zelditch, Morris. Jr. 1964. "Cross-cultural analysis of family structure." Pp. 462–500 in Harold T. Christensen (ed.), *Handbook of Marriage and the Family*. Chicago: Rand McNally.

Zimmerman, Carle C. 1947. *Family and Civilization*. New York: Harper & Bros.

———. 1949. *The Family of Tomorrow: The Cultural Crisis and the Way Out*. New York: Harper & Bros.

————. 1970. ''The atomistic family—fact or fiction.'' *Journal of Comparative Family Studies* 1:5–16.

Zimmerman, Carle C., and Merle E. Frampton. 1966. ''Theories of Frederic Le Play.'' Pp. 14–23 in Bernard Farber (ed.), *Kinship and Family Organization*. New York: John Wiley & Sons.

Zorbaugh, Harvey W. 1929. *The Gold Coast and the Slum*. Chicago: University of Chicago Press.

Photo Credits

AUTHOR INDEX

SUBJECT INDEX